THE TRIAL OF THOR

THOR: TRUTH OF HISTORY

WRITER & PENCILER **ALAN DAVIS**
INKER **MARK FARMER**
COLORIST **ROB SCHWAGER**
LETTERER **VC's JOE CARAMAGNA**
COVER ART **ALAN DAVIS, MARK FARMER
& ROB SCHWAGER**

THOR: WOLVES OF THE NORTH

WRITER **MIKE CAREY**
ARTIST **MIKE PERKINS**
COLORIST **DAN BROWN**
LETTERER **DAVE SHARPE**
COVER ART **MIKE PERKINS** & **LAURA MARTIN**

SPECIAL THANKS TO
TOM BREVOORT & ALEJANDRO ARBONA

THOR: THE TRIAL OF THOR

WRITER **PETER MILLIGAN**
ARTIST **CARY NORD**
COLORIST **CHRISTINA STRAIN**
LETTERER **VC's JOE CARAMAGNA**
COVER ART **CARY NORD** & **CHRISTINA STRAIN**

THOR: THE RAGE OF THOR

WRITER **PETER MILLIGAN**
ARTIST **MICO SUAYAN**
COLORIST **MATT MILLA**
LETTERER **VC's JOE SABINO**
COVER ART **MICO SUAYAN** & **IAN HANNIN**

THOR CREATED BY **STAN LEE, LARRY LIEBER** & **JACK KIRBY**

COLLECTION EDITOR **MARK D. BEAZLEY** • ASSISTANT EDITOR **CAITLIN O'CONNELL**
ASSOCIATE MANAGING EDITOR **KATERI WOODY** • ASSOCIATE MANAGER, DIGITAL ASSETS **JOE HOCHSTEIN**
SENIOR EDITOR, SPECIAL PROJECTS **JENNIFER GRÜNWALD** • VP PRODUCTION & SPECIAL PROJECTS **JEFF YOUNGQUIST**
RESEARCH **DARON JENSEN** • LAYOUT **JEPH YORK** • PRODUCTION **SALENA JOHNSON** • BOOK DESIGNER **JAY BOWEN**
SVP PRINT, SALES & MARKETING **DAVID GABRIEL**

EDITOR IN CHIEF **AXEL ALONSO** • CHIEF CREATIVE OFFICER **JOE QUESADA**
PRESIDENT **DAN BUCKLEY** • EXECUTIVE PRODUCER **ALAN FINE**

SPECIAL THANKS TO **MIKE HANSEN**

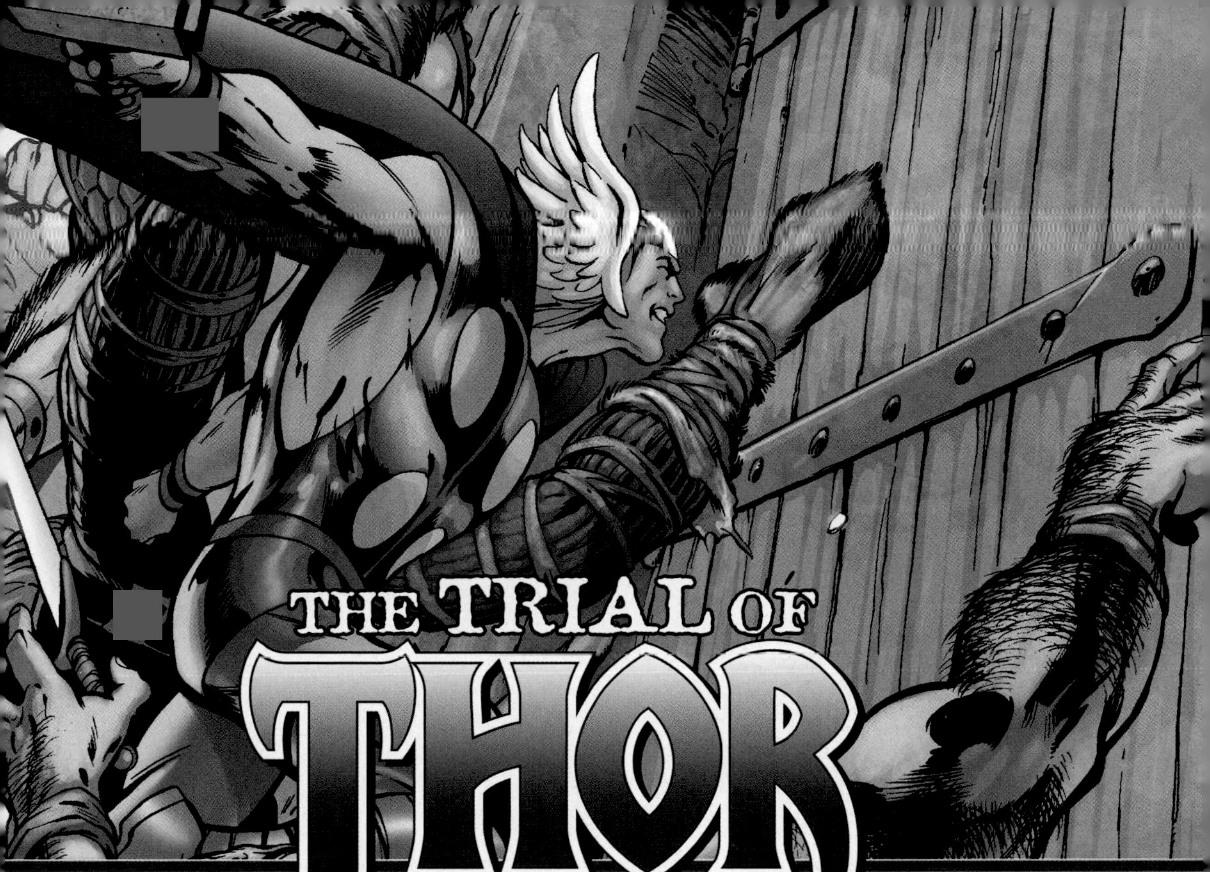

THE TRIAL OF THOR

THOR ANNUAL (2009) #1

WRITER **PETER MILLIGAN**
ARTIST (CELESTIAL HELIOPOLIS) **MICO SUAYAN**
ARTISTS (EARTH) **TOM GRINDBERG**
WITH **STEFANO GAUDIANO**
COLORISTS **EDGAR DELGADO**
& **SOTOCOLOR'S J. ROBERTS**
LETTERER **VC's JOE CARAMAGNA**
COVER ART **MARKO DJURDJEVIC**

DARK REIGN: THE CABAL

WRITER **PETER MILLIGAN**
ARTIST **TONCI ZONJIC**
COLORIST **JOSE VILLARRUBIA**
LETTERER **BLAMBOT'S NATE PIEKOS**
COVER ART **DANIEL ACUÑA**

THOR: HEAVEN & EARTH

WRITER: **PAUL JENKINS**
ARTISTS: **ARIEL OLIVETTI** (#1), **MARK TEXEIRA** (#2),
PASCAL ALIXE (#3) & **LAN MEDINA** (#4)
COLORISTS: **ARIEL OLIVETTI** (#1),
SOTOCOLOR (#2-3) & **CHRIS SOTOMAYOR** (#4)
LETTERER: **DAVE SHARPE**
COVER ART: **ARIEL OLIVETTI** (#1),
MARK TEXEIRA (#2),
AGUSTIN PADILLA & **CHRIS SOTOMAYOR** (#3),
STÉPHANE PERGER (#4)

ASSISTANT EDITOR **ALEJANDRO ARBONA**
EDITORS **WARREN SIMONS,**
MICHAEL HORWITZ & **CHARLIE BECKERMAN**
WITH **ALEJANDRO ARBONA** & **JAKE THOMAS**
SENIOR EDITORS **RALPH MACCHIO**
& **MARK PANICCIA**
EXECUTIVE EDITOR (*DARK REIGN: THE CABAL*)
TOM BREVOORT

THOR: THE TRIAL OF THOR. Contains material originally published in magazine form as THOR: TRUTH OF HISTORY ONE-SHOT, THOR: WOLVES OF THE NORTH #1, THOR: THE TRIAL OF THOR ONE SHOT, THOR: THE RAGE OF THOR #1, THOR ANNUAL #1, THOR: HEAVEN & EARTH #1-4 and DARK REIGN: THE CABAL ONE-SHOT. First printing 2017. ISBN# 978-1-302-90795-2. Published by MARVEL WORLDWIDE, INC., a subsidiary of MARVEL ENTERTAINMENT, LLC. OFFICE OF PUBLICATION: 135 West 50th Street, New York, NY 10020. **Printed in the U.S.A.** DAN BUCKLEY, President, Marvel Entertainment; JOE QUESADA, Chief Creative Officer; TOM BREVOORT, SVP of Publishing; DAVID BOGART, SVP of Business Affairs & Operations, Publishing & Partnership; C.B. CEBULSKI, VP of Brand Management & Development, Asia; DAVID GABRIEL, SVP of Sales & Marketing, Publishing; JEFF YOUNGQUIST, VP of Production & Special Projects; DAN CARR, Executive Director of Publishing Technology; ALEX MORALES, Director of Publishing Operations; SUSAN CRESPI, Production Manager; STAN LEE, Chairman Emeritus. For information regarding advertising in Marvel Comics or on Marvel.com, please contact Vit DeBellis, Integrated Sales Manager, at vdebellis@marvel.com. For Marvel subscription inquiries, please call 888-511-5480. **Manufactured between 7/28/2017 and 8/29/2017 by LSC COMMUNICATIONS INC., KENDALLVILLE, IN, USA.**

10 9 8 7 6 5 4 3 2 1

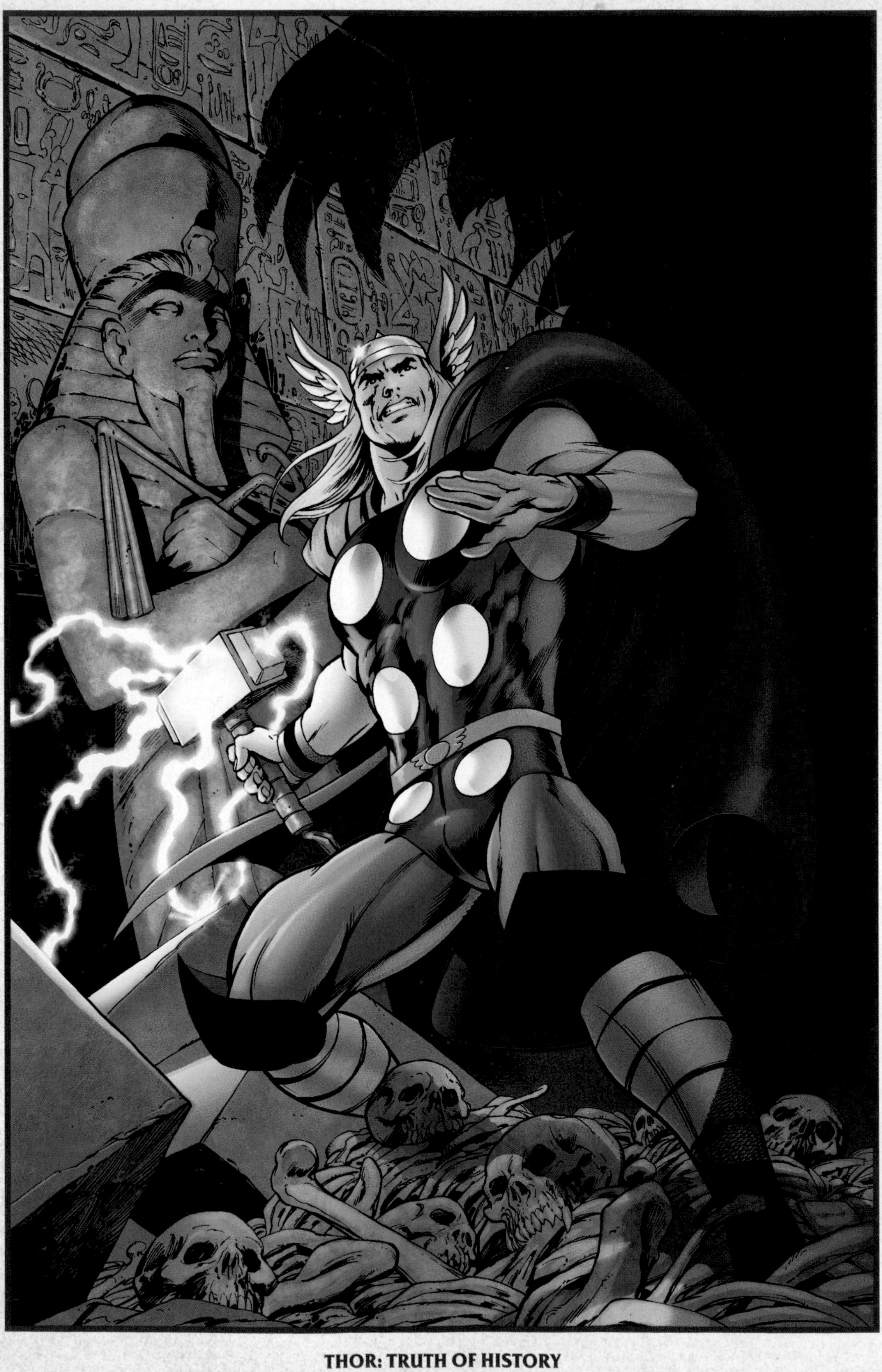

THOR: TRUTH OF HISTORY

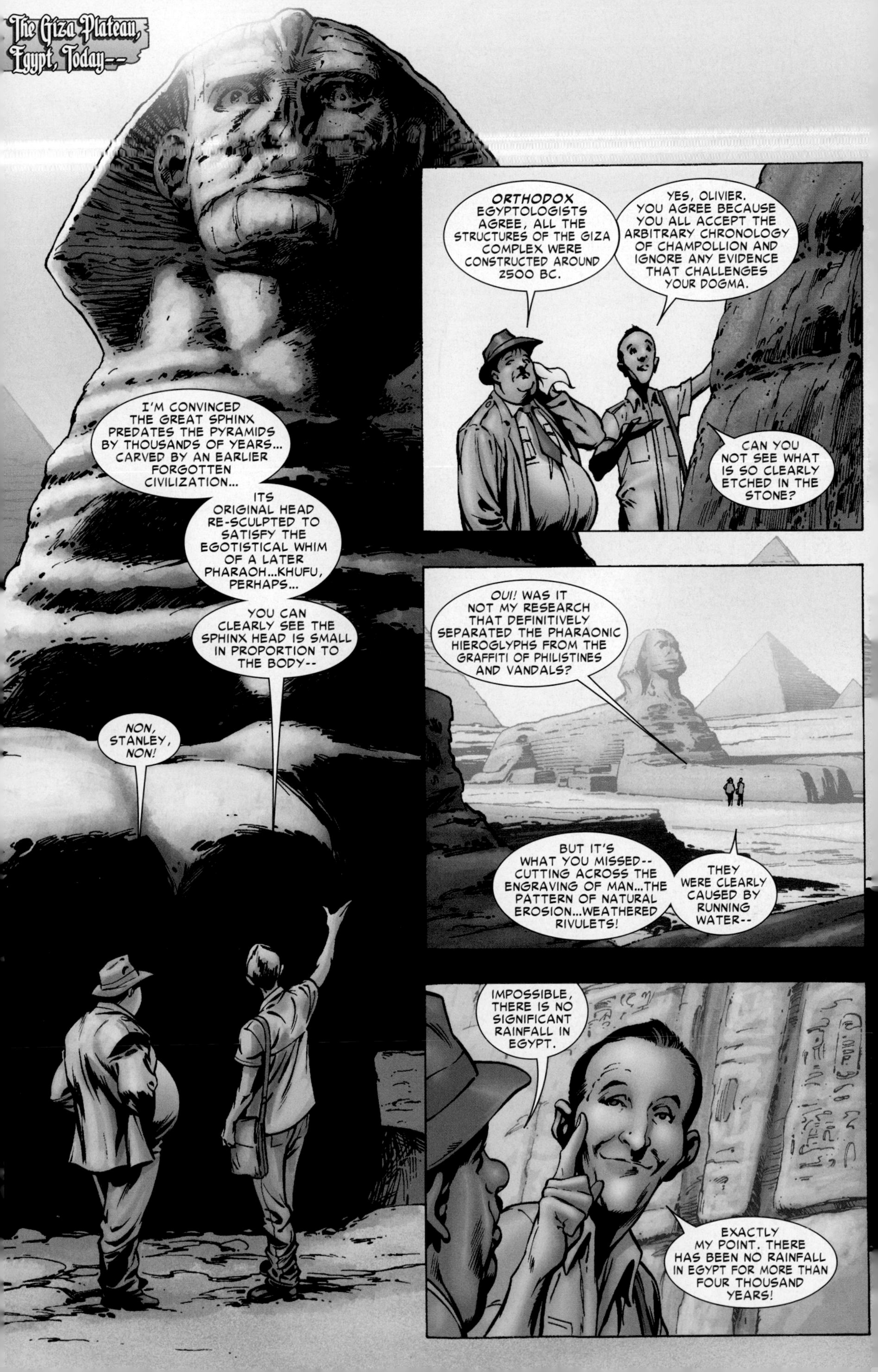
The Giza Plateau, Egypt, Today--
I'M CONVINCED THE GREAT SPHINX PREDATES THE PYRAMIDS BY THOUSANDS OF YEARS... CARVED BY AN EARLIER FORGOTTEN CIVILIZATION...
ITS ORIGINAL HEAD RE-SCULPTED TO SATISFY THE EGOTISTICAL WHIM OF A LATER PHARAOH...KHUFU, PERHAPS...
YOU CAN CLEARLY SEE THE SPHINX HEAD IS SMALL IN PROPORTION TO THE BODY--
NON, STANLEY, NON!
ORTHODOX EGYPTOLOGISTS AGREE, ALL THE STRUCTURES OF THE GIZA COMPLEX WERE CONSTRUCTED AROUND 2500 BC.
YES, OLIVIER. YOU AGREE BECAUSE YOU ALL ACCEPT THE ARBITRARY CHRONOLOGY OF CHAMPOLLION AND IGNORE ANY EVIDENCE THAT CHALLENGES YOUR DOGMA.
CAN YOU NOT SEE WHAT IS SO CLEARLY ETCHED IN THE STONE?
OUI! WAS IT NOT MY RESEARCH THAT DEFINITIVELY SEPARATED THE PHARAONIC HIEROGLYPHS FROM THE GRAFFITI OF PHILISTINES AND VANDALS?
BUT IT'S WHAT YOU MISSED-- CUTTING ACROSS THE ENGRAVING OF MAN...THE PATTERN OF NATURAL EROSION...WEATHERED RIVULETS!
THEY WERE CLEARLY CAUSED BY RUNNING WATER--
IMPOSSIBLE, THERE IS NO SIGNIFICANT RAINFALL IN EGYPT.
EXACTLY MY POINT. THERE HAS BEEN NO RAINFALL IN EGYPT FOR MORE THAN FOUR THOUSAND YEARS!

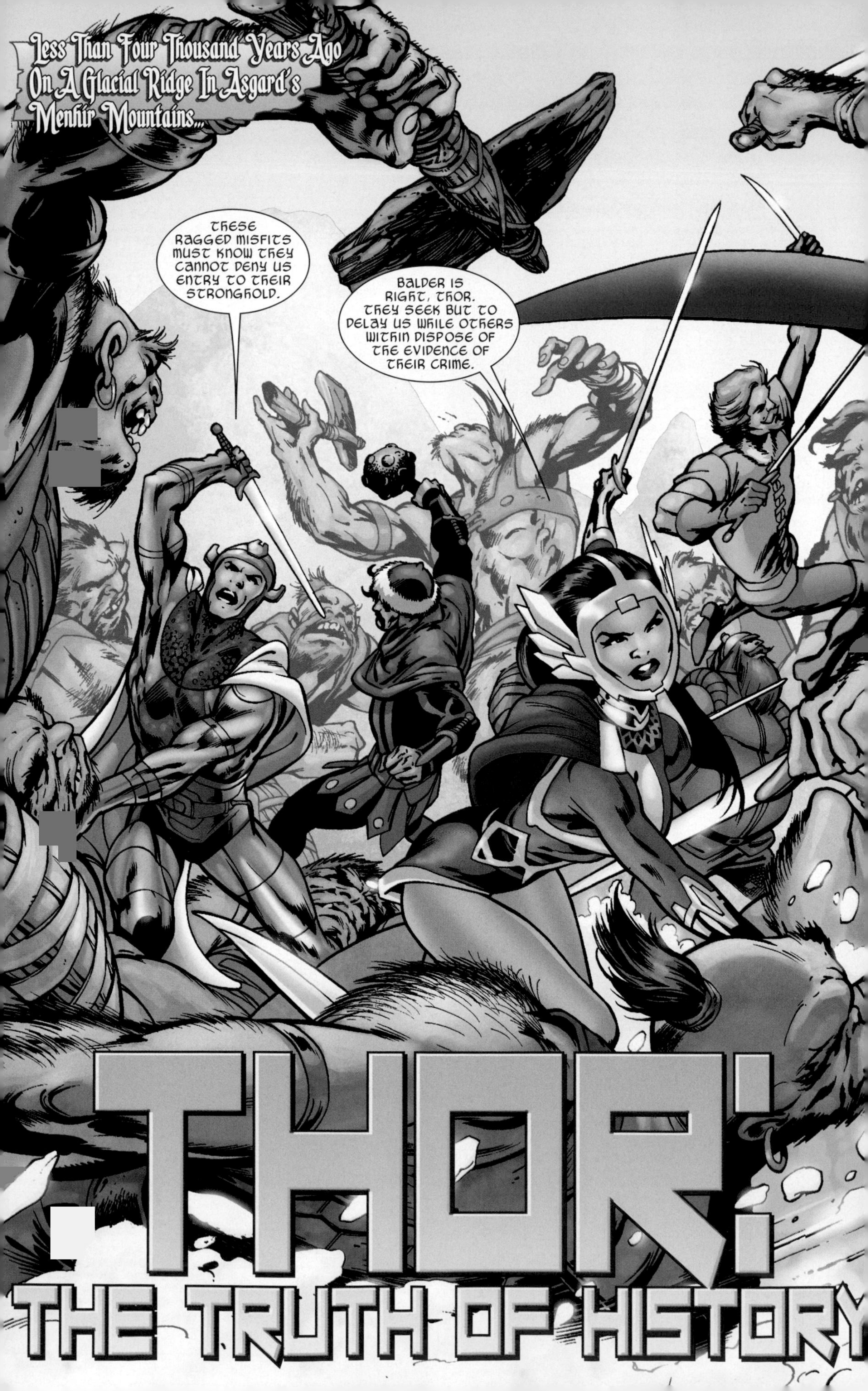
Less Than Four Thousand Years Ago On A Glacial Ridge In Asgard's Menhir Mountains...
THESE RAGGED MISFITS MUST KNOW THEY CANNOT DENY US ENTRY TO THEIR STRONGHOLD.
BALDER IS RIGHT, THOR. THEY SEEK BUT TO DELAY US WHILE OTHERS WITHIN DISPOSE OF THE EVIDENCE OF THEIR CRIME.
THOR: THE TRUTH OF HISTORY

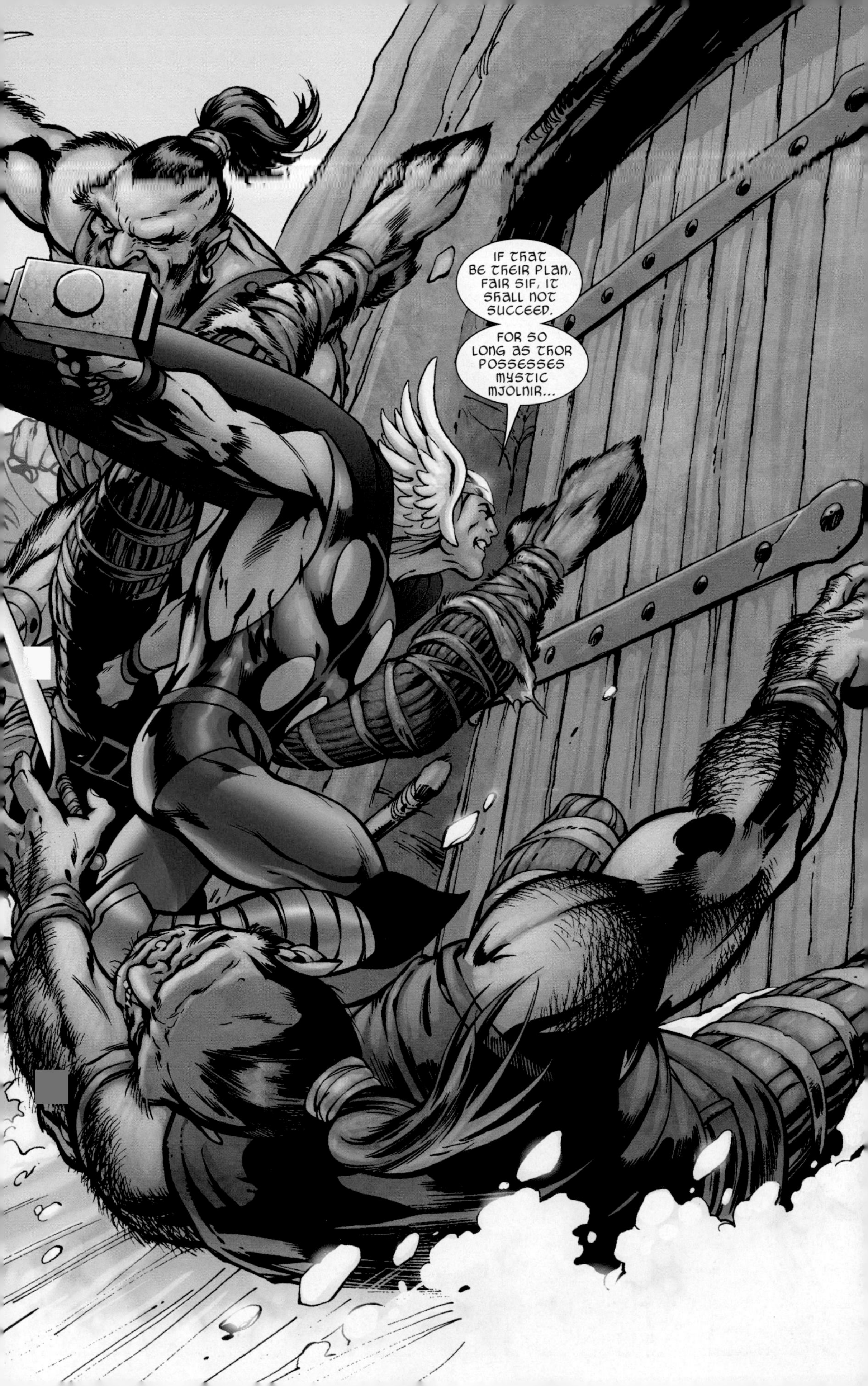
IF THAT BE THEIR PLAN, FAIR SIF, IT SHALL NOT SUCCEED.
FOR SO LONG AS THOR POSSESSES MYSTIC MJOLNIR...

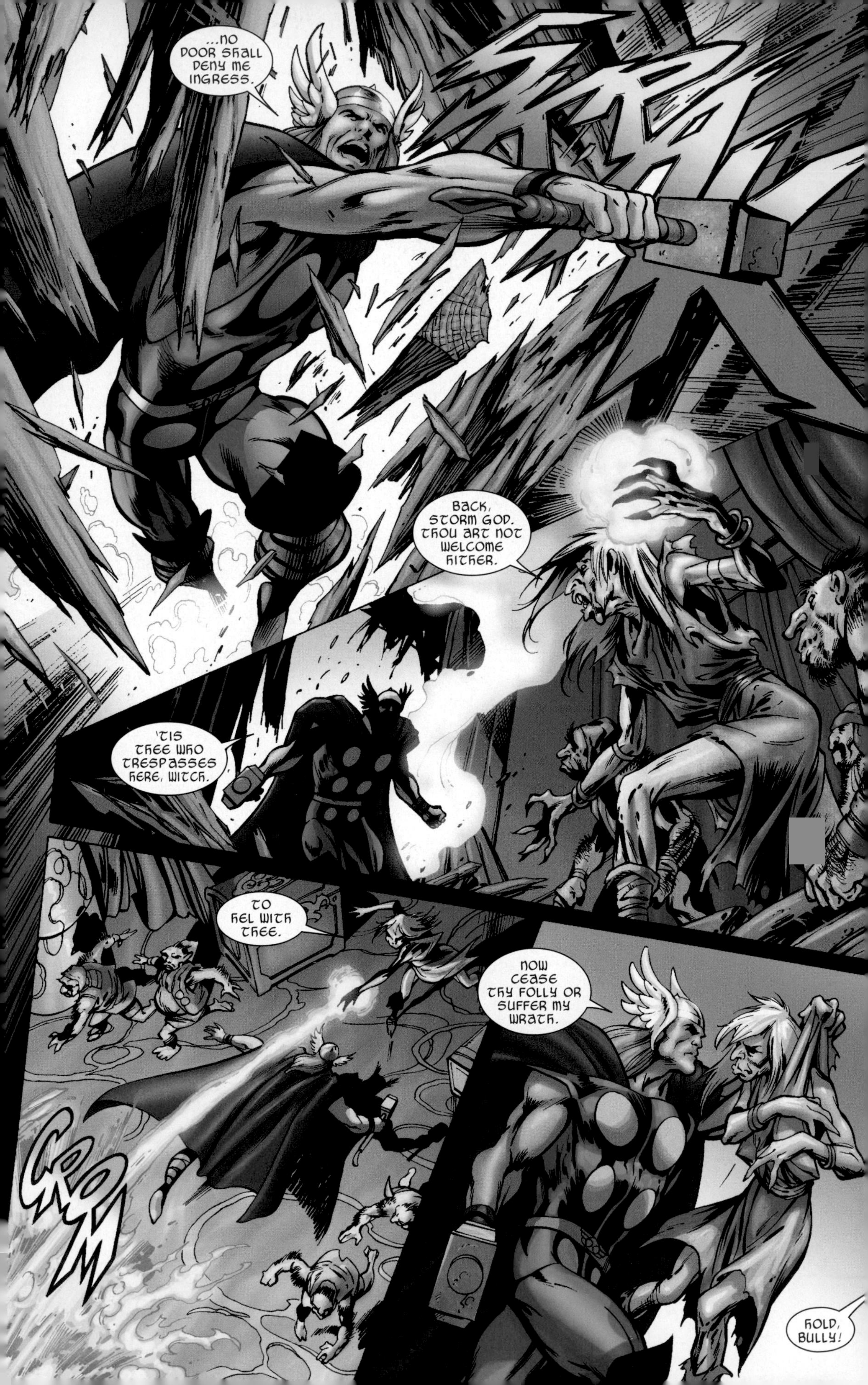
...NO DOOR SHALL DENY ME INGRESS.
BACK, STORM GOD. THOU ART NOT WELCOME HITHER.
'TIS THEE WHO TRESPASSES HERE, WITCH.
TO HEL WITH THEE.
NOW CEASE THY FOLLY OR SUFFER MY WRATH.
HOLD, BULLY!

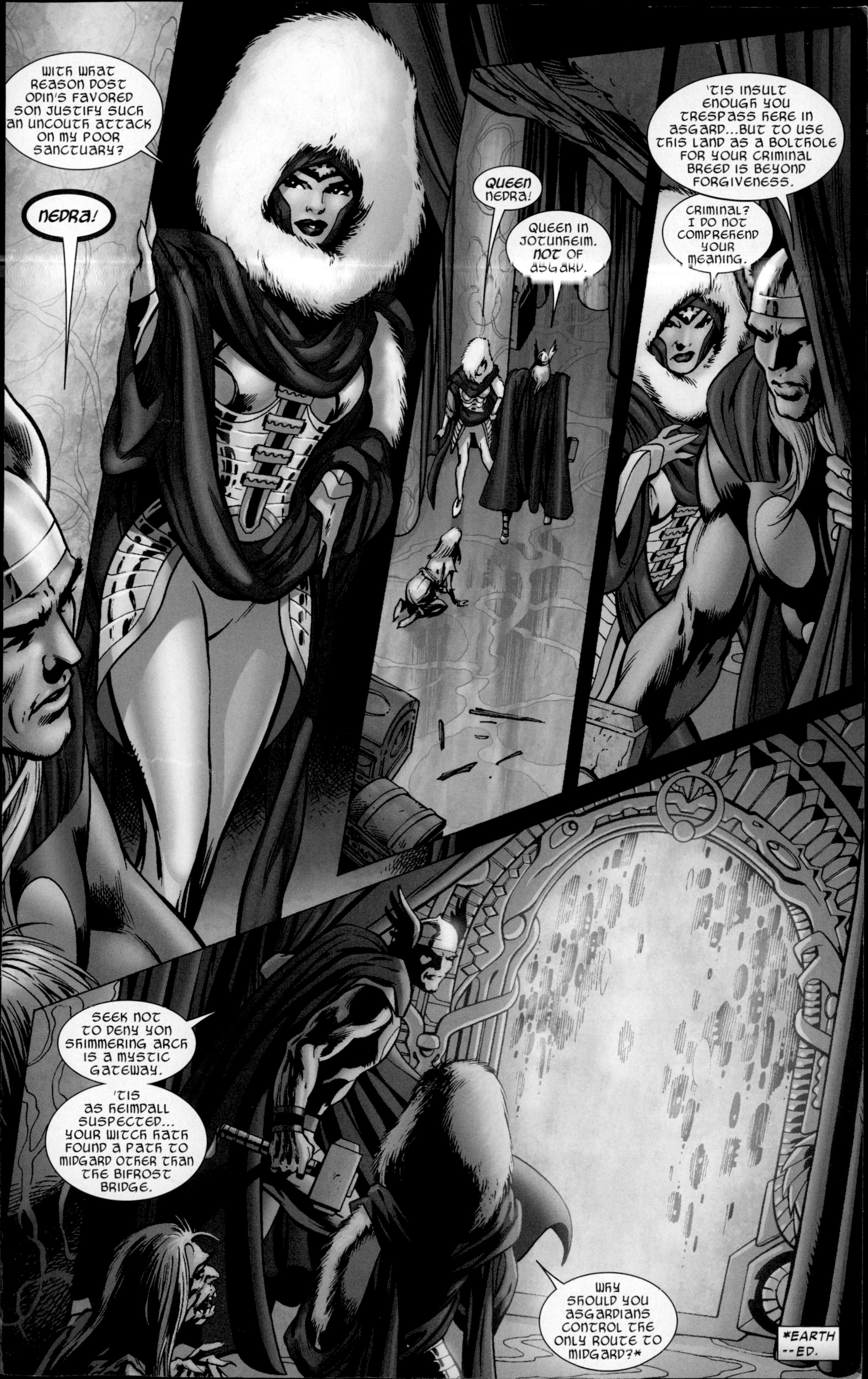
WITH WHAT REASON DOST ODIN'S FAVORED SON JUSTIFY SUCH AN UNCOUTH ATTACK ON MY POOR SANCTUARY?
NEDRA!
QUEEN NEDRA!
QUEEN IN JOTUNHEIM. NOT OF ASGARD.
'TIS INSULT ENOUGH YOU TRESPASS HERE IN ASGARD...BUT TO USE THIS LAND AS A BOLTHOLE FOR YOUR CRIMINAL BREED IS BEYOND FORGIVENESS.
CRIMINAL? I DO NOT COMPREHEND YOUR MEANING.
SEEK NOT TO DENY YON SHIMMERING ARCH IS A MYSTIC GATEWAY.
'TIS AS HEIMDALL SUSPECTED... YOUR WITCH HATH FOUND A PATH TO MIDGARD OTHER THAN THE BIFROST BRIDGE.
WHY SHOULD YOU ASGARDIANS CONTROL THE ONLY ROUTE TO MIDGARD?*
*EARTH --ED.

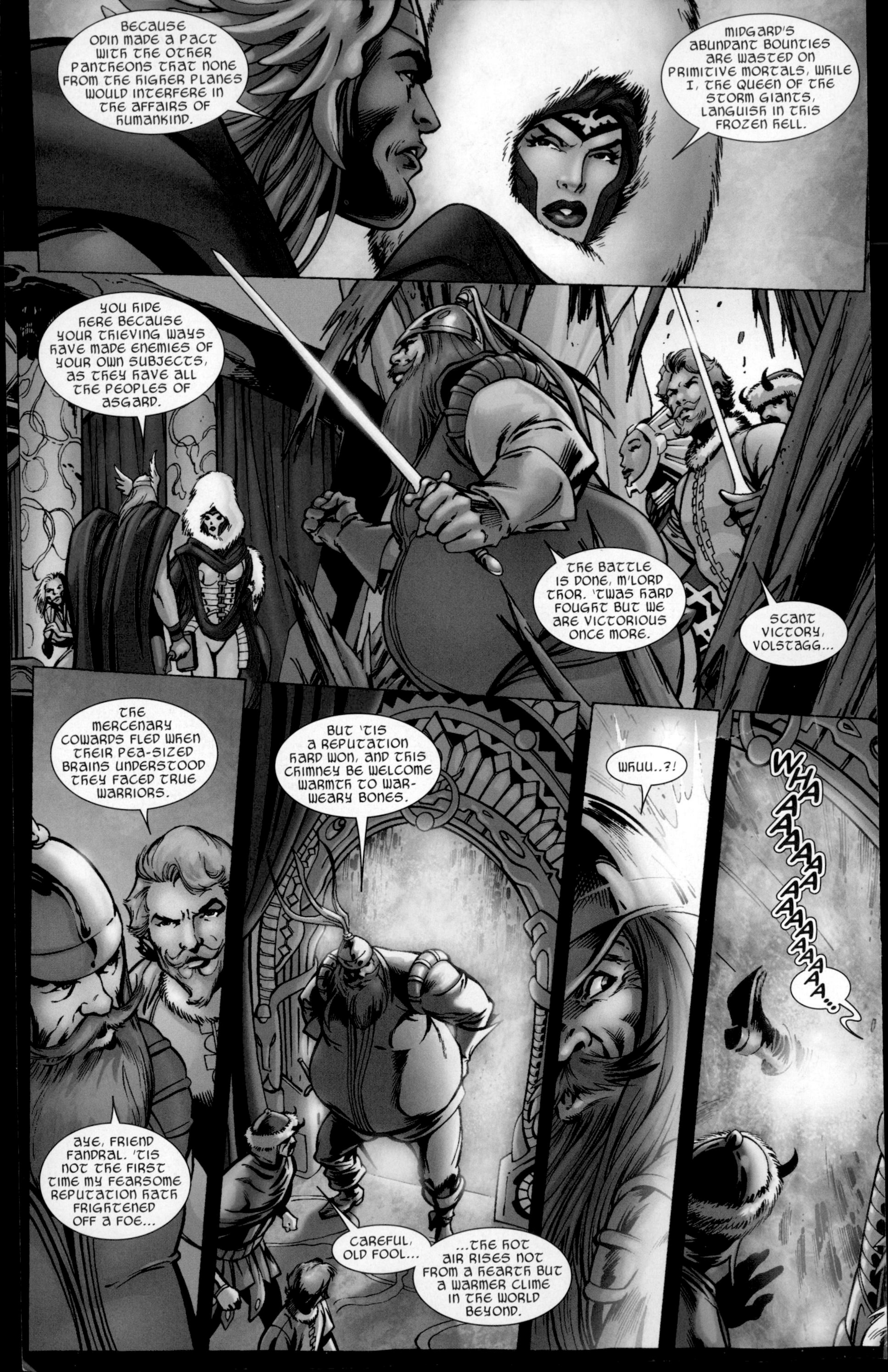
BECAUSE ODIN MADE A PACT WITH THE OTHER PANTHEONS THAT NONE FROM THE HIGHER PLANES WOULD INTERFERE IN THE AFFAIRS OF HUMANKIND.
MIDGARD'S ABUNDANT BOUNTIES ARE WASTED ON PRIMITIVE MORTALS, WHILE I, THE QUEEN OF THE STORM GIANTS, LANGUISH IN THIS FROZEN HELL.
YOU HIDE HERE BECAUSE YOUR THIEVING WAYS HAVE MADE ENEMIES OF YOUR OWN SUBJECTS, AS THEY HAVE ALL THE PEOPLES OF ASGARD.
THE BATTLE IS DONE, M'LORD THOR. 'TWAS HARD FOUGHT BUT WE ARE VICTORIOUS ONCE MORE.
SCANT VICTORY, VOLSTAGG...
THE MERCENARY COWARDS FLED WHEN THEIR PEA-SIZED BRAINS UNDERSTOOD THEY FACED TRUE WARRIORS.
AYE, FRIEND FANDRAL. 'TIS NOT THE FIRST TIME MY FEARSOME REPUTATION HATH FRIGHTENED OFF A FOE...
BUT 'TIS A REPUTATION HARD WON, AND THIS CHIMNEY BE WELCOME WARMTH TO WAR-WEARY BONES.
CAREFUL, OLD FOOL...
...THE HOT AIR RISES NOT FROM A HEARTH BUT A WARMER CLIME IN THE WORLD BEYOND.
WHUU..?!
WHAAAAAAAAAAAAAAAA...

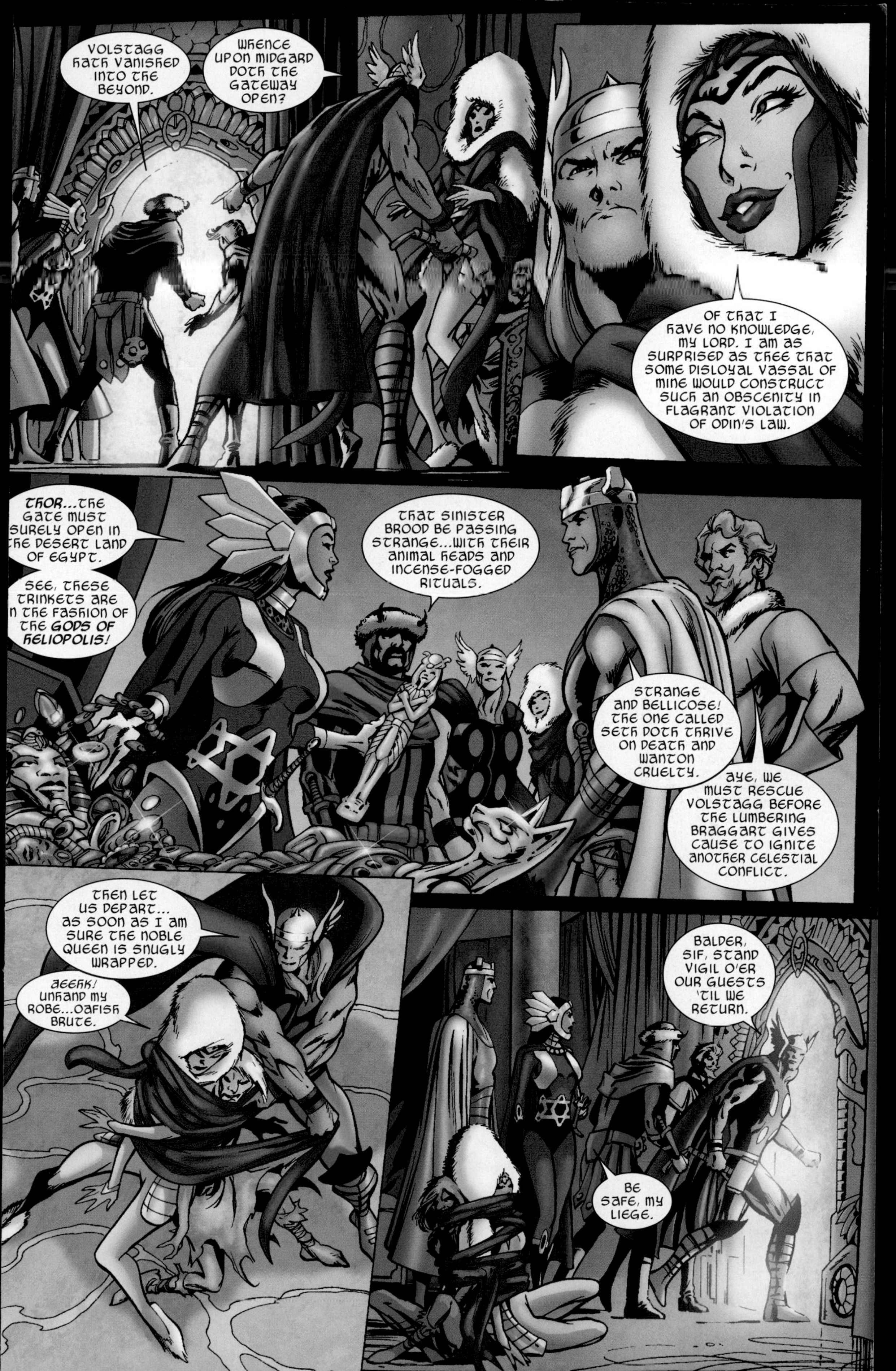
VOLSTAGG HATH VANISHED INTO THE BEYOND.
WHENCE UPON MIDGARD DOTH THE GATEWAY OPEN?
OF THAT I HAVE NO KNOWLEDGE, MY LORD. I AM AS SURPRISED AS THEE THAT SOME DISLOYAL VASSAL OF MINE WOULD CONSTRUCT SUCH AN OBSCENITY IN FLAGRANT VIOLATION OF ODIN'S LAW.
THOR...THE GATE MUST SURELY OPEN IN THE DESERT LAND OF EGYPT.
SEE, THESE TRINKETS ARE IN THE FASHION OF THE GODS OF HELIOPOLIS!
THAT SINISTER BROOD BE PASSING STRANGE...WITH THEIR ANIMAL HEADS AND INCENSE-FOGGED RITUALS.
STRANGE AND BELLICOSE! THE ONE CALLED SETH DOTH THRIVE ON DEATH AND WANTON CRUELTY.
AYE, WE MUST RESCUE VOLSTAGG BEFORE THE LUMBERING BRAGGART GIVES CAUSE TO IGNITE ANOTHER CELESTIAL CONFLICT.
THEN LET US DEPART... AS SOON AS I AM SURE THE NOBLE QUEEN IS SNUGLY WRAPPED.
AEEKK! UNHAND MY ROBE...OAFISH BRUTE.
BALDER, SIF, STAND VIGIL O'ER OUR GUESTS 'TIL WE RETURN.
BE SAFE, MY LIEGE.

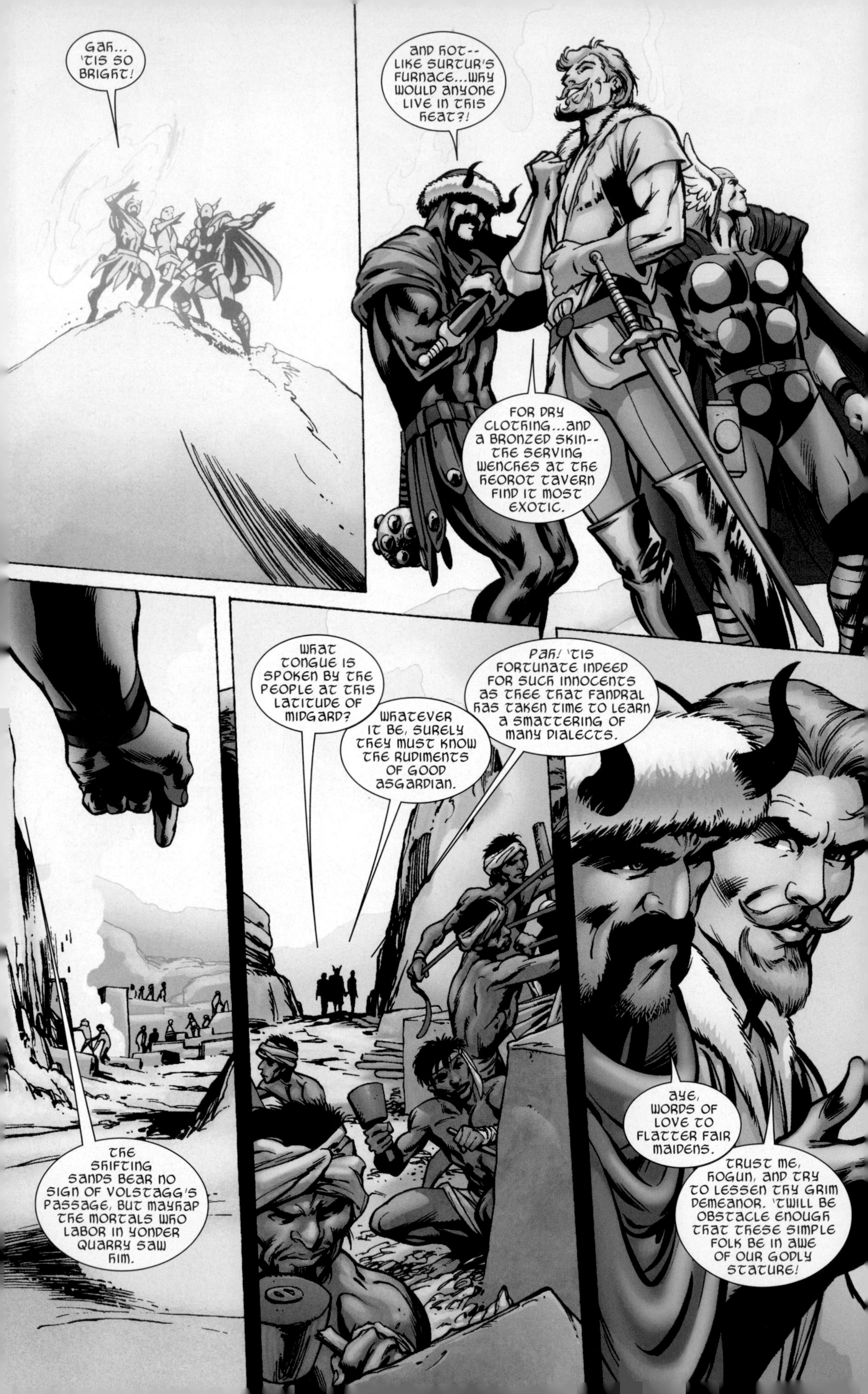
GAH... 'TIS SO BRIGHT!
AND HOT-- LIKE SURTUR'S FURNACE...WHY WOULD ANYONE LIVE IN THIS HEAT?!
FOR DRY CLOTHING...AND A BRONZED SKIN-- THE SERVING WENCHES AT THE HEOROT TAVERN FIND IT MOST EXOTIC.
THE SHIFTING SANDS BEAR NO SIGN OF VOLSTAGG'S PASSAGE, BUT MAYHAP THE MORTALS WHO LABOR IN YONDER QUARRY SAW HIM.
WHAT TONGUE IS SPOKEN BY THE PEOPLE AT THIS LATITUDE OF MIDGARD?
WHATEVER IT BE, SURELY THEY MUST KNOW THE RUDIMENTS OF GOOD ASGARDIAN.
PAH! 'TIS FORTUNATE INDEED FOR SUCH INNOCENTS AS THEE THAT FANDRAL HAS TAKEN TIME TO LEARN A SMATTERING OF MANY DIALECTS.
AYE, WORDS OF LOVE TO FLATTER FAIR MAIDENS.
TRUST ME, HOGUN, AND TRY TO LESSEN THY GRIM DEMEANOR. 'TWILL BE OBSTACLE ENOUGH THAT THESE SIMPLE FOLK BE IN AWE OF OUR GODLY STATURE!

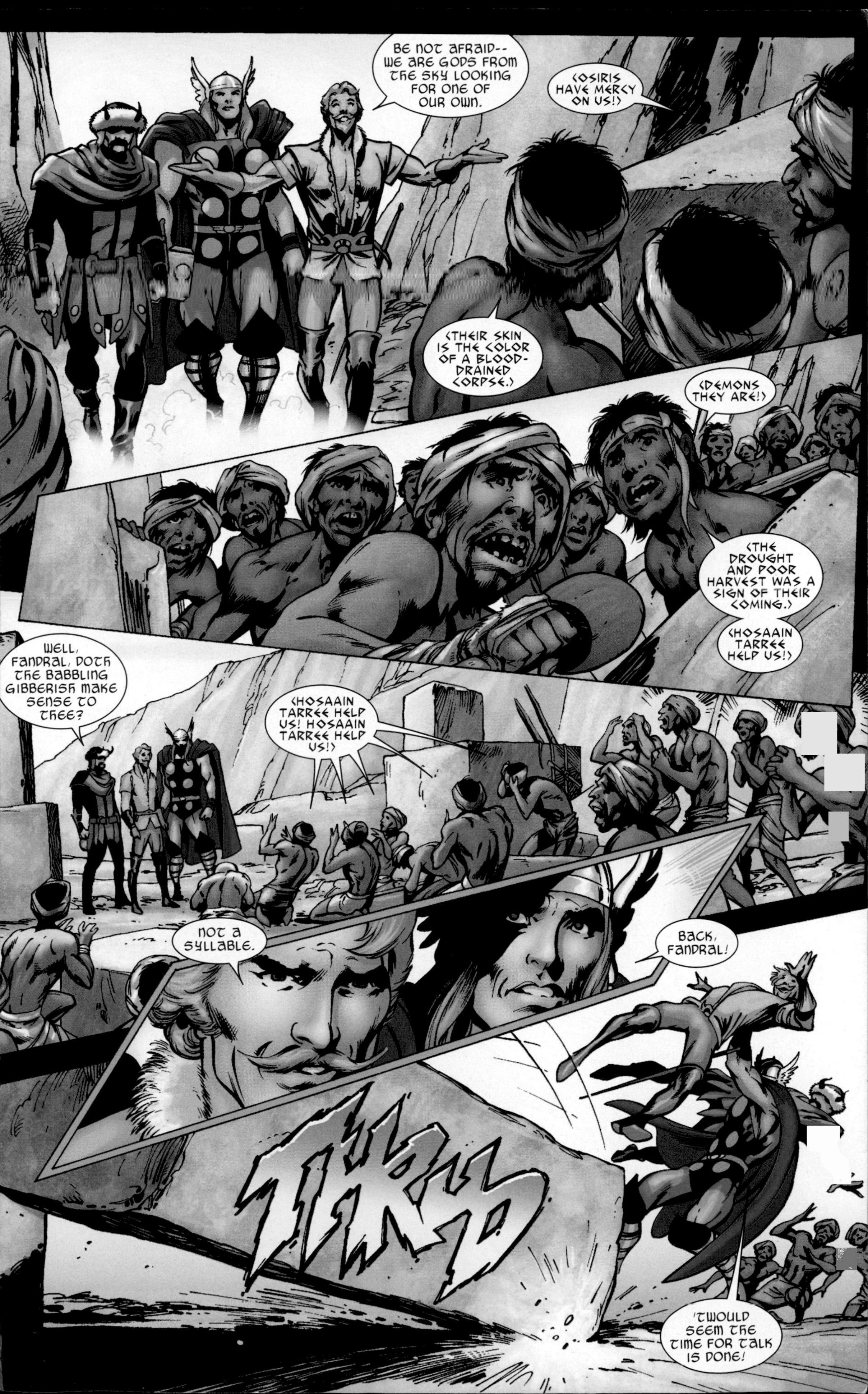
BE NOT AFRAID-- WE ARE GODS FROM THE SKY LOOKING FOR ONE OF OUR OWN.
<OSIRIS HAVE MERCY ON US!>
<THEIR SKIN IS THE COLOR OF A BLOOD-DRAINED CORPSE.>
<DEMONS THEY ARE!>
<THE DROUGHT AND POOR HARVEST WAS A SIGN OF THEIR COMING.>
<HOSAAIN TARREE HELP US!>
WELL, FANDRAL, DOTH THE BABBLING GIBBERISH MAKE SENSE TO THEE?
<HOSAAIN TARREE HELP US! HOSAAIN TARREE HELP US!>
NOT A SYLLABLE.
BACK, FANDRAL!
'TWOULD SEEM THE TIME FOR TALK IS DONE!

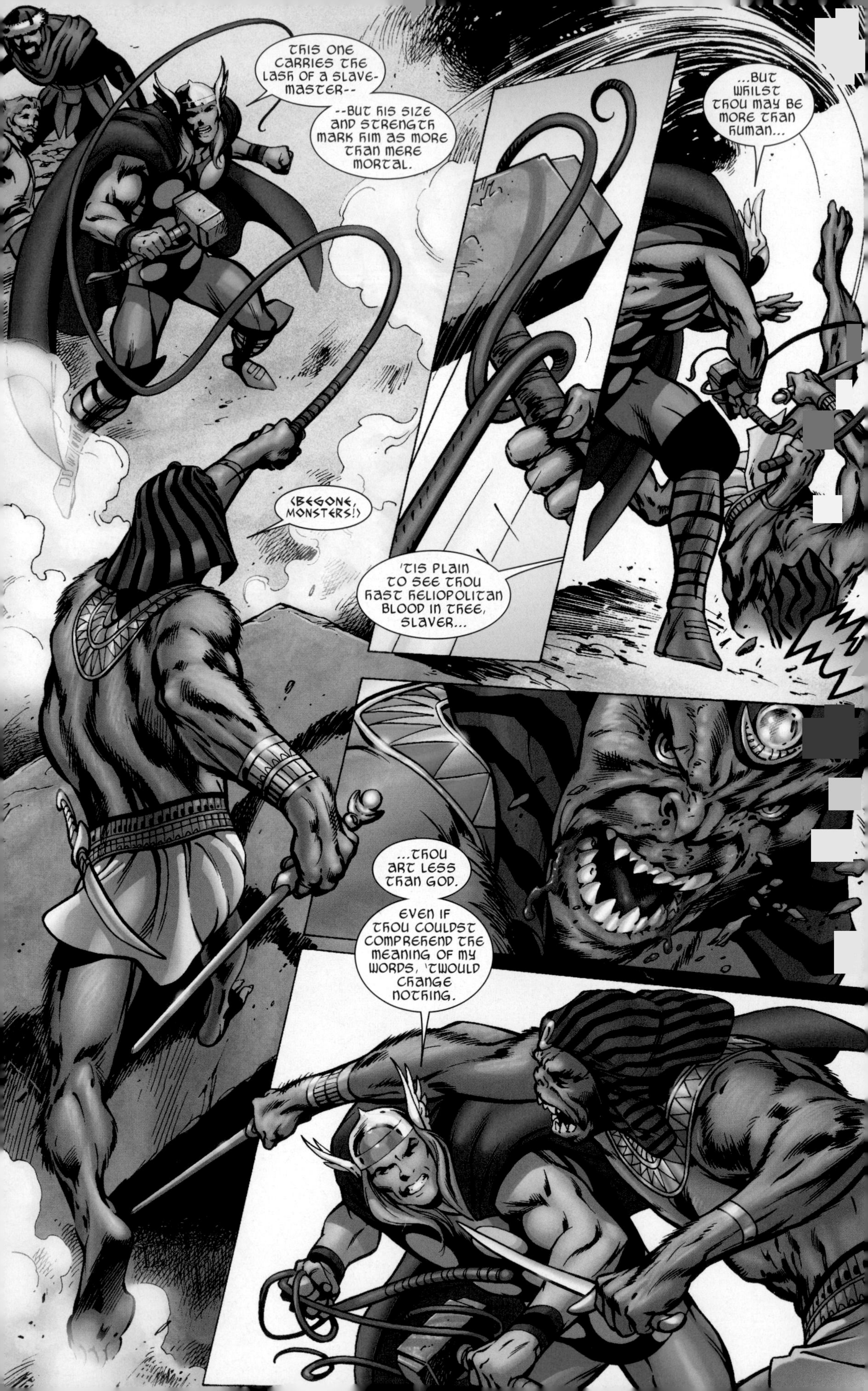
THIS ONE CARRIES THE LASH OF A SLAVE-MASTER--
--BUT HIS SIZE AND STRENGTH MARK HIM AS MORE THAN MERE MORTAL.
<BEGONE, MONSTERS!>
'TIS PLAIN TO SEE THOU HAST HELIOPOLITAN BLOOD IN THEE, SLAVER...
...BUT WHILST THOU MAY BE MORE THAN HUMAN...
...THOU ART LESS THAN GOD.
EVEN IF THOU COULDST COMPREHEND THE MEANING OF MY WORDS, 'TWOULD CHANGE NOTHING.

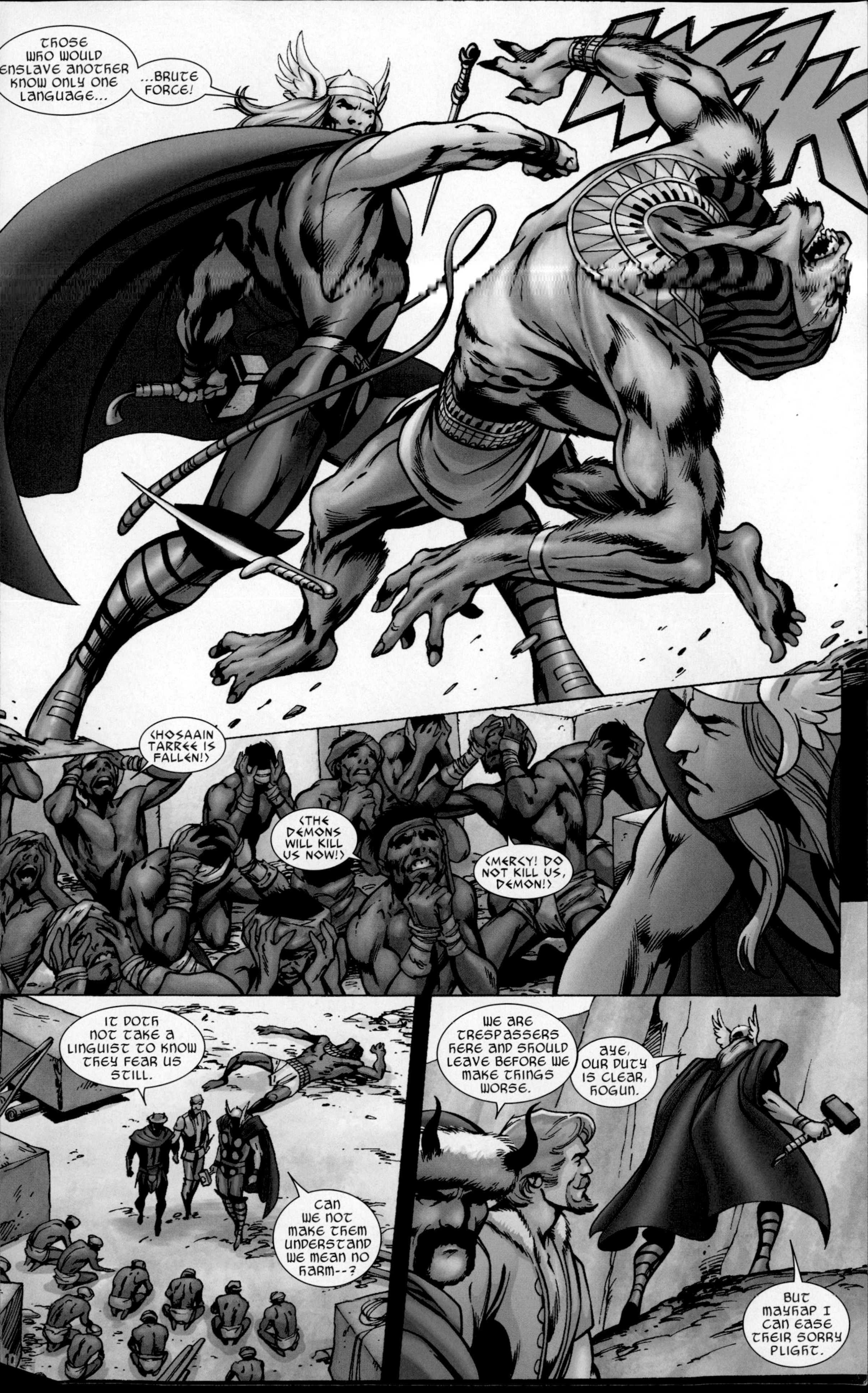
THOSE WHO WOULD ENSLAVE ANOTHER KNOW ONLY ONE LANGUAGE...
...BRUTE FORCE!
<HOSAAIN TARREE IS FALLEN!>
<THE DEMONS WILL KILL US NOW!>
<MERCY! DO NOT KILL US, DEMON!>
IT DOTH NOT TAKE A LINGUIST TO KNOW THEY FEAR US STILL.
CAN WE NOT MAKE THEM UNDERSTAND WE MEAN NO HARM--?
WE ARE TRESPASSERS HERE AND SHOULD LEAVE BEFORE WE MAKE THINGS WORSE.
AYE, OUR DUTY IS CLEAR, HOGUN.
BUT MAYHAP I CAN EASE THEIR SORRY PLIGHT.

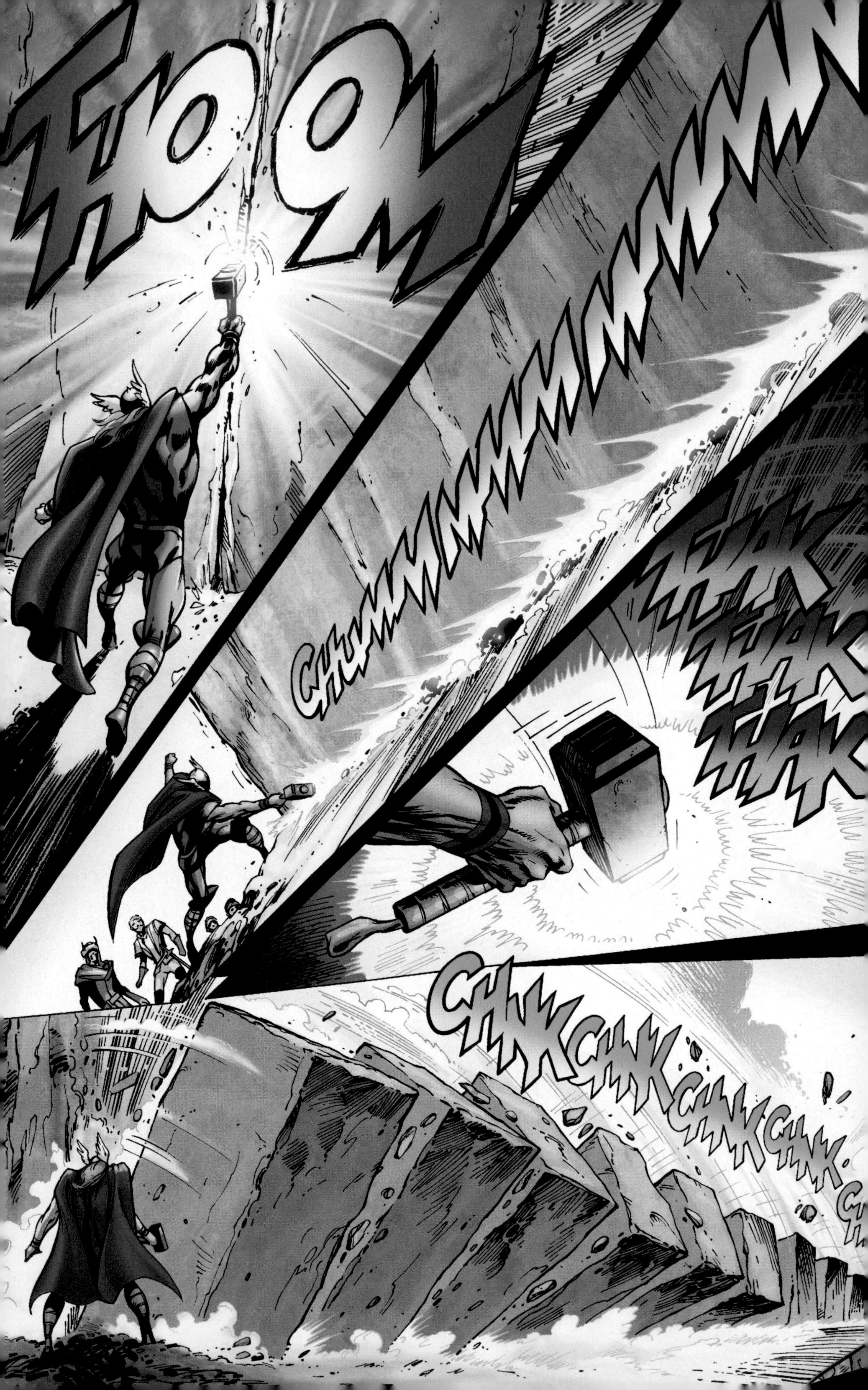

FTOOM
CHUMMMMMMMMMMMN
THAK THAK THAK THAK
CHNK CHNK CHNK CHNK CHNK CH

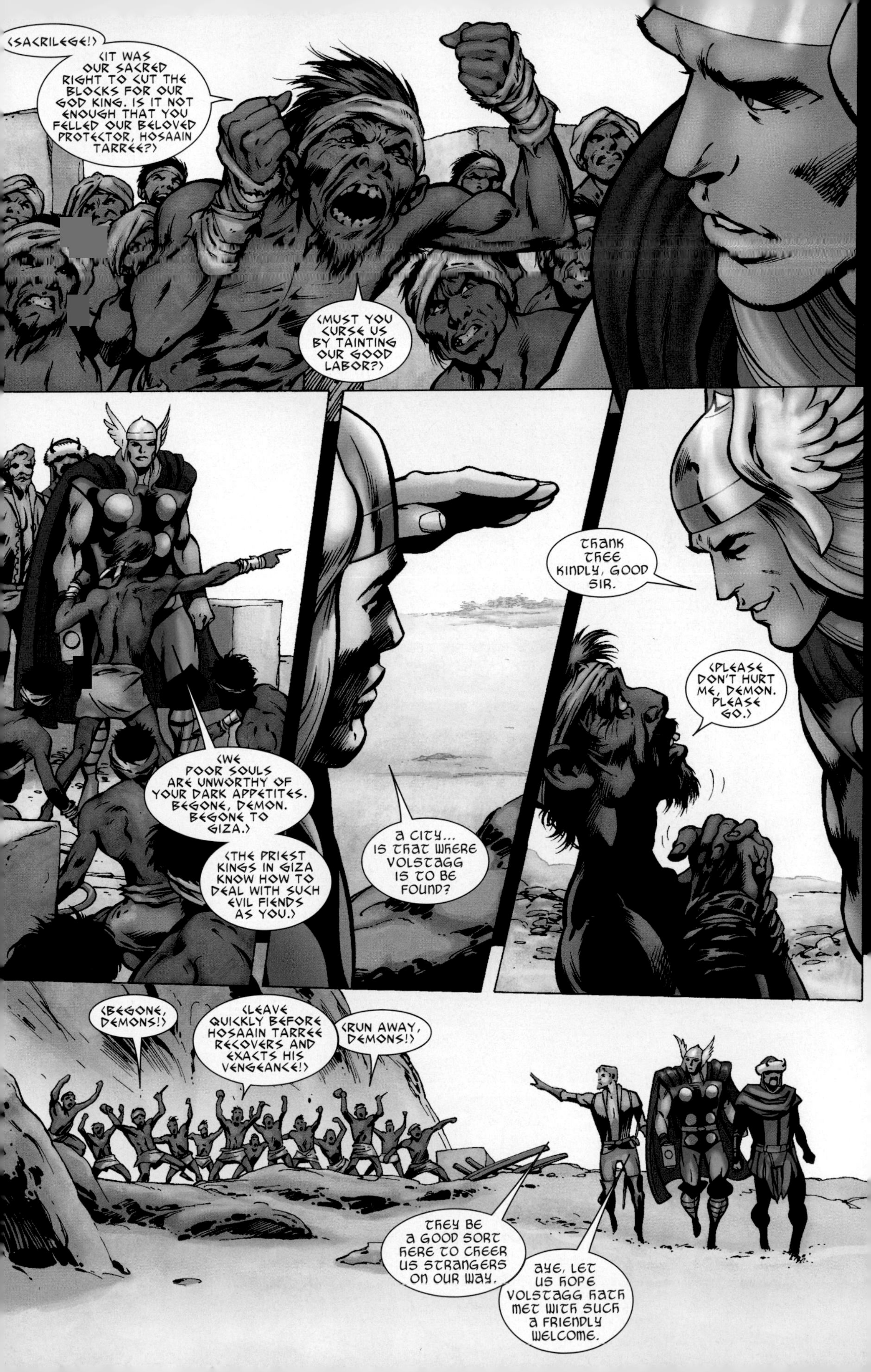

<SACRILEGE!>
<IT WAS OUR SACRED RIGHT TO CUT THE BLOCKS FOR OUR GOD KING. IS IT NOT ENOUGH THAT YOU FELLED OUR BELOVED PROTECTOR, HOSAAIN TARREE?>
<MUST YOU CURSE US BY TAINTING OUR GOOD LABOR?>
<WE POOR SOULS ARE UNWORTHY OF YOUR DARK APPETITES. BEGONE, DEMON. BEGONE TO GIZA.>
<THE PRIEST KINGS IN GIZA KNOW HOW TO DEAL WITH SUCH EVIL FIENDS AS YOU.>
A CITY... IS THAT WHERE VOLSTAGG IS TO BE FOUND?
THANK THEE KINDLY, GOOD SIR.
<PLEASE DON'T HURT ME, DEMON. PLEASE GO.>
<BEGONE, DEMONS!>
<LEAVE QUICKLY BEFORE HOSAAIN TARREE RECOVERS AND EXACTS HIS VENGEANCE!>
<RUN AWAY, DEMONS!>
THEY BE A GOOD SORT HERE TO CHEER US STRANGERS ON OUR WAY.
AYE, LET US HOPE VOLSTAGG HATH MET WITH SUCH A FRIENDLY WELCOME.

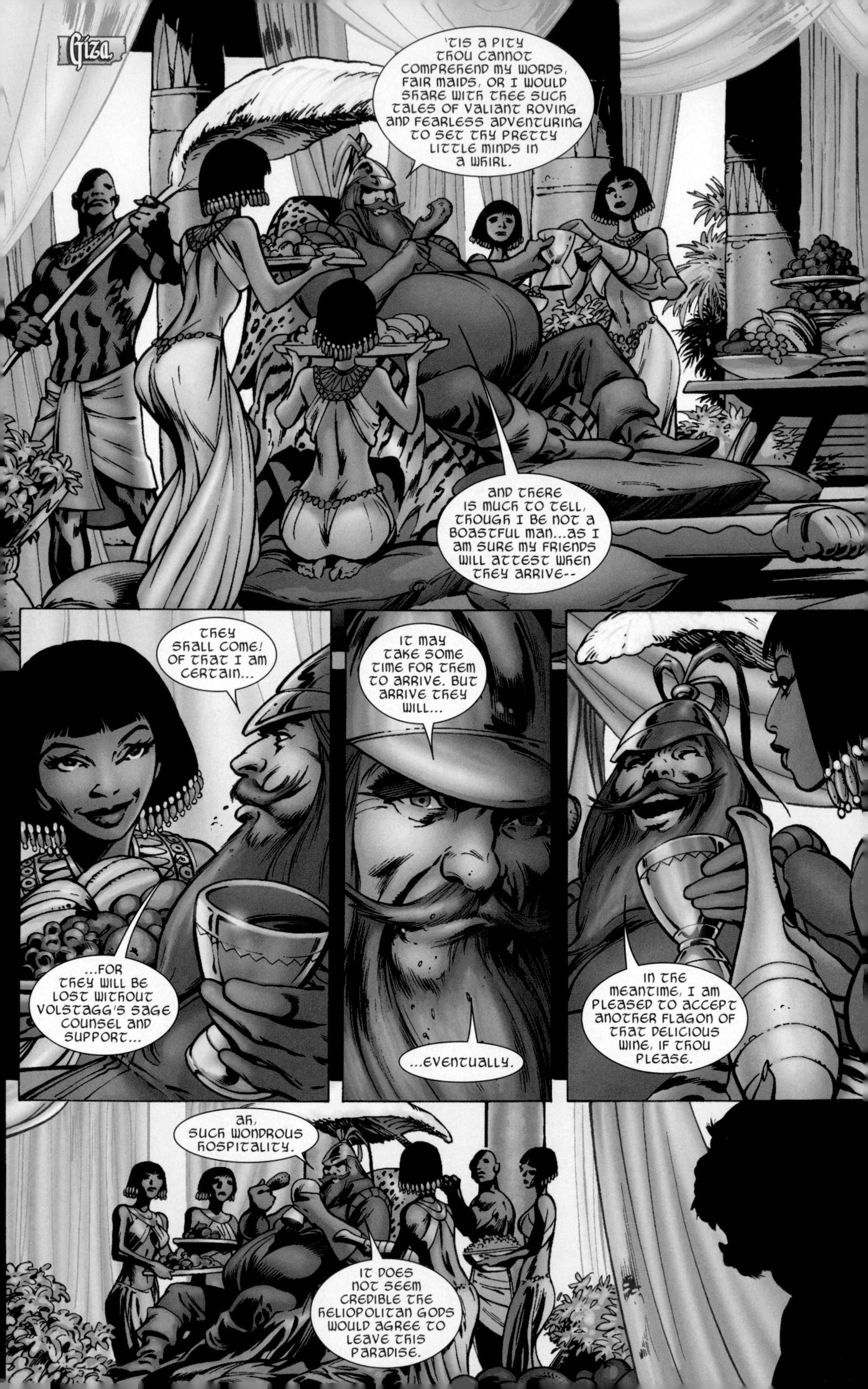
Giza
'TIS A PITY THOU CANNOT COMPREHEND MY WORDS, FAIR MAIDS, OR I WOULD SHARE WITH THEE SUCH TALES OF VALIANT ROVING AND FEARLESS ADVENTURING TO SET THY PRETTY LITTLE MINDS IN A WHIRL.
AND THERE IS MUCH TO TELL, THOUGH I BE NOT A BOASTFUL MAN...AS I AM SURE MY FRIENDS WILL ATTEST WHEN THEY ARRIVE--
THEY SHALL COME! OF THAT I AM CERTAIN...
...FOR THEY WILL BE LOST WITHOUT VOLSTAGG'S SAGE COUNSEL AND SUPPORT...
IT MAY TAKE SOME TIME FOR THEM TO ARRIVE. BUT ARRIVE THEY WILL...
...EVENTUALLY.
IN THE MEANTIME, I AM PLEASED TO ACCEPT ANOTHER FLAGON OF THAT DELICIOUS WINE, IF THOU PLEASE.
AH, SUCH WONDROUS HOSPITALITY.
IT DOES NOT SEEM CREDIBLE THE HELIOPOLITAN GODS WOULD AGREE TO LEAVE THIS PARADISE.

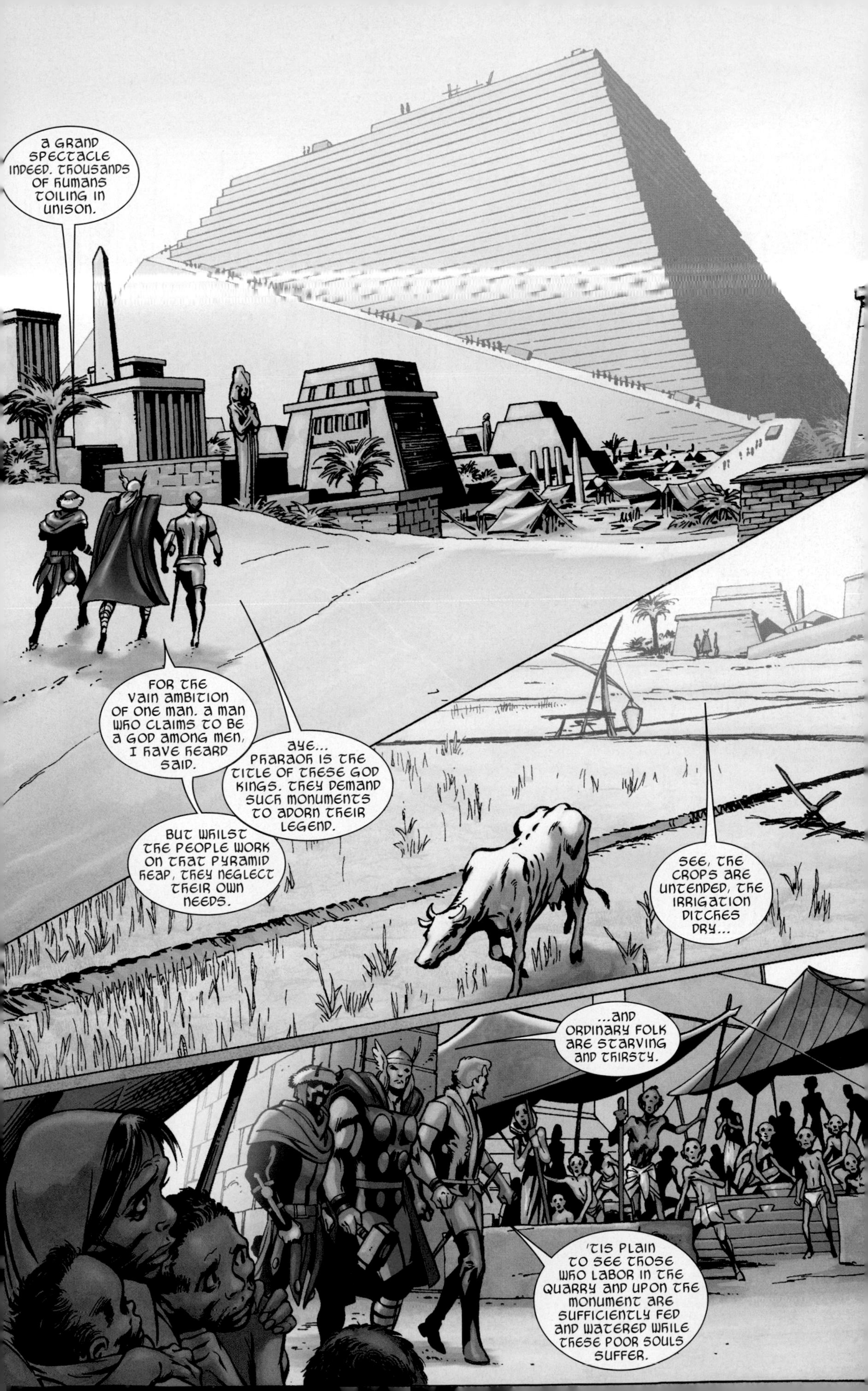
A GRAND SPECTACLE INDEED. THOUSANDS OF HUMANS TOILING IN UNISON.
FOR THE VAIN AMBITION OF ONE MAN. A MAN WHO CLAIMS TO BE A GOD AMONG MEN, I HAVE HEARD SAID.
AYE... PHARAOH IS THE TITLE OF THESE GOD KINGS. THEY DEMAND SUCH MONUMENTS TO ADORN THEIR LEGEND.
BUT WHILST THE PEOPLE WORK ON THAT PYRAMID HEAP, THEY NEGLECT THEIR OWN NEEDS.
SEE, THE CROPS ARE UNTENDED, THE IRRIGATION DITCHES DRY...
...AND ORDINARY FOLK ARE STARVING AND THIRSTY.
'TIS PLAIN TO SEE THOSE WHO LABOR IN THE QUARRY AND UPON THE MONUMENT ARE SUFFICIENTLY FED AND WATERED WHILE THESE POOR SOULS SUFFER.

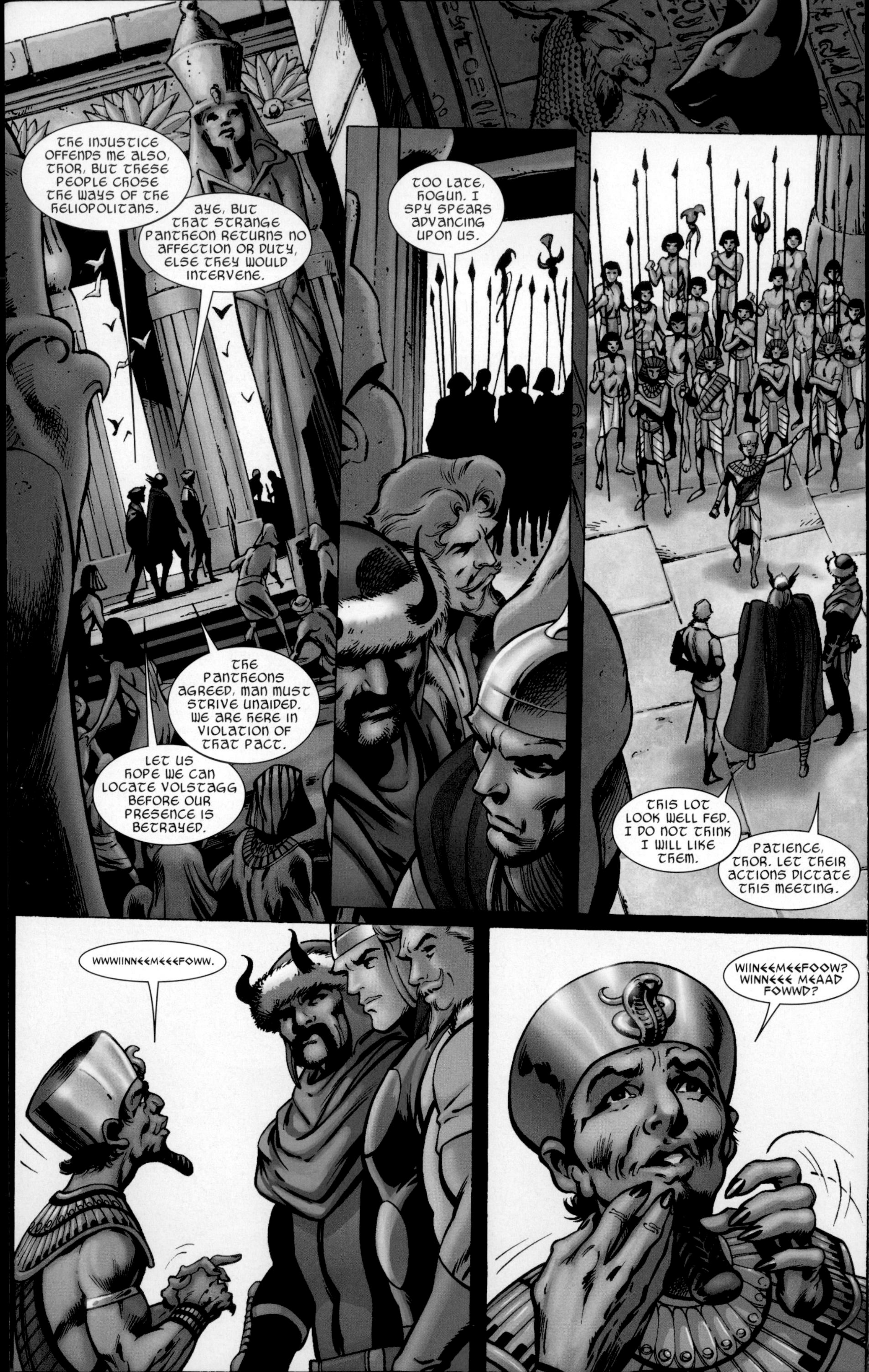
THE INJUSTICE OFFENDS ME ALSO, THOR, BUT THESE PEOPLE CHOSE THE WAYS OF THE HELIOPOLITANS.
AYE, BUT THAT STRANGE PANTHEON RETURNS NO AFFECTION OR DUTY, ELSE THEY WOULD INTERVENE.
THE PANTHEONS AGREED, MAN MUST STRIVE UNAIDED. WE ARE HERE IN VIOLATION OF THAT PACT.
LET US HOPE WE CAN LOCATE VOLSTAGG BEFORE OUR PRESENCE IS BETRAYED.
TOO LATE, HOGUN. I SPY SPEARS ADVANCING UPON US.
THIS LOT LOOK WELL FED. I DO NOT THINK I WILL LIKE THEM.
PATIENCE, THOR. LET THEIR ACTIONS DICTATE THIS MEETING.
WWWIINNEEMEEEFOWW.
WIINEEMEEFOOW? WINNEEE MEAAD FOWWD?

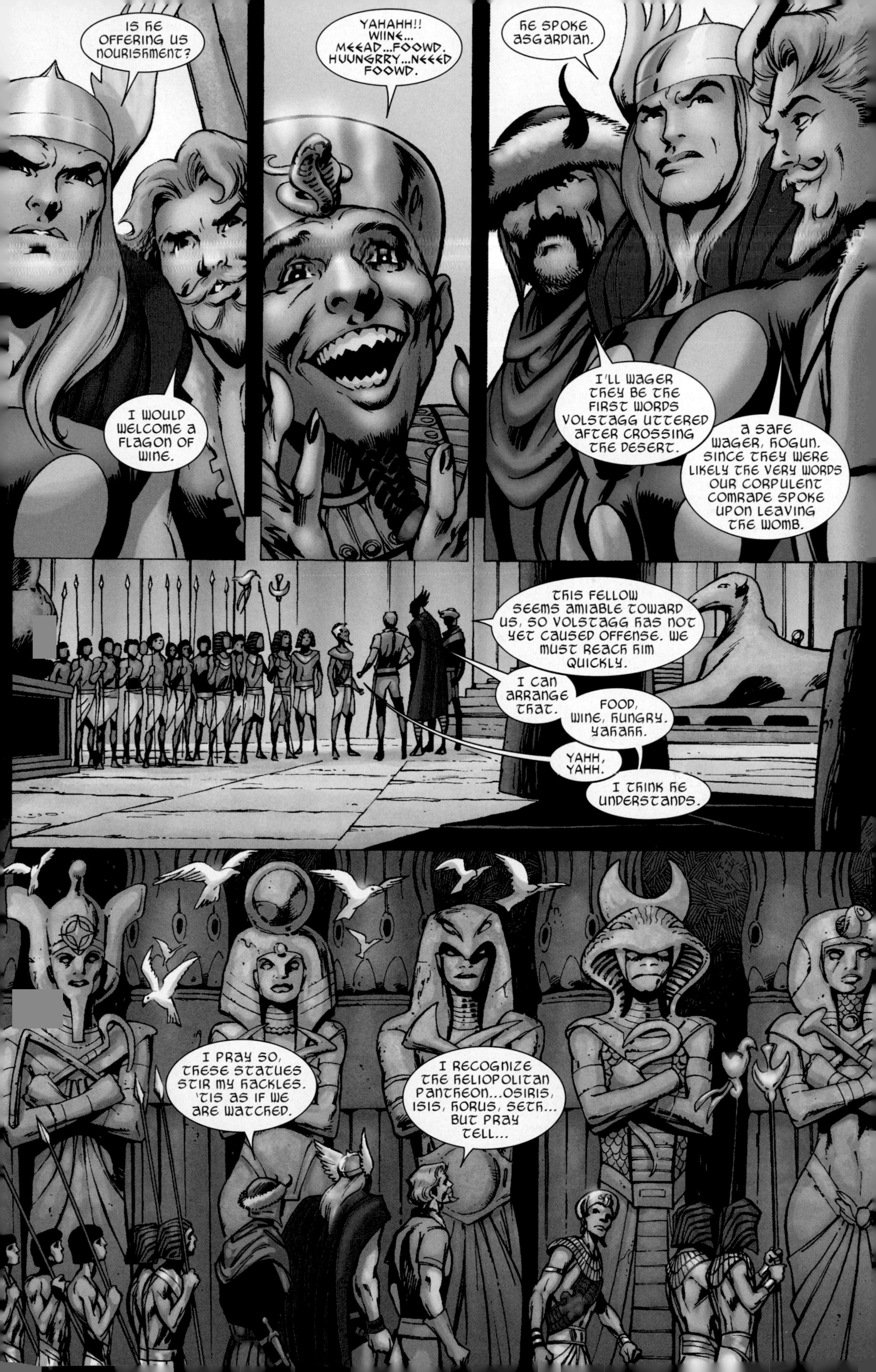
IS HE OFFERING US NOURISHMENT?
I WOULD WELCOME A FLAGON OF WINE.
YAHAHH!! WIINE... MEEAD...FOOWD. HUUNGRRY...NEEED FOOWD.
HE SPOKE ASGARDIAN.
I'LL WAGER THEY BE THE FIRST WORDS VOLSTAGG UTTERED AFTER CROSSING THE DESERT.
A SAFE WAGER, HOGUN. SINCE THEY WERE LIKELY THE VERY WORDS OUR CORPULENT COMRADE SPOKE UPON LEAVING THE WOMB.
THIS FELLOW SEEMS AMIABLE TOWARD US, SO VOLSTAGG HAS NOT YET CAUSED OFFENSE. WE MUST REACH HIM QUICKLY.
I CAN ARRANGE THAT.
FOOD, WINE, HUNGRY. YAHAHH.
YAHH, YAHH.
I THINK HE UNDERSTANDS.
I PRAY SO, THESE STATUES STIR MY HACKLES. 'TIS AS IF WE ARE WATCHED.
I RECOGNIZE THE HELIOPOLITAN PANTHEON...OSIRIS, ISIS, HORUS, SETH... BUT PRAY TELL...

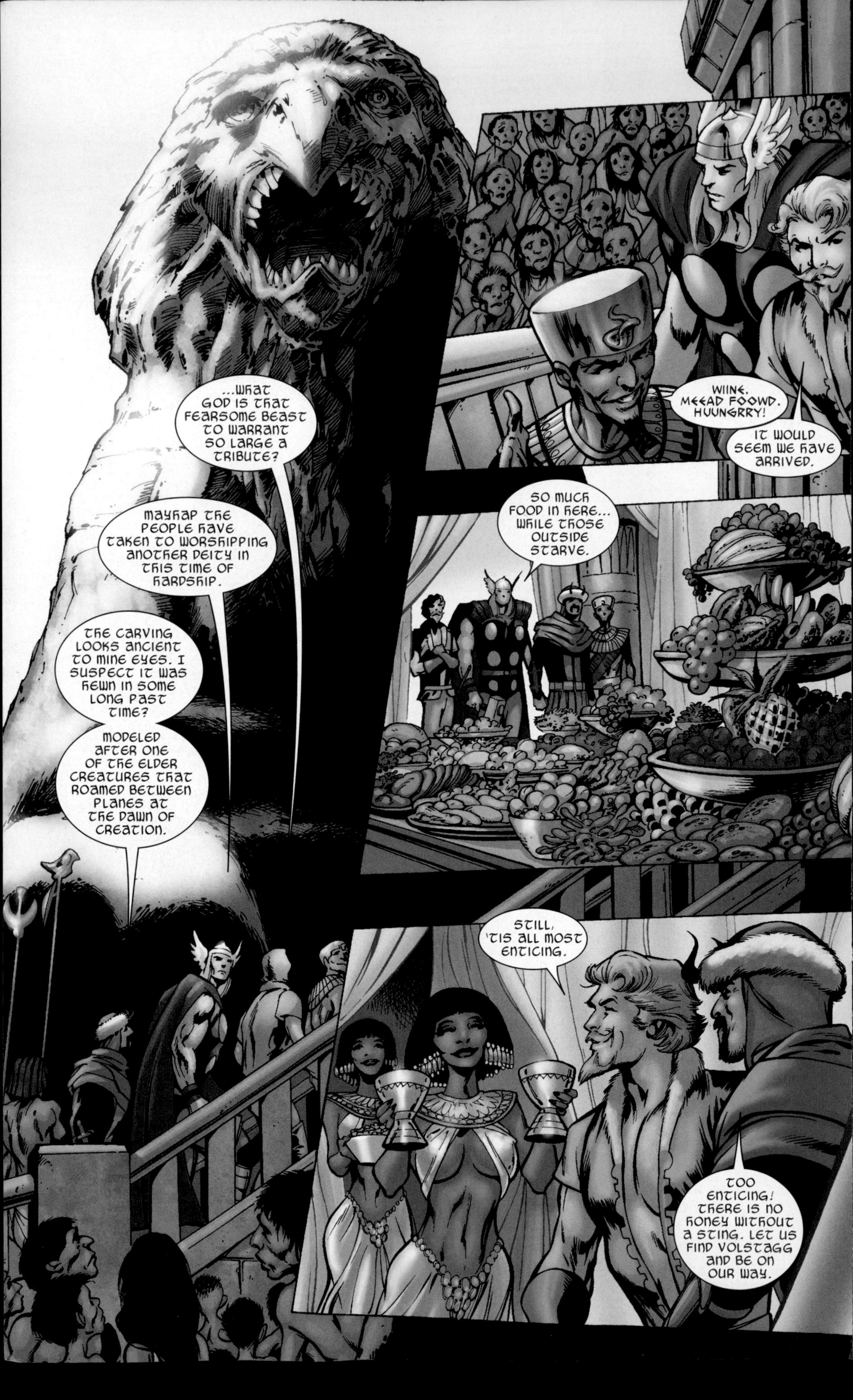

...WHAT GOD IS THAT FEARSOME BEAST TO WARRANT SO LARGE A TRIBUTE?
MAYHAP THE PEOPLE HAVE TAKEN TO WORSHIPPING ANOTHER DEITY IN THIS TIME OF HARDSHIP.
THE CARVING LOOKS ANCIENT TO MINE EYES. I SUSPECT IT WAS HEWN IN SOME LONG PAST TIME?
MODELED AFTER ONE OF THE ELDER CREATURES THAT ROAMED BETWEEN PLANES AT THE DAWN OF CREATION.
WIINE. MEEAD FOOWD. HUUNGRRY!
IT WOULD SEEM WE HAVE ARRIVED.
SO MUCH FOOD IN HERE... WHILE THOSE OUTSIDE STARVE.
STILL, 'TIS ALL MOST ENTICING.
TOO ENTICING! THERE IS NO HONEY WITHOUT A STING. LET US FIND VOLSTAGG AND BE ON OUR WAY.

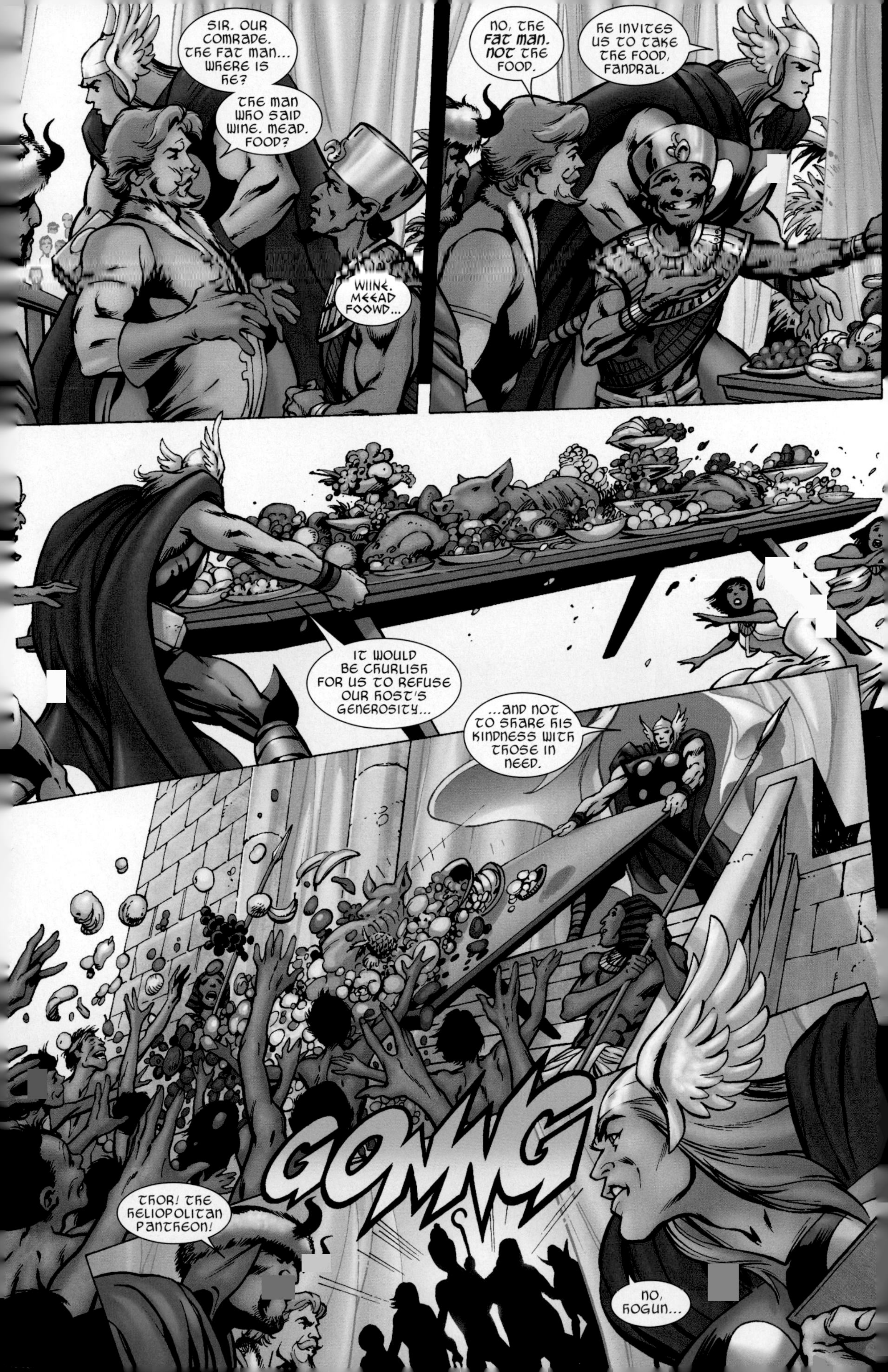
SIR. OUR COMRADE. THE FAT MAN... WHERE IS HE?
THE MAN WHO SAID WINE. MEAD. FOOD?
WIINE. MEEAD FOOWD...
NO, THE FAT MAN. NOT THE FOOD.
HE INVITES US TO TAKE THE FOOD, FANDRAL.
IT WOULD BE CHURLISH FOR US TO REFUSE OUR HOST'S GENEROSITY...
...AND NOT TO SHARE HIS KINDNESS WITH THOSE IN NEED.
GONNG
THOR! THE HELIOPOLITAN PANTHEON!
NO, HOGUN...

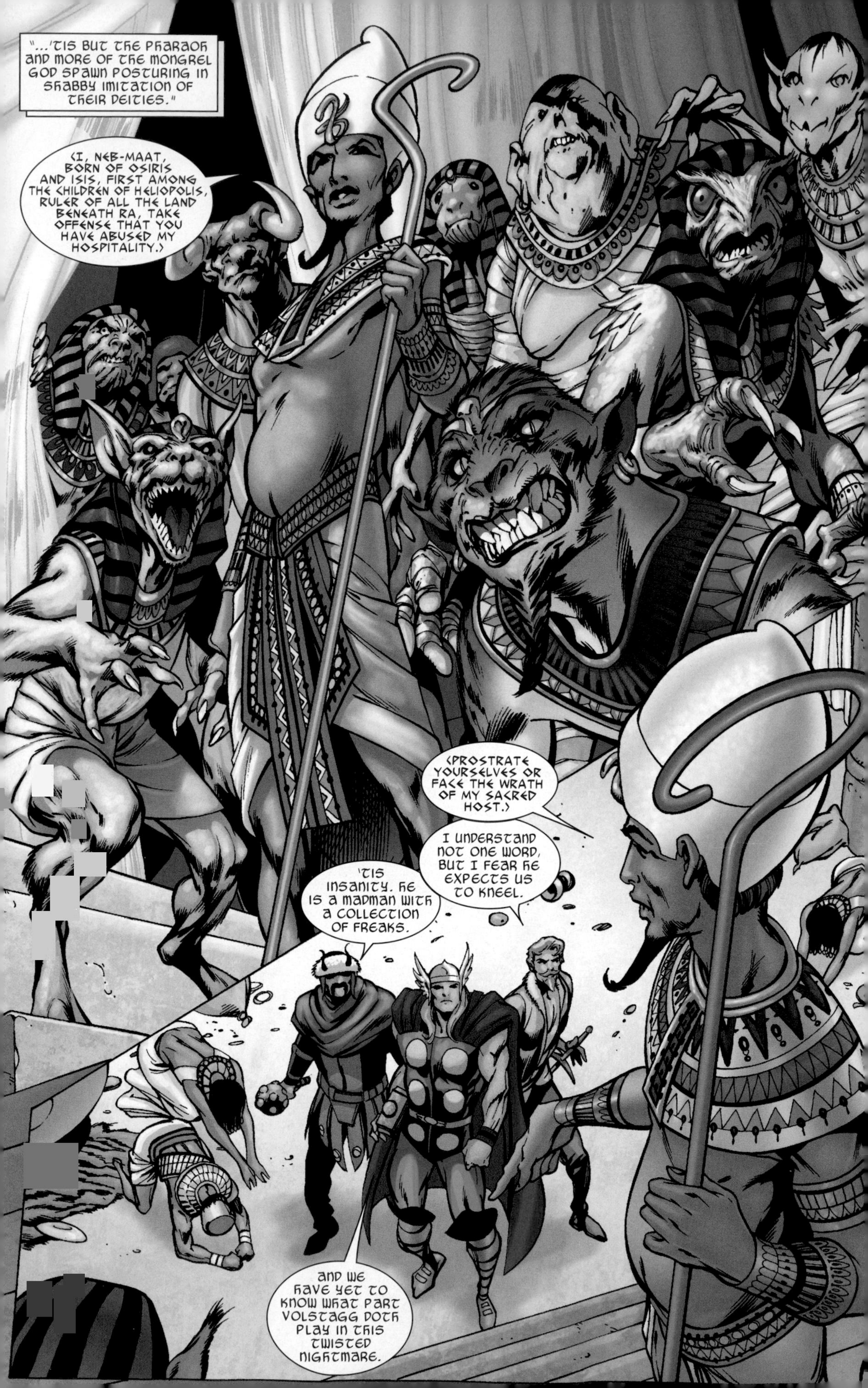
"...'TIS BUT THE PHARAOH AND MORE OF THE MONGREL GOD SPAWN POSTURING IN SHABBY IMITATION OF THEIR DEITIES."
‹I, NEB-MAAT, BORN OF OSIRIS AND ISIS, FIRST AMONG THE CHILDREN OF HELIOPOLIS, RULER OF ALL THE LAND BENEATH RA, TAKE OFFENSE THAT YOU HAVE ABUSED MY HOSPITALITY.›
‹PROSTRATE YOURSELVES OR FACE THE WRATH OF MY SACRED HOST.›
I UNDERSTAND NOT ONE WORD, BUT I FEAR HE EXPECTS US TO KNEEL.
'TIS INSANITY. HE IS A MADMAN WITH A COLLECTION OF FREAKS.
AND WE HAVE YET TO KNOW WHAT PART VOLSTAGG DOTH PLAY IN THIS TWISTED NIGHTMARE.

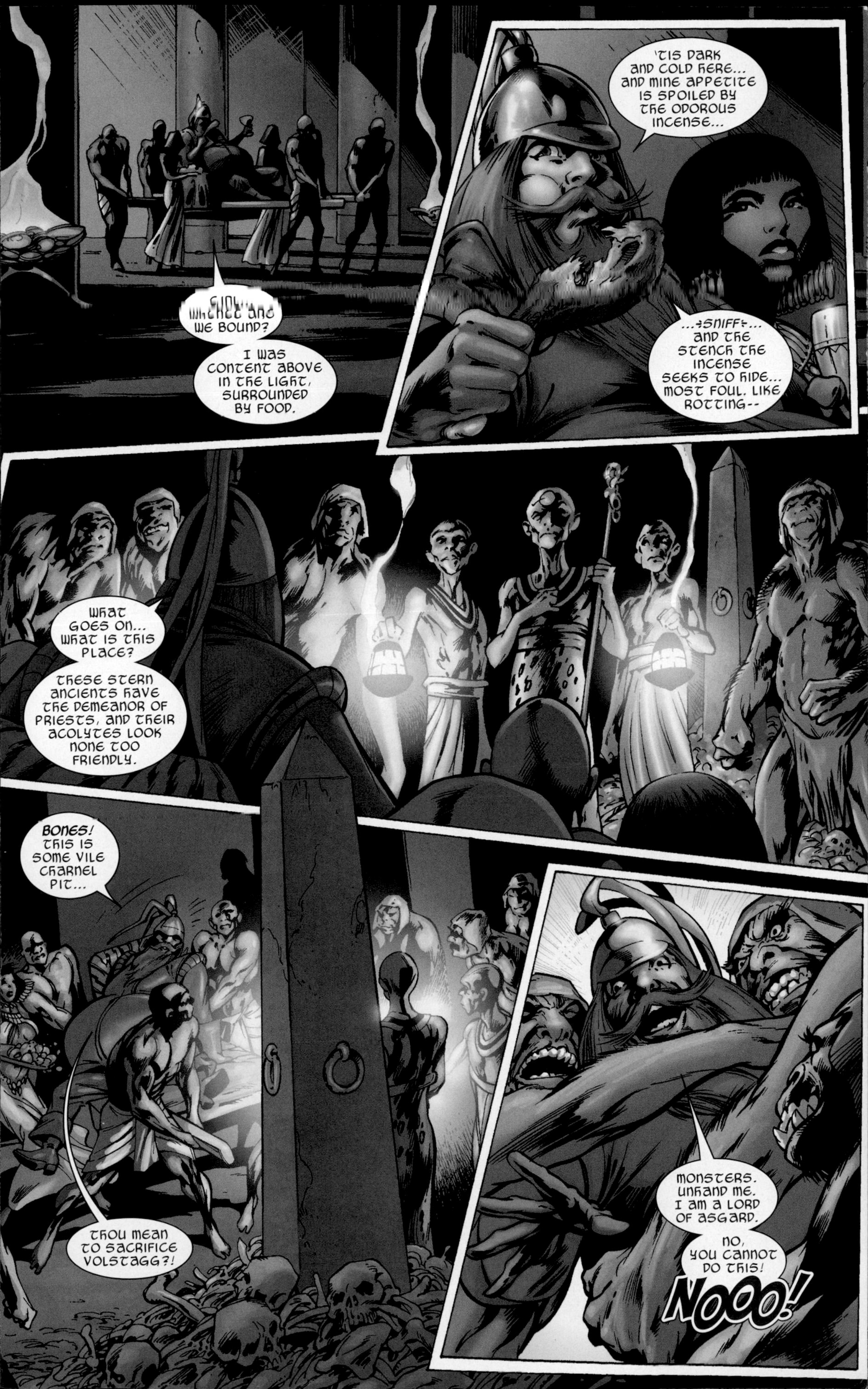

WE BOUND?
I WAS CONTENT ABOVE IN THE LIGHT, SURROUNDED BY FOOD.
'TIS DARK AND COLD HERE... AND MINE APPETITE IS SPOILED BY THE ODOROUS INCENSE...
...SNIFF... AND THE STENCH THE INCENSE SEEKS TO HIDE... MOST FOUL. LIKE ROTTING--
WHAT GOES ON... WHAT IS THIS PLACE?
THESE STERN ANCIENTS HAVE THE DEMEANOR OF PRIESTS, AND THEIR ACOLYTES LOOK NONE TOO FRIENDLY.
BONES! THIS IS SOME VILE CHARNEL PIT...
THOU MEAN TO SACRIFICE VOLSTAGG?!
MONSTERS. UNHAND ME. I AM A LORD OF ASGARD.
NO, YOU CANNOT DO THIS!
NOOO!

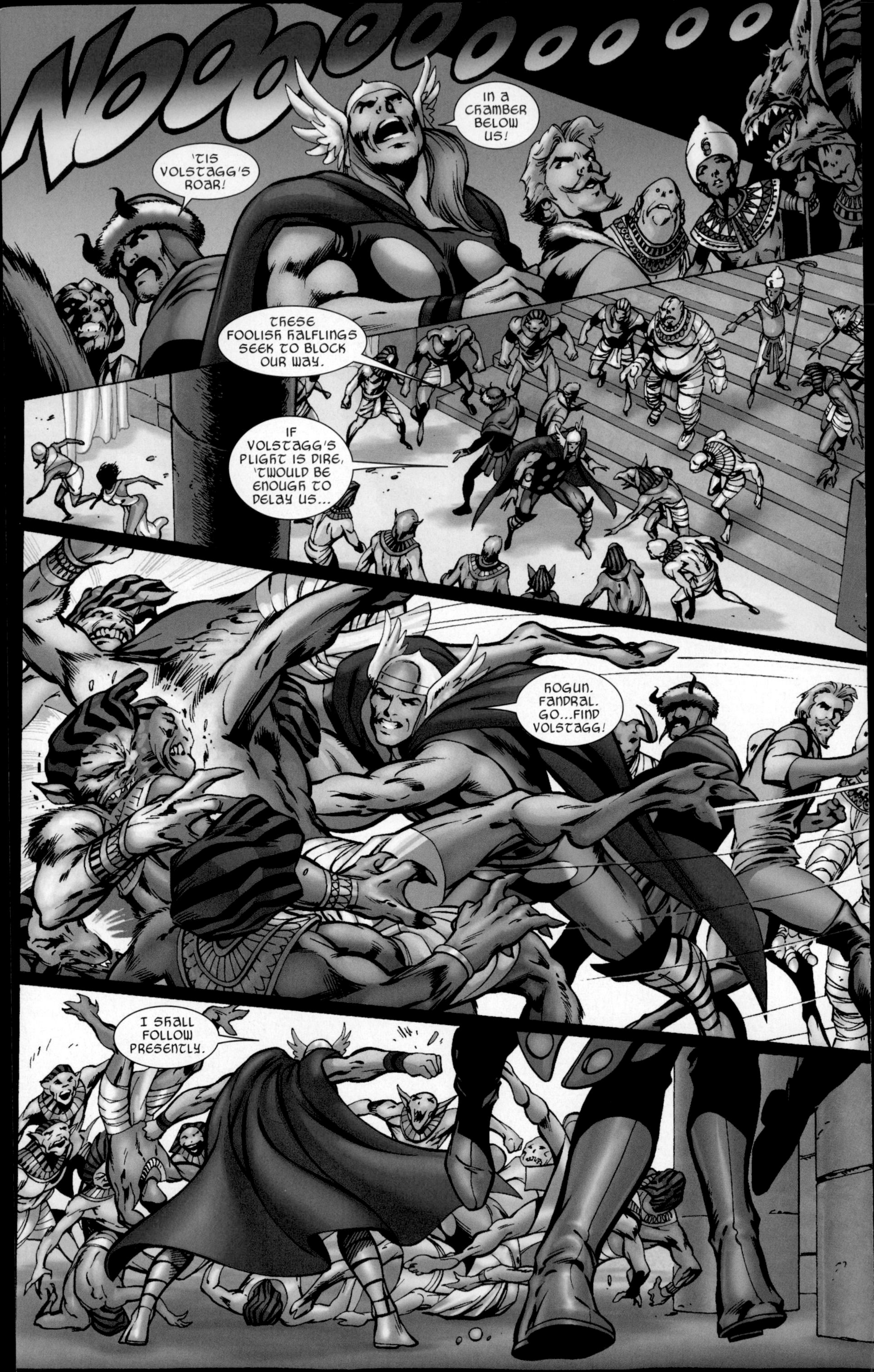
NOOOOOOOOOOOO
'TIS VOLSTAGG'S ROAR!
IN A CHAMBER BELOW US!
THESE FOOLISH HALFLINGS SEEK TO BLOCK OUR WAY.
IF VOLSTAGG'S PLIGHT IS DIRE, 'TWOULD BE ENOUGH TO DELAY US...
HOGUN. FANDRAL. GO...FIND VOLSTAGG!
I SHALL FOLLOW PRESENTLY.

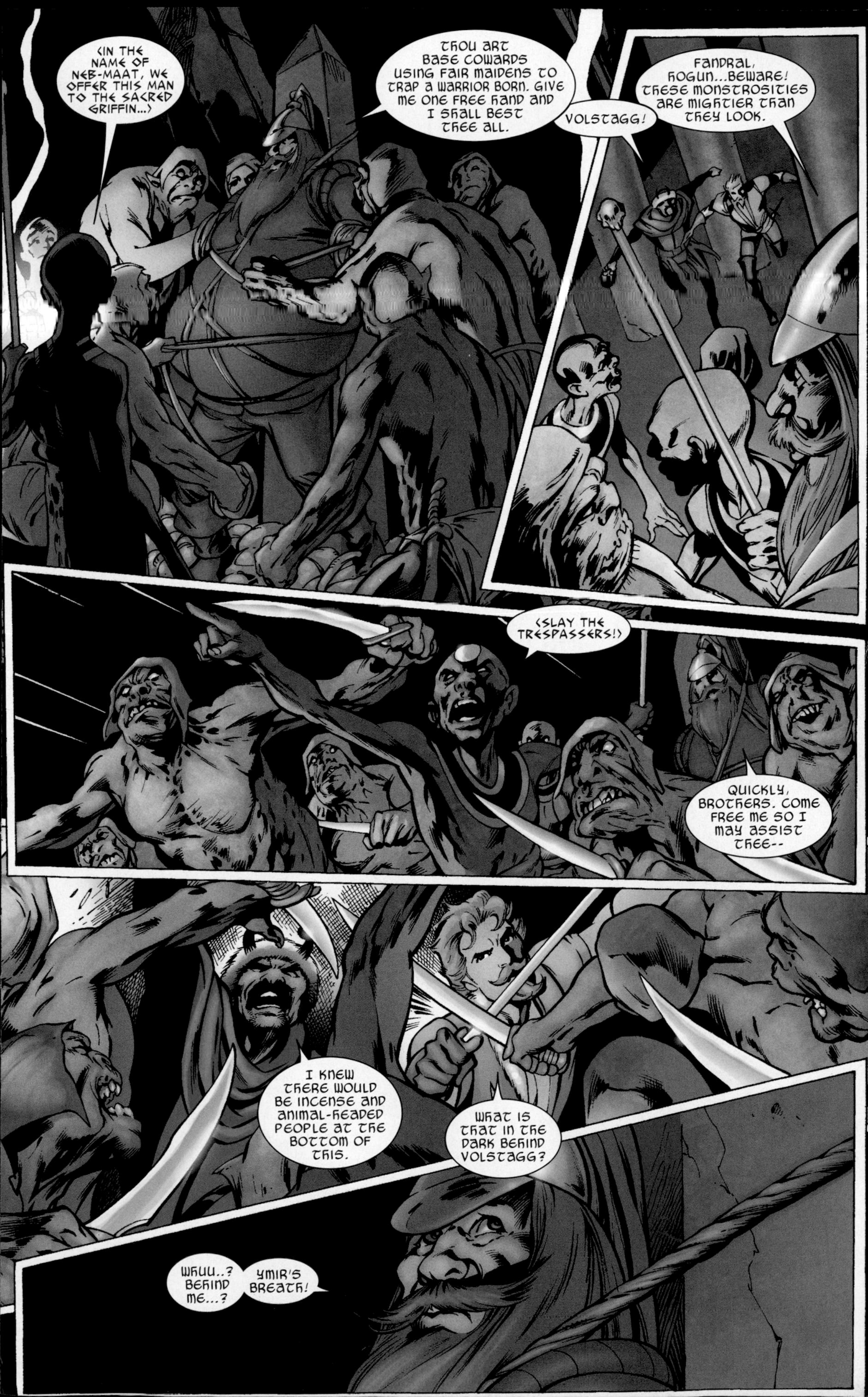
<IN THE NAME OF NEB-MAAT, WE OFFER THIS MAN TO THE SACRED GRIFFIN...>
THOU ART BASE COWARDS USING FAIR MAIDENS TO TRAP A WARRIOR BORN. GIVE ME ONE FREE HAND AND I SHALL BEST THEE ALL.
VOLSTAGG!
FANDRAL, HOGUN...BEWARE! THESE MONSTROSITIES ARE MIGHTIER THAN THEY LOOK.
<SLAY THE TRESPASSERS!>
QUICKLY, BROTHERS. COME FREE ME SO I MAY ASSIST THEE--
I KNEW THERE WOULD BE INCENSE AND ANIMAL-HEADED PEOPLE AT THE BOTTOM OF THIS.
WHAT IS THAT IN THE DARK BEHIND VOLSTAGG?
WHUU..? BEHIND ME...?
YMIR'S BREATH!

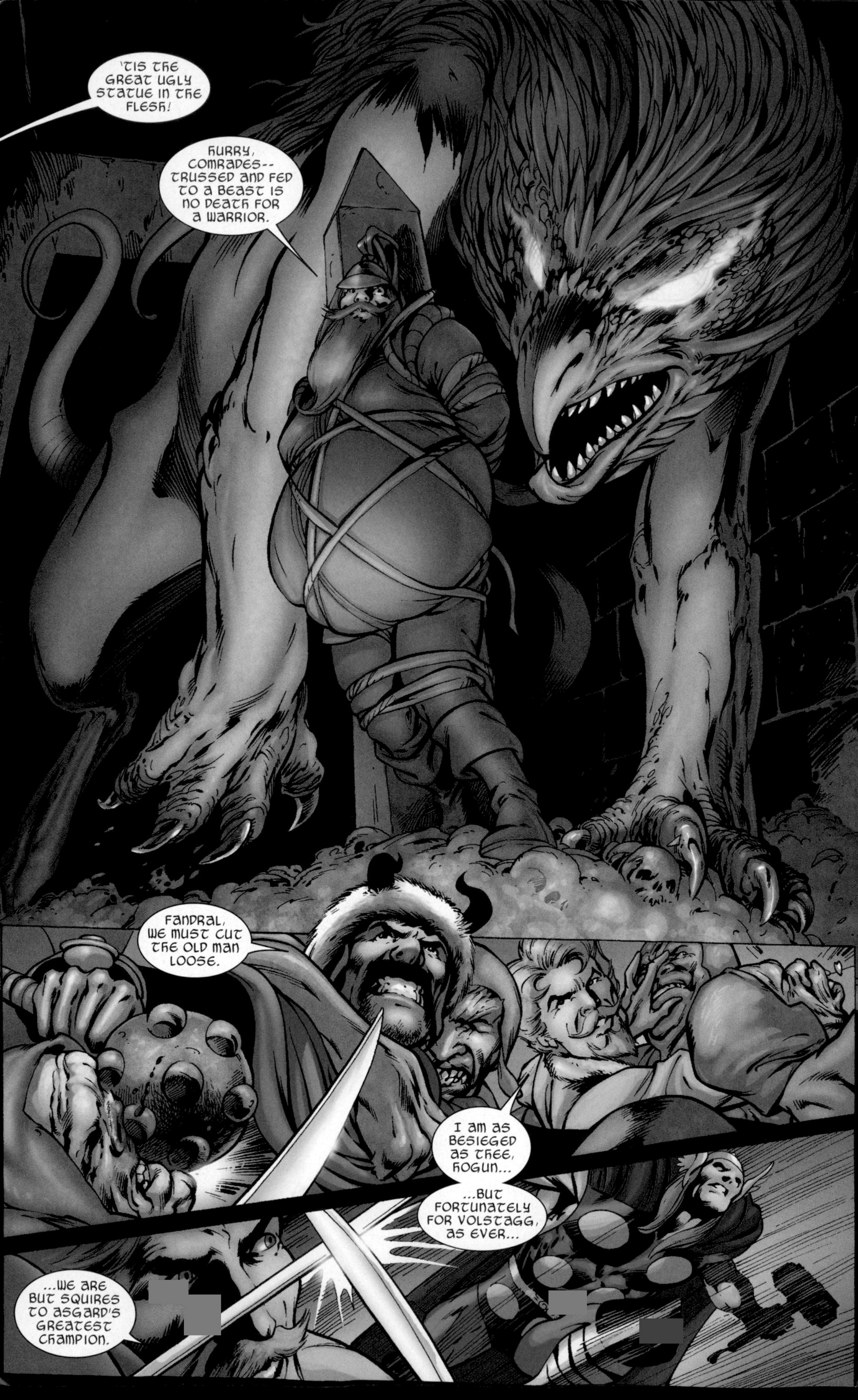
'TIS THE GREAT UGLY STATUE IN THE FLESH!
HURRY, COMRADES-- TRUSSED AND FED TO A BEAST IS NO DEATH FOR A WARRIOR.
FANDRAL, WE MUST CUT THE OLD MAN LOOSE.
I AM AS BESIEGED AS THEE, HOGUN...
...BUT FORTUNATELY FOR VOLSTAGG, AS EVER...
...WE ARE BUT SQUIRES TO ASGARD'S GREATEST CHAMPION.

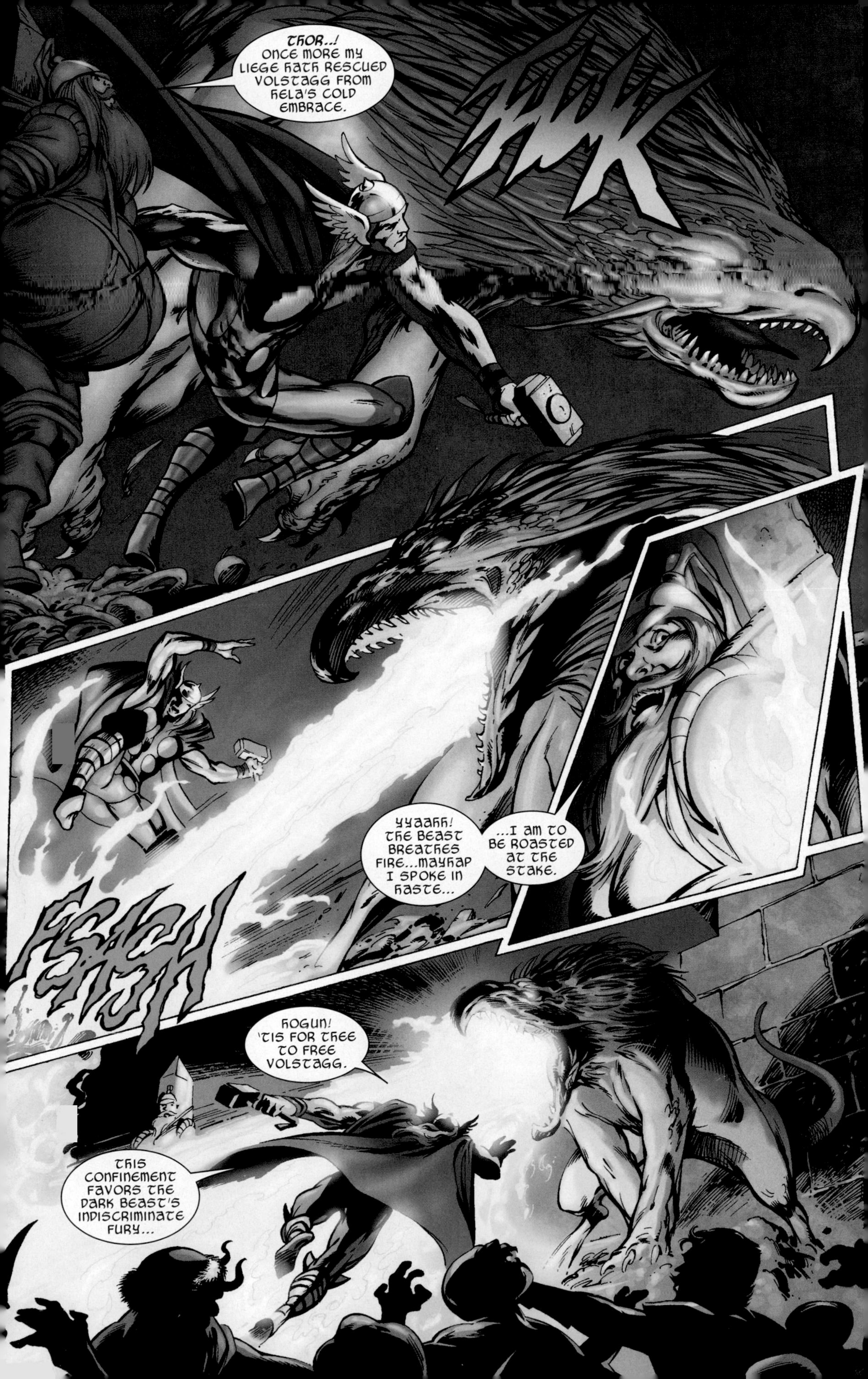
THOR..! ONCE MORE MY LIEGE HATH RESCUED VOLSTAGG FROM HELA'S COLD EMBRACE.
YYAAHH! THE BEAST BREATHES FIRE...MAYHAP I SPOKE IN HASTE...
...I AM TO BE ROASTED AT THE STAKE.
HOGUN! 'TIS FOR THEE TO FREE VOLSTAGG.
THIS CONFINEMENT FAVORS THE DARK BEAST'S INDISCRIMINATE FURY...

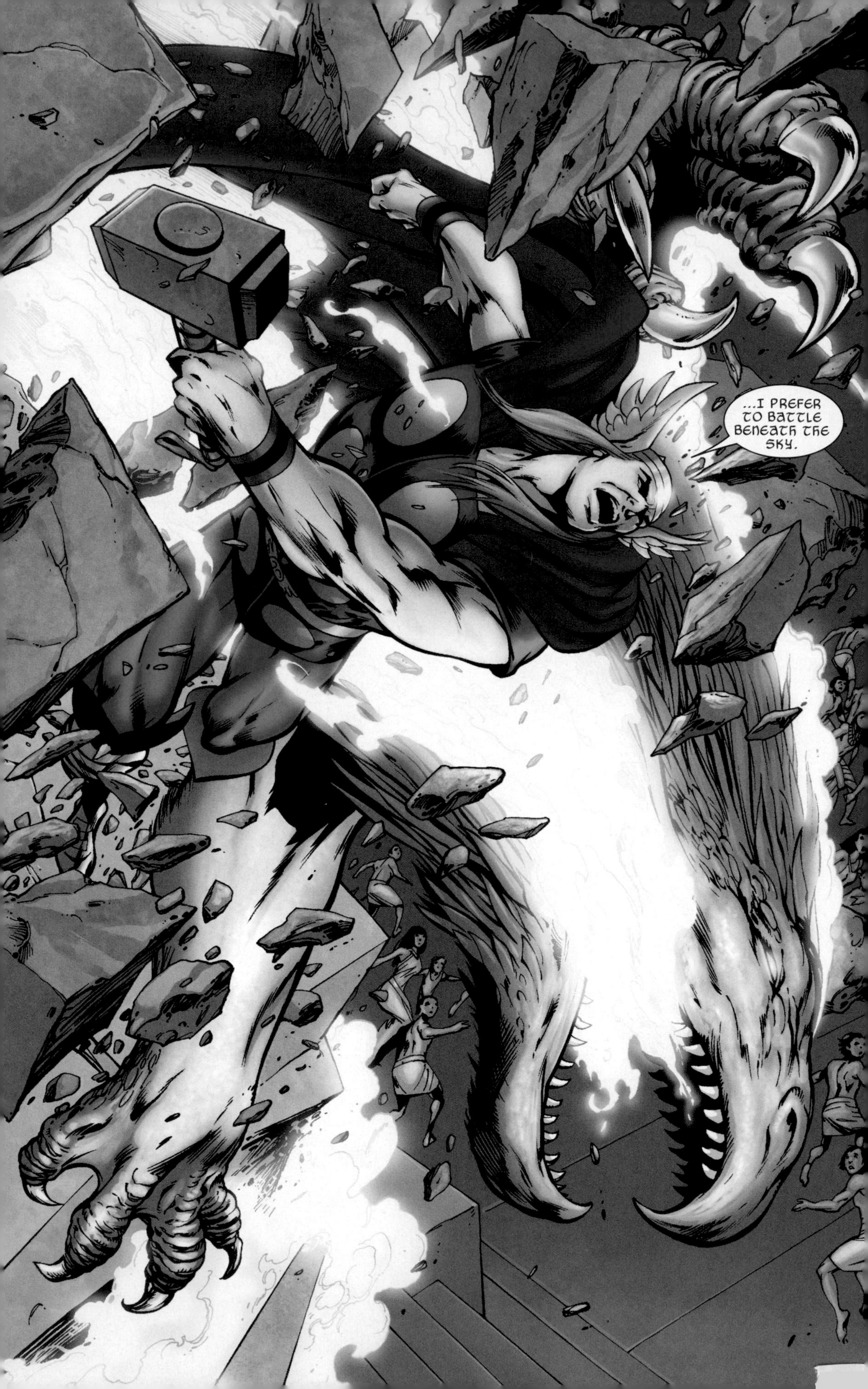
...I PREFER TO BATTLE BENEATH THE SKY.

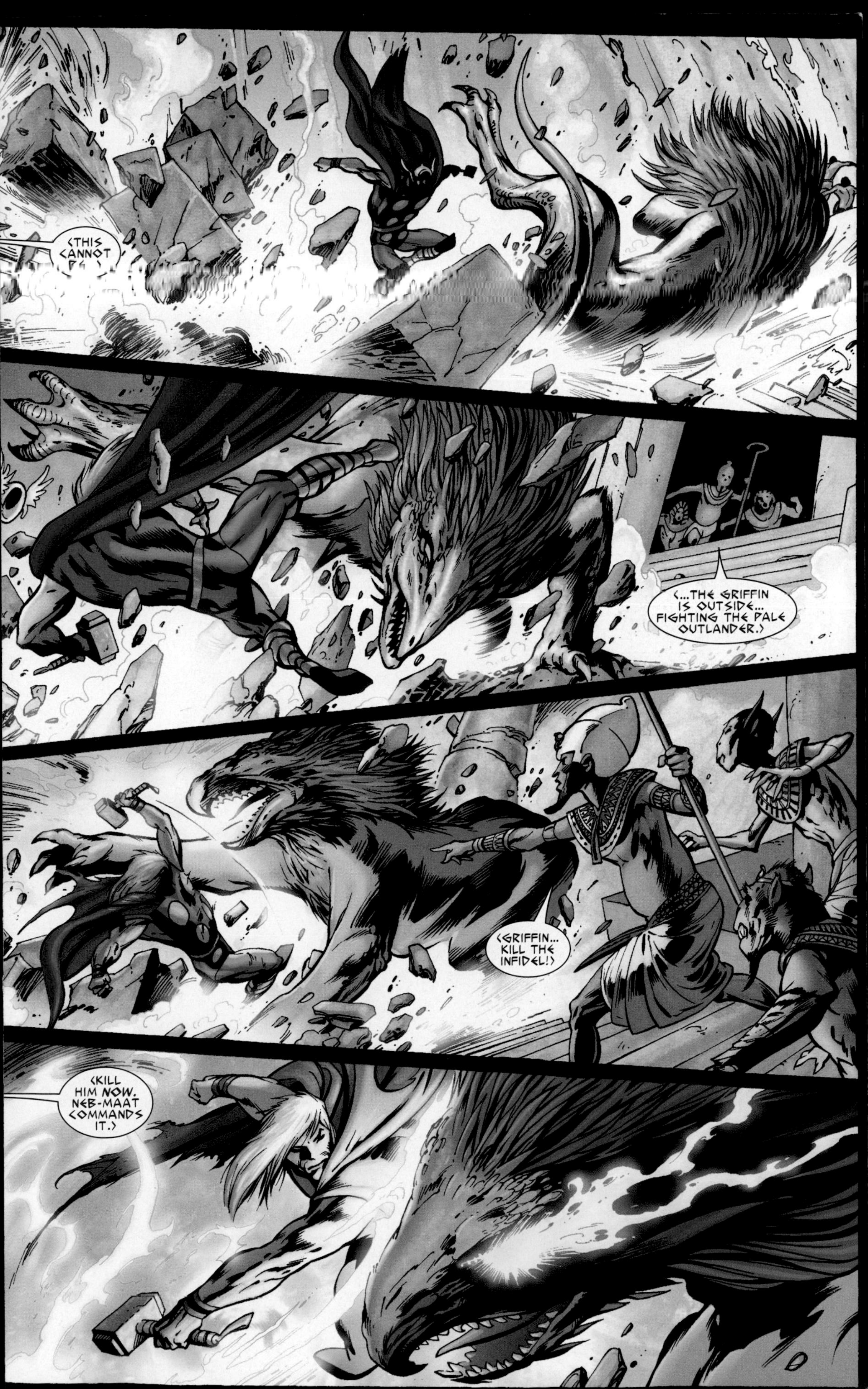
‹THIS CANNOT BE!›
‹...THE GRIFFIN IS OUTSIDE... FIGHTING THE PALE OUTLANDER.›
‹GRIFFIN... KILL THE INFIDEL!›
‹KILL HIM NOW. NEB-MAAT COMMANDS IT.›

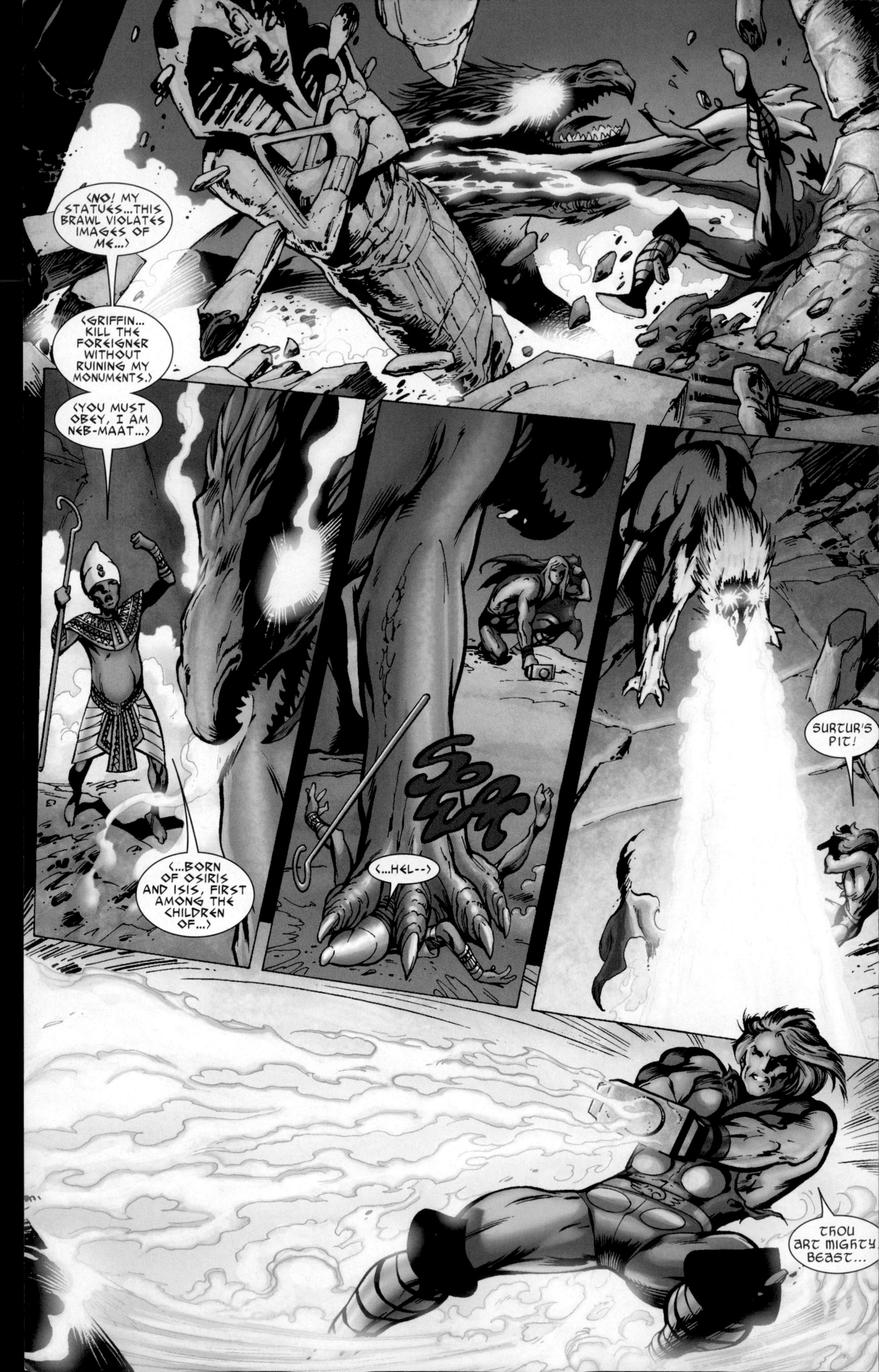
‹NO! MY STATUES...THIS BRAWL VIOLATES IMAGES OF ME...›
‹GRIFFIN... KILL THE FOREIGNER WITHOUT RUINING MY MONUMENTS.›
‹YOU MUST OBEY, I AM NEB-MAAT...›
‹...BORN OF OSIRIS AND ISIS, FIRST AMONG THE CHILDREN OF...›
‹...HEL--›
SURTUR'S PIT!
THOU ART MIGHTY, BEAST...

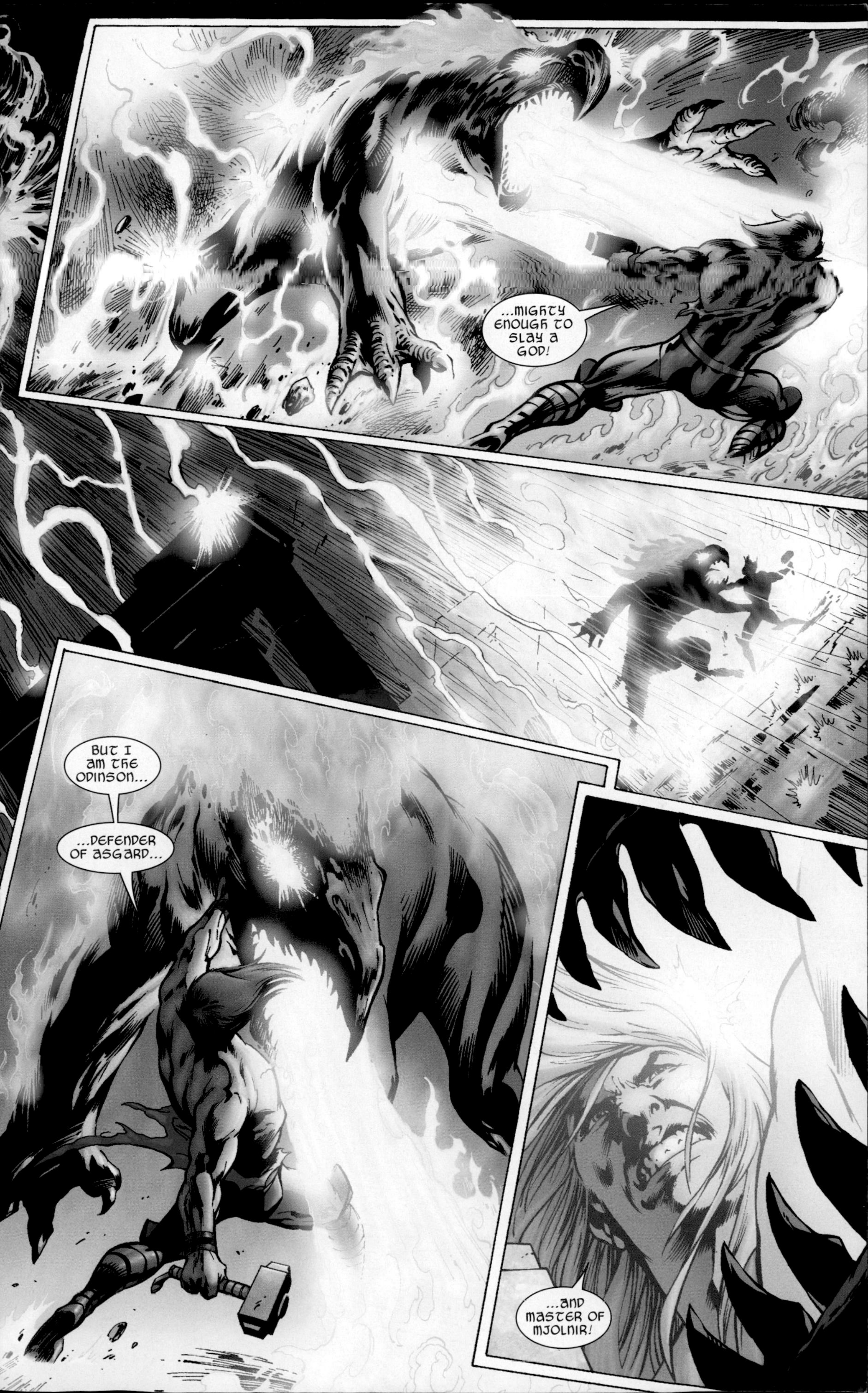
...MIGHTY ENOUGH TO SLAY A GOD!
BUT I AM THE ODINSON...
...DEFENDER OF ASGARD...
...AND MASTER OF MJOLNIR!

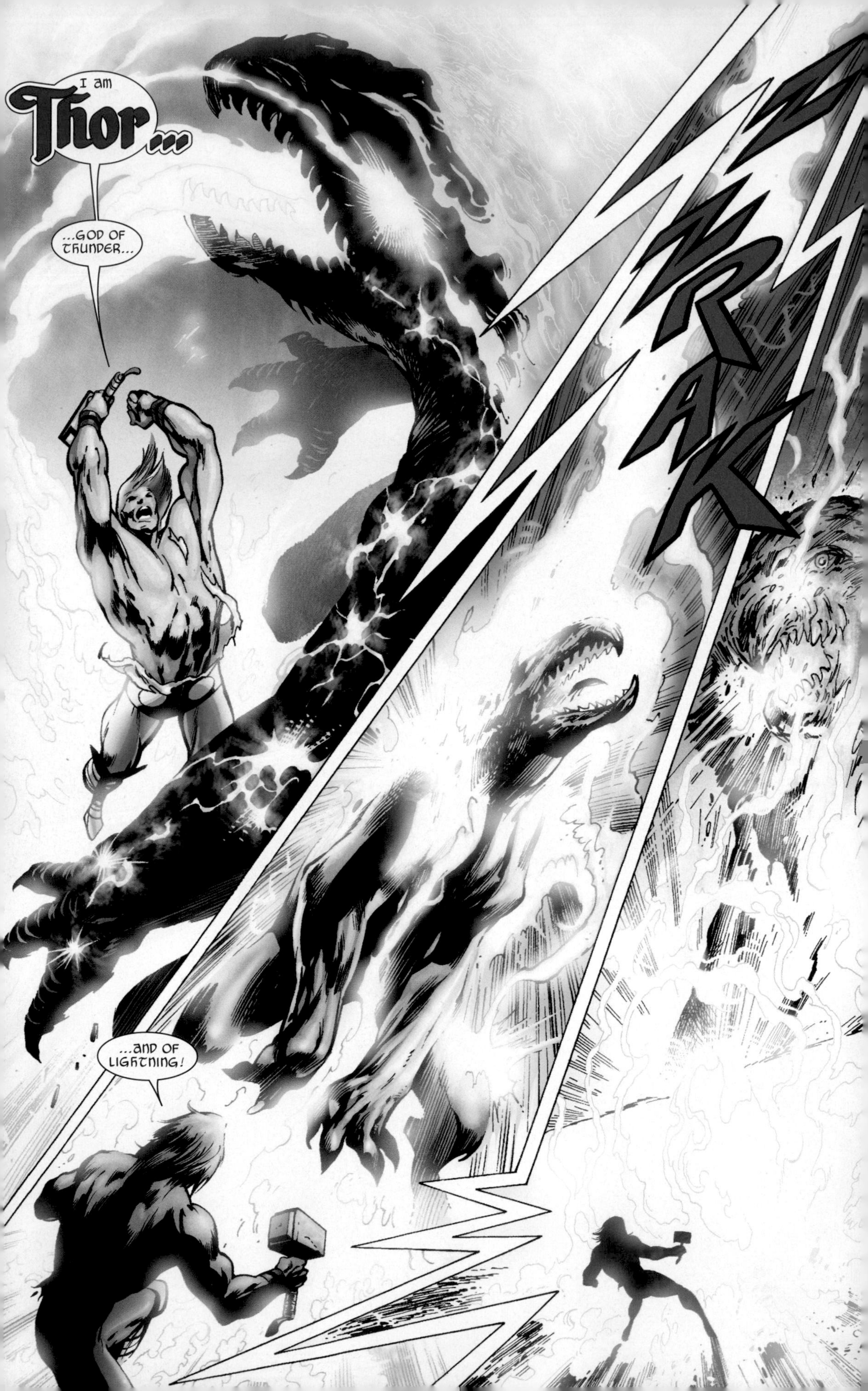
I am Thor...
...GOD OF THUNDER...
...AND OF LIGHTNING!
KRAKK

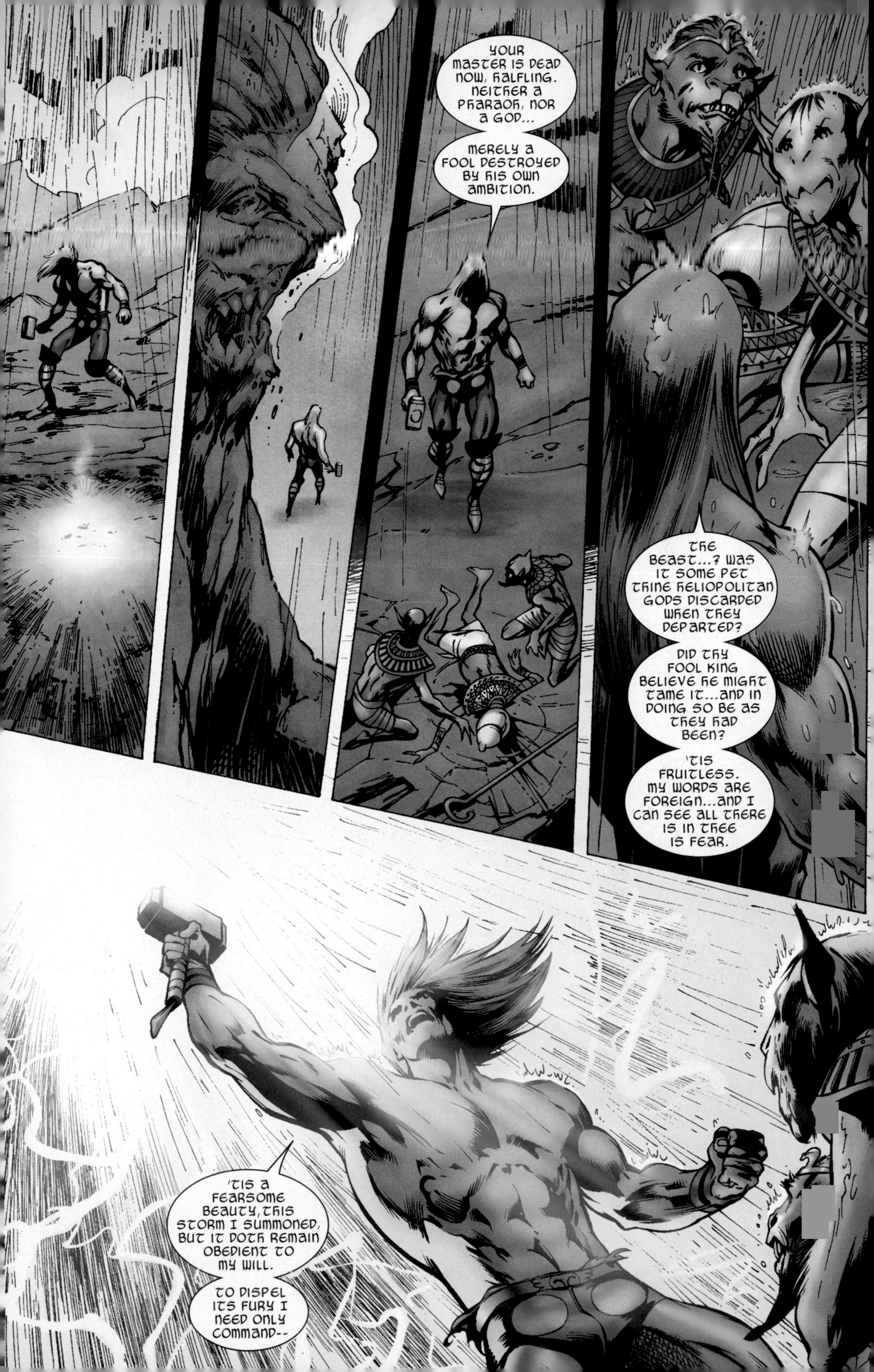
YOUR MASTER IS DEAD NOW, HALFLING. NEITHER A PHARAOH, NOR A GOD...
MERELY A FOOL DESTROYED BY HIS OWN AMBITION.
THE BEAST...? WAS IT SOME PET THINE HELIOPOLITAN GODS DISCARDED WHEN THEY DEPARTED?
DID THY FOOL KING BELIEVE HE MIGHT TAME IT...AND IN DOING SO BE AS THEY HAD BEEN?
'TIS FRUITLESS. MY WORDS ARE FOREIGN...AND I CAN SEE ALL THERE IS IN THEE IS FEAR.
'TIS A FEARSOME BEAUTY, THIS STORM I SUMMONED, BUT IT DOTH REMAIN OBEDIENT TO MY WILL.
TO DISPEL ITS FURY I NEED ONLY COMMAND--

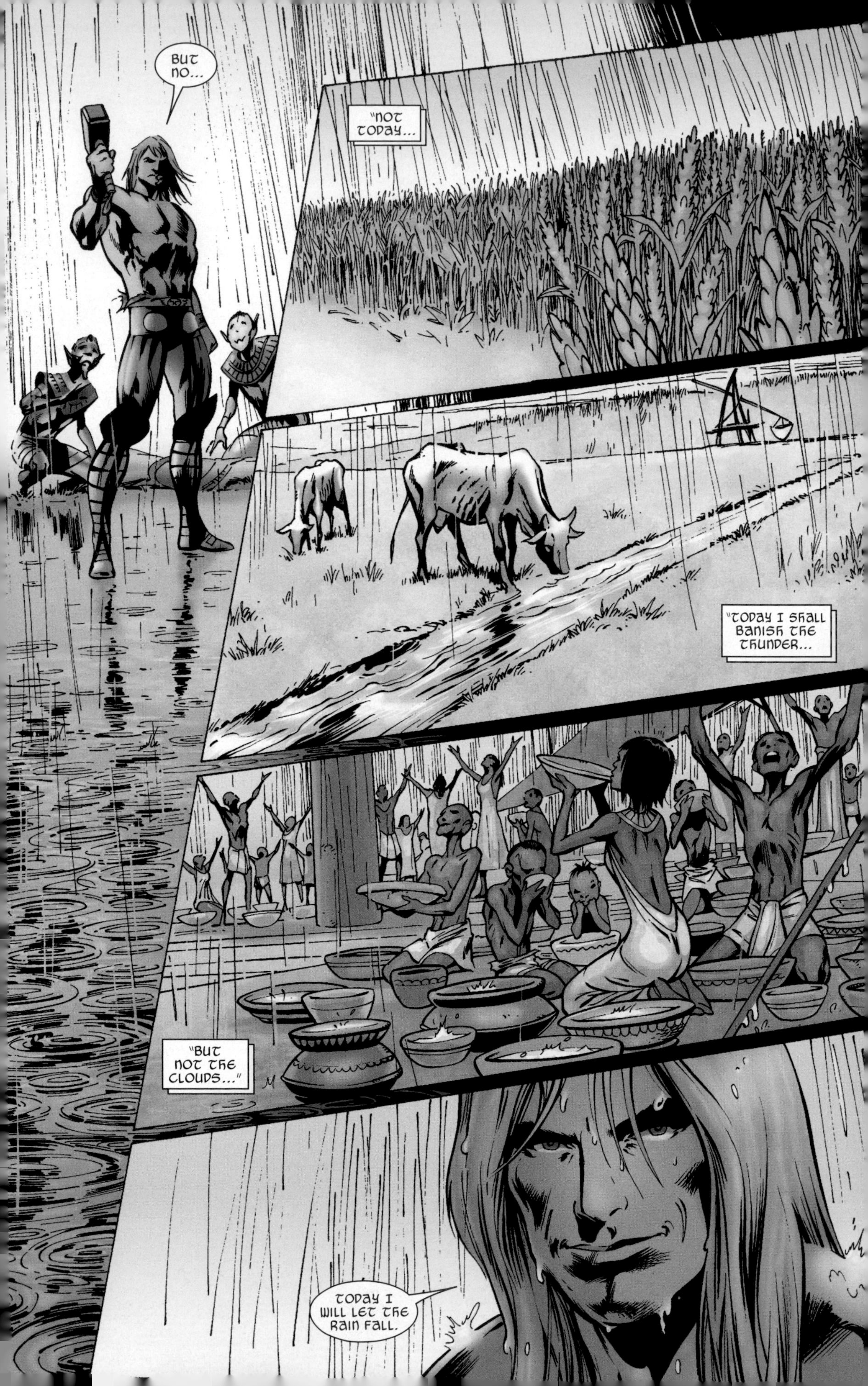

BUT NO...
"NOT TODAY...
"TODAY I SHALL BANISH THE THUNDER...
"BUT NOT THE CLOUDS..."
TODAY I WILL LET THE RAIN FALL.

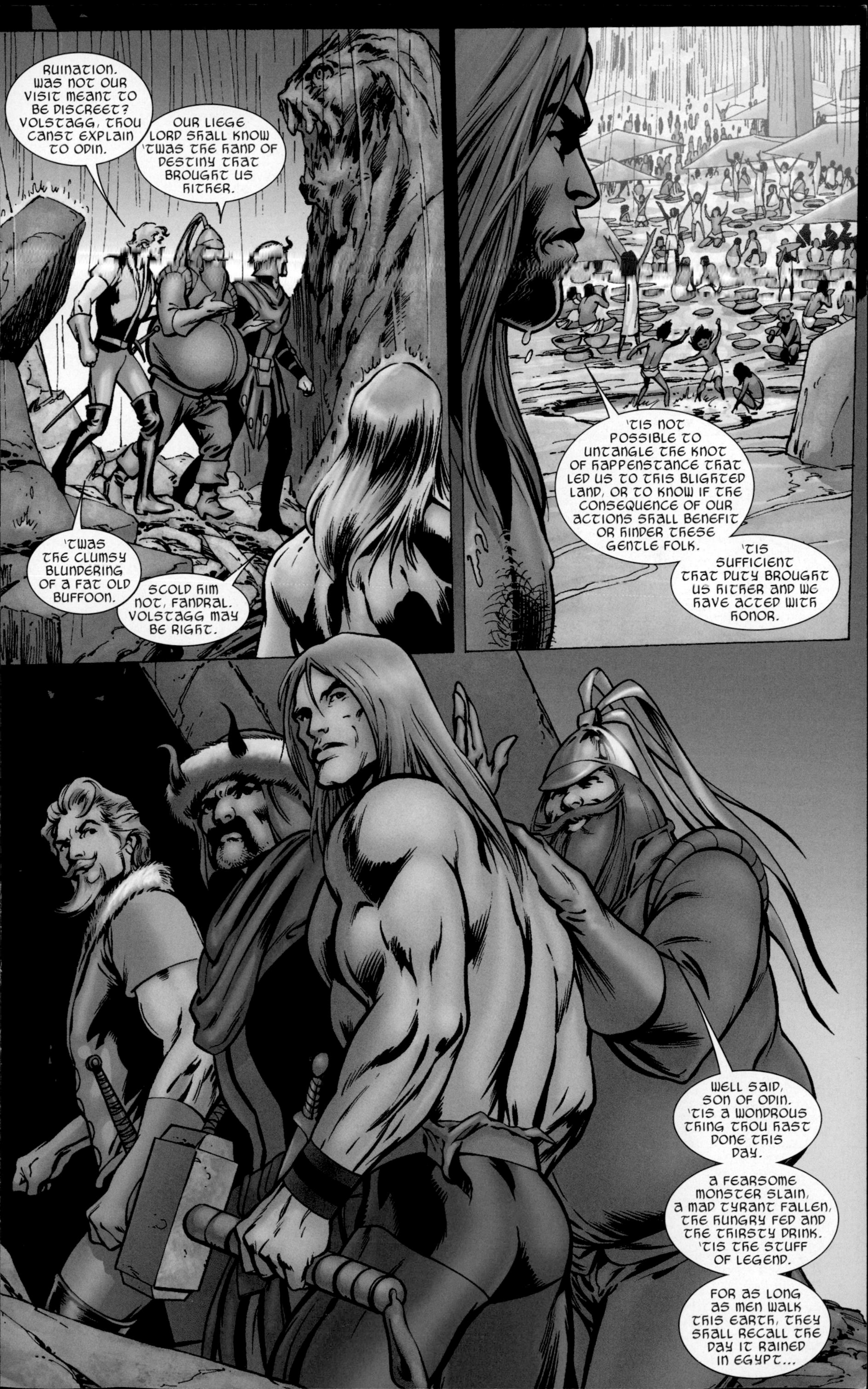
RUINATION. WAS NOT OUR VISIT MEANT TO BE DISCREET? VOLSTAGG, THOU CANST EXPLAIN TO ODIN.
OUR LIEGE LORD SHALL KNOW 'TWAS THE HAND OF DESTINY THAT BROUGHT US HITHER.
'TWAS THE CLUMSY BLUNDERING OF A FAT OLD BUFFOON.
SCOLD HIM NOT, FANDRAL. VOLSTAGG MAY BE RIGHT.
'TIS NOT POSSIBLE TO UNTANGLE THE KNOT OF HAPPENSTANCE THAT LED US TO THIS BLIGHTED LAND, OR TO KNOW IF THE CONSEQUENCE OF OUR ACTIONS SHALL BENEFIT OR HINDER THESE GENTLE FOLK.
'TIS SUFFICIENT THAT DUTY BROUGHT US HITHER AND WE HAVE ACTED WITH HONOR.
WELL SAID, SON OF ODIN. 'TIS A WONDROUS THING THOU HAST DONE THIS DAY.
A FEARSOME MONSTER SLAIN, A MAD TYRANT FALLEN, THE HUNGRY FED AND THE THIRSTY DRINK. 'TIS THE STUFF OF LEGEND.
FOR AS LONG AS MEN WALK THIS EARTH, THEY SHALL RECALL THE DAY IT RAINED IN EGYPT...

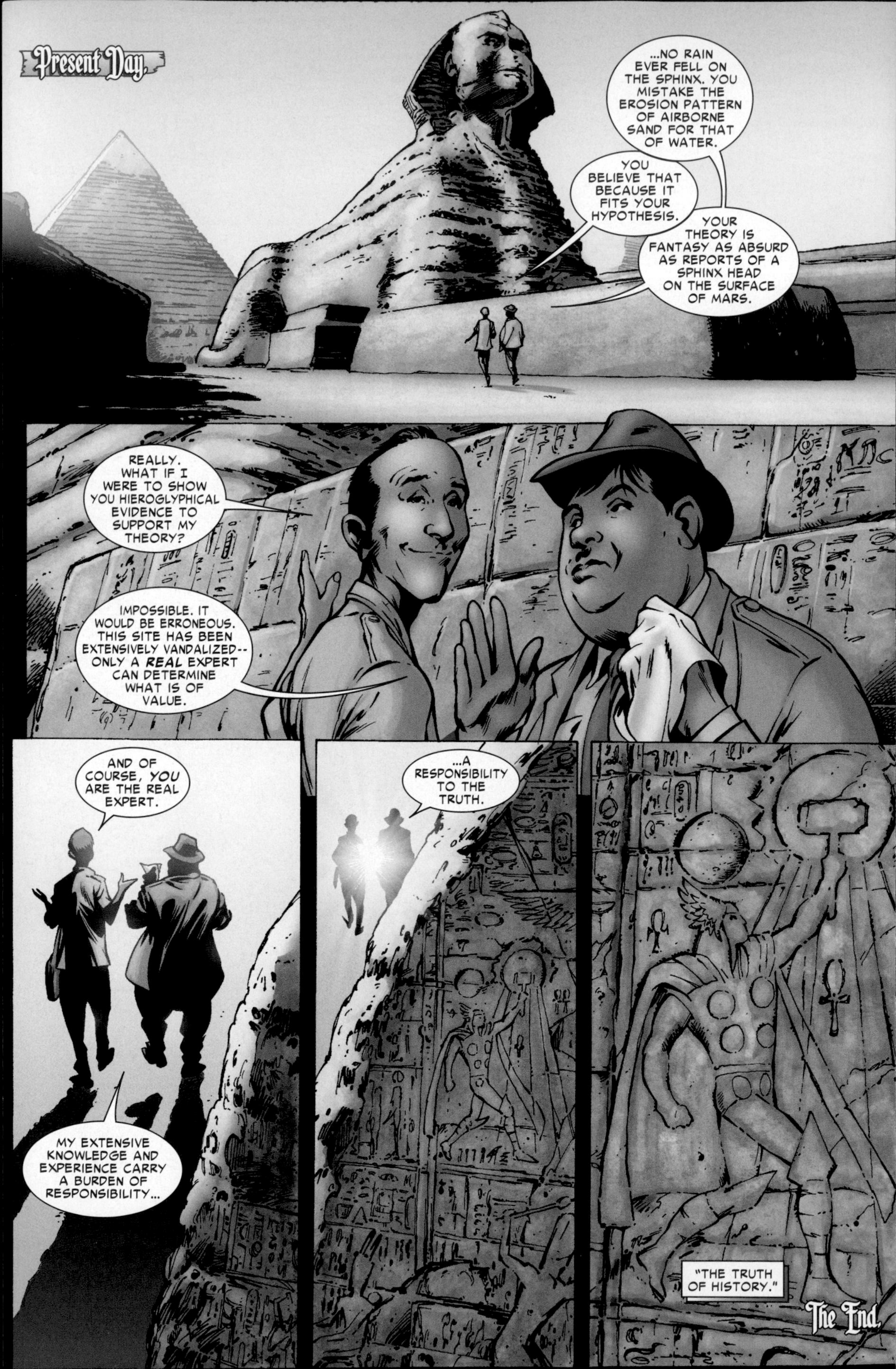
Present Day.
...NO RAIN EVER FELL ON THE SPHINX. YOU MISTAKE THE EROSION PATTERN OF AIRBORNE SAND FOR THAT OF WATER.
YOU BELIEVE THAT BECAUSE IT FITS YOUR HYPOTHESIS.
YOUR THEORY IS FANTASY AS ABSURD AS REPORTS OF A SPHINX HEAD ON THE SURFACE OF MARS.
REALLY. WHAT IF I WERE TO SHOW YOU HIEROGLYPHICAL EVIDENCE TO SUPPORT MY THEORY?
IMPOSSIBLE. IT WOULD BE ERRONEOUS. THIS SITE HAS BEEN EXTENSIVELY VANDALIZED--ONLY A REAL EXPERT CAN DETERMINE WHAT IS OF VALUE.
AND OF COURSE, YOU ARE THE REAL EXPERT.
MY EXTENSIVE KNOWLEDGE AND EXPERIENCE CARRY A BURDEN OF RESPONSIBILITY...
...A RESPONSIBILITY TO THE TRUTH.
"THE TRUTH OF HISTORY."
The End.

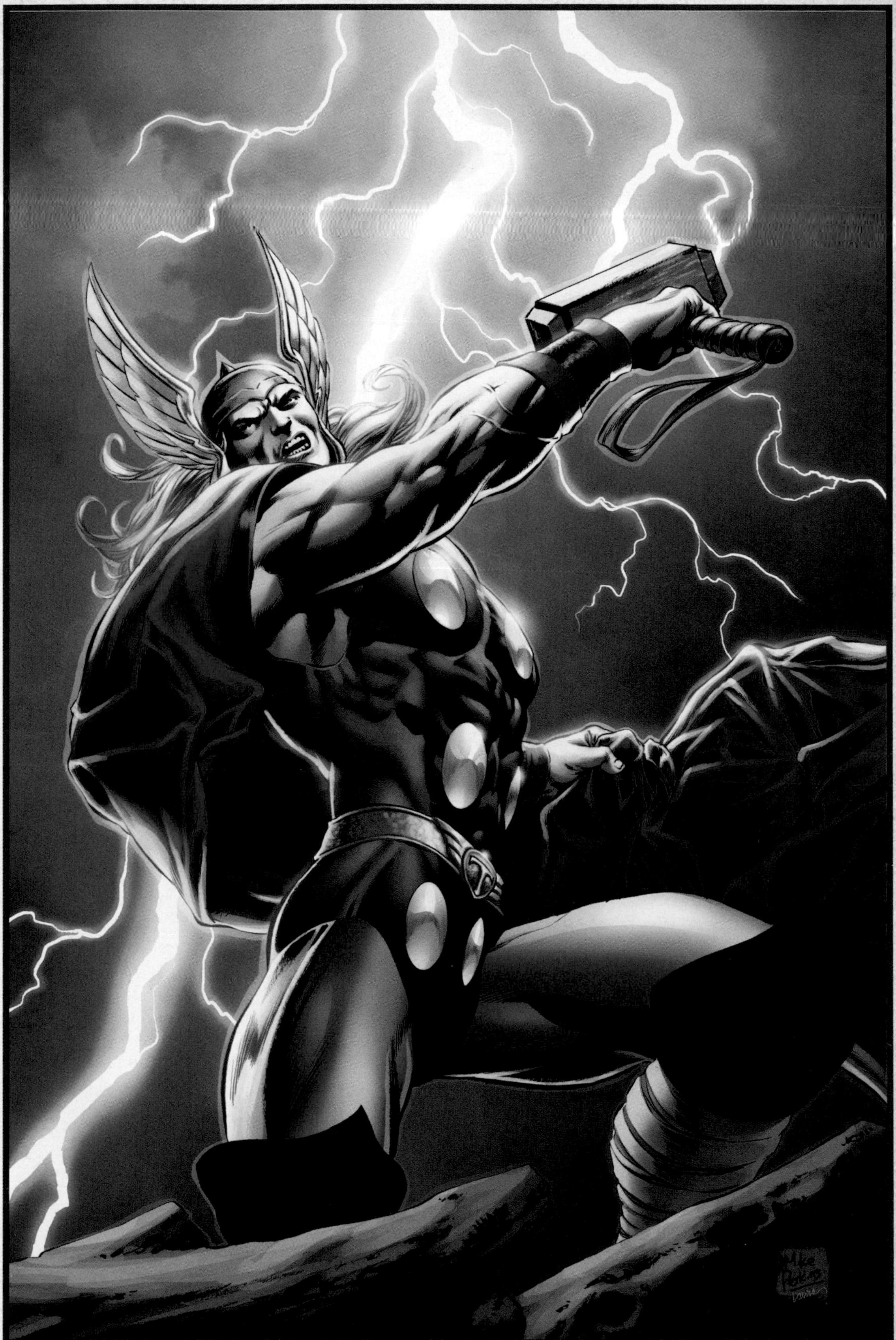

THOR: WOLVES OF THE NORTH

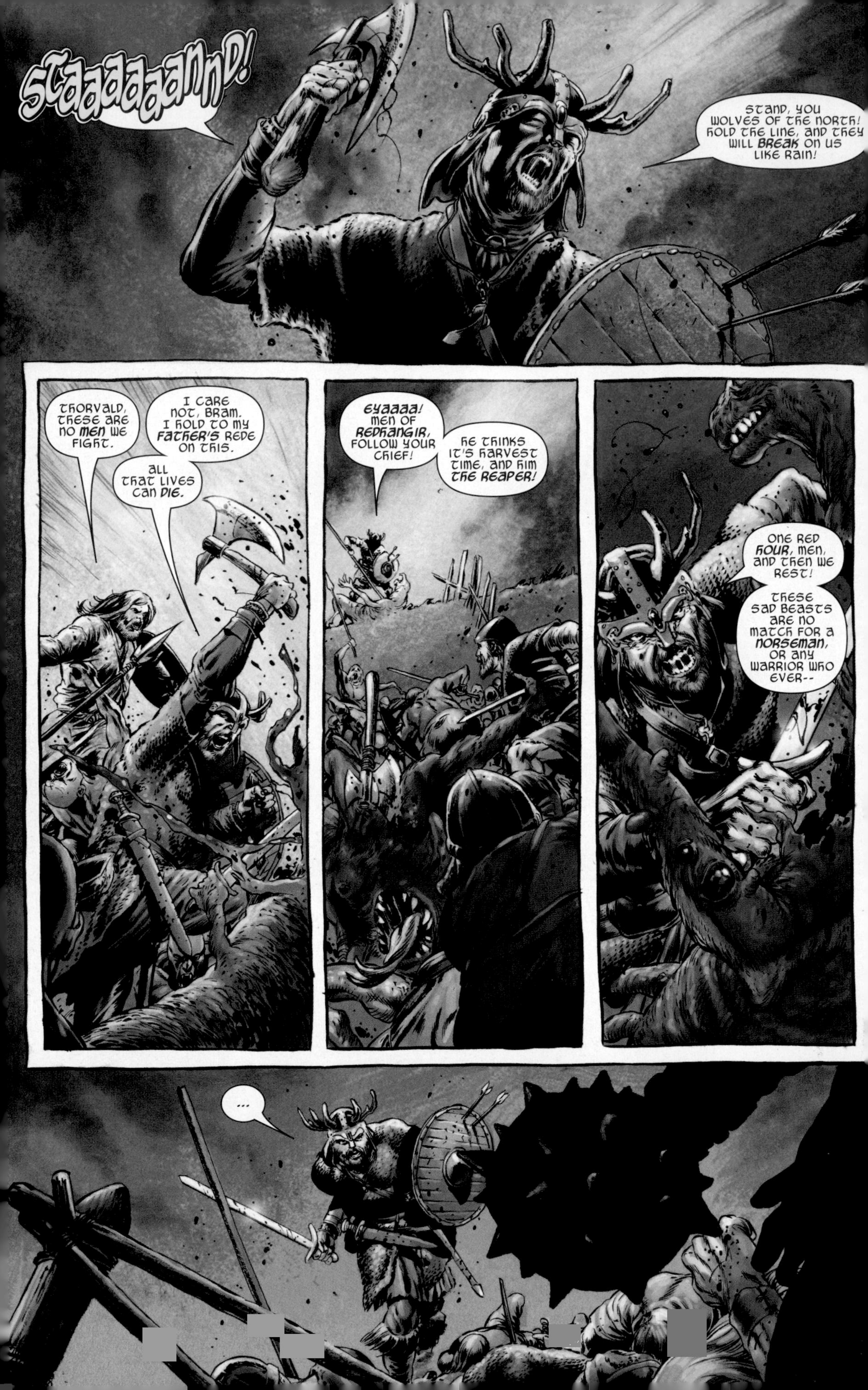
STAAAAAAANND!
STAND, YOU WOLVES OF THE NORTH! HOLD THE LINE, AND THEY WILL BREAK ON US LIKE RAIN!
THORVALD, THESE ARE NO MEN WE FIGHT.
I CARE NOT, BRAM. I HOLD TO MY FATHER'S REDE ON THIS.
ALL THAT LIVES CAN DIE.
EYAAAA! MEN OF REDHANGIR, FOLLOW YOUR CHIEF!
HE THINKS IT'S HARVEST TIME, AND HIM THE REAPER!
ONE RED HOUR, MEN, AND THEN WE REST!
THESE SAD BEASTS ARE NO MATCH FOR A NORSEMAN, OR ANY WARRIOR WHO EVER--
...

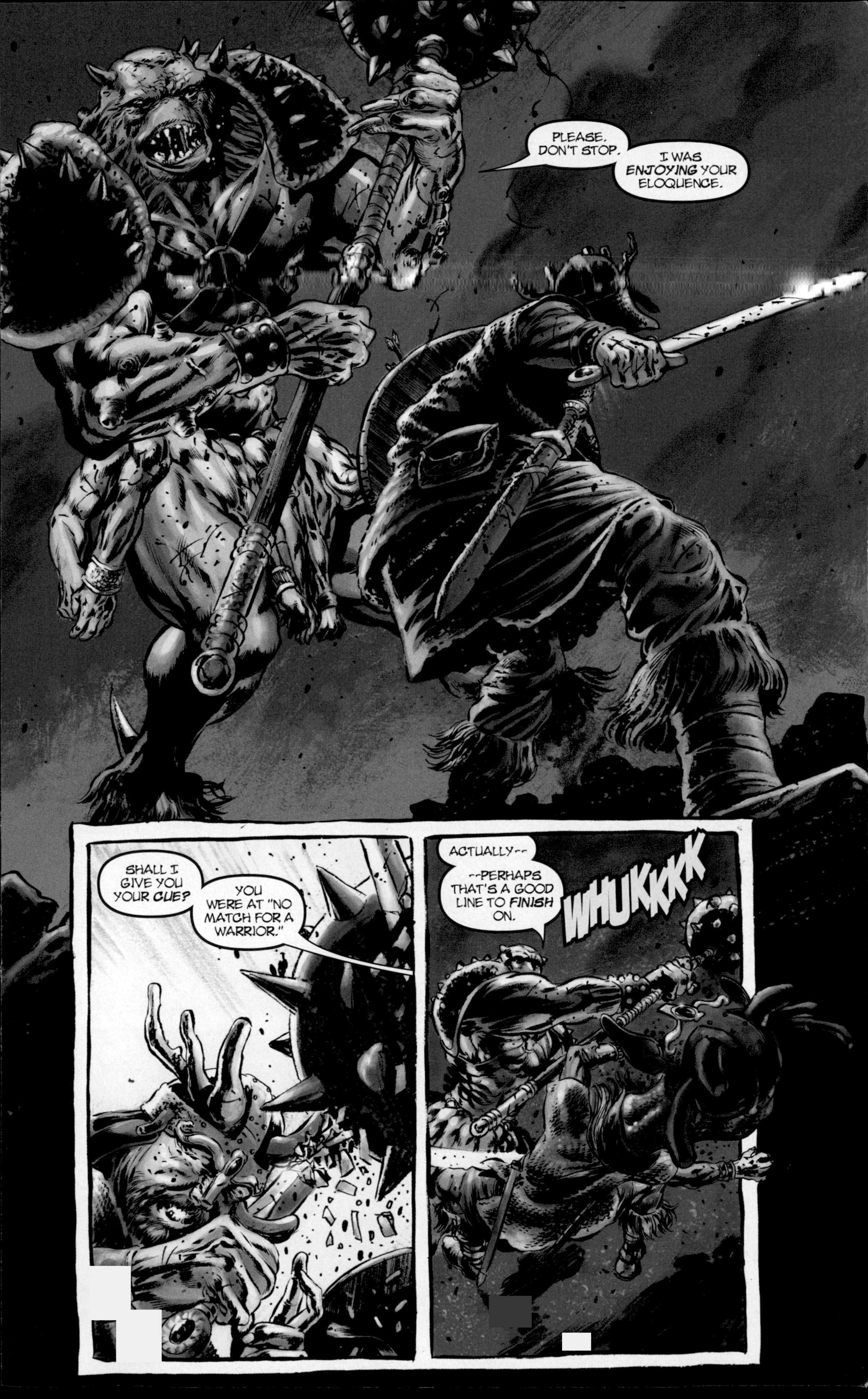
PLEASE. DON'T STOP.
I WAS ENJOYING YOUR ELOQUENCE.
SHALL I GIVE YOU YOUR CUE?
YOU WERE AT "NO MATCH FOR A WARRIOR."
ACTUALLY--
--PERHAPS THAT'S A GOOD LINE TO FINISH ON.
WHUKKKK

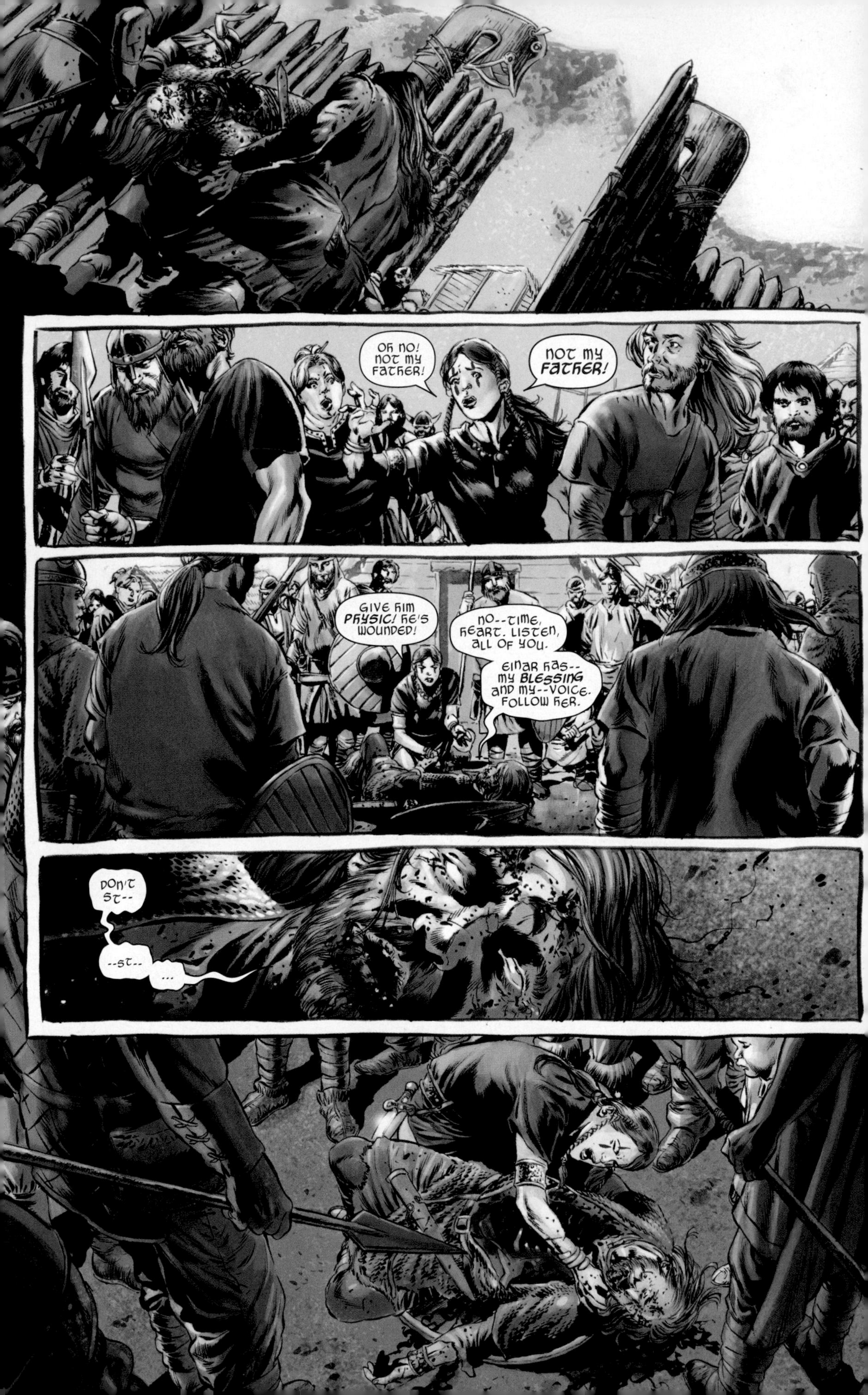
OH NO! NOT MY FATHER!
NOT MY FATHER!
GIVE HIM PHYSIC! HE'S WOUNDED!
NO--TIME, HEART. LISTEN, ALL OF YOU.
EINAR HAS--MY BLESSING AND MY--VOICE. FOLLOW HER.
DON'T ST--
--ST--
...

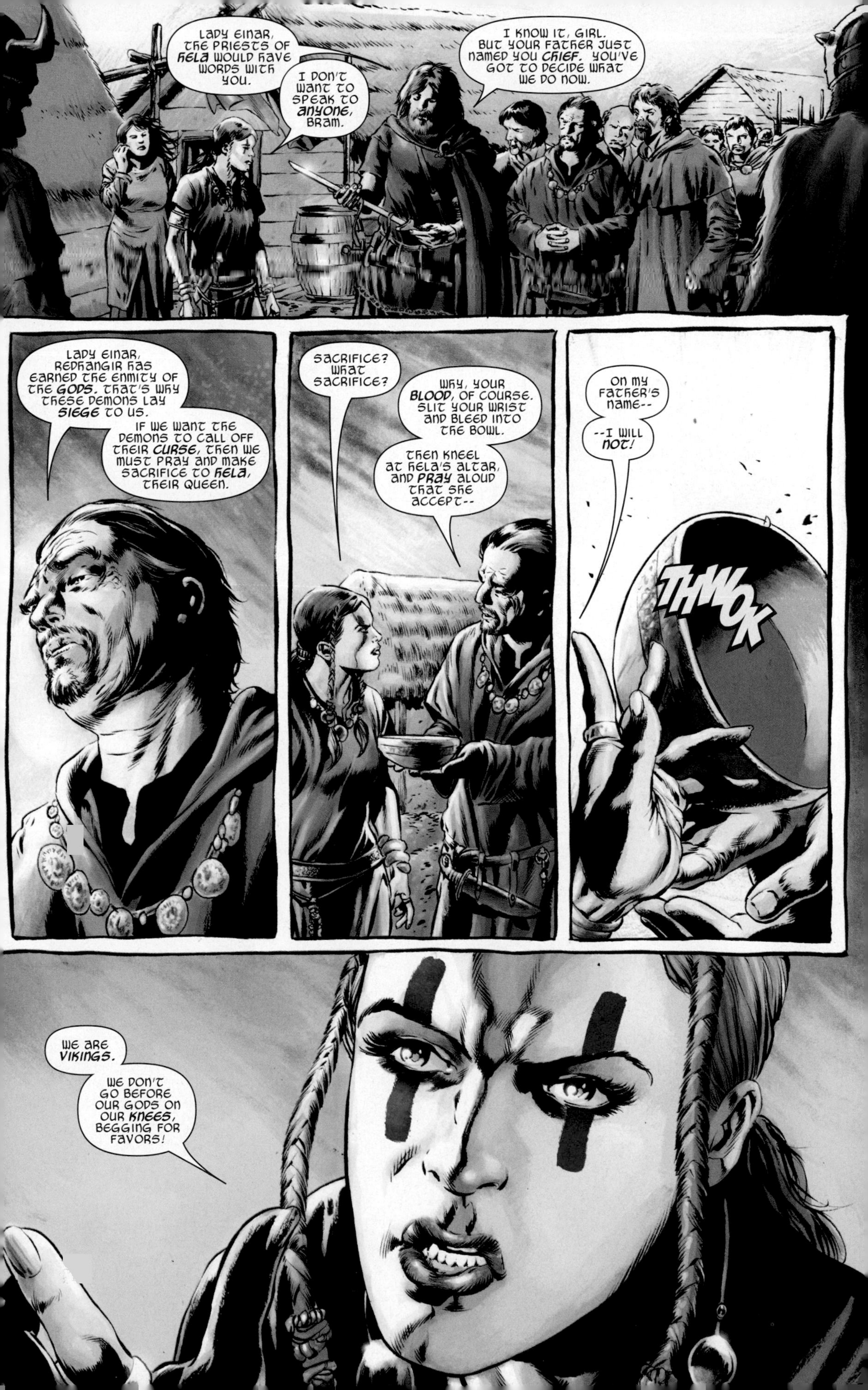

Lady Einar, the priests of Hela would have words with you.
I don't want to speak to anyone, Bram.
I know it, girl. But your father just named you chief. You've got to decide what we do now.
Lady Einar, Redhangir has earned the enmity of the gods. That's why these demons lay siege to us.
If we want the demons to call off their curse, then we must pray and make sacrifice to Hela, their queen.
Sacrifice? What sacrifice?
Why, your blood, of course. Slit your wrist and bleed into the bowl.
Then kneel at Hela's altar, and pray aloud that she accept--
On my father's name--
--I will not!
THWOK
We are Vikings.
We don't go before our gods on our knees, begging for favors!

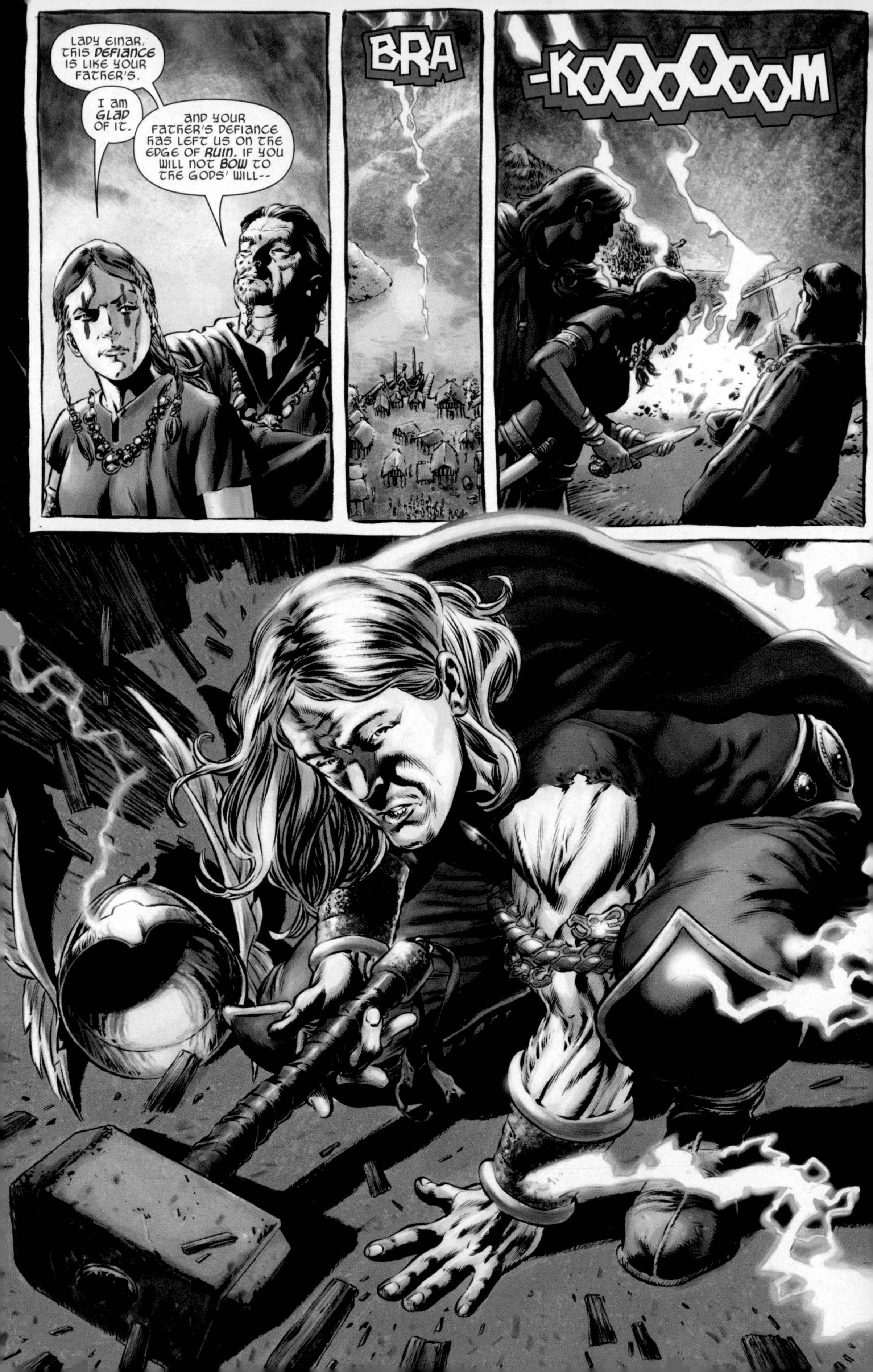

LADY EINAR, THIS DEFIANCE IS LIKE YOUR FATHER'S.
I AM GLAD OF IT.
AND YOUR FATHER'S DEFIANCE HAS LEFT US ON THE EDGE OF RUIN. IF YOU WILL NOT BOW TO THE GODS' WILL--
BRA
-KOOOOOOM

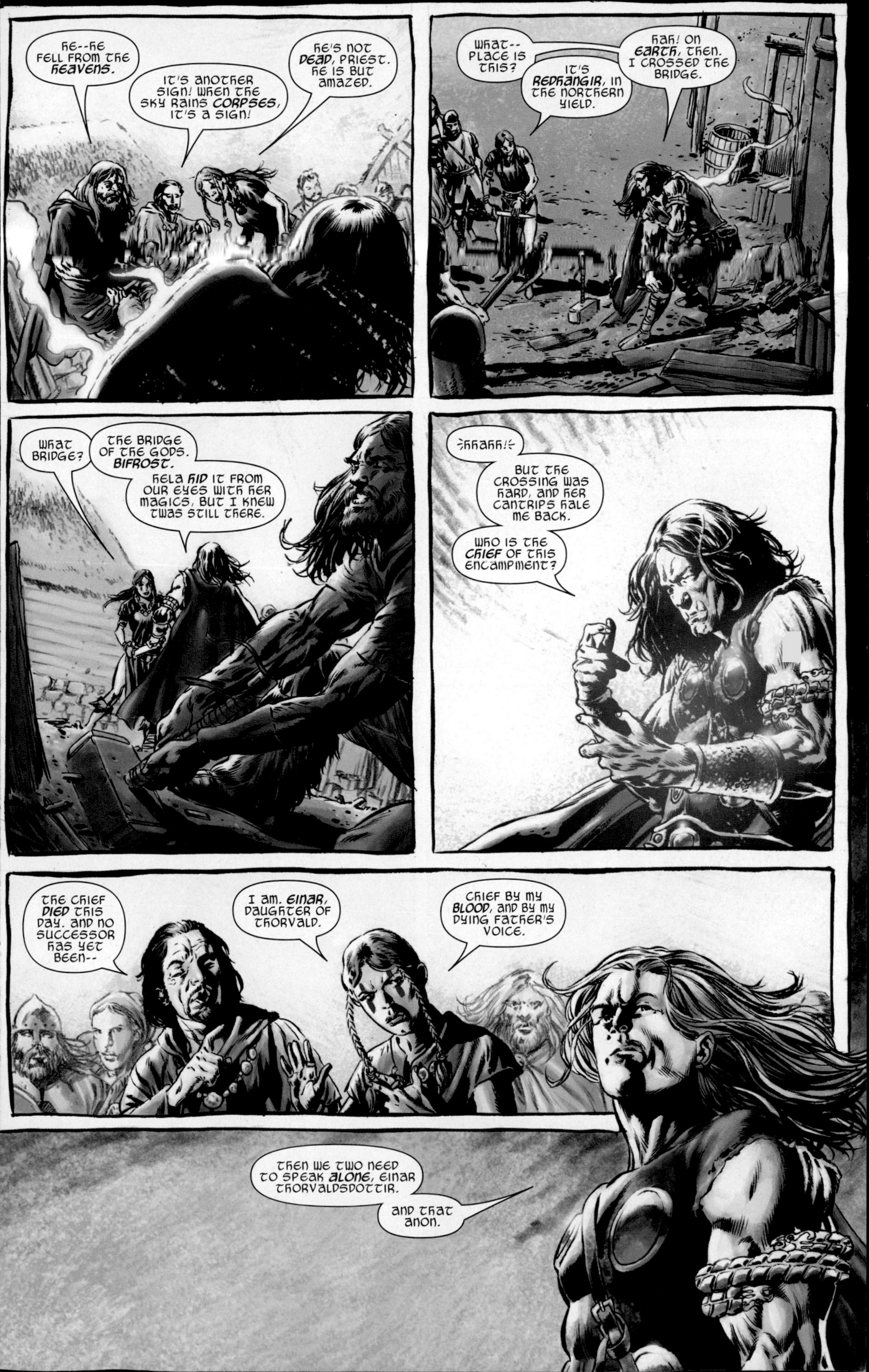
HE--HE FELL FROM THE HEAVENS.
IT'S ANOTHER SIGN! WHEN THE SKY RAINS CORPSES, IT'S A SIGN!
HE'S NOT DEAD, PRIEST. HE IS BUT AMAZED.
WHAT-- PLACE IS THIS?
IT'S REDHANGIR, IN THE NORTHERN YIELD.
HAH! ON EARTH, THEN. I CROSSED THE BRIDGE.
WHAT BRIDGE?
THE BRIDGE OF THE GODS. BIFROST.
HELA HID IT FROM OUR EYES WITH HER MAGICS, BUT I KNEW TWAS STILL THERE.
HHAHH!
BUT THE CROSSING WAS HARD, AND HER CANTRIPS HALE ME BACK.
WHO IS THE CHIEF OF THIS ENCAMPMENT?
THE CHIEF DIED THIS DAY. AND NO SUCCESSOR HAS YET BEEN--
I AM. EINAR, DAUGHTER OF THORVALD.
CHIEF BY MY BLOOD, AND BY MY DYING FATHER'S VOICE.
THEN WE TWO NEED TO SPEAK ALONE, EINAR THORVALDSDOTTIR.
AND THAT ANON.

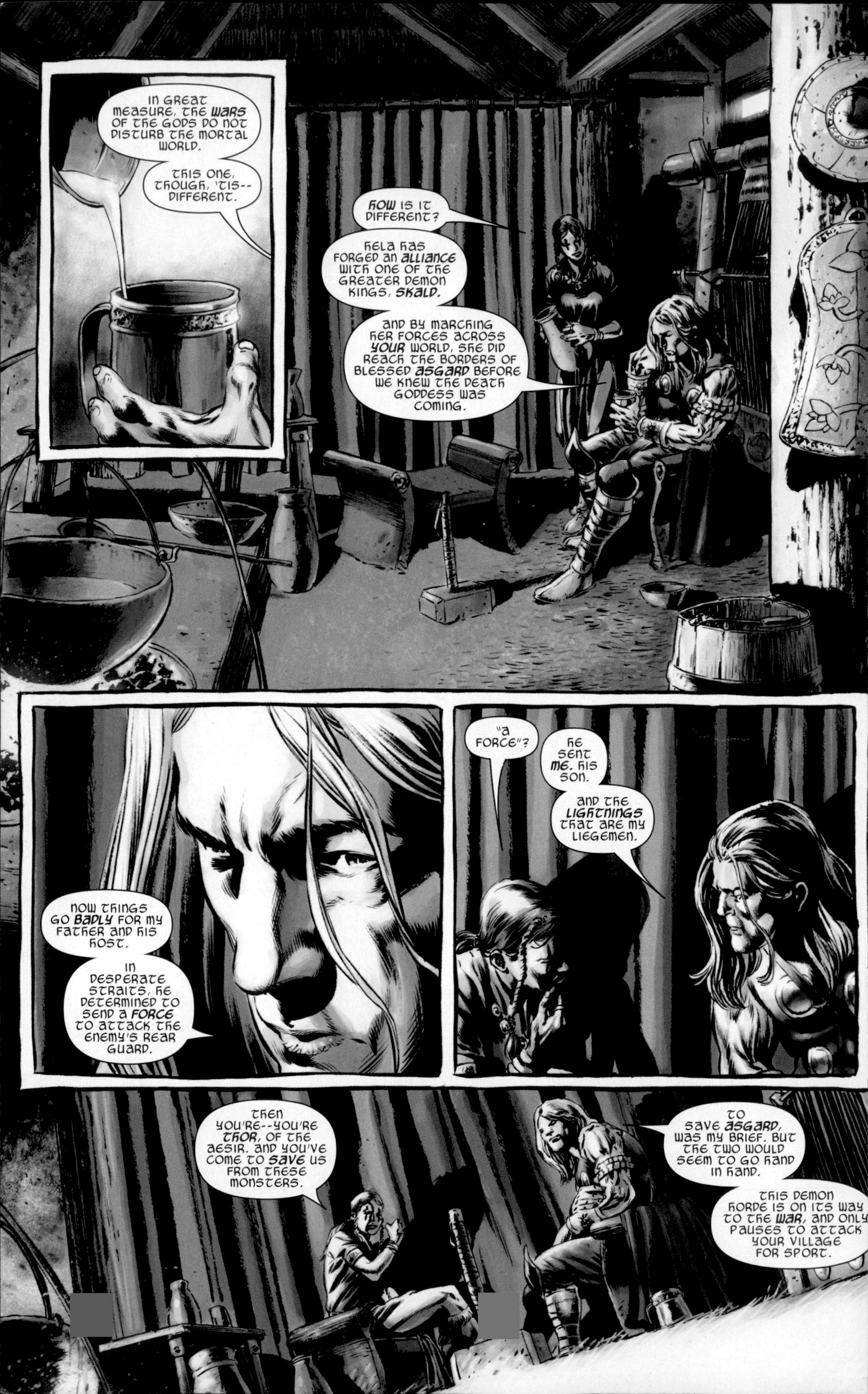

IN GREAT MEASURE, THE WARS OF THE GODS DO NOT DISTURB THE MORTAL WORLD.
THIS ONE, THOUGH, 'TIS-- DIFFERENT.
HOW IS IT DIFFERENT?
HELA HAS FORGED AN ALLIANCE WITH ONE OF THE GREATER DEMON KINGS, SKALD.
AND BY MARCHING HER FORCES ACROSS YOUR WORLD, SHE DID REACH THE BORDERS OF BLESSED ASGARD BEFORE WE KNEW THE DEATH GODDESS WAS COMING.
NOW THINGS GO BADLY FOR MY FATHER AND HIS HOST.
IN DESPERATE STRAITS, HE DETERMINED TO SEND A FORCE TO ATTACK THE ENEMY'S REAR GUARD.
"A FORCE"?
HE SENT ME. HIS SON.
AND THE LIGHTNINGS THAT ARE MY LIEGEMEN.
THEN YOU'RE--YOU'RE THOR, OF THE AESIR. AND YOU'VE COME TO SAVE US FROM THESE MONSTERS.
TO SAVE ASGARD, WAS MY BRIEF. BUT THE TWO WOULD SEEM TO GO HAND IN HAND.
THIS DEMON HORDE IS ON ITS WAY TO THE WAR, AND ONLY PAUSES TO ATTACK YOUR VILLAGE FOR SPORT.

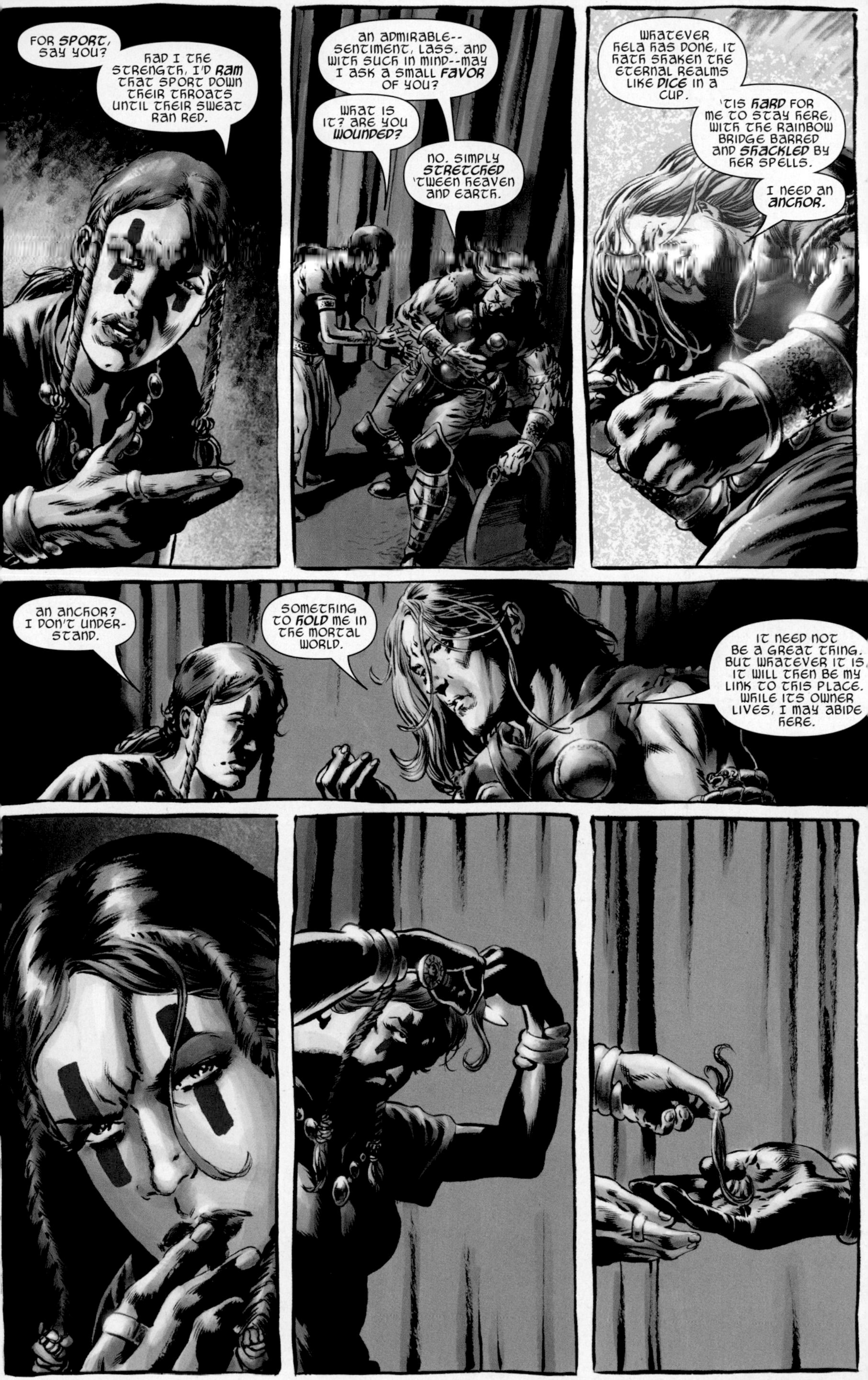

FOR SPORT, SAY YOU?
HAD I THE STRENGTH, I'D RAM THAT SPORT DOWN THEIR THROATS UNTIL THEIR SWEAT RAN RED.
AN ADMIRABLE--SENTIMENT, LASS. AND WITH SUCH IN MIND--MAY I ASK A SMALL FAVOR OF YOU?
WHAT IS IT? ARE YOU WOUNDED?
NO. SIMPLY STRETCHED 'TWEEN HEAVEN AND EARTH.
WHATEVER HELA HAS DONE, IT HATH SHAKEN THE ETERNAL REALMS LIKE DICE IN A CUP.
'TIS HARD FOR ME TO STAY HERE, WITH THE RAINBOW BRIDGE BARRED AND SHACKLED BY HER SPELLS.
I NEED AN ANCHOR.
AN ANCHOR? I DON'T UNDERSTAND.
SOMETHING TO HOLD ME IN THE MORTAL WORLD.
IT NEED NOT BE A GREAT THING. BUT WHATEVER IT IS IT WILL THEN BE MY LINK TO THIS PLACE. WHILE ITS OWNER LIVES, I MAY ABIDE HERE.

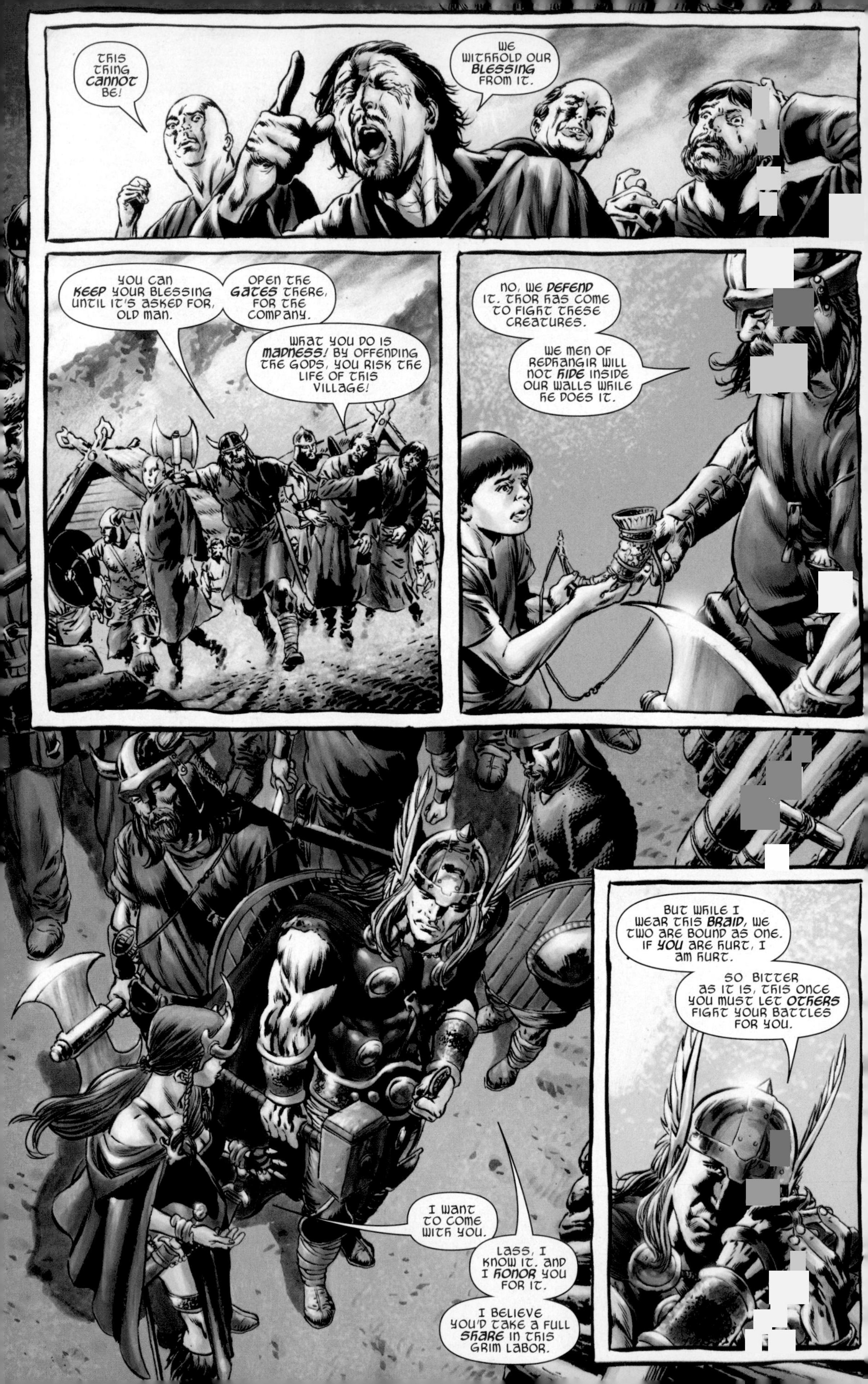
THIS THING CANNOT BE!
WE WITHHOLD OUR BLESSING FROM IT.
YOU CAN KEEP YOUR BLESSING UNTIL IT'S ASKED FOR, OLD MAN.
OPEN THE GATES THERE, FOR THE COMPANY.
WHAT YOU DO IS MADNESS! BY OFFENDING THE GODS, YOU RISK THE LIFE OF THIS VILLAGE!
NO, WE DEFEND IT. THOR HAS COME TO FIGHT THESE CREATURES.
WE MEN OF REDHANGIR WILL NOT HIDE INSIDE OUR WALLS WHILE HE DOES IT.
I WANT TO COME WITH YOU.
LASS, I KNOW IT. AND I HONOR YOU FOR IT.
I BELIEVE YOU'D TAKE A FULL SHARE IN THIS GRIM LABOR.
BUT WHILE I WEAR THIS BRAID, WE TWO ARE BOUND AS ONE. IF YOU ARE HURT, I AM HURT.
SO BITTER AS IT IS, THIS ONCE YOU MUST LET OTHERS FIGHT YOUR BATTLES FOR YOU.

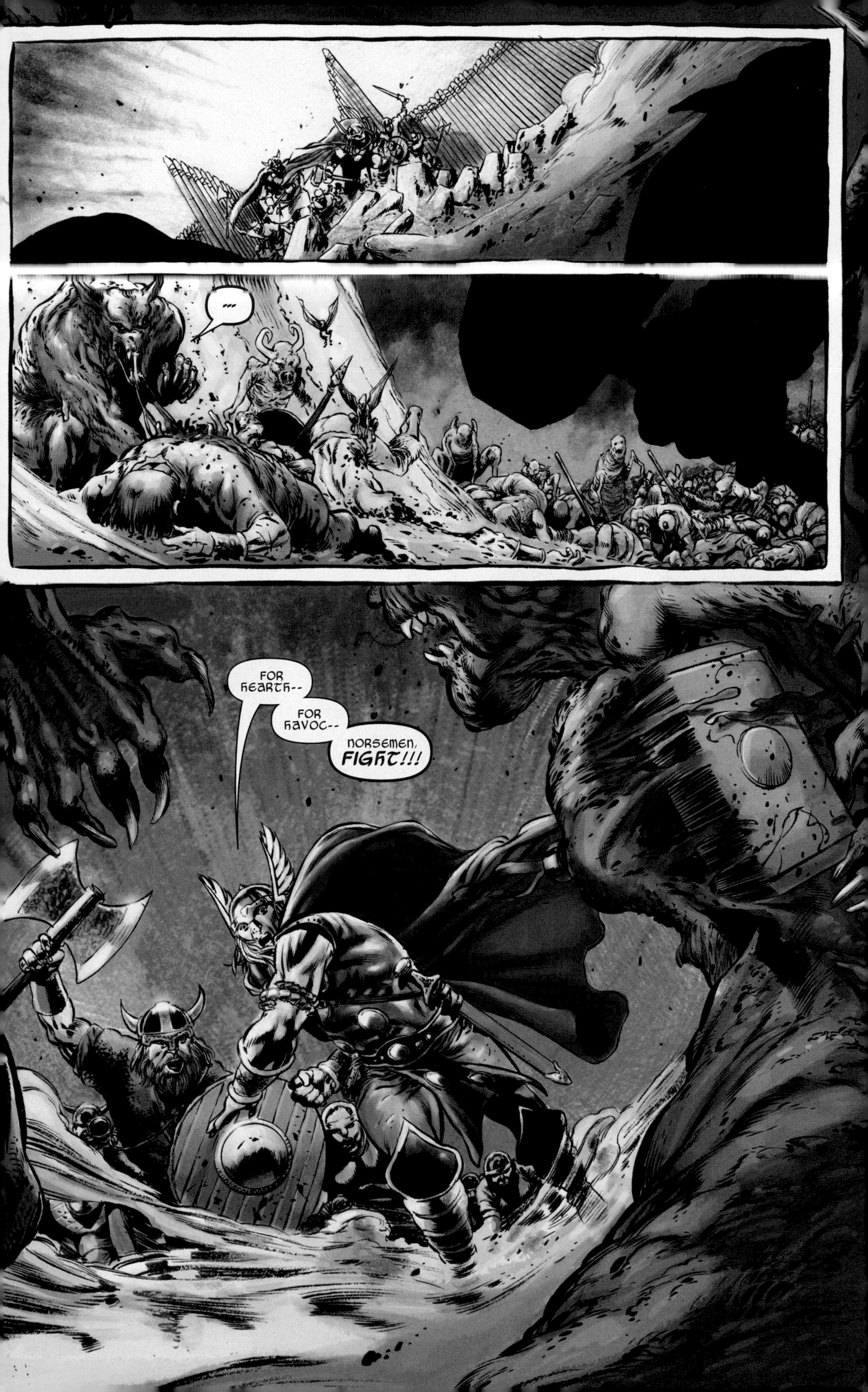
...
FOR HEARTH--
FOR HAVOC--
NORSEMEN, FIGHT!!!

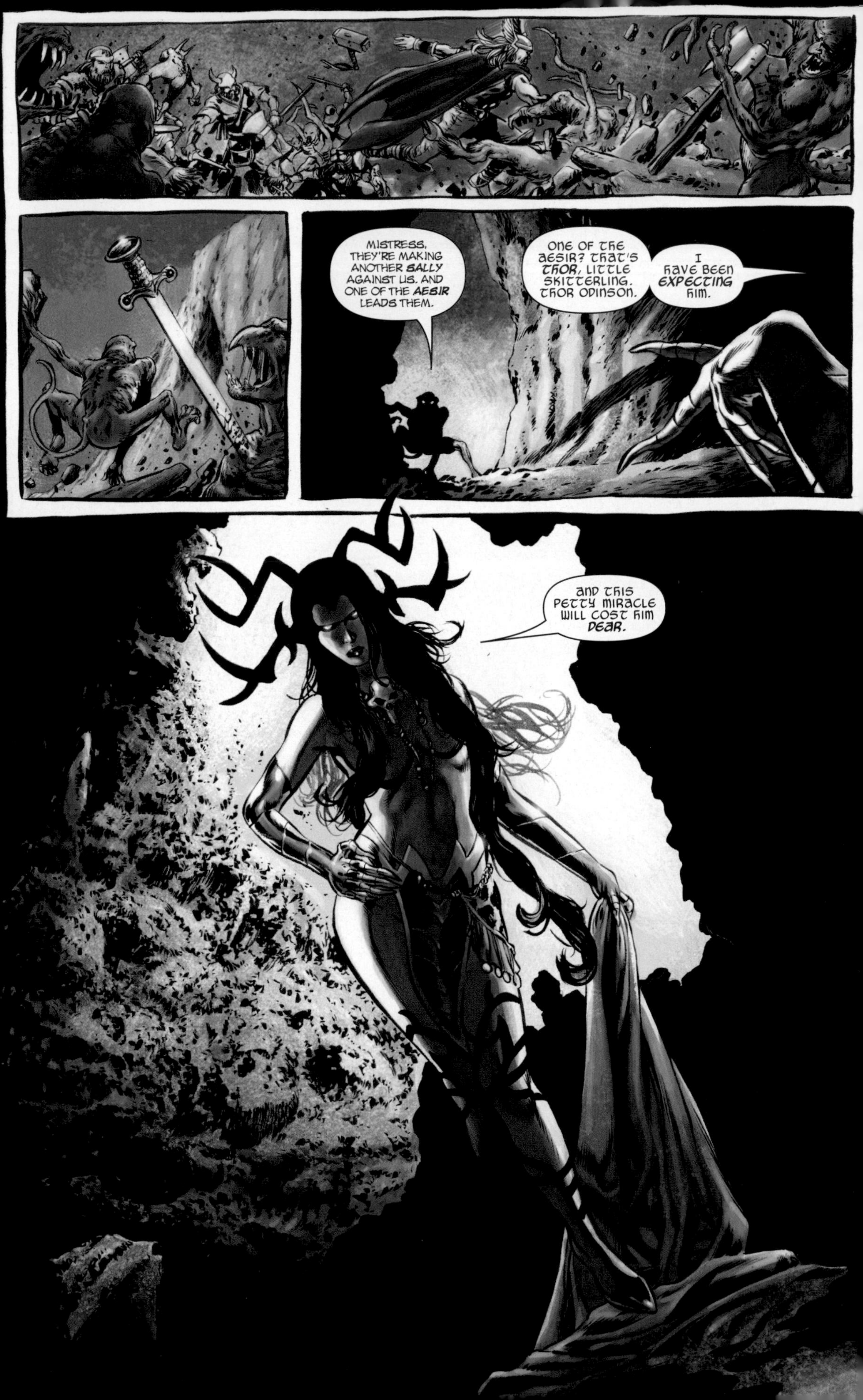

MISTRESS, THEY'RE MAKING ANOTHER **SALLY** AGAINST US. AND ONE OF THE **AESIR** LEADS THEM.
ONE OF THE AESIR? THAT'S **THOR**, LITTLE SKITTERLING. THOR ODINSON.
I HAVE BEEN **EXPECTING** HIM.
AND THIS PETTY MIRACLE WILL COST HIM **DEAR.**

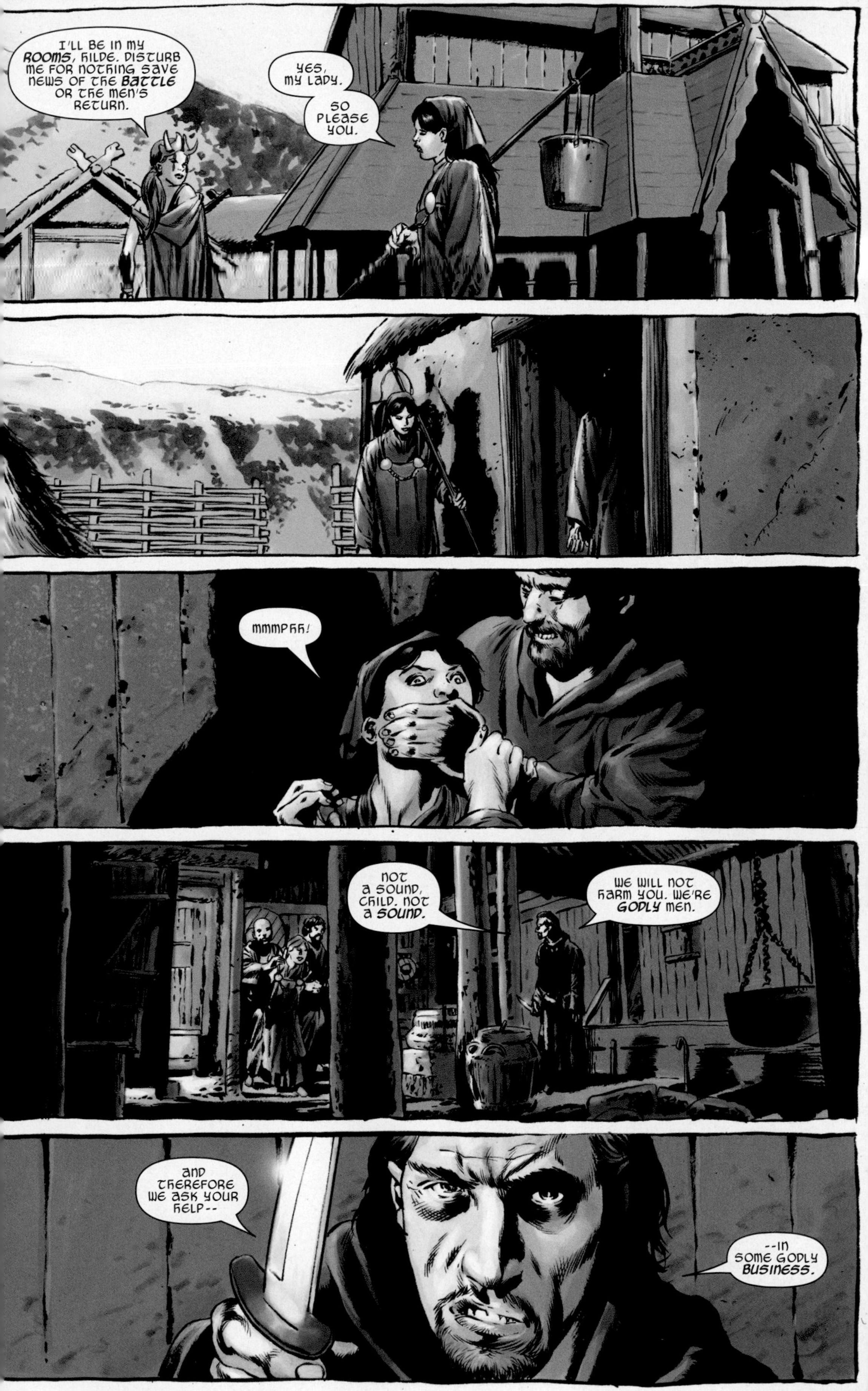
I'LL BE IN MY ROOMS, HILDE. DISTURB ME FOR NOTHING SAVE NEWS OF THE BATTLE OR THE MEN'S RETURN.
YES, MY LADY.
SO PLEASE YOU.
MMMPHH!
NOT A SOUND, CHILD. NOT A SOUND.
WE WILL NOT HARM YOU. WE'RE GODLY MEN.
AND THEREFORE WE ASK YOUR HELP--
--IN SOME GODLY BUSINESS.

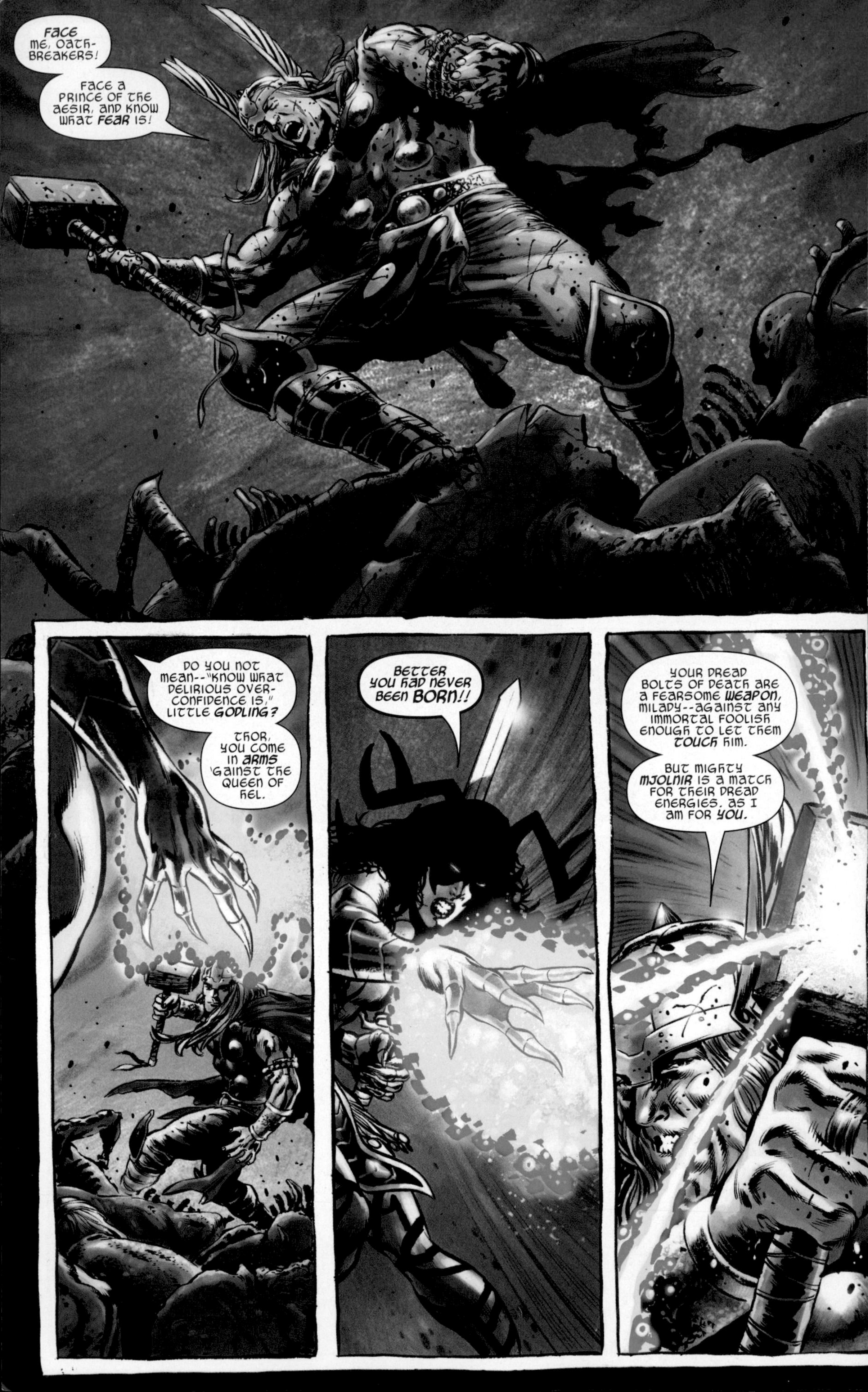
FACE ME, OATH-BREAKERS!
FACE A PRINCE OF THE AESIR, AND KNOW WHAT FEAR IS!
DO YOU NOT MEAN--"KNOW WHAT DELIRIOUS OVER-CONFIDENCE IS," LITTLE GODLING?
THOR, YOU COME IN ARMS 'GAINST THE QUEEN OF HEL.
BETTER YOU HAD NEVER BEEN BORN!!
YOUR DREAD BOLTS OF DEATH ARE A FEARSOME WEAPON, MILADY--AGAINST ANY IMMORTAL FOOLISH ENOUGH TO LET THEM TOUCH HIM.
BUT MIGHTY MJOLNIR IS A MATCH FOR THEIR DREAD ENERGIES. AS I AM FOR YOU.

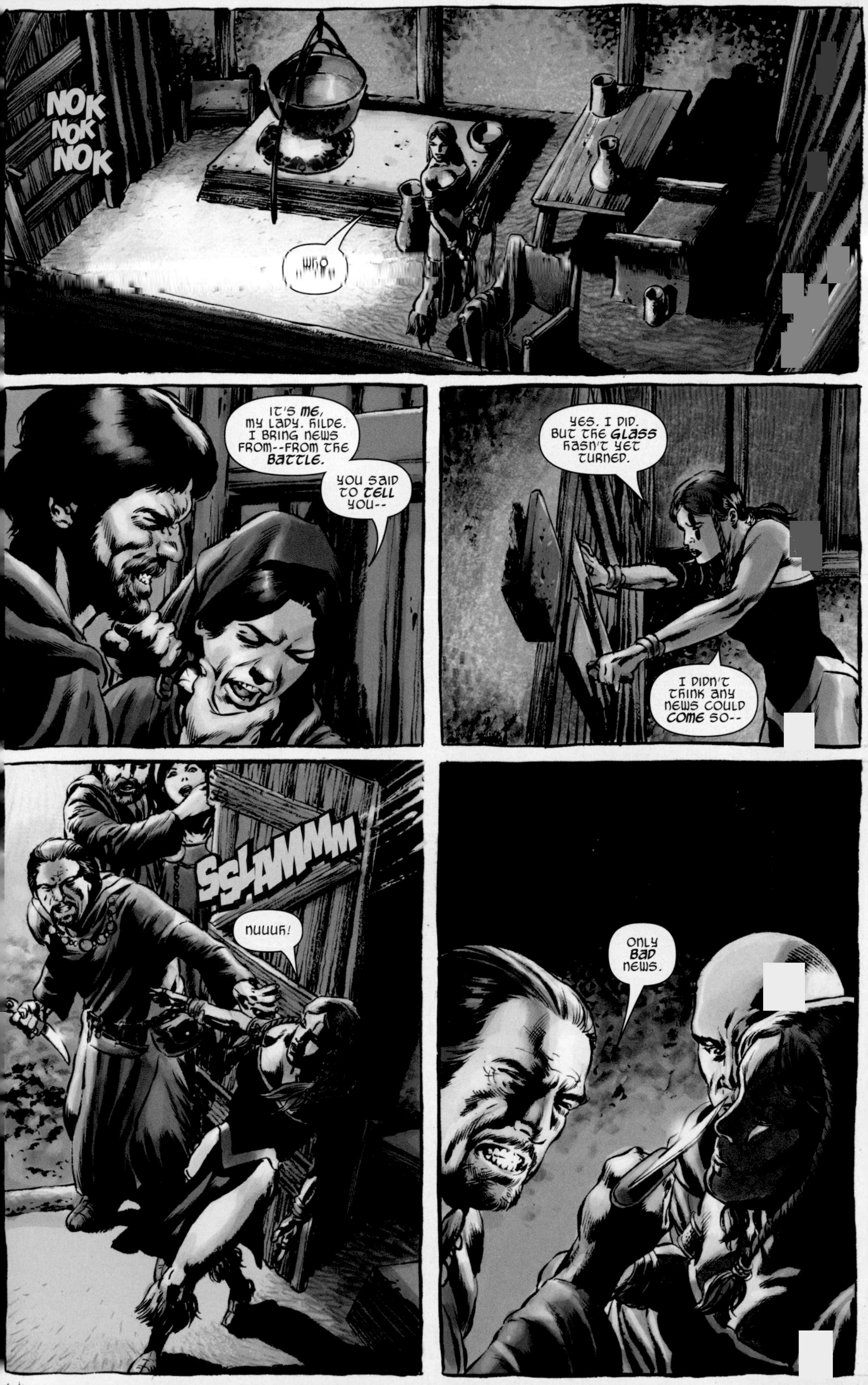
NOK NOK NOK
WHO
IT'S ME, MY LADY. HILDE. I BRING NEWS FROM--FROM THE BATTLE.
YOU SAID TO TELL YOU--
YES. I DID. BUT THE GLASS HASN'T YET TURNED.
I DIDN'T THINK ANY NEWS COULD COME SO--
SSLAMMMM
NUUUH!
ONLY BAD NEWS.

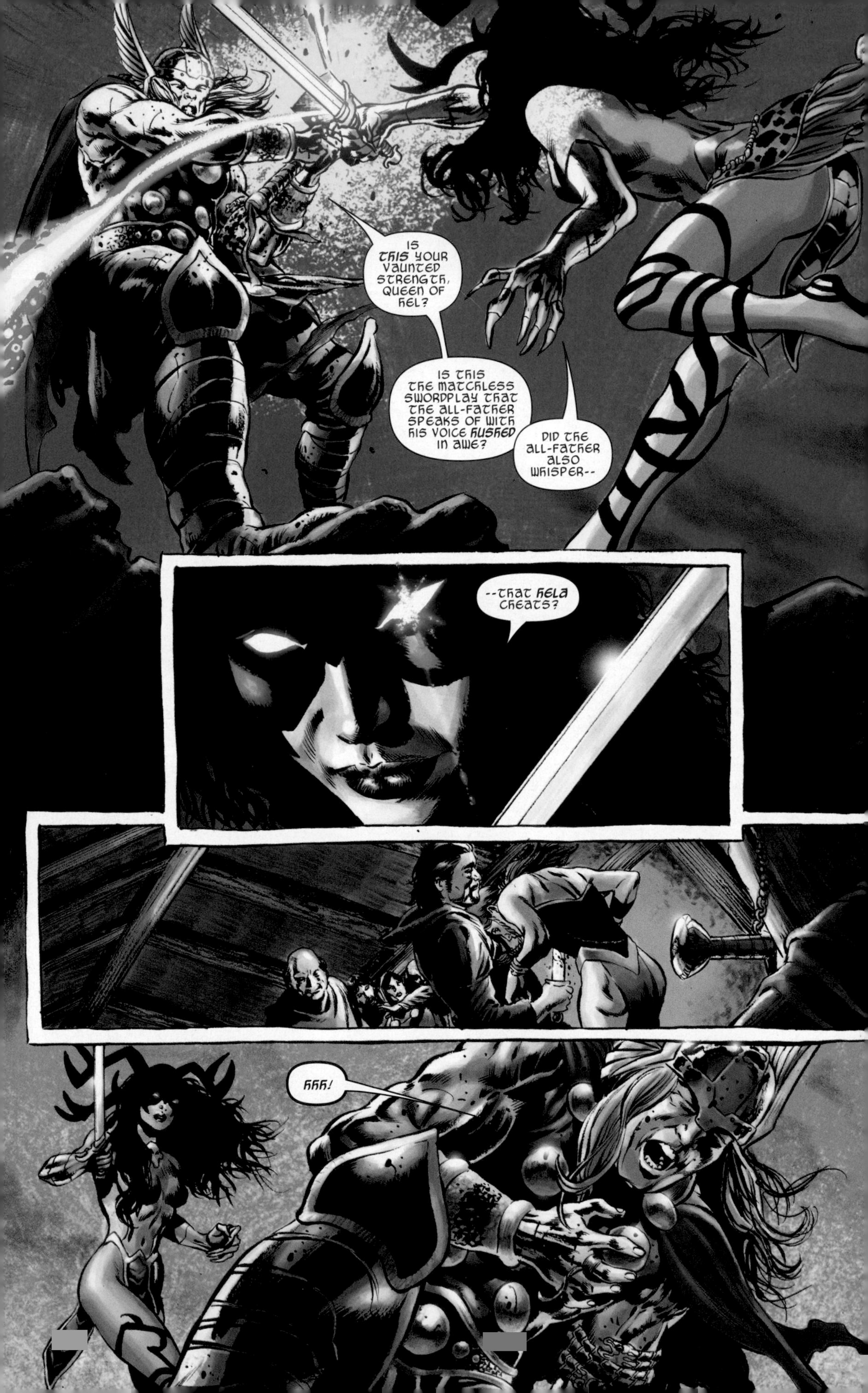

IS THIS YOUR VAUNTED STRENGTH, QUEEN OF HEL?
IS THIS THE MATCHLESS SWORDPLAY THAT THE ALL-FATHER SPEAKS OF WITH HIS VOICE HUSHED IN AWE?
DID THE ALL-FATHER ALSO WHISPER--
--THAT HELA CHEATS?
HHH!

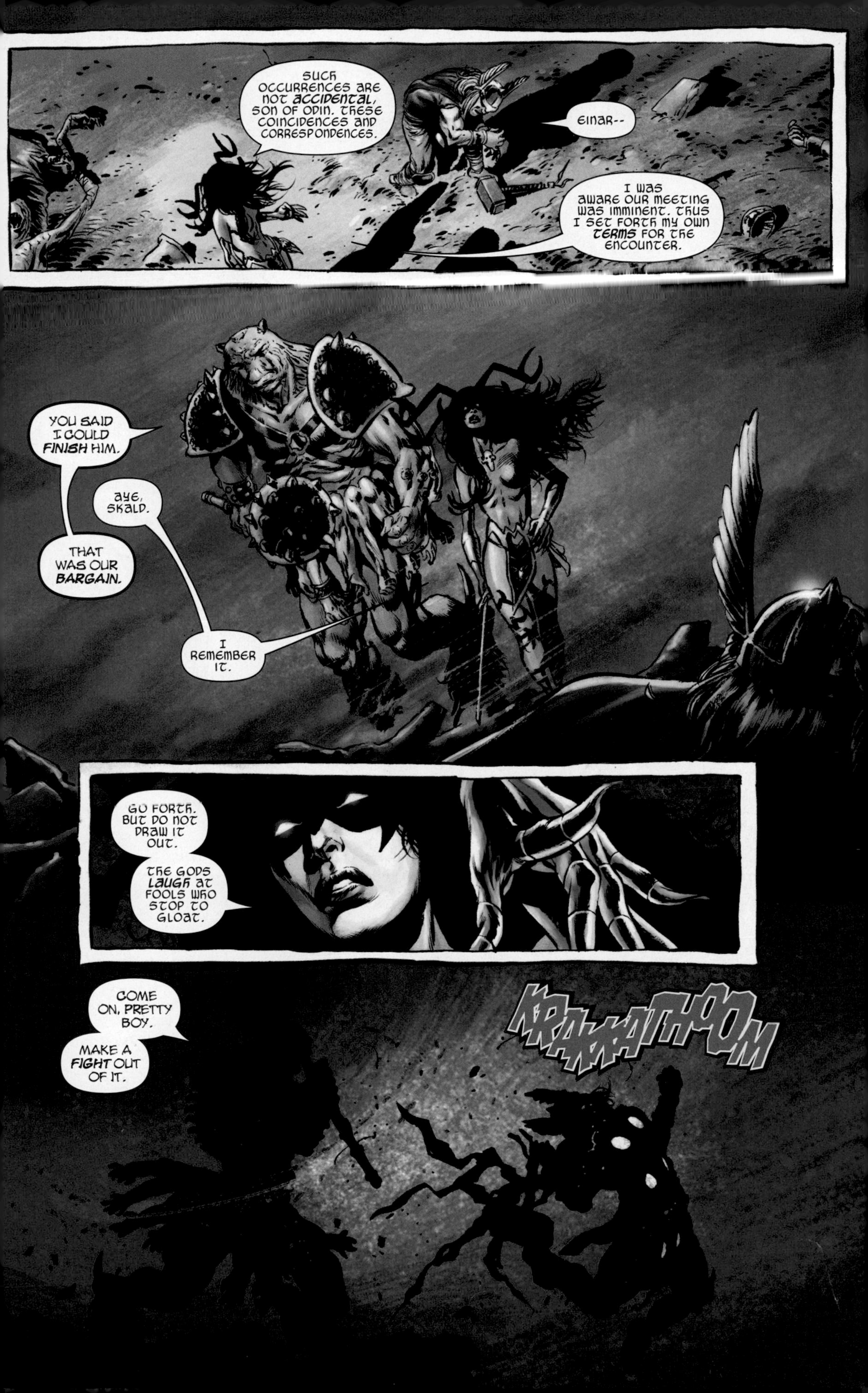
SUCH OCCURRENCES ARE NOT ACCIDENTAL, SON OF ODIN. THESE COINCIDENCES AND CORRESPONDENCES.
EINAR--
I WAS AWARE OUR MEETING WAS IMMINENT. THUS I SET FORTH MY OWN TERMS FOR THE ENCOUNTER.
YOU SAID I COULD FINISH HIM.
THAT WAS OUR BARGAIN.
AYE, SKALD.
I REMEMBER IT.
GO FORTH. BUT DO NOT DRAW IT OUT.
THE GODS LAUGH AT FOOLS WHO STOP TO GLOAT.
COME ON, PRETTY BOY.
MAKE A FIGHT OUT OF IT.
KRAKAKATHOOM

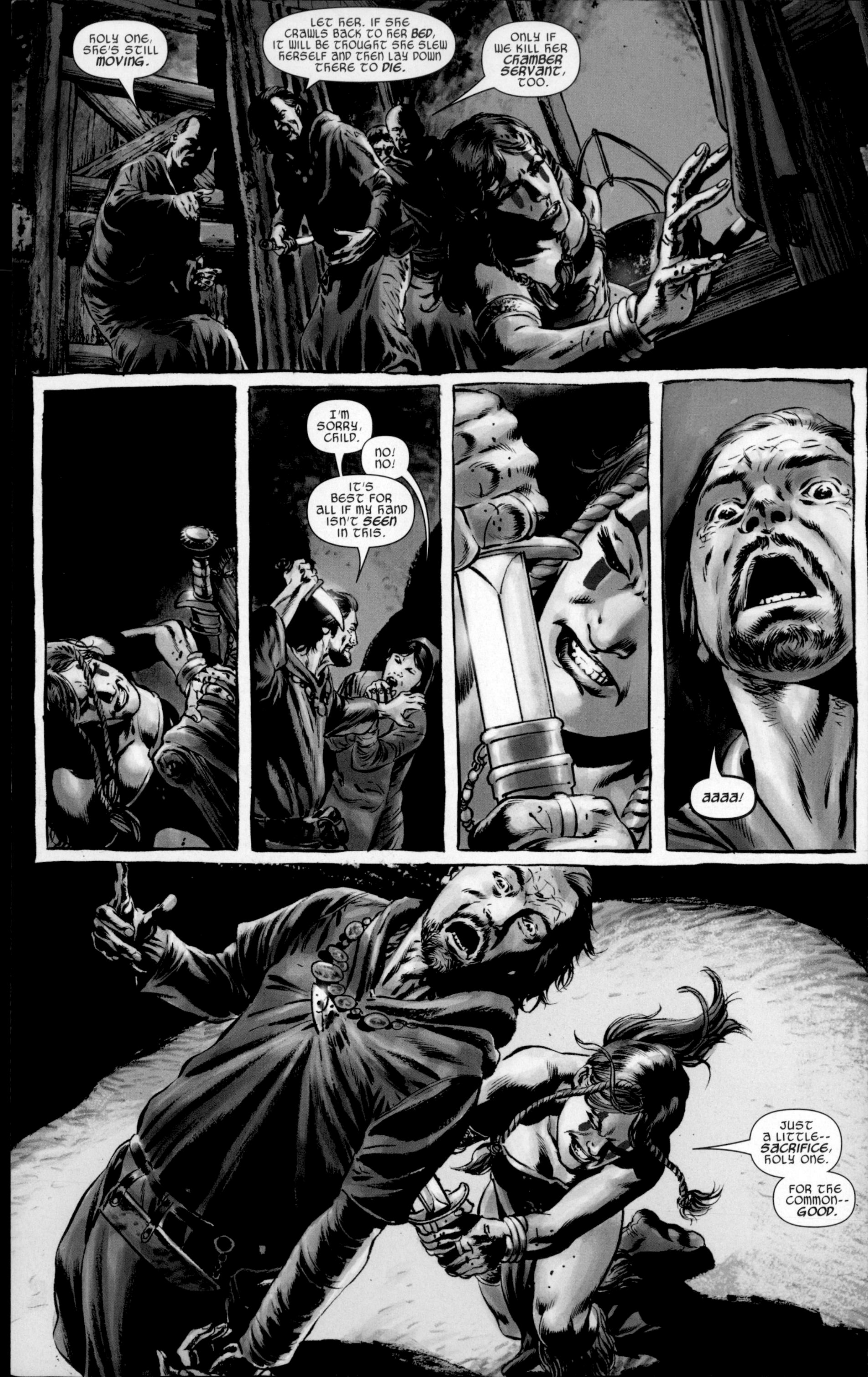
HOLY ONE, SHE'S STILL MOVING.
LET HER. IF SHE CRAWLS BACK TO HER BED, IT WILL BE THOUGHT SHE SLEW HERSELF AND THEN LAY DOWN THERE TO DIE.
ONLY IF WE KILL HER CHAMBER SERVANT, TOO.
I'M SORRY, CHILD.
NO! NO!
IT'S BEST FOR ALL IF MY HAND ISN'T SEEN IN THIS.
AAAA!
JUST A LITTLE-- SACRIFICE, HOLY ONE.
FOR THE COMMON-- GOOD.

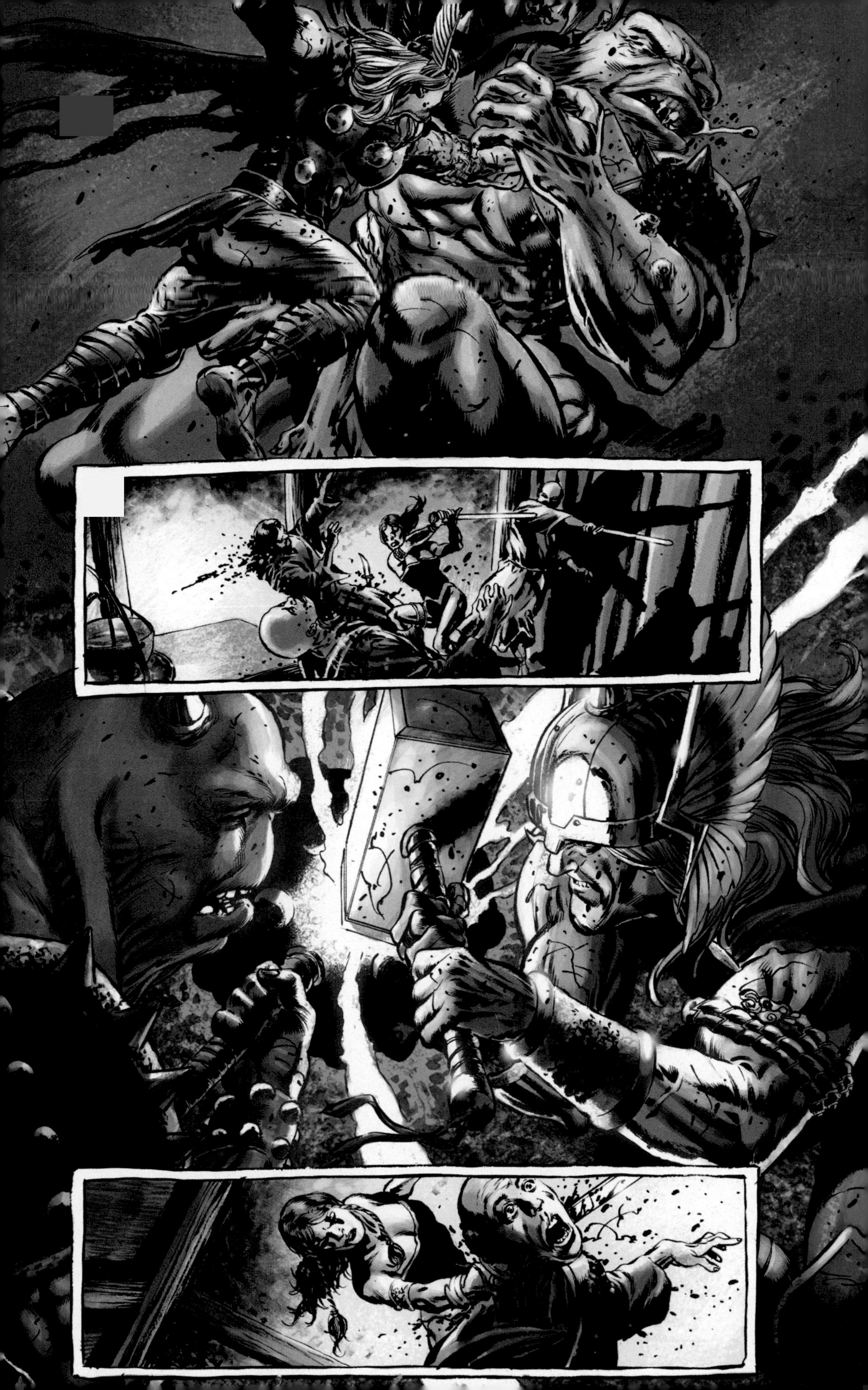

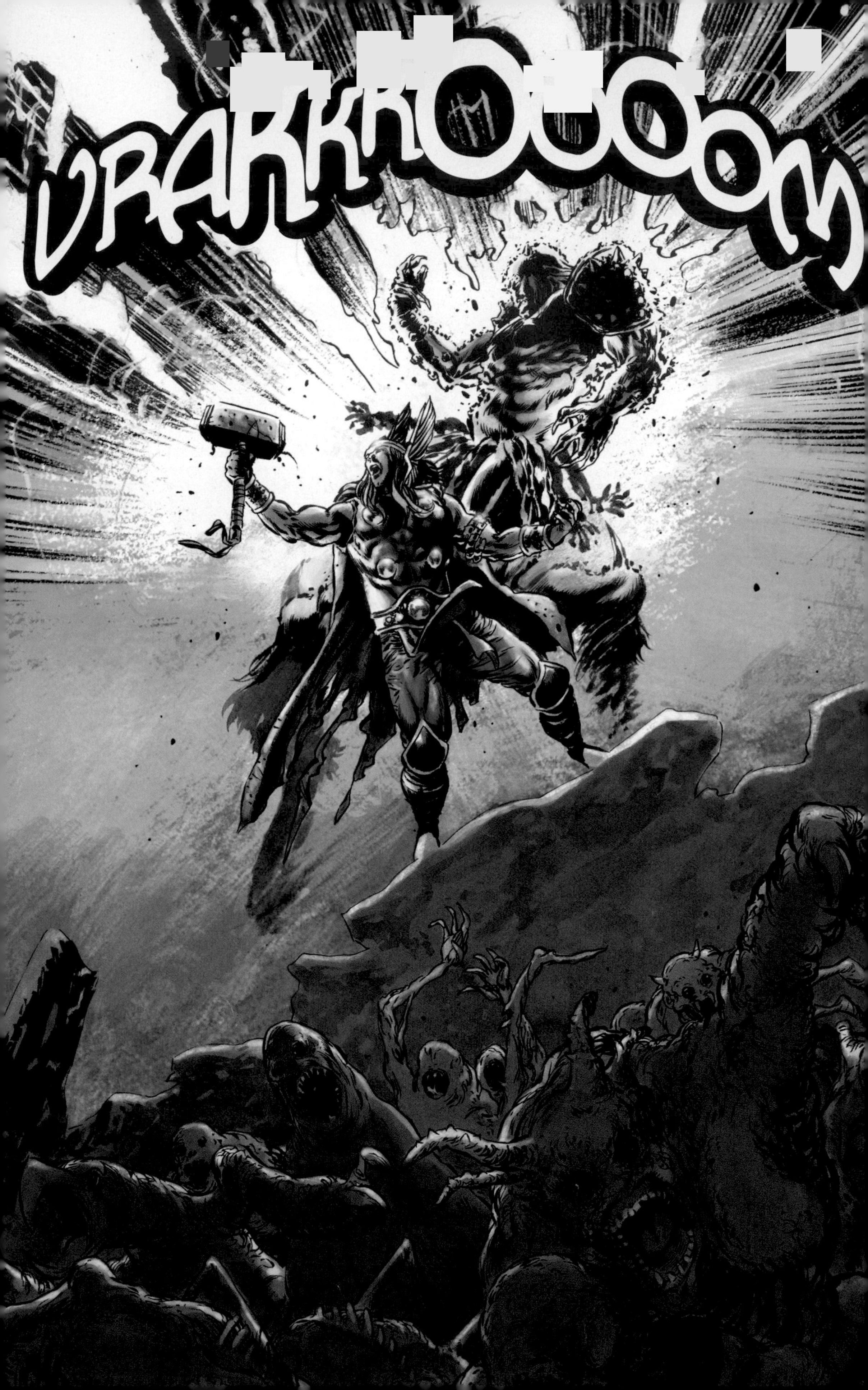
VRAKKROOOOM

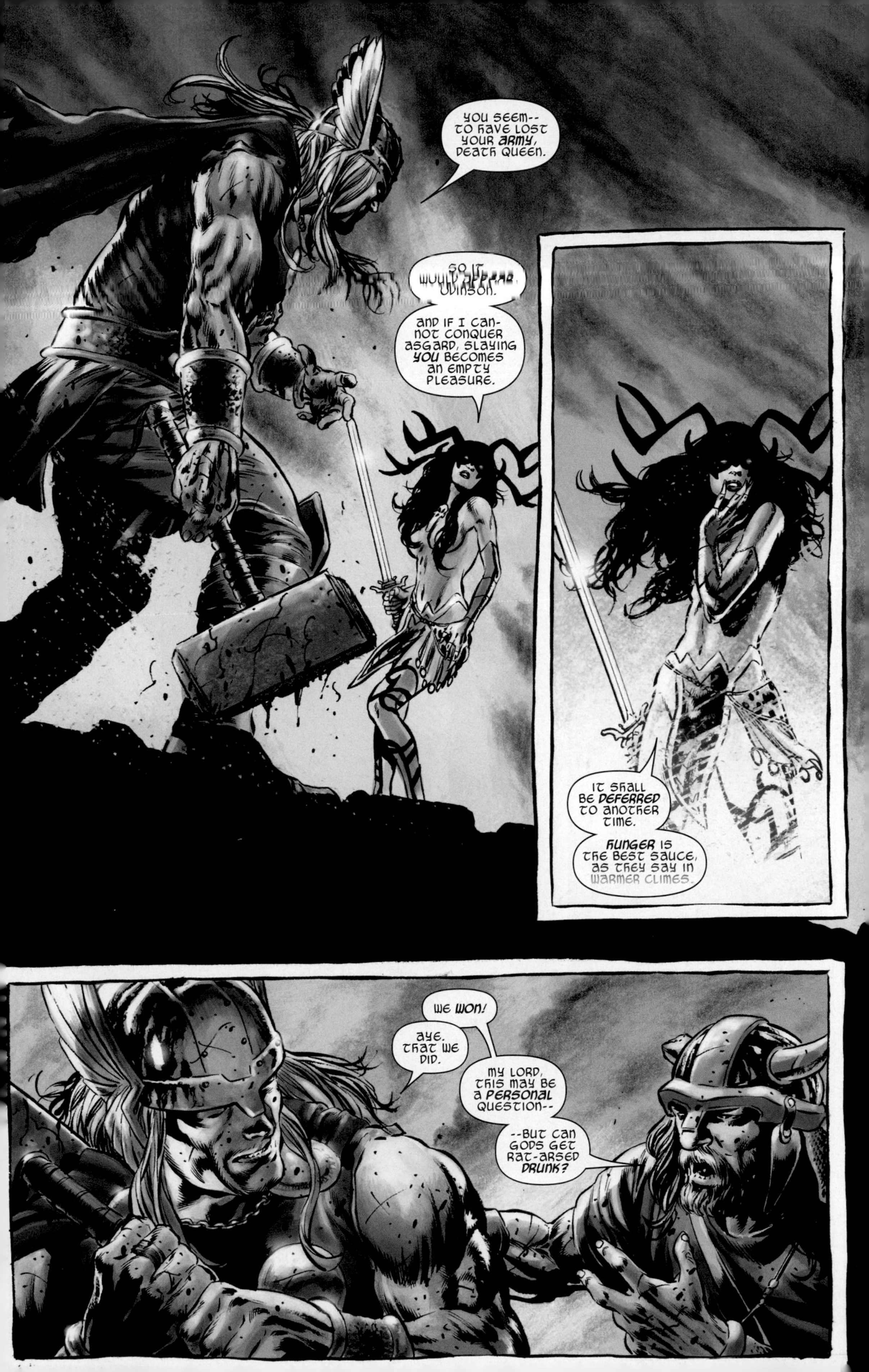
YOU SEEM-- TO HAVE LOST YOUR ARMY, DEATH QUEEN.
SO IT WOULD APPEAR, ODINSON.
AND IF I CAN-NOT CONQUER ASGARD, SLAYING YOU BECOMES AN EMPTY PLEASURE.
IT SHALL BE DEFERRED TO ANOTHER TIME.
HUNGER IS THE BEST SAUCE, AS THEY SAY IN WARMER CLIMES.
WE WON!
AYE. THAT WE DID.
MY LORD, THIS MAY BE A PERSONAL QUESTION--
--BUT CAN GODS GET RAT-ARSED DRUNK?

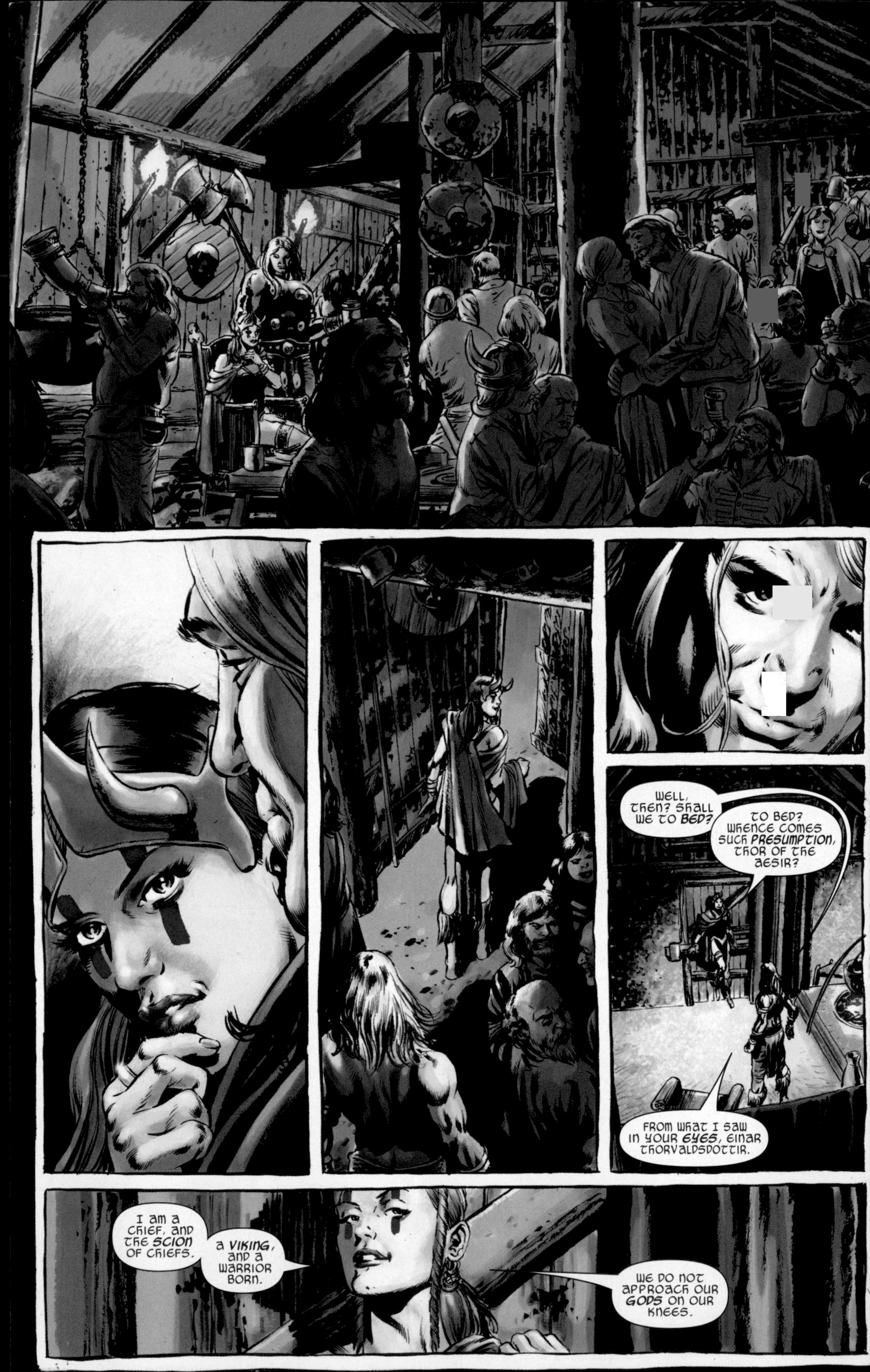

WELL, THEN? SHALL WE TO BED?
TO BED? WHENCE COMES SUCH PRESUMPTION, THOR OF THE AESIR?
FROM WHAT I SAW IN YOUR EYES, EINAR THORVALDSDOTTIR.
I AM A CHIEF, AND THE SCION OF CHIEFS.
A VIKING, AND A WARRIOR BORN.
WE DO NOT APPROACH OUR GODS ON OUR KNEES.

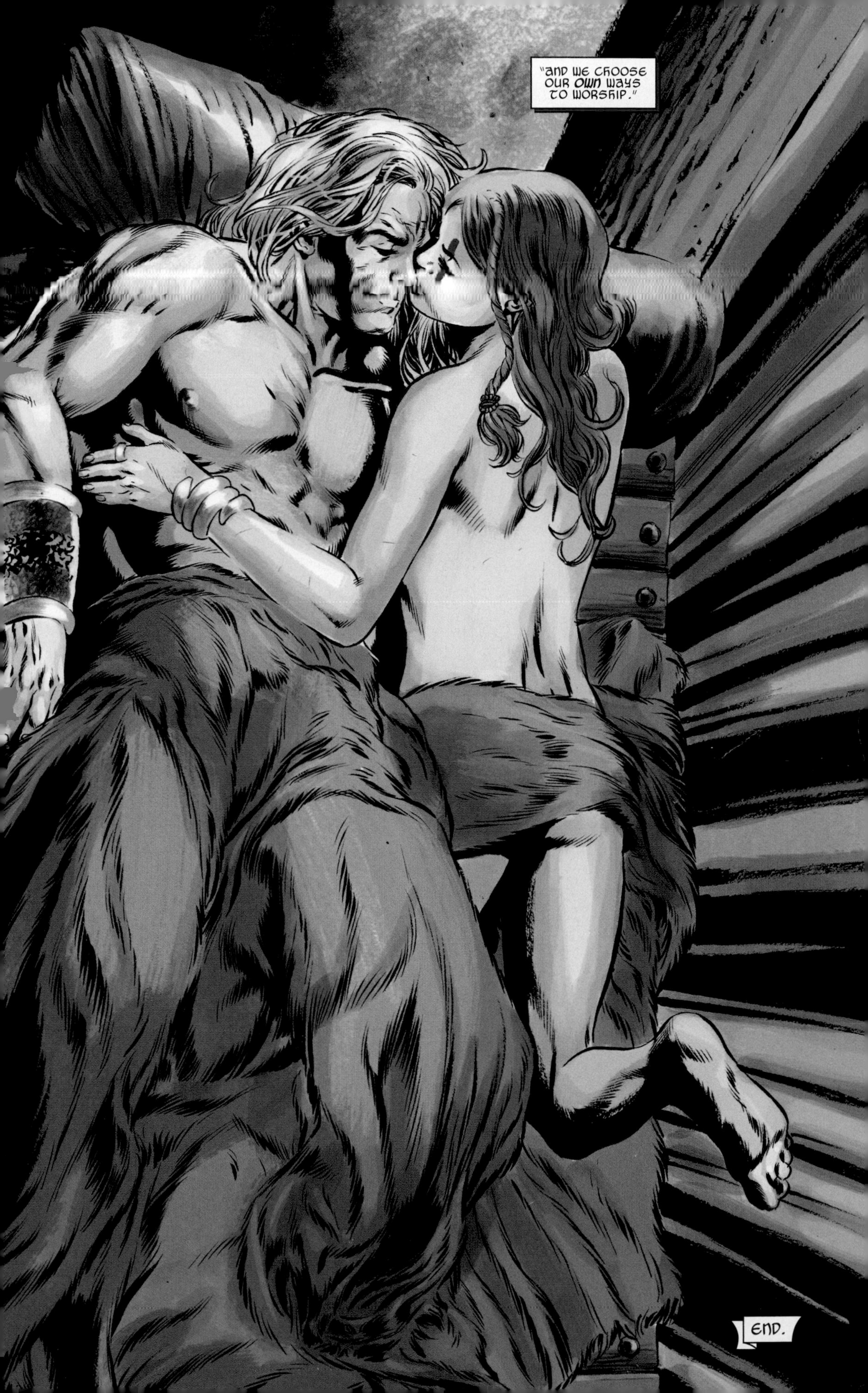
"AND WE CHOOSE OUR OWN WAYS TO WORSHIP."
END.

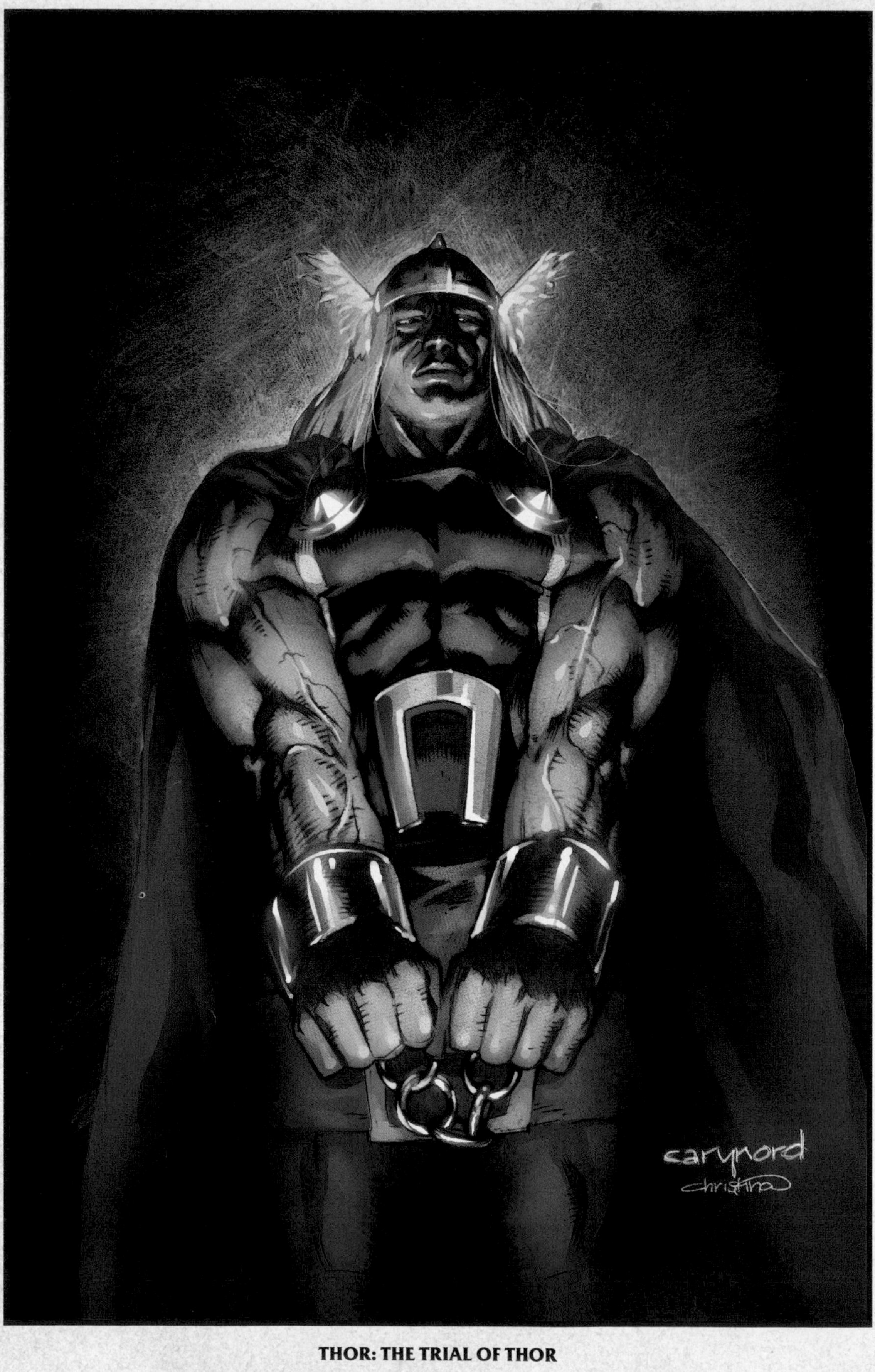
carynord
christina

THOR: THE TRIAL OF THOR

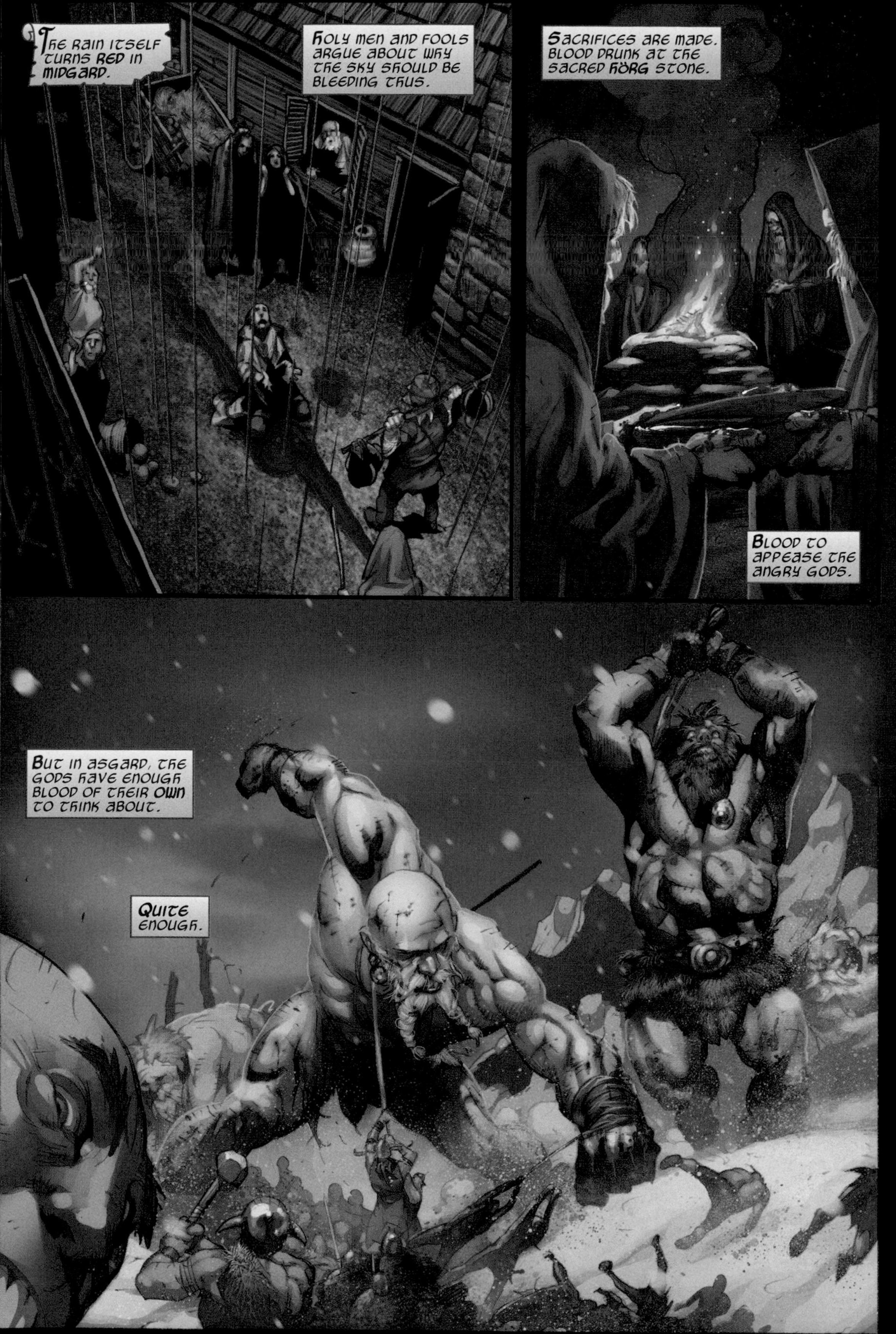
The rain itself turns red in Midgard.
Holy men and fools argue about why the sky should be bleeding thus.
Sacrifices are made. Blood drunk at the sacred Hörg stone.
Blood to appease the angry gods.
But in Asgard, the gods have enough blood of their own to think about.
Quite enough.

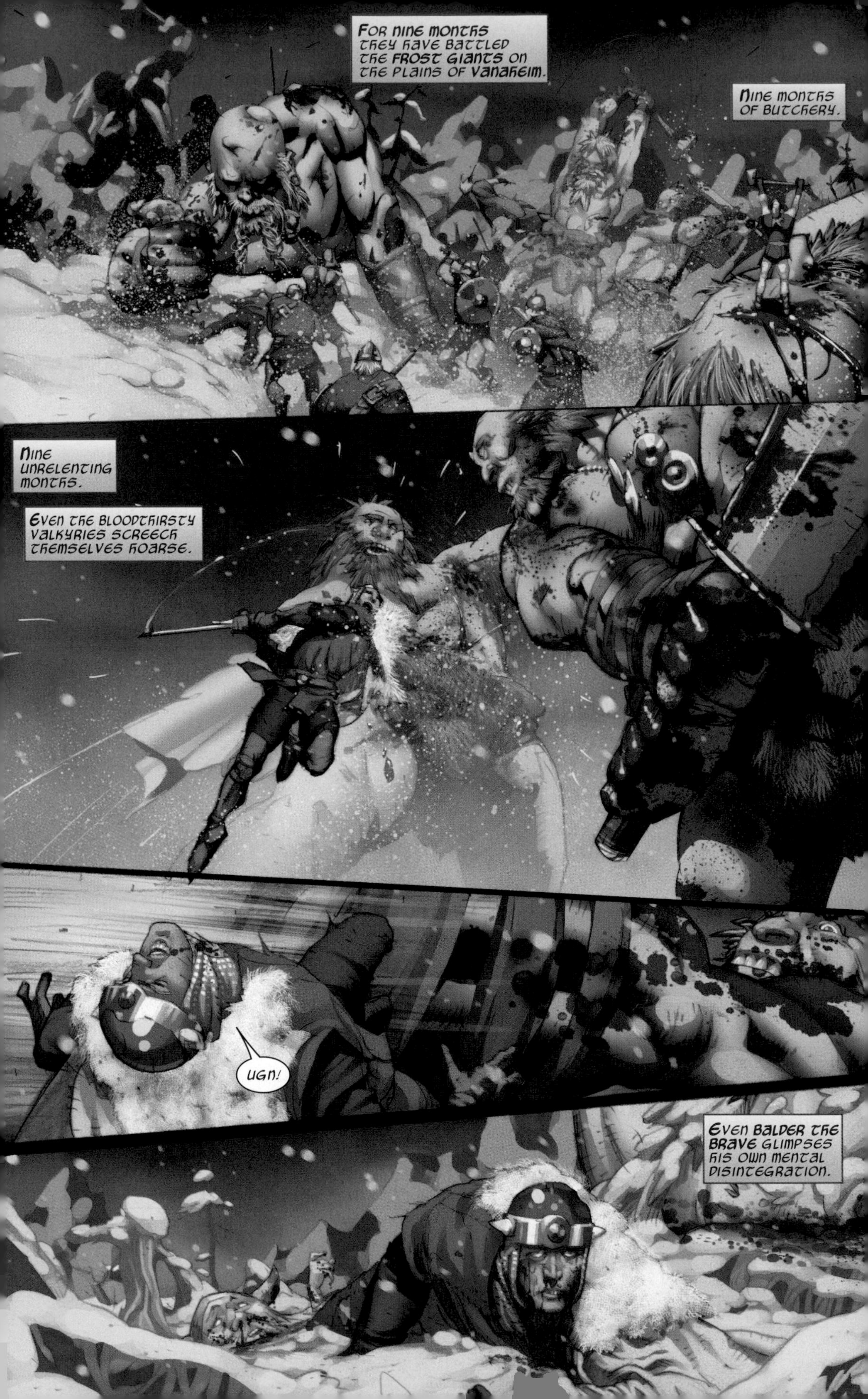
For nine months they have battled the Frost Giants on the plains of Vanaheim.
Nine months of butchery.
Nine unrelenting months.
Even the bloodthirsty Valkyries screech themselves hoarse.
UGN!
Even Balder the Brave glimpses his own mental disintegration.

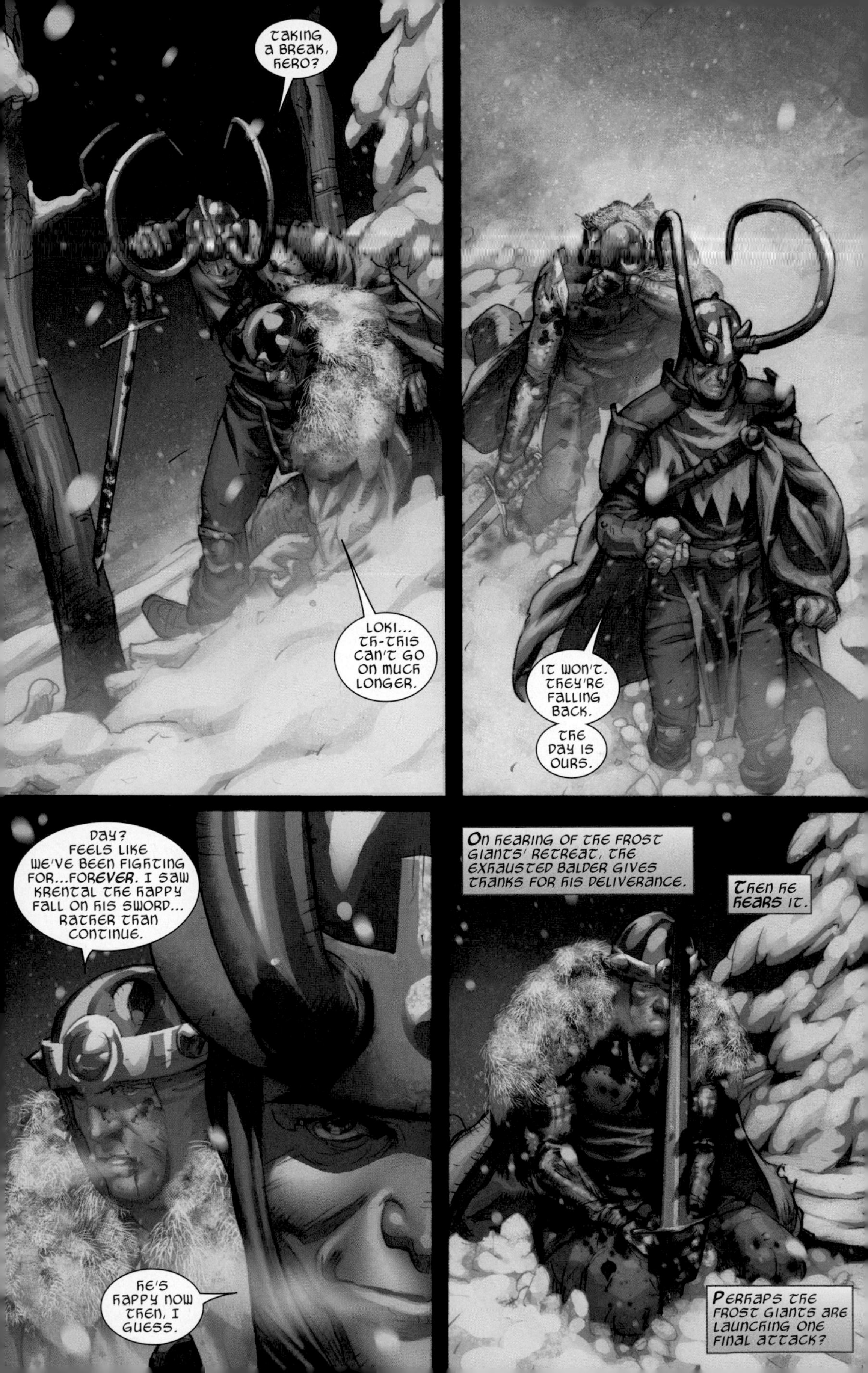
TAKING A BREAK, HERO?
LOKI... TH-THIS CAN'T GO ON MUCH LONGER.
IT WON'T. THEY'RE FALLING BACK.
THE DAY IS OURS.
DAY? FEELS LIKE WE'VE BEEN FIGHTING FOR...FOREVER. I SAW KRENTAL THE HAPPY FALL ON HIS SWORD... RATHER THAN CONTINUE.
HE'S HAPPY NOW THEN, I GUESS.
ON HEARING OF THE FROST GIANTS' RETREAT, THE EXHAUSTED BALDER GIVES THANKS FOR HIS DELIVERANCE.
THEN HE HEARS IT.
PERHAPS THE FROST GIANTS ARE LAUNCHING ONE FINAL ATTACK?

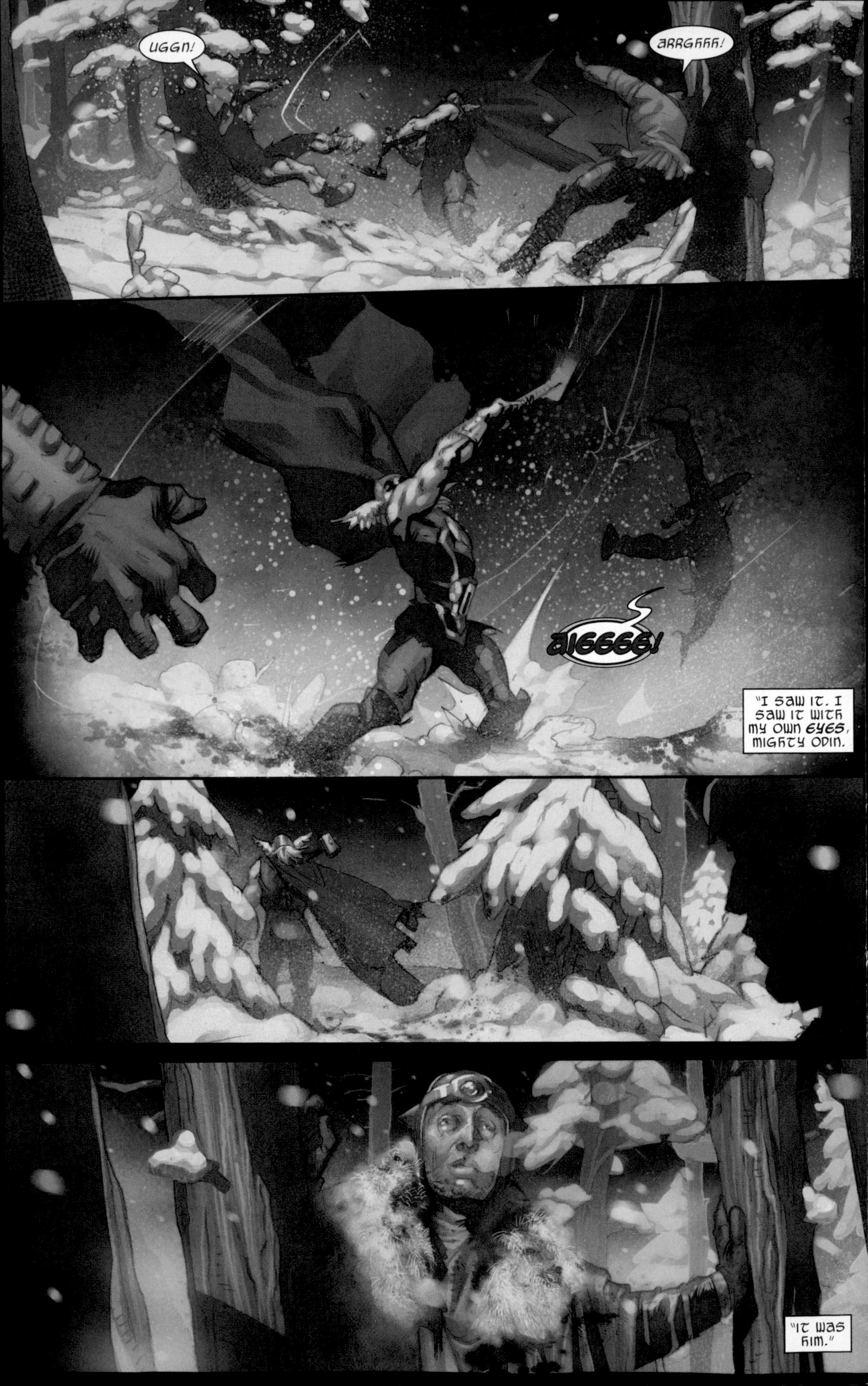
UGGN!
ARRGHHH!
AIGGGG!
"I SAW IT. I SAW IT WITH MY OWN EYES, MIGHTY ODIN.
"IT WAS HIM."

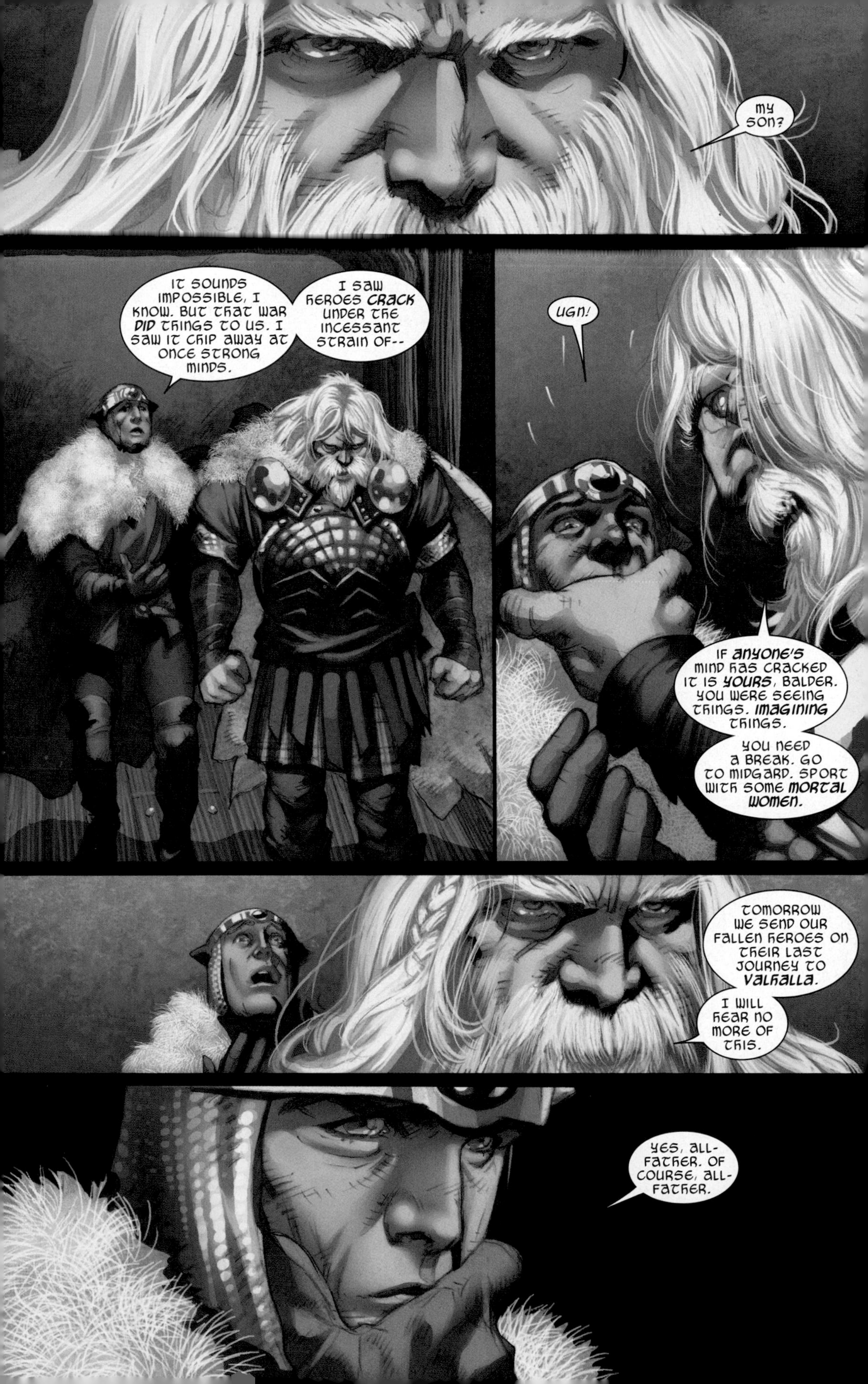
MY SON?
IT SOUNDS IMPOSSIBLE, I KNOW. BUT THAT WAR DID THINGS TO US. I SAW IT CHIP AWAY AT ONCE STRONG MINDS.
I SAW HEROES CRACK UNDER THE INCESSANT STRAIN OF--
UGN!
IF ANYONE'S MIND HAS CRACKED IT IS YOURS, BALDER. YOU WERE SEEING THINGS. IMAGINING THINGS.
YOU NEED A BREAK. GO TO MIDGARD. SPORT WITH SOME MORTAL WOMEN.
TOMORROW WE SEND OUR FALLEN HEROES ON THEIR LAST JOURNEY TO VALHALLA.
I WILL HEAR NO MORE OF THIS.
YES, ALL-FATHER. OF COURSE, ALL-FATHER.

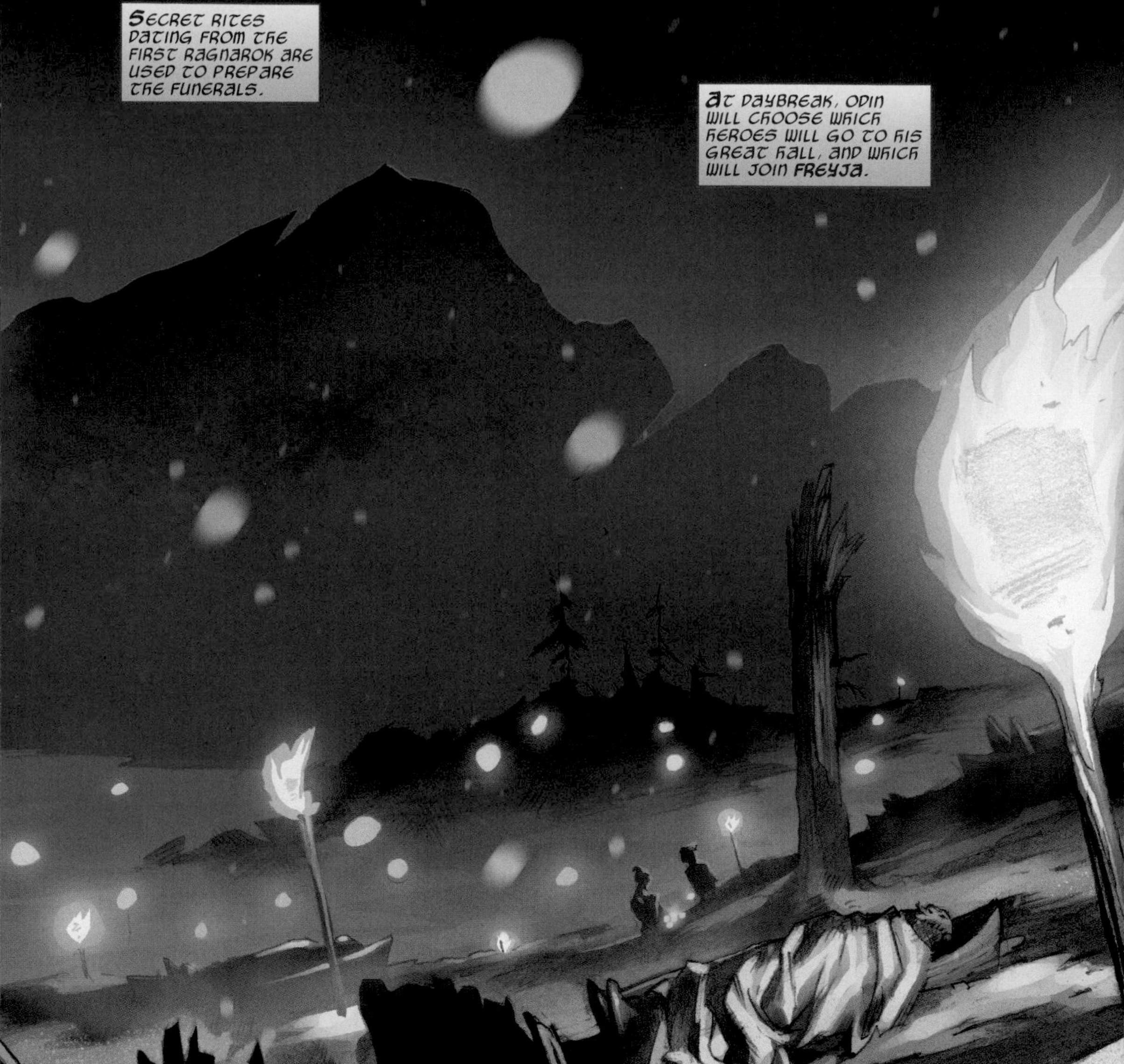
Secret rites dating from the first Ragnarok are used to prepare the funerals.
At daybreak, Odin will choose which heroes will go to his great hall, and which will join Freyja.

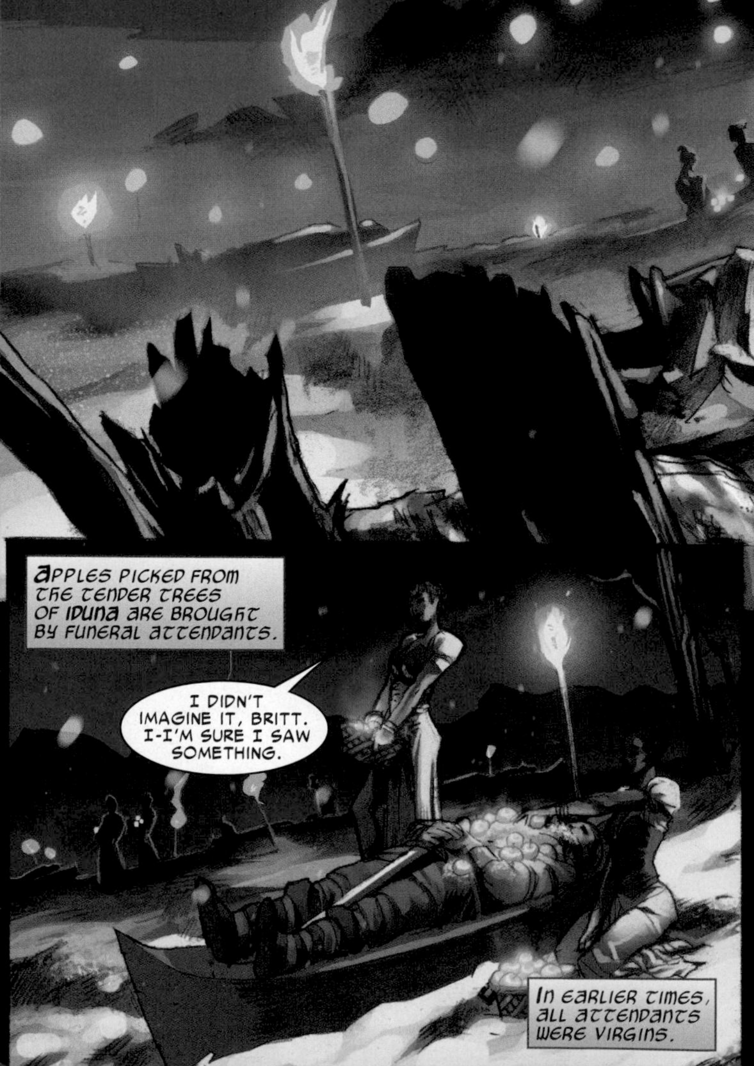
Apples picked from the tender trees of Iduna are brought by funeral attendants.
I DIDN'T IMAGINE IT, BRITT. I-I'M SURE I SAW SOMETHING.
In earlier times, all attendants were virgins.

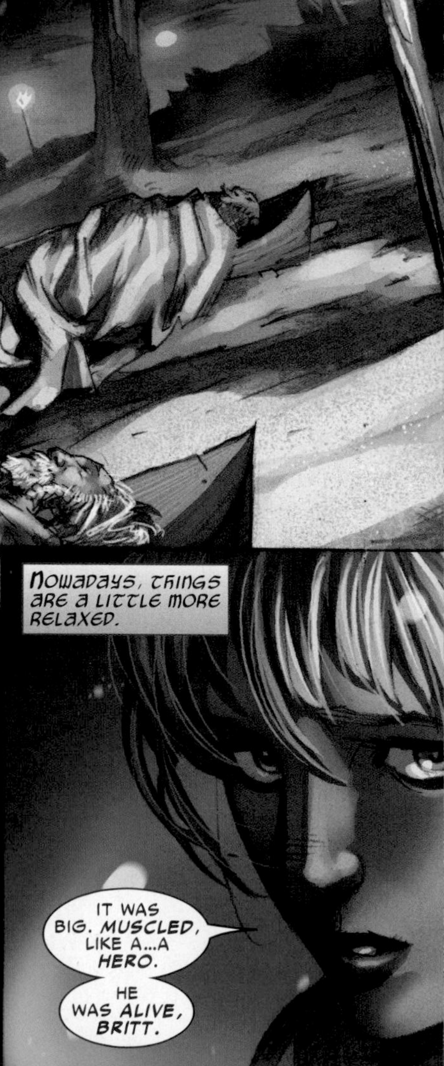
Nowadays, things are a little more relaxed.
IT WAS BIG. MUSCLED, LIKE A...A HERO.
HE WAS ALIVE, BRITT.

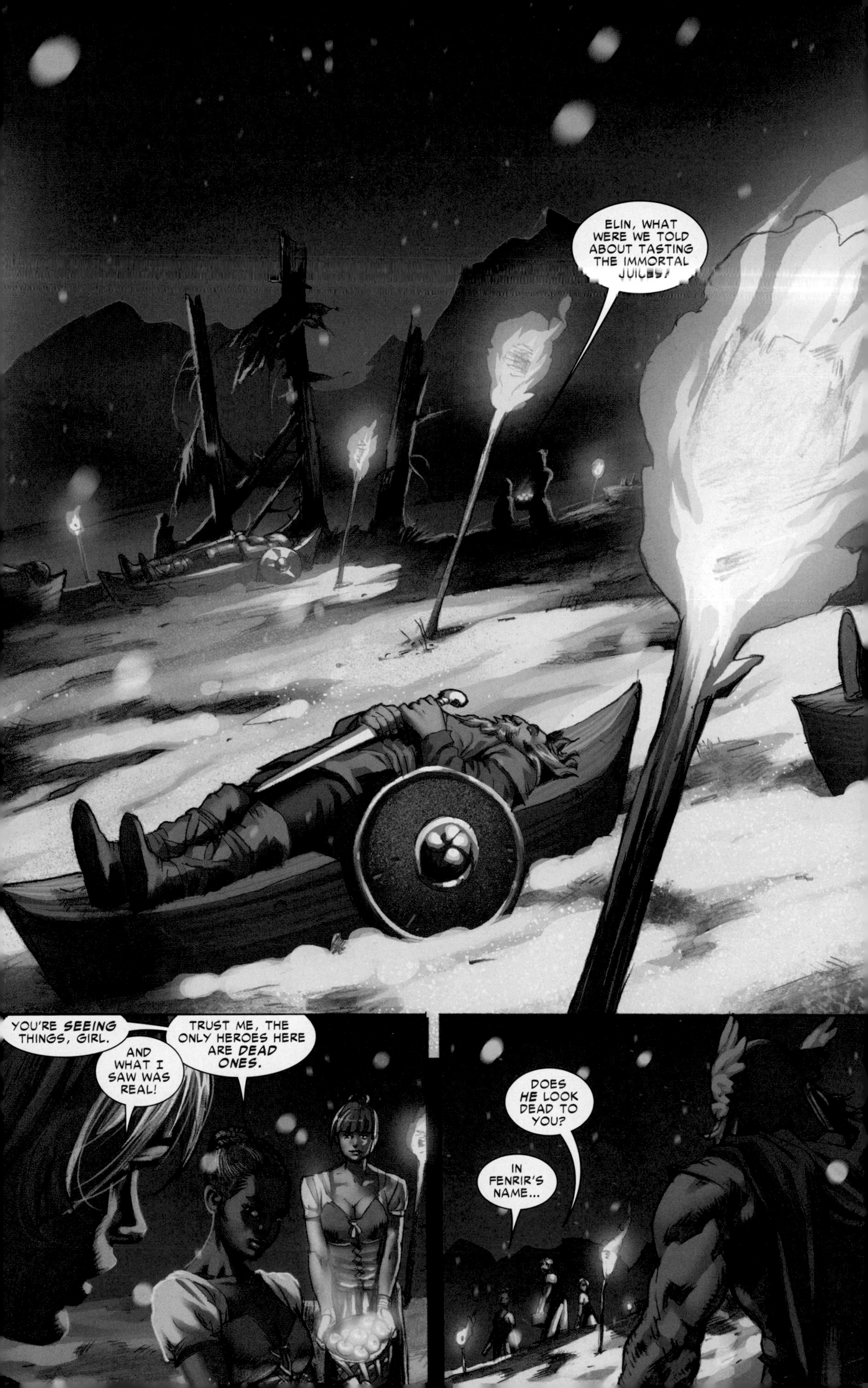
ELIN, WHAT WERE WE TOLD ABOUT TASTING THE IMMORTAL JUICES?
YOU'RE *SEEING* THINGS, GIRL.
TRUST ME, THE ONLY HEROES HERE ARE *DEAD ONES*.
AND WHAT I SAW WAS REAL!
DOES *HE* LOOK DEAD TO YOU?
IN FENRIR'S NAME...

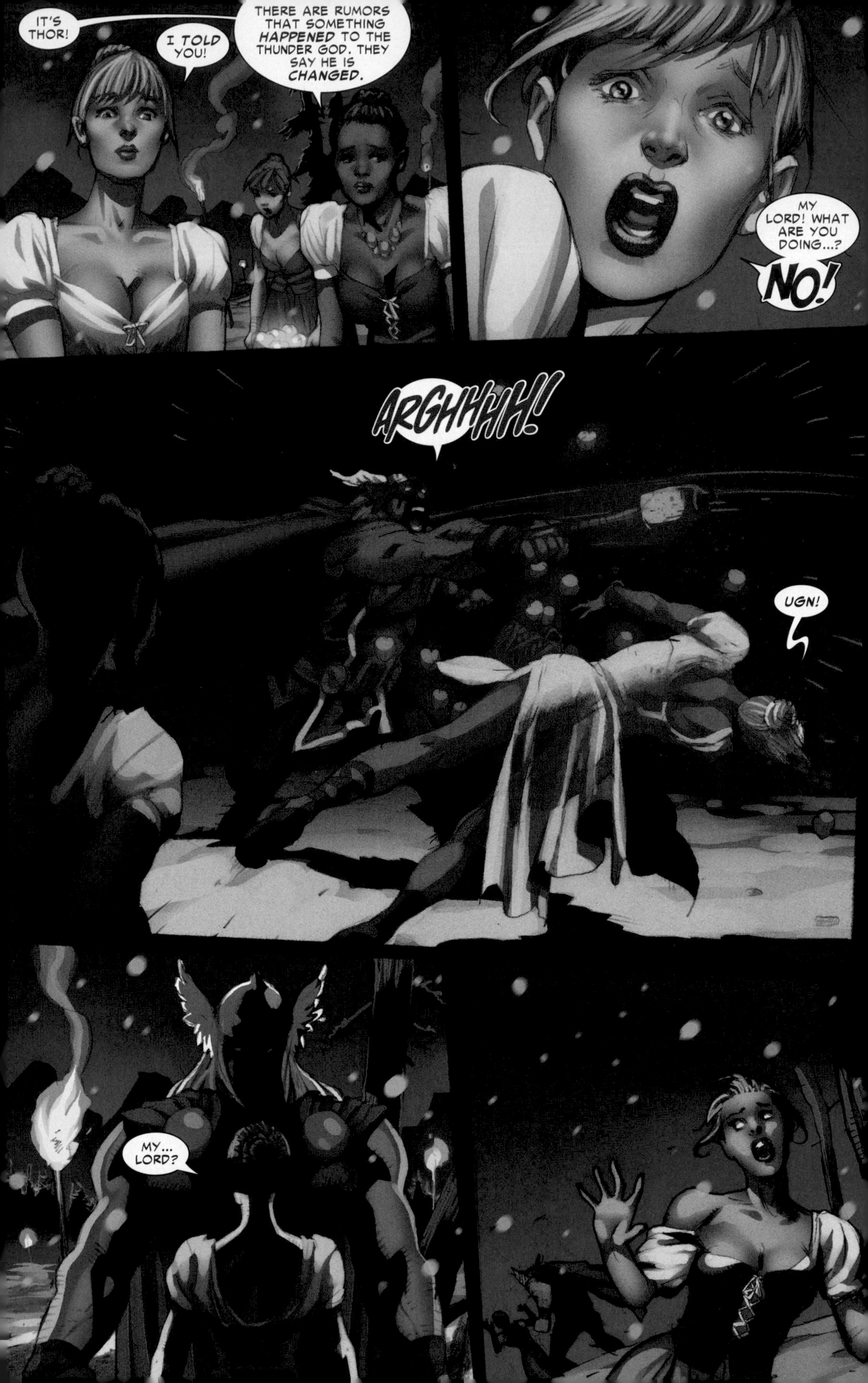
IT'S THOR!
I TOLD YOU!
THERE ARE RUMORS THAT SOMETHING HAPPENED TO THE THUNDER GOD. THEY SAY HE IS CHANGED.
MY LORD! WHAT ARE YOU DOING...?
NO!
ARGHHHH!
UGN!
MY... LORD?

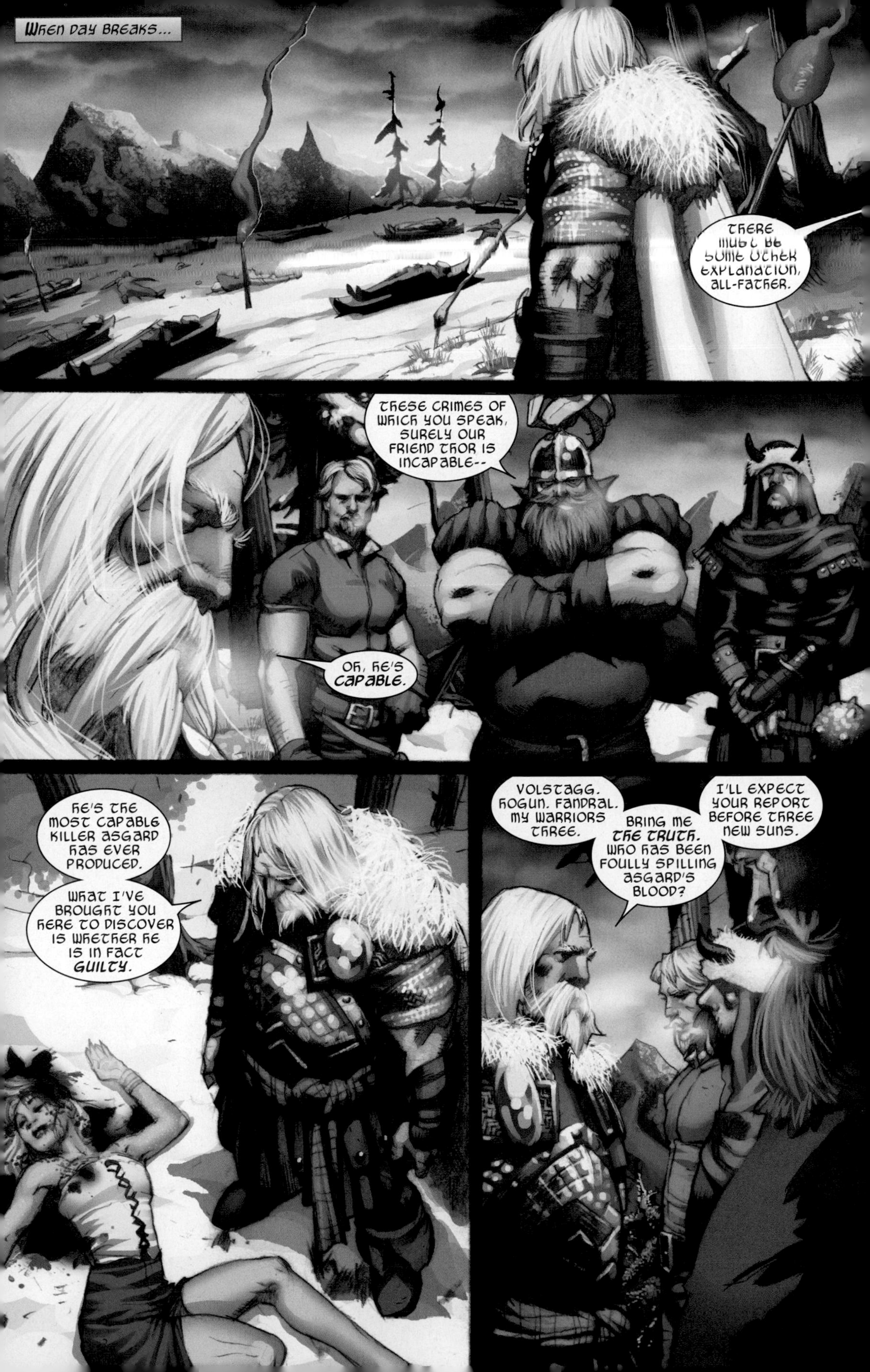
WHEN DAY BREAKS...
THERE MUST BE SOME OTHER EXPLANATION, ALL-FATHER.
THESE CRIMES OF WHICH YOU SPEAK, SURELY OUR FRIEND THOR IS INCAPABLE--
OH, HE'S CAPABLE.
HE'S THE MOST CAPABLE KILLER ASGARD HAS EVER PRODUCED.
WHAT I'VE BROUGHT YOU HERE TO DISCOVER IS WHETHER HE IS IN FACT GUILTY.
VOLSTAGG. HOGUN. FANDRAL. MY WARRIORS THREE.
BRING ME THE TRUTH. WHO HAS BEEN FOULLY SPILLING ASGARD'S BLOOD?
I'LL EXPECT YOUR REPORT BEFORE THREE NEW SUNS.

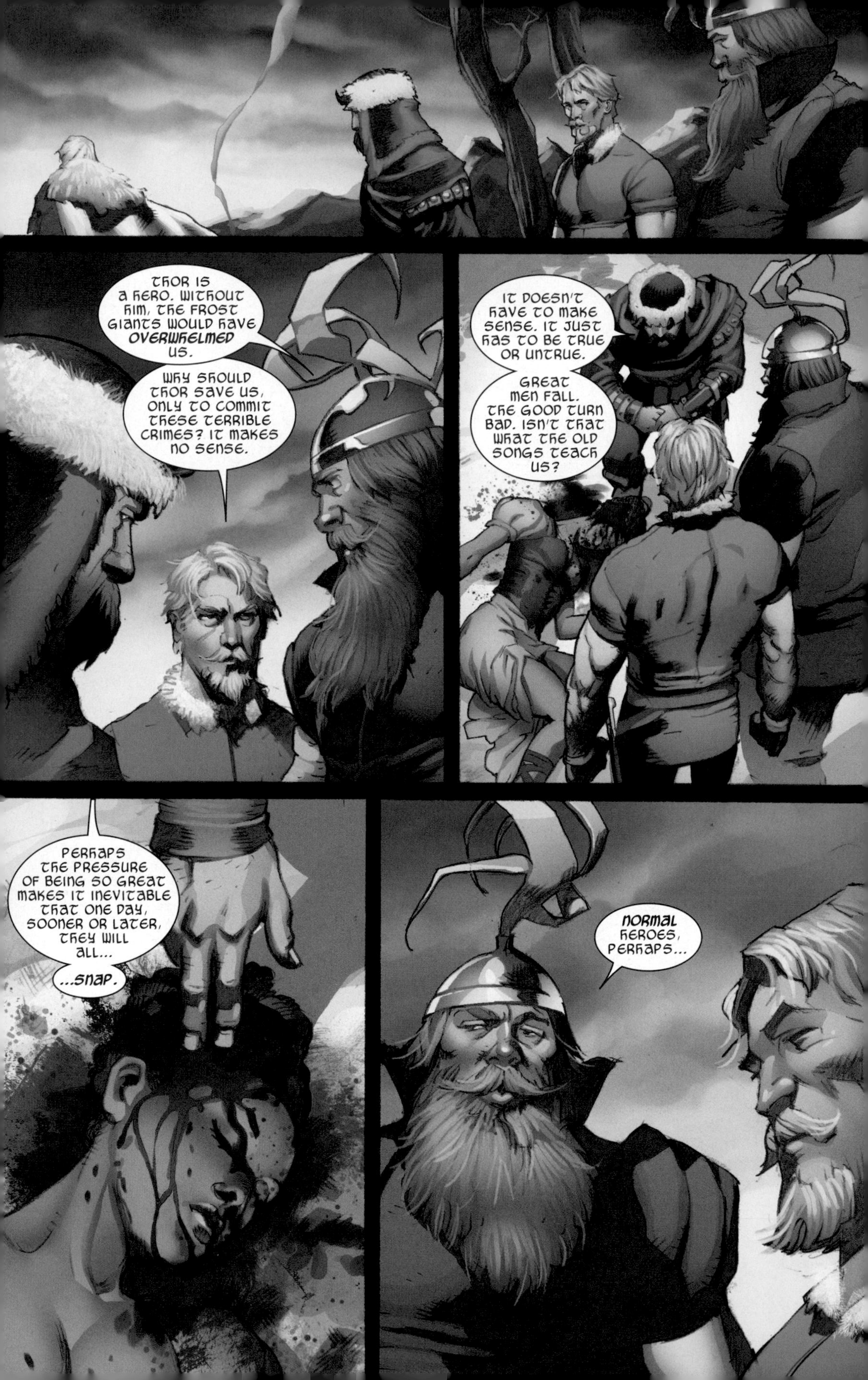

THOR IS A HERO. WITHOUT HIM, THE FROST GIANTS WOULD HAVE **OVERWHELMED** US.
WHY SHOULD THOR SAVE US, ONLY TO COMMIT THESE TERRIBLE CRIMES? IT MAKES NO SENSE.
IT DOESN'T HAVE TO MAKE SENSE. IT JUST HAS TO BE TRUE OR UNTRUE.
GREAT MEN FALL. THE GOOD TURN BAD. ISN'T THAT WHAT THE OLD SONGS TEACH US?
PERHAPS THE PRESSURE OF BEING SO GREAT MAKES IT INEVITABLE THAT ONE DAY, SOONER OR LATER, THEY WILL ALL...
...*SNAP*.
NORMAL HEROES, PERHAPS...

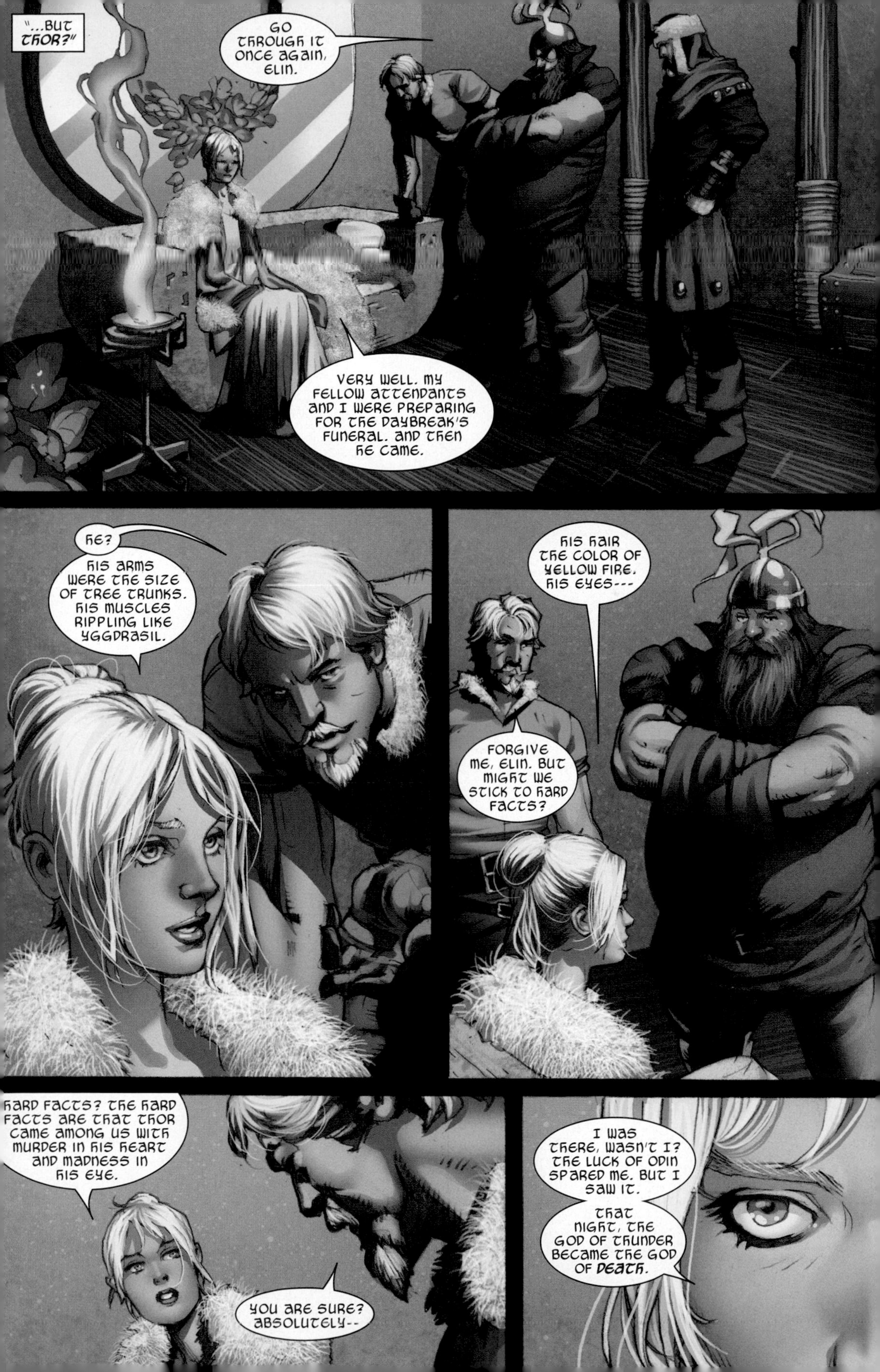
"...BUT THOR?"
GO THROUGH IT ONCE AGAIN, ELIN.
VERY WELL. MY FELLOW ATTENDANTS AND I WERE PREPARING FOR THE DAYBREAK'S FUNERAL. AND THEN HE CAME.
HE?
HIS ARMS WERE THE SIZE OF TREE TRUNKS. HIS MUSCLES RIPPLING LIKE YGGDRASIL.
HIS HAIR THE COLOR OF YELLOW FIRE. HIS EYES---
FORGIVE ME, ELIN. BUT MIGHT WE STICK TO HARD FACTS?
HARD FACTS? THE HARD FACTS ARE THAT THOR CAME AMONG US WITH MURDER IN HIS HEART AND MADNESS IN HIS EYE.
YOU ARE SURE? ABSOLUTELY--
I WAS THERE, WASN'T I? THE LUCK OF ODIN SPARED ME. BUT I SAW IT.
THAT NIGHT, THE GOD OF THUNDER BECAME THE GOD OF DEATH.

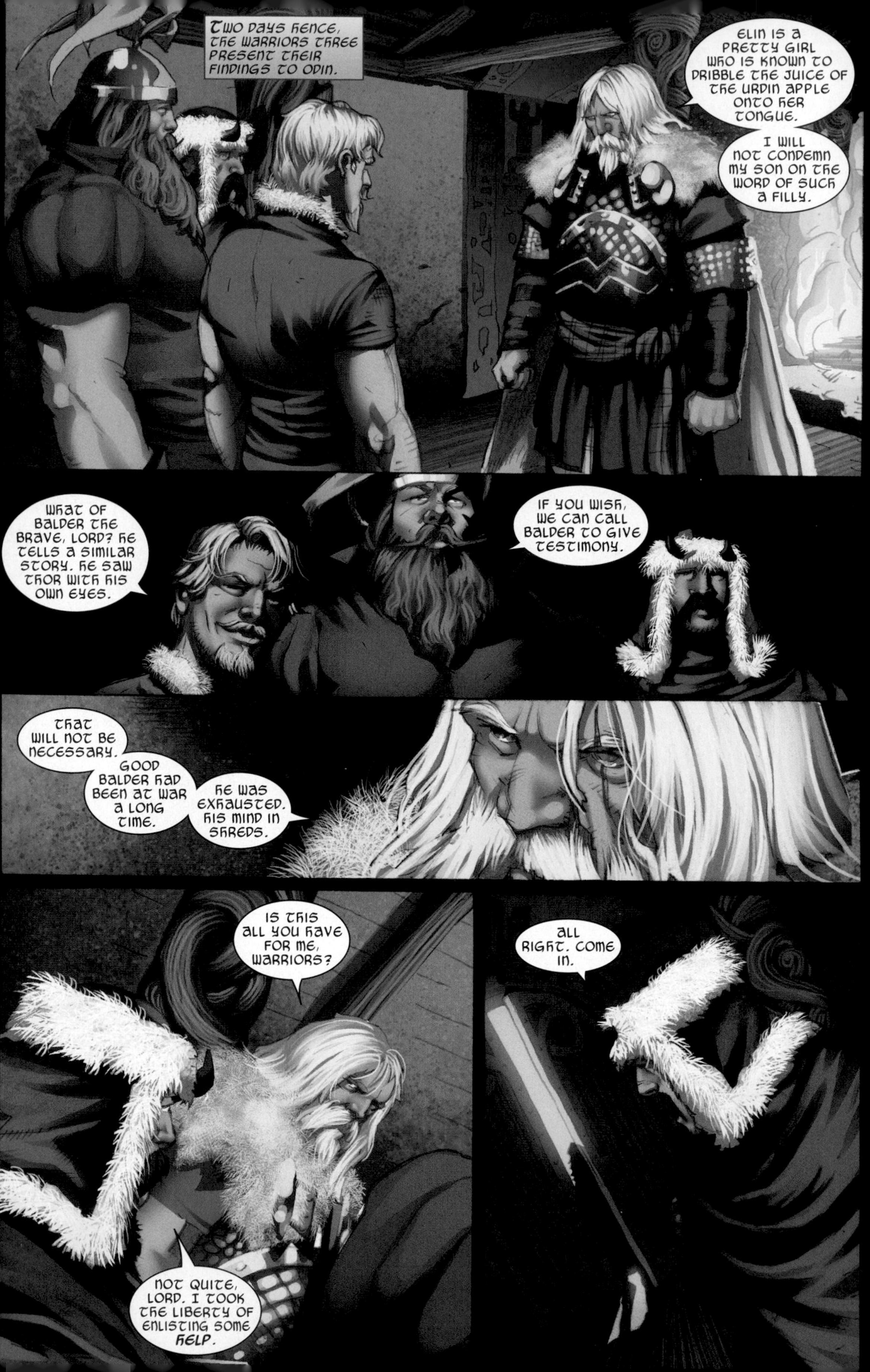
TWO DAYS HENCE, THE WARRIORS THREE PRESENT THEIR FINDINGS TO ODIN.
ELIN IS A PRETTY GIRL WHO IS KNOWN TO DRIBBLE THE JUICE OF THE URDIN APPLE ONTO HER TONGUE.
I WILL NOT CONDEMN MY SON ON THE WORD OF SUCH A FILLY.
WHAT OF BALDER THE BRAVE, LORD? HE TELLS A SIMILAR STORY. HE SAW THOR WITH HIS OWN EYES.
IF YOU WISH, WE CAN CALL BALDER TO GIVE TESTIMONY.
THAT WILL NOT BE NECESSARY.
GOOD BALDER HAD BEEN AT WAR A LONG TIME.
HE WAS EXHAUSTED. HIS MIND IN SHREDS.
IS THIS ALL YOU HAVE FOR ME, WARRIORS?
NOT QUITE, LORD. I TOOK THE LIBERTY OF ENLISTING SOME HELP.
ALL RIGHT. COME IN.

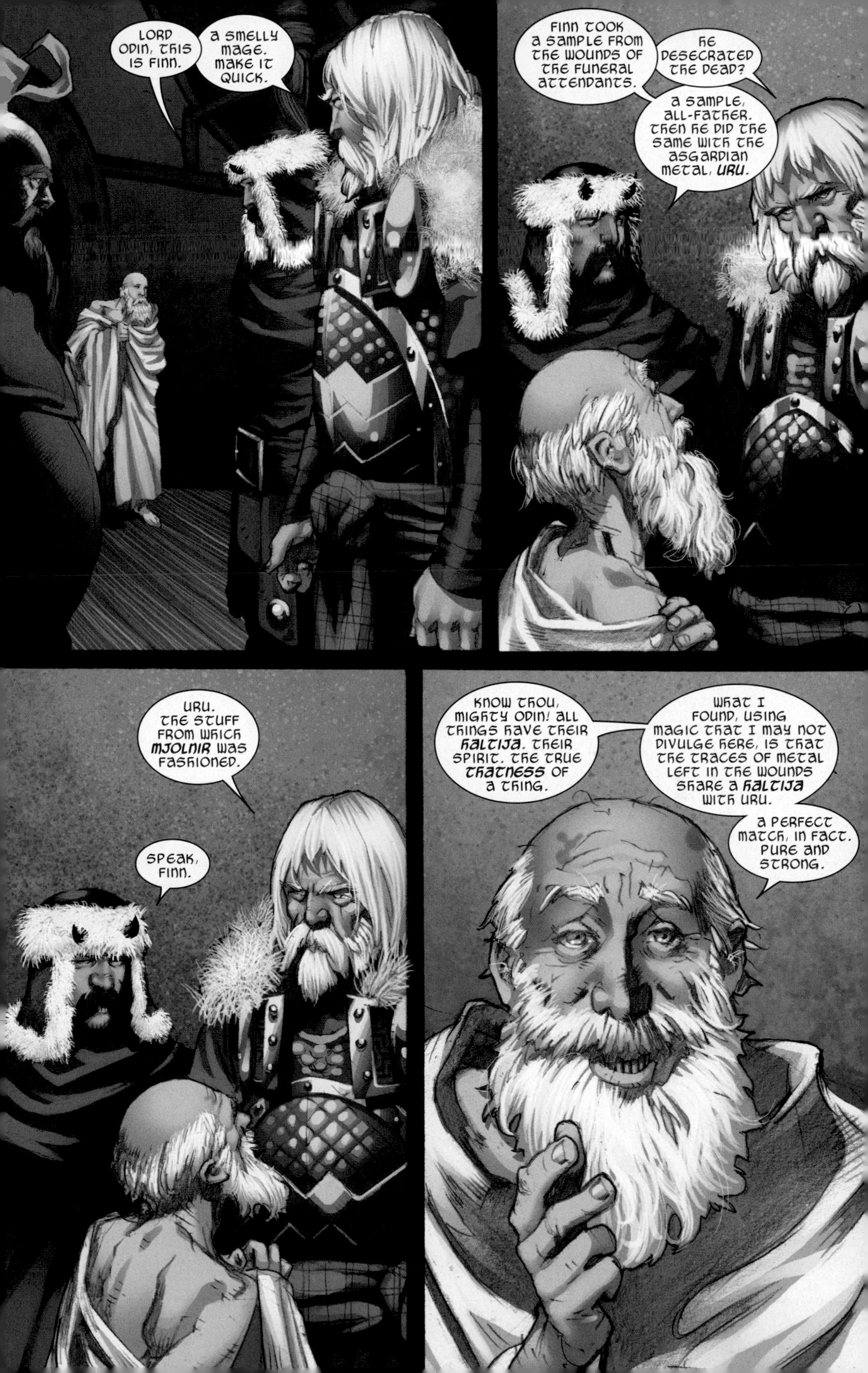
LORD ODIN, THIS IS FINN.
A SMELLY MAGE. MAKE IT QUICK.
FINN TOOK A SAMPLE FROM THE WOUNDS OF THE FUNERAL ATTENDANTS.
HE DESECRATED THE DEAD?
A SAMPLE, ALL-FATHER. THEN HE DID THE SAME WITH THE ASGARDIAN METAL, URU.
URU. THE STUFF FROM WHICH MJOLNIR WAS FASHIONED.
SPEAK, FINN.
KNOW THOU, MIGHTY ODIN! ALL THINGS HAVE THEIR HALTIJA. THEIR SPIRIT. THE TRUE THATNESS OF A THING.
WHAT I FOUND, USING MAGIC THAT I MAY NOT DIVULGE HERE, IS THAT THE TRACES OF METAL LEFT IN THE WOUNDS SHARE A HALTIJA WITH URU.
A PERFECT MATCH, IN FACT. PURE AND STRONG.

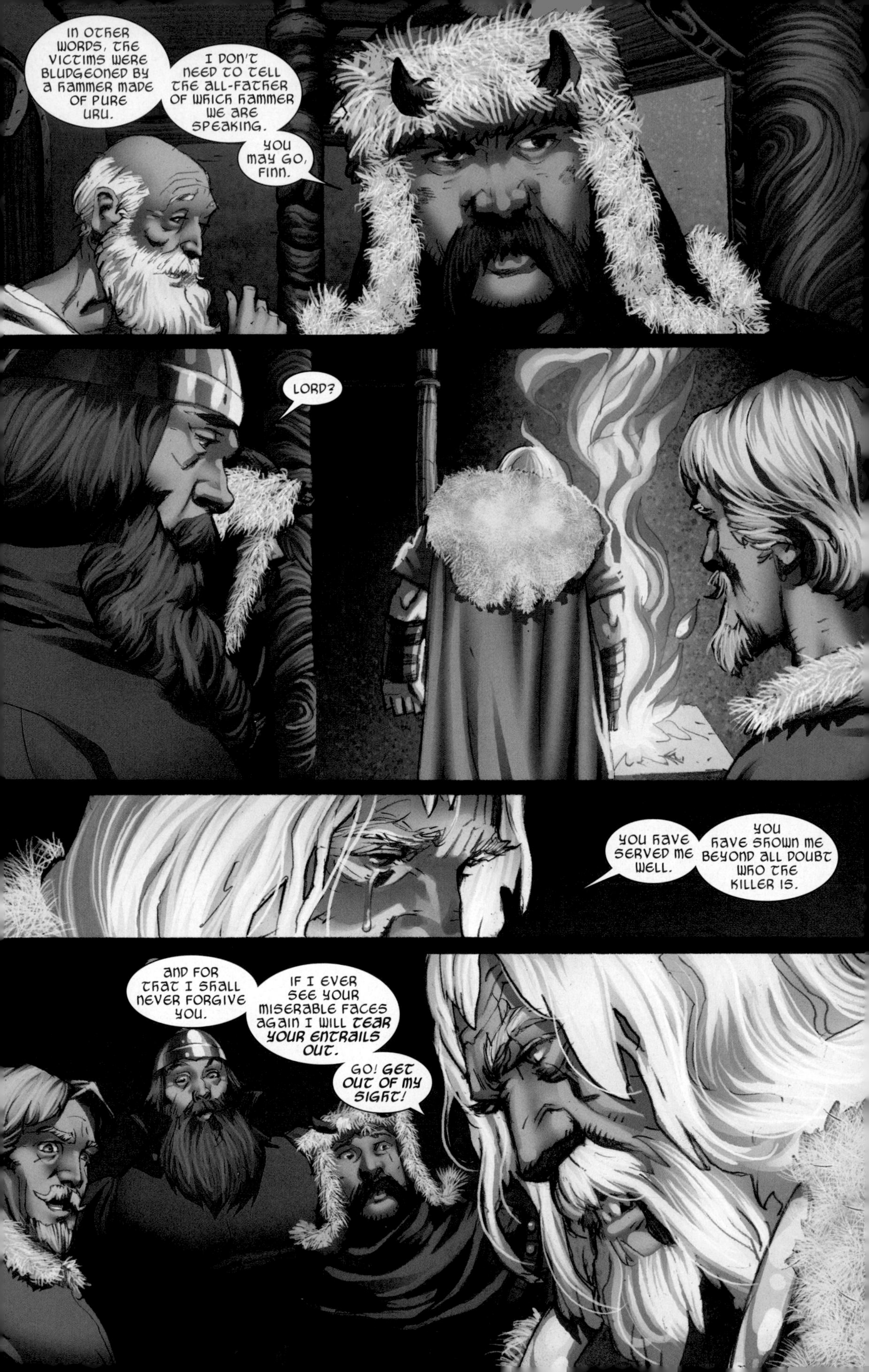
IN OTHER WORDS, THE VICTIMS WERE BLUDGEONED BY A HAMMER MADE OF PURE URU.
I DON'T NEED TO TELL THE ALL-FATHER OF WHICH HAMMER WE ARE SPEAKING.
YOU MAY GO, FINN.
LORD?
YOU HAVE SERVED ME WELL.
YOU HAVE SHOWN ME BEYOND ALL DOUBT WHO THE KILLER IS.
AND FOR THAT I SHALL NEVER FORGIVE YOU.
IF I EVER SEE YOUR MISERABLE FACES AGAIN I WILL *TEAR YOUR ENTRAILS OUT.*
GO! *GET OUT OF MY SIGHT!*

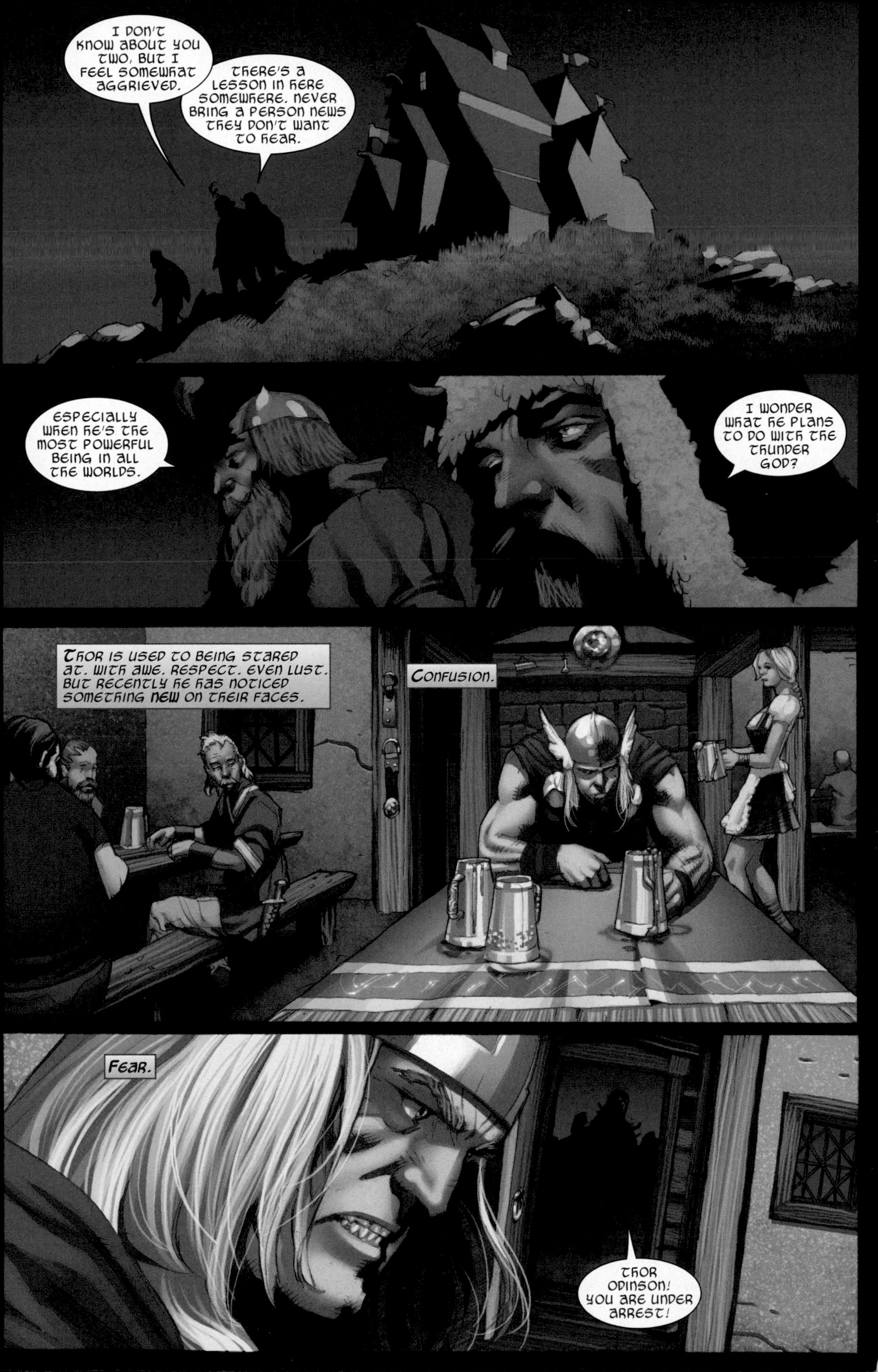
I DON'T KNOW ABOUT YOU TWO, BUT I FEEL SOMEWHAT AGGRIEVED.
THERE'S A LESSON IN HERE SOMEWHERE. NEVER BRING A PERSON NEWS THEY DON'T WANT TO HEAR.
ESPECIALLY WHEN HE'S THE MOST POWERFUL BEING IN ALL THE WORLDS.
I WONDER WHAT HE PLANS TO DO WITH THE THUNDER GOD?
THOR IS USED TO BEING STARED AT. WITH AWE. RESPECT. EVEN LUST. BUT RECENTLY HE HAS NOTICED SOMETHING NEW ON THEIR FACES.
CONFUSION.
FEAR.
THOR ODINSON! YOU ARE UNDER ARREST!

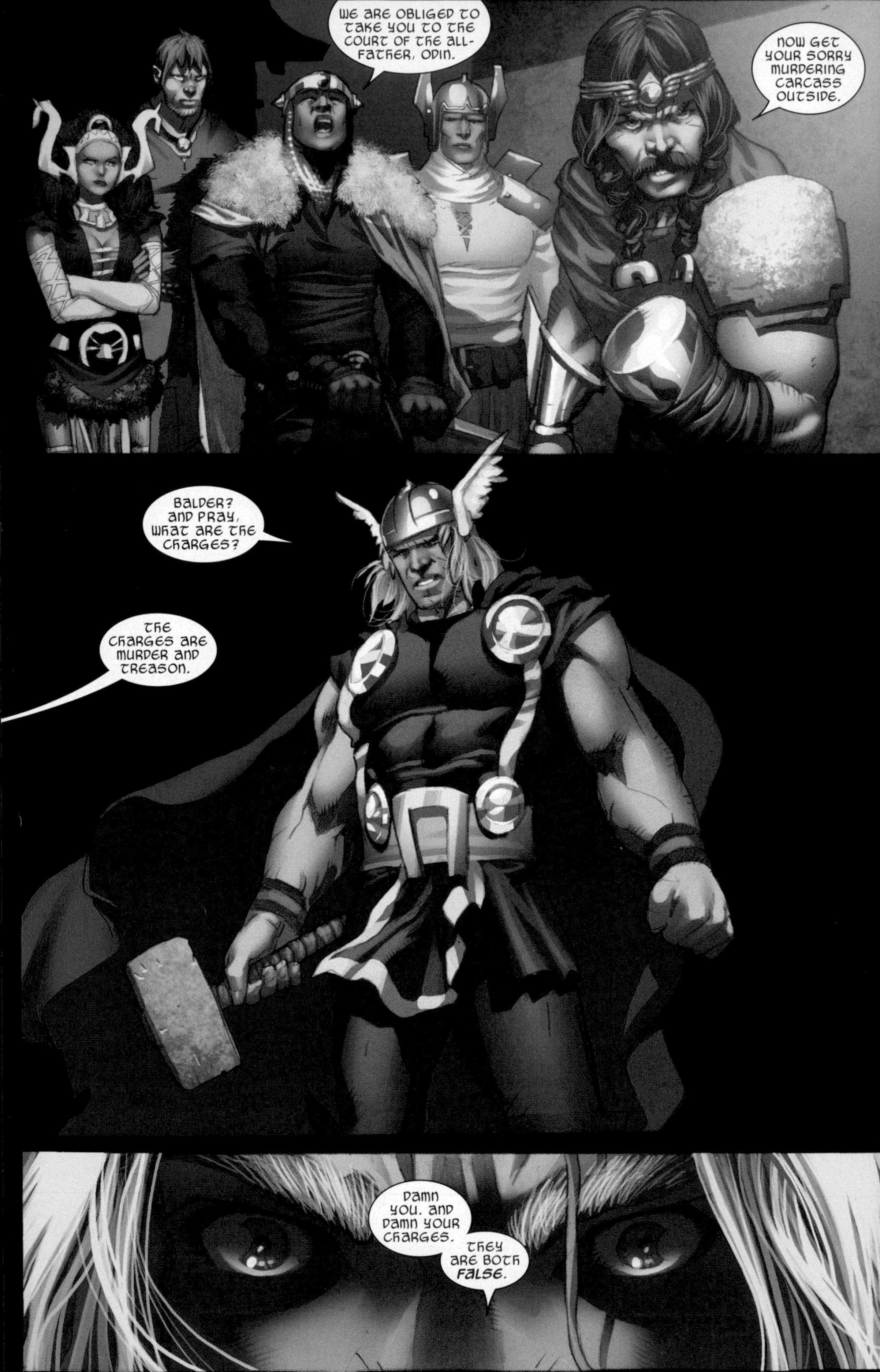
WE ARE OBLIGED TO TAKE YOU TO THE COURT OF THE ALL-FATHER, ODIN.
NOW GET YOUR SORRY MURDERING CARCASS OUTSIDE.
BALDER? AND PRAY, WHAT ARE THE CHARGES?
THE CHARGES ARE MURDER AND TREASON.
DAMN YOU. AND DAMN YOUR CHARGES.
THEY ARE BOTH FALSE.

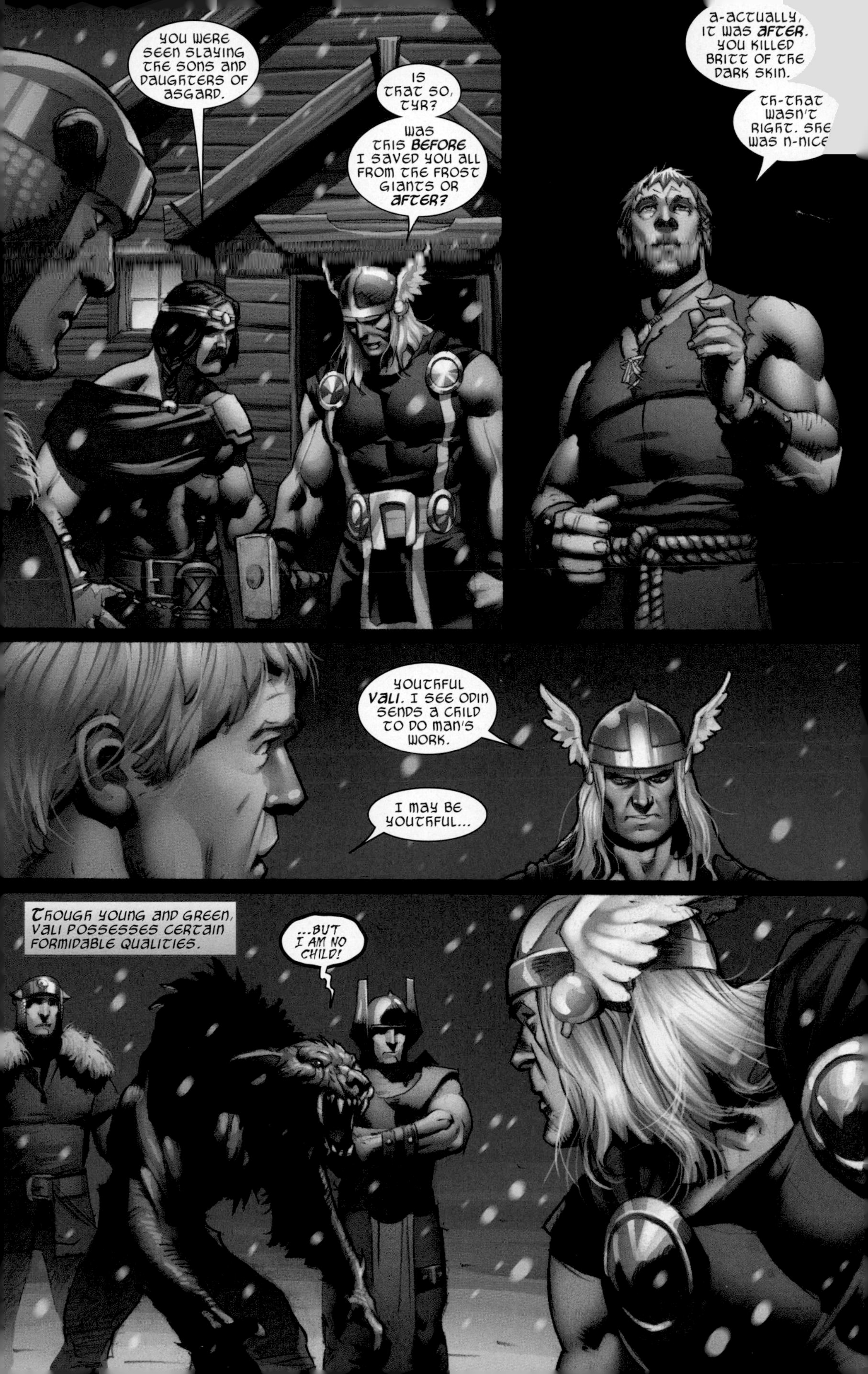
YOU WERE SEEN SLAYING THE SONS AND DAUGHTERS OF ASGARD.
IS THAT SO, TYR?
WAS THIS BEFORE I SAVED YOU ALL FROM THE FROST GIANTS OR AFTER?
A-ACTUALLY, IT WAS AFTER. YOU KILLED BRITT OF THE DARK SKIN.
TH-THAT WASN'T RIGHT. SHE WAS N-NICE
YOUTHFUL VALI. I SEE ODIN SENDS A CHILD TO DO MAN'S WORK.
I MAY BE YOUTHFUL...
THOUGH YOUNG AND GREEN, VALI POSSESSES CERTAIN FORMIDABLE QUALITIES.
...BUT I AM NO CHILD!

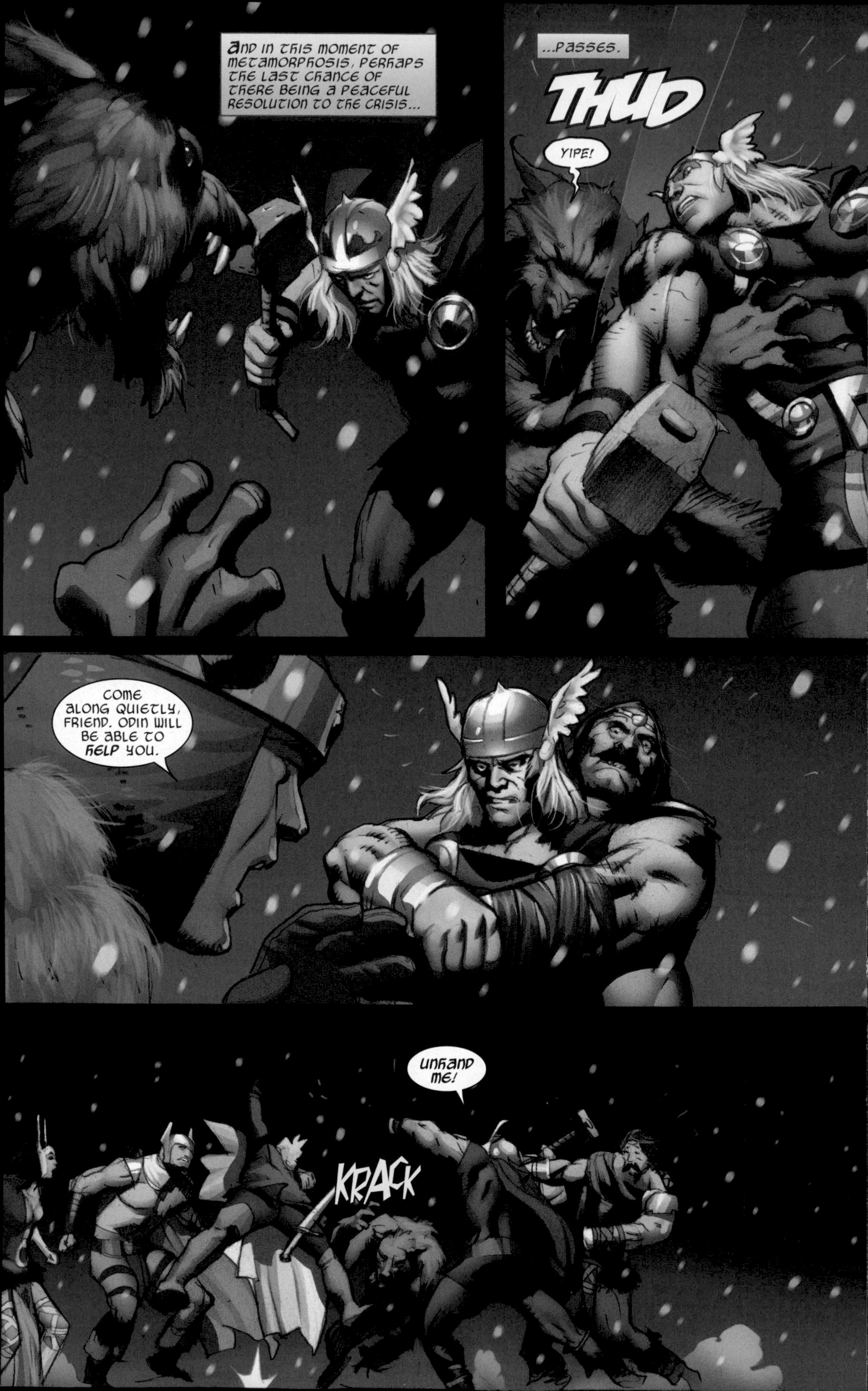
AND IN THIS MOMENT OF METAMORPHOSIS, PERHAPS THE LAST CHANCE OF THERE BEING A PEACEFUL RESOLUTION TO THE CRISIS...
...PASSES.
THUD
YIPE!
COME ALONG QUIETLY, FRIEND. ODIN WILL BE ABLE TO HELP YOU.
UNHAND ME!
KRACK

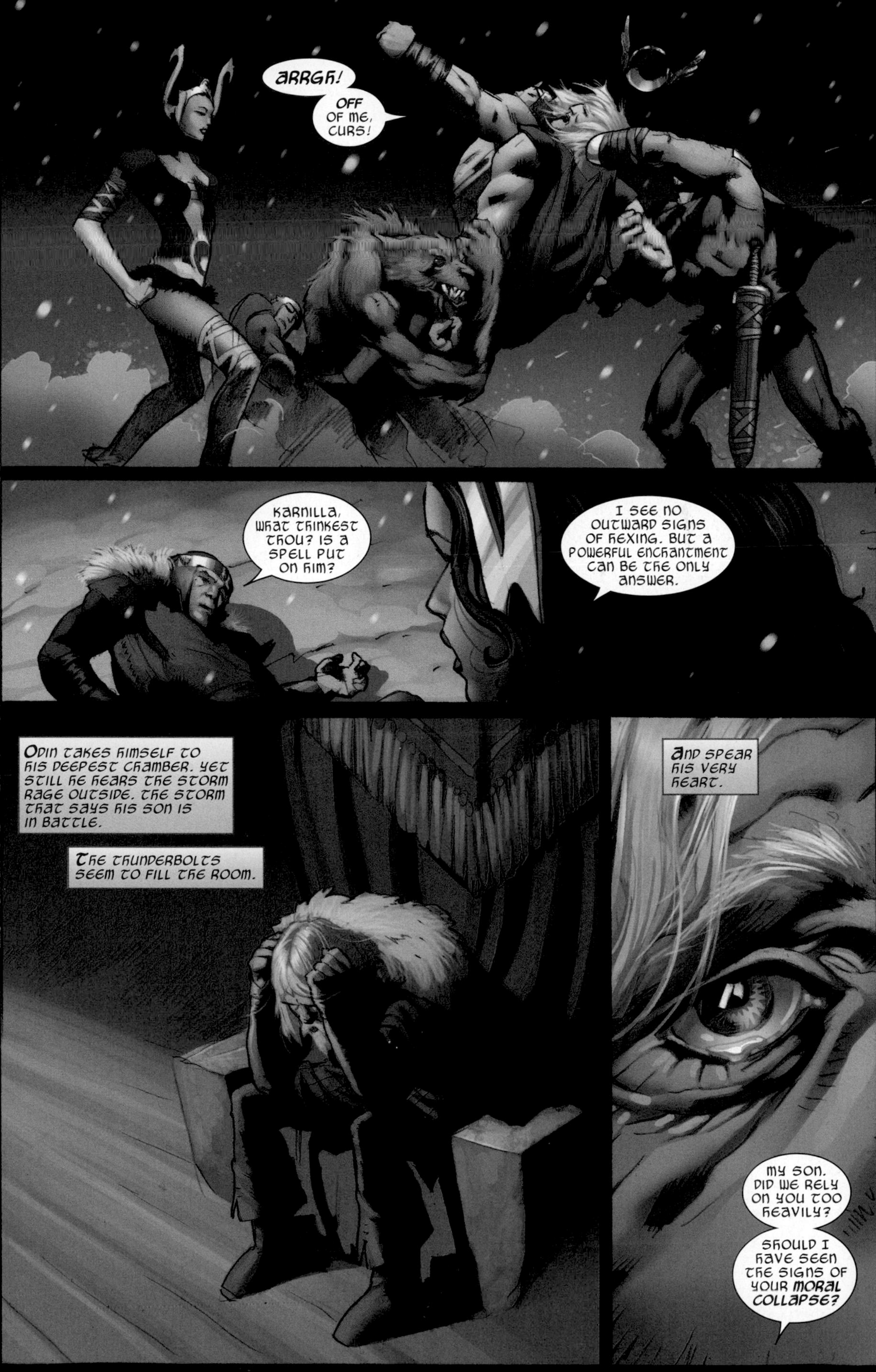
ARRGH!
OFF OF ME, CURS!
KARNILLA, WHAT THINKEST THOU? IS A SPELL PUT ON HIM?
I SEE NO OUTWARD SIGNS OF HEXING. BUT A POWERFUL ENCHANTMENT CAN BE THE ONLY ANSWER.
ODIN TAKES HIMSELF TO HIS DEEPEST CHAMBER. YET STILL HE HEARS THE STORM RAGE OUTSIDE. THE STORM THAT SAYS HIS SON IS IN BATTLE.
THE THUNDERBOLTS SEEM TO FILL THE ROOM.
AND SPEAR HIS VERY HEART.
MY SON. DID WE RELY ON YOU TOO HEAVILY?
SHOULD I HAVE SEEN THE SIGNS OF YOUR MORAL COLLAPSE?

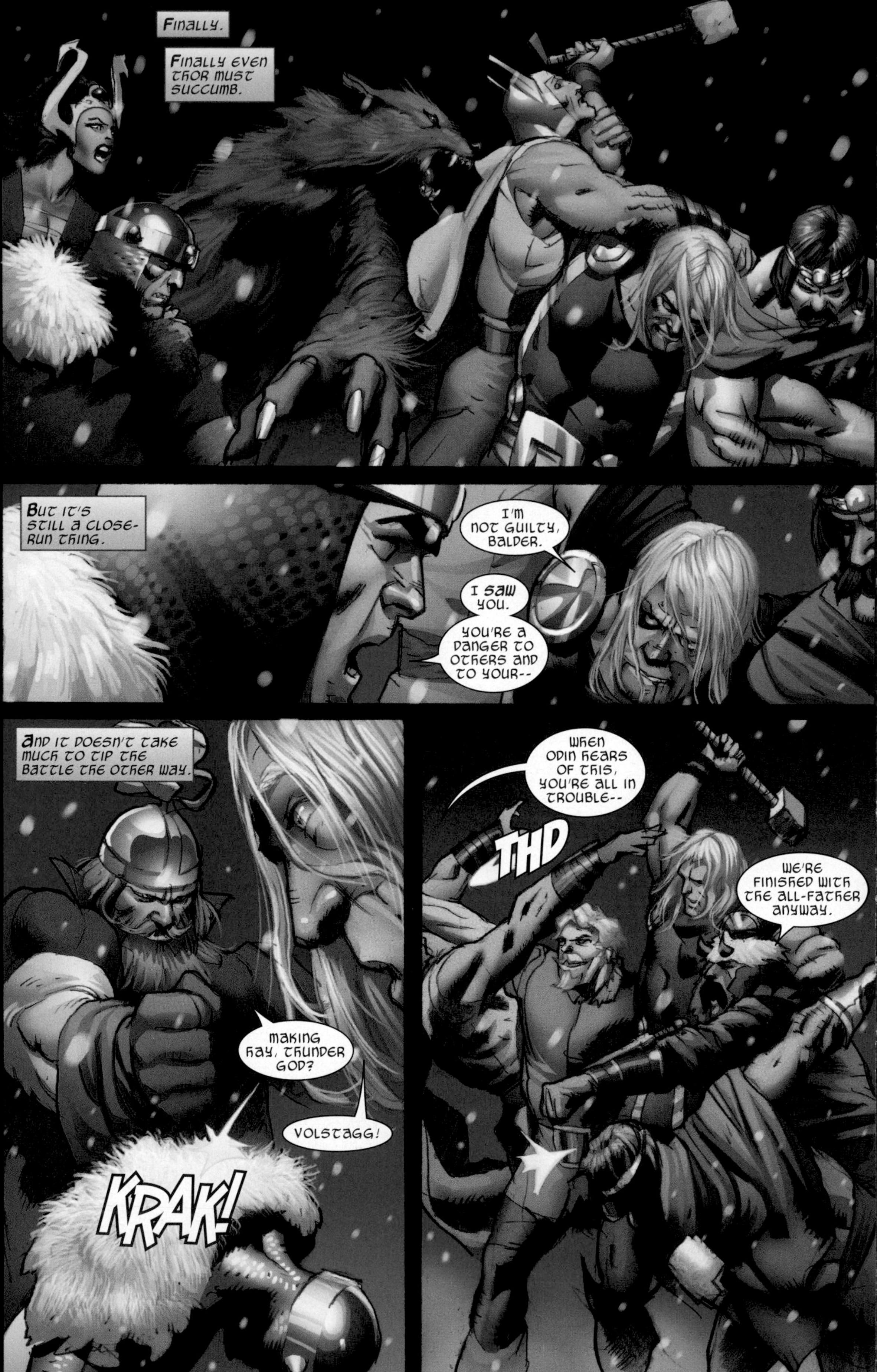
FINALLY.
FINALLY EVEN THOR MUST SUCCUMB.
BUT IT'S STILL A CLOSE-RUN THING.
I'M NOT GUILTY, BALDER.
I SAW YOU.
YOU'RE A DANGER TO OTHERS AND TO YOUR--
AND IT DOESN'T TAKE MUCH TO TIP THE BATTLE THE OTHER WAY.
MAKING HAY, THUNDER GOD?
VOLSTAGG!
KRAK!
WHEN ODIN HEARS OF THIS, YOU'RE ALL IN TROUBLE--
THD
WE'RE FINISHED WITH THE ALL-FATHER ANYWAY.

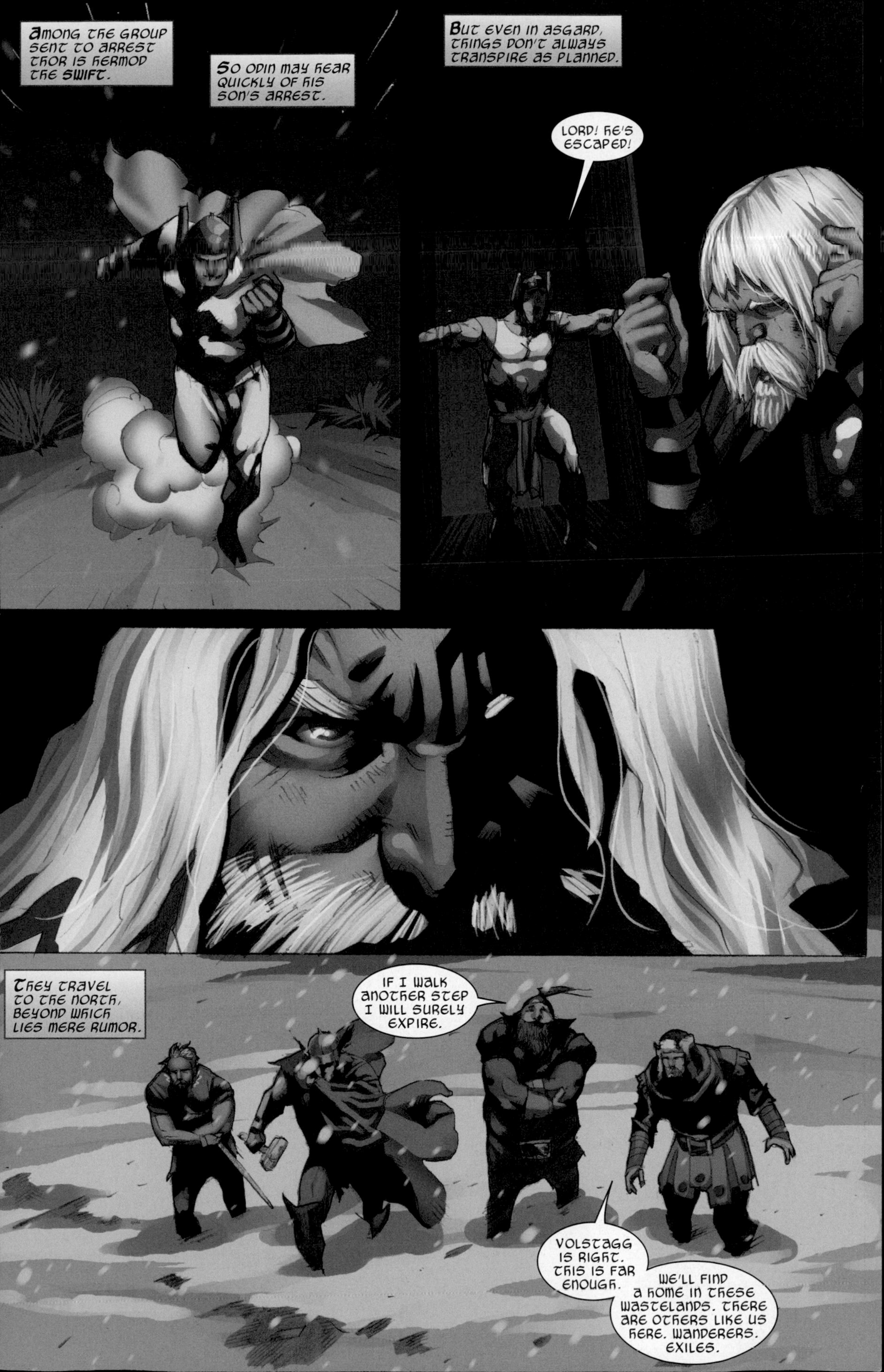
AMONG THE GROUP SENT TO ARREST THOR IS HERMOD THE SWIFT.
SO ODIN MAY HEAR QUICKLY OF HIS SON'S ARREST.
BUT EVEN IN ASGARD, THINGS DON'T ALWAYS TRANSPIRE AS PLANNED.
LORD! HE'S ESCAPED!
THEY TRAVEL TO THE NORTH, BEYOND WHICH LIES MERE RUMOR.
IF I WALK ANOTHER STEP I WILL SURELY EXPIRE.
VOLSTAGG IS RIGHT. THIS IS FAR ENOUGH.
WE'LL FIND A HOME IN THESE WASTELANDS. THERE ARE OTHERS LIKE US HERE. WANDERERS. EXILES.

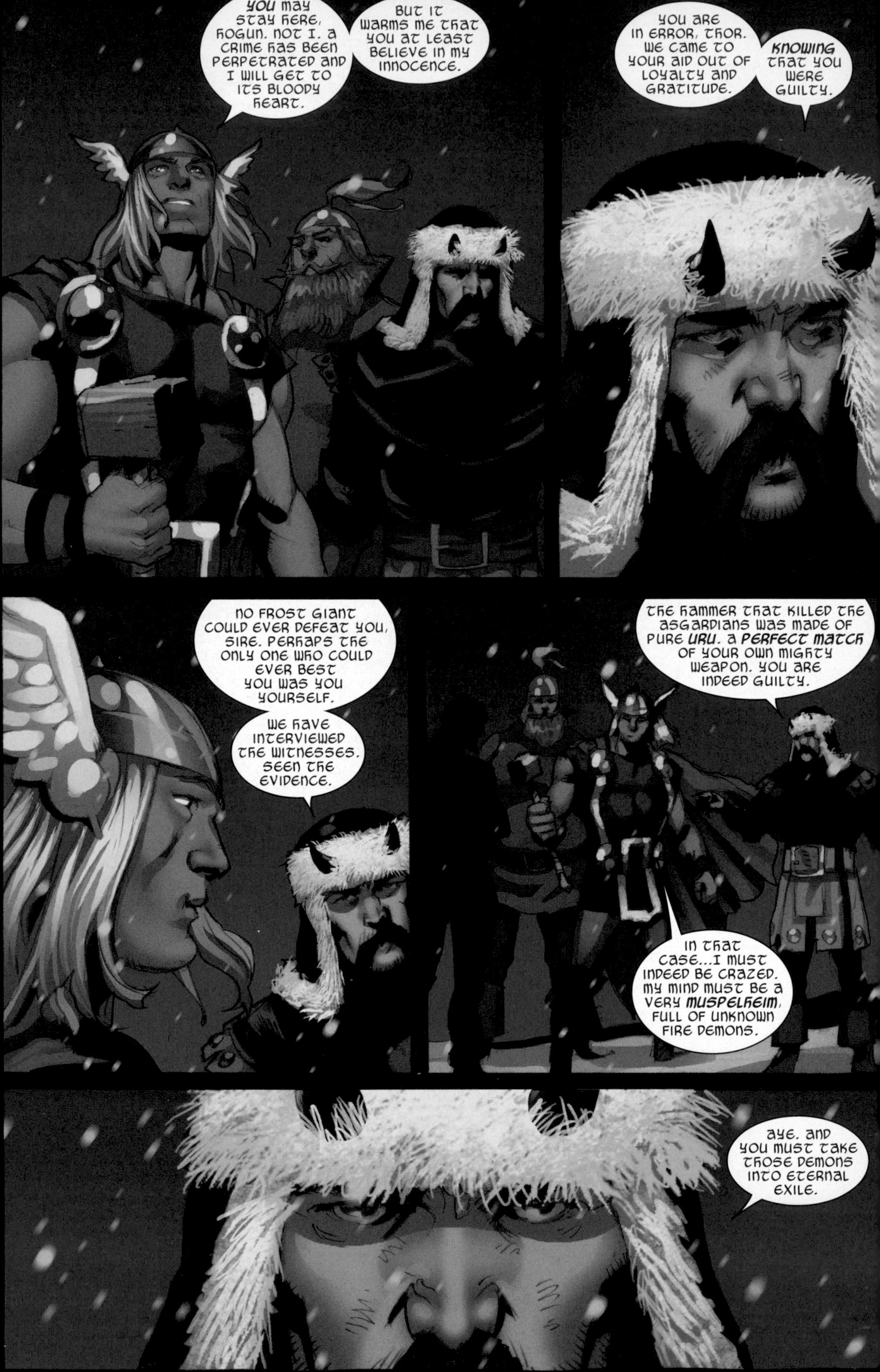
YOU MAY STAY HERE, HOGUN. NOT I. A CRIME HAS BEEN PERPETRATED AND I WILL GET TO ITS BLOODY HEART.
BUT IT WARMS ME THAT YOU AT LEAST BELIEVE IN MY INNOCENCE.
YOU ARE IN ERROR, THOR. WE CAME TO YOUR AID OUT OF LOYALTY AND GRATITUDE.
KNOWING THAT YOU WERE GUILTY.
NO FROST GIANT COULD EVER DEFEAT YOU, SIRE. PERHAPS THE ONLY ONE WHO COULD EVER BEST YOU WAS YOU YOURSELF.
WE HAVE INTERVIEWED THE WITNESSES. SEEN THE EVIDENCE.
THE HAMMER THAT KILLED THE ASGARDIANS WAS MADE OF PURE URU. A PERFECT MATCH OF YOUR OWN MIGHTY WEAPON. YOU ARE INDEED GUILTY.
IN THAT CASE...I MUST INDEED BE CRAZED. MY MIND MUST BE A VERY MUSPELHEIM, FULL OF UNKNOWN FIRE DEMONS.
AYE. AND YOU MUST TAKE THOSE DEMONS INTO ETERNAL EXILE.

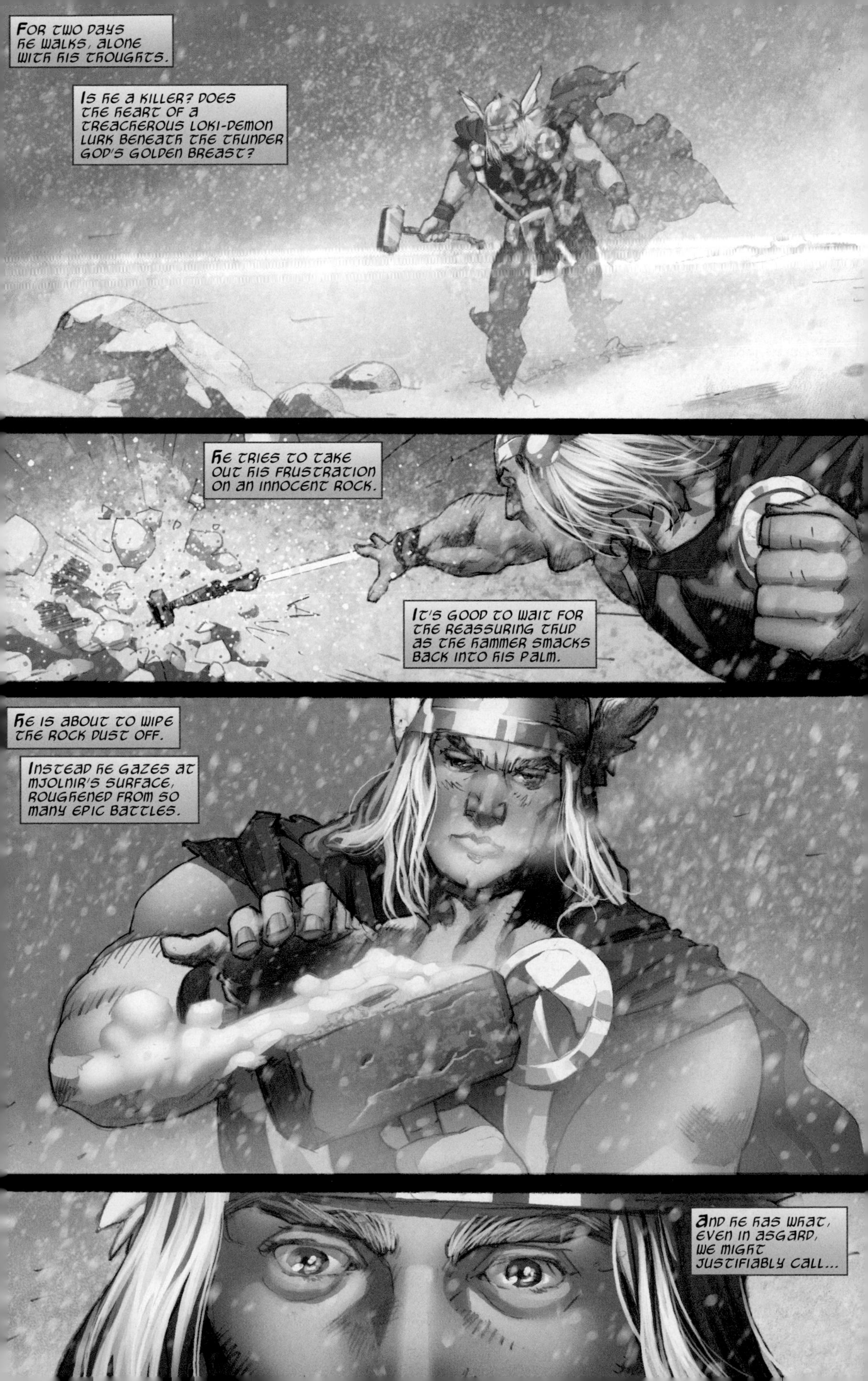
For two days he walks, alone with his thoughts.
Is he a killer? Does the heart of a treacherous Loki-demon lurk beneath the thunder god's golden breast?
He tries to take out his frustration on an innocent rock.
It's good to wait for the reassuring thud as the hammer smacks back into his palm.
He is about to wipe the rock dust off.
Instead he gazes at Mjolnir's surface, roughened from so many epic battles.
And he has what, even in Asgard, we might justifiably call...

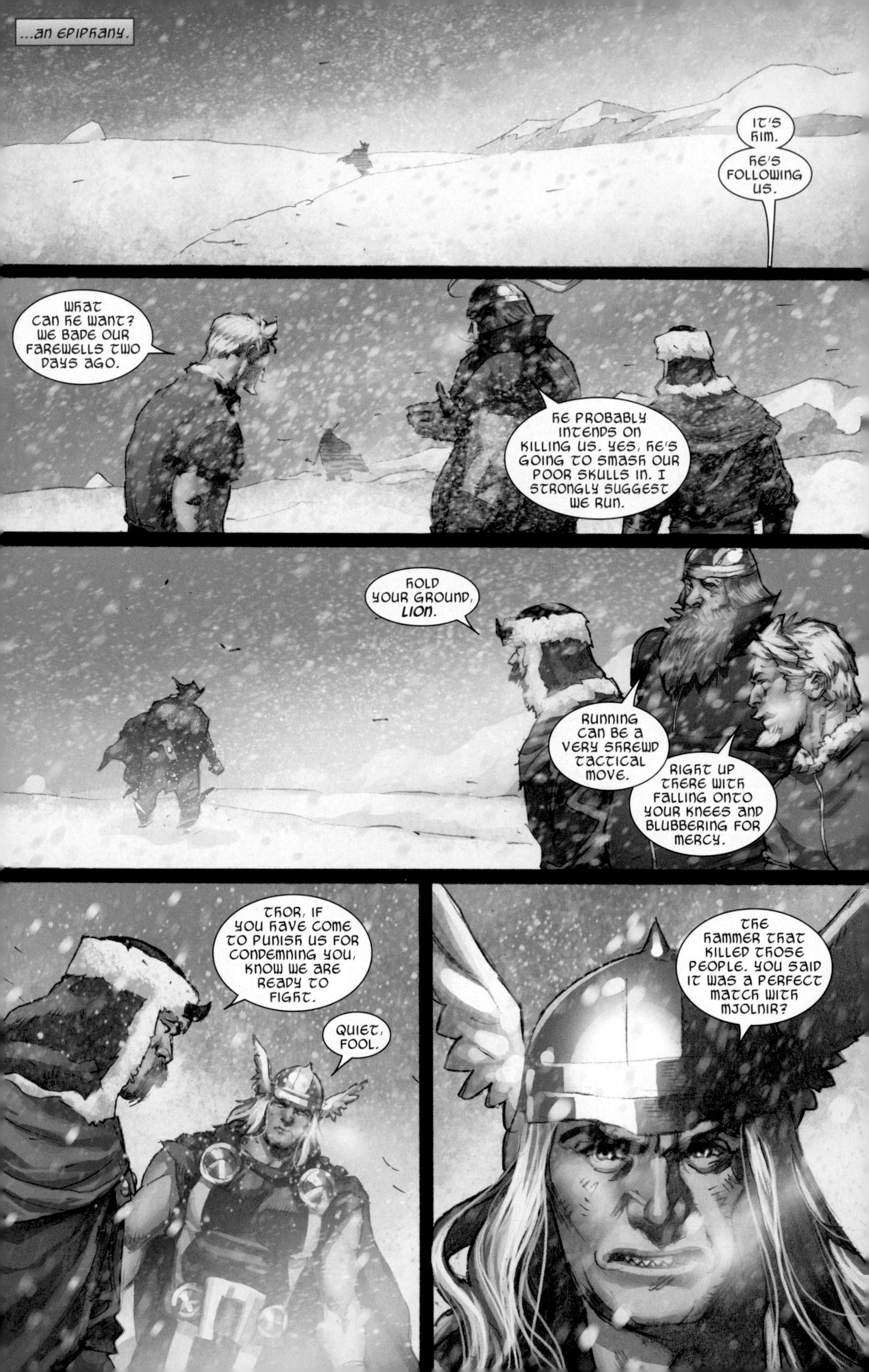

...AN EPIPHANY.
IT'S HIM.
HE'S FOLLOWING US.
WHAT CAN HE WANT? WE BADE OUR FAREWELLS TWO DAYS AGO.
HE PROBABLY INTENDS ON KILLING US. YES, HE'S GOING TO SMASH OUR POOR SKULLS IN. I STRONGLY SUGGEST WE RUN.
HOLD YOUR GROUND, LION.
RUNNING CAN BE A VERY SHREWD TACTICAL MOVE.
RIGHT UP THERE WITH FALLING ONTO YOUR KNEES AND BLUBBERING FOR MERCY.
THOR, IF YOU HAVE COME TO PUNISH US FOR CONDEMNING YOU, KNOW WE ARE READY TO FIGHT.
QUIET, FOOL.
THE HAMMER THAT KILLED THOSE PEOPLE. YOU SAID IT WAS A PERFECT MATCH WITH MJOLNIR?

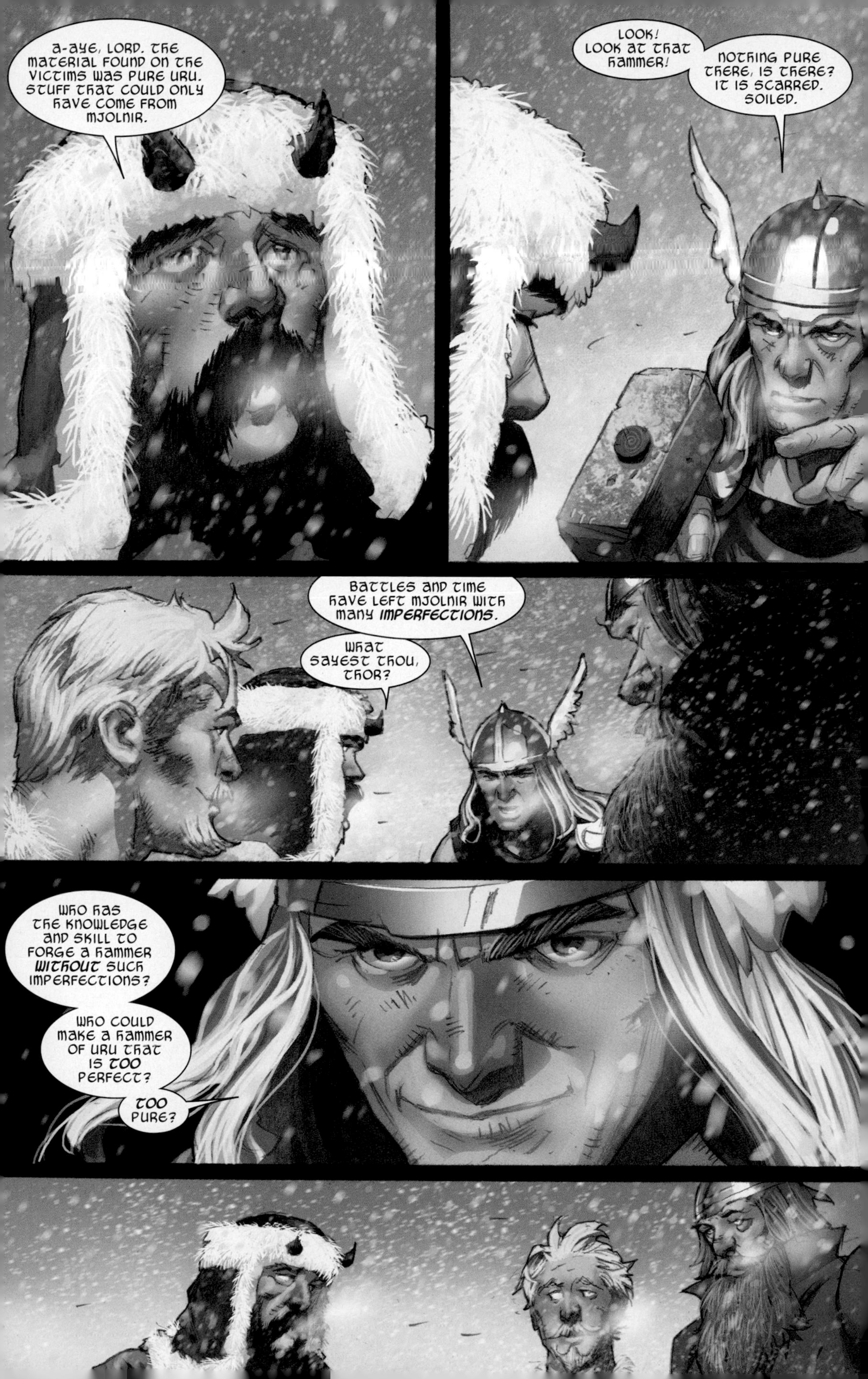
A-AYE, LORD. THE MATERIAL FOUND ON THE VICTIMS WAS PURE URU. STUFF THAT COULD ONLY HAVE COME FROM MJOLNIR.
LOOK! LOOK AT THAT HAMMER!
NOTHING PURE THERE, IS THERE? IT IS SCARRED. SOILED.
BATTLES AND TIME HAVE LEFT MJOLNIR WITH MANY IMPERFECTIONS.
WHAT SAYEST THOU, THOR?
WHO HAS THE KNOWLEDGE AND SKILL TO FORGE A HAMMER WITHOUT SUCH IMPERFECTIONS?
WHO COULD MAKE A HAMMER OF URU THAT IS TOO PERFECT?
TOO PURE?

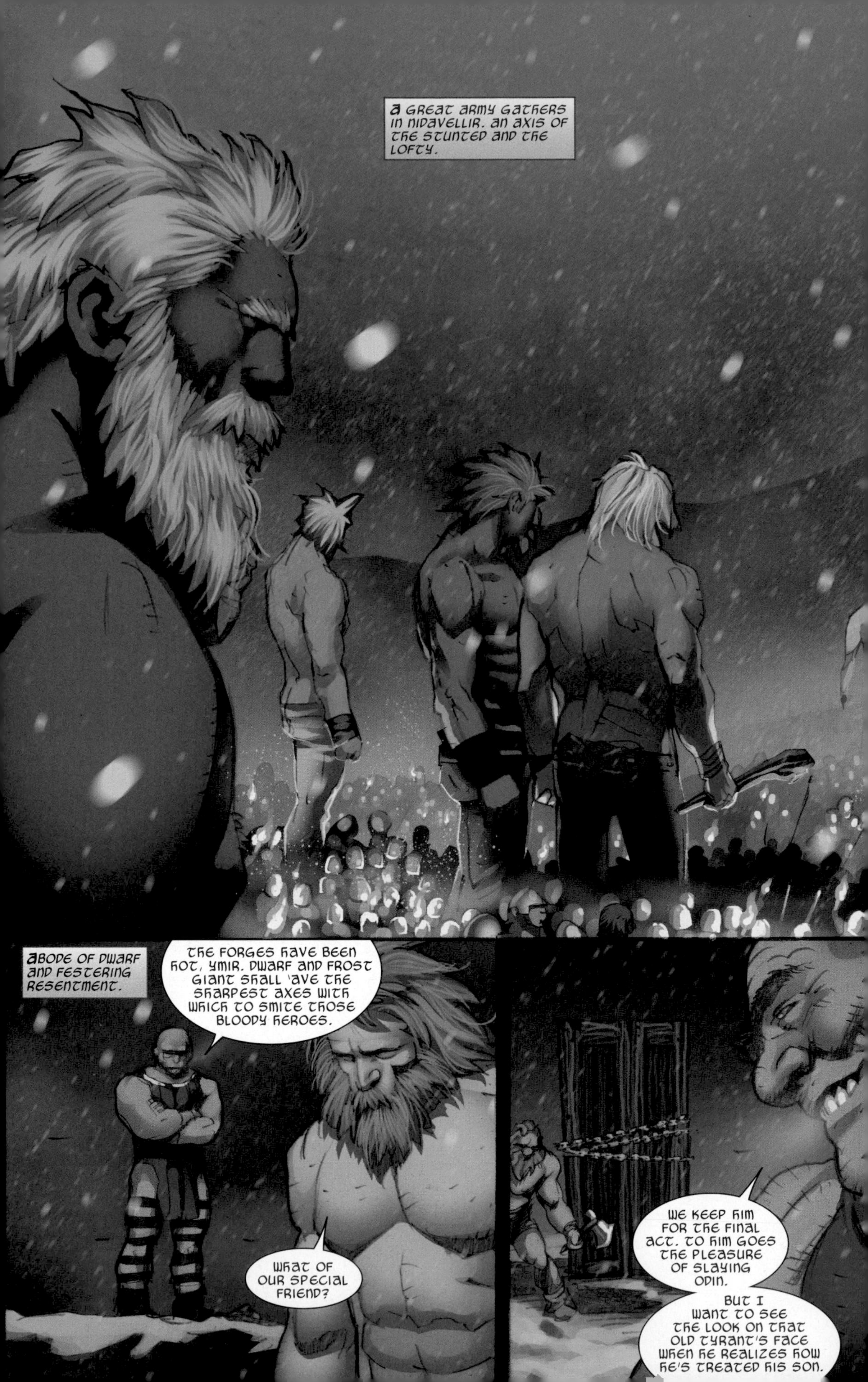
A GREAT ARMY GATHERS IN NIDAVELLIR. AN AXIS OF THE STUNTED AND THE LOFTY.
ABODE OF DWARF AND FESTERING RESENTMENT.
THE FORGES HAVE BEEN HOT, YMIR. DWARF AND FROST GIANT SHALL 'AVE THE SHARPEST AXES WITH WHICH TO SMITE THOSE BLOODY HEROES.
WHAT OF OUR SPECIAL FRIEND?
WE KEEP HIM FOR THE FINAL ACT. TO HIM GOES THE PLEASURE OF SLAYING ODIN.
BUT I WANT TO SEE THE LOOK ON THAT OLD TYRANT'S FACE WHEN HE REALIZES HOW HE'S TREATED HIS SON.

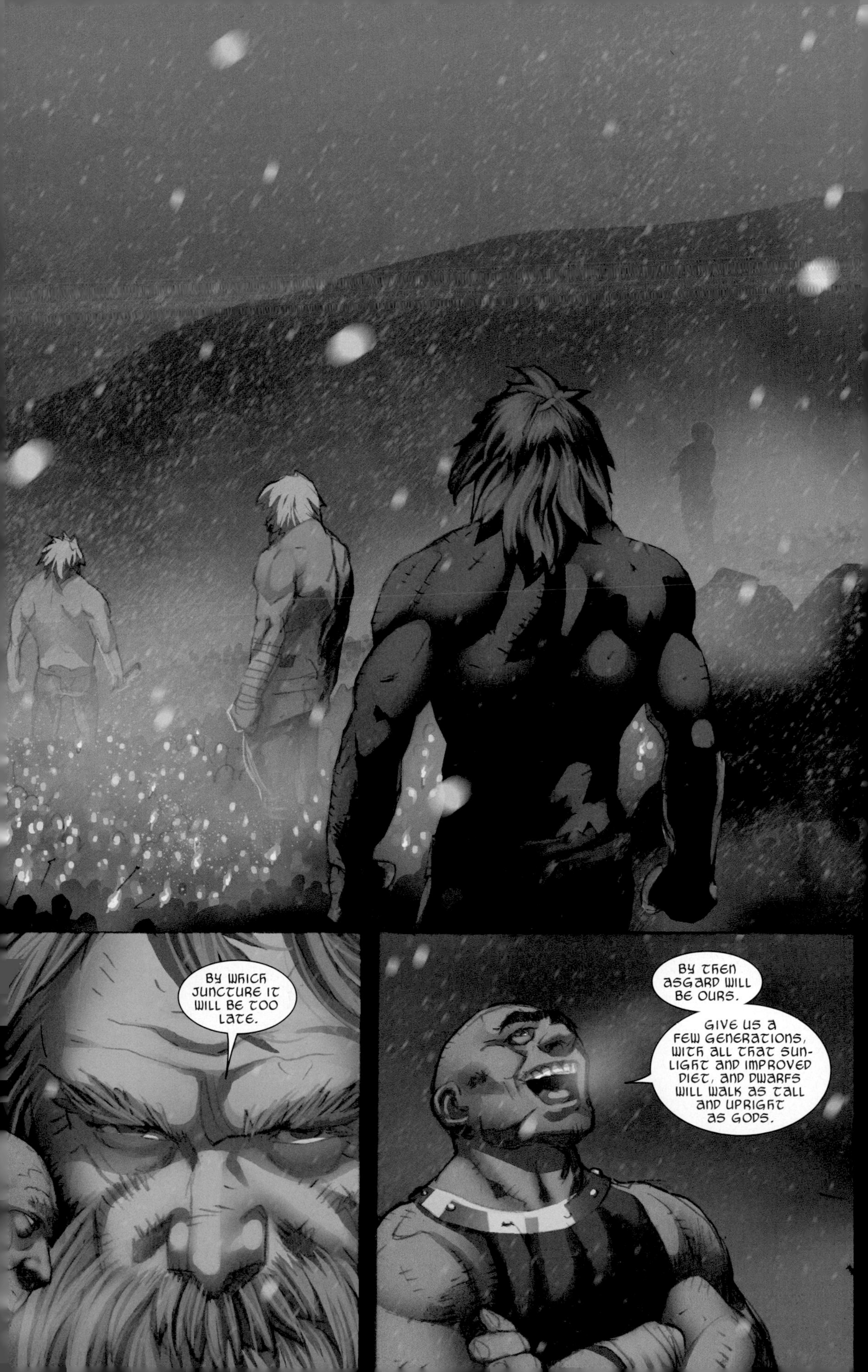
BY WHICH JUNCTURE IT WILL BE TOO LATE.
BY THEN ASGARD WILL BE OURS.
GIVE US A FEW GENERATIONS, WITH ALL THAT SUN-LIGHT AND IMPROVED DIET, AND DWARFS WILL WALK AS TALL AND UPRIGHT AS GODS.

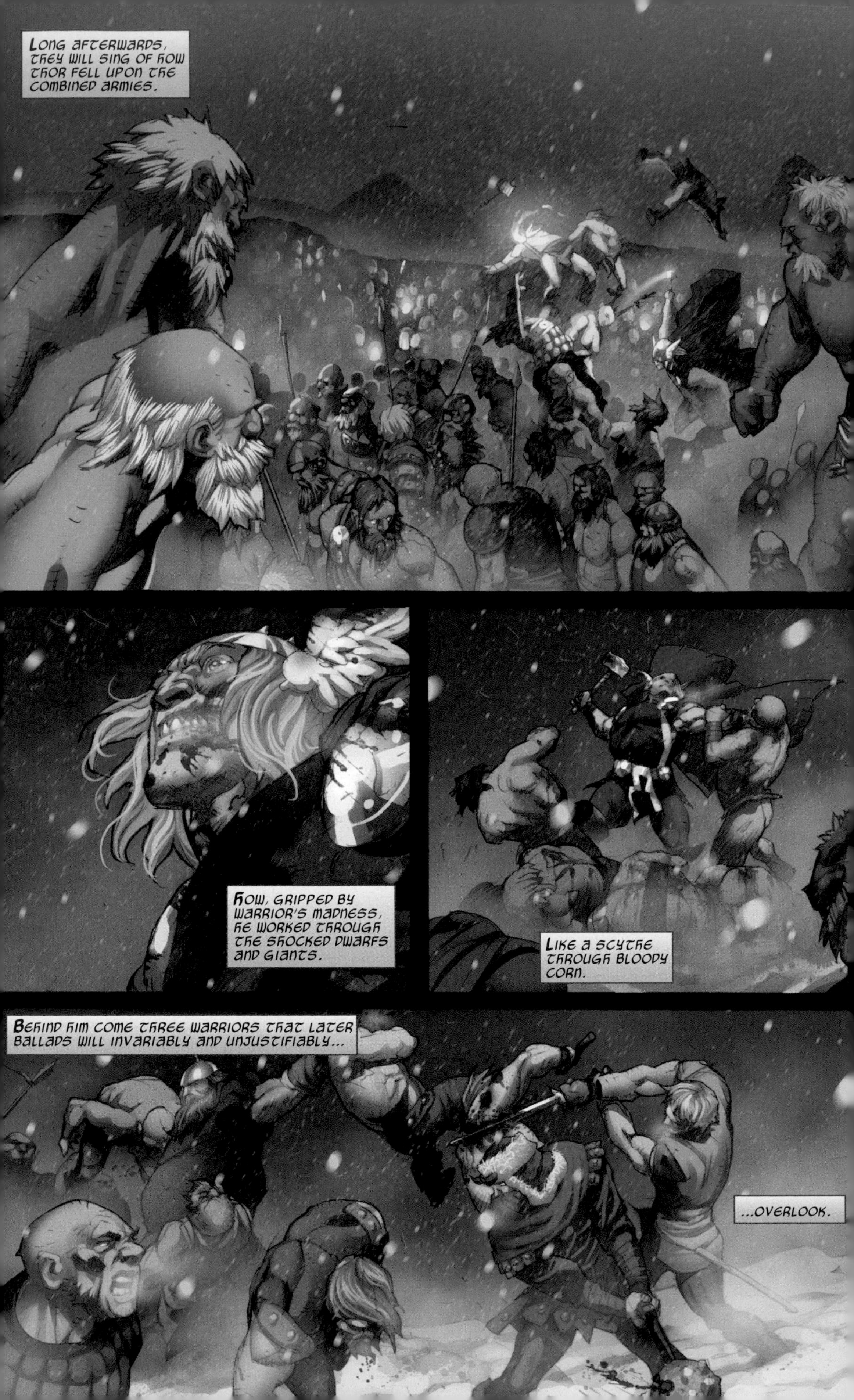
LONG AFTERWARDS, THEY WILL SING OF HOW THOR FELL UPON THE COMBINED ARMIES.
HOW, GRIPPED BY WARRIOR'S MADNESS, HE WORKED THROUGH THE SHOCKED DWARFS AND GIANTS.
LIKE A SCYTHE THROUGH BLOODY CORN.
BEHIND HIM COME THREE WARRIORS THAT LATER BALLADS WILL INVARIABLY AND UNJUSTIFIABLY...
...OVERLOOK.

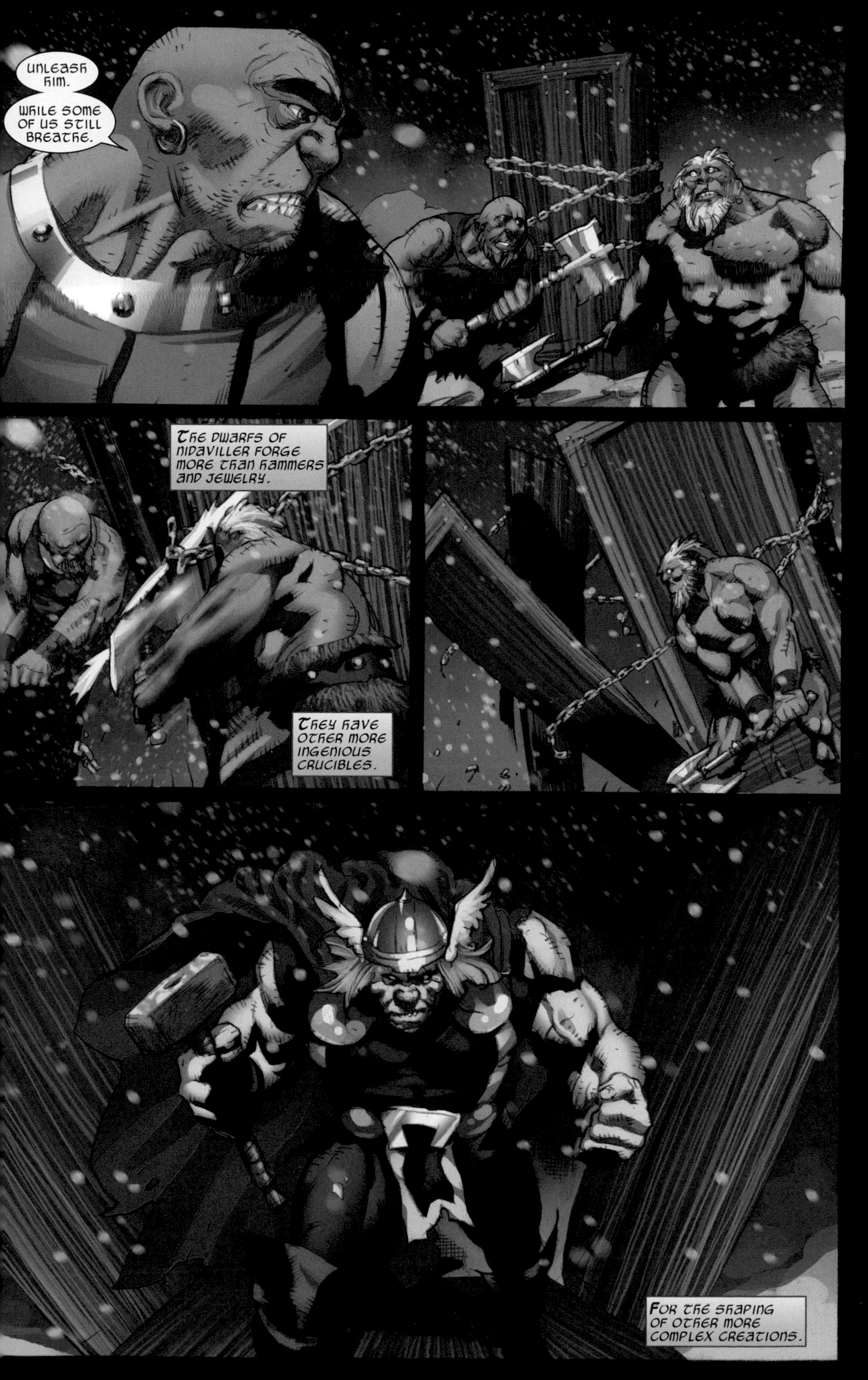
UNLEASH HIM.
WHILE SOME OF US STILL BREATHE.
THE DWARFS OF NIDAVILLER FORGE MORE THAN HAMMERS AND JEWELRY.
THEY HAVE OTHER MORE INGENIOUS CRUCIBLES.
FOR THE SHAPING OF OTHER MORE COMPLEX CREATIONS.

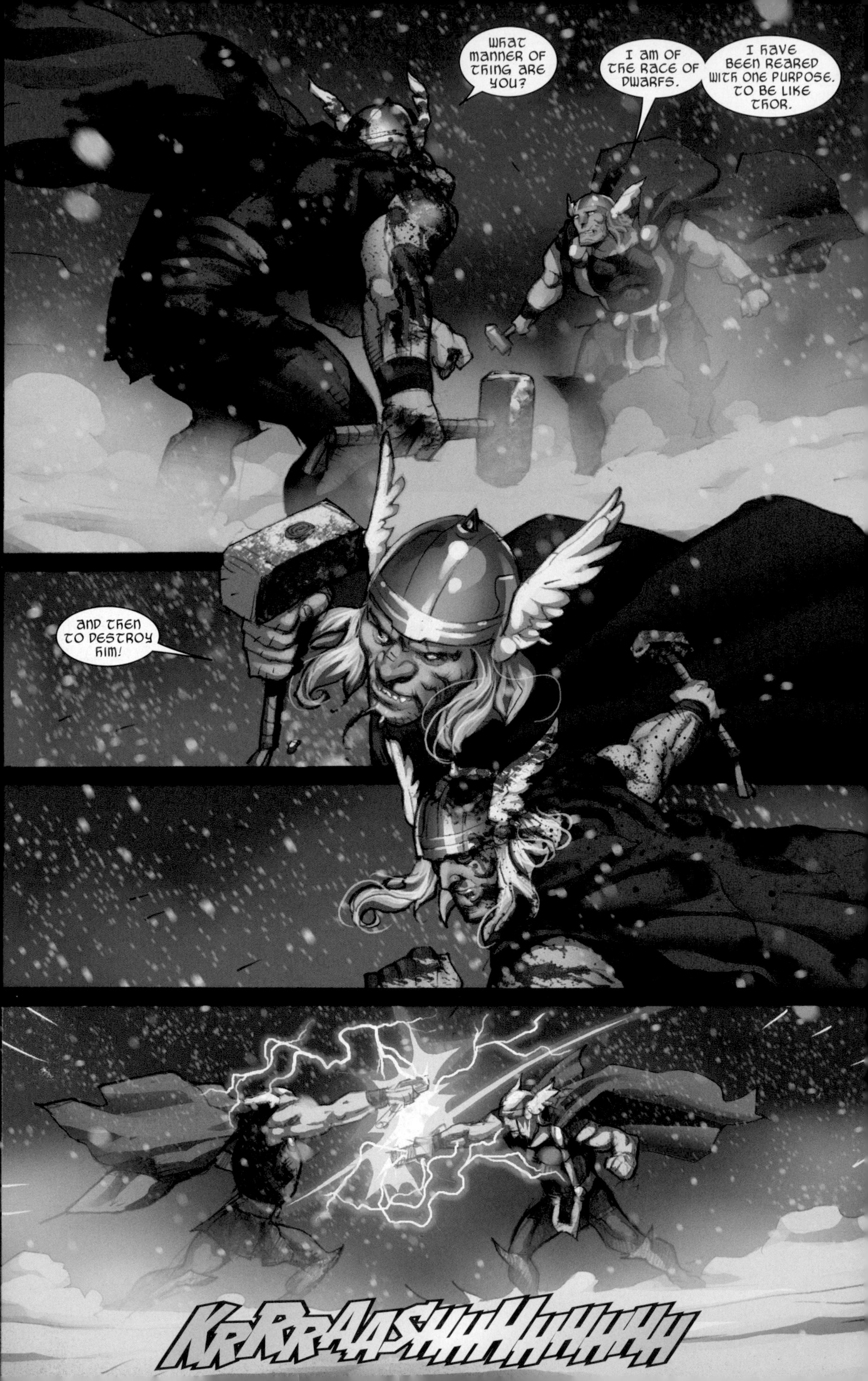
WHAT MANNER OF THING ARE YOU?
I AM OF THE RACE OF DWARFS.
I HAVE BEEN REARED WITH ONE PURPOSE. TO BE LIKE THOR.
AND THEN TO DESTROY HIM!
KRRRRAASHHHHHHHHH

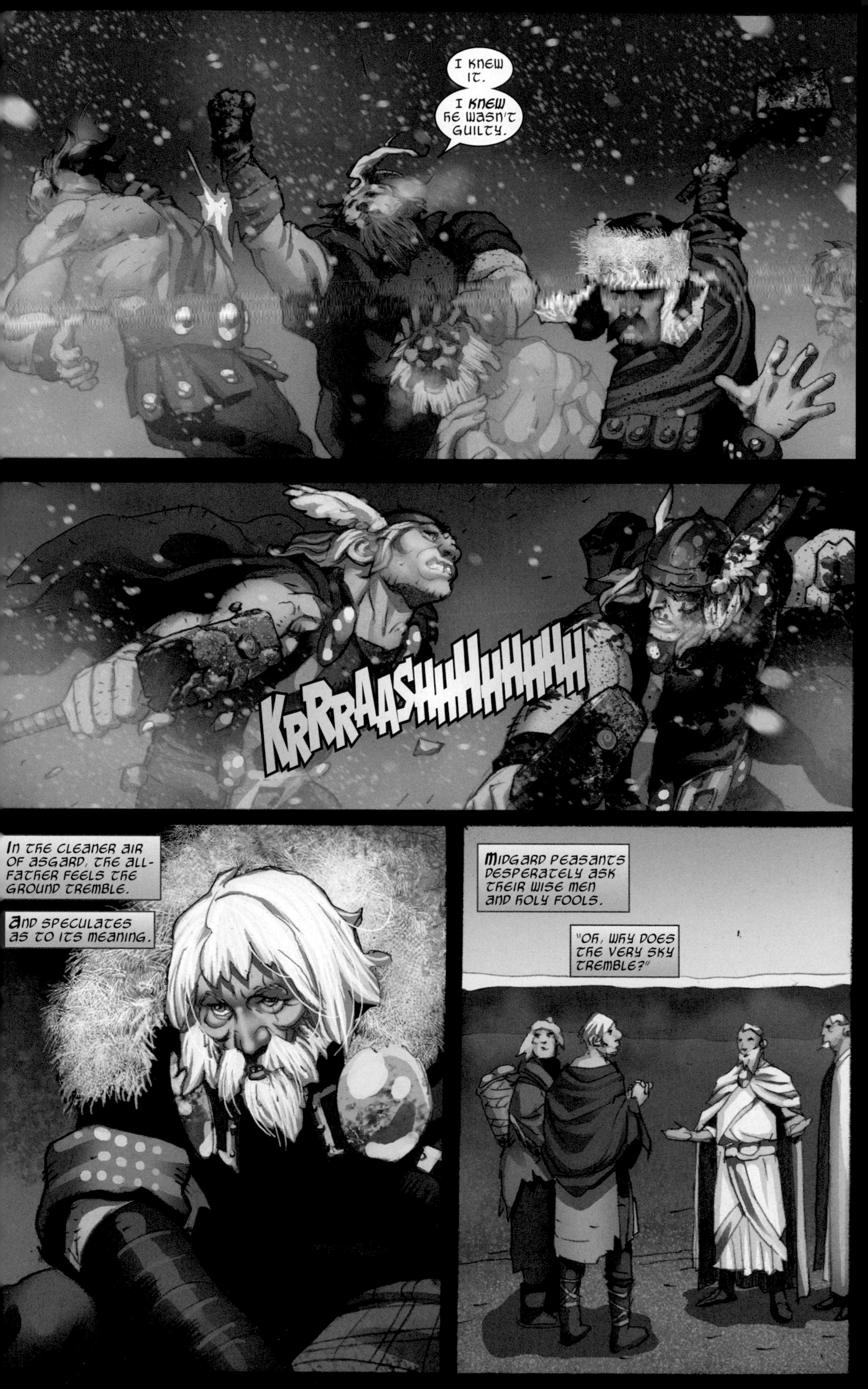
I KNEW IT.
I KNEW HE WASN'T GUILTY.
KRRRAASHHHHHHHH
IN THE CLEANER AIR OF ASGARD, THE ALL-FATHER FEELS THE GROUND TREMBLE.
AND SPECULATES AS TO ITS MEANING.
MIDGARD PEASANTS DESPERATELY ASK THEIR WISE MEN AND HOLY FOOLS.
"OH, WHY DOES THE VERY SKY TREMBLE?"

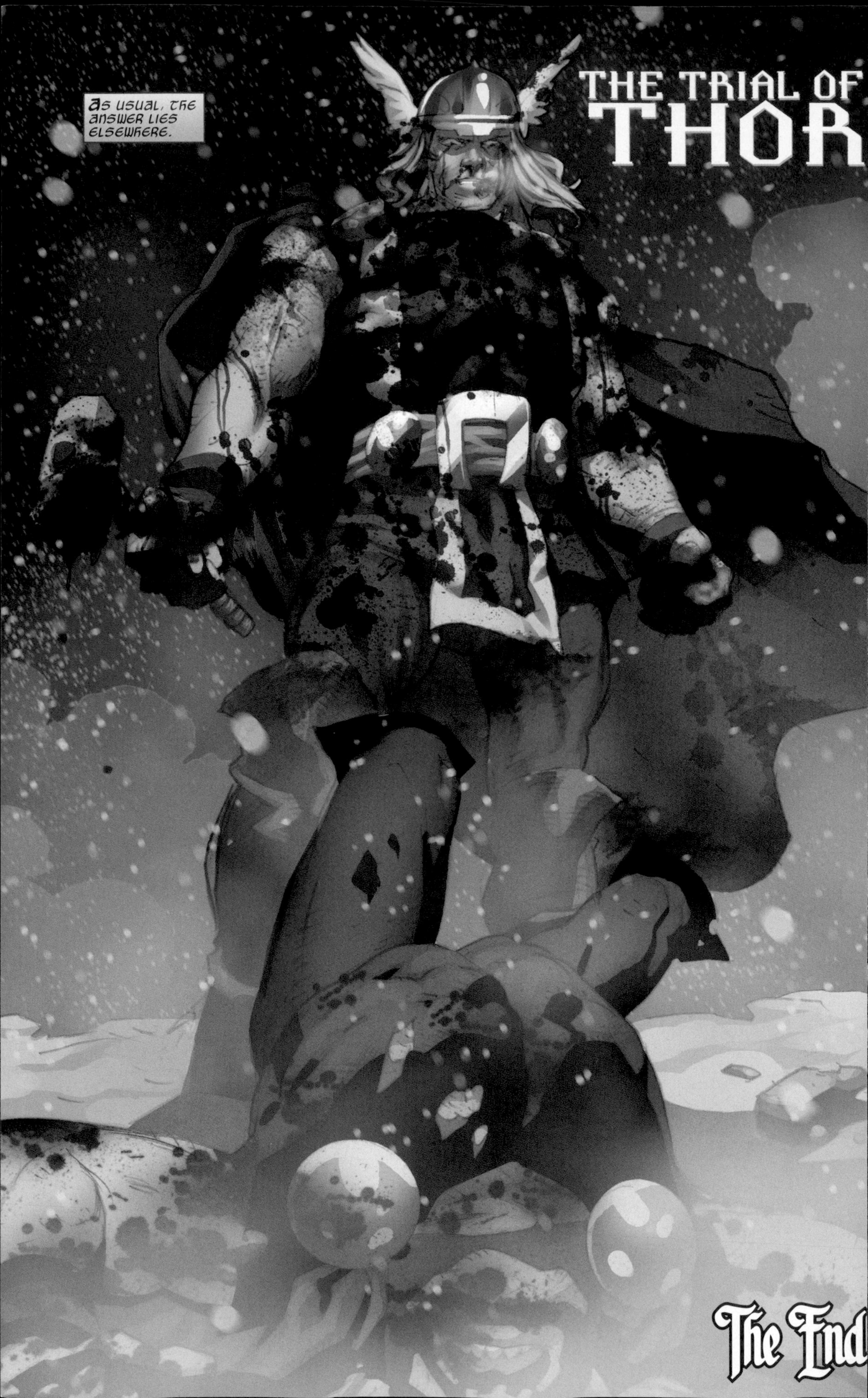

As usual, the answer lies elsewhere.
THE TRIAL OF THOR
The End

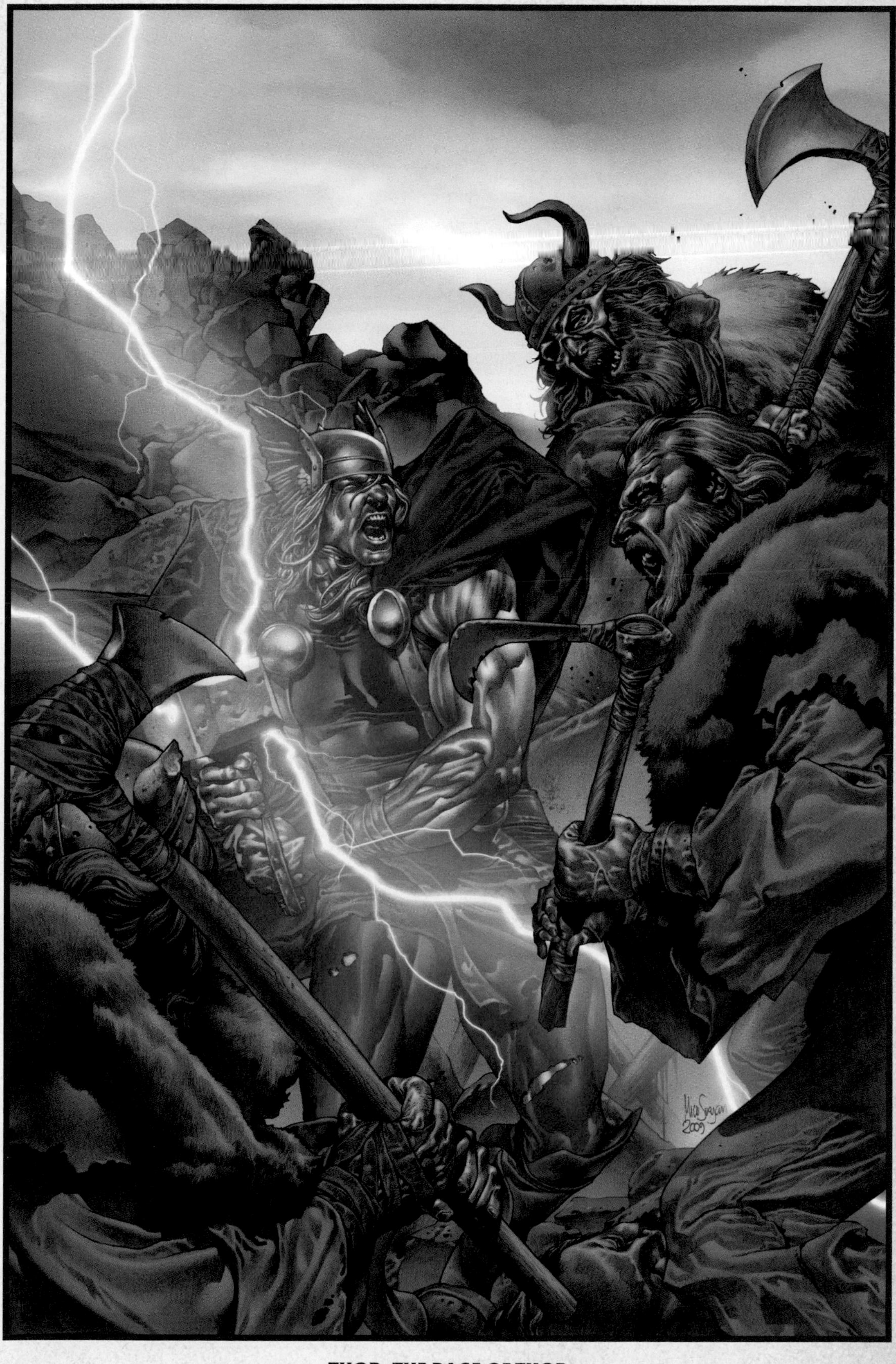

THOR: THE RAGE OF THOR

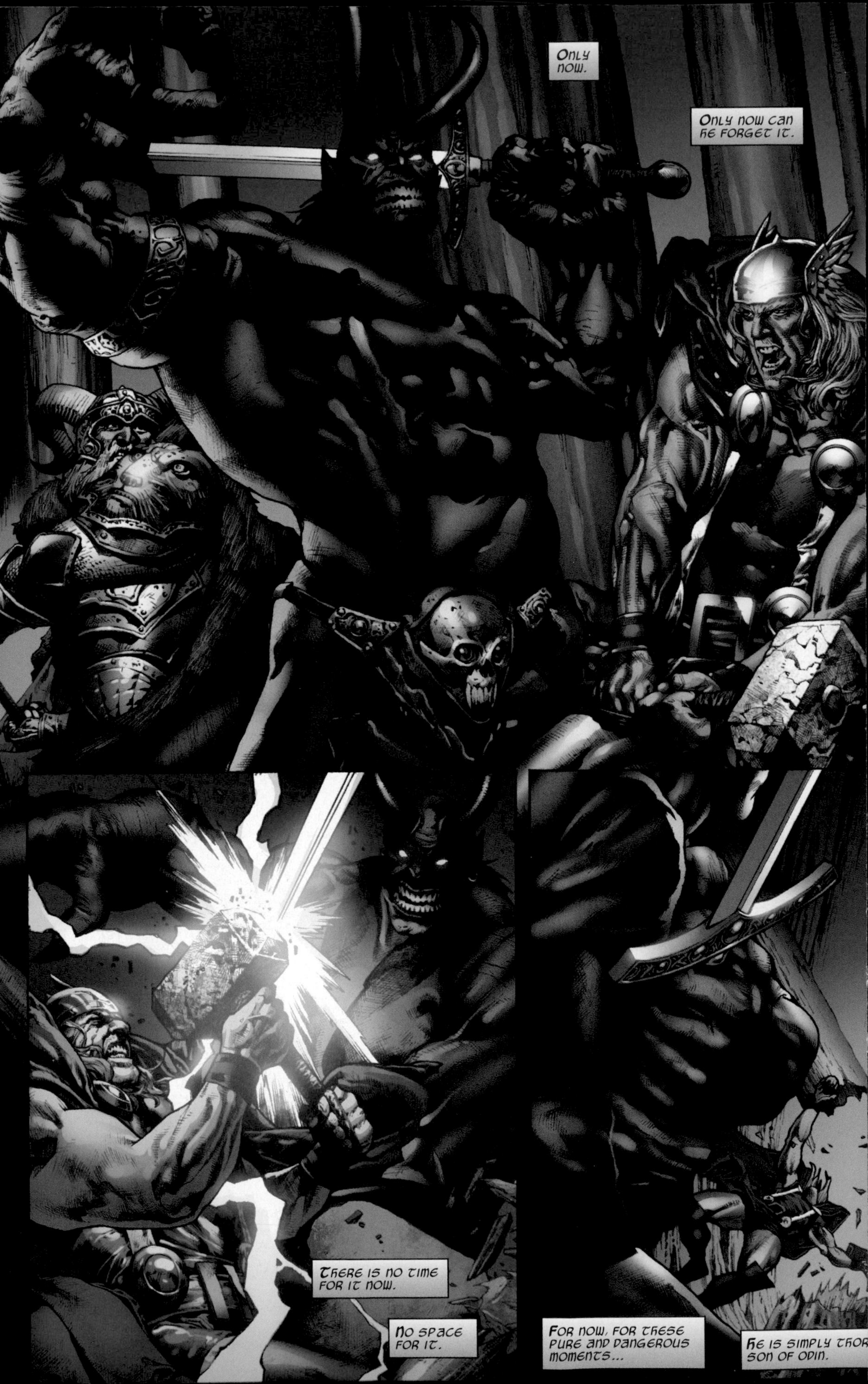
Only now.
Only now can he forget it.
There is no time for it now.
No space for it.
For now, for these pure and dangerous moments...
He is simply Thor, son of Odin.

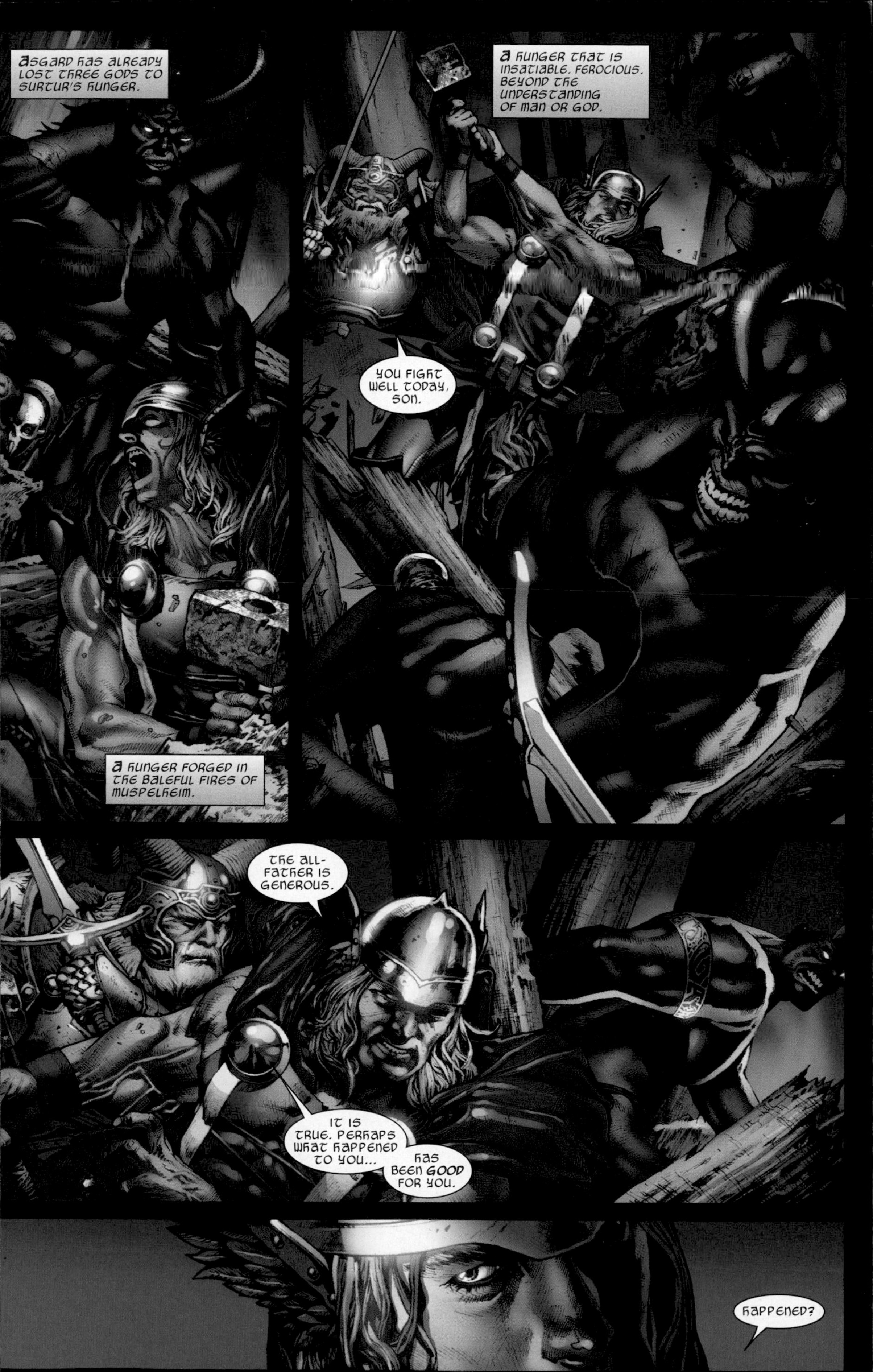
Asgard has already lost three gods to Surtur's hunger.
A hunger that is insatiable. Ferocious. Beyond the understanding of man or god.
You fight well today, son.
A hunger forged in the baleful fires of Muspelheim.
The All-Father is generous.
It is true. Perhaps what happened to you...
Has been GOOD for you.
Happened?

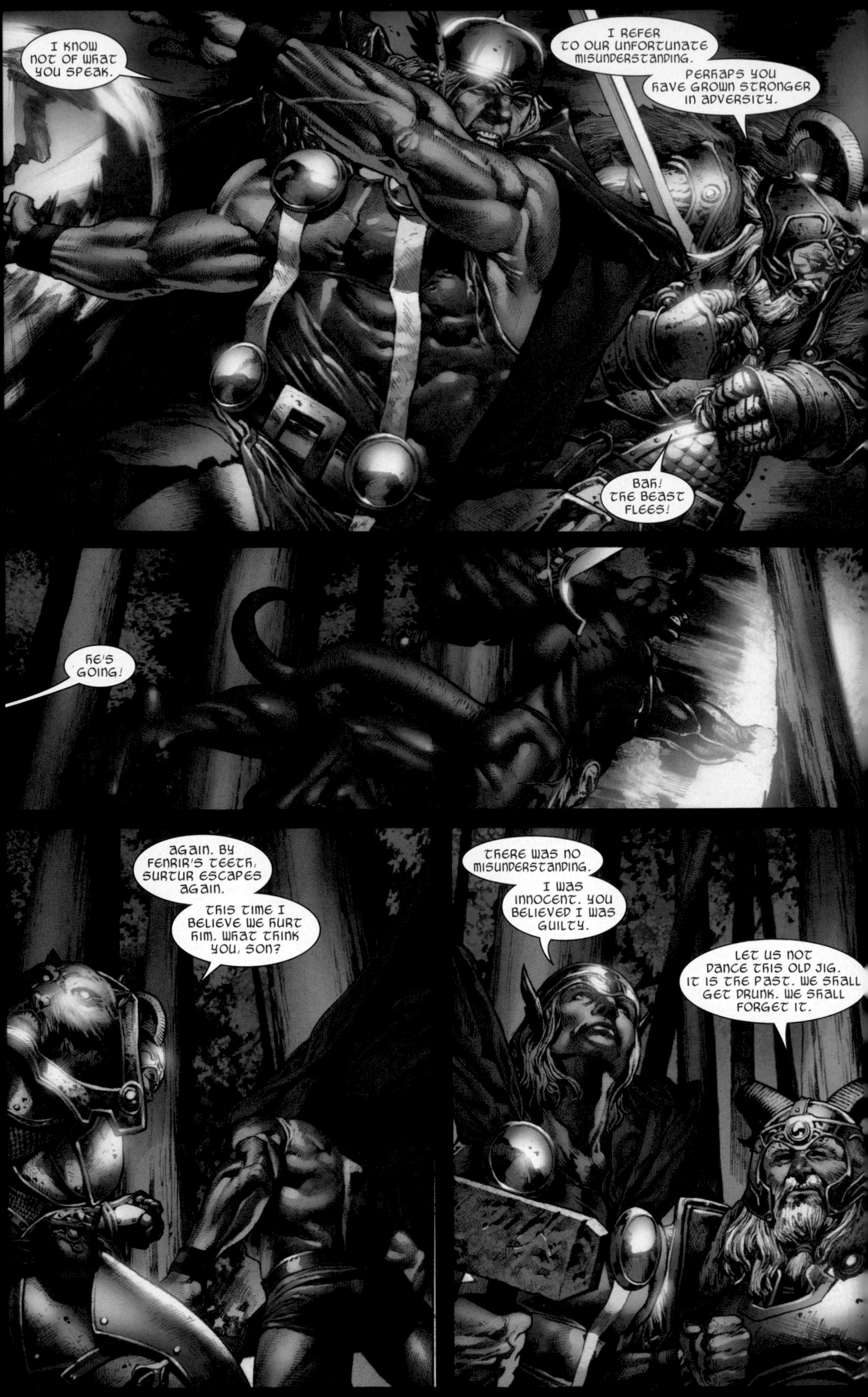
I KNOW NOT OF WHAT YOU SPEAK.
I REFER TO OUR UNFORTUNATE MISUNDERSTANDING.
PERHAPS YOU HAVE GROWN STRONGER IN ADVERSITY.
BAH! THE BEAST FLEES!
HE'S GOING!
AGAIN. BY FENRIR'S TEETH, SURTUR ESCAPES AGAIN.
THIS TIME I BELIEVE WE HURT HIM. WHAT THINK YOU, SON?
THERE WAS NO MISUNDERSTANDING.
I WAS INNOCENT. YOU BELIEVED I WAS GUILTY.
LET US NOT DANCE THIS OLD JIG. IT IS THE PAST. WE SHALL GET DRUNK. WE SHALL FORGET IT.

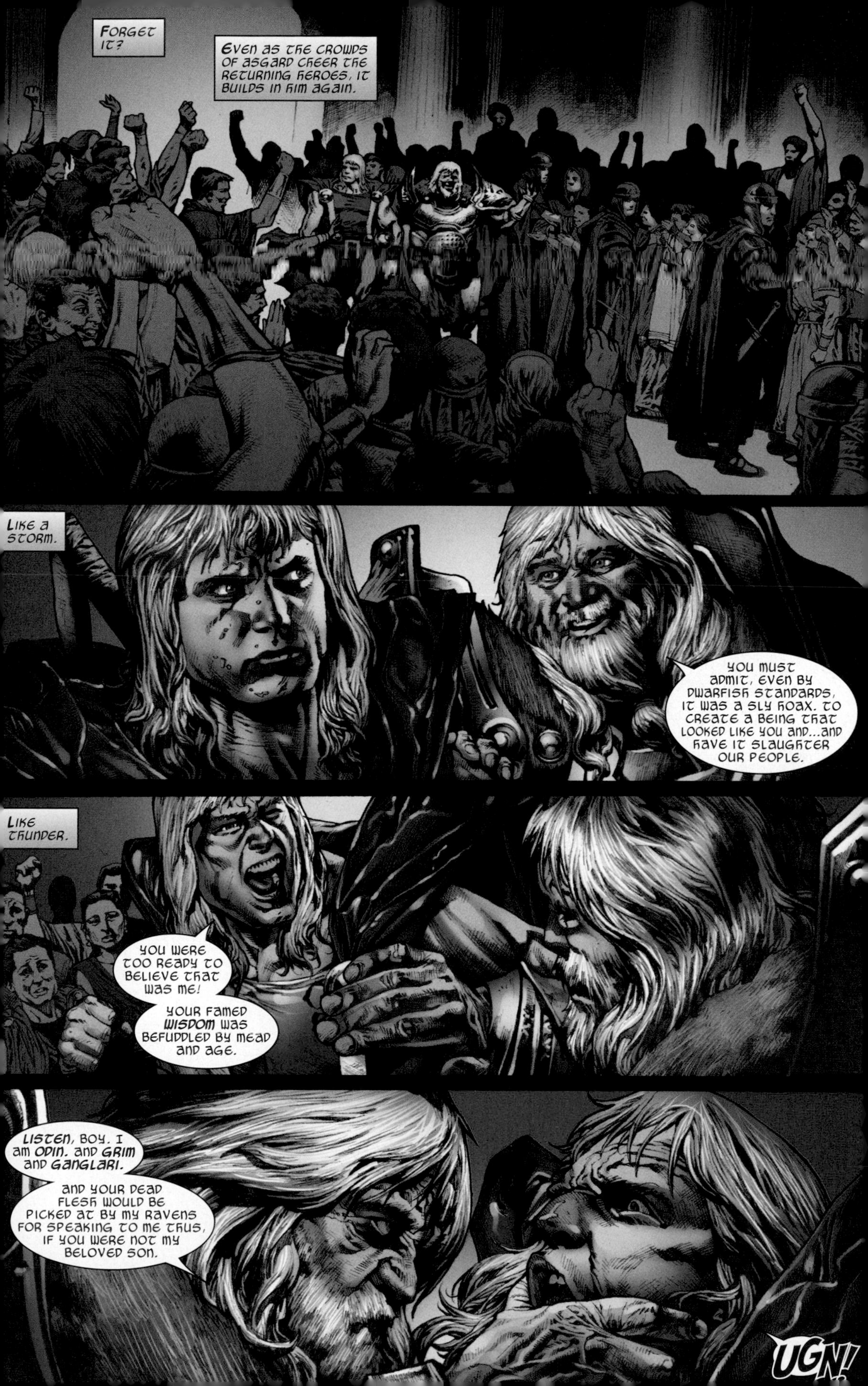
FORGET IT?
EVEN AS THE CROWDS OF ASGARD CHEER THE RETURNING HEROES, IT BUILDS IN HIM AGAIN.
LIKE A STORM.
YOU MUST ADMIT, EVEN BY DWARFISH STANDARDS, IT WAS A SLY HOAX. TO CREATE A BEING THAT LOOKED LIKE YOU AND...AND HAVE IT SLAUGHTER OUR PEOPLE.
LIKE THUNDER.
YOU WERE TOO READY TO BELIEVE THAT WAS ME!
YOUR FAMED WISDOM WAS BEFUDDLED BY MEAD AND AGE.
LISTEN, BOY. I AM ODIN. AND GRIM AND GANGLARI.
AND YOUR DEAD FLESH WOULD BE PICKED AT BY MY RAVENS FOR SPEAKING TO ME THUS, IF YOU WERE NOT MY BELOVED SON.
UGN!

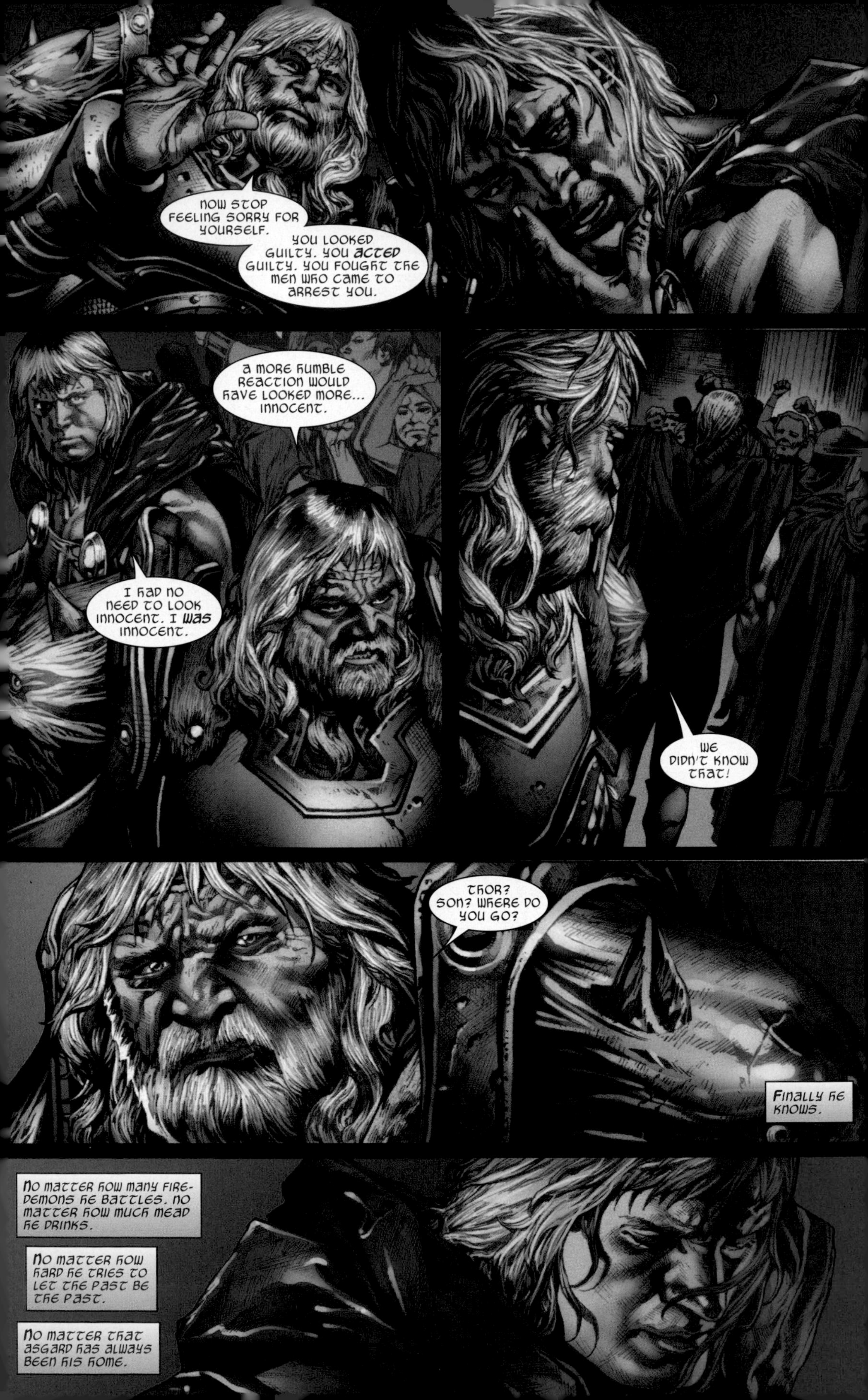
NOW STOP FEELING SORRY FOR YOURSELF.
YOU LOOKED GUILTY. YOU ACTED GUILTY. YOU FOUGHT THE MEN WHO CAME TO ARREST YOU.
A MORE HUMBLE REACTION WOULD HAVE LOOKED MORE... INNOCENT.
I HAD NO NEED TO LOOK INNOCENT. I WAS INNOCENT.
WE DIDN'T KNOW THAT!
THOR? SON? WHERE DO YOU GO?
FINALLY HE KNOWS.
NO MATTER HOW MANY FIRE-DEMONS HE BATTLES. NO MATTER HOW MUCH MEAD HE DRINKS.
NO MATTER HOW HARD HE TRIES TO LET THE PAST BE THE PAST.
NO MATTER THAT ASGARD HAS ALWAYS BEEN HIS HOME.

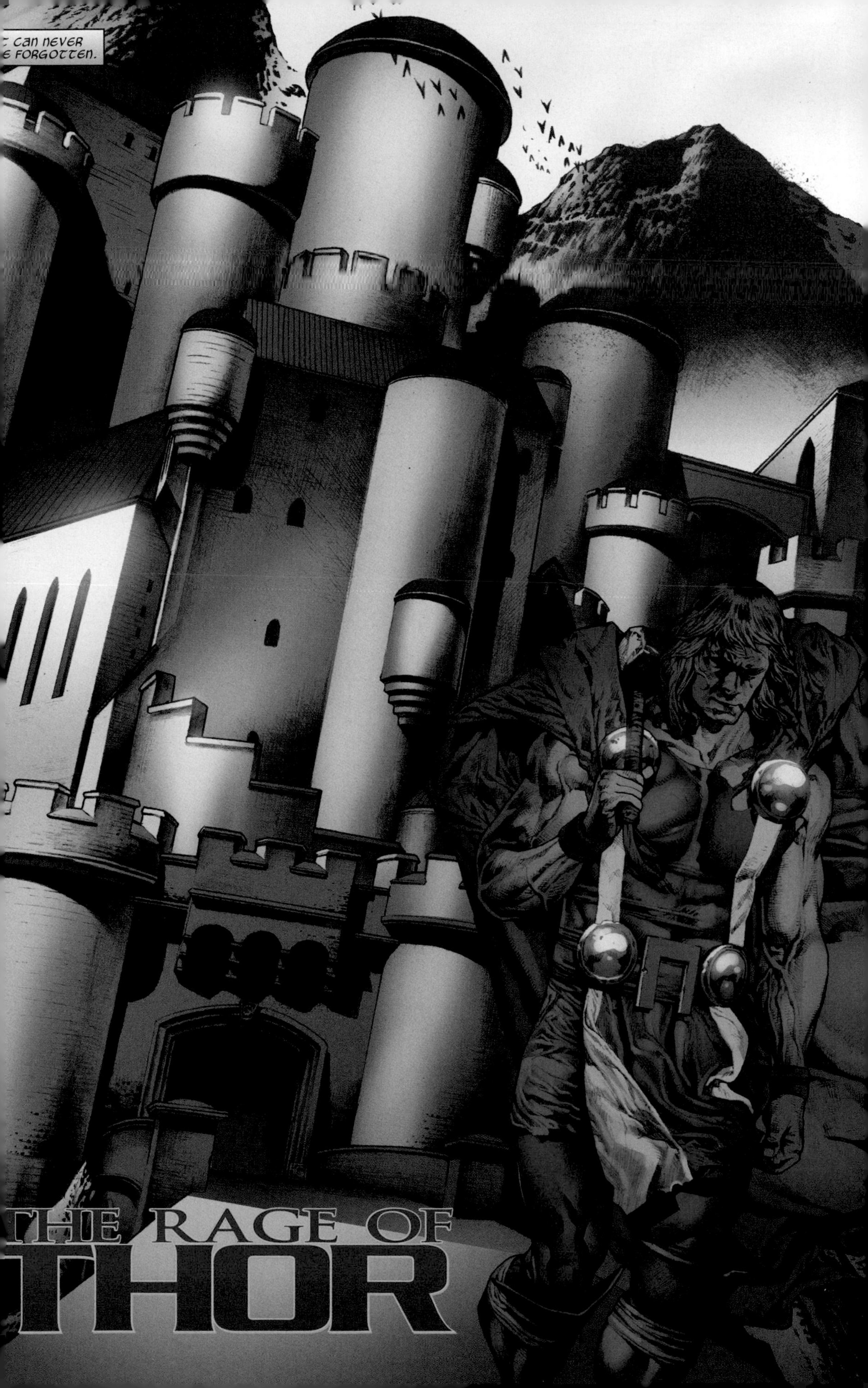
T CAN NEVER
E FORGOTTEN.
THE RAGE OF
THOR

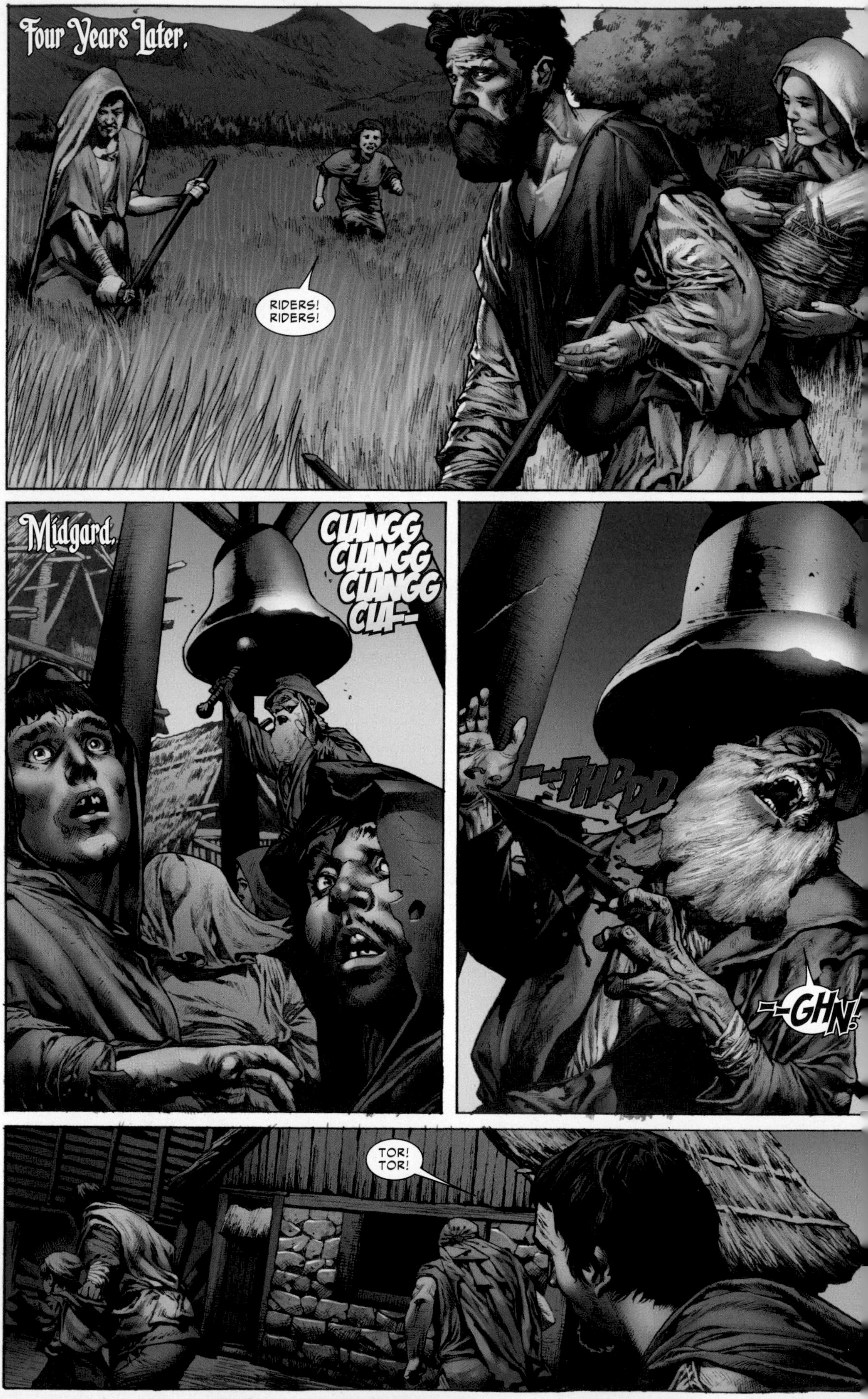
Four Years Later,
RIDERS! RIDERS!
Midgard,
CLANGG CLANGG CLANGG CLA--
--THDDD
--GHN!
TOR! TOR!

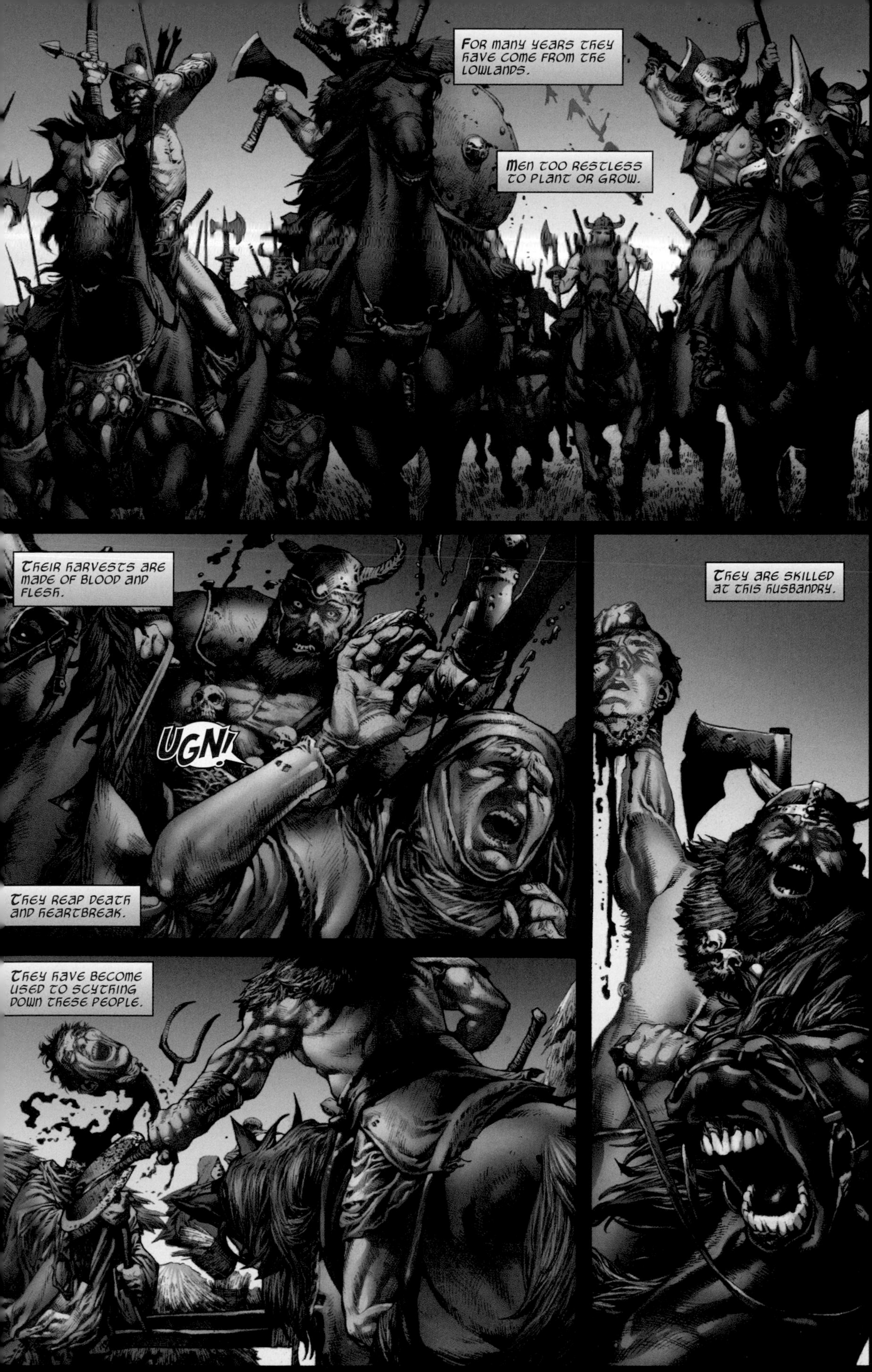
For many years they have come from the lowlands.
Men too restless to plant or grow.
Their harvests are made of blood and flesh.
UGN!
They reap death and heartbreak.
They are skilled at this husbandry.
They have become used to scything down these people.

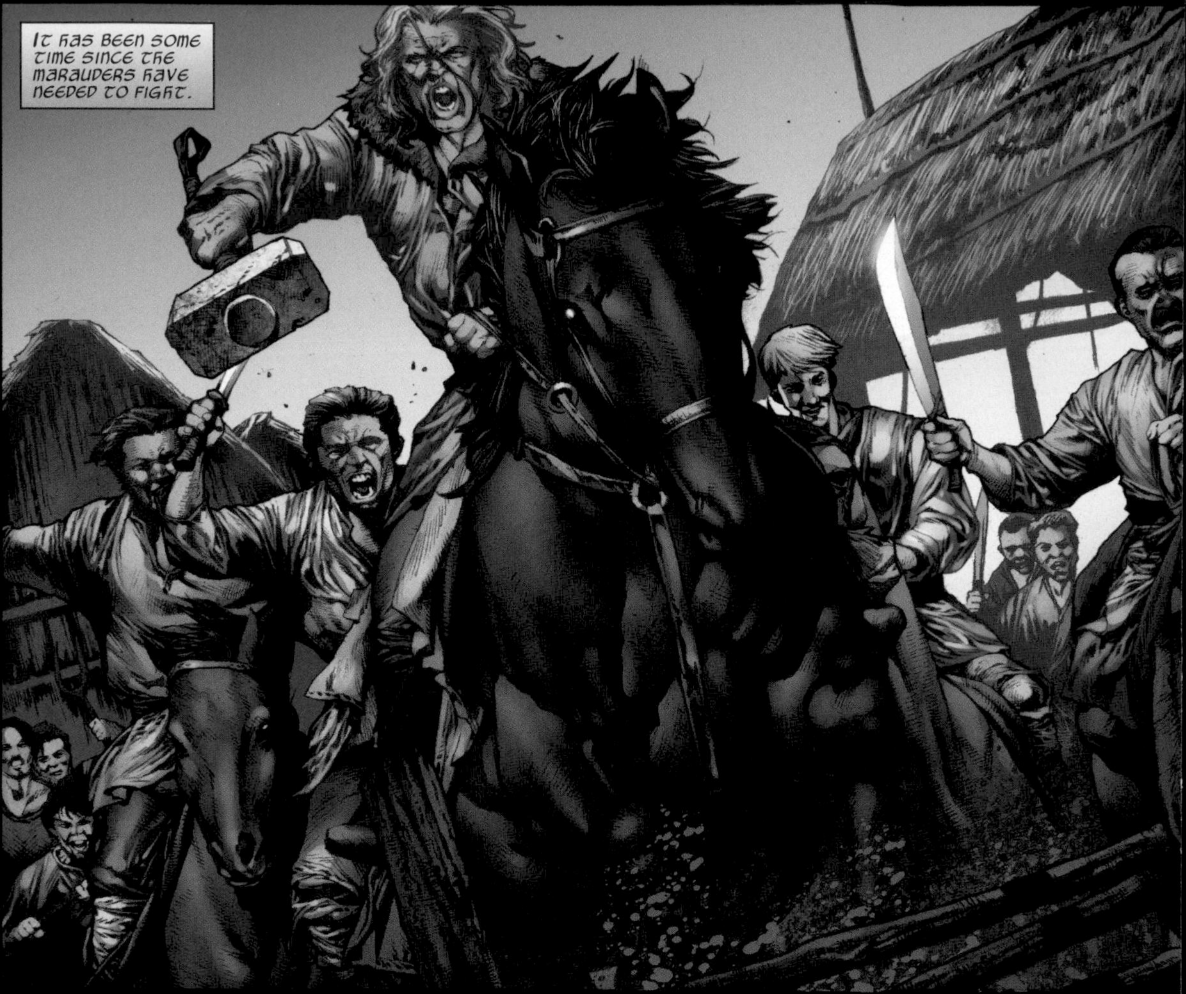
It has been some time since the marauders have needed to fight.

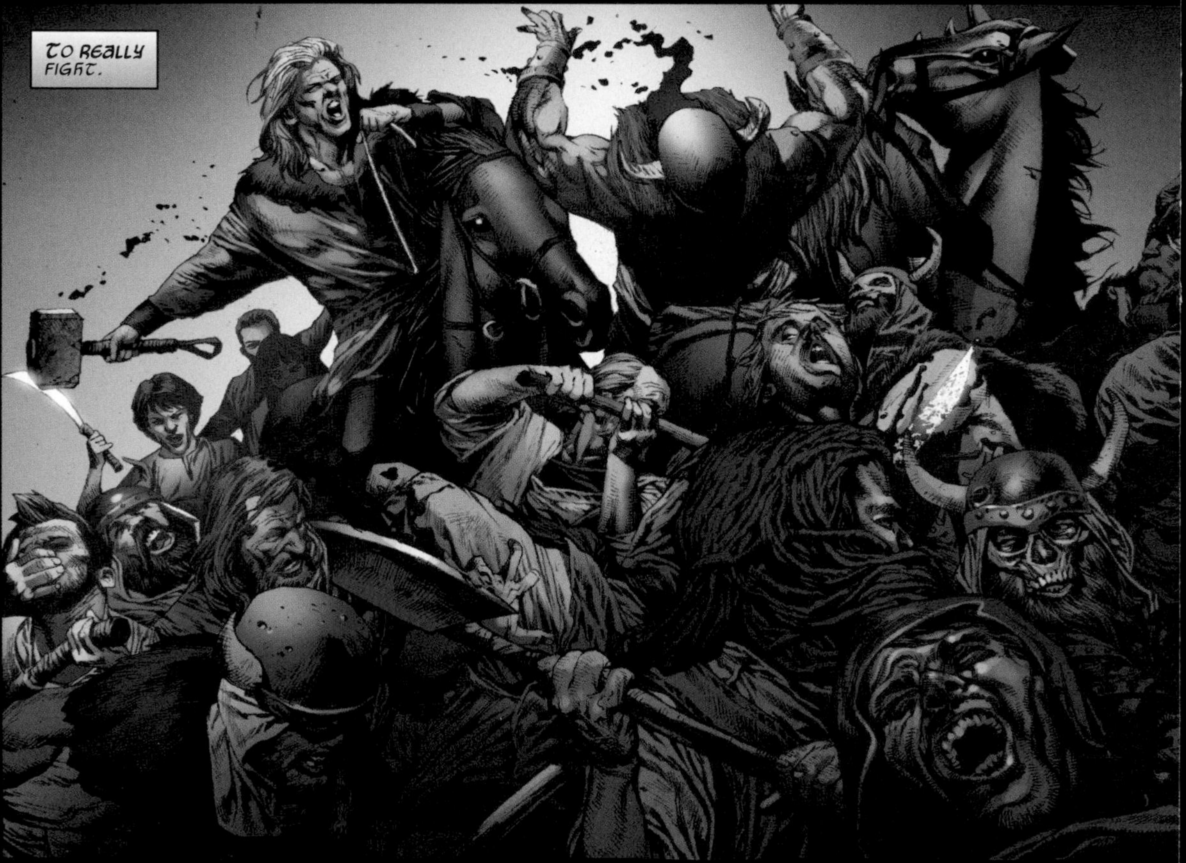
To really fight.

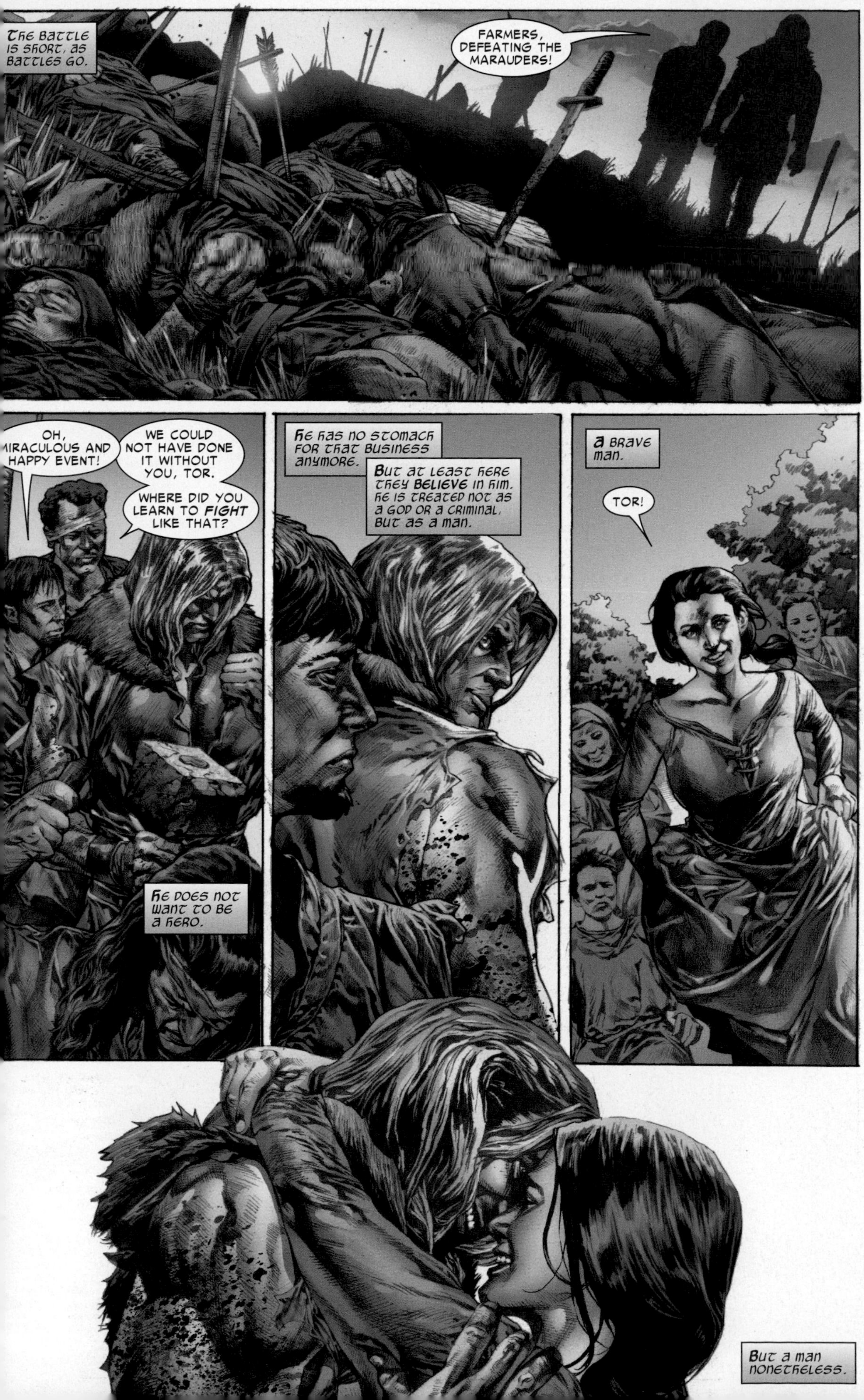
The battle is short, as battles go.
Farmers, defeating the marauders!
Oh, miraculous and happy event!
We could not have done it without you, Tor.
Where did you learn to *fight* like that?
He does not want to be a hero.
He has no stomach for that business anymore.
But at least here they **believe** in him. He is treated not as a god or a criminal, but as a man.
A brave man.
Tor!
But a man nonetheless.

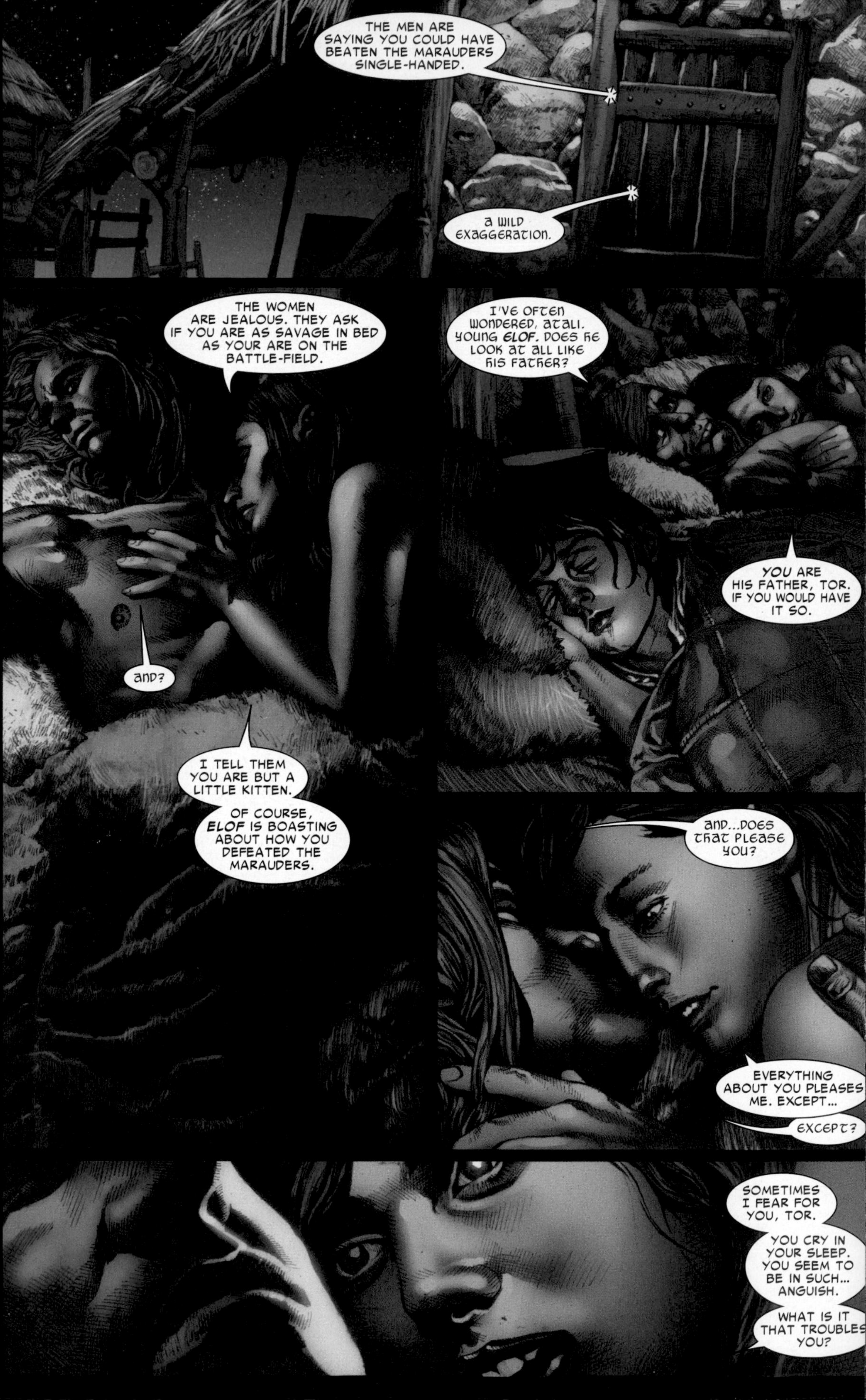
THE MEN ARE SAYING YOU COULD HAVE BEATEN THE MARAUDERS SINGLE-HANDED.
A WILD EXAGGERATION.
THE WOMEN ARE JEALOUS. THEY ASK IF YOU ARE AS SAVAGE IN BED AS YOUR ARE ON THE BATTLE-FIELD.
AND?
I TELL THEM YOU ARE BUT A LITTLE KITTEN.
OF COURSE, ELOF IS BOASTING ABOUT HOW YOU DEFEATED THE MARAUDERS.
I'VE OFTEN WONDERED, ATALI. YOUNG ELOF. DOES HE LOOK AT ALL LIKE HIS FATHER?
YOU ARE HIS FATHER, TOR. IF YOU WOULD HAVE IT SO.
AND...DOES THAT PLEASE YOU?
EVERYTHING ABOUT YOU PLEASES ME. EXCEPT...
EXCEPT?
SOMETIMES I FEAR FOR YOU, TOR.
YOU CRY IN YOUR SLEEP. YOU SEEM TO BE IN SUCH... ANGUISH.
WHAT IS IT THAT TROUBLES YOU?

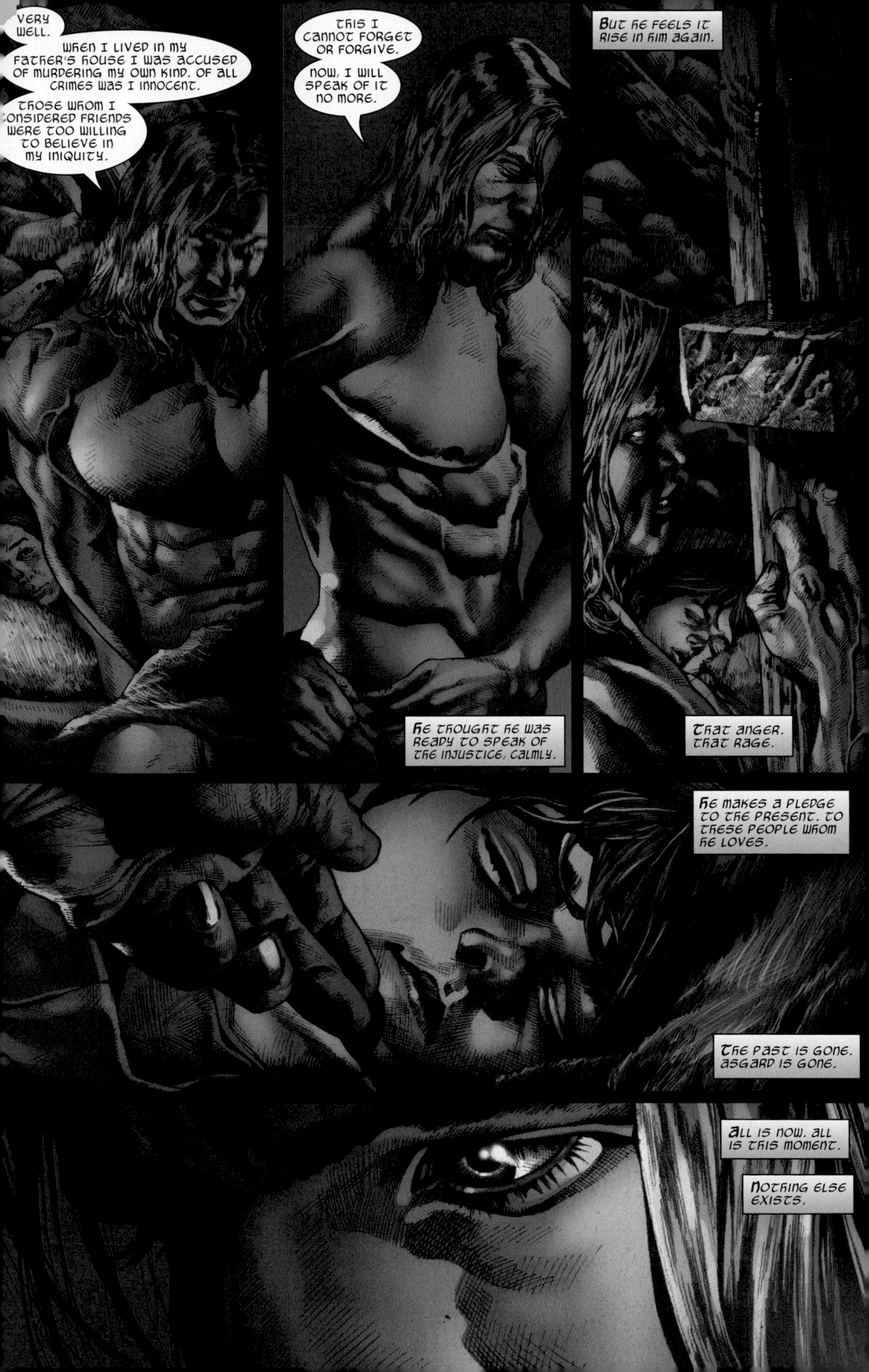

VERY WELL.
WHEN I LIVED IN MY FATHER'S HOUSE I WAS ACCUSED OF MURDERING MY OWN KIND. OF ALL CRIMES WAS I INNOCENT.
THOSE WHOM I CONSIDERED FRIENDS WERE TOO WILLING TO BELIEVE IN MY INIQUITY.
THIS I CANNOT FORGET OR FORGIVE.
NOW, I WILL SPEAK OF IT NO MORE.
HE THOUGHT HE WAS READY TO SPEAK OF THE INJUSTICE, CALMLY.
BUT HE FEELS IT RISE IN HIM AGAIN.
THAT ANGER. THAT RAGE.
HE MAKES A PLEDGE TO THE PRESENT. TO THESE PEOPLE WHOM HE LOVES.
THE PAST IS GONE. ASGARD IS GONE.
ALL IS NOW. ALL IS THIS MOMENT.
NOTHING ELSE EXISTS.

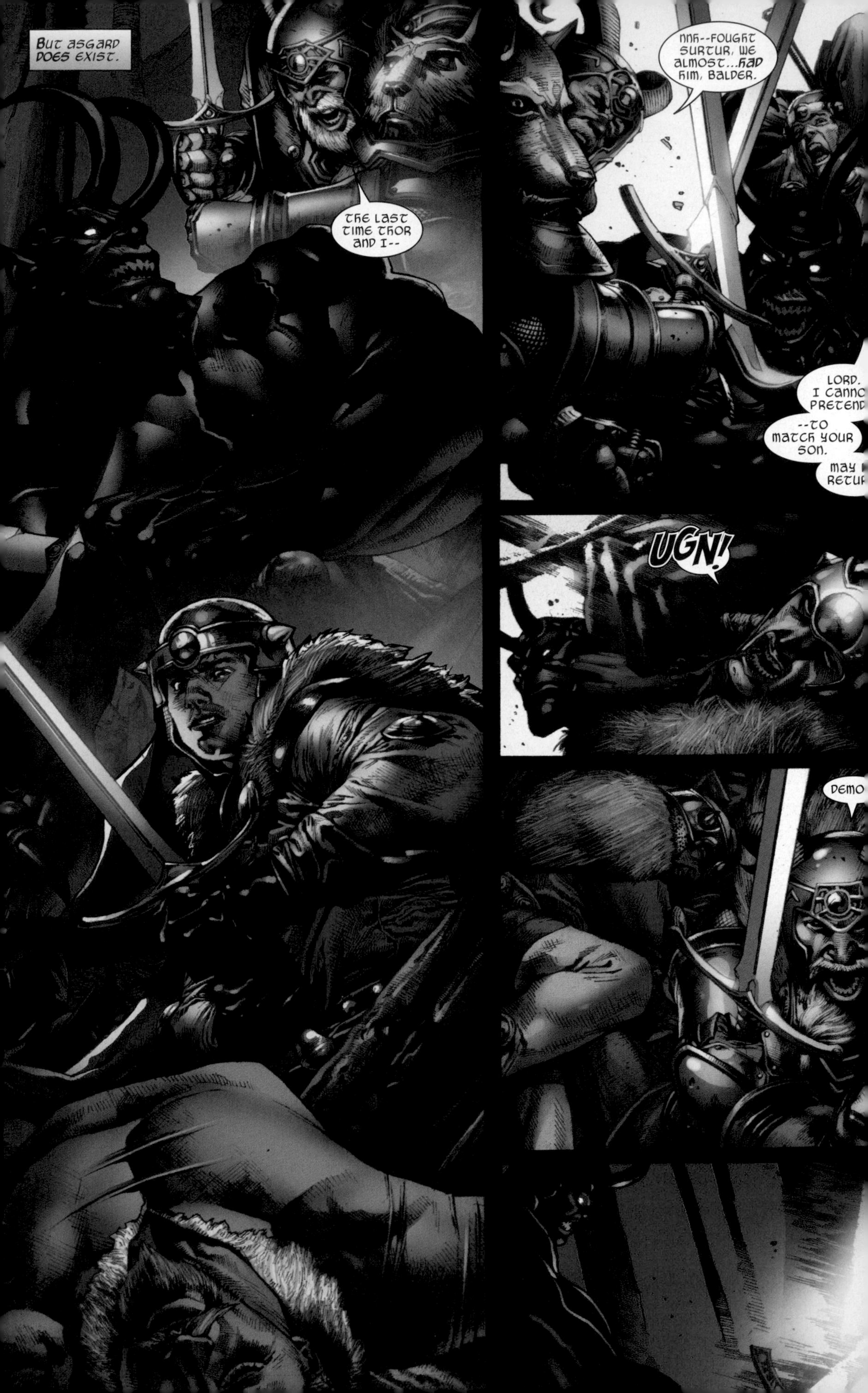
BUT ASGARD DOES EXIST.
THE LAST TIME THOR AND I--
NNH--FOUGHT SURTUR, WE ALMOST...HAD HIM, BALDER.
LORD. I CANNO PRETEND
--TO MATCH YOUR SON.
MAY RETUR
UGN!
DEMO

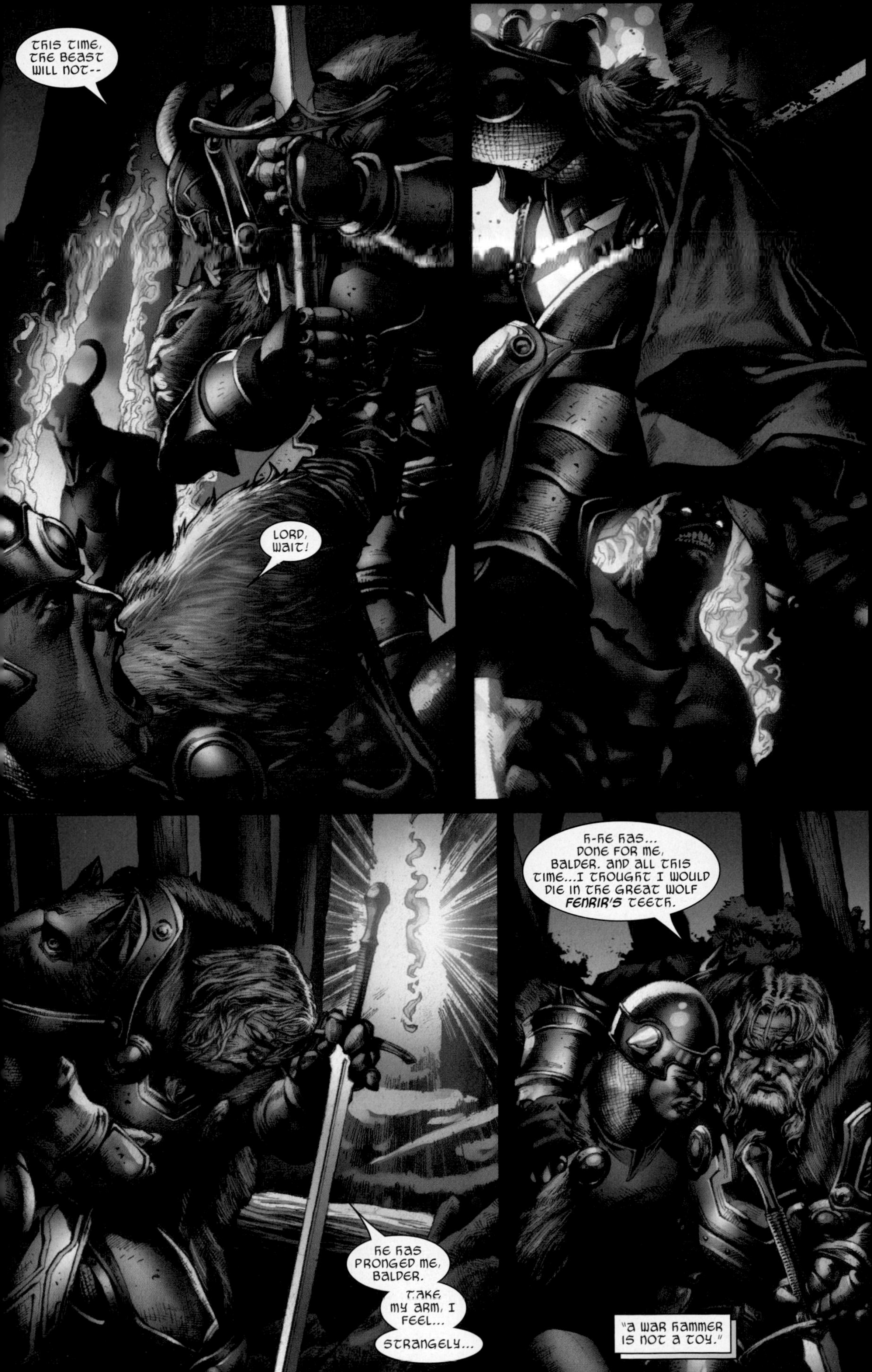
THIS TIME, THE BEAST WILL NOT--
LORD, WAIT!
HE HAS PRONGED ME, BALDER.
TAKE MY ARM. I FEEL...
STRANGELY...
H-HE HAS... DONE FOR ME, BALDER. AND ALL THIS TIME...I THOUGHT I WOULD DIE IN THE GREAT WOLF FENRIR'S TEETH.
"A WAR HAMMER IS NOT A TOY."

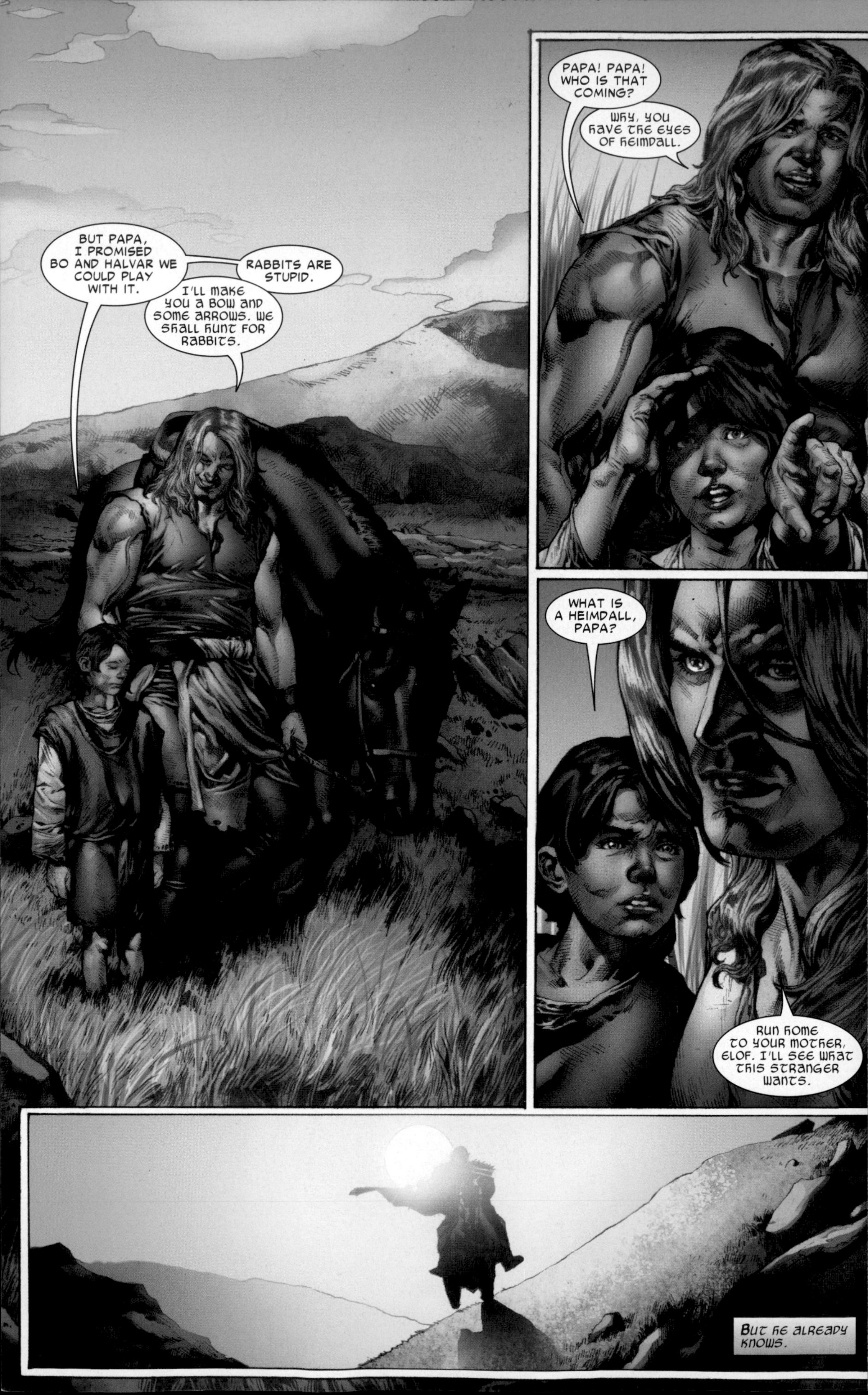
BUT PAPA, I PROMISED BO AND HALVAR WE COULD PLAY WITH IT.
RABBITS ARE STUPID.
I'LL MAKE YOU A BOW AND SOME ARROWS. WE SHALL HUNT FOR RABBITS.
PAPA! PAPA! WHO IS THAT COMING?
WHY, YOU HAVE THE EYES OF HEIMDALL.
WHAT IS A HEIMDALL, PAPA?
RUN HOME TO YOUR MOTHER, ELOF. I'LL SEE WHAT THIS STRANGER WANTS.
BUT HE ALREADY KNOWS.

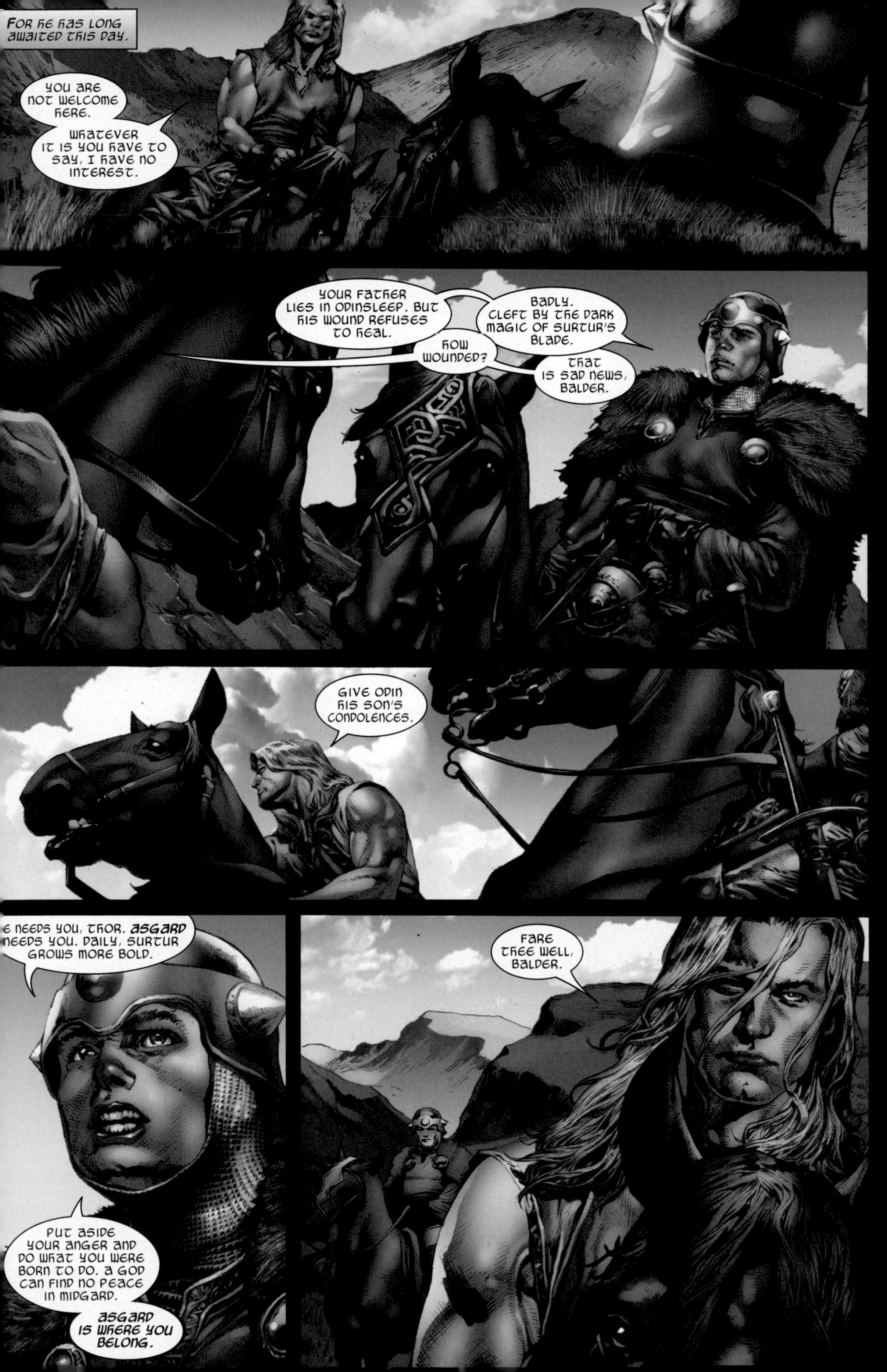
FOR HE HAS LONG AWAITED THIS DAY.
YOU ARE NOT WELCOME HERE.
WHATEVER IT IS YOU HAVE TO SAY, I HAVE NO INTEREST.
YOUR FATHER LIES IN ODINSLEEP. BUT HIS WOUND REFUSES TO HEAL.
HOW WOUNDED?
BADLY. CLEFT BY THE DARK MAGIC OF SURTUR'S BLADE.
THAT IS SAD NEWS, BALDER.
GIVE ODIN HIS SON'S CONDOLENCES.
E NEEDS YOU, THOR. ASGARD NEEDS YOU. DAILY, SURTUR GROWS MORE BOLD.
PUT ASIDE YOUR ANGER AND DO WHAT YOU WERE BORN TO DO. A GOD CAN FIND NO PEACE IN MIDGARD.
ASGARD IS WHERE YOU BELONG.
FARE THEE WELL, BALDER.

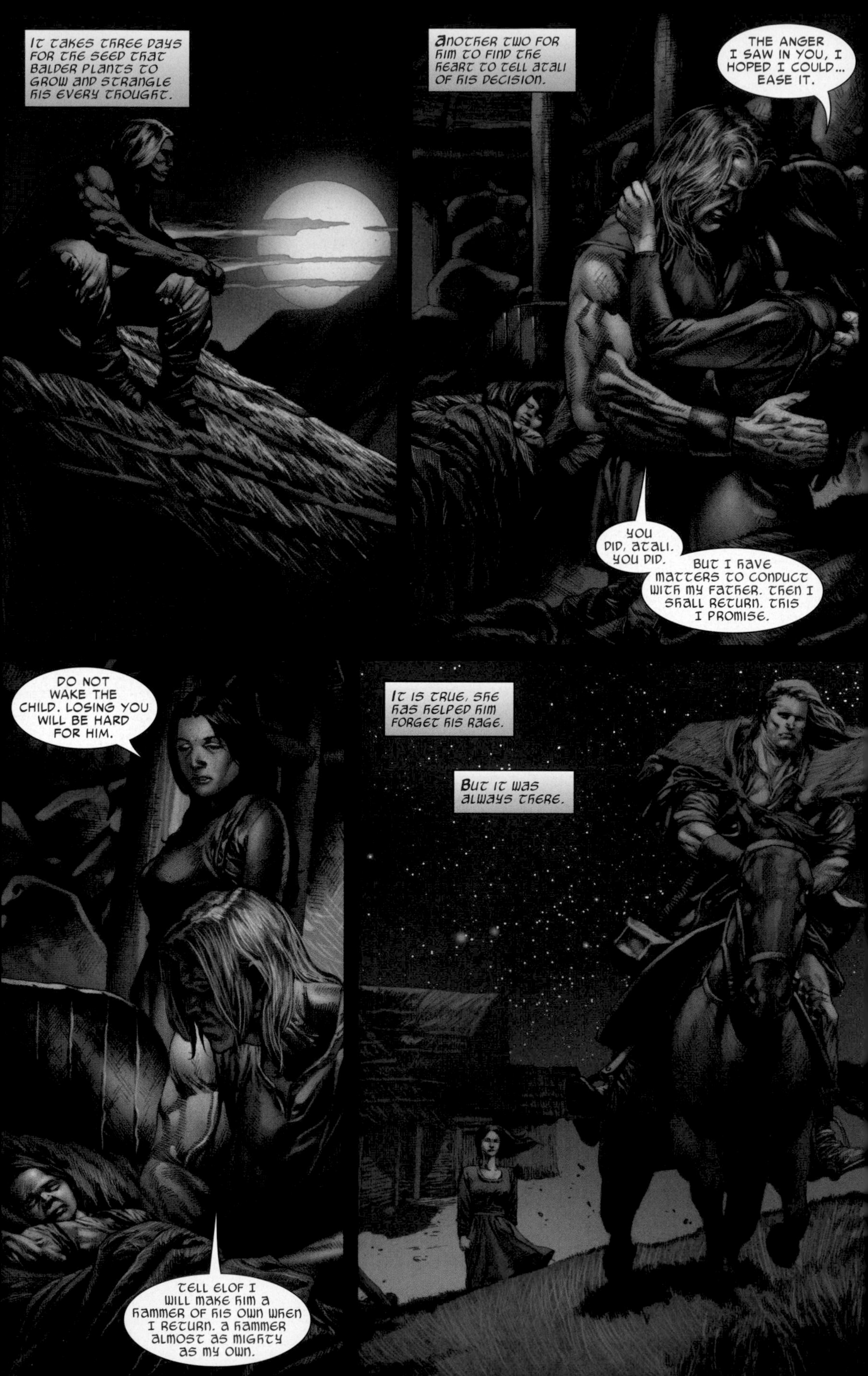
It takes three days for the seed that Balder plants to grow and strangle his every thought.
Another two for him to find the heart to tell Atali of his decision.
THE ANGER I SAW IN YOU, I HOPED I COULD... EASE IT.
You did, Atali. You did.
But I have matters to conduct with my father. Then I shall return. This I PROMISE.
DO NOT WAKE THE CHILD. LOSING YOU WILL BE HARD FOR HIM.
Tell Elof I will make him a hammer of his own when I return. A hammer almost as mighty as my own.
It is true, she has helped him forget his rage.
But it was always there.

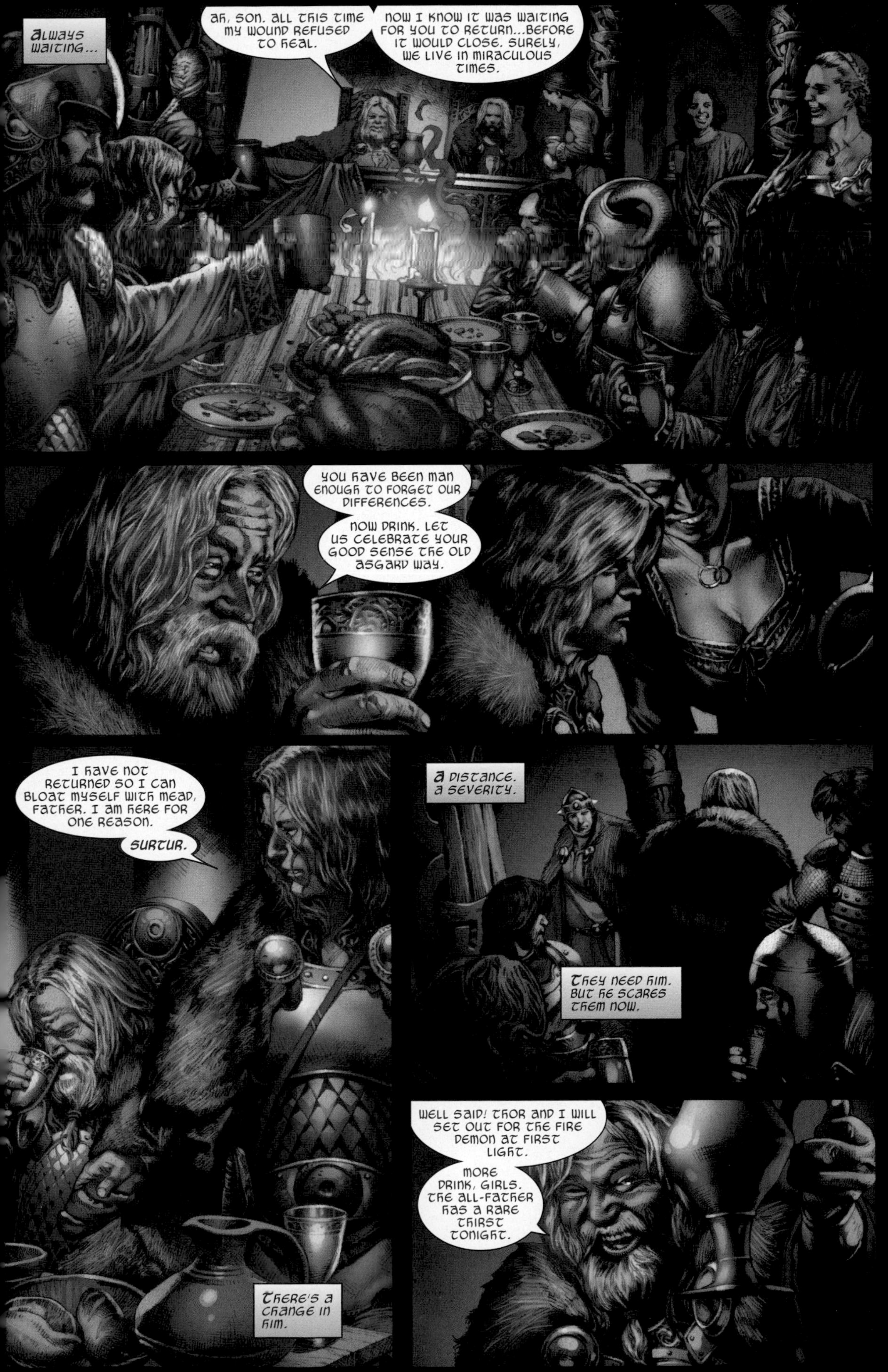
ALWAYS WAITING...
AH, SON. ALL THIS TIME MY WOUND REFUSED TO HEAL.
NOW I KNOW IT WAS WAITING FOR YOU TO RETURN...BEFORE IT WOULD CLOSE. SURELY, WE LIVE IN MIRACULOUS TIMES.
YOU HAVE BEEN MAN ENOUGH TO FORGET OUR DIFFERENCES.
NOW DRINK. LET US CELEBRATE YOUR GOOD SENSE THE OLD ASGARD WAY.
I HAVE NOT RETURNED SO I CAN BLOAT MYSELF WITH MEAD, FATHER. I AM HERE FOR ONE REASON.
SURTUR.
THERE'S A CHANGE IN HIM.
A DISTANCE. A SEVERITY.
THEY NEED HIM. BUT HE SCARES THEM NOW.
WELL SAID! THOR AND I WILL SET OUT FOR THE FIRE DEMON AT FIRST LIGHT.
MORE DRINK, GIRLS. THE ALL-FATHER HAS A RARE THIRST TONIGHT.

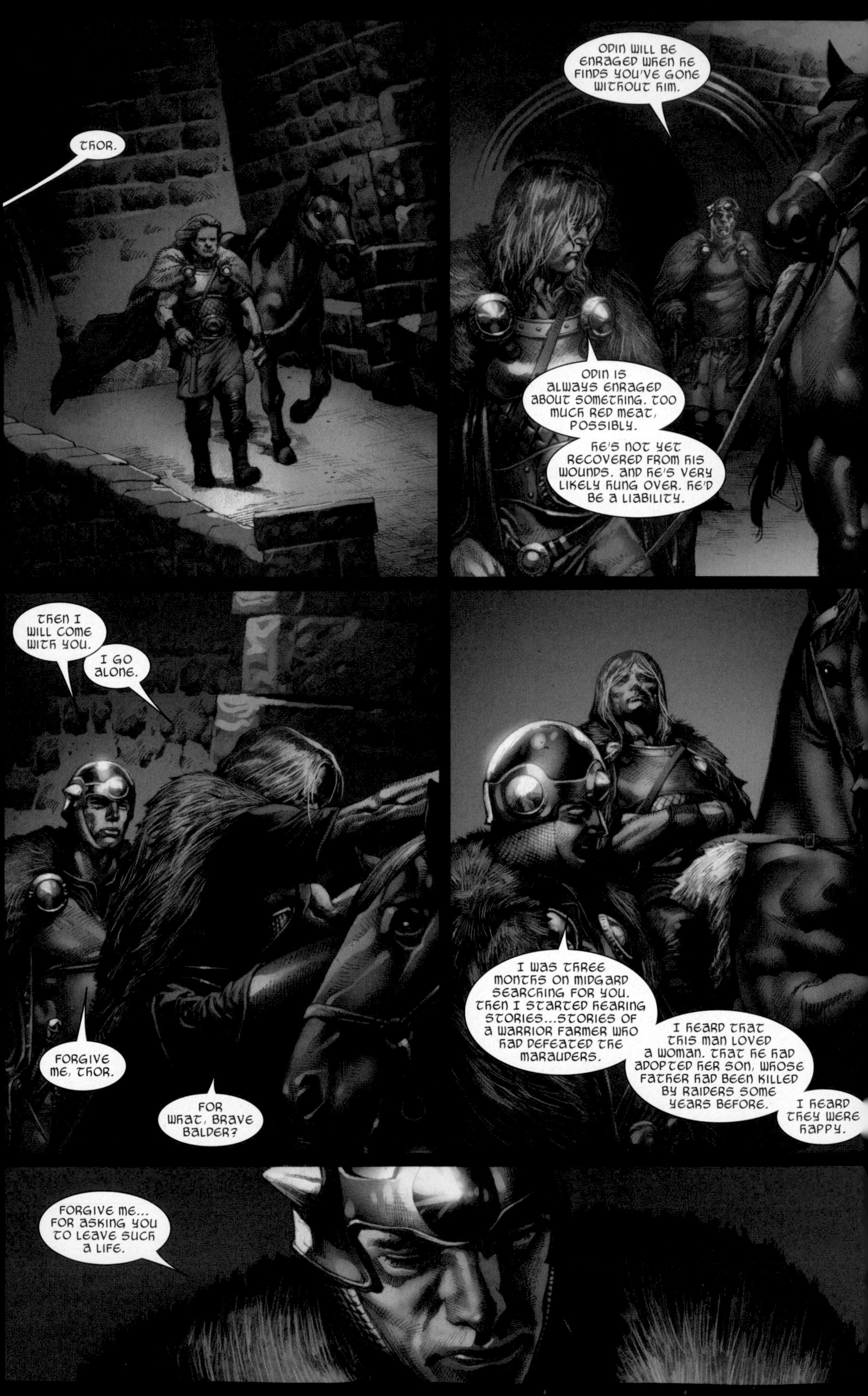
THOR.
ODIN WILL BE ENRAGED WHEN HE FINDS YOU'VE GONE WITHOUT HIM.
ODIN IS ALWAYS ENRAGED ABOUT SOMETHING. TOO MUCH RED MEAT, POSSIBLY.
HE'S NOT YET RECOVERED FROM HIS WOUNDS. AND HE'S VERY LIKELY HUNG OVER. HE'D BE A LIABILITY.
THEN I WILL COME WITH YOU.
I GO ALONE.
FORGIVE ME, THOR.
FOR WHAT, BRAVE BALDER?
I WAS THREE MONTHS ON MIDGARD SEARCHING FOR YOU. THEN I STARTED HEARING STORIES...STORIES OF A WARRIOR FARMER WHO HAD DEFEATED THE MARAUDERS.
I HEARD THAT THIS MAN LOVED A WOMAN. THAT HE HAD ADOPTED HER SON, WHOSE FATHER HAD BEEN KILLED BY RAIDERS SOME YEARS BEFORE.
I HEARD THEY WERE HAPPY.
FORGIVE ME... FOR ASKING YOU TO LEAVE SUCH A LIFE.

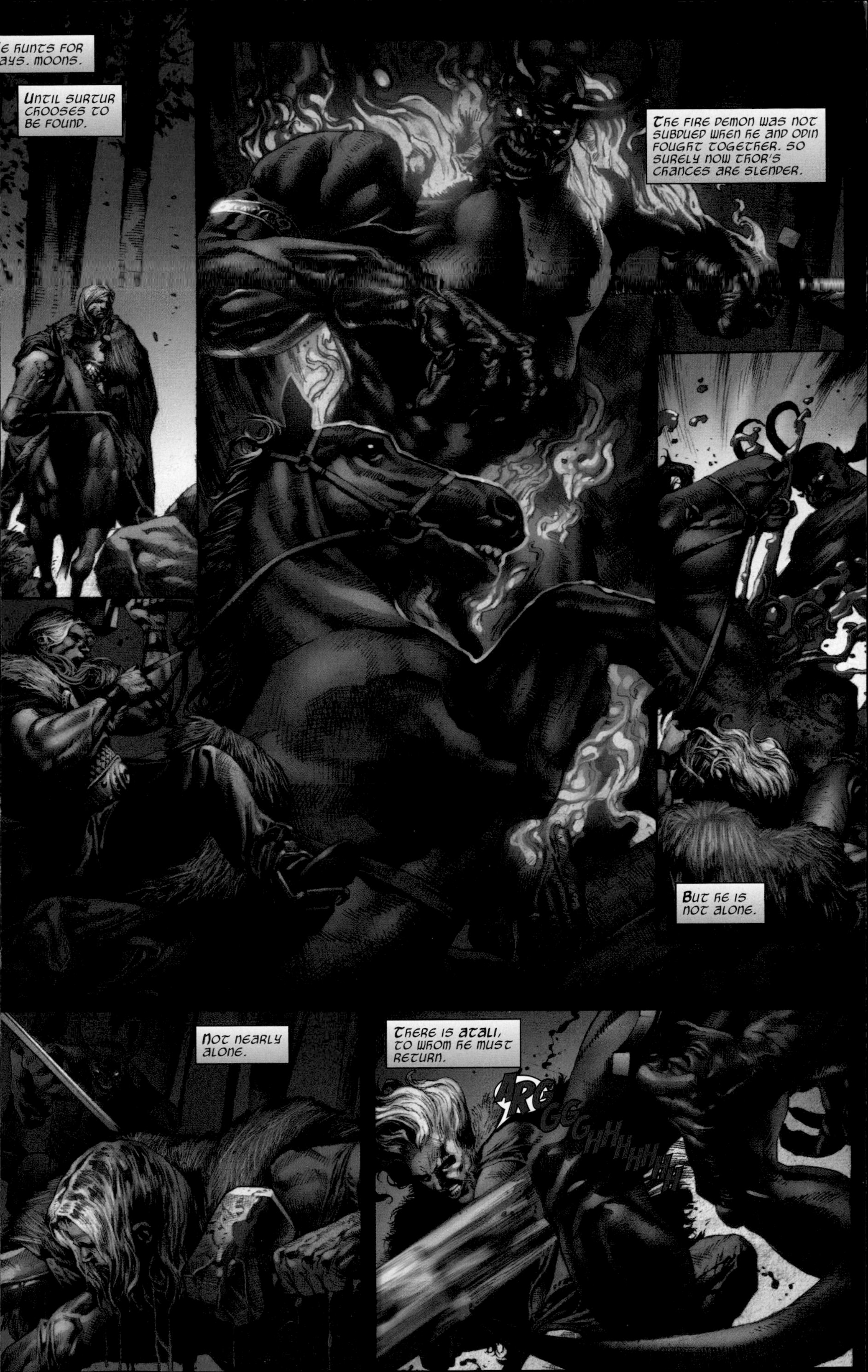
E HUNTS FOR
AYS. MOONS.
UNTIL SURTUR CHOOSES TO BE FOUND.
THE FIRE DEMON WAS NOT SUBDUED WHEN HE AND ODIN FOUGHT TOGETHER. SO SURELY NOW THOR'S CHANCES ARE SLENDER.
BUT HE IS NOT ALONE.
NOT NEARLY ALONE.
THERE IS ATALI, TO WHOM HE MUST RETURN.
ARGGGHHHHHHHH

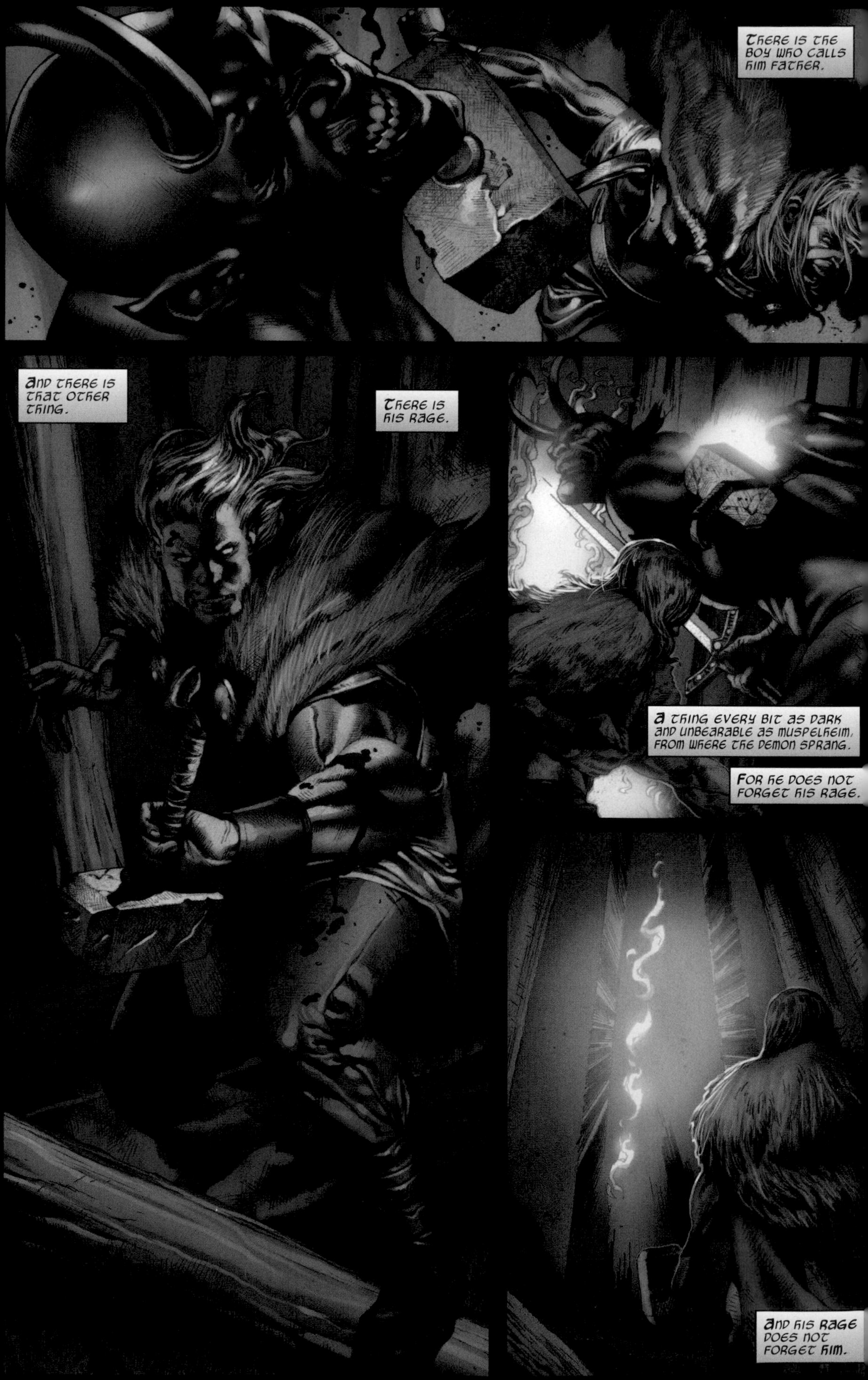

THERE IS THE BOY WHO CALLS HIM FATHER.
AND THERE IS THAT OTHER THING.
THERE IS HIS RAGE.
A THING EVERY BIT AS DARK AND UNBEARABLE AS MUSPELHEIM, FROM WHERE THE DEMON SPRANG.
FOR HE DOES NOT FORGET HIS RAGE.
AND HIS RAGE DOES NOT FORGET HIM.

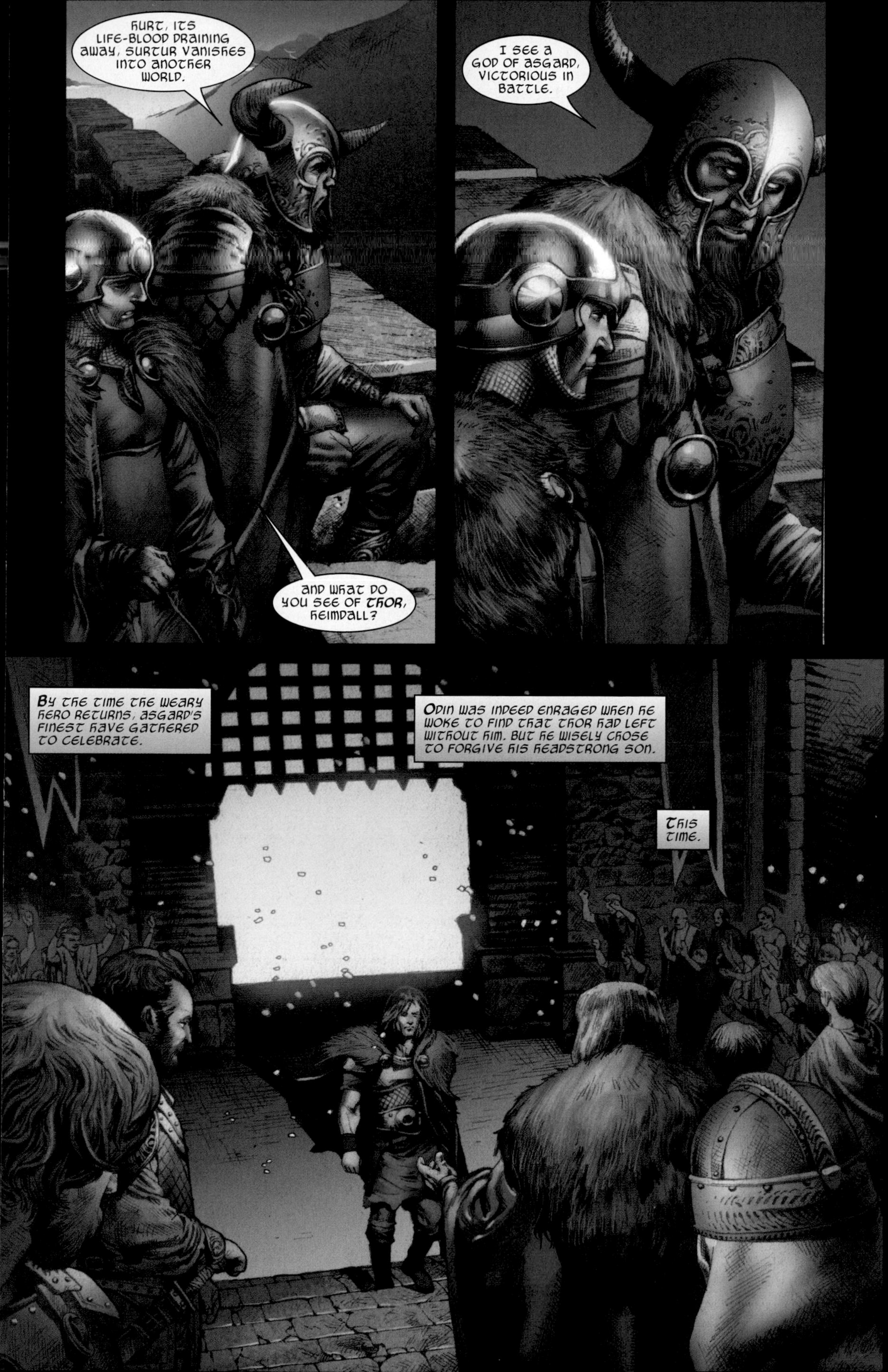
HURT, ITS LIFE-BLOOD DRAINING AWAY, SURTUR VANISHES INTO ANOTHER WORLD.
AND WHAT DO YOU SEE OF THOR, HEIMDALL?
I SEE A GOD OF ASGARD, VICTORIOUS IN BATTLE.
BY THE TIME THE WEARY HERO RETURNS, ASGARD'S FINEST HAVE GATHERED TO CELEBRATE.
ODIN WAS INDEED ENRAGED WHEN HE WOKE TO FIND THAT THOR HAD LEFT WITHOUT HIM. BUT HE WISELY CHOSE TO FORGIVE HIS HEADSTRONG SON.
THIS TIME.

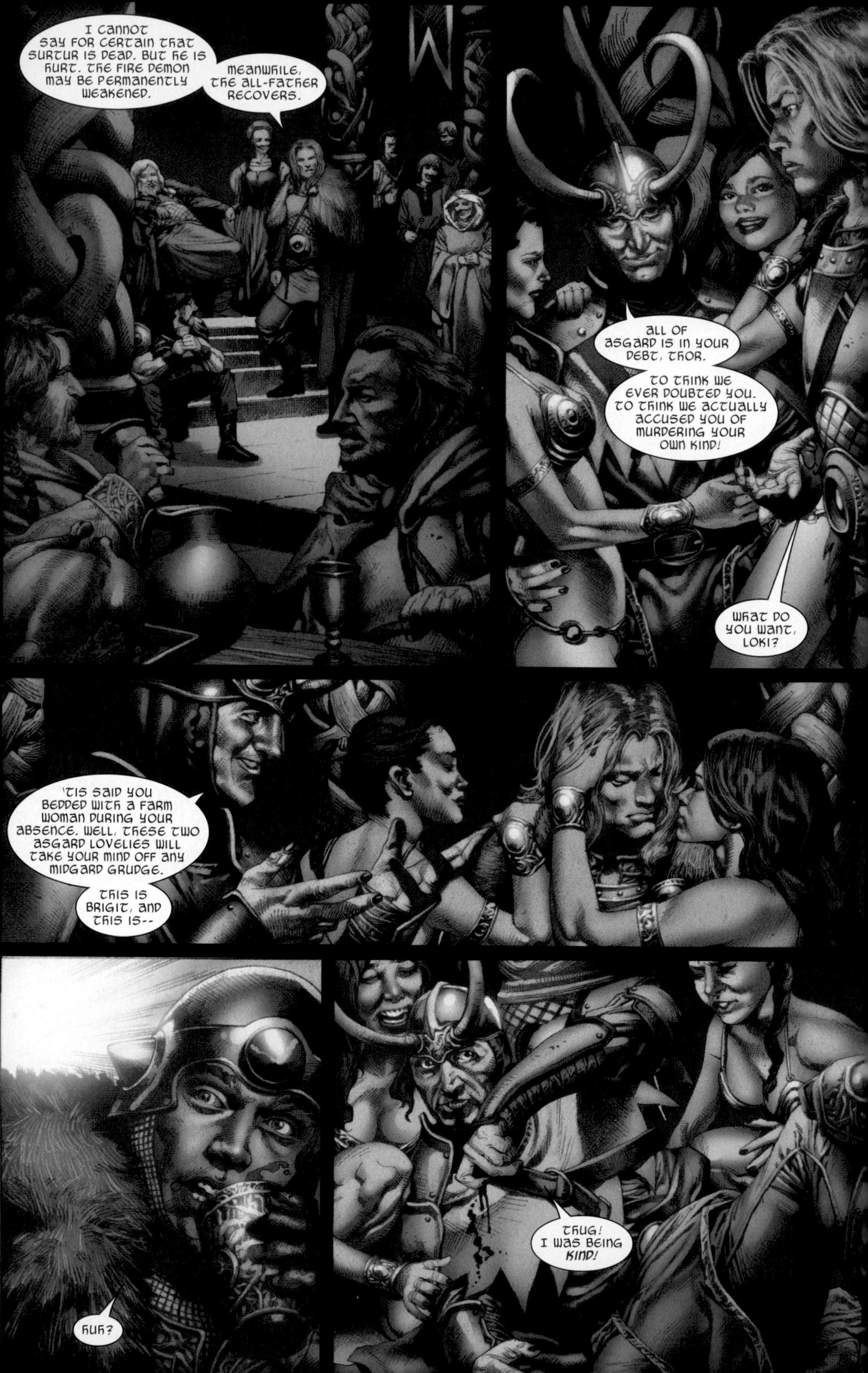

I CANNOT SAY FOR CERTAIN THAT SURTUR IS DEAD. BUT HE IS HURT. THE FIRE DEMON MAY BE PERMANENTLY WEAKENED.
MEANWHILE, THE ALL-FATHER RECOVERS.
ALL OF ASGARD IS IN YOUR DEBT, THOR.
TO THINK WE EVER DOUBTED YOU. TO THINK WE ACTUALLY ACCUSED YOU OF MURDERING YOUR OWN KIND!
WHAT DO YOU WANT, LOKI?
'TIS SAID YOU BEDDED WITH A FARM WOMAN DURING YOUR ABSENCE. WELL, THESE TWO ASGARD LOVELIES WILL TAKE YOUR MIND OFF ANY MIDGARD GRUDGE.
THIS IS BRIGIT, AND THIS IS--
HUH?
THUG! I WAS BEING KIND!

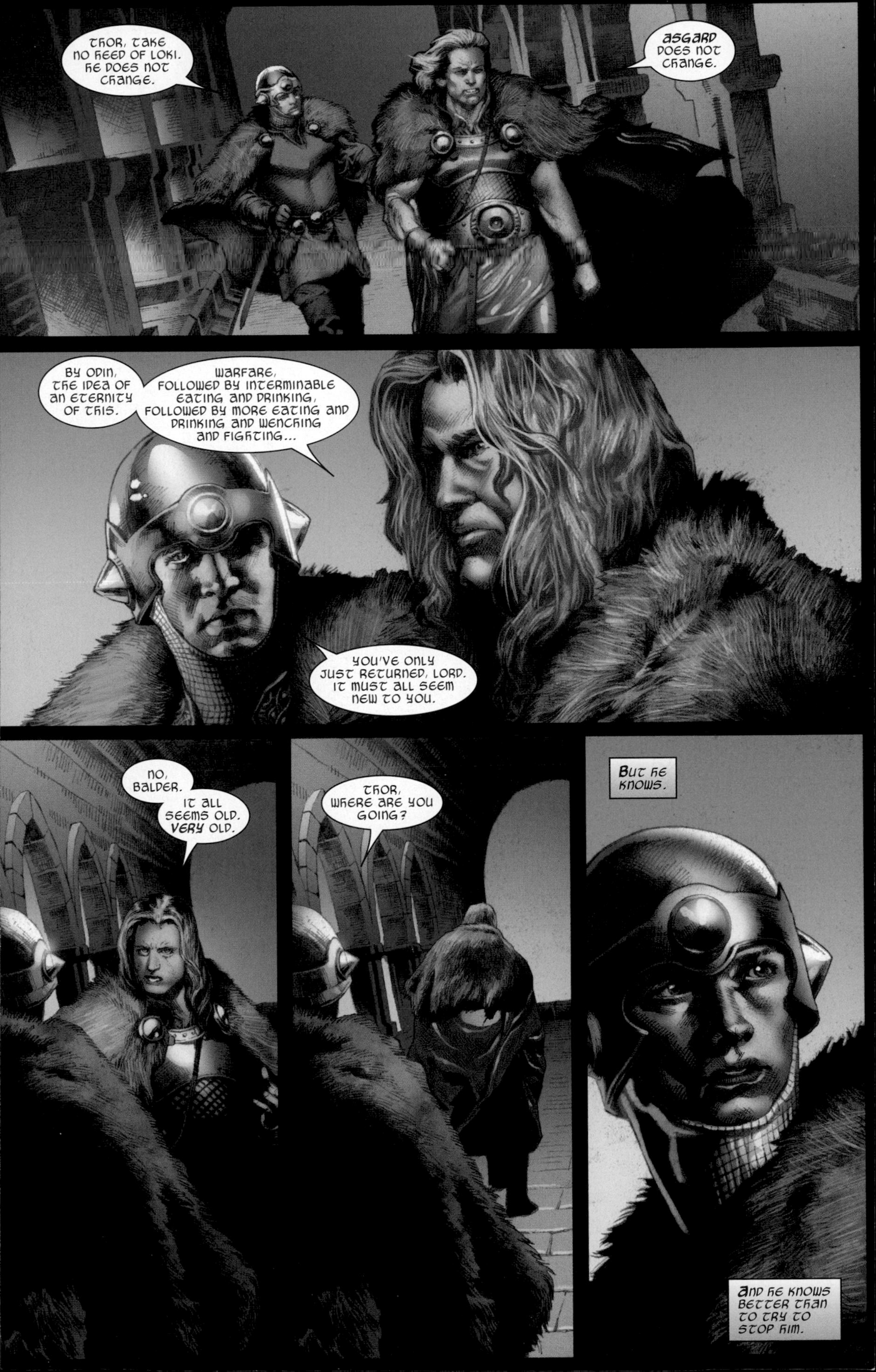

THOR, TAKE NO HEED OF LOKI. HE DOES NOT CHANGE.
ASGARD DOES NOT CHANGE.
BY ODIN, THE IDEA OF AN ETERNITY OF THIS.
WARFARE, FOLLOWED BY INTERMINABLE EATING AND DRINKING, FOLLOWED BY MORE EATING AND DRINKING AND WENCHING AND FIGHTING...
YOU'VE ONLY JUST RETURNED, LORD. IT MUST ALL SEEM NEW TO YOU.
NO, BALDER.
IT ALL SEEMS OLD. VERY OLD.
THOR, WHERE ARE YOU GOING?
BUT HE KNOWS.
AND HE KNOWS BETTER THAN TO TRY TO STOP HIM.

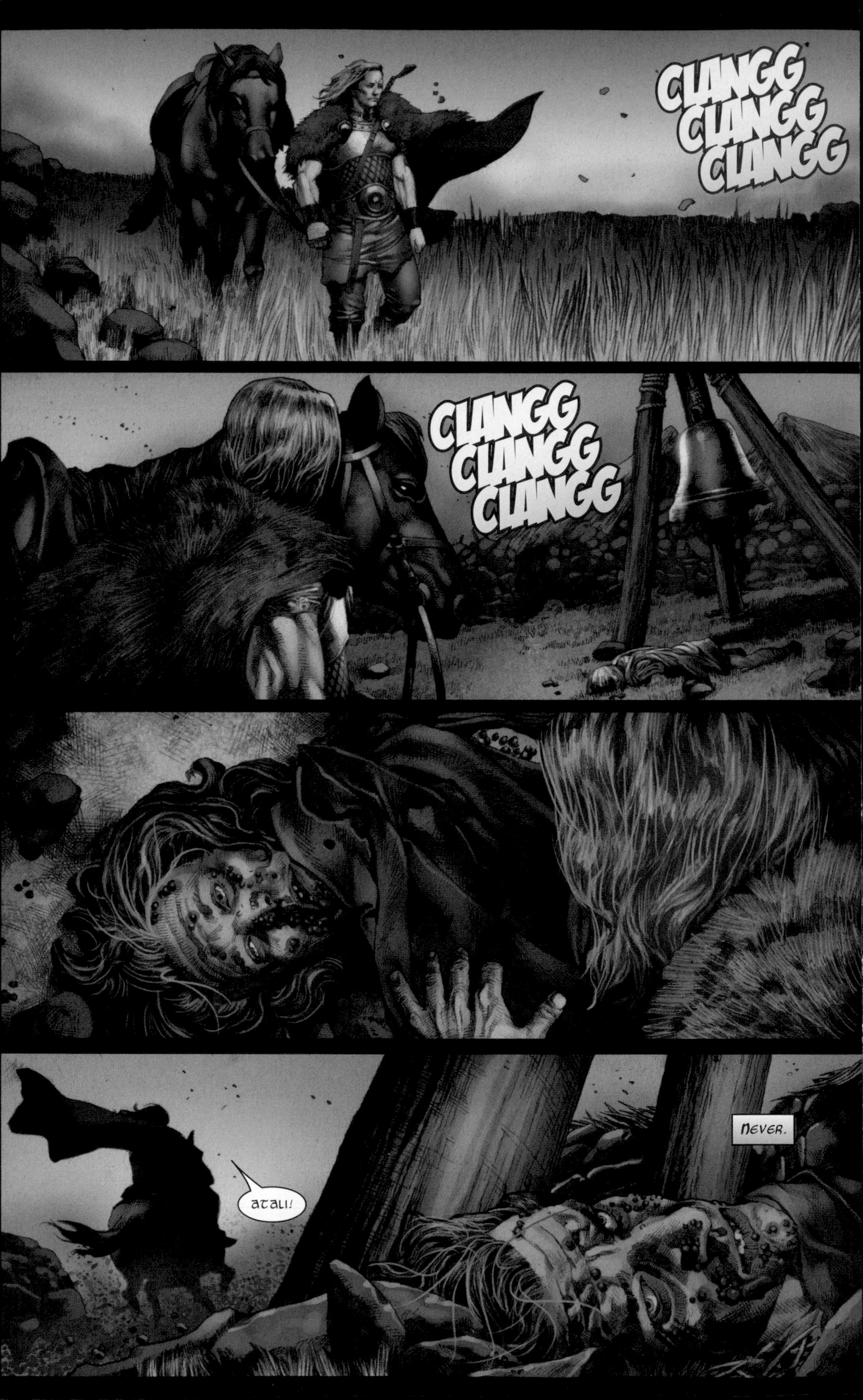
CLANGG
CLANGG
CLANGG
CLANGG
CLANGG
CLANGG
ATALI!
NEVER.

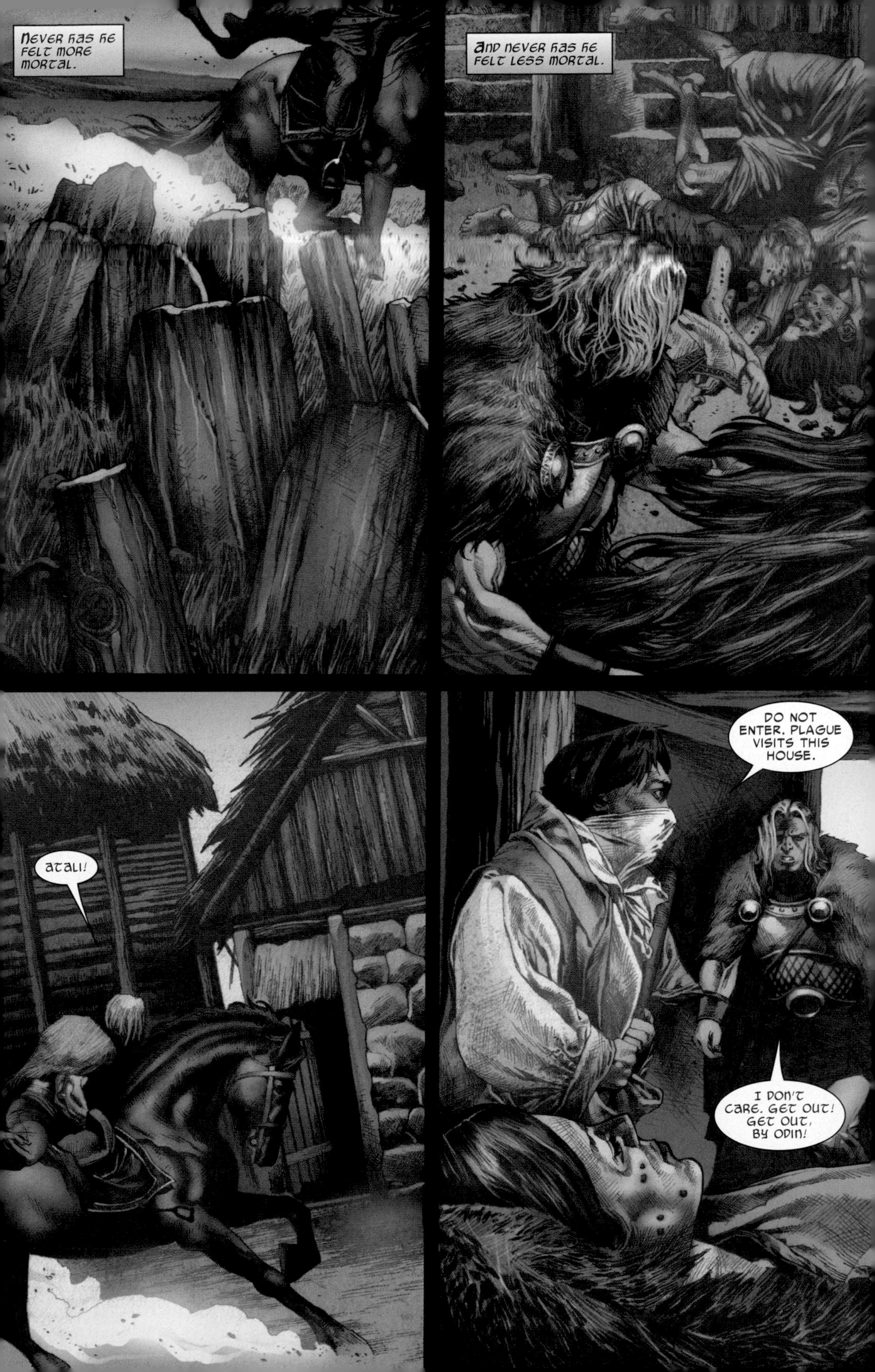

Never has he felt more mortal.
And never has he felt less mortal.
Atali!
Do not enter. Plague visits this house.
I don't care. Get out! Get out, by Odin!

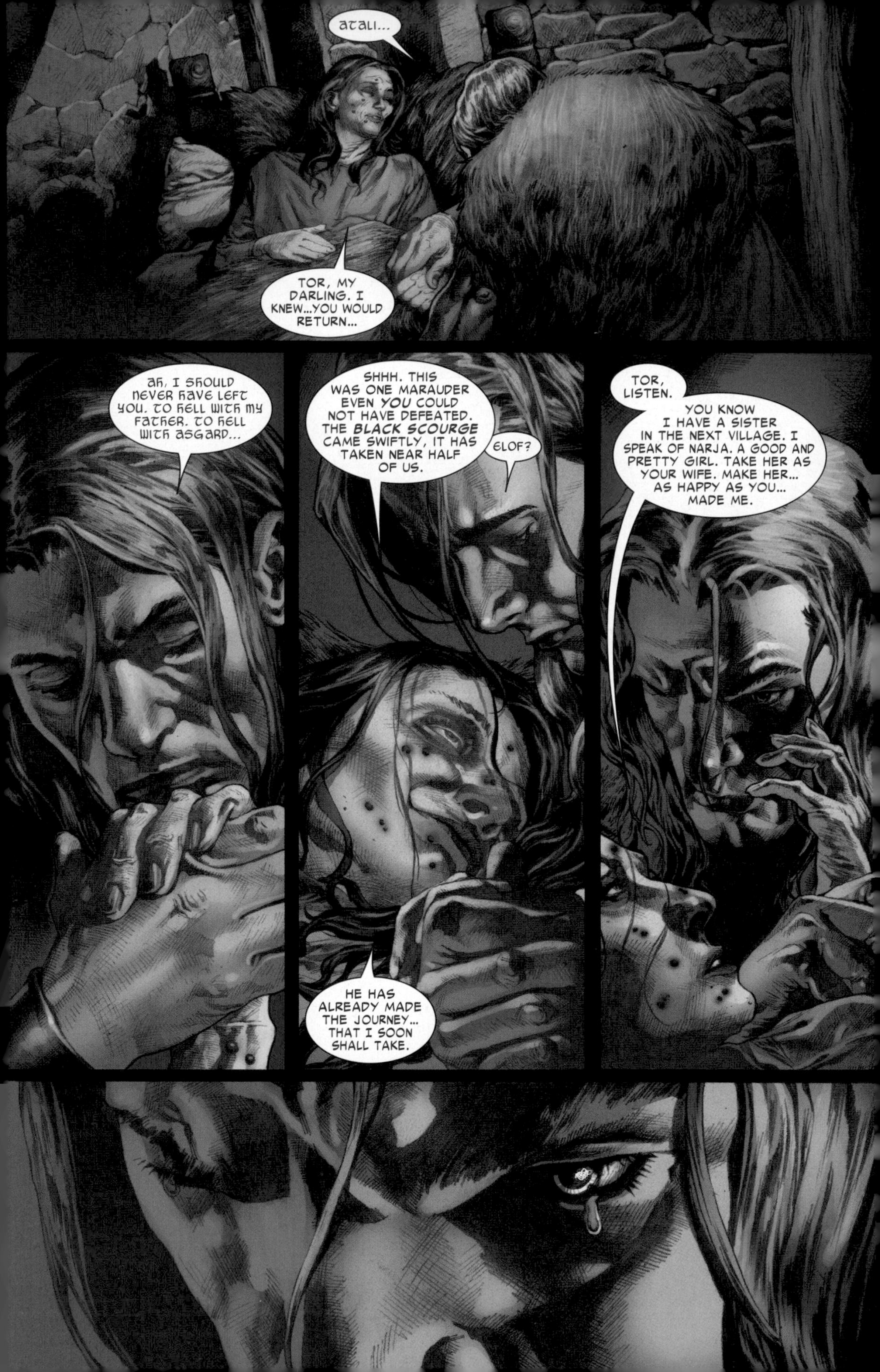
ATALI...
TOR, MY DARLING. I KNEW...YOU WOULD RETURN...
AH, I SHOULD NEVER HAVE LEFT YOU. TO HELL WITH MY FATHER. TO HELL WITH ASGARD...
SHHH. THIS WAS ONE MARAUDER EVEN *YOU* COULD NOT HAVE DEFEATED. THE *BLACK SCOURGE* CAME SWIFTLY, IT HAS TAKEN NEAR HALF OF US.
ELOF?
HE HAS ALREADY MADE THE JOURNEY... THAT I SOON SHALL TAKE.
TOR, LISTEN.
YOU KNOW I HAVE A SISTER IN THE NEXT VILLAGE. I SPEAK OF NARJA. A GOOD AND PRETTY GIRL. TAKE HER AS YOUR WIFE. MAKE HER... AS HAPPY AS YOU... MADE ME.

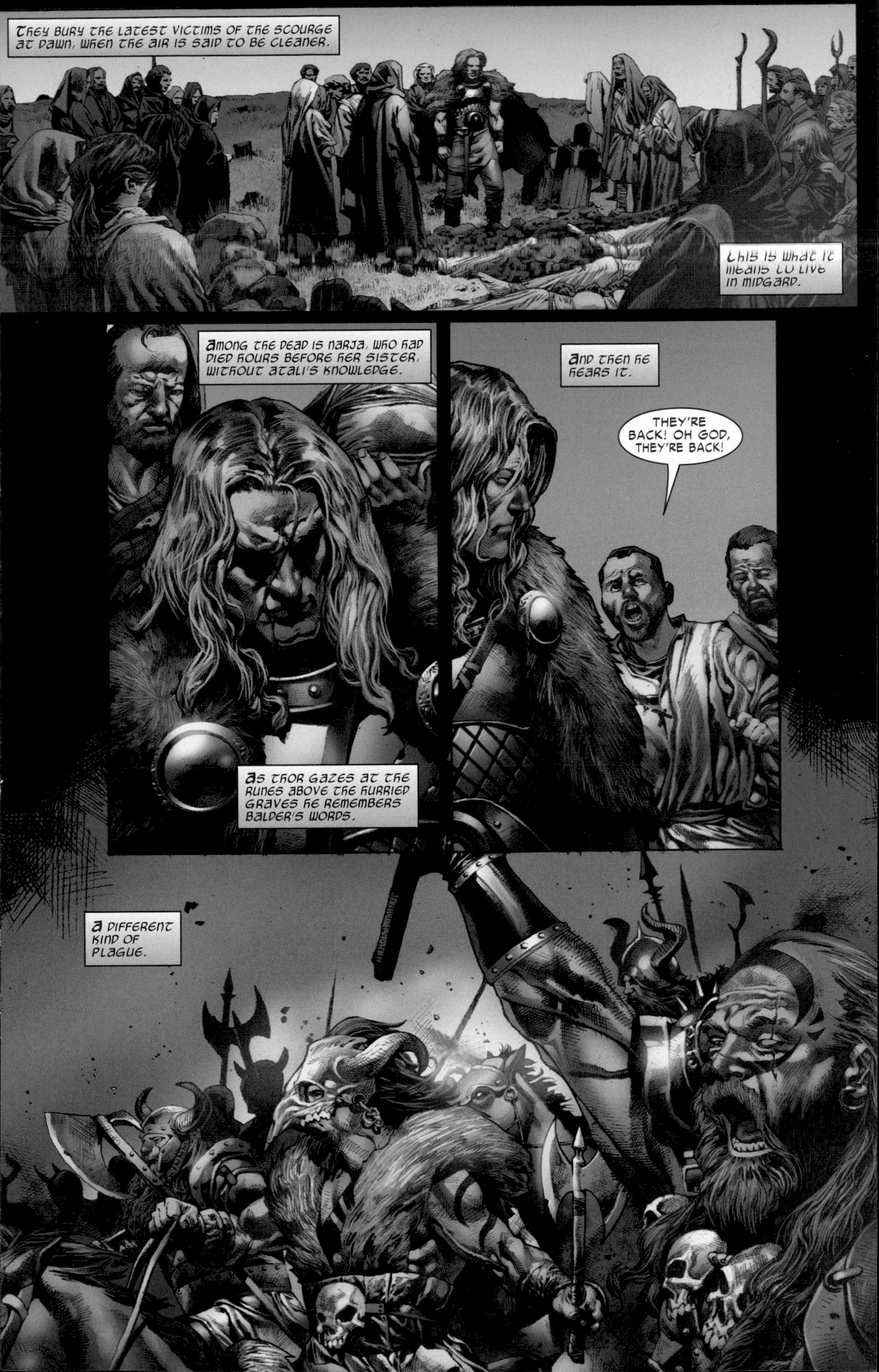
They bury the latest victims of the scourge at dawn, when the air is said to be cleaner.
This is what it means to live in Midgard.
Among the dead is Narja, who had died hours before her sister, without Atali's knowledge.
As Thor gazes at the runes above the hurried graves he remembers Balder's words.
And then he hears it.
THEY'RE BACK! OH GOD, THEY'RE BACK!
A different kind of plague.

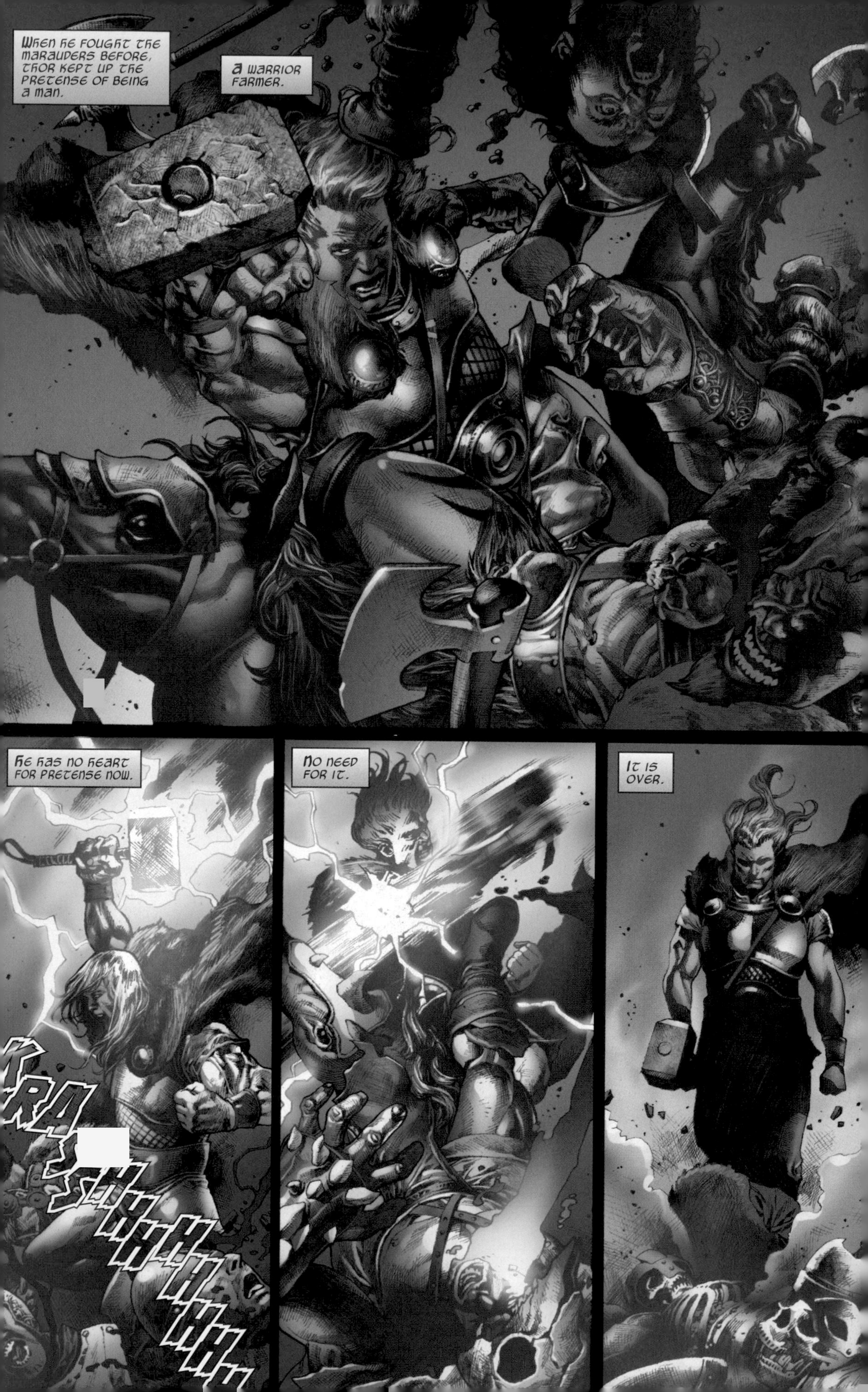
When he fought the marauders before, Thor kept up the pretense of being a man.
A warrior farmer.
He has no heart for pretense now.
No need for it.
It is over.

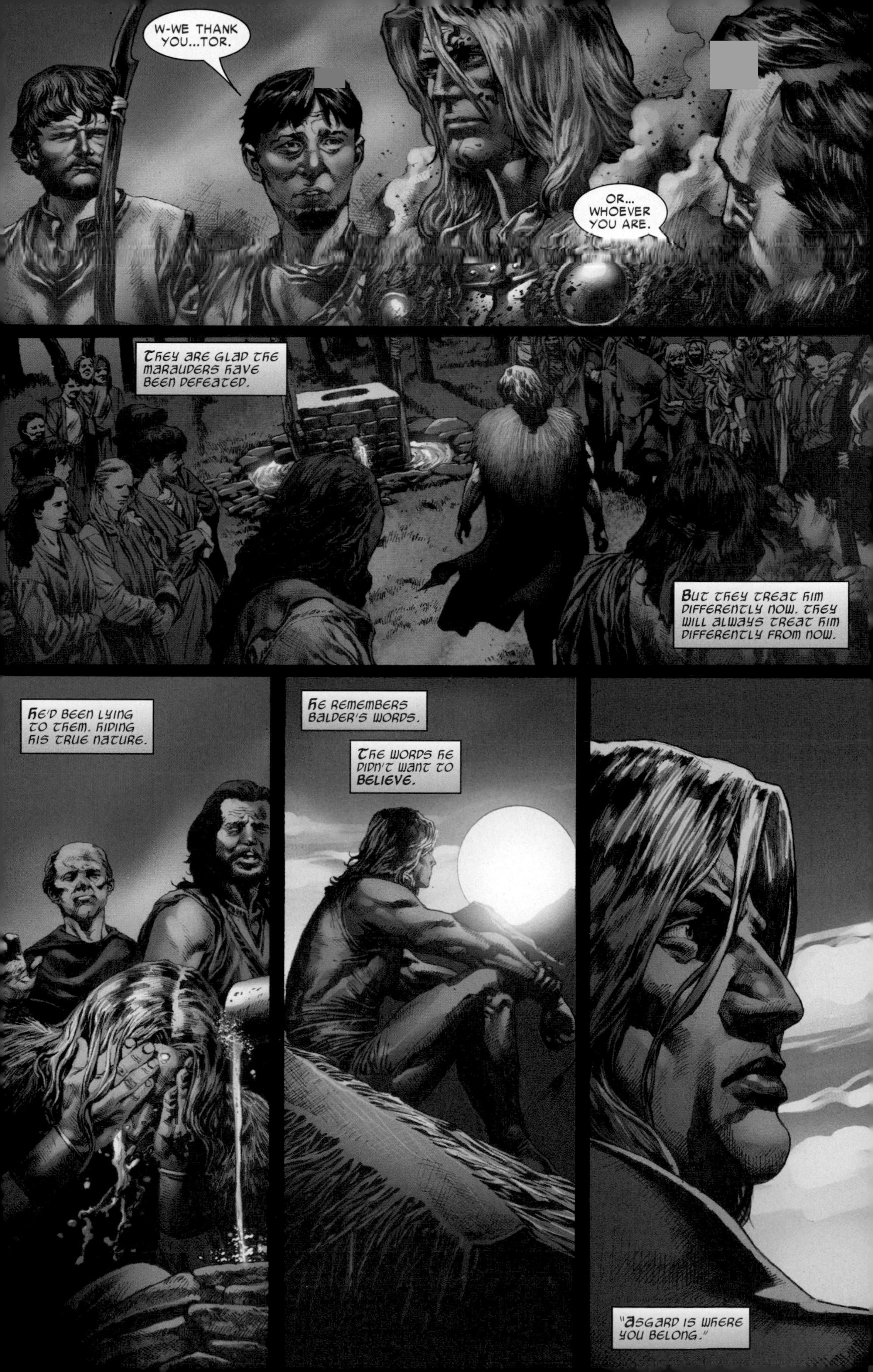
W-WE THANK YOU...TOR.
OR... WHOEVER YOU ARE.
THEY ARE GLAD THE MARAUDERS HAVE BEEN DEFEATED.
BUT THEY TREAT HIM DIFFERENTLY NOW. THEY WILL ALWAYS TREAT HIM DIFFERENTLY FROM NOW.
HE'D BEEN LYING TO THEM. HIDING HIS TRUE NATURE.
HE REMEMBERS BALDER'S WORDS.
THE WORDS HE DIDN'T WANT TO BELIEVE.
"ASGARD IS WHERE YOU BELONG."

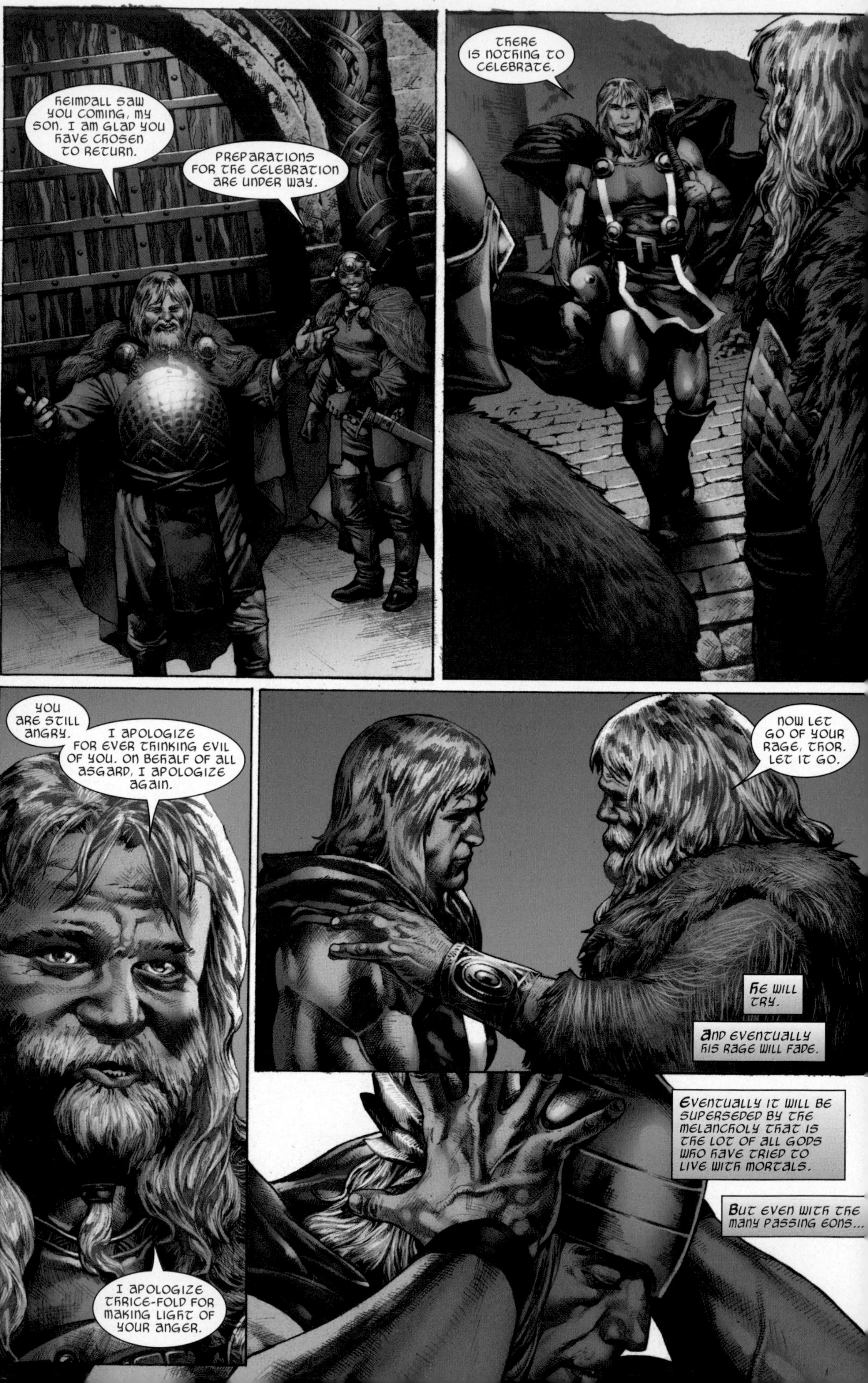
HEIMDALL SAW YOU COMING, MY SON. I AM GLAD YOU HAVE CHOSEN TO RETURN.
PREPARATIONS FOR THE CELEBRATION ARE UNDER WAY.
THERE IS NOTHING TO CELEBRATE.
YOU ARE STILL ANGRY.
I APOLOGIZE FOR EVER THINKING EVIL OF YOU. ON BEHALF OF ALL ASGARD, I APOLOGIZE AGAIN.
I APOLOGIZE THRICE-FOLD FOR MAKING LIGHT OF YOUR ANGER.
NOW LET GO OF YOUR RAGE, THOR. LET IT GO.
HE WILL TRY.
AND EVENTUALLY HIS RAGE WILL FADE.
EVENTUALLY IT WILL BE SUPERSEDED BY THE MELANCHOLY THAT IS THE LOT OF ALL GODS WHO HAVE TRIED TO LIVE WITH MORTALS.
BUT EVEN WITH THE MANY PASSING EONS...

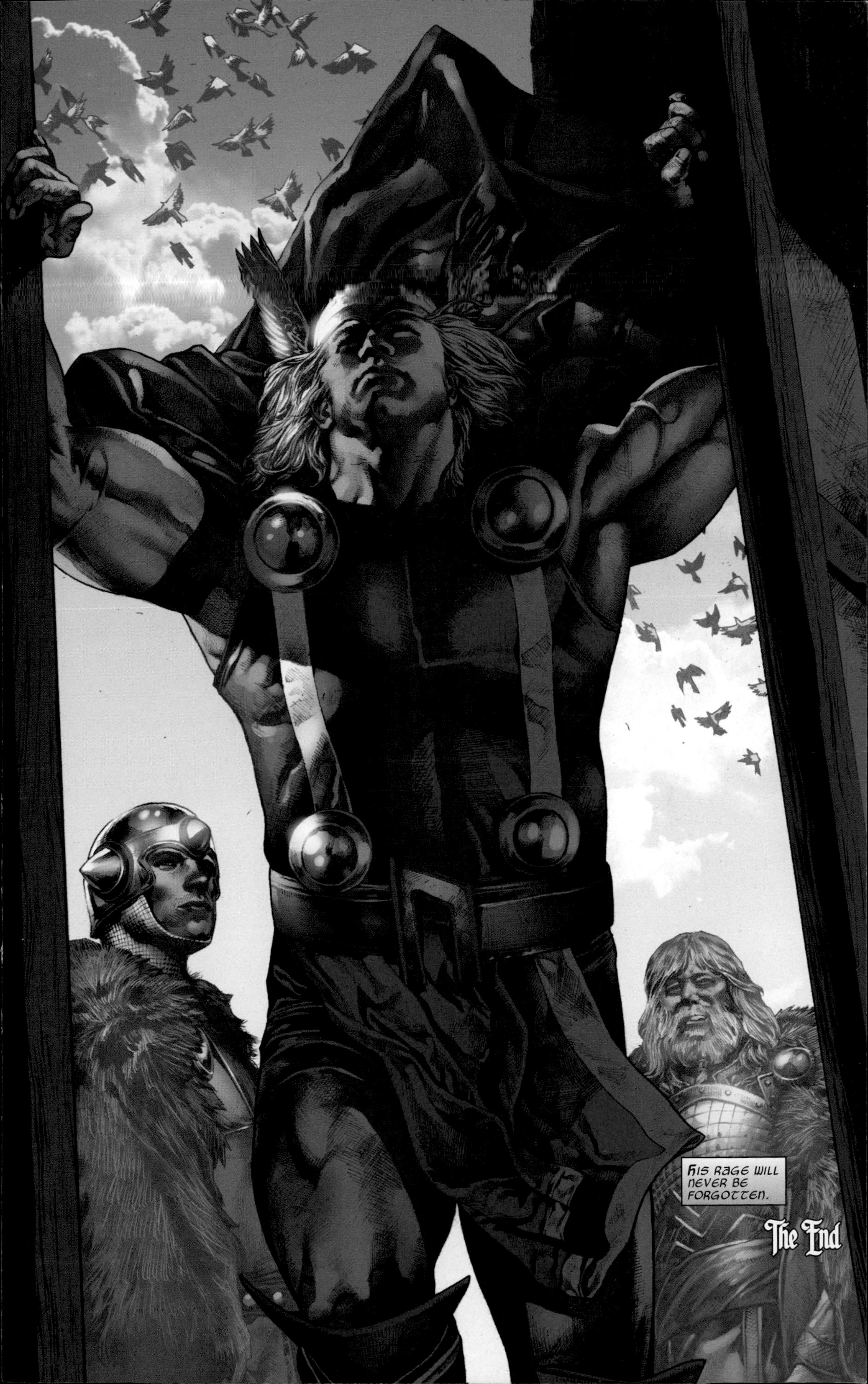
HIS RAGE WILL NEVER BE FORGOTTEN.
The End

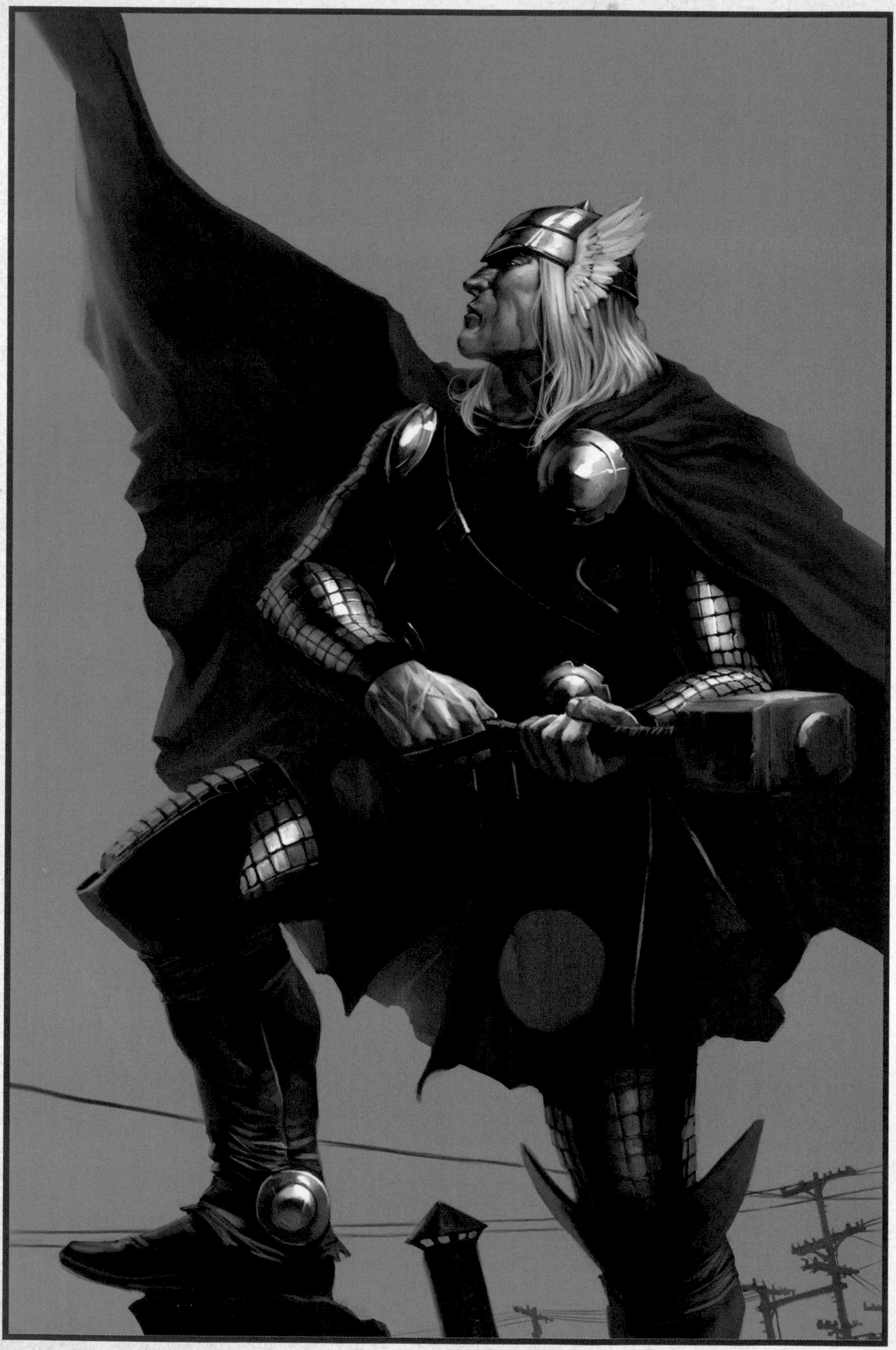

THOR ANNUAL (2009) #1

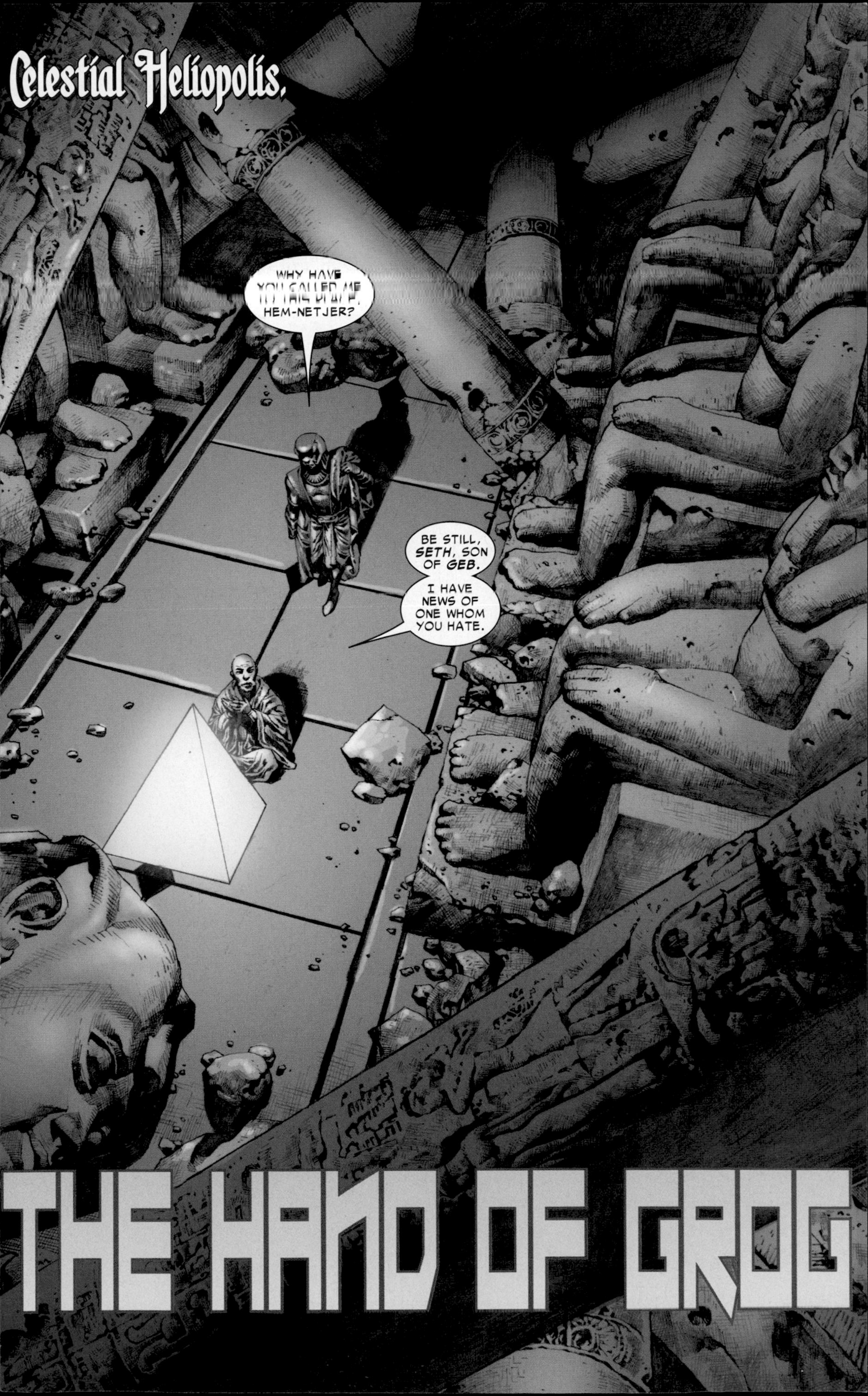
Celestial Heliopolis.
WHY HAVE YOU CALLED ME TO THIS PLACE, HEM-NETJER?
BE STILL, SETH, SON OF GEB.
I HAVE NEWS OF ONE WHOM YOU HATE.
THE HAND OF GROG

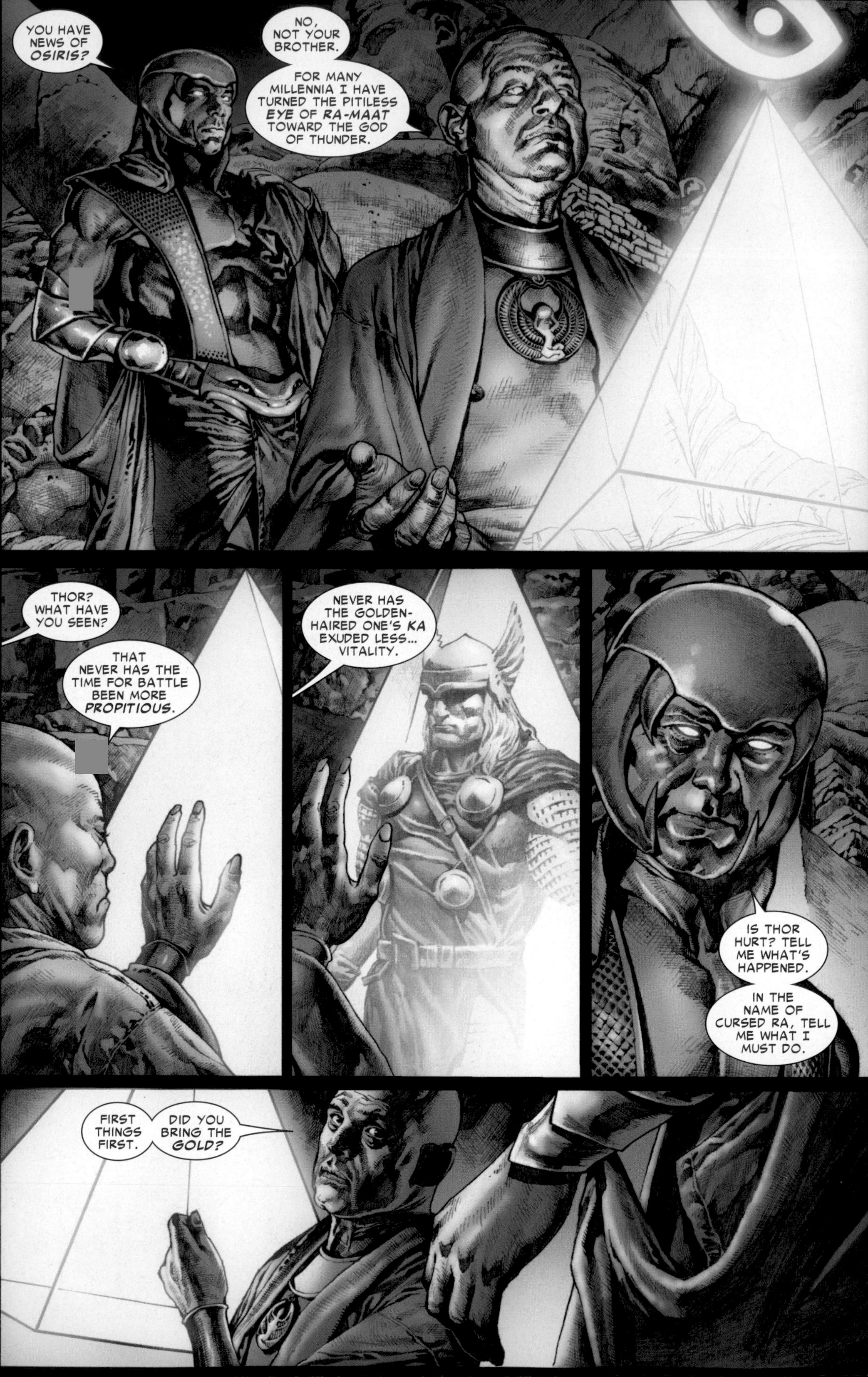
YOU HAVE NEWS OF OSIRIS?
NO, NOT YOUR BROTHER.
FOR MANY MILLENNIA I HAVE TURNED THE PITILESS EYE OF RA-MAAT TOWARD THE GOD OF THUNDER.
THOR? WHAT HAVE YOU SEEN?
THAT NEVER HAS THE TIME FOR BATTLE BEEN MORE PROPITIOUS.
NEVER HAS THE GOLDEN-HAIRED ONE'S KA EXUDED LESS... VITALITY.
IS THOR HURT? TELL ME WHAT'S HAPPENED.
IN THE NAME OF CURSED RA, TELL ME WHAT I MUST DO.
FIRST THINGS FIRST.
DID YOU BRING THE GOLD?

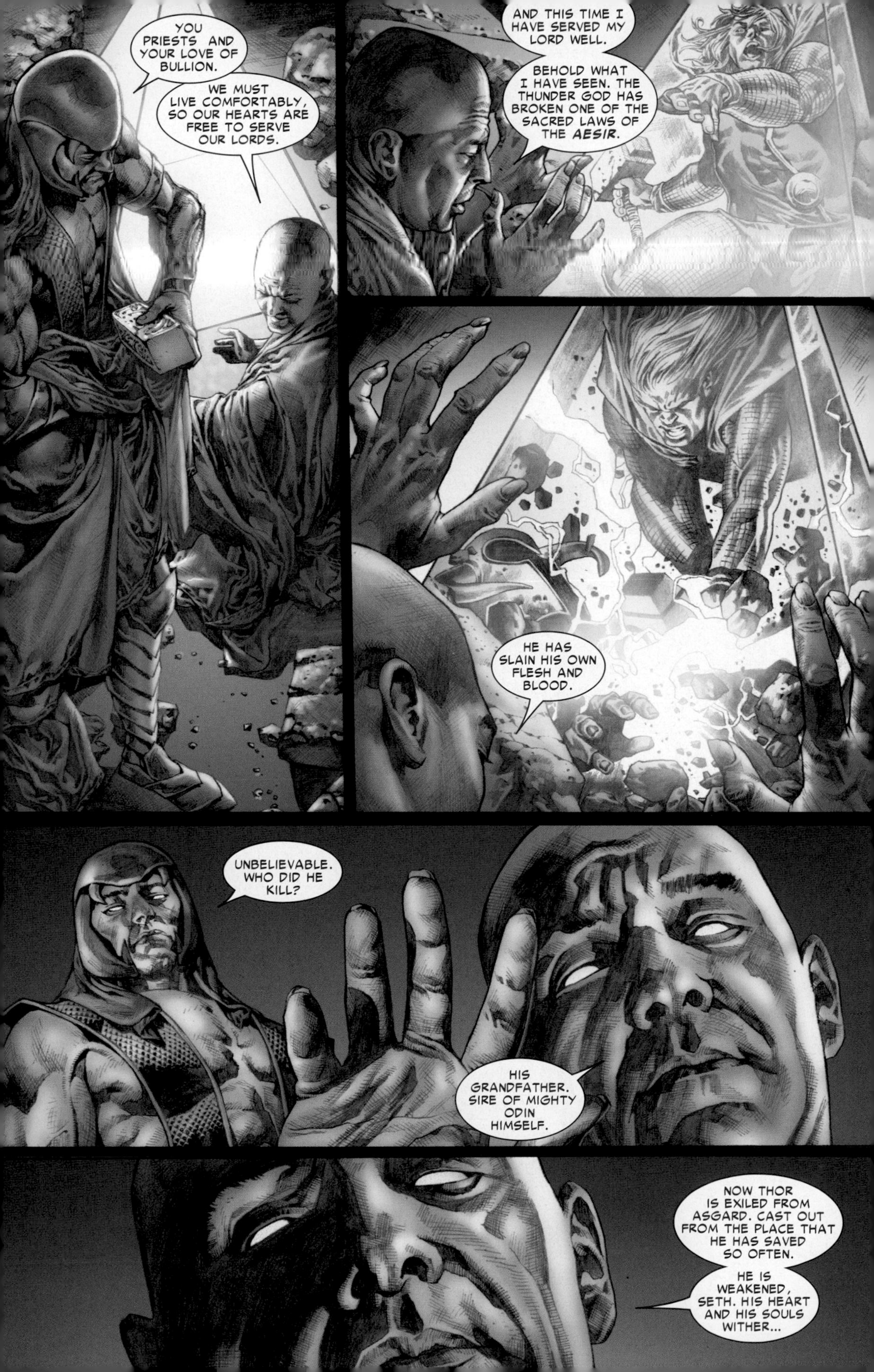
YOU PRIESTS AND YOUR LOVE OF BULLION.
WE MUST LIVE COMFORTABLY, SO OUR HEARTS ARE FREE TO SERVE OUR LORDS.
AND THIS TIME I HAVE SERVED MY LORD WELL.
BEHOLD WHAT I HAVE SEEN. THE THUNDER GOD HAS BROKEN ONE OF THE SACRED LAWS OF THE *AESIR*.
HE HAS SLAIN HIS OWN FLESH AND BLOOD.
UNBELIEVABLE. WHO DID HE KILL?
HIS GRANDFATHER. SIRE OF MIGHTY ODIN HIMSELF.
NOW THOR IS EXILED FROM ASGARD. CAST OUT FROM THE PLACE THAT HE HAS SAVED SO OFTEN.
HE IS WEAKENED, SETH. HIS HEART AND HIS SOULS WITHER...

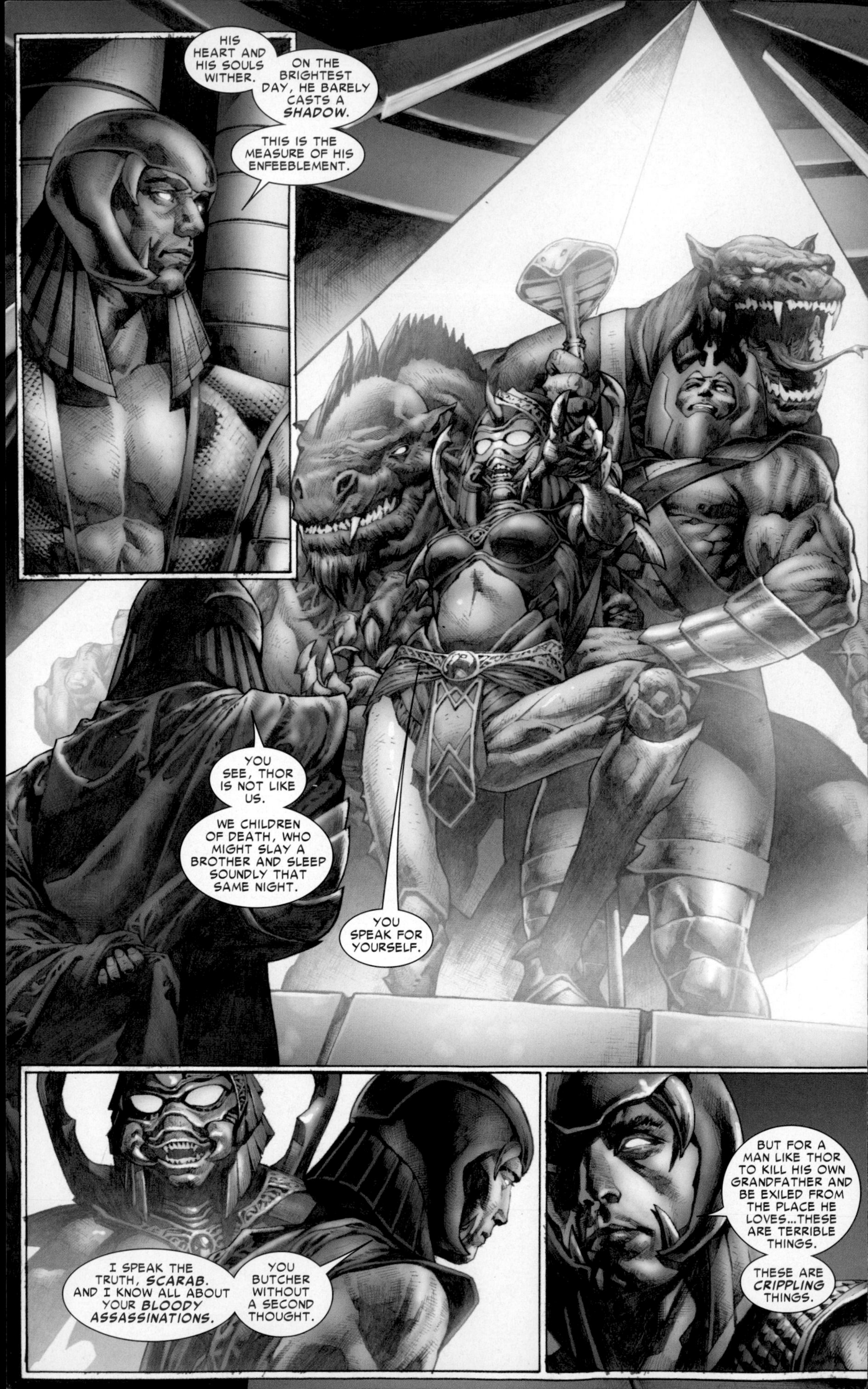

HIS HEART AND HIS SOULS WITHER.
ON THE BRIGHTEST DAY, HE BARELY CASTS A *SHADOW*.
THIS IS THE MEASURE OF HIS ENFEEBLEMENT.
YOU SEE, THOR IS NOT LIKE US.
WE CHILDREN OF DEATH, WHO MIGHT SLAY A BROTHER AND SLEEP SOUNDLY THAT SAME NIGHT.
YOU SPEAK FOR YOURSELF.
YOU BUTCHER WITHOUT A SECOND THOUGHT.
I SPEAK THE TRUTH, *SCARAB*. AND I KNOW ALL ABOUT YOUR *BLOODY ASSASSINATIONS*.
BUT FOR A MAN LIKE THOR TO KILL HIS OWN GRANDFATHER AND BE EXILED FROM THE PLACE HE LOVES...THESE ARE TERRIBLE THINGS.
THESE ARE *CRIPPLING* THINGS.

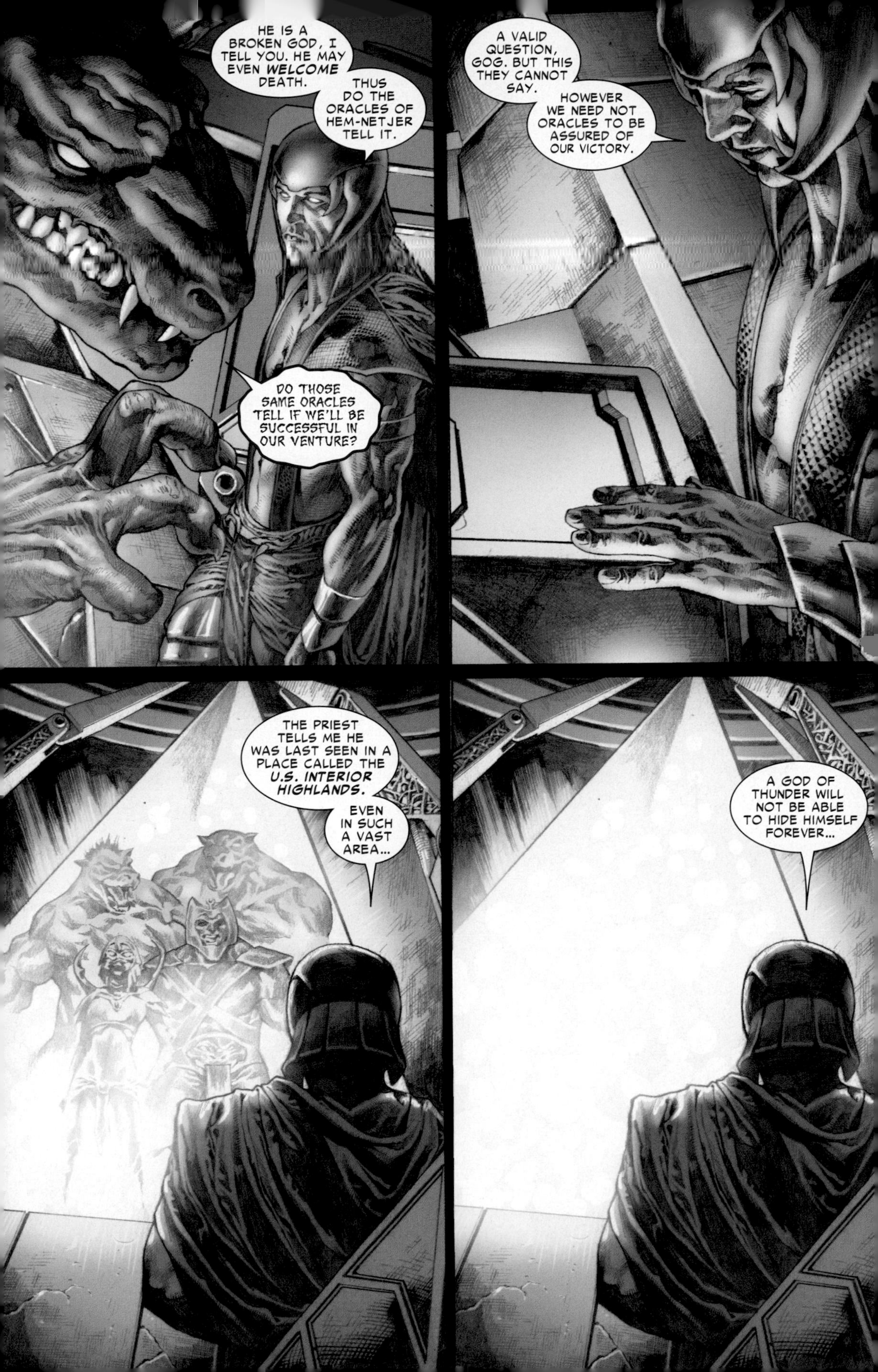
HE IS A BROKEN GOD, I TELL YOU. HE MAY EVEN WELCOME DEATH.
THUS DO THE ORACLES OF HEM-NETJER TELL IT.
DO THOSE SAME ORACLES TELL IF WE'LL BE SUCCESSFUL IN OUR VENTURE?
A VALID QUESTION, GOG. BUT THIS THEY CANNOT SAY.
HOWEVER WE NEED NOT ORACLES TO BE ASSURED OF OUR VICTORY.
THE PRIEST TELLS ME HE WAS LAST SEEN IN A PLACE CALLED THE U.S. INTERIOR HIGHLANDS.
EVEN IN SUCH A VAST AREA...
A GOD OF THUNDER WILL NOT BE ABLE TO HIDE HIMSELF FOREVER...

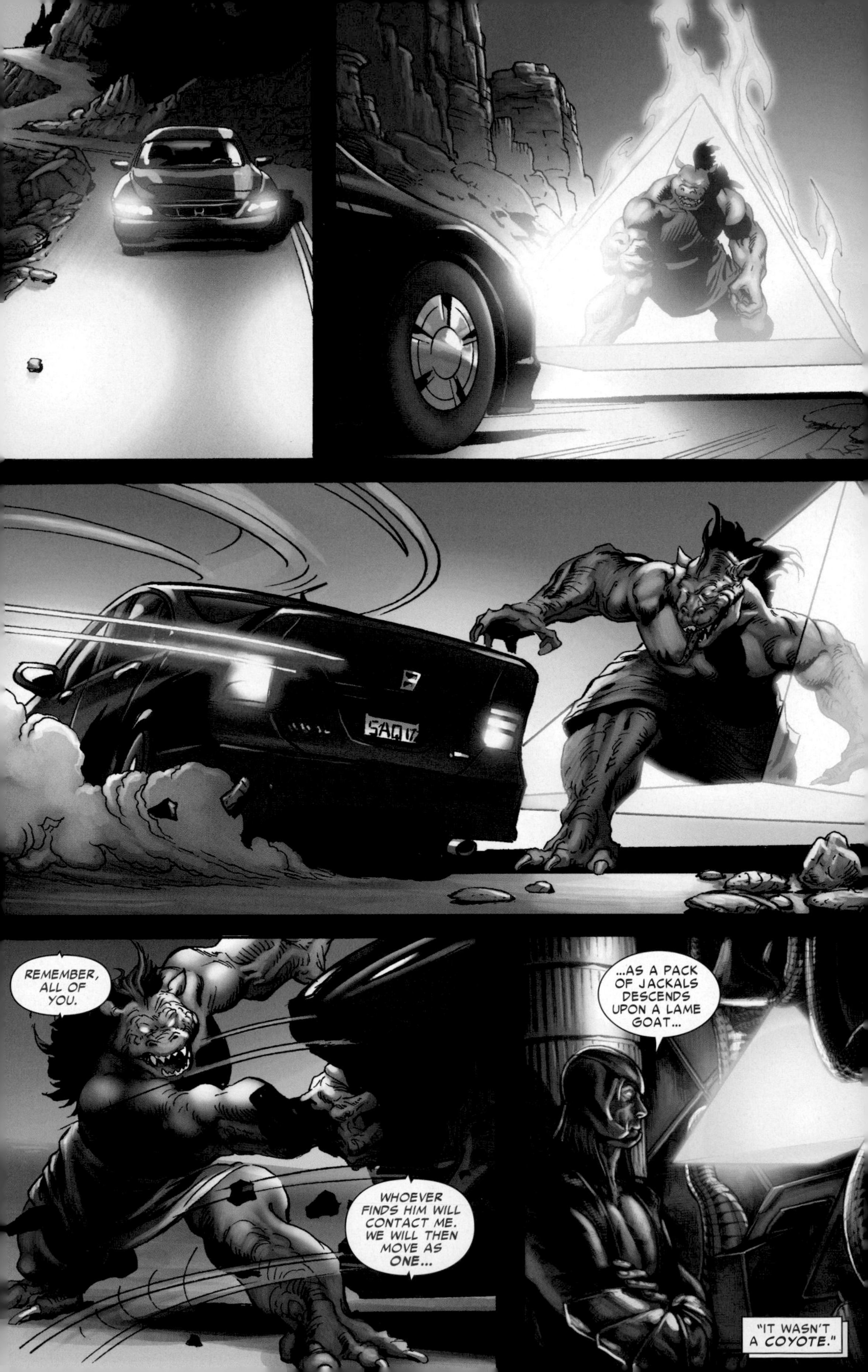

REMEMBER, ALL OF YOU.
WHOEVER FINDS HIM WILL CONTACT ME. WE WILL THEN MOVE AS ONE...
...AS A PACK OF JACKALS DESCENDS UPON A LAME GOAT...
"IT WASN'T A COYOTE."

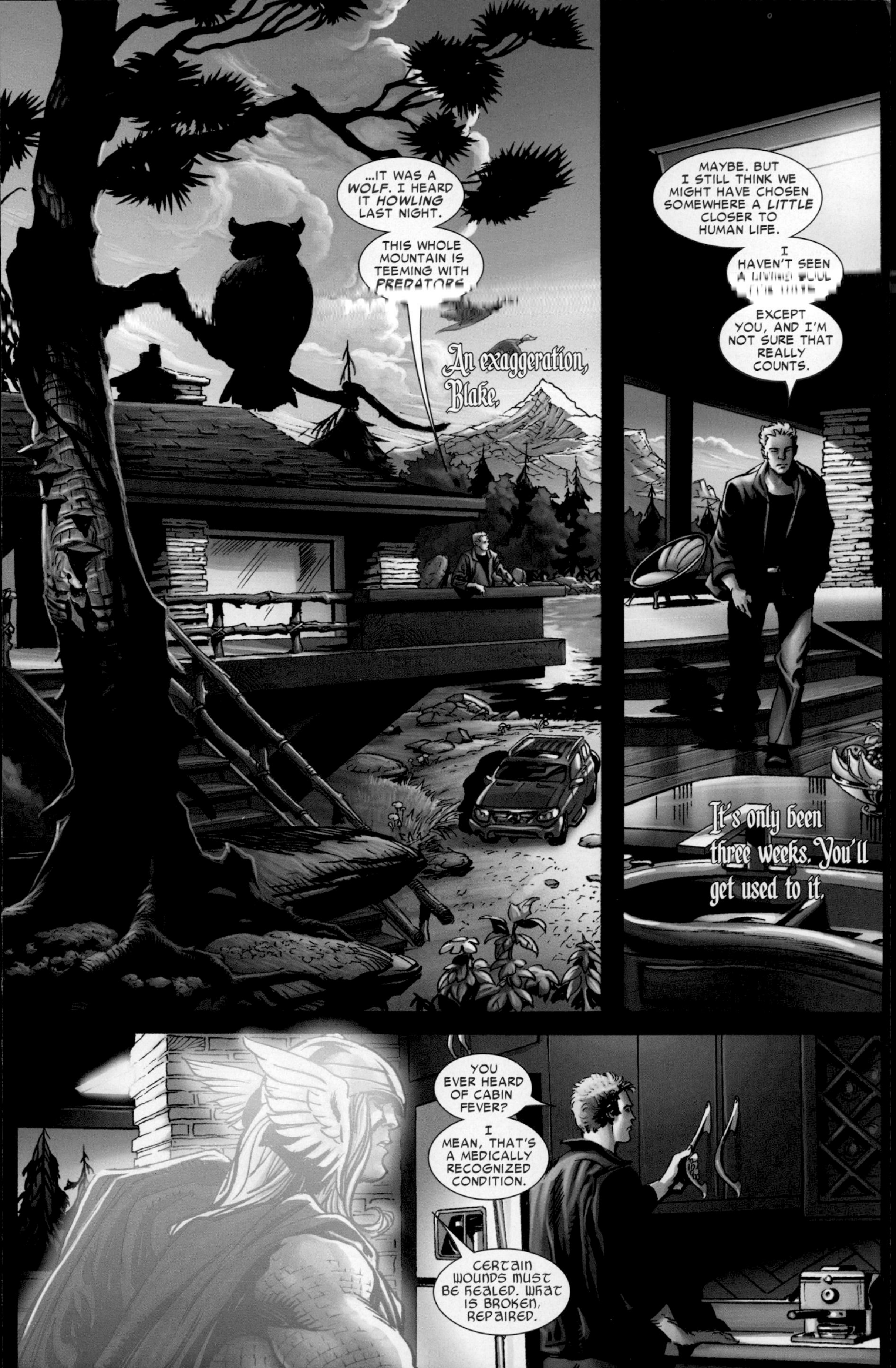
...IT WAS A WOLF. I HEARD IT HOWLING LAST NIGHT.
THIS WHOLE MOUNTAIN IS TEEMING WITH
An exaggeration, Blake.
MAYBE. BUT I STILL THINK WE MIGHT HAVE CHOSEN SOMEWHERE A LITTLE CLOSER TO HUMAN LIFE.
I HAVEN'T SEEN
EXCEPT YOU, AND I'M NOT SURE THAT REALLY COUNTS.
It's only been three weeks. You'll get used to it.
YOU EVER HEARD OF CABIN FEVER?
I MEAN, THAT'S A MEDICALLY RECOGNIZED CONDITION.
CERTAIN WOUNDS MUST BE HEALED. WHAT IS BROKEN, REPAIRED.

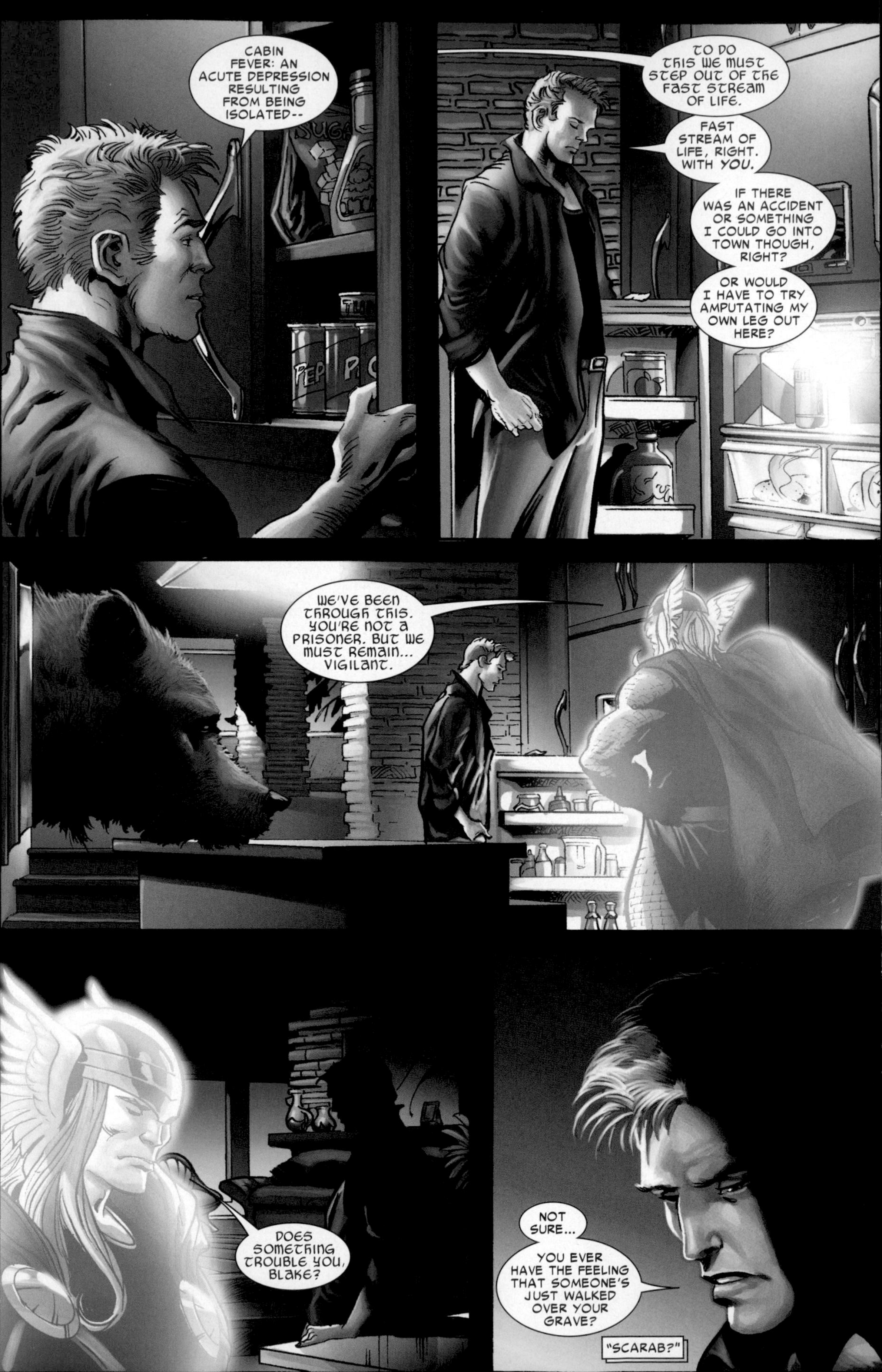
CABIN FEVER: AN ACUTE DEPRESSION RESULTING FROM BEING ISOLATED--
TO DO THIS WE MUST STEP OUT OF THE FAST STREAM OF LIFE.
FAST STREAM OF LIFE, RIGHT. WITH YOU.
IF THERE WAS AN ACCIDENT OR SOMETHING I COULD GO INTO TOWN THOUGH, RIGHT?
OR WOULD I HAVE TO TRY AMPUTATING MY OWN LEG OUT HERE?
WE'VE BEEN THROUGH THIS. YOU'RE NOT A PRISONER. BUT WE MUST REMAIN... VIGILANT.
DOES SOMETHING TROUBLE YOU, BLAKE?
NOT SURE...
YOU EVER HAVE THE FEELING THAT SOMEONE'S JUST WALKED OVER YOUR GRAVE?
"SCARAB?"

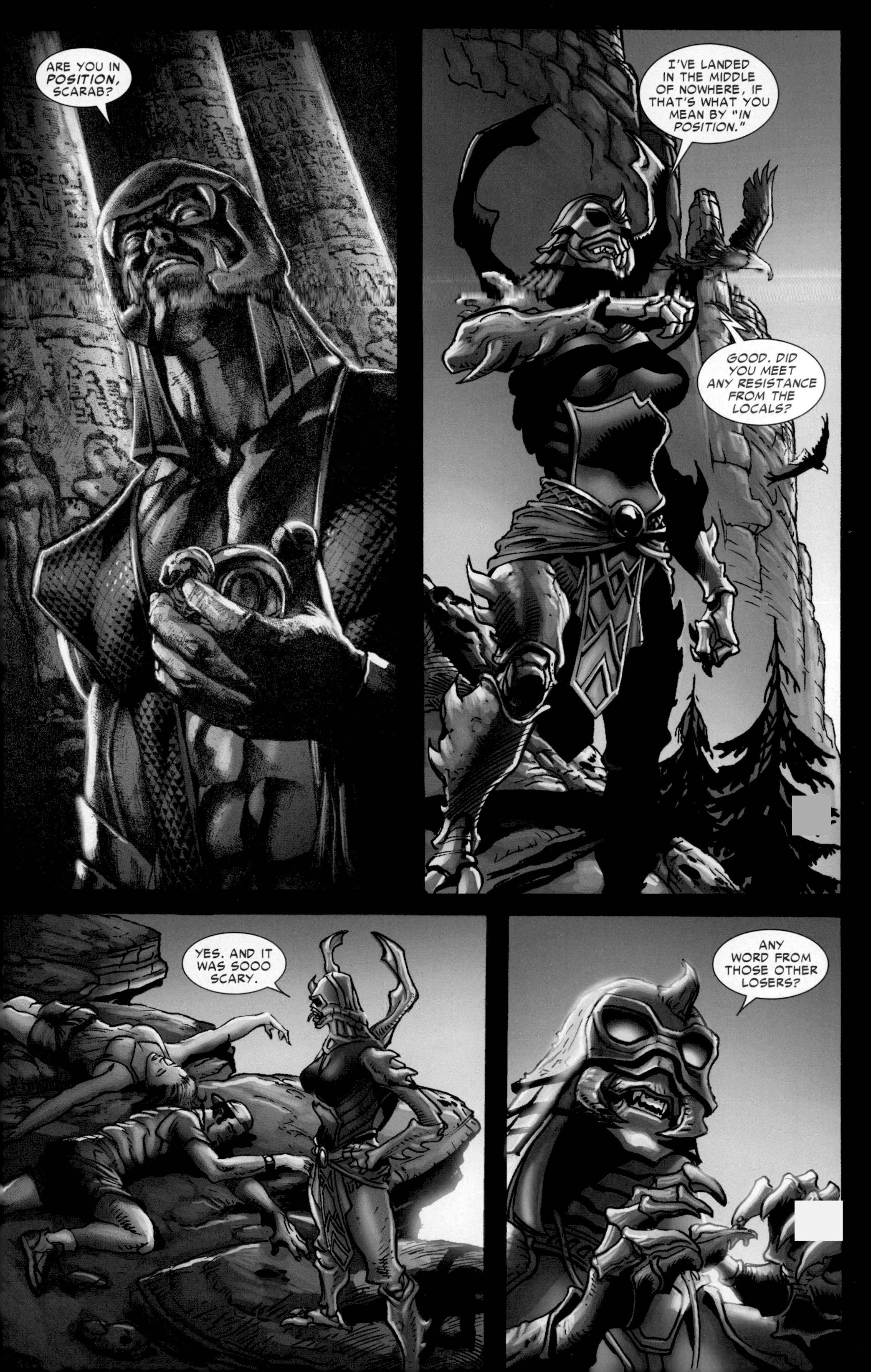
ARE YOU IN POSITION, SCARAB?
I'VE LANDED IN THE MIDDLE OF NOWHERE, IF THAT'S WHAT YOU MEAN BY "IN POSITION."
GOOD. DID YOU MEET ANY RESISTANCE FROM THE LOCALS?
YES. AND IT WAS SOOO SCARY.
ANY WORD FROM THOSE OTHER LOSERS?

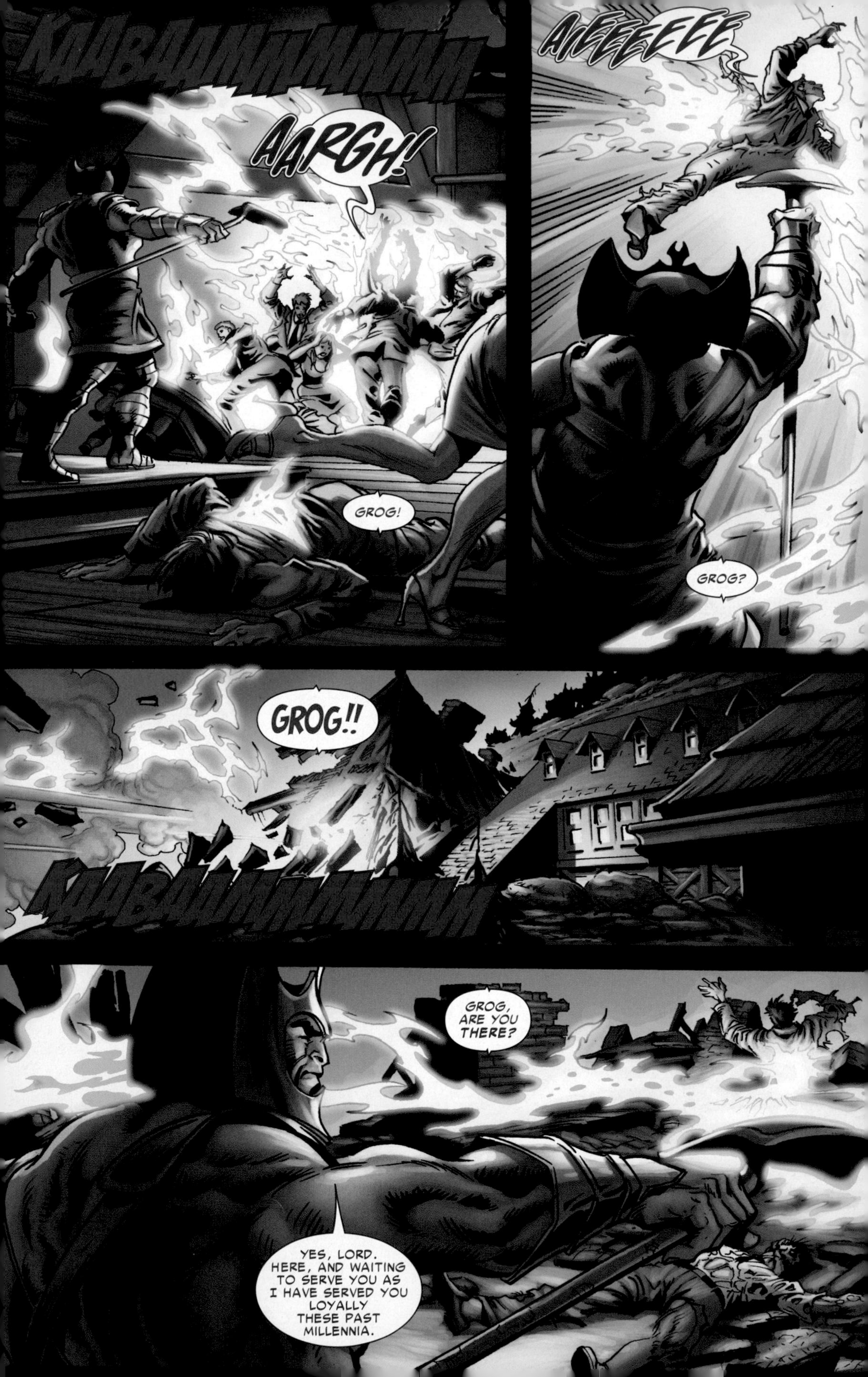
KAABAAMMMMMMM
AARGH!
GROG!
AIEEEEEEE
GROG?
GROG!!
KAABAAMMMMMMM
GROG, ARE YOU THERE?
YES, LORD. HERE, AND WAITING TO SERVE YOU AS I HAVE SERVED YOU LOYALLY THESE PAST MILLENNIA.

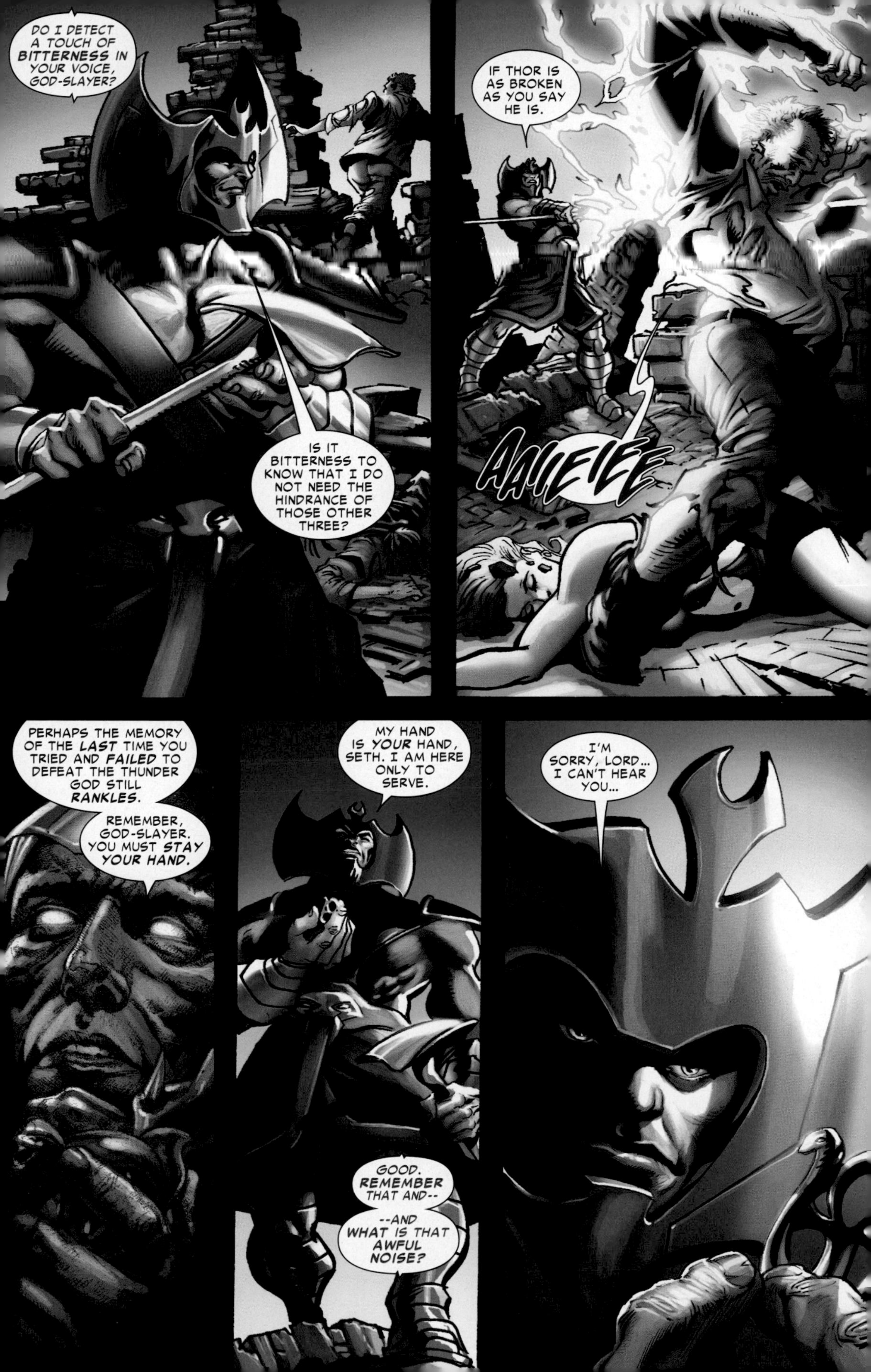
DO I DETECT A TOUCH OF BITTERNESS IN YOUR VOICE, GOD-SLAYER?
IS IT BITTERNESS TO KNOW THAT I DO NOT NEED THE HINDRANCE OF THOSE OTHER THREE?
IF THOR IS AS BROKEN AS YOU SAY HE IS.
AAIIEICE
PERHAPS THE MEMORY OF THE LAST TIME YOU TRIED AND FAILED TO DEFEAT THE THUNDER GOD STILL RANKLES.
REMEMBER, GOD-SLAYER. YOU MUST STAY YOUR HAND.
MY HAND IS YOUR HAND, SETH. I AM HERE ONLY TO SERVE.
GOOD. REMEMBER THAT AND--
--AND WHAT IS THAT AWFUL NOISE?
I'M SORRY, LORD... I CAN'T HEAR YOU...

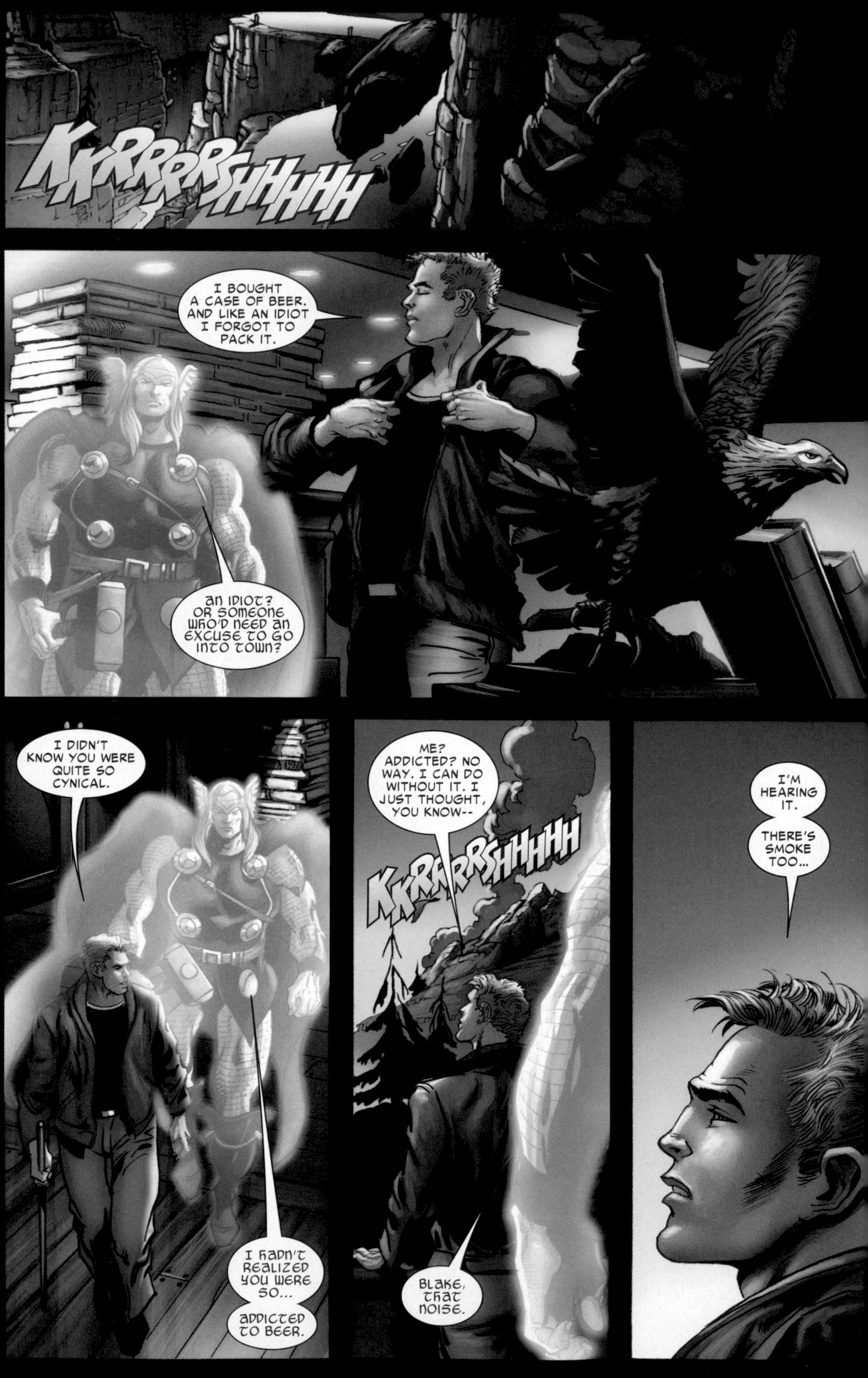
KKRRRRSHHHHH
I BOUGHT A CASE OF BEER. AND LIKE AN IDIOT I FORGOT TO PACK IT.
AN IDIOT? OR SOMEONE WHO'D NEED AN EXCUSE TO GO INTO TOWN?
I DIDN'T KNOW YOU WERE QUITE SO CYNICAL.
I HADN'T REALIZED YOU WERE SO...
ADDICTED TO BEER.
ME? ADDICTED? NO WAY. I CAN DO WITHOUT IT. I JUST THOUGHT, YOU KNOW--
KKRRRRSHHHHH
BLAKE, THAT NOISE.
I'M HEARING IT.
THERE'S SMOKE TOO...

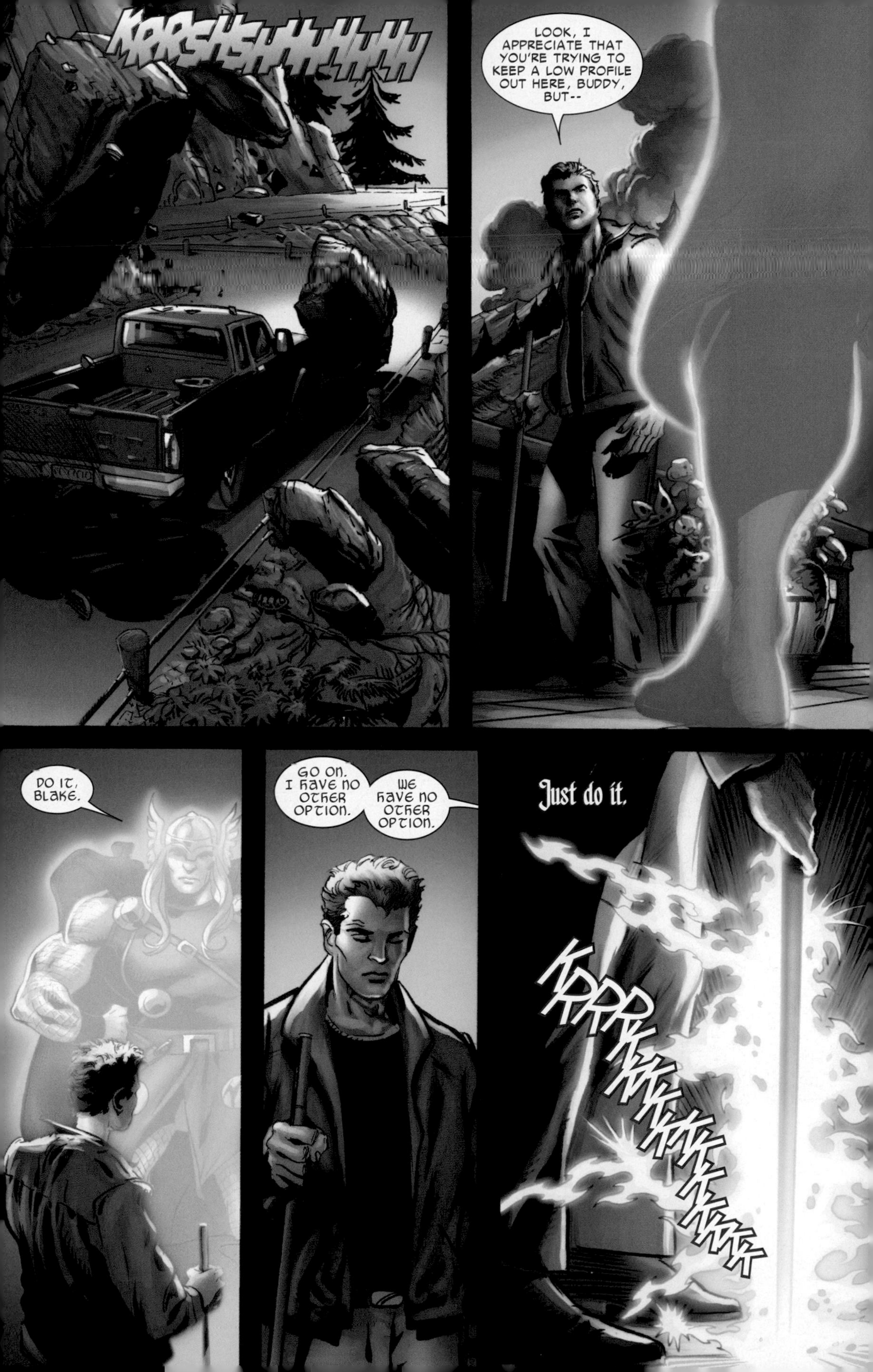
KRRSHSHHHHHH
LOOK, I APPRECIATE THAT YOU'RE TRYING TO KEEP A LOW PROFILE OUT HERE, BUDDY, BUT--
DO IT, BLAKE.
GO ON. I HAVE NO OTHER OPTION.
WE HAVE NO OTHER OPTION.
Just do it.
KRRRKKKKKKKKKKK

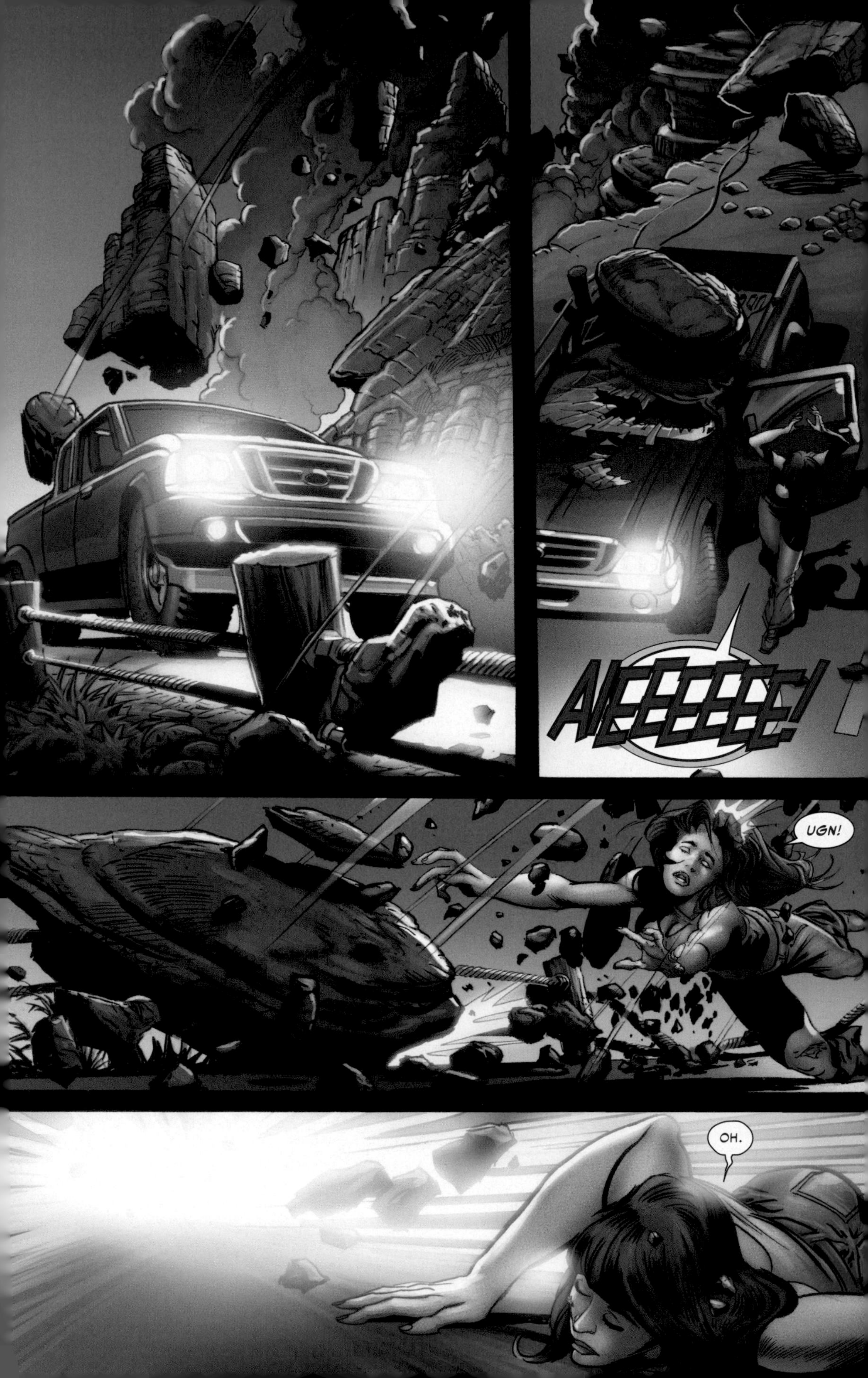
AIEEEEEEE!
UGN!
OH.

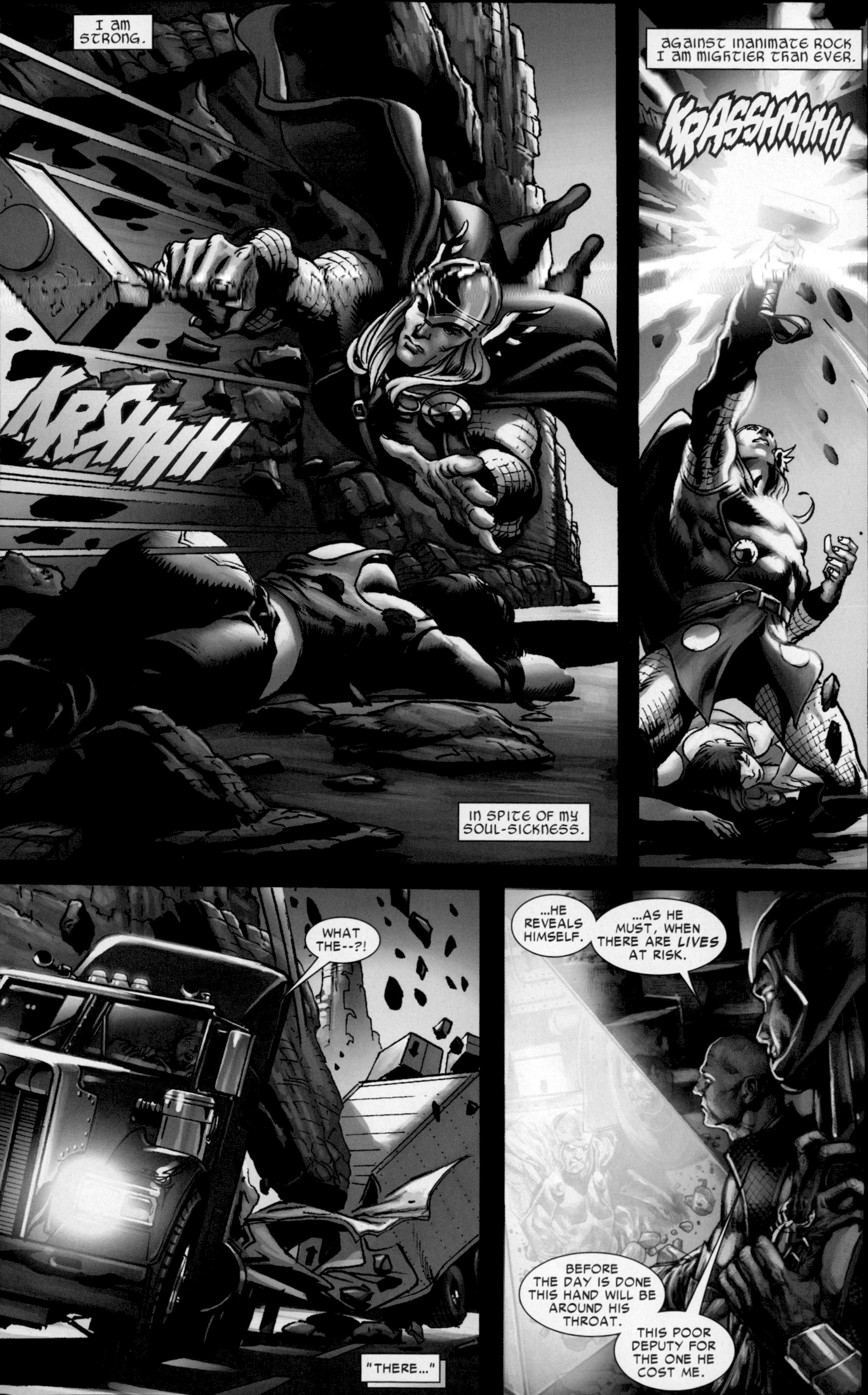
I AM STRONG.
KRSHHH
IN SPITE OF MY SOUL-SICKNESS.
AGAINST INANIMATE ROCK I AM MIGHTIER THAN EVER.
KRASHHHHH
WHAT THE--?!
"THERE..."
...HE REVEALS HIMSELF.
...AS HE MUST, WHEN THERE ARE LIVES AT RISK.
BEFORE THE DAY IS DONE THIS HAND WILL BE AROUND HIS THROAT.
THIS POOR DEPUTY FOR THE ONE HE COST ME.

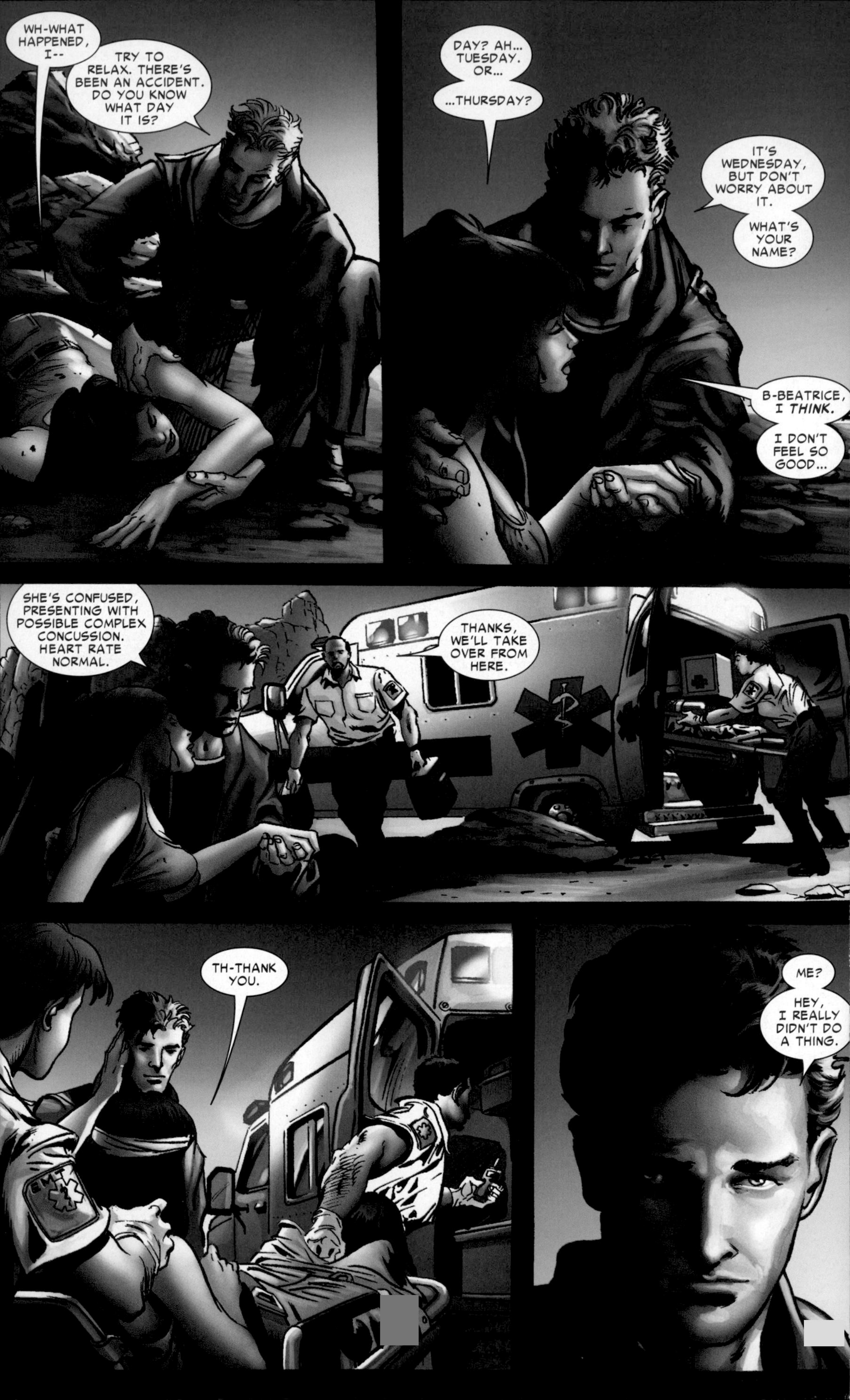
WH-WHAT HAPPENED, I--
TRY TO RELAX. THERE'S BEEN AN ACCIDENT. DO YOU KNOW WHAT DAY IT IS?
DAY? AH... TUESDAY. OR...
...THURSDAY?
IT'S WEDNESDAY, BUT DON'T WORRY ABOUT IT.
WHAT'S YOUR NAME?
B-BEATRICE, I *THINK.*
I DON'T FEEL SO GOOD...
SHE'S CONFUSED, PRESENTING WITH POSSIBLE COMPLEX CONCUSSION. HEART RATE NORMAL.
THANKS, WE'LL TAKE OVER FROM HERE.
TH-THANK YOU.
ME?
HEY, I REALLY DIDN'T DO A THING.

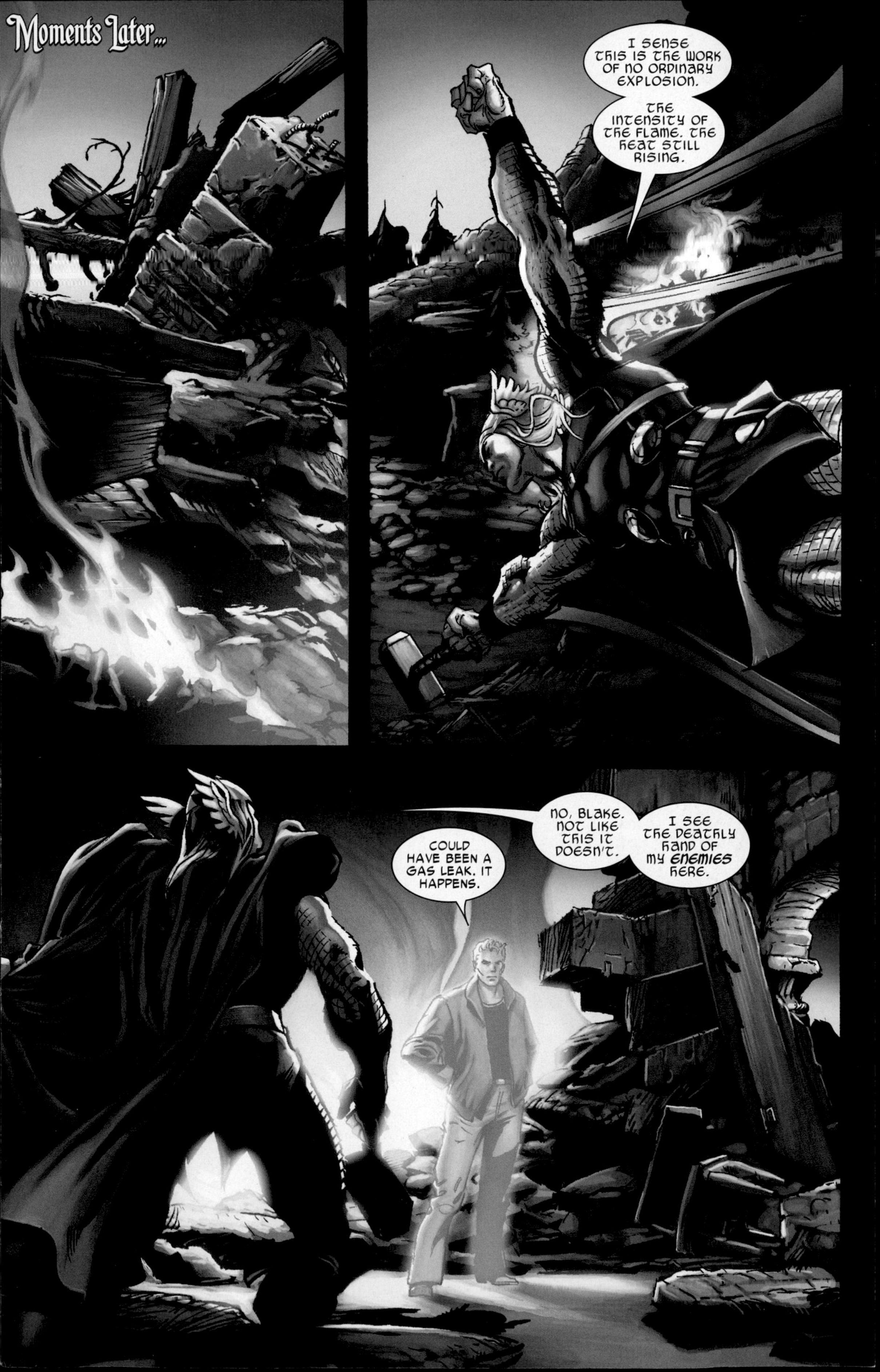
Moments Later...
I SENSE THIS IS THE WORK OF NO ORDINARY EXPLOSION.
THE INTENSITY OF THE FLAME. THE HEAT STILL RISING.
COULD HAVE BEEN A GAS LEAK. IT HAPPENS.
NO, BLAKE. NOT LIKE THIS IT DOESN'T.
I SEE THE DEATHLY HAND OF MY ENEMIES HERE.

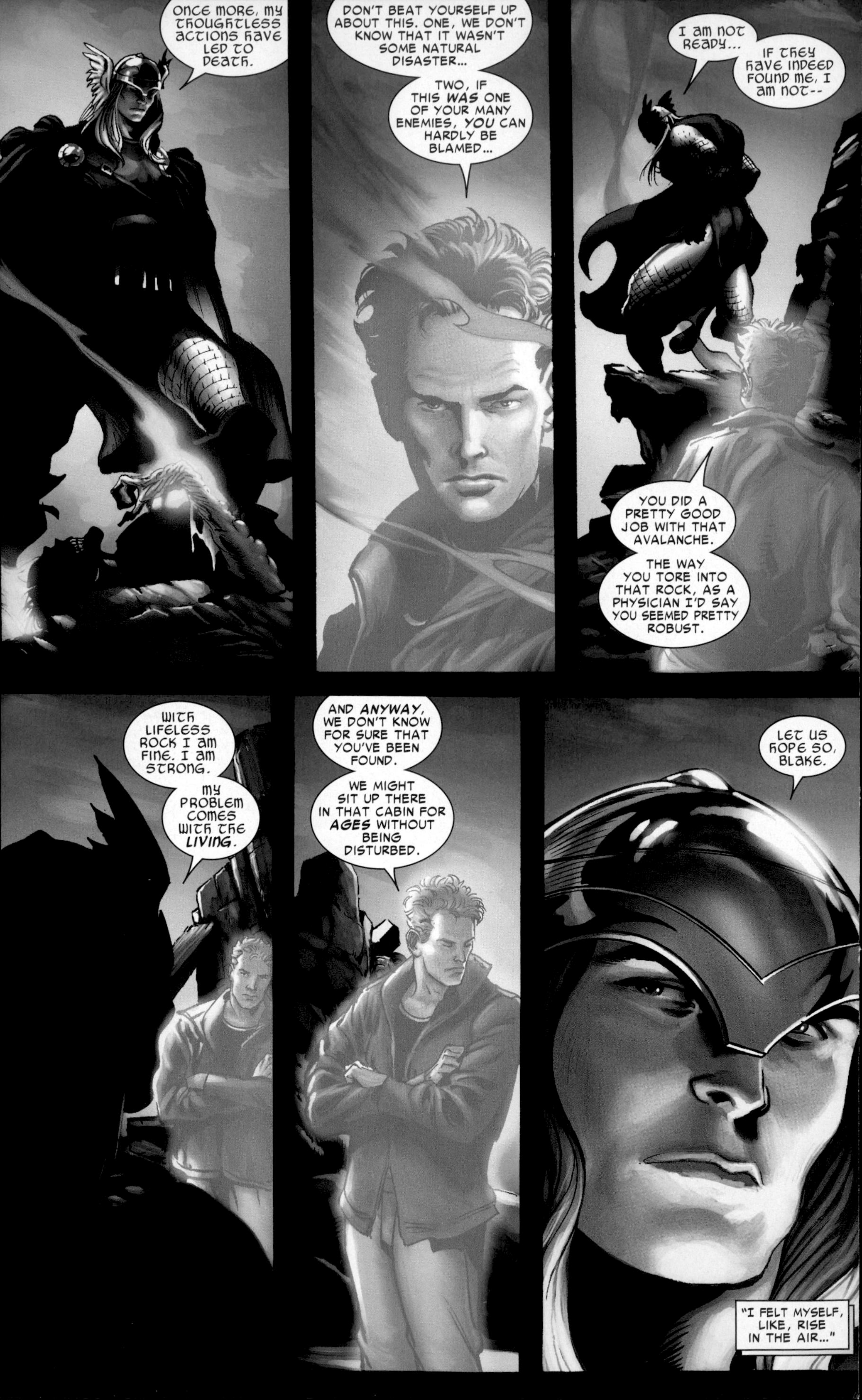
ONCE MORE, MY THOUGHTLESS ACTIONS HAVE LED TO DEATH.
DON'T BEAT YOURSELF UP ABOUT THIS. ONE, WE DON'T KNOW THAT IT WASN'T SOME NATURAL DISASTER...
TWO, IF THIS WAS ONE OF YOUR MANY ENEMIES, YOU CAN HARDLY BE BLAMED...
I AM NOT READY...
IF THEY HAVE INDEED FOUND ME, I AM NOT--
YOU DID A PRETTY GOOD JOB WITH THAT AVALANCHE.
THE WAY YOU TORE INTO THAT ROCK, AS A PHYSICIAN I'D SAY YOU SEEMED PRETTY ROBUST.
WITH LIFELESS ROCK I AM FINE. I AM STRONG.
MY PROBLEM COMES WITH THE LIVING.
AND ANYWAY, WE DON'T KNOW FOR SURE THAT YOU'VE BEEN FOUND.
WE MIGHT SIT UP THERE IN THAT CABIN FOR AGES WITHOUT BEING DISTURBED.
LET US HOPE SO, BLAKE.
"I FELT MYSELF, LIKE, RISE IN THE AIR..."

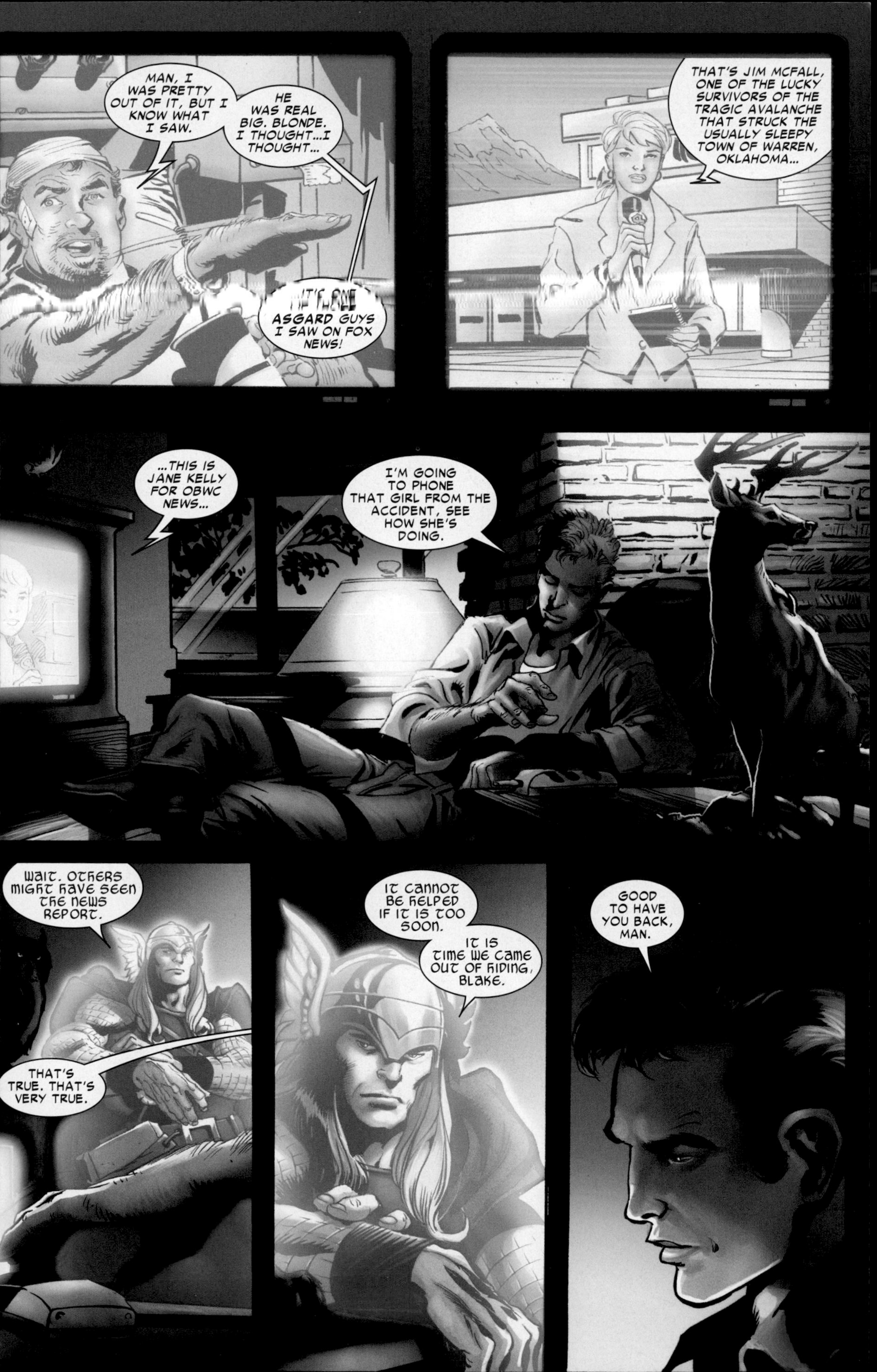

MAN, I WAS PRETTY OUT OF IT, BUT I KNOW WHAT I SAW.
HE WAS REAL BIG. BLONDE. I THOUGHT...I THOUGHT...
ASGARD GUYS I SAW ON FOX NEWS!
THAT'S JIM MCFALL, ONE OF THE LUCKY SURVIVORS OF THE TRAGIC AVALANCHE THAT STRUCK THE USUALLY SLEEPY TOWN OF WARREN, OKLAHOMA...
...THIS IS JANE KELLY FOR OBWC NEWS...
I'M GOING TO PHONE THAT GIRL FROM THE ACCIDENT, SEE HOW SHE'S DOING.
WAIT. OTHERS MIGHT HAVE SEEN THE NEWS REPORT.
THAT'S TRUE. THAT'S VERY TRUE.
IT CANNOT BE HELPED IF IT IS TOO SOON.
IT IS TIME WE CAME OUT OF HIDING, BLAKE.
GOOD TO HAVE YOU BACK, MAN.

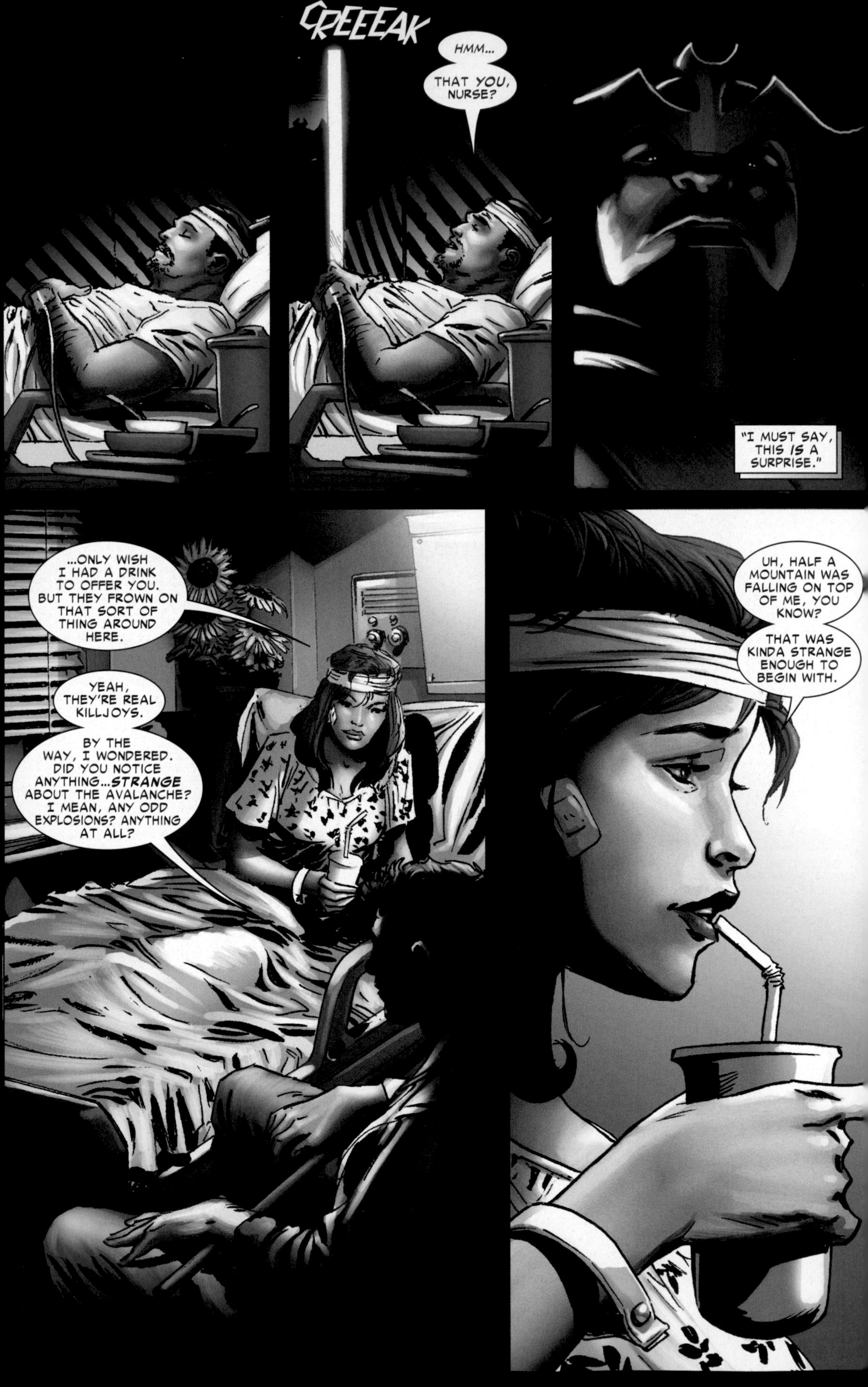
CREEEAK
HMM...
THAT YOU, NURSE?
"I MUST SAY, THIS IS A SURPRISE."
...ONLY WISH I HAD A DRINK TO OFFER YOU. BUT THEY FROWN ON THAT SORT OF THING AROUND HERE.
YEAH, THEY'RE REAL KILLJOYS.
BY THE WAY, I WONDERED. DID YOU NOTICE ANYTHING...STRANGE ABOUT THE AVALANCHE? I MEAN, ANY ODD EXPLOSIONS? ANYTHING AT ALL?
UH, HALF A MOUNTAIN WAS FALLING ON TOP OF ME, YOU KNOW?
THAT WAS KINDA STRANGE ENOUGH TO BEGIN WITH.

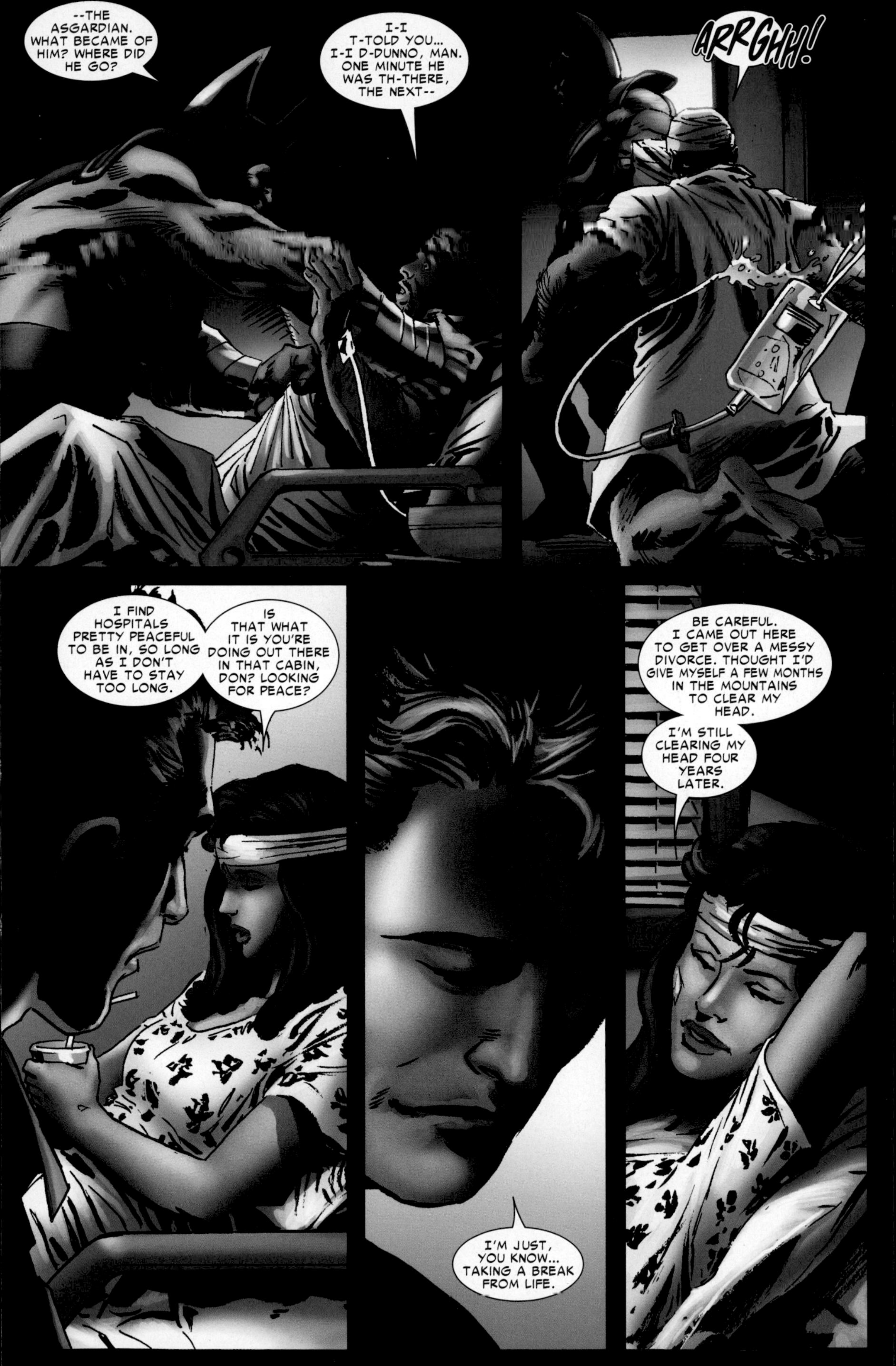
--THE ASGARDIAN. WHAT BECAME OF HIM? WHERE DID HE GO?
I-I T-TOLD YOU... I-I D-DUNNO, MAN. ONE MINUTE HE WAS TH-THERE, THE NEXT--
ARRGHH!
I FIND HOSPITALS PRETTY PEACEFUL TO BE IN, SO LONG AS I DON'T HAVE TO STAY TOO LONG.
IS THAT WHAT IT IS YOU'RE DOING OUT THERE IN THAT CABIN, DON? LOOKING FOR PEACE?
I'M JUST, YOU KNOW... TAKING A BREAK FROM LIFE.
BE CAREFUL. I CAME OUT HERE TO GET OVER A MESSY DIVORCE. THOUGHT I'D GIVE MYSELF A FEW MONTHS IN THE MOUNTAINS TO CLEAR MY HEAD.
I'M STILL CLEARING MY HEAD FOUR YEARS LATER.

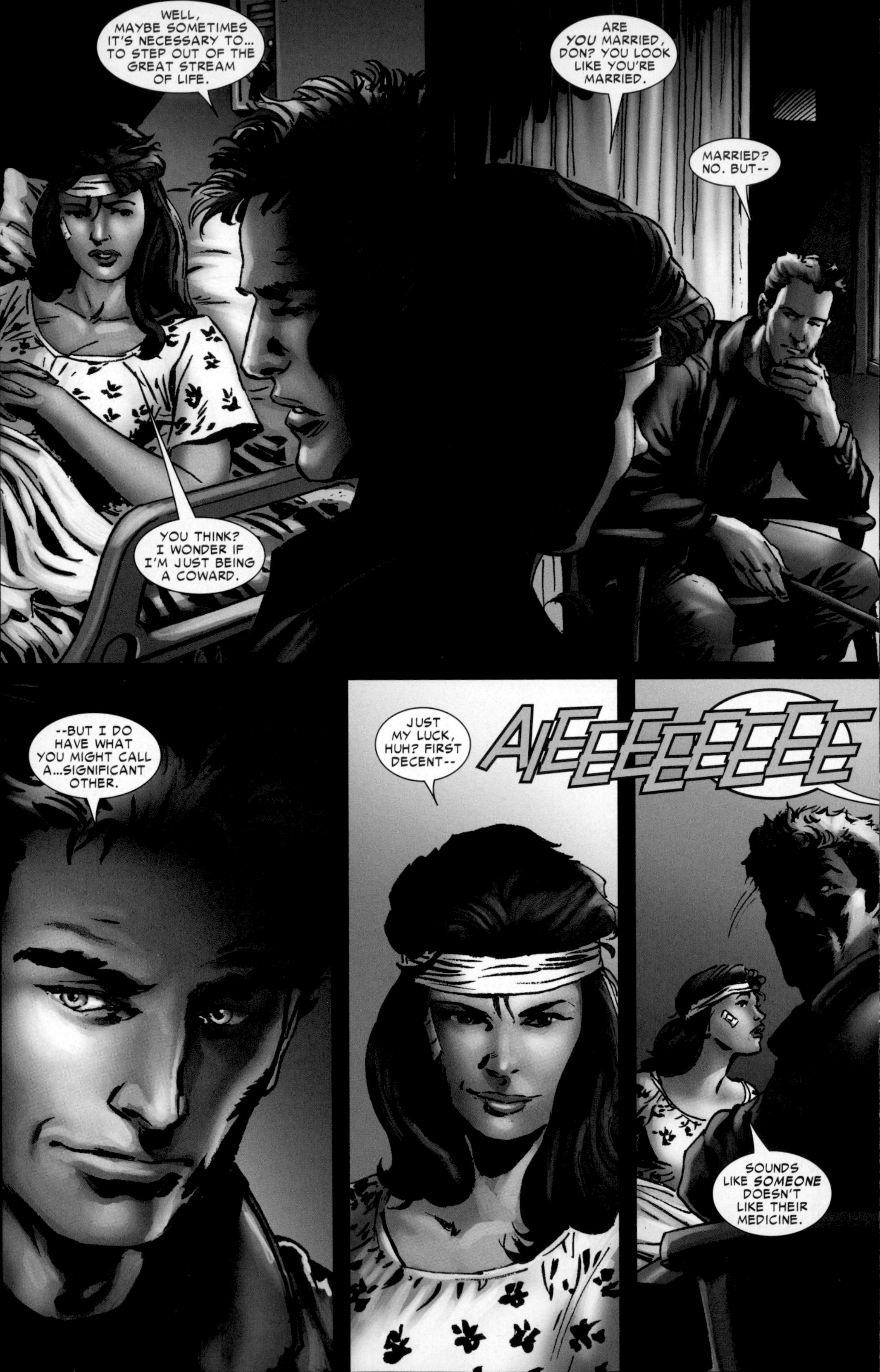
WELL, MAYBE SOMETIMES IT'S NECESSARY TO... TO STEP OUT OF THE GREAT STREAM OF LIFE.
YOU THINK? I WONDER IF I'M JUST BEING A COWARD.
ARE YOU MARRIED, DON? YOU LOOK LIKE YOU'RE MARRIED.
MARRIED? NO. BUT--
--BUT I DO HAVE WHAT YOU MIGHT CALL A...SIGNIFICANT OTHER.
JUST MY LUCK, HUH? FIRST DECENT--
AIEEEEEEEEEE
SOUNDS LIKE SOMEONE DOESN'T LIKE THEIR MEDICINE.

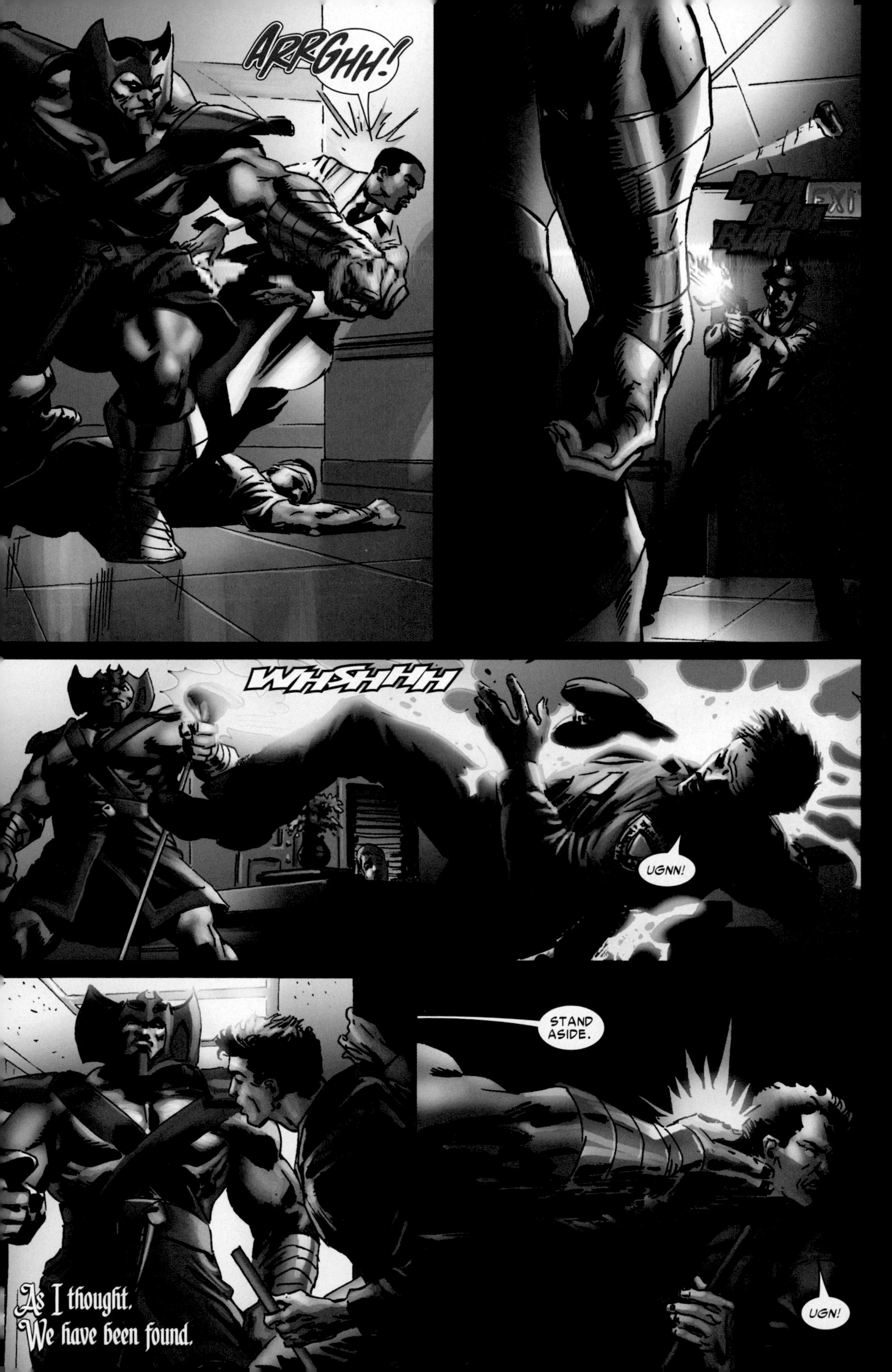
ARRGHH!
BLAM BLAM BLAM
EXI
WHSHHH
UGNN!
STAND ASIDE.
As I thought.
We have been found.
UGN!

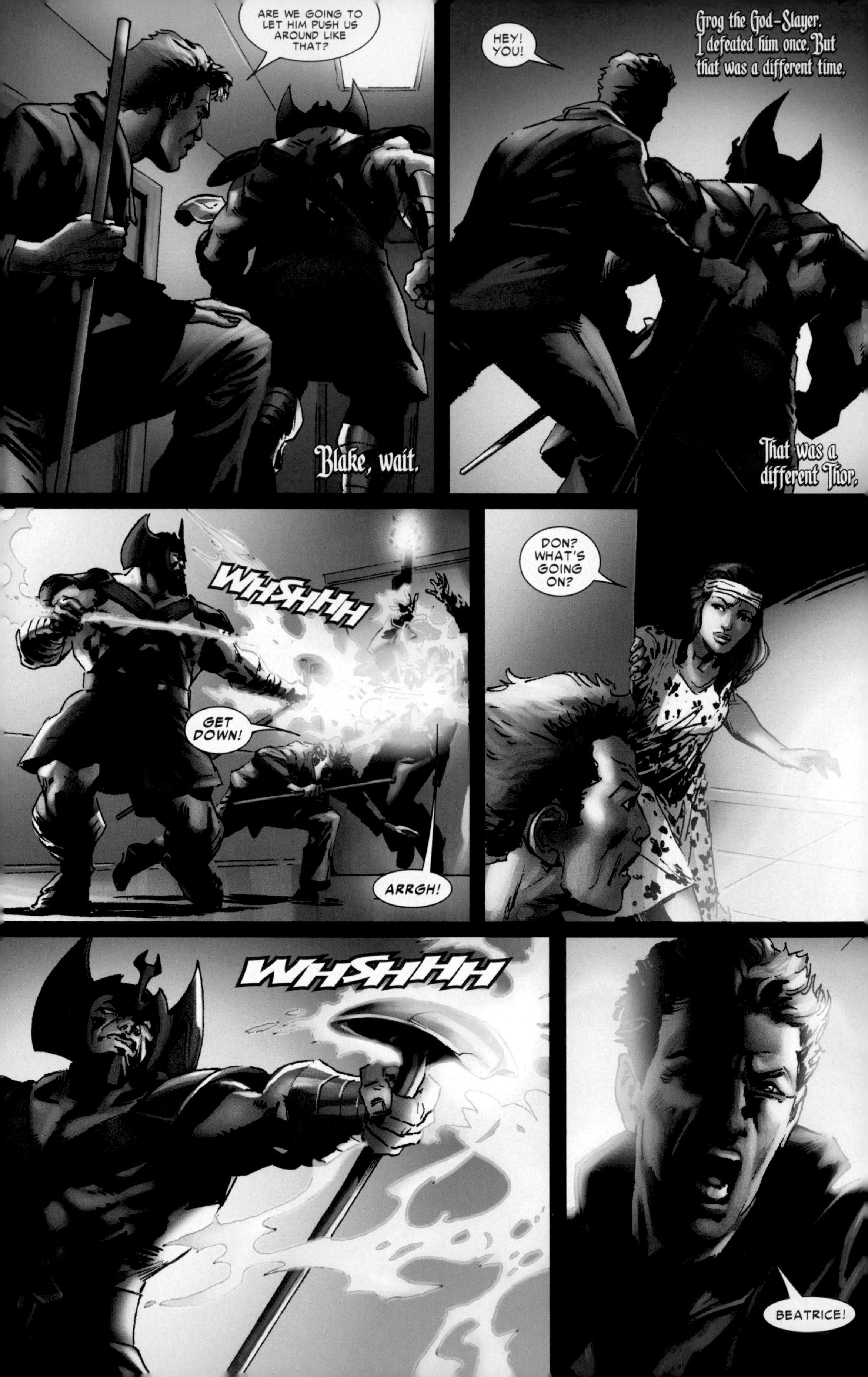

ARE WE GOING TO LET HIM PUSH US AROUND LIKE THAT?
Blake, wait.
HEY! YOU!
Grog the God-Slayer. I defeated him once. But that was a different time.
That was a different Thor.
WHSHHH
GET DOWN!
ARRGH!
DON? WHAT'S GOING ON?
WHSHHH
BEATRICE!

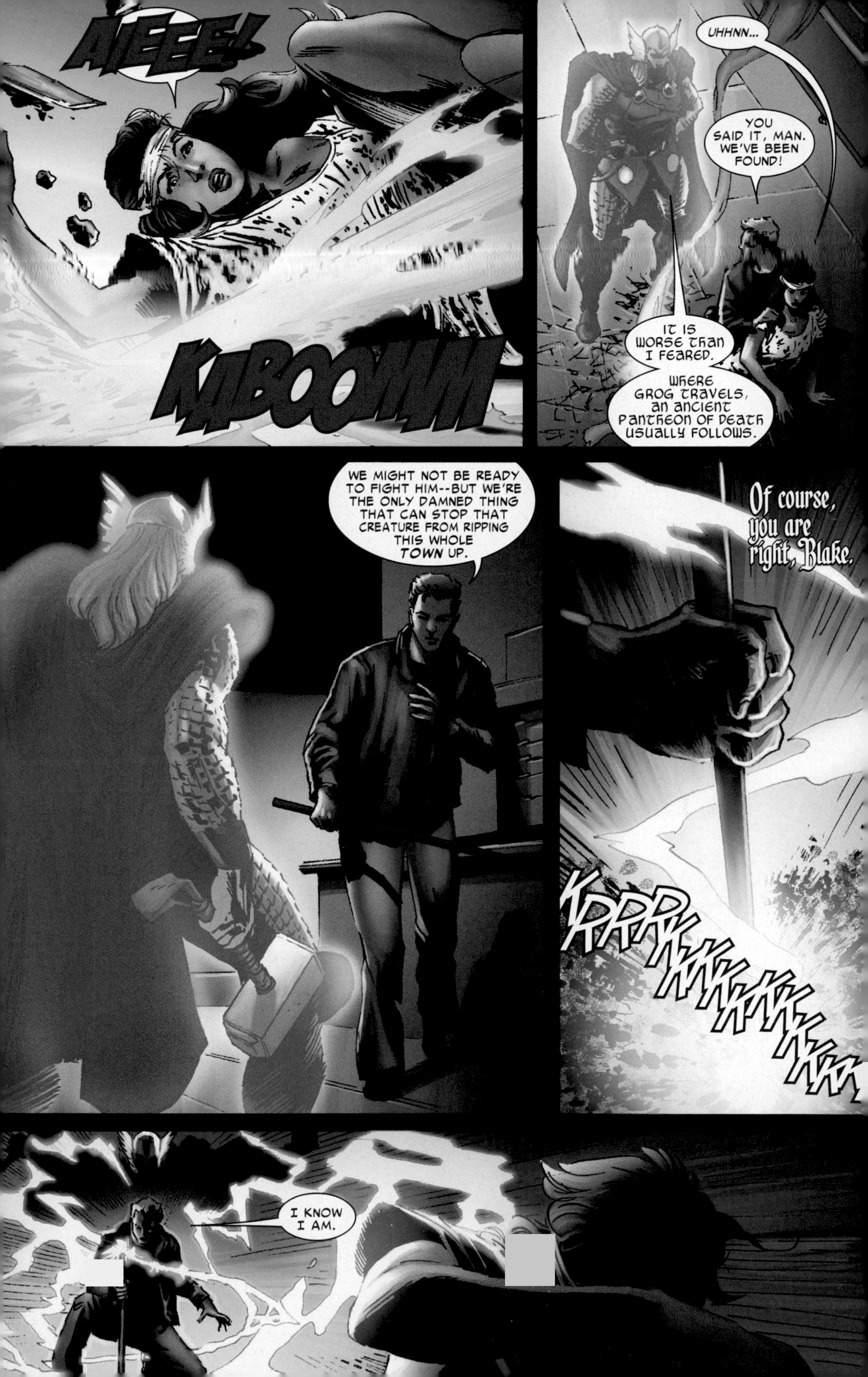
AIEEE!
KABOOMM
UHHNN...
YOU SAID IT, MAN. WE'VE BEEN FOUND!
IT IS WORSE THAN I FEARED.
WHERE GROG TRAVELS, AN ANCIENT PANTHEON OF DEATH USUALLY FOLLOWS.
WE MIGHT NOT BE READY TO FIGHT HIM--BUT WE'RE THE ONLY DAMNED THING THAT CAN STOP THAT CREATURE FROM RIPPING THIS WHOLE TOWN UP.
Of course, you are right, Blake.
KRRRKKKKKKKKKKKRR
I KNOW I AM.

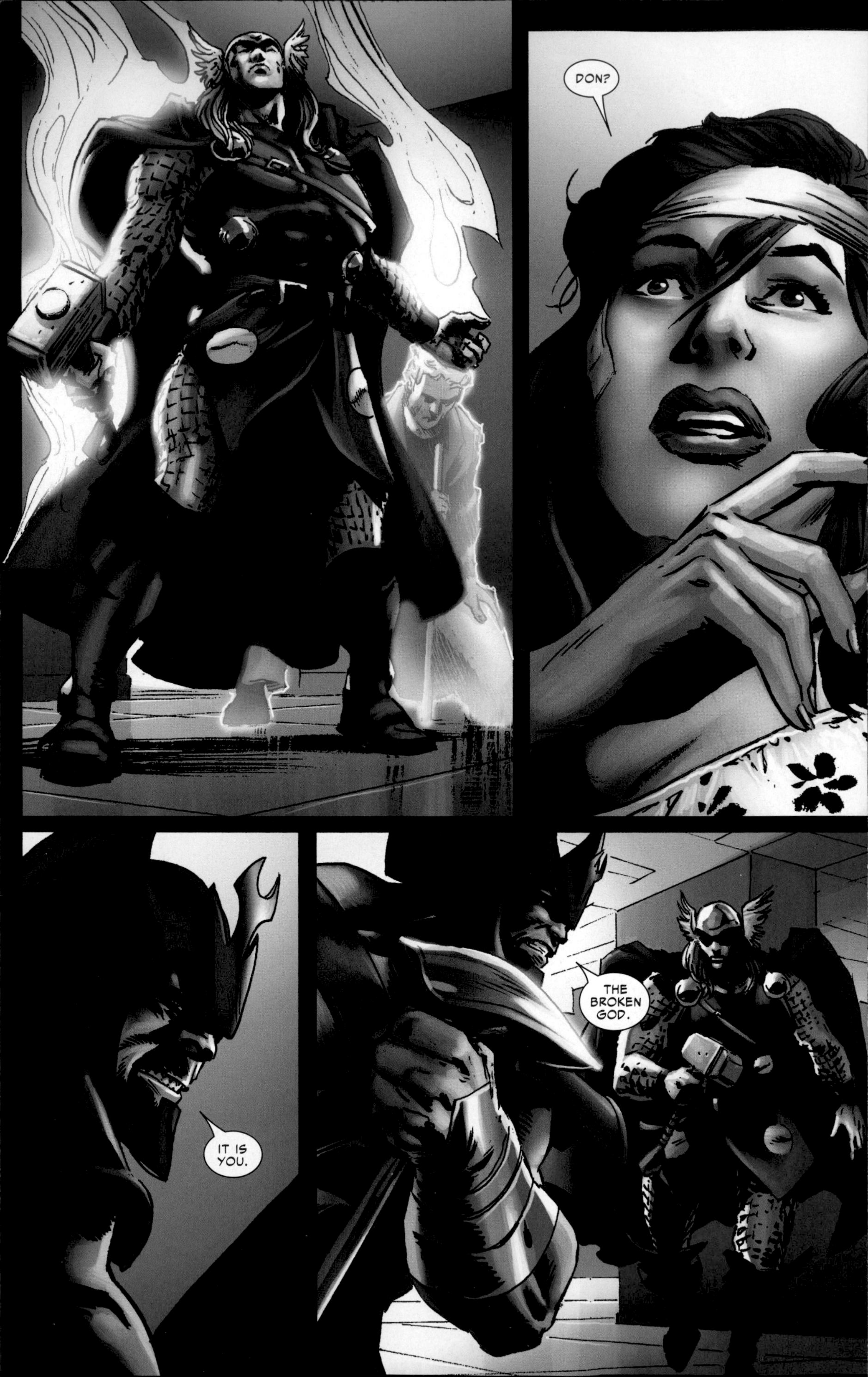
DON?
IT IS YOU.
THE BROKEN GOD.

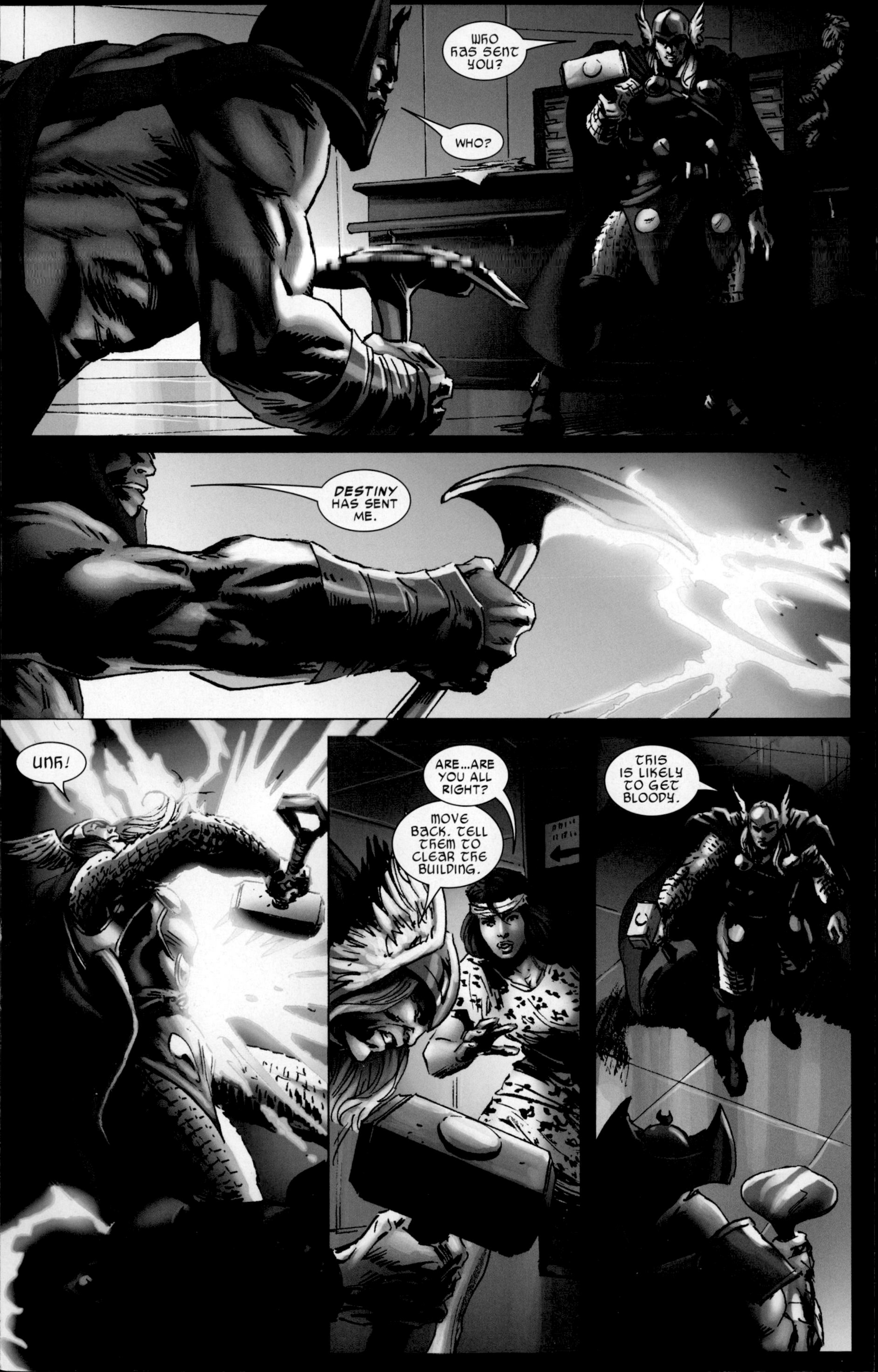
WHO HAS SENT YOU?
WHO?
DESTINY HAS SENT ME.
UNH!
ARE...ARE YOU ALL RIGHT?
MOVE BACK. TELL THEM TO CLEAR THE BUILDING.
THIS IS LIKELY TO GET BLOODY.

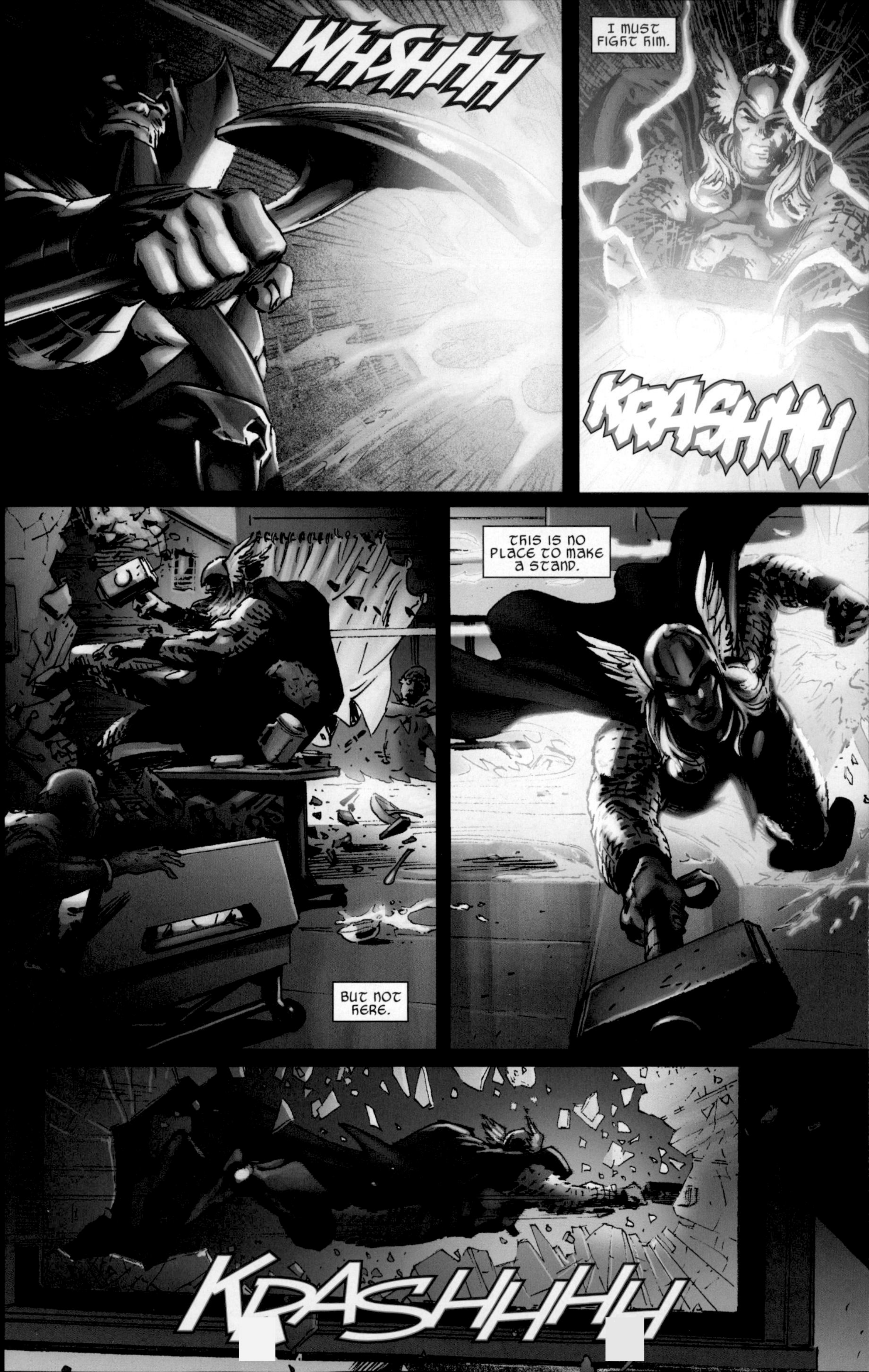
WHSHHH
I MUST FIGHT HIM.
KRASHHH
THIS IS NO PLACE TO MAKE A STAND.
BUT NOT HERE.
KRASHHHH

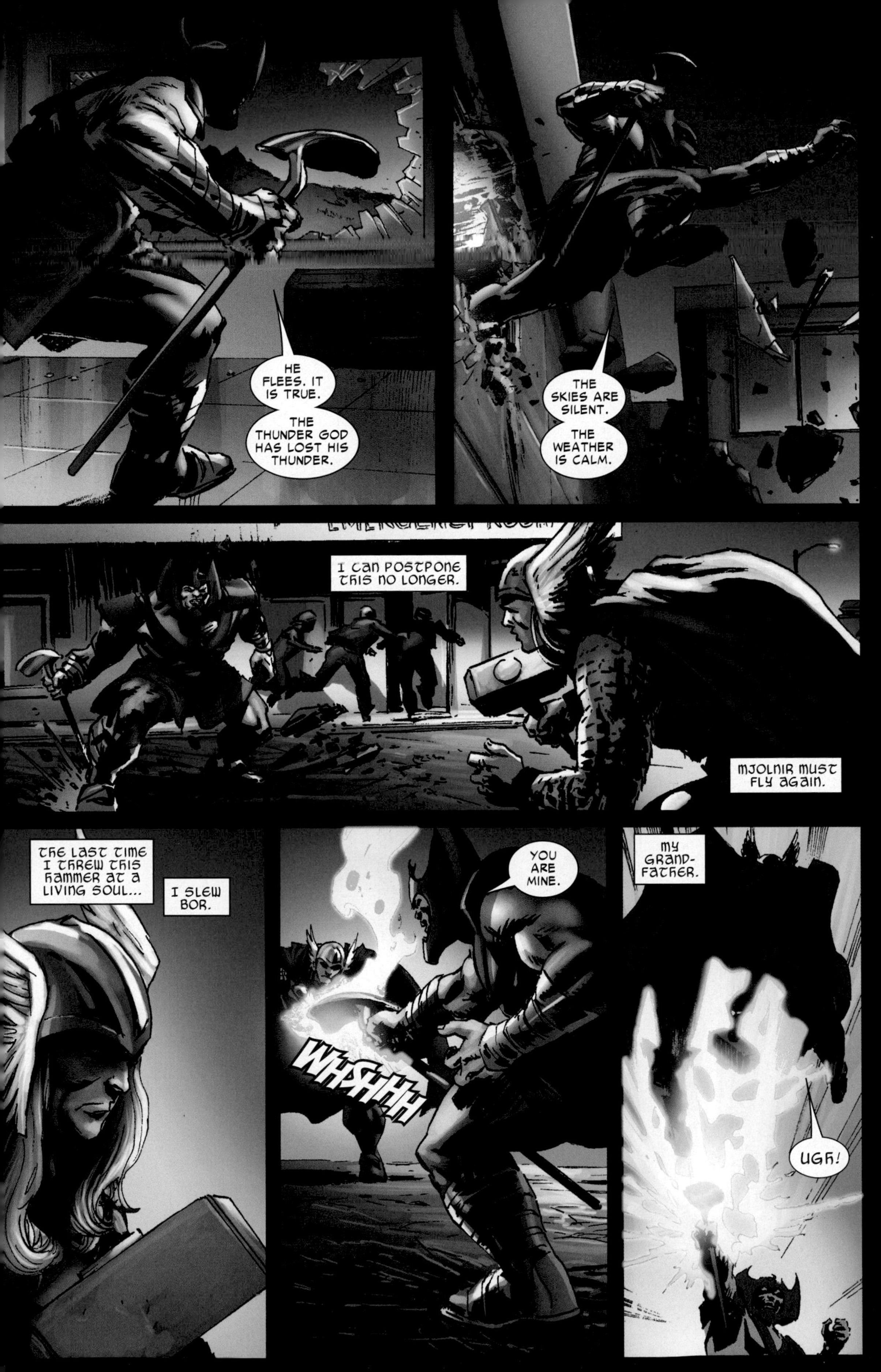
HE FLEES. IT IS TRUE.
THE THUNDER GOD HAS LOST HIS THUNDER.
THE SKIES ARE SILENT.
THE WEATHER IS CALM.
I CAN POSTPONE THIS NO LONGER.
MJOLNIR MUST FLY AGAIN.
THE LAST TIME I THREW THIS HAMMER AT A LIVING SOUL...
I SLEW BOR.
YOU ARE MINE.
WHSHHH
MY GRAND-FATHER.
UGH!

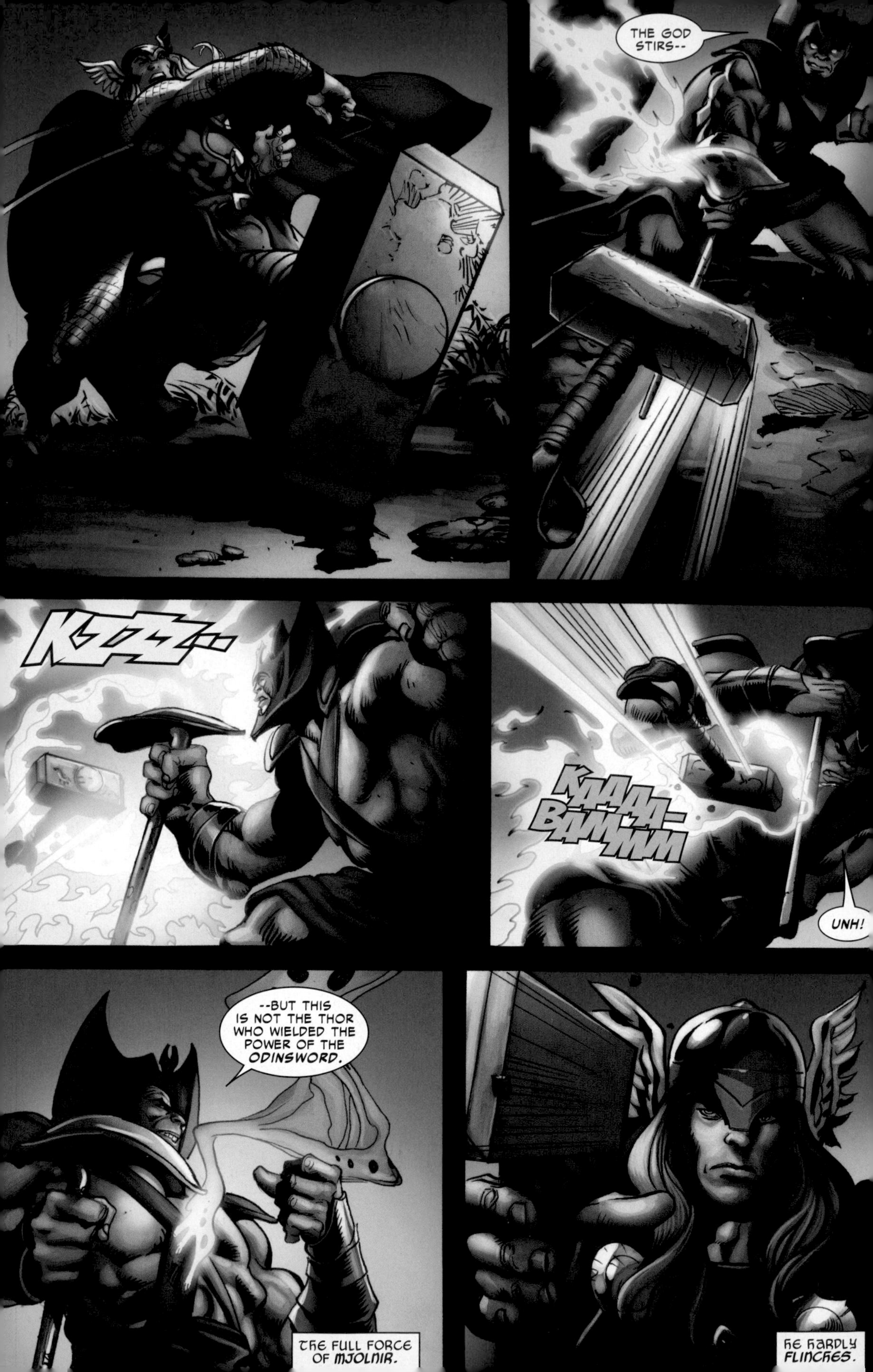

THE GOD STIRS--
KZZZ--
KAAAA-BAMMM
UNH!
--BUT THIS IS NOT THE THOR WHO WIELDED THE POWER OF THE ODINSWORD.
THE FULL FORCE OF MJOLNIR.
HE HARDLY FLINCHES.

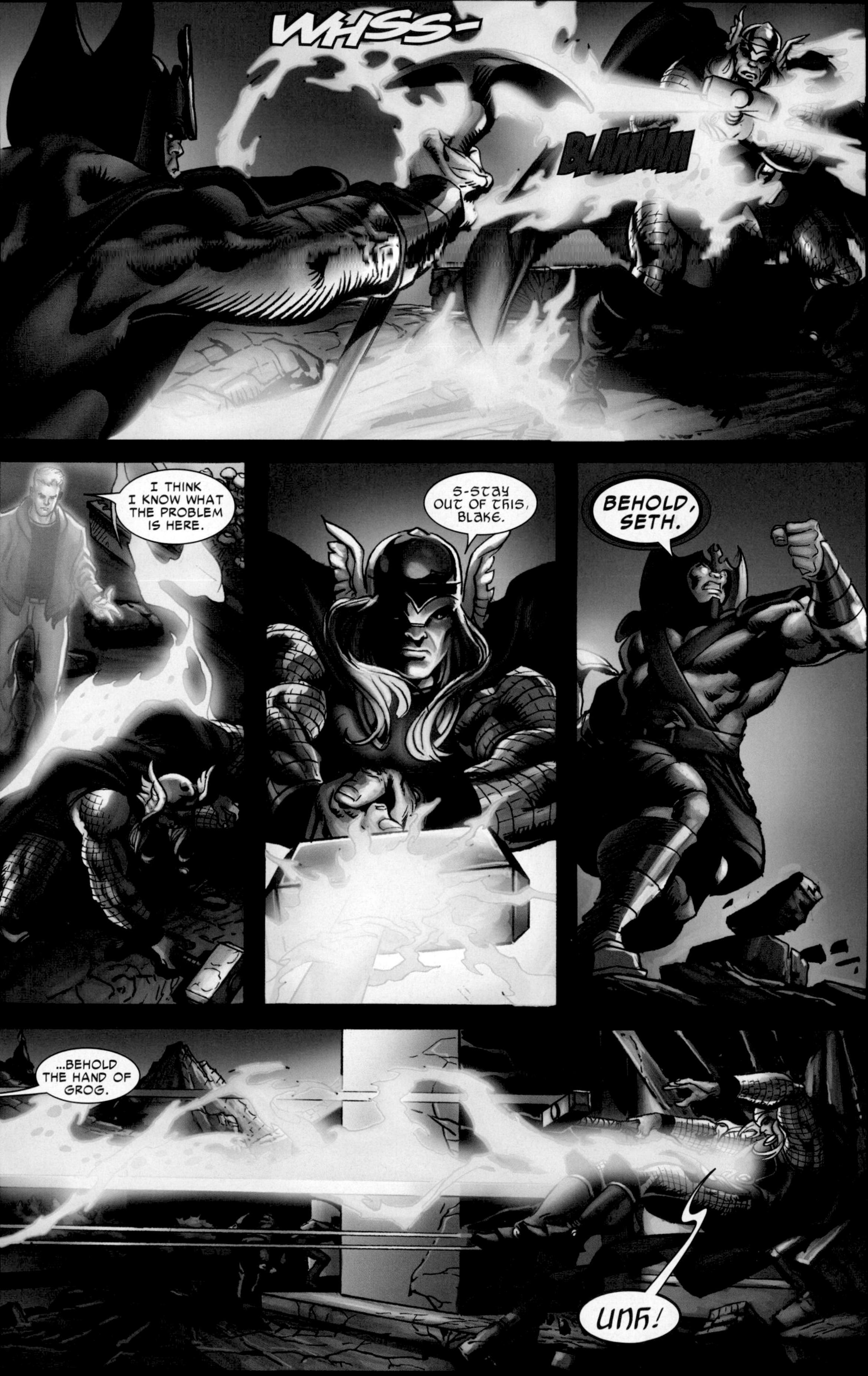
WHSS-
BLAMMM
I THINK I KNOW WHAT THE PROBLEM IS HERE.
S-STAY OUT OF THIS, BLAKE.
BEHOLD, SETH.
...BEHOLD THE HAND OF GROG.
UNH!

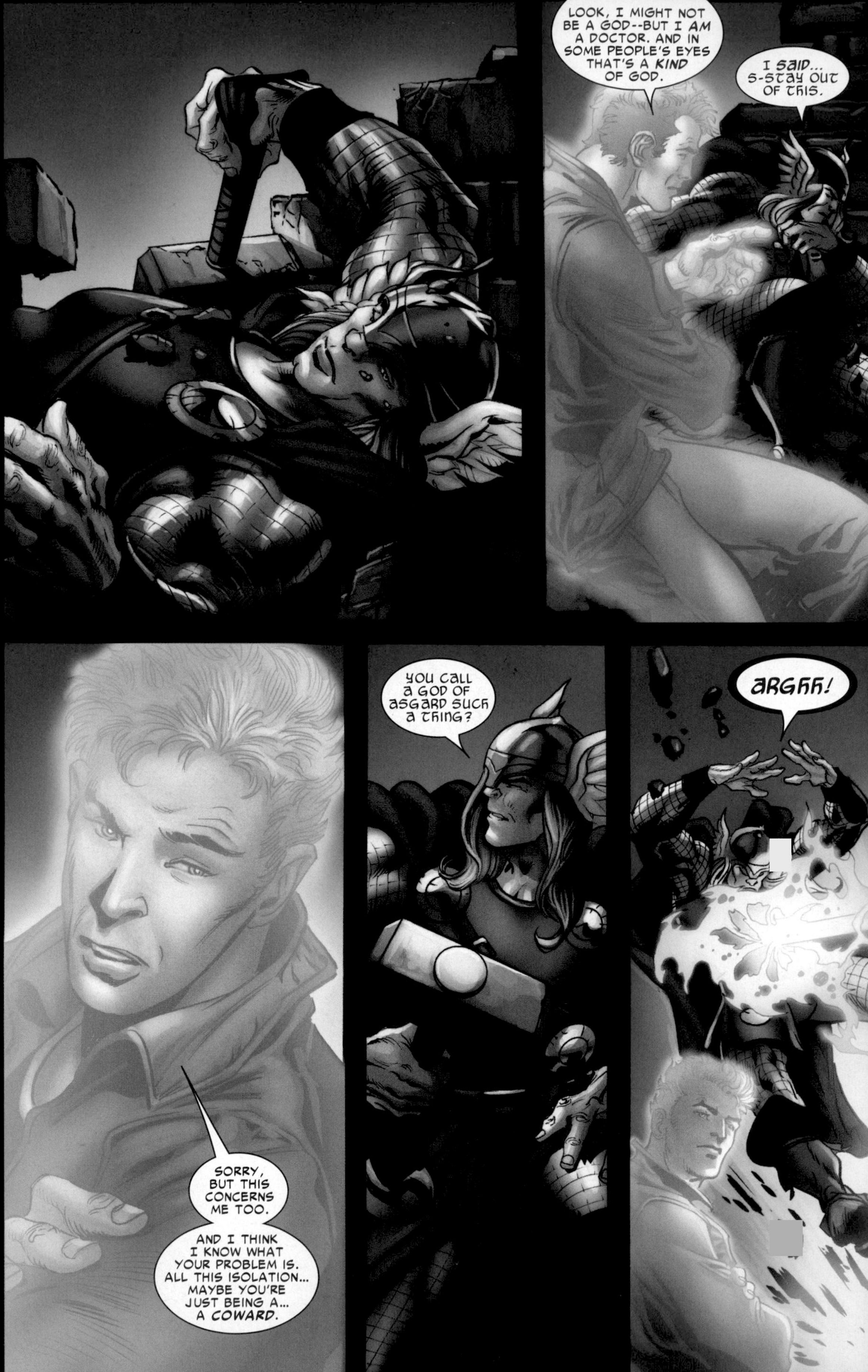
LOOK, I MIGHT NOT BE A GOD--BUT I AM A DOCTOR. AND IN SOME PEOPLE'S EYES THAT'S A KIND OF GOD.
I SAID... S-STAY OUT OF THIS.
SORRY, BUT THIS CONCERNS ME TOO.
AND I THINK I KNOW WHAT YOUR PROBLEM IS. ALL THIS ISOLATION... MAYBE YOU'RE JUST BEING A... A COWARD.
YOU CALL A GOD OF ASGARD SUCH A THING?
ARGHH!

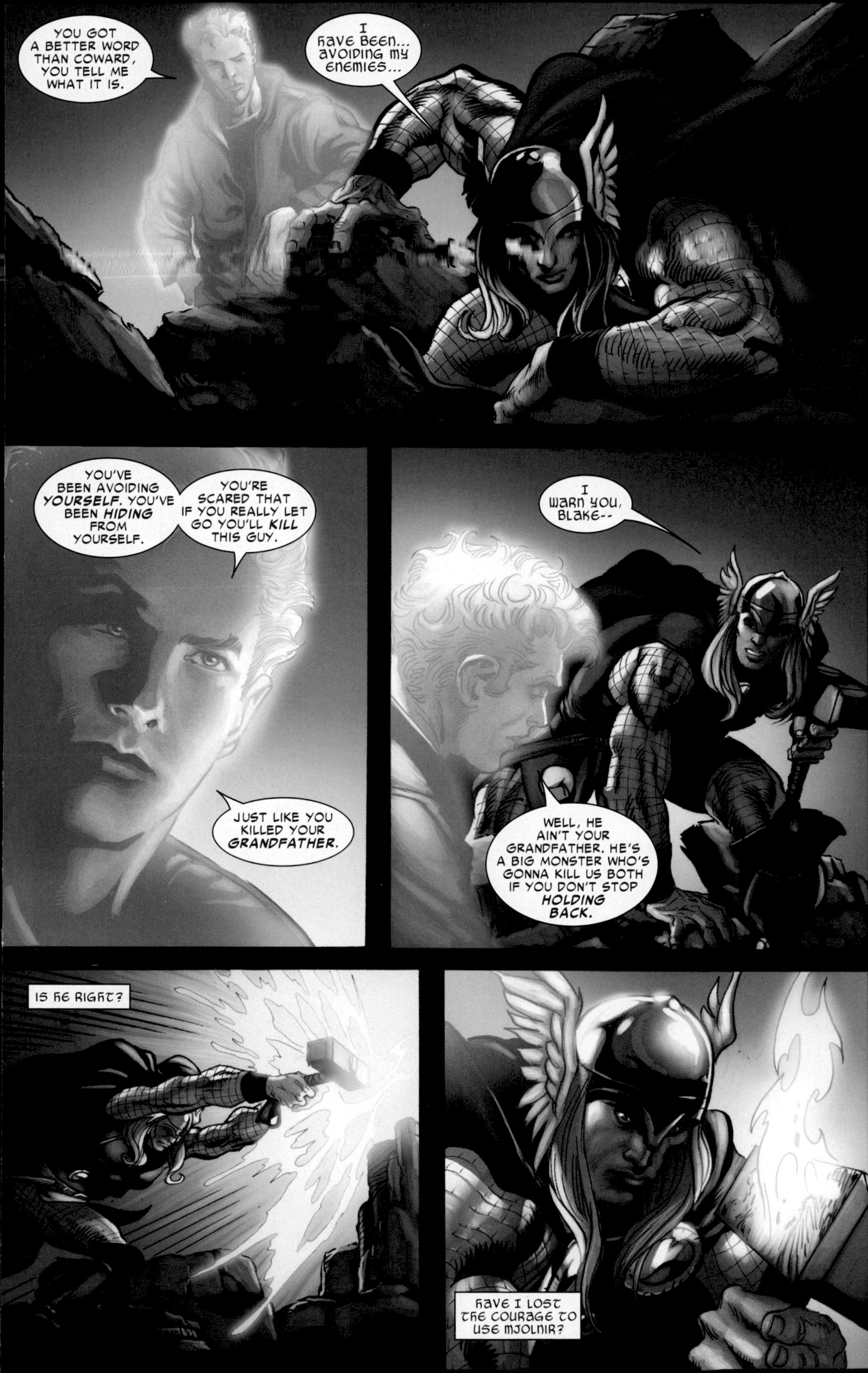
YOU GOT A BETTER WORD THAN COWARD, YOU TELL ME WHAT IT IS.
I HAVE BEEN... AVOIDING MY ENEMIES...
YOU'VE BEEN AVOIDING YOURSELF. YOU'VE BEEN HIDING FROM YOURSELF.
YOU'RE SCARED THAT IF YOU REALLY LET GO YOU'LL KILL THIS GUY.
JUST LIKE YOU KILLED YOUR GRANDFATHER.
I WARN YOU, BLAKE--
WELL, HE AIN'T YOUR GRANDFATHER. HE'S A BIG MONSTER WHO'S GONNA KILL US BOTH IF YOU DON'T STOP HOLDING BACK.
IS HE RIGHT?
HAVE I LOST THE COURAGE TO USE MJOLNIR?

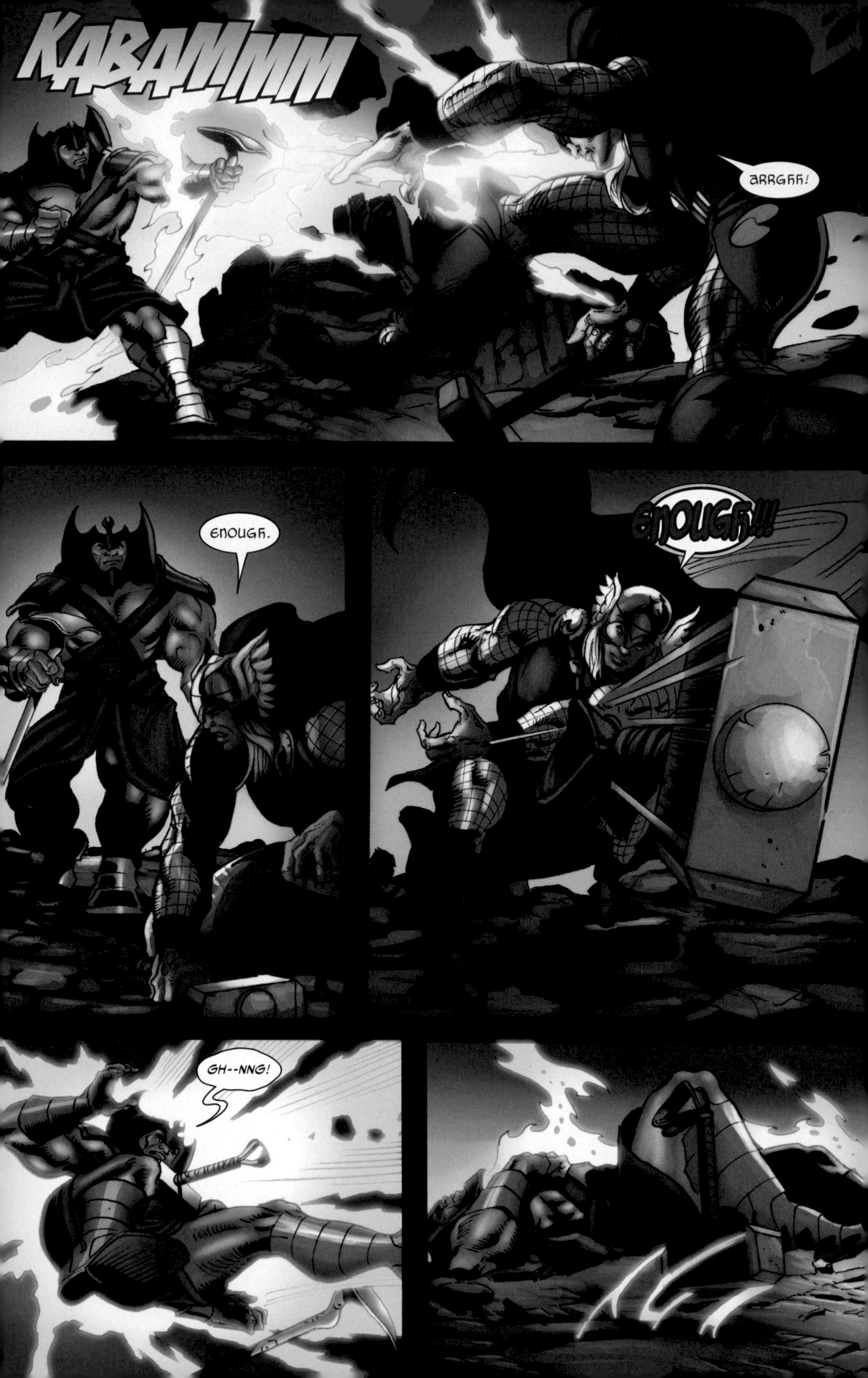
KABAMMMM
ARRGHH!
ENOUGH.
ENOUGH!!!
GH--NNG!

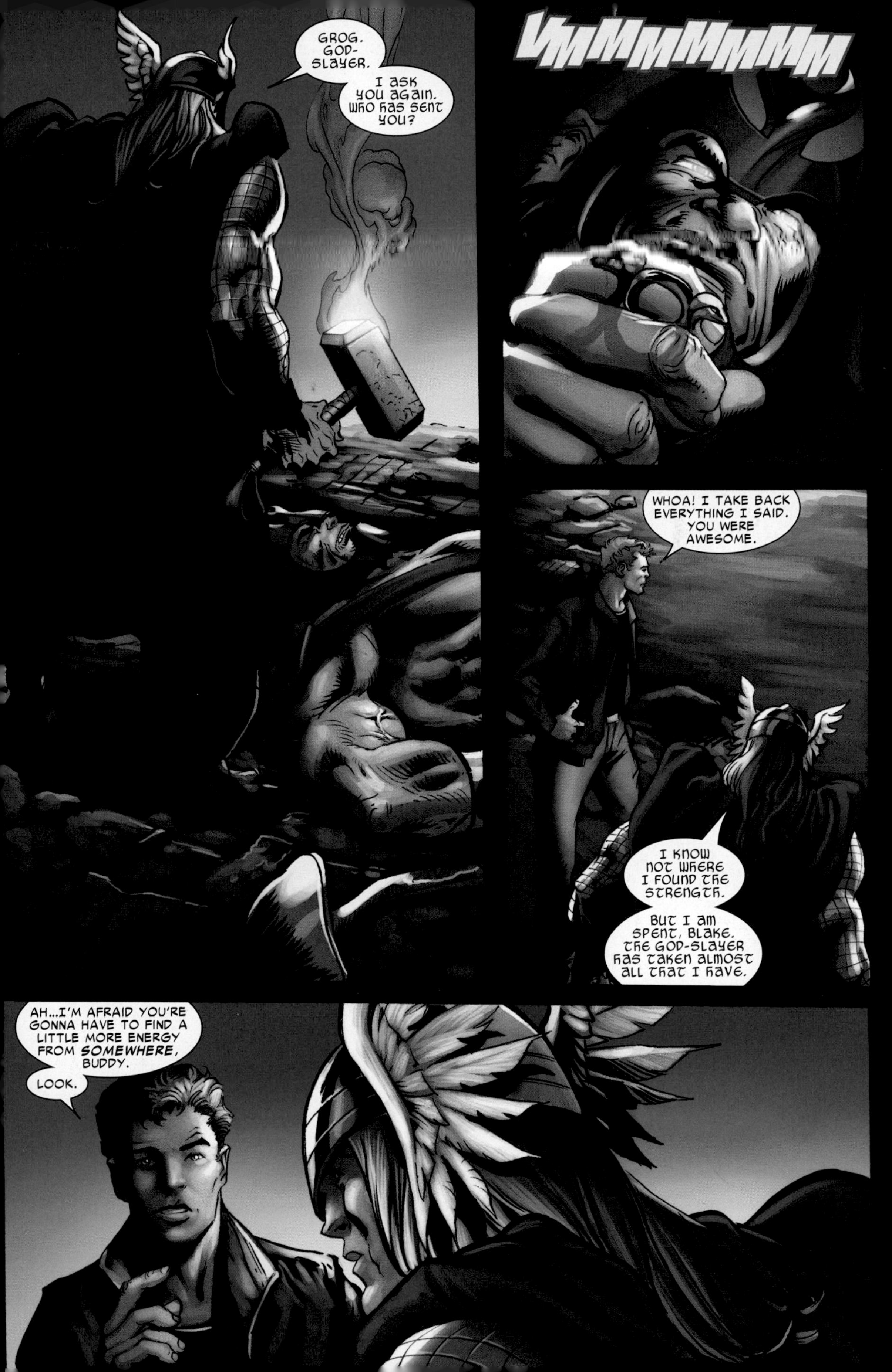
GROG. GOD-SLAYER.
I ASK YOU AGAIN. WHO HAS SENT YOU?
VMMMMMMMM
WHOA! I TAKE BACK EVERYTHING I SAID. YOU WERE AWESOME.
I KNOW NOT WHERE I FOUND THE STRENGTH.
BUT I AM SPENT, BLAKE. THE GOD-SLAYER HAS TAKEN ALMOST ALL THAT I HAVE.
AH...I'M AFRAID YOU'RE GONNA HAVE TO FIND A LITTLE MORE ENERGY FROM SOMEWHERE, BUDDY.
LOOK.

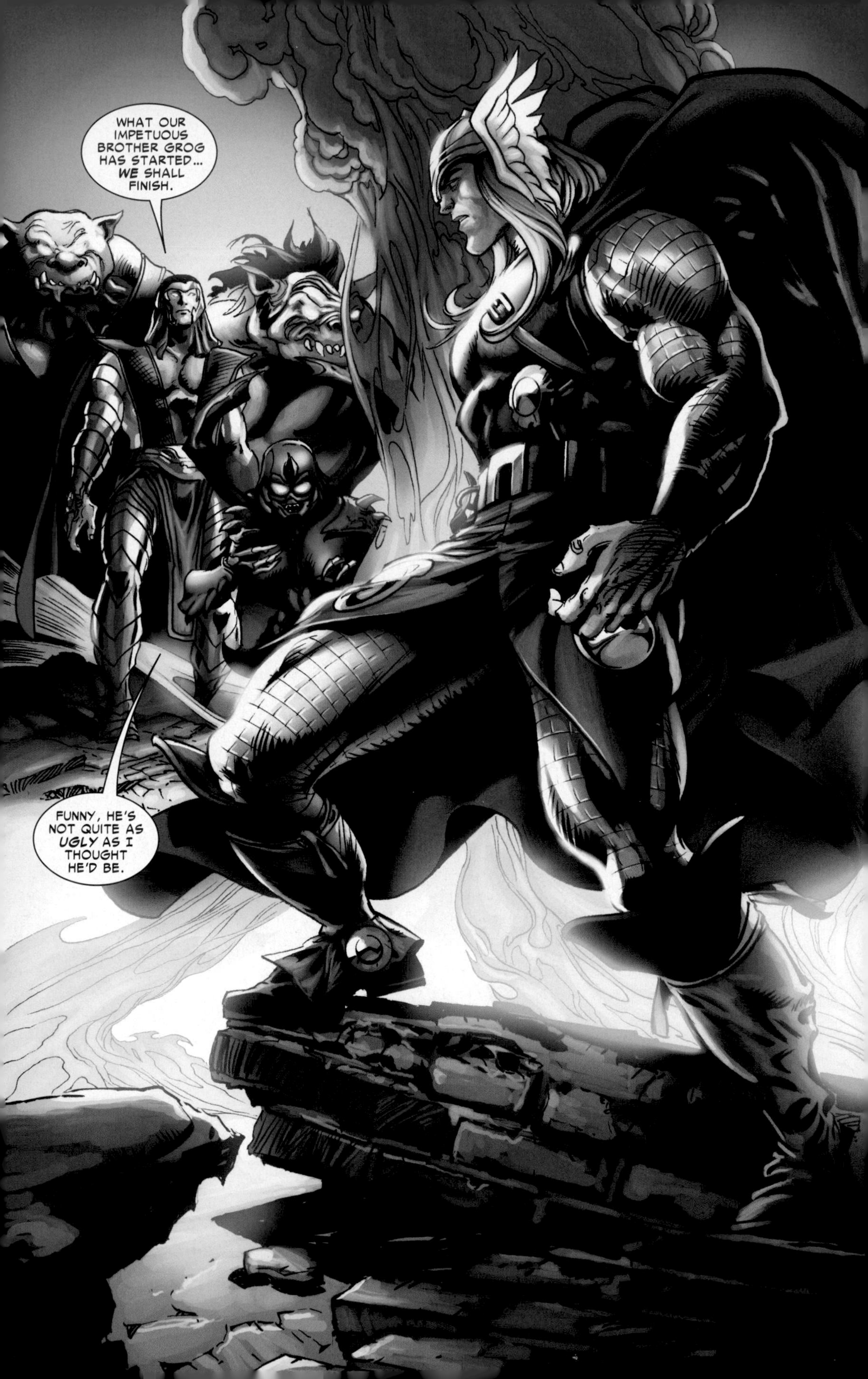
WHAT OUR IMPETUOUS BROTHER GROG HAS STARTED... WE SHALL FINISH.
FUNNY, HE'S NOT QUITE AS UGLY AS I THOUGHT HE'D BE.

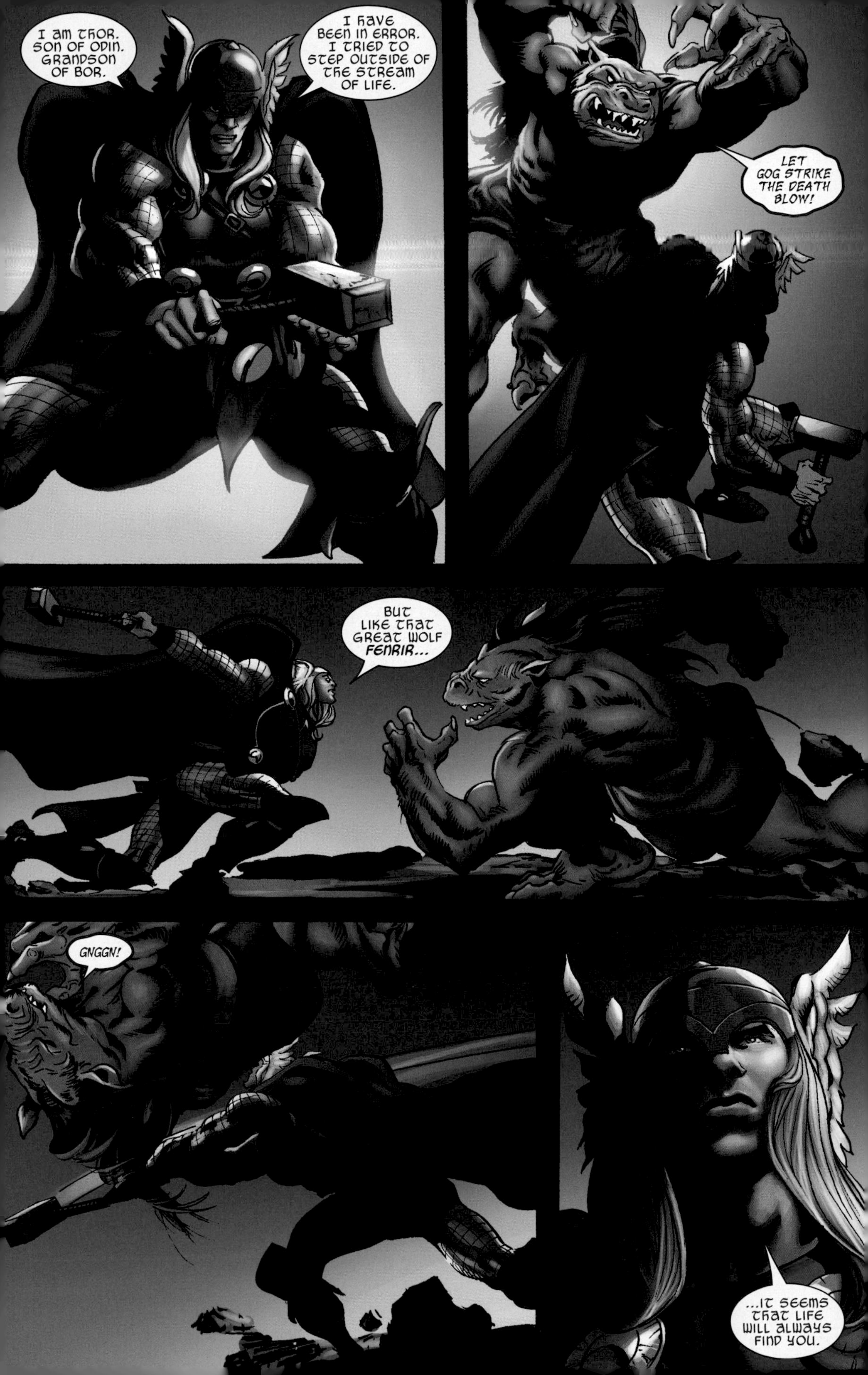
I AM THOR. SON OF ODIN. GRANDSON OF BOR.
I HAVE BEEN IN ERROR. I TRIED TO STEP OUTSIDE OF THE STREAM OF LIFE.
LET GOG STRIKE THE DEATH BLOW!
BUT LIKE THAT GREAT WOLF FENRIR...
GNGGN!
...IT SEEMS THAT LIFE WILL ALWAYS FIND YOU.

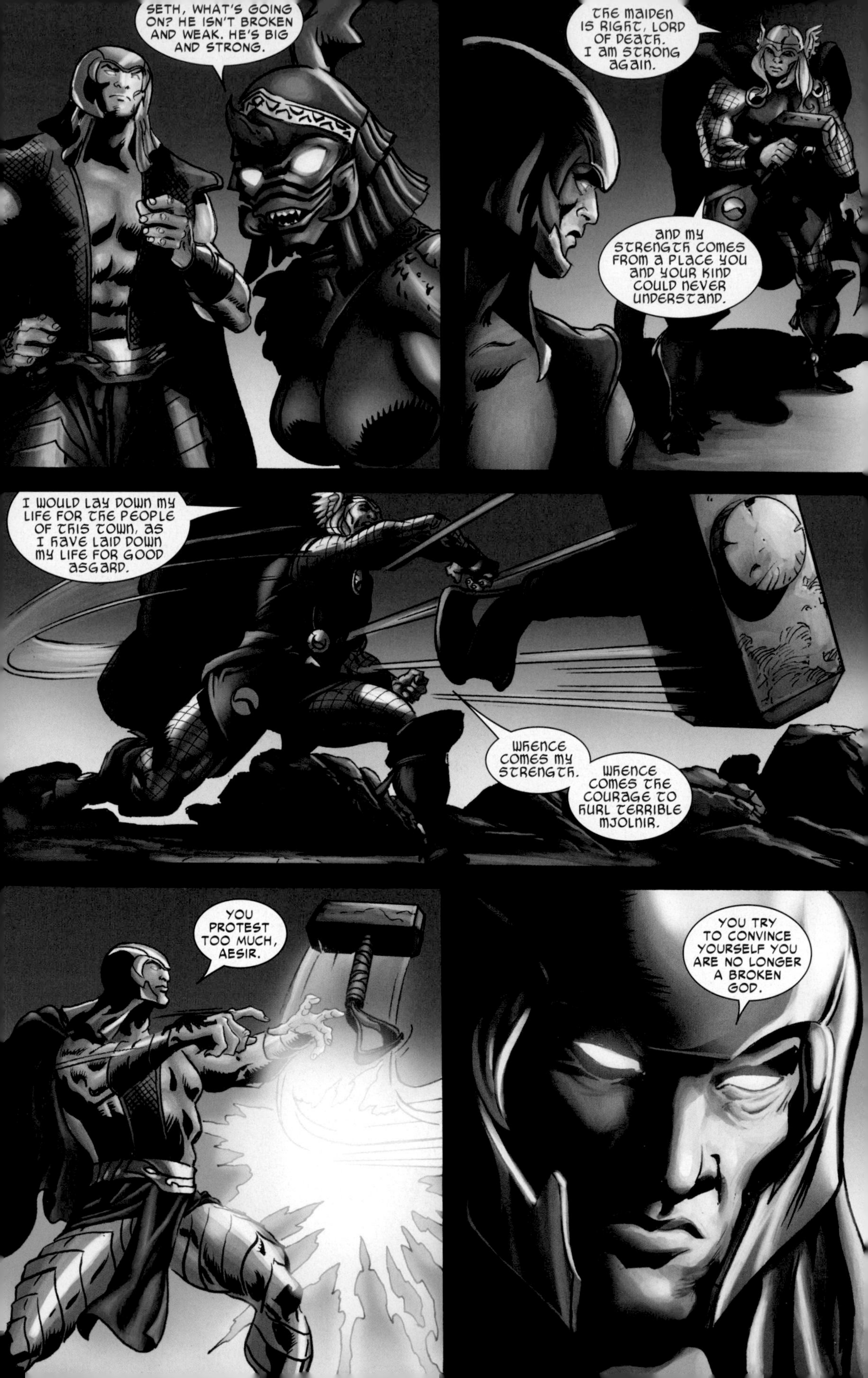
SETH, WHAT'S GOING ON? HE ISN'T BROKEN AND WEAK. HE'S BIG AND STRONG.
THE MAIDEN IS RIGHT, LORD OF DEATH. I AM STRONG AGAIN.
AND MY STRENGTH COMES FROM A PLACE YOU AND YOUR KIND COULD NEVER UNDERSTAND.
I WOULD LAY DOWN MY LIFE FOR THE PEOPLE OF THIS TOWN, AS I HAVE LAID DOWN MY LIFE FOR GOOD ASGARD.
WHENCE COMES MY STRENGTH.
WHENCE COMES THE COURAGE TO HURL TERRIBLE MJOLNIR.
YOU PROTEST TOO MUCH, AESIR.
YOU TRY TO CONVINCE YOURSELF YOU ARE NO LONGER A BROKEN GOD.

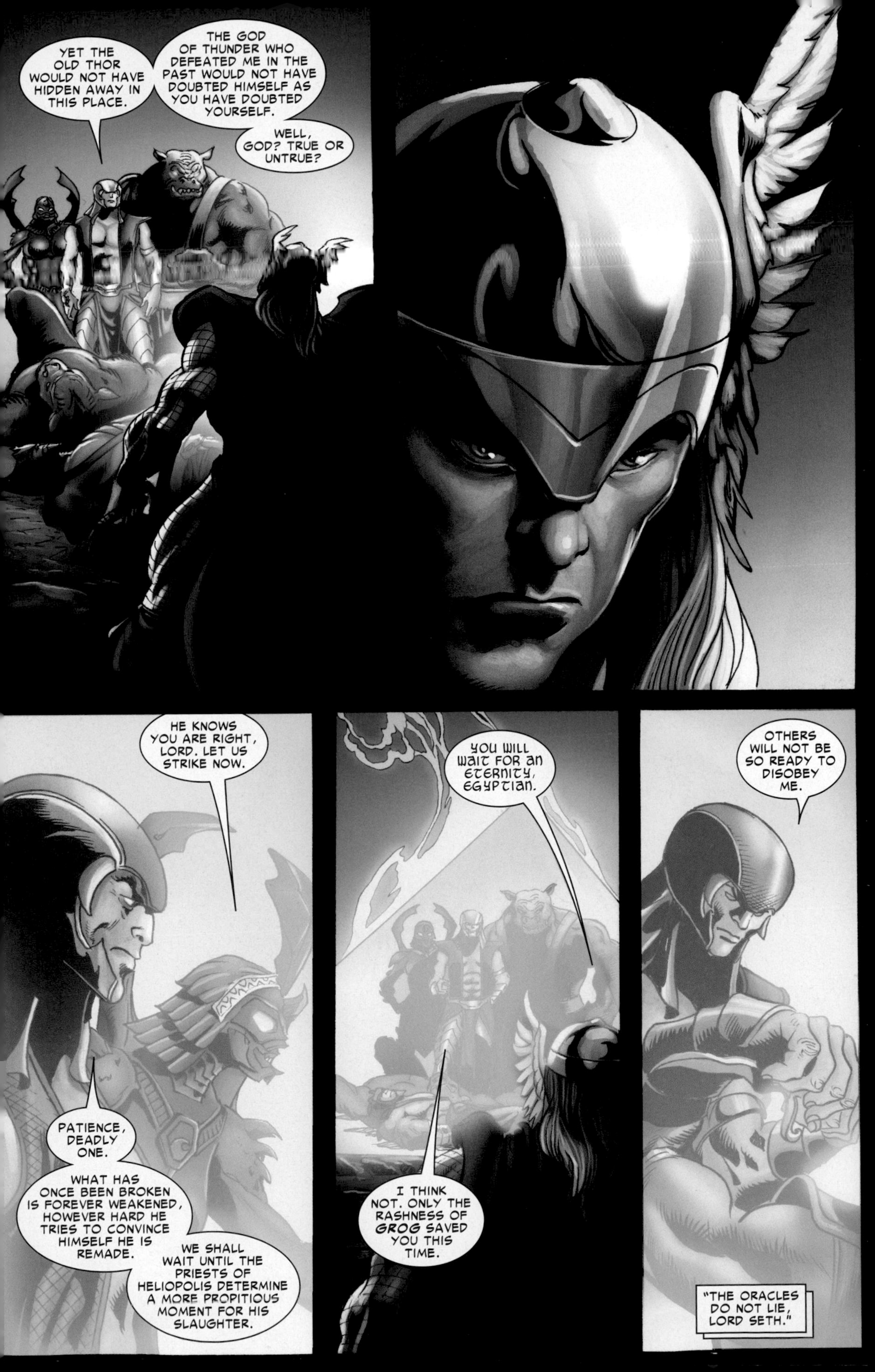
YET THE OLD THOR WOULD NOT HAVE HIDDEN AWAY IN THIS PLACE.
THE GOD OF THUNDER WHO DEFEATED ME IN THE PAST WOULD NOT HAVE DOUBTED HIMSELF AS YOU HAVE DOUBTED YOURSELF.
WELL, GOD? TRUE OR UNTRUE?
HE KNOWS YOU ARE RIGHT, LORD. LET US STRIKE NOW.
PATIENCE, DEADLY ONE.
WHAT HAS ONCE BEEN BROKEN IS FOREVER WEAKENED, HOWEVER HARD HE TRIES TO CONVINCE HIMSELF HE IS REMADE.
WE SHALL WAIT UNTIL THE PRIESTS OF HELIOPOLIS DETERMINE A MORE PROPITIOUS MOMENT FOR HIS SLAUGHTER.
YOU WILL WAIT FOR AN ETERNITY, EGYPTIAN.
I THINK NOT. ONLY THE RASHNESS OF GROG SAVED YOU THIS TIME.
OTHERS WILL NOT BE SO READY TO DISOBEY ME.
"THE ORACLES DO NOT LIE, LORD SETH."

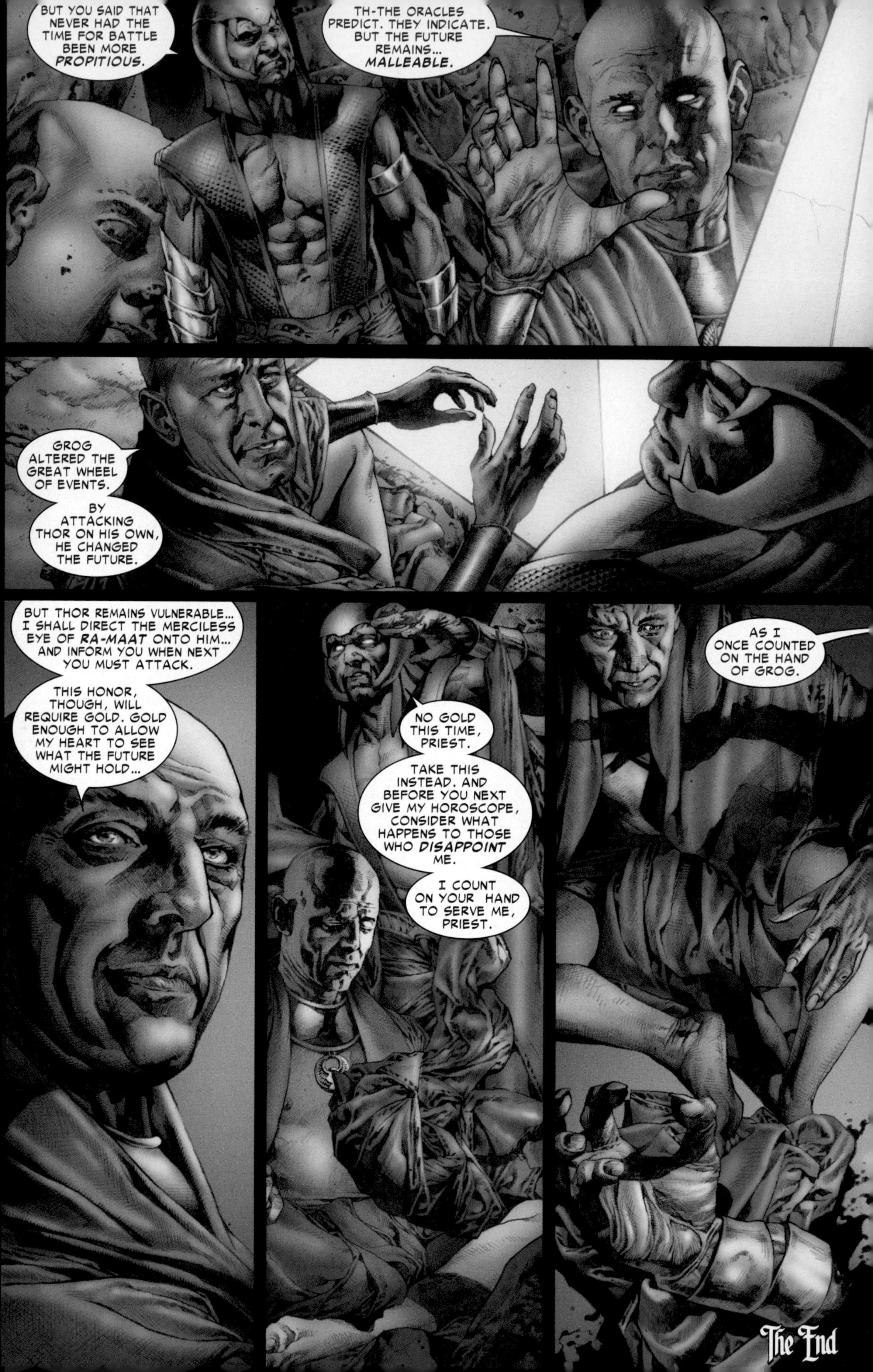

BUT YOU SAID THAT NEVER HAD THE TIME FOR BATTLE BEEN MORE *PROPITIOUS*.
TH-THE ORACLES PREDICT. THEY INDICATE. BUT THE FUTURE REMAINS... *MALLEABLE*.
GROG ALTERED THE GREAT WHEEL OF EVENTS.
BY ATTACKING THOR ON HIS OWN, HE CHANGED THE FUTURE.
BUT THOR REMAINS VULNERABLE... I SHALL DIRECT THE MERCILESS EYE OF *RA-MAAT* ONTO HIM... AND INFORM YOU WHEN NEXT YOU MUST ATTACK.
THIS HONOR, THOUGH, WILL REQUIRE GOLD. GOLD ENOUGH TO ALLOW MY HEART TO SEE WHAT THE FUTURE MIGHT HOLD...
NO GOLD THIS TIME, PRIEST.
TAKE THIS INSTEAD. AND BEFORE YOU NEXT GIVE MY HOROSCOPE, CONSIDER WHAT HAPPENS TO THOSE WHO *DISAPPOINT* ME.
I COUNT ON YOUR HAND TO SERVE ME, PRIEST.
AS I ONCE COUNTED ON THE HAND OF GROG.
The End

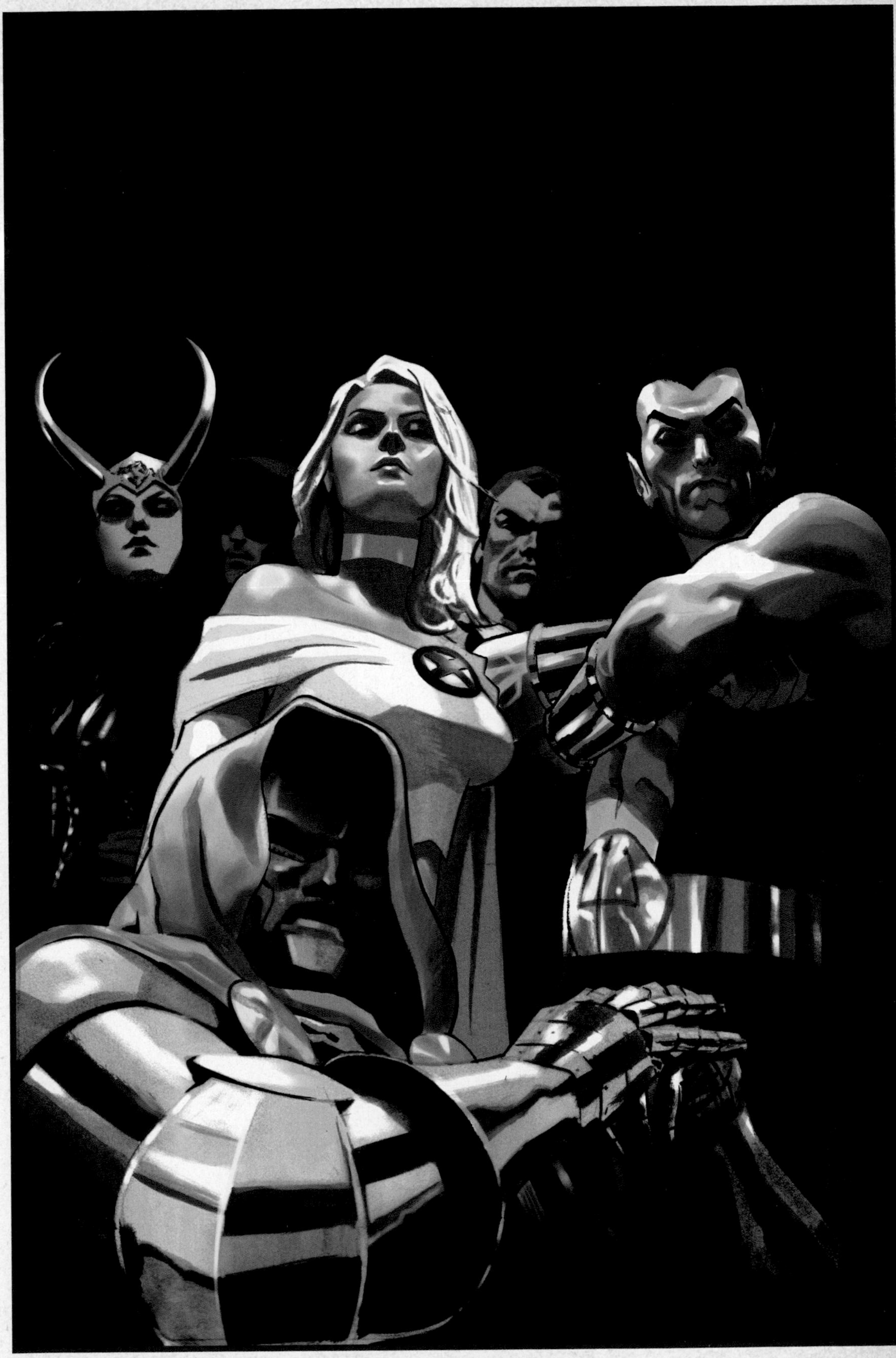

DARK REIGN: THE CABAL

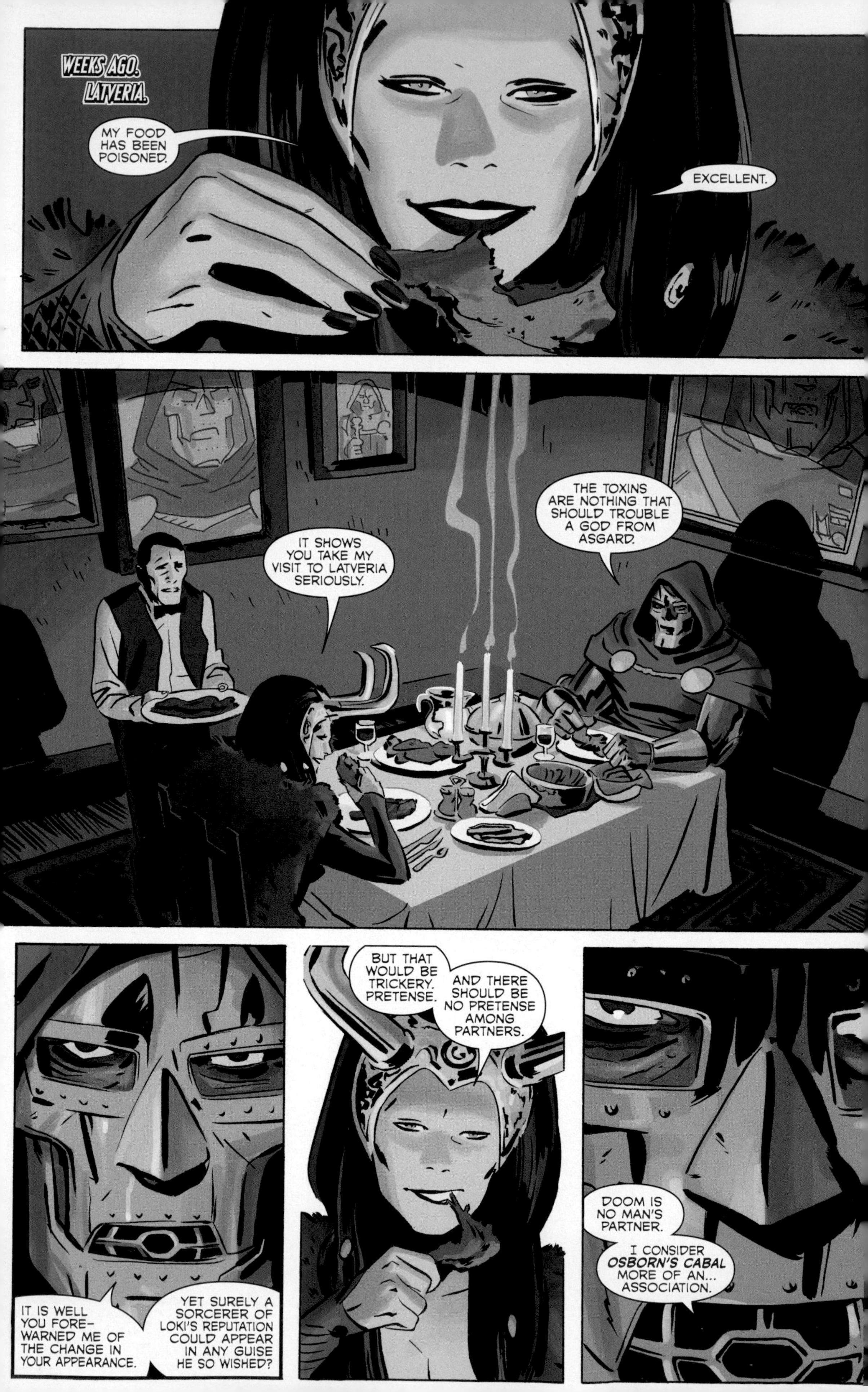
WEEKS AGO. LATVERIA.
MY FOOD HAS BEEN POISONED.
EXCELLENT.
IT SHOWS YOU TAKE MY VISIT TO LATVERIA SERIOUSLY.
THE TOXINS ARE NOTHING THAT SHOULD TROUBLE A GOD FROM ASGARD.
IT IS WELL YOU FORE-WARNED ME OF THE CHANGE IN YOUR APPEARANCE.
YET SURELY A SORCERER OF LOKI'S REPUTATION COULD APPEAR IN ANY GUISE HE SO WISHED?
BUT THAT WOULD BE TRICKERY. PRETENSE.
AND THERE SHOULD BE NO PRETENSE AMONG PARTNERS.
DOOM IS NO MAN'S PARTNER.
I CONSIDER OSBORN'S CABAL MORE OF AN... ASSOCIATION.

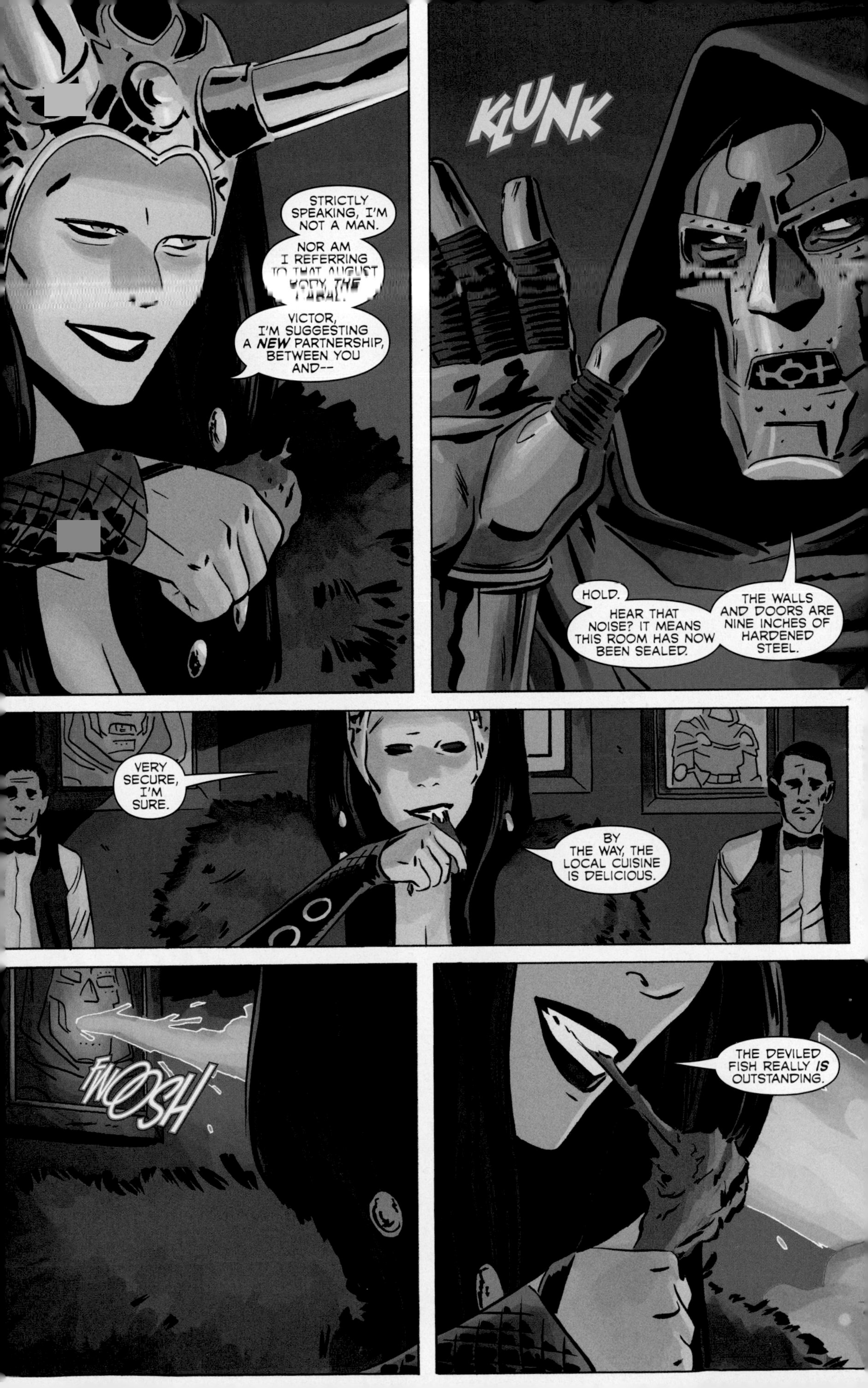
STRICTLY SPEAKING, I'M NOT A MAN.
NOR AM I REFERRING TO THAT AUGUST
VICTOR, I'M SUGGESTING A ***NEW*** PARTNERSHIP, BETWEEN YOU AND--
KLUNK
HOLD.
HEAR THAT NOISE? IT MEANS THIS ROOM HAS NOW BEEN SEALED.
THE WALLS AND DOORS ARE NINE INCHES OF HARDENED STEEL.
VERY SECURE, I'M SURE.
BY THE WAY, THE LOCAL CUISINE IS DELICIOUS.
FWOOSH
THE DEVILED FISH REALLY ***IS*** OUTSTANDING.

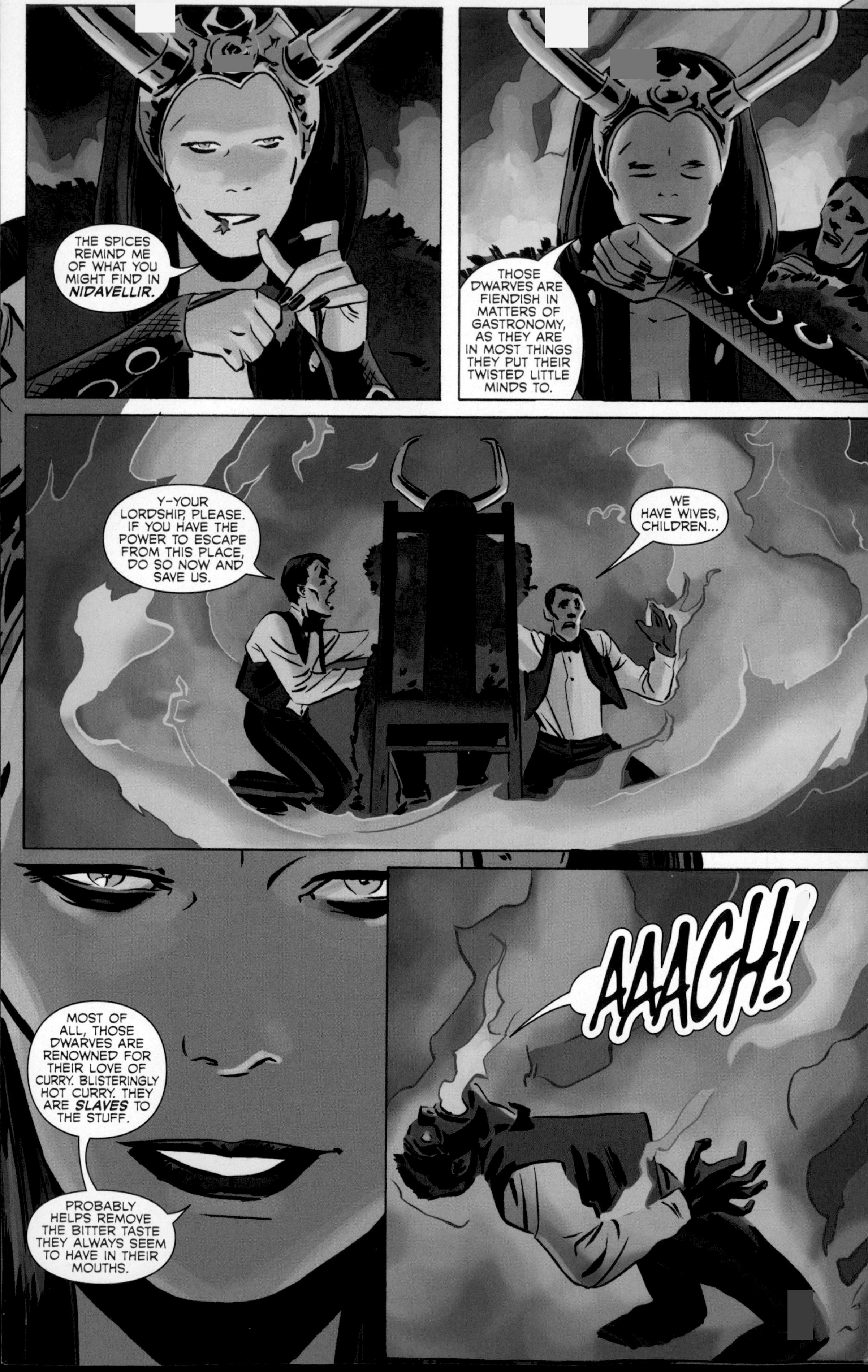
THE SPICES REMIND ME OF WHAT YOU MIGHT FIND IN NIDAVELLIR.
THOSE DWARVES ARE FIENDISH IN MATTERS OF GASTRONOMY, AS THEY ARE IN MOST THINGS THEY PUT THEIR TWISTED LITTLE MINDS TO.
Y-YOUR LORDSHIP, PLEASE. IF YOU HAVE THE POWER TO ESCAPE FROM THIS PLACE, DO SO NOW AND SAVE US.
WE HAVE WIVES, CHILDREN...
MOST OF ALL, THOSE DWARVES ARE RENOWNED FOR THEIR LOVE OF CURRY. BLISTERINGLY HOT CURRY. THEY ARE SLAVES TO THE STUFF.
PROBABLY HELPS REMOVE THE BITTER TASTE THEY ALWAYS SEEM TO HAVE IN THEIR MOUTHS.
AAAGH!

Hmm.

WELL, DON'T MIND ME.

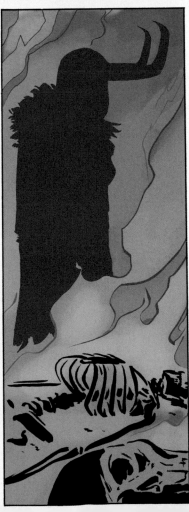

I'M **USED** TO TALKING TO MYSELF.

I PRESUME YOU'RE WATCHING THIS, DOOM.

ARE YOU **CONVINCED** YET?

AN IMMUNITY TO POISON AND PAIN. A CALLOUS DISREGARD FOR HUMAN LIFE.

I AM WILLING TO CONCEDE THAT YOU ARE LOKI. MAKE YOUR WAY THROUGH THE LOCKED DOOR.

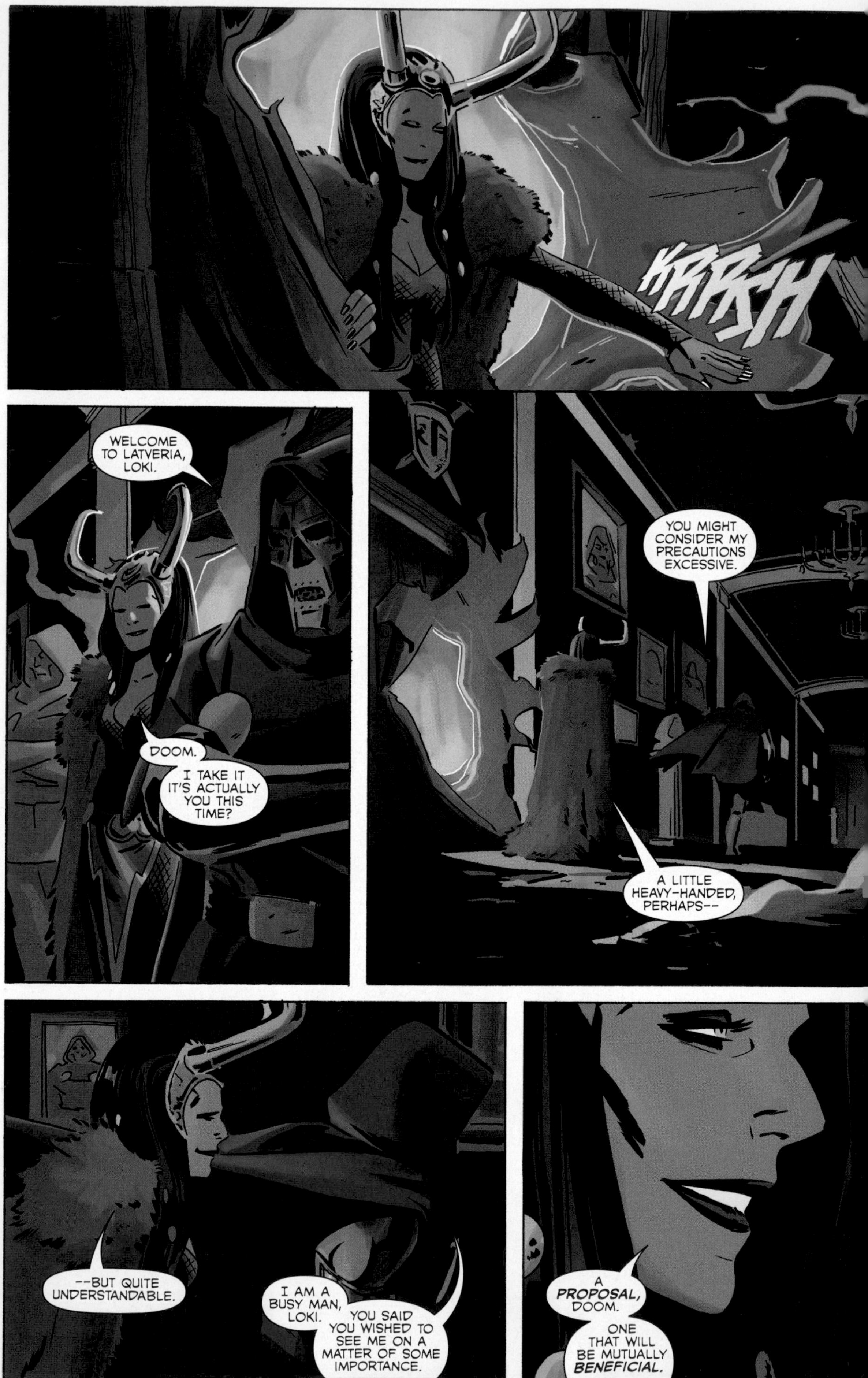
KRRSH
WELCOME TO LATVERIA, LOKI.
DOOM.
I TAKE IT IT'S ACTUALLY YOU THIS TIME?
YOU MIGHT CONSIDER MY PRECAUTIONS EXCESSIVE.
A LITTLE HEAVY-HANDED, PERHAPS--
--BUT QUITE UNDERSTANDABLE.
I AM A BUSY MAN, LOKI.
YOU SAID YOU WISHED TO SEE ME ON A MATTER OF SOME IMPORTANCE.
A *PROPOSAL,* DOOM.
ONE THAT WILL BE MUTUALLY *BENEFICIAL.*

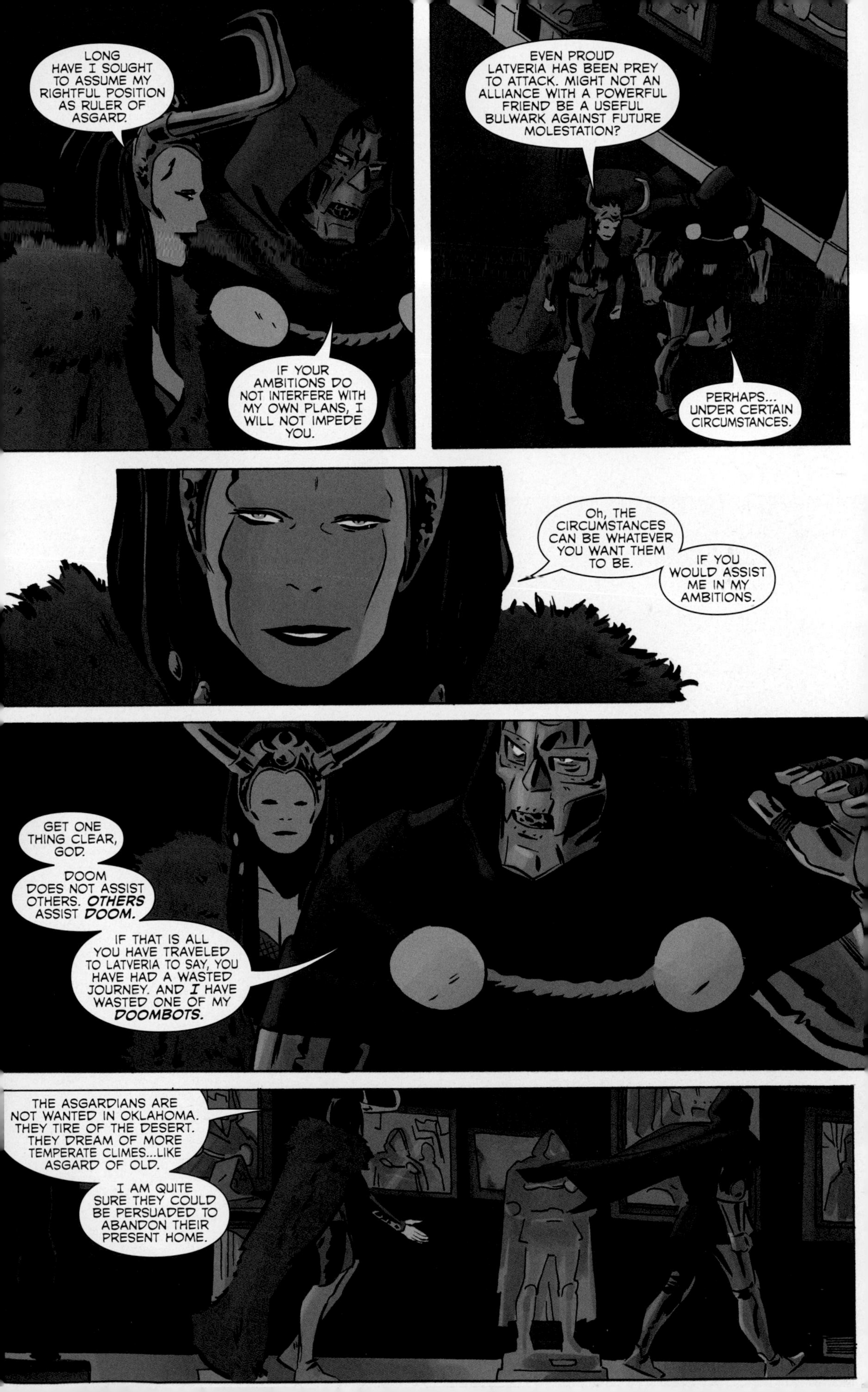
LONG HAVE I SOUGHT TO ASSUME MY RIGHTFUL POSITION AS RULER OF ASGARD.
IF YOUR AMBITIONS DO NOT INTERFERE WITH MY OWN PLANS, I WILL NOT IMPEDE YOU.
EVEN PROUD LATVERIA HAS BEEN PREY TO ATTACK. MIGHT NOT AN ALLIANCE WITH A POWERFUL FRIEND BE A USEFUL BULWARK AGAINST FUTURE MOLESTATION?
PERHAPS... UNDER CERTAIN CIRCUMSTANCES.
Oh, THE CIRCUMSTANCES CAN BE WHATEVER YOU WANT THEM TO BE.
IF YOU WOULD ASSIST ME IN MY AMBITIONS.
GET ONE THING CLEAR, GOD.
DOOM DOES NOT ASSIST OTHERS. *OTHERS* ASSIST *DOOM.*
IF THAT IS ALL YOU HAVE TRAVELED TO LATVERIA TO SAY, YOU HAVE HAD A WASTED JOURNEY. AND *I* HAVE WASTED ONE OF MY *DOOMBOTS.*
THE ASGARDIANS ARE NOT WANTED IN OKLAHOMA. THEY TIRE OF THE DESERT. THEY DREAM OF MORE TEMPERATE CLIMES...LIKE ASGARD OF OLD.
I AM QUITE SURE THEY COULD BE PERSUADED TO ABANDON THEIR PRESENT HOME.

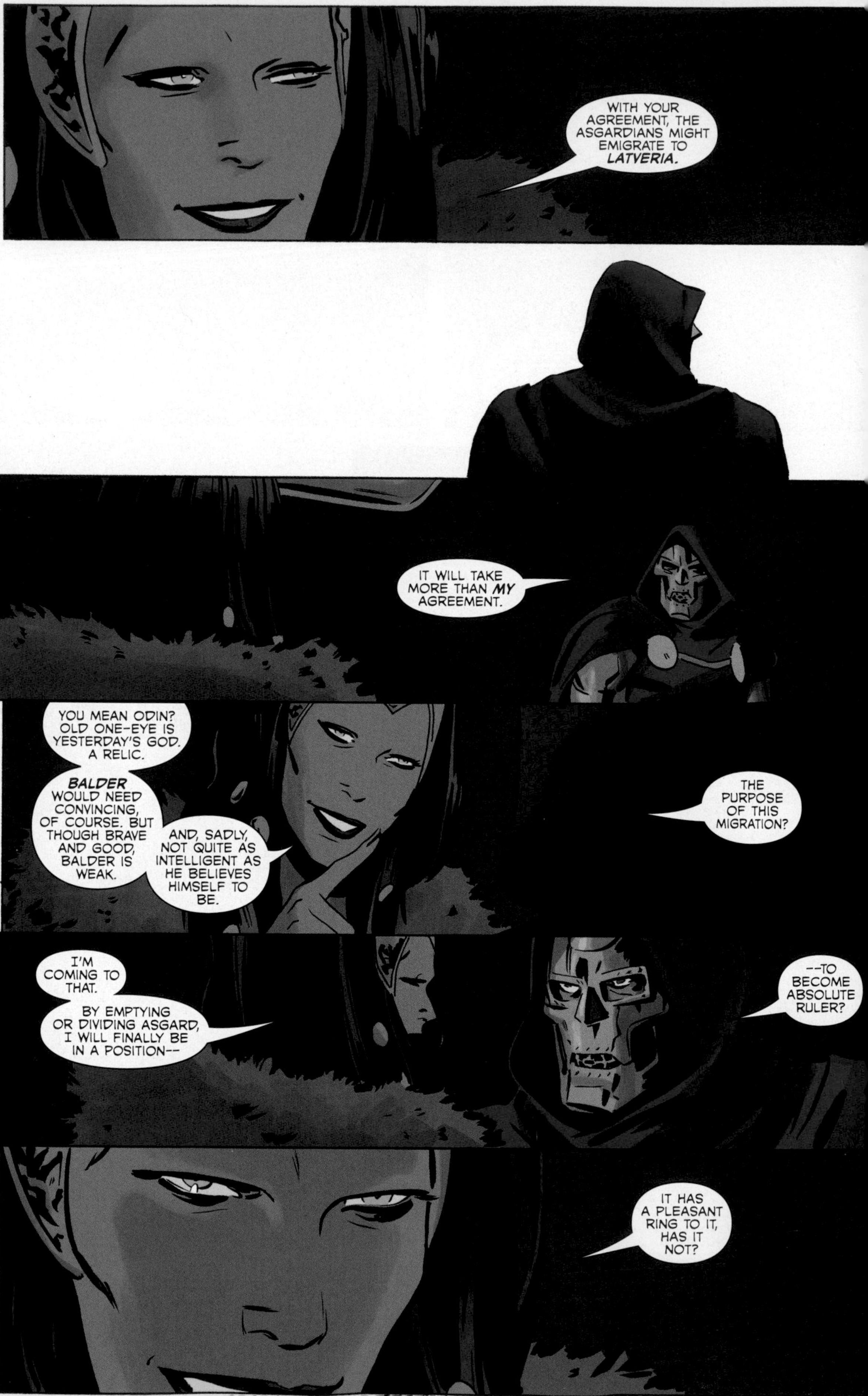
WITH YOUR AGREEMENT, THE ASGARDIANS MIGHT EMIGRATE TO LATVERIA.
IT WILL TAKE MORE THAN MY AGREEMENT.
YOU MEAN ODIN? OLD ONE-EYE IS YESTERDAY'S GOD. A RELIC.
BALDER WOULD NEED CONVINCING, OF COURSE. BUT THOUGH BRAVE AND GOOD, BALDER IS WEAK.
AND, SADLY, NOT QUITE AS INTELLIGENT AS HE BELIEVES HIMSELF TO BE.
THE PURPOSE OF THIS MIGRATION?
I'M COMING TO THAT.
BY EMPTYING OR DIVIDING ASGARD, I WILL FINALLY BE IN A POSITION--
--TO BECOME ABSOLUTE RULER?
IT HAS A PLEASANT RING TO IT, HAS IT NOT?

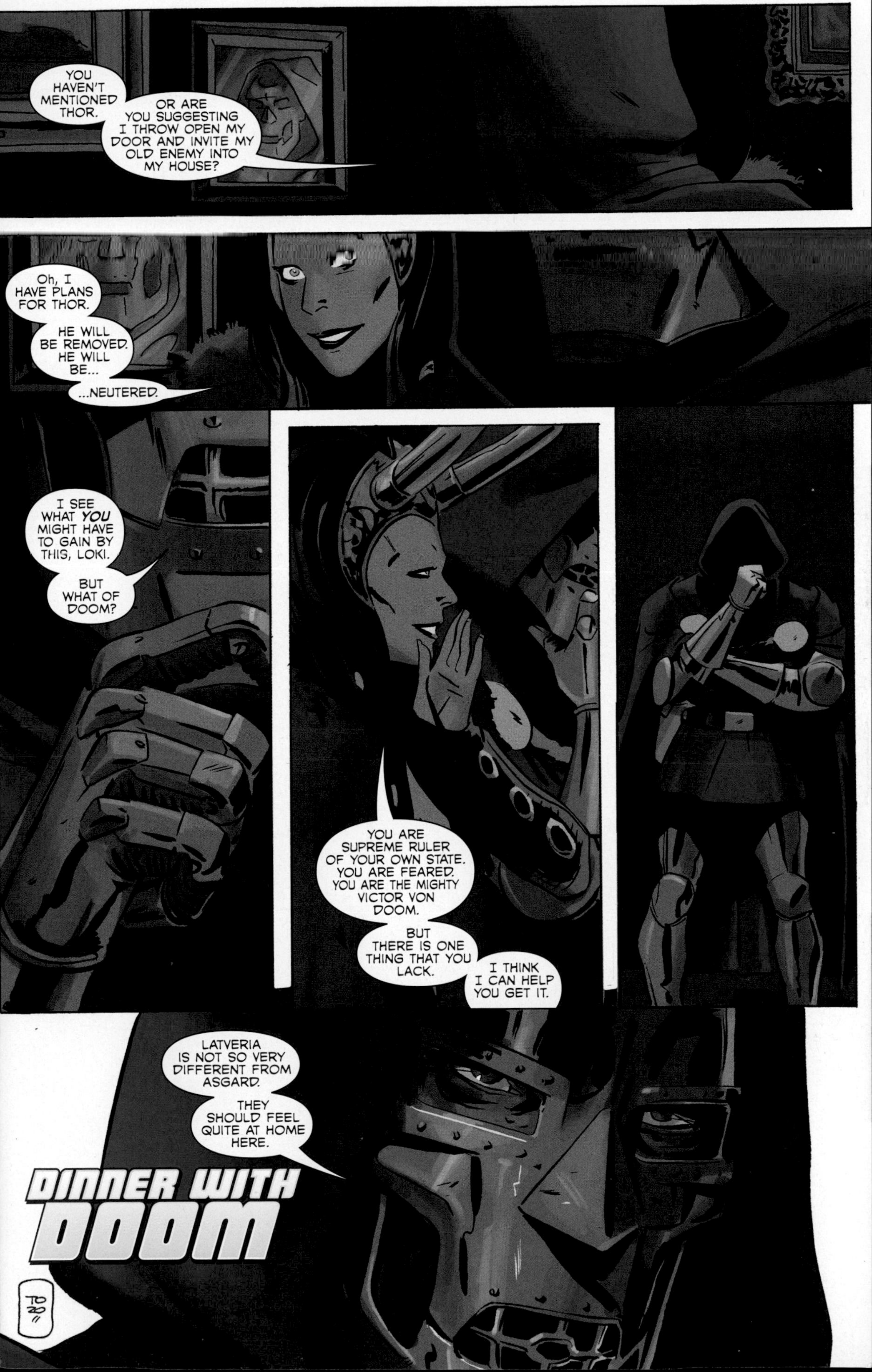
YOU HAVEN'T MENTIONED THOR.
OR ARE YOU SUGGESTING I THROW OPEN MY DOOR AND INVITE MY OLD ENEMY INTO MY HOUSE?
Oh, I HAVE PLANS FOR THOR.
HE WILL BE REMOVED. HE WILL BE...
...NEUTERED.
I SEE WHAT *YOU* MIGHT HAVE TO GAIN BY THIS, LOKI.
BUT WHAT OF DOOM?
YOU ARE SUPREME RULER OF YOUR OWN STATE. YOU ARE FEARED. YOU ARE THE MIGHTY VICTOR VON DOOM.
BUT THERE IS ONE THING THAT YOU LACK.
I THINK I CAN HELP YOU GET IT.
LATVERIA IS NOT SO VERY DIFFERENT FROM ASGARD.
THEY SHOULD FEEL QUITE AT HOME HERE.
DINNER WITH DOOM

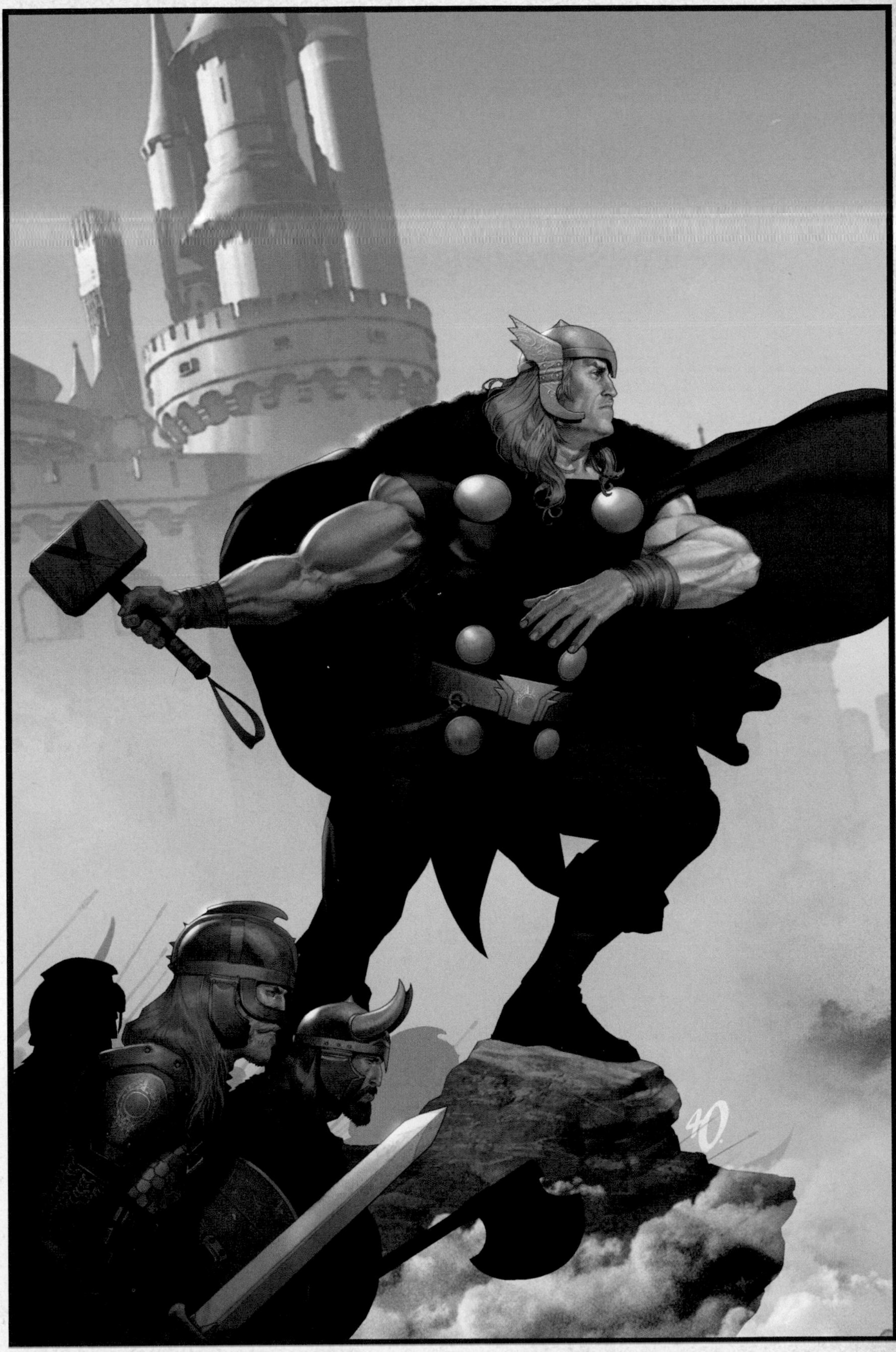

THOR: HEAVEN & EARTH #1

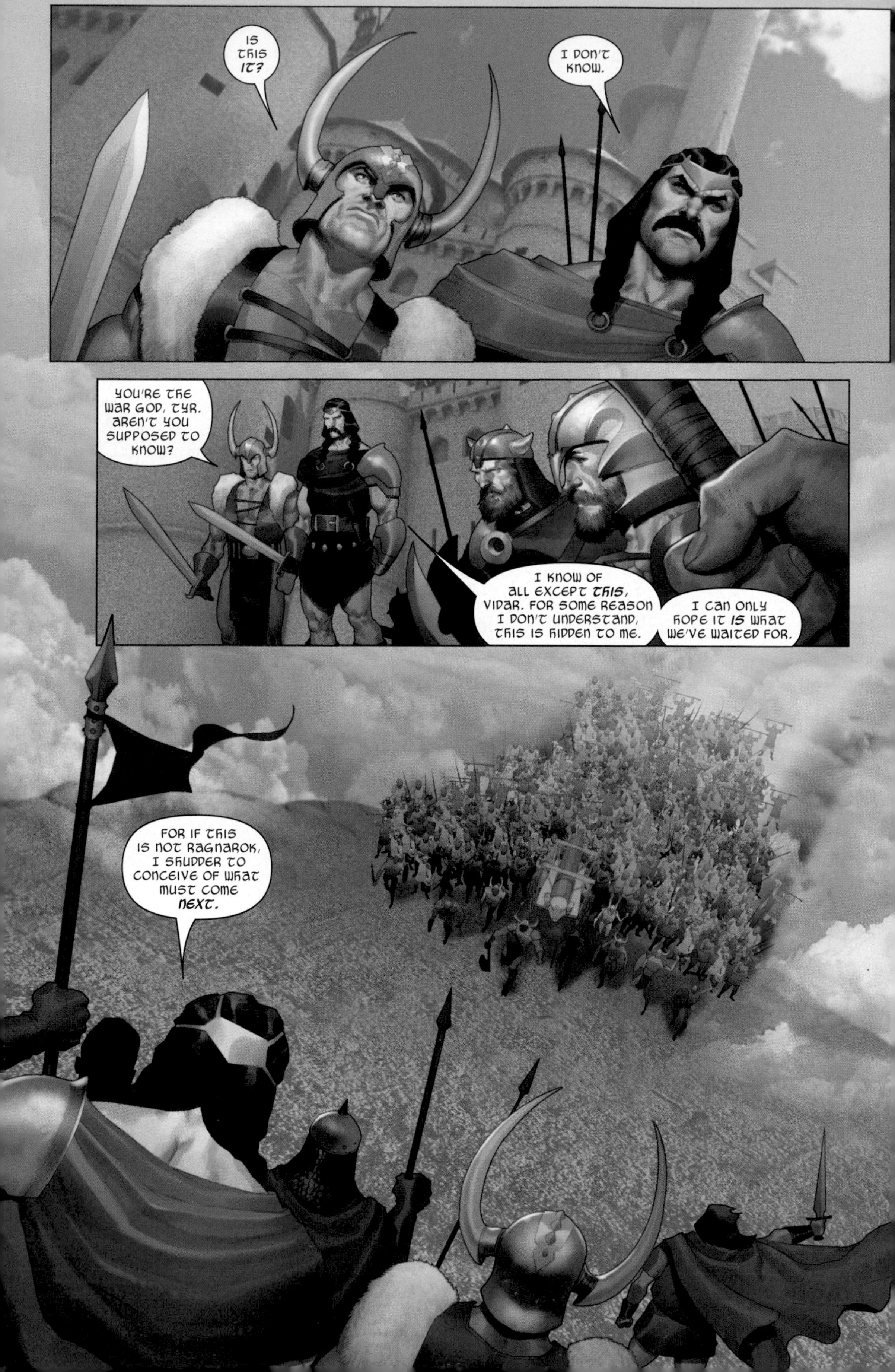
IS THIS IT?
I DON'T KNOW.
YOU'RE THE WAR GOD, TYR. AREN'T YOU SUPPOSED TO KNOW?
I KNOW OF ALL EXCEPT THIS, VIDAR. FOR SOME REASON I DON'T UNDERSTAND, THIS IS HIDDEN TO ME.
I CAN ONLY HOPE IT IS WHAT WE'VE WAITED FOR.
FOR IF THIS IS NOT RAGNAROK, I SHUDDER TO CONCEIVE OF WHAT MUST COME NEXT.

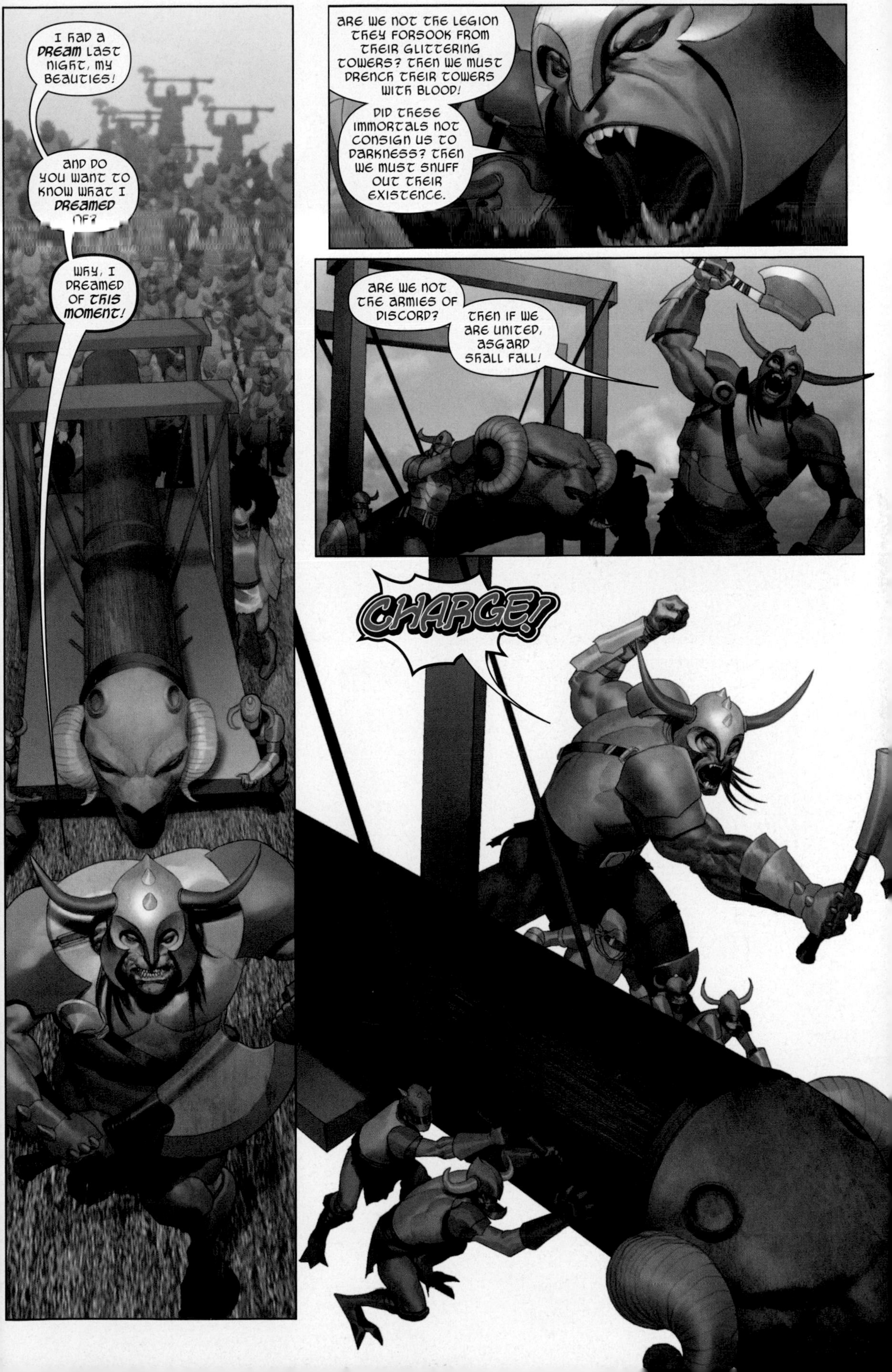
I HAD A DREAM LAST NIGHT, MY BEAUTIES!
AND DO YOU WANT TO KNOW WHAT I DREAMED OF?
WHY, I DREAMED OF THIS MOMENT!
ARE WE NOT THE LEGION THEY FORSOOK FROM THEIR GLITTERING TOWERS? THEN WE MUST DRENCH THEIR TOWERS WITH BLOOD!
DID THESE IMMORTALS NOT CONSIGN US TO DARKNESS? THEN WE MUST SNUFF OUT THEIR EXISTENCE.
ARE WE NOT THE ARMIES OF DISCORD?
THEN IF WE ARE UNITED, ASGARD SHALL FALL!
CHARGE!

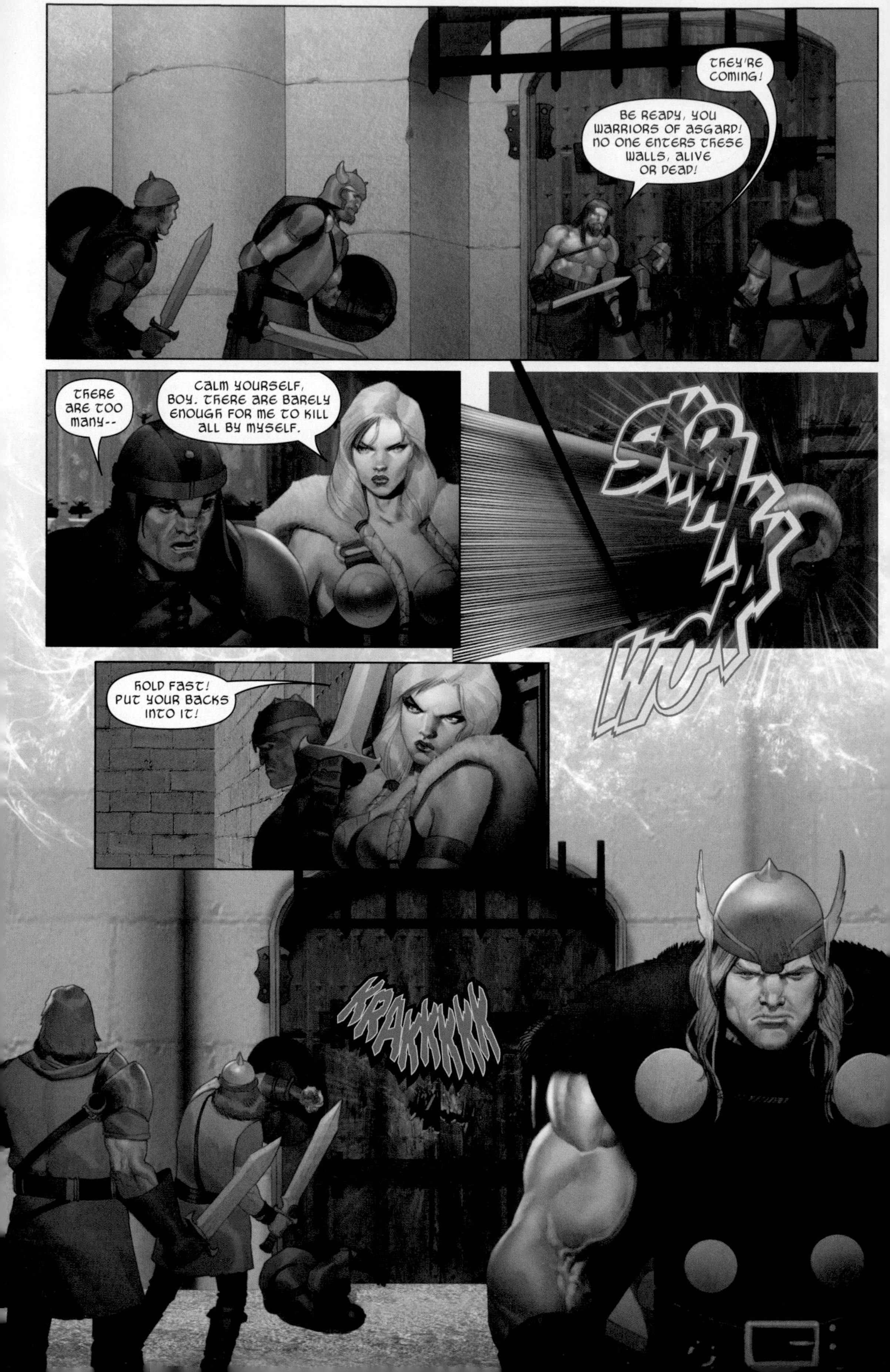
THEY'RE COMING!
BE READY, YOU WARRIORS OF ASGARD! NO ONE ENTERS THESE WALLS, ALIVE OR DEAD!
THERE ARE TOO MANY--
CALM YOURSELF, BOY. THERE ARE BARELY ENOUGH FOR ME TO KILL ALL BY MYSELF.
HOLD FAST! PUT YOUR BACKS INTO IT!
KRAKKKKK

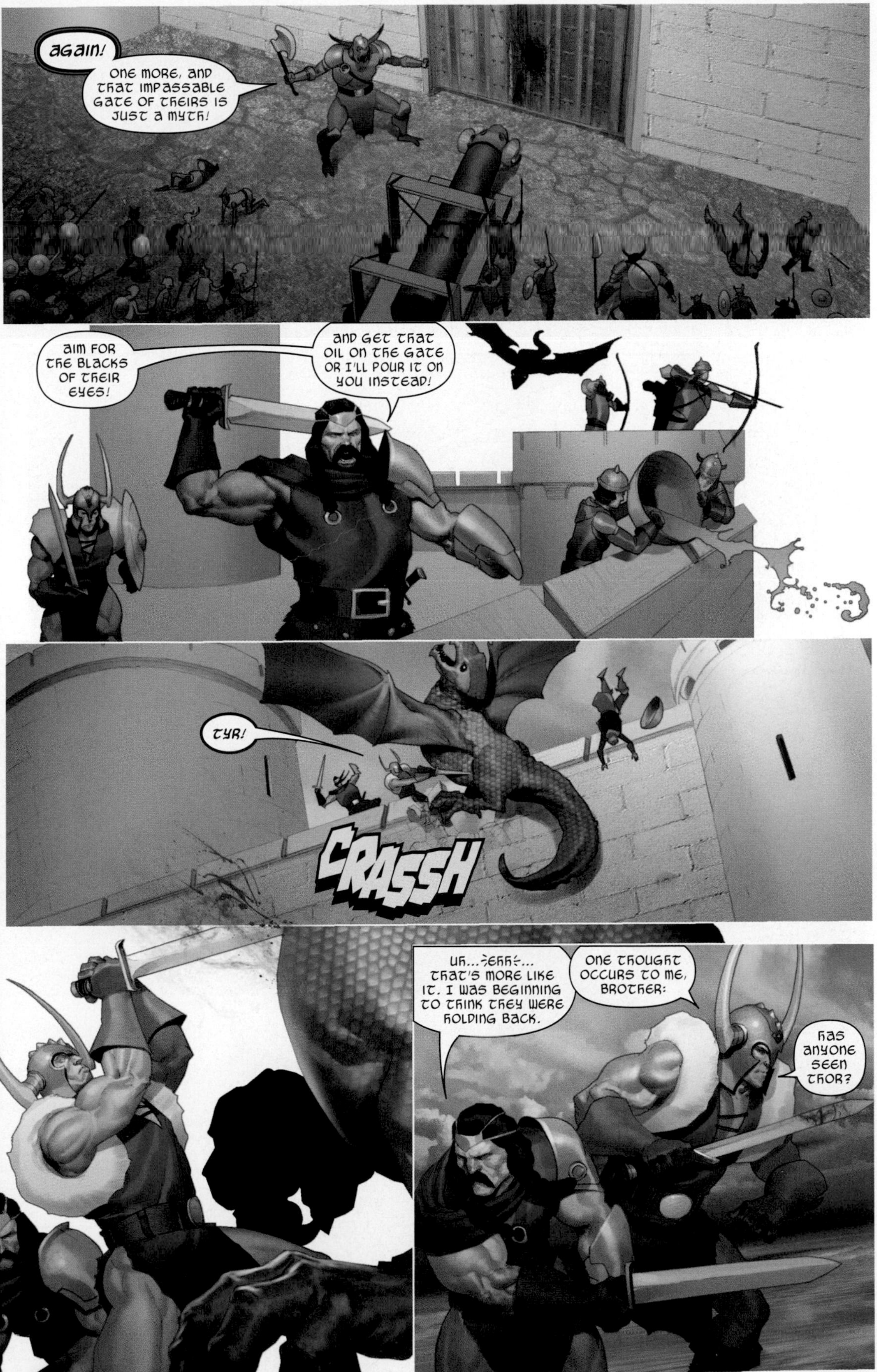
AGAIN!
ONE MORE, AND THAT IMPASSABLE GATE OF THEIRS IS JUST A MYTH!
AIM FOR THE BLACKS OF THEIR EYES!
AND GET THAT OIL ON THE GATE OR I'LL POUR IT ON YOU INSTEAD!
TYR!
CRASSH
UH... EHH... THAT'S MORE LIKE IT. I WAS BEGINNING TO THINK THEY WERE HOLDING BACK.
ONE THOUGHT OCCURS TO ME, BROTHER:
HAS ANYONE SEEN THOR?

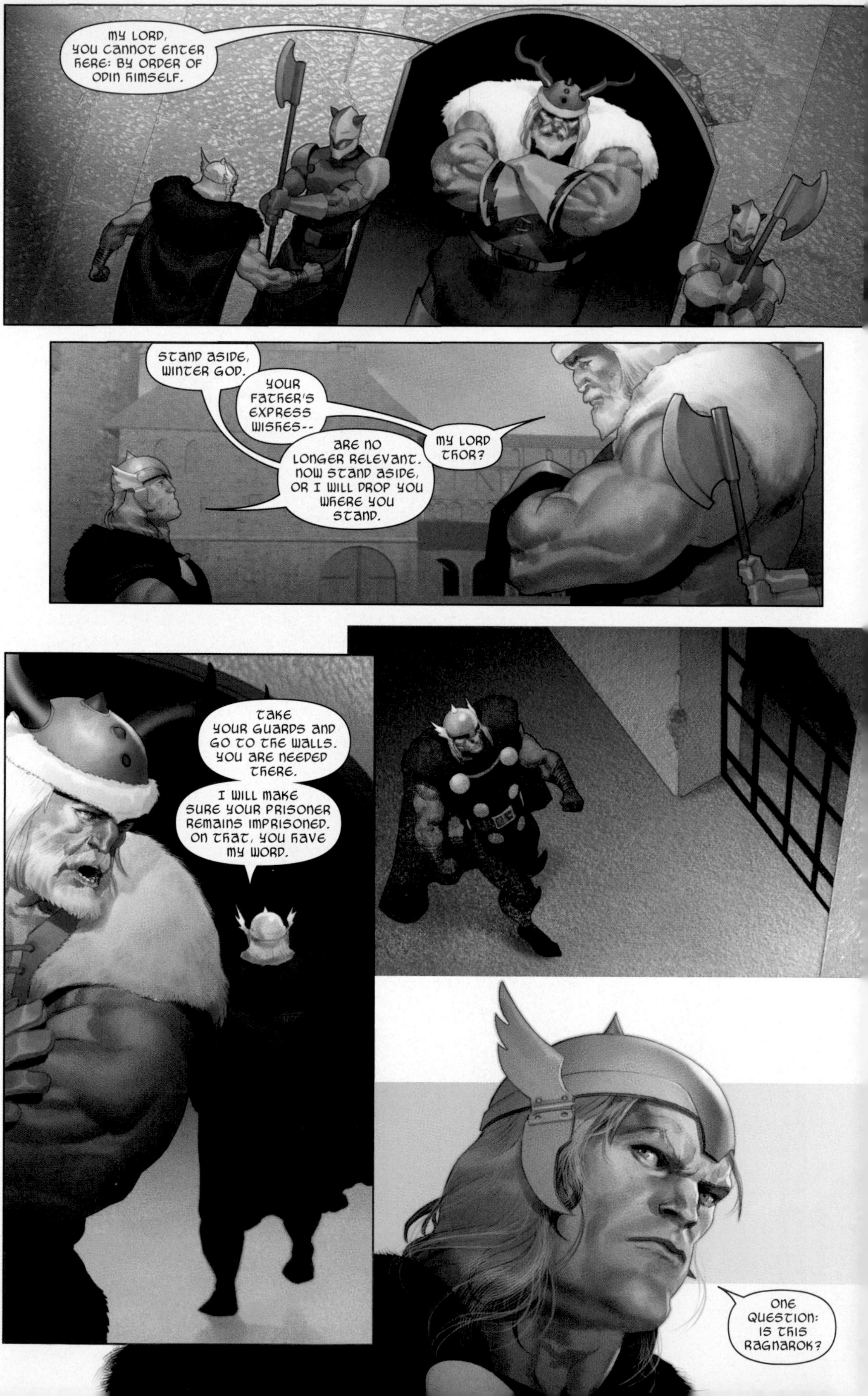
MY LORD, YOU CANNOT ENTER HERE: BY ORDER OF ODIN HIMSELF.
STAND ASIDE, WINTER GOD.
YOUR FATHER'S EXPRESS WISHES--
ARE NO LONGER RELEVANT. NOW STAND ASIDE, OR I WILL DROP YOU WHERE YOU STAND.
MY LORD THOR?
TAKE YOUR GUARDS AND GO TO THE WALLS. YOU ARE NEEDED THERE.
I WILL MAKE SURE YOUR PRISONER REMAINS IMPRISONED. ON THAT, YOU HAVE MY WORD.
ONE QUESTION: IS THIS RAGNAROK?

THE DAY BEFORE WINTER
BROTHER DEAREST.
I DON'T THINK YOU'D BELIEVE ME NO MATTER WHAT MY ANSWER.

OF COURSE, IF YOU WERE TO SEE YOUR WAY TO UNTYING THESE BINDINGS I MIGHT BE PERSUADED TO *TALK.* AS LONG AS WE BOTH AGREE WHATEVER I SAY IS PROBABLY A *LIE.*

BUT SINCE LIES SERVE TO ILLUMINATE THE TRUTH, MAYBE YOU CAN FIGURE IT OUT FOR YOURSELF.

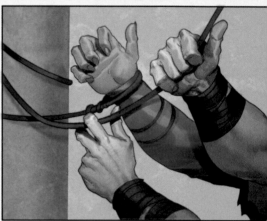

I HOPED YOU'D COME TO YOUR SENSES, THOR. WE ARE ABOUT TO ENDURE THE INEVITABLE. YOU MAY AS WELL BE ON MY SIDE WHEN IT COMES.

THOUGH THIS IS NOT RAGNAROK. IF IT WERE, I WOULD BE THE ONE OUTSIDE THE GATES, KNOCKING TO COME IN.

THIS IS JUST A TEST OF ASGARD'S DEFENSES--

BLUK

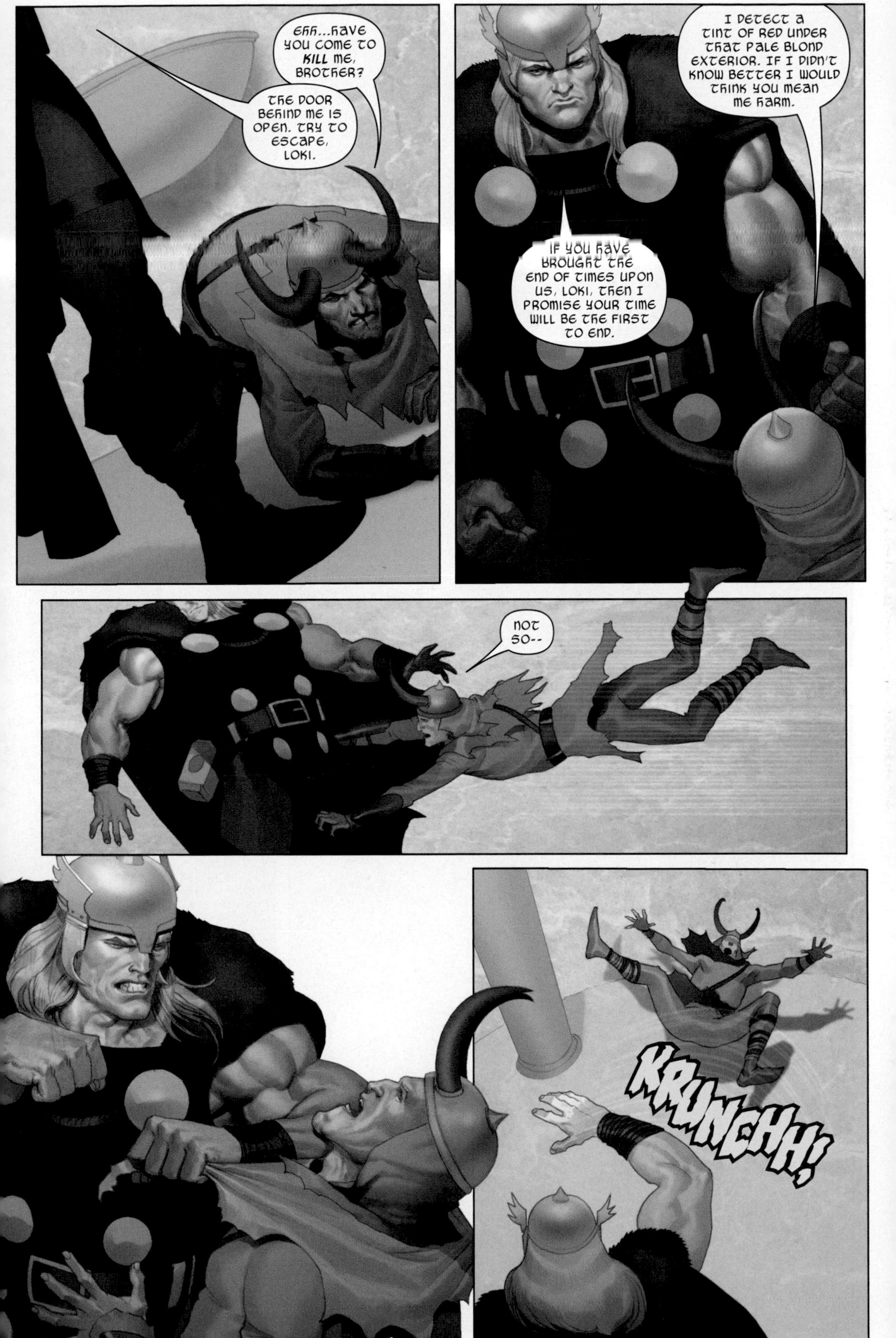

EHH...HAVE YOU COME TO KILL ME, BROTHER?
THE DOOR BEHIND ME IS OPEN. TRY TO ESCAPE, LOKI.
I DETECT A TINT OF RED UNDER THAT PALE BLOND EXTERIOR. IF I DIDN'T KNOW BETTER I WOULD THINK YOU MEAN ME HARM.
IF YOU HAVE BROUGHT THE END OF TIMES UPON US, LOKI, THEN I PROMISE YOUR TIME WILL BE THE FIRST TO END.
NOT SO--
KRUNCHH!

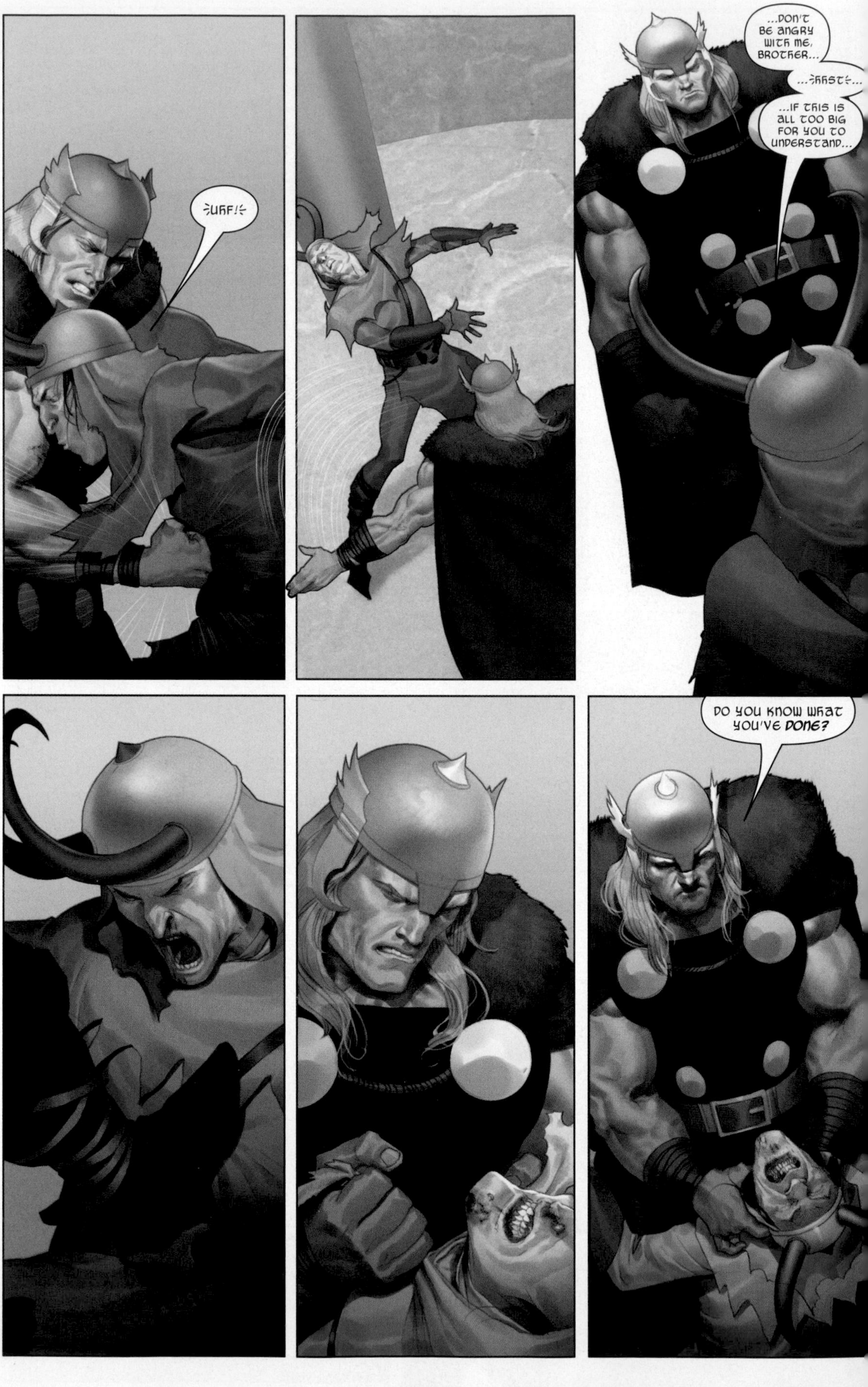
UHF!
...DON'T BE ANGRY WITH ME, BROTHER...
...HHST...
...IF THIS IS ALL TOO BIG FOR YOU TO UNDERSTAND...
DO YOU KNOW WHAT YOU'VE DONE?

I HAVEN'T DONE ANYTHING. YOU'RE JUST UPSET BECAUSE OF WHAT SOME GRUDGE-BEARING OLD HAG SAYS I'M *GOING* TO DO.

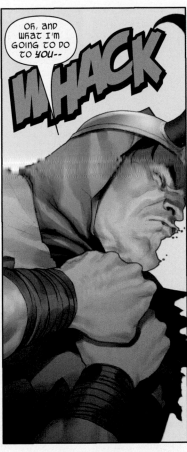

OH, AND WHAT I'M GOING TO DO TO *YOU*--

WHACK

I HAVE THOUGHT LONG ON THOSE PROPHECIES, BROTHER: THAT YOU WOULD BRING ABOUT THE END OF TIMES; THAT YOU MUST ONE DAY LEAD THE ARMIES OF DISCORD AGAINST ASGARD.

WHAT SAY WE TEST THE STRENGTH OF THE PROPHECY HERE BY ENDING IT BEFORE IT BEGINS?

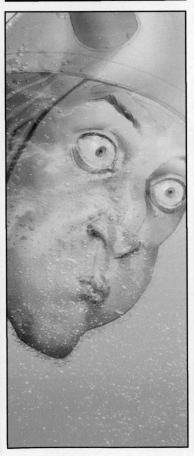

A-AHH!

IS IT THE END OF TIMES THAT UPSETS YOU?

OR DOES IT SCARE YOU THAT JUST FOR ONCE I MIGHT BE TELLING THE *TRUTH*?

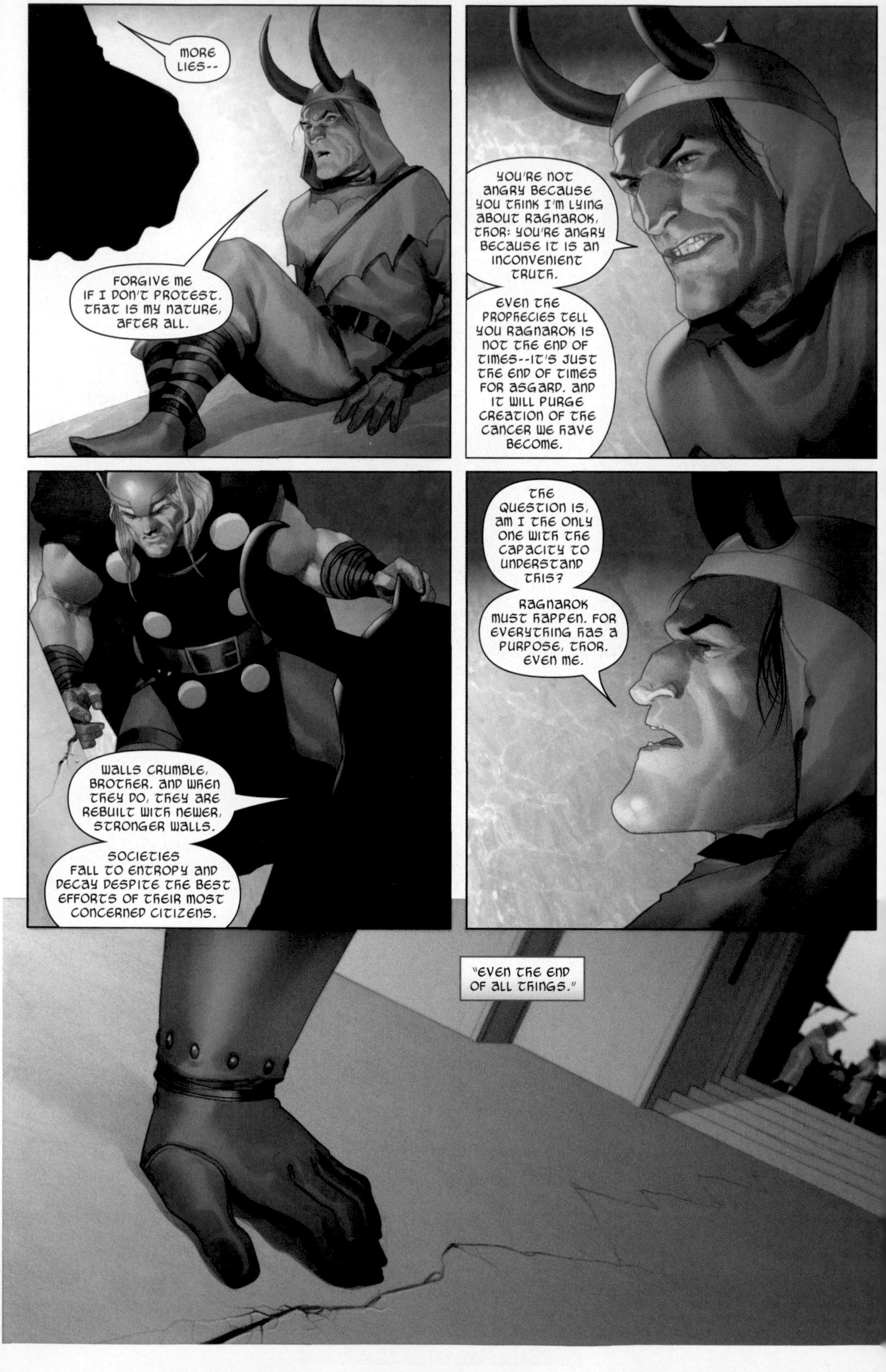
MORE LIES--
FORGIVE ME IF I DON'T PROTEST. THAT IS MY NATURE, AFTER ALL.
YOU'RE NOT ANGRY BECAUSE YOU THINK I'M LYING ABOUT RAGNAROK, THOR: YOU'RE ANGRY BECAUSE IT IS AN INCONVENIENT TRUTH.
EVEN THE PROPHECIES TELL YOU RAGNAROK IS NOT THE END OF TIMES--IT'S JUST THE END OF TIMES FOR ASGARD. AND IT WILL PURGE CREATION OF THE CANCER WE HAVE BECOME.
WALLS CRUMBLE, BROTHER. AND WHEN THEY DO, THEY ARE REBUILT WITH NEWER, STRONGER WALLS.
SOCIETIES FALL TO ENTROPY AND DECAY DESPITE THE BEST EFFORTS OF THEIR MOST CONCERNED CITIZENS.
THE QUESTION IS, AM I THE ONLY ONE WITH THE CAPACITY TO UNDERSTAND THIS?
RAGNAROK MUST HAPPEN. FOR EVERYTHING HAS A PURPOSE, THOR. EVEN ME.
"EVEN THE END OF ALL THINGS."

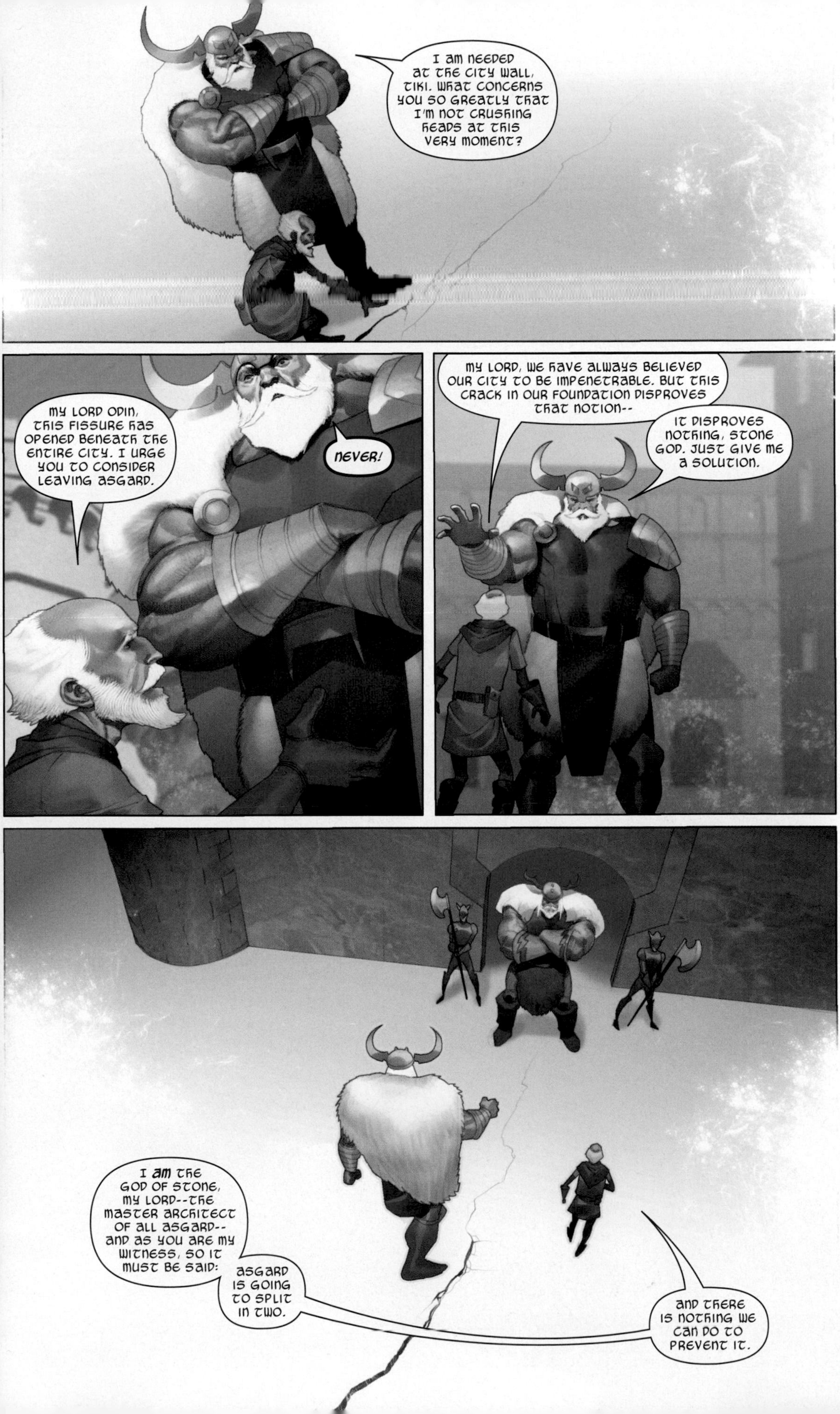
I AM NEEDED AT THE CITY WALL, TIKI. WHAT CONCERNS YOU SO GREATLY THAT I'M NOT CRUSHING HEADS AT THIS VERY MOMENT?
MY LORD ODIN, THIS FISSURE HAS OPENED BENEATH THE ENTIRE CITY. I URGE YOU TO CONSIDER LEAVING ASGARD.
NEVER!
MY LORD, WE HAVE ALWAYS BELIEVED OUR CITY TO BE IMPENETRABLE. BUT THIS CRACK IN OUR FOUNDATION DISPROVES THAT NOTION--
IT DISPROVES NOTHING, STONE GOD. JUST GIVE ME A SOLUTION.
I AM THE GOD OF STONE, MY LORD--THE MASTER ARCHITECT OF ALL ASGARD--AND AS YOU ARE MY WITNESS, SO IT MUST BE SAID:
ASGARD IS GOING TO SPLIT IN TWO.
AND THERE IS NOTHING WE CAN DO TO PREVENT IT.

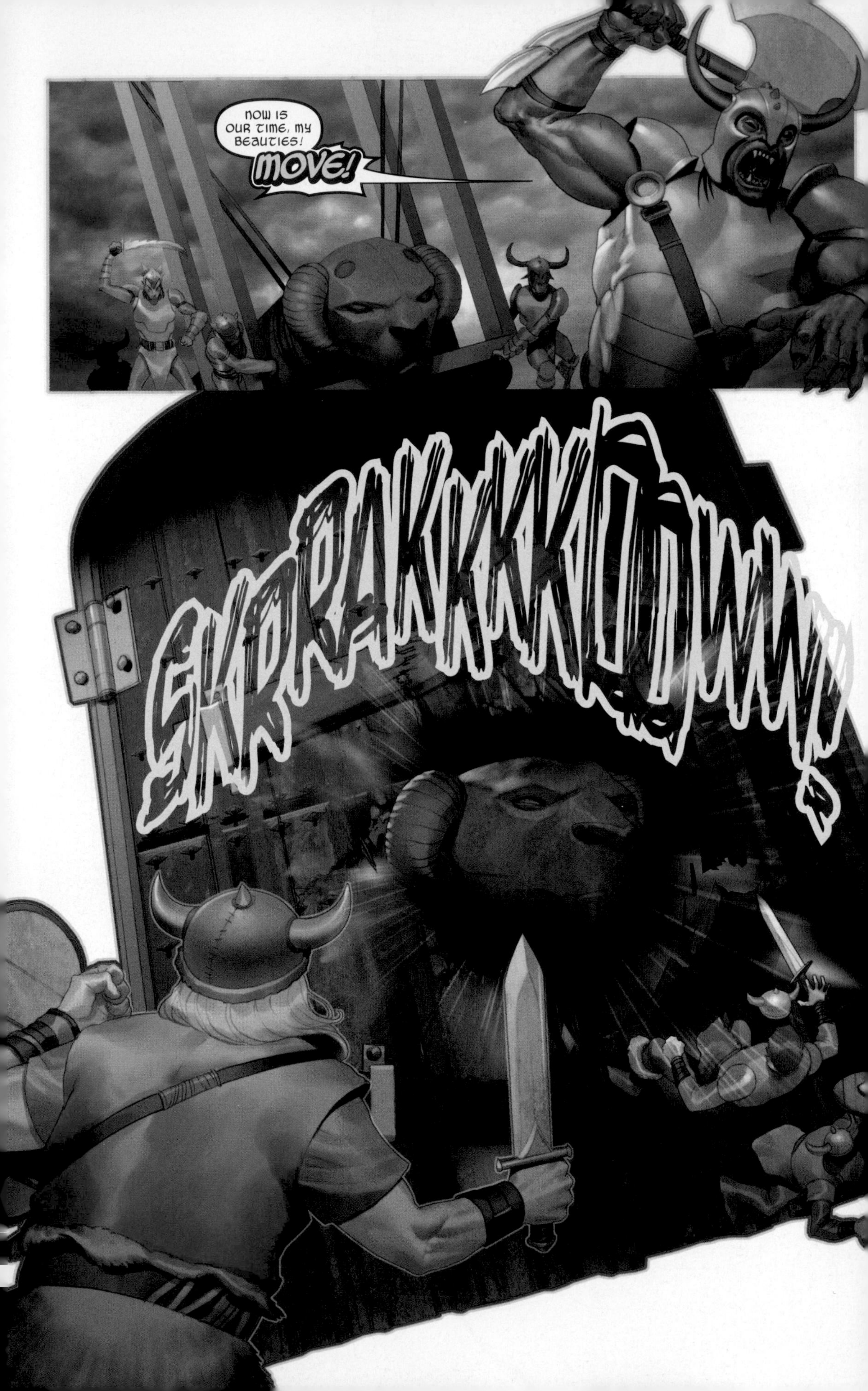
NOW IS OUR TIME, MY BEAUTIES!
MOVE!

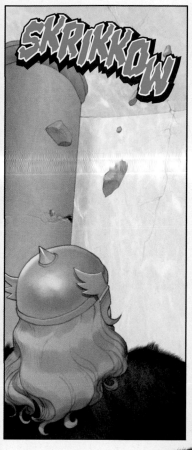

SKRIKKOW

THIS ATTACK ON ASGARD IS NOT THE END. NEITHER WILL RAGNAROK BE. IT'S JUST THE DESTINY OF MAN AND GOD ALIKE.

ALL THAT LIVE MUST DIE... AND ALL THAT DIE SHALL LIVE.

A LIAR I MAY BE. BUT I'D RATHER BE A LIAR THAN ONE WHO REFUSES TO LISTEN TO THE TRUTH.

AND WHAT ABOUT YOU? WHAT WOULD YOU BE?

YOU SAY THIS MURDEROUS INSANITY HAS A PURPOSE, LOKI. BUT AS EVER, YOUR CLAIMS SEEM REASONABLE UNTIL WE STAND AT THE CENTER OF THE DEBRIS AND WONDER HOW WE ARRIVED.

NO GOOD CAN COME OF ASGARD'S FALL, AS NO GOOD CAN COME OF YOUR INCESSANT LIES.

AND WHAT IF I PROVED THAT SOME GOOD COULD COME OF LIES?

WOULD THAT SWAY YOUR MIND ON RAGNAROK?

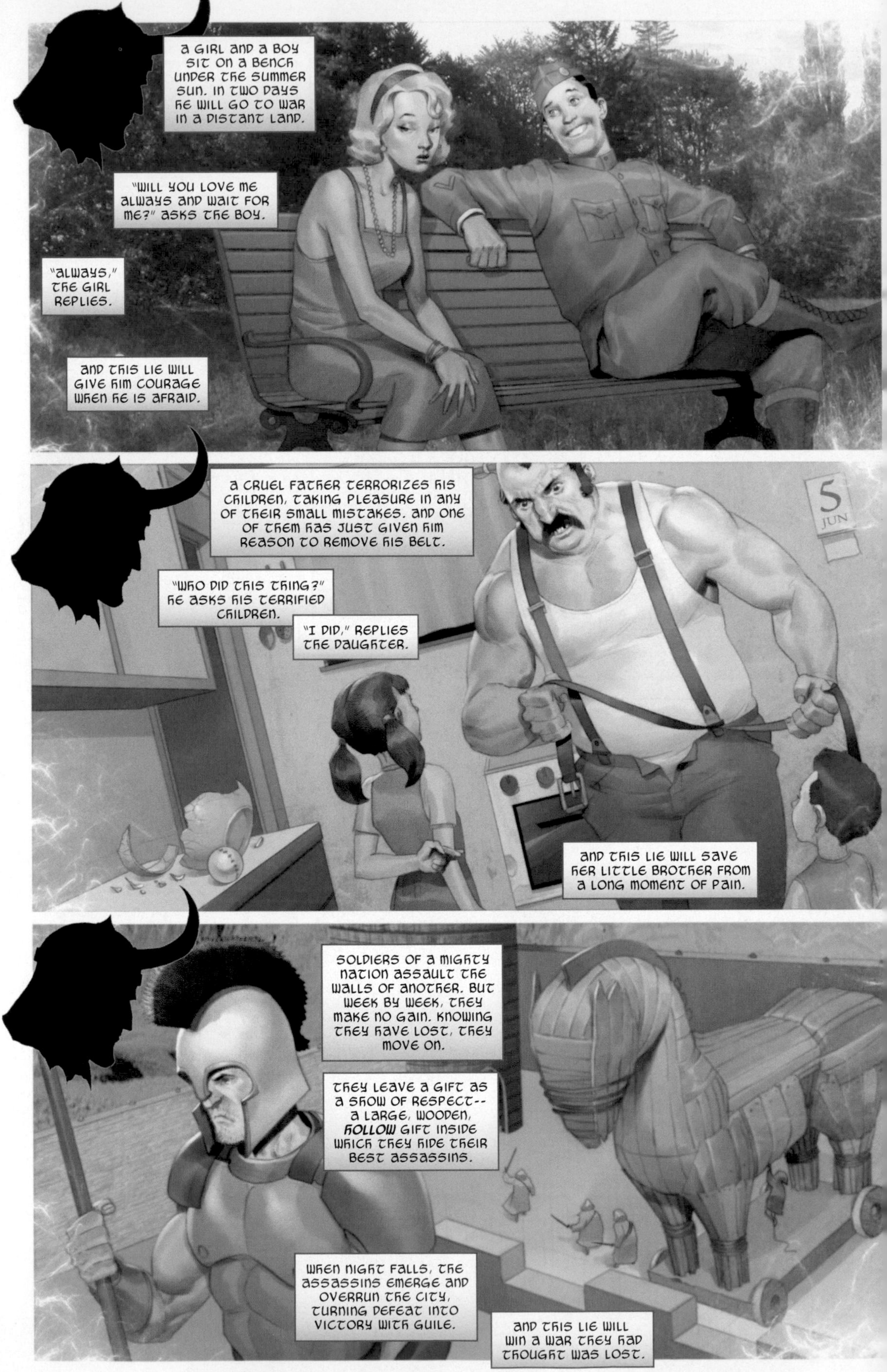
A GIRL AND A BOY SIT ON A BENCH UNDER THE SUMMER SUN. IN TWO DAYS HE WILL GO TO WAR IN A DISTANT LAND.
"WILL YOU LOVE ME ALWAYS AND WAIT FOR ME?" ASKS THE BOY.
"ALWAYS," THE GIRL REPLIES.
AND THIS LIE WILL GIVE HIM COURAGE WHEN HE IS AFRAID.
A CRUEL FATHER TERRORIZES HIS CHILDREN, TAKING PLEASURE IN ANY OF THEIR SMALL MISTAKES. AND ONE OF THEM HAS JUST GIVEN HIM REASON TO REMOVE HIS BELT.
5 JUN
"WHO DID THIS THING?" HE ASKS HIS TERRIFIED CHILDREN.
"I DID," REPLIES THE DAUGHTER.
AND THIS LIE WILL SAVE HER LITTLE BROTHER FROM A LONG MOMENT OF PAIN.
SOLDIERS OF A MIGHTY NATION ASSAULT THE WALLS OF ANOTHER. BUT WEEK BY WEEK, THEY MAKE NO GAIN. KNOWING THEY HAVE LOST, THEY MOVE ON.
THEY LEAVE A GIFT AS A SHOW OF RESPECT-- A LARGE, WOODEN, **HOLLOW** GIFT INSIDE WHICH THEY HIDE THEIR BEST ASSASSINS.
WHEN NIGHT FALLS, THE ASSASSINS EMERGE AND OVERRUN THE CITY, TURNING DEFEAT INTO VICTORY WITH GUILE.
AND THIS LIE WILL WIN A WAR THEY HAD THOUGHT WAS LOST.

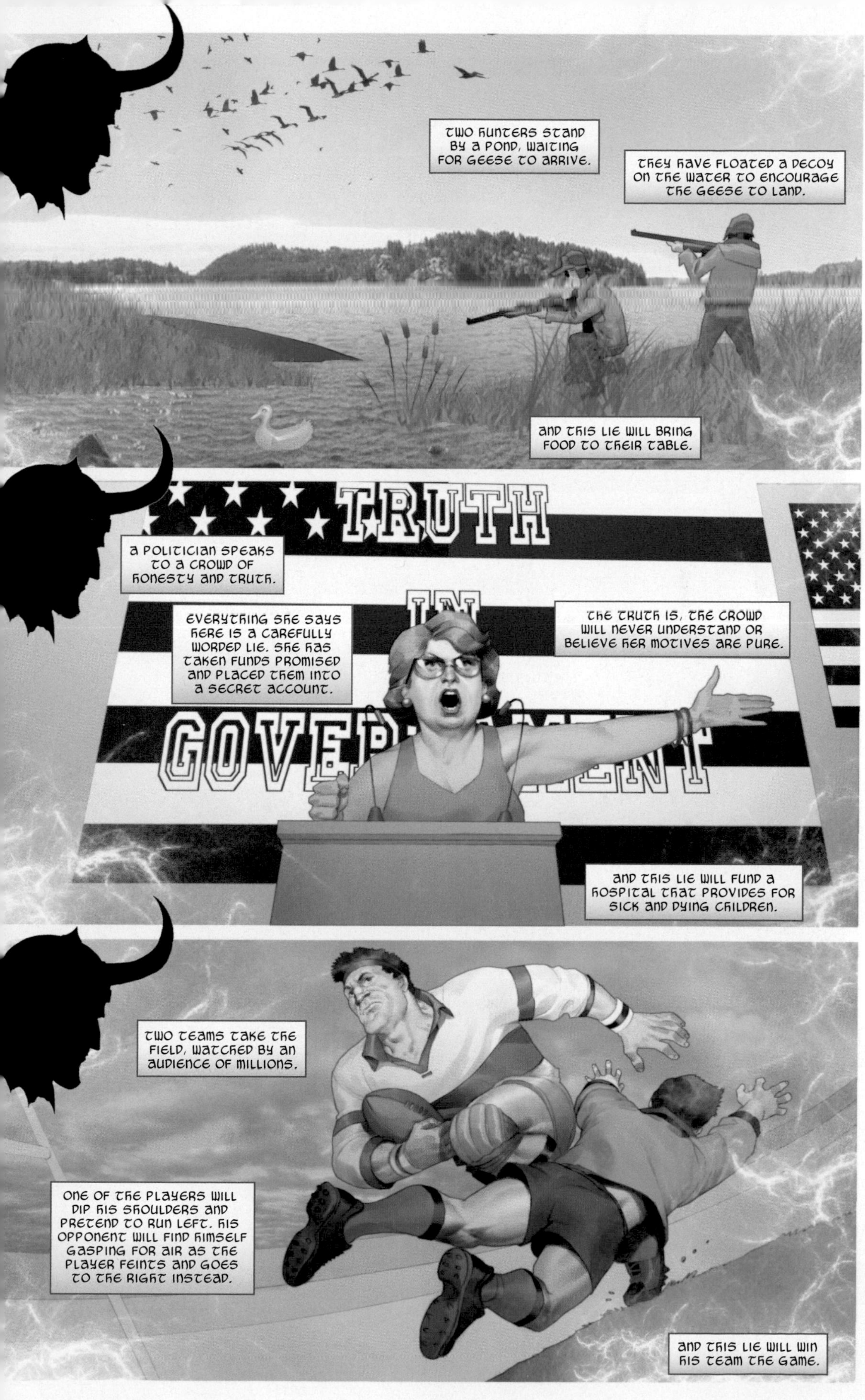
TWO HUNTERS STAND BY A POND, WAITING FOR GEESE TO ARRIVE.
THEY HAVE FLOATED A DECOY ON THE WATER TO ENCOURAGE THE GEESE TO LAND.
AND THIS LIE WILL BRING FOOD TO THEIR TABLE.
TRUTH
IN
GOVE
A POLITICIAN SPEAKS TO A CROWD OF HONESTY AND TRUTH.
EVERYTHING SHE SAYS HERE IS A CAREFULLY WORDED LIE. SHE HAS TAKEN FUNDS PROMISED AND PLACED THEM INTO A SECRET ACCOUNT.
THE TRUTH IS, THE CROWD WILL NEVER UNDERSTAND OR BELIEVE HER MOTIVES ARE PURE.
AND THIS LIE WILL FUND A HOSPITAL THAT PROVIDES FOR SICK AND DYING CHILDREN.
TWO TEAMS TAKE THE FIELD, WATCHED BY AN AUDIENCE OF MILLIONS.
ONE OF THE PLAYERS WILL DIP HIS SHOULDERS AND PRETEND TO RUN LEFT. HIS OPPONENT WILL FIND HIMSELF GASPING FOR AIR AS THE PLAYER FEINTS AND GOES TO THE RIGHT INSTEAD.
AND THIS LIE WILL WIN HIS TEAM THE GAME.

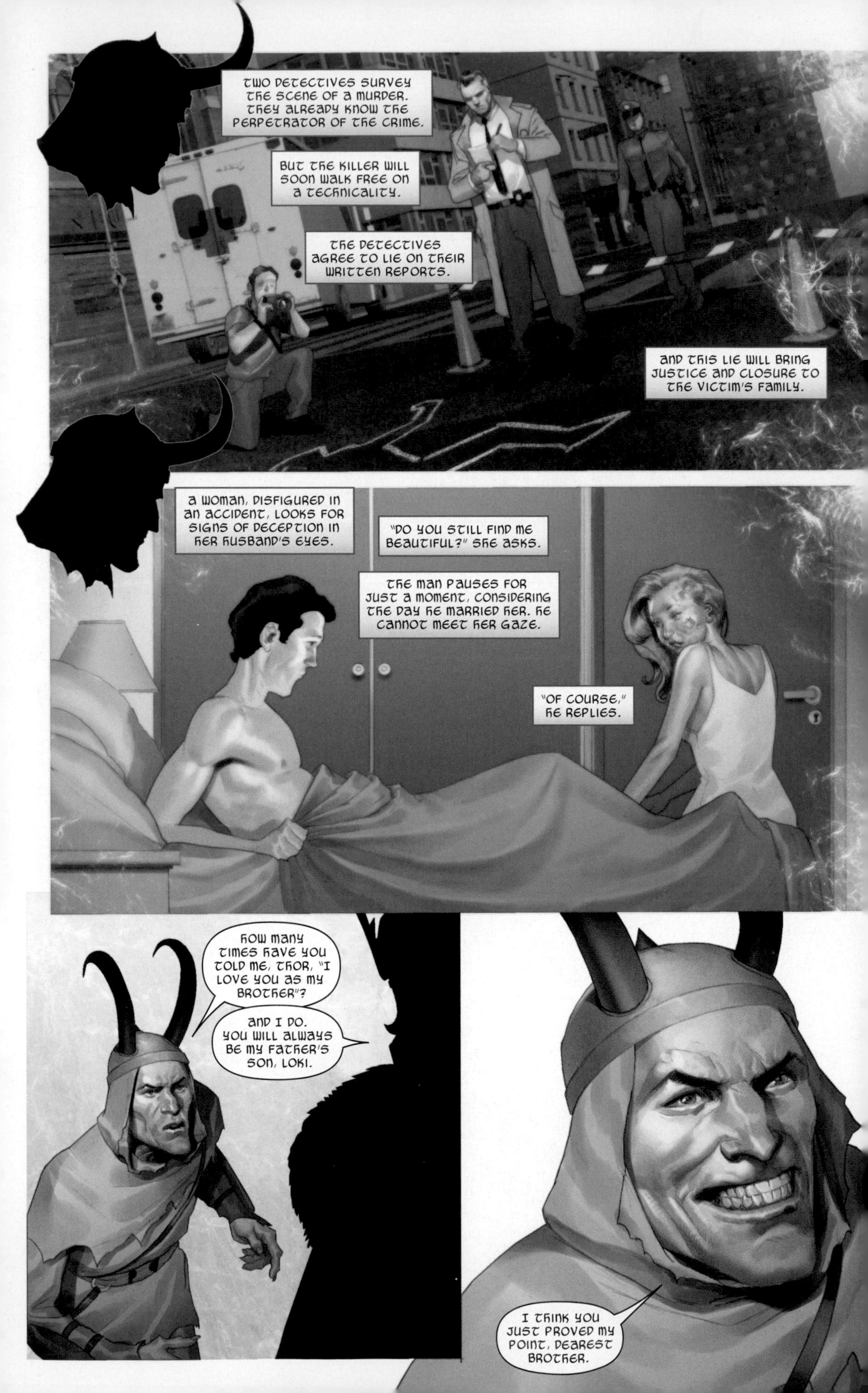
TWO DETECTIVES SURVEY THE SCENE OF A MURDER. THEY ALREADY KNOW THE PERPETRATOR OF THE CRIME.
BUT THE KILLER WILL SOON WALK FREE ON A TECHNICALITY.
THE DETECTIVES AGREE TO LIE ON THEIR WRITTEN REPORTS.
AND THIS LIE WILL BRING JUSTICE AND CLOSURE TO THE VICTIM'S FAMILY.
A WOMAN, DISFIGURED IN AN ACCIDENT, LOOKS FOR SIGNS OF DECEPTION IN HER HUSBAND'S EYES.
"DO YOU STILL FIND ME BEAUTIFUL?" SHE ASKS.
THE MAN PAUSES FOR JUST A MOMENT, CONSIDERING THE DAY HE MARRIED HER. HE CANNOT MEET HER GAZE.
"OF COURSE," HE REPLIES.
HOW MANY TIMES HAVE YOU TOLD ME, THOR, "I LOVE YOU AS MY BROTHER"?
AND I DO. YOU WILL ALWAYS BE MY FATHER'S SON, LOKI.
I THINK YOU JUST PROVED MY POINT, DEAREST BROTHER.

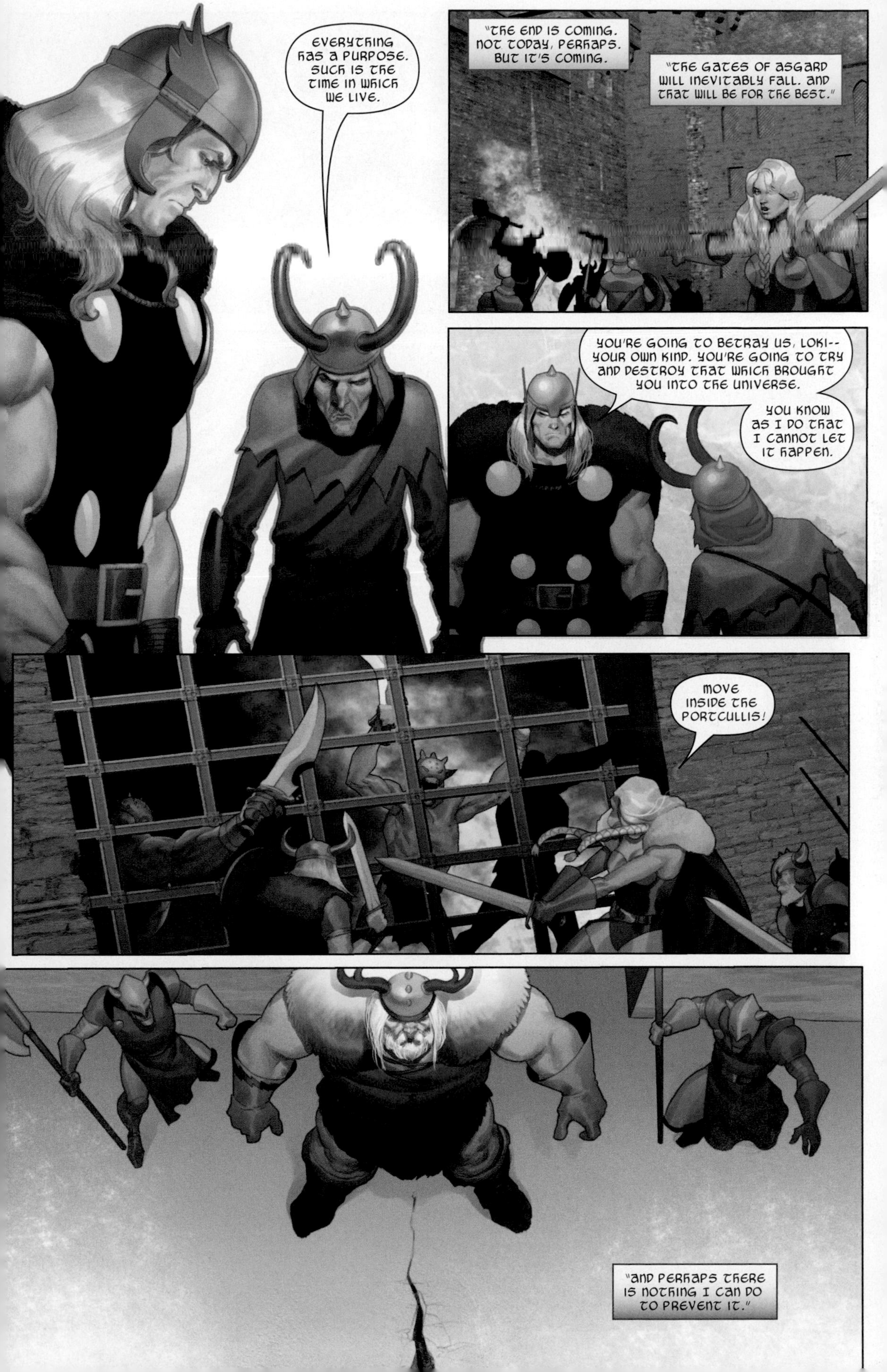

EVERYTHING HAS A PURPOSE. SUCH IS THE TIME IN WHICH WE LIVE.
"THE END IS COMING. NOT TODAY, PERHAPS. BUT IT'S COMING.
"THE GATES OF ASGARD WILL INEVITABLY FALL. AND THAT WILL BE FOR THE BEST."
YOU'RE GOING TO BETRAY US, LOKI-- YOUR OWN KIND. YOU'RE GOING TO TRY AND DESTROY THAT WHICH BROUGHT YOU INTO THE UNIVERSE.
YOU KNOW AS I DO THAT I CANNOT LET IT HAPPEN.
MOVE INSIDE THE PORTCULLIS!
"AND PERHAPS THERE IS NOTHING I CAN DO TO PREVENT IT."

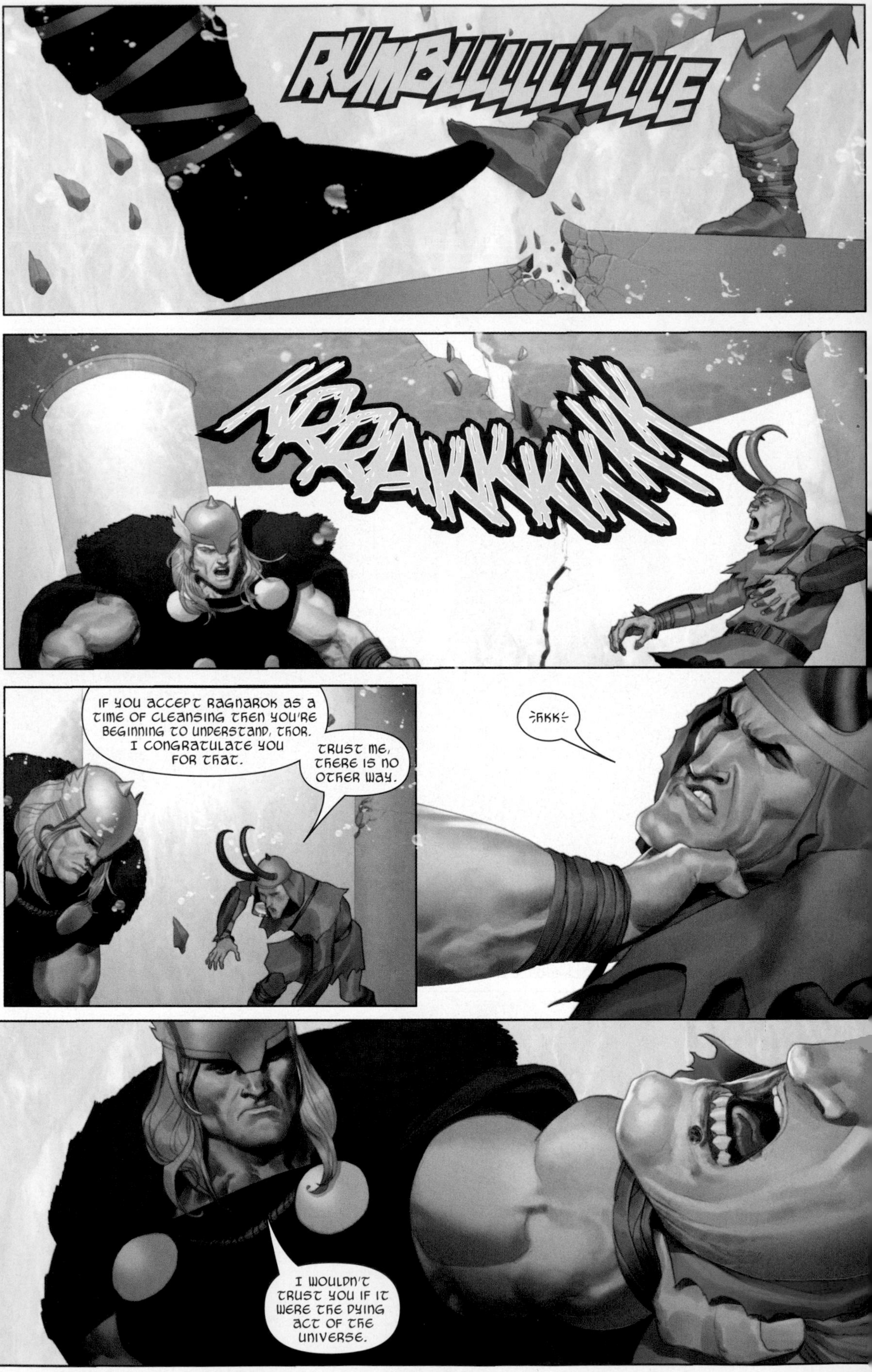
RUMBLLLLLLLLLE
KRRAKKKKK
IF YOU ACCEPT RAGNAROK AS A TIME OF CLEANSING THEN YOU'RE BEGINNING TO UNDERSTAND, THOR. I CONGRATULATE YOU FOR THAT.
TRUST ME, THERE IS NO OTHER WAY.
AKK
I WOULDN'T TRUST YOU IF IT WERE THE DYING ACT OF THE UNIVERSE.

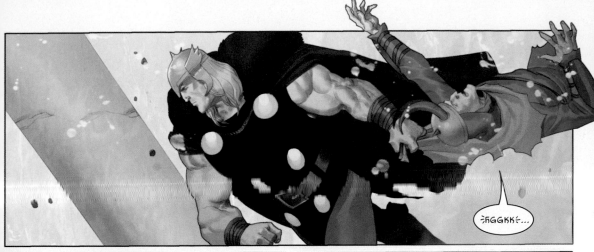

ЋGGKKҌ...

YOU HAD BETTER HOPE YOUR INCONVENIENT TRUTH IS A LIE, LOKI.

ARE YOU SO OBTUSE, EVEN NOW? DID I NOT SHOW YOU HOW LITTLE YOU REALLY KNOW, YOU DOLT?

MAYBE I AM TOO HARD-HEADED TO UNDERSTAND. BUT ONE THING I DO KNOW:

YOU HAD BETTER PRAY THAT ASGARD IS NOT TORN IN TWO, AS THE PROPHECIES FORETELL.

BECAUSE AS ASGARD GOES, SO GO YOU.

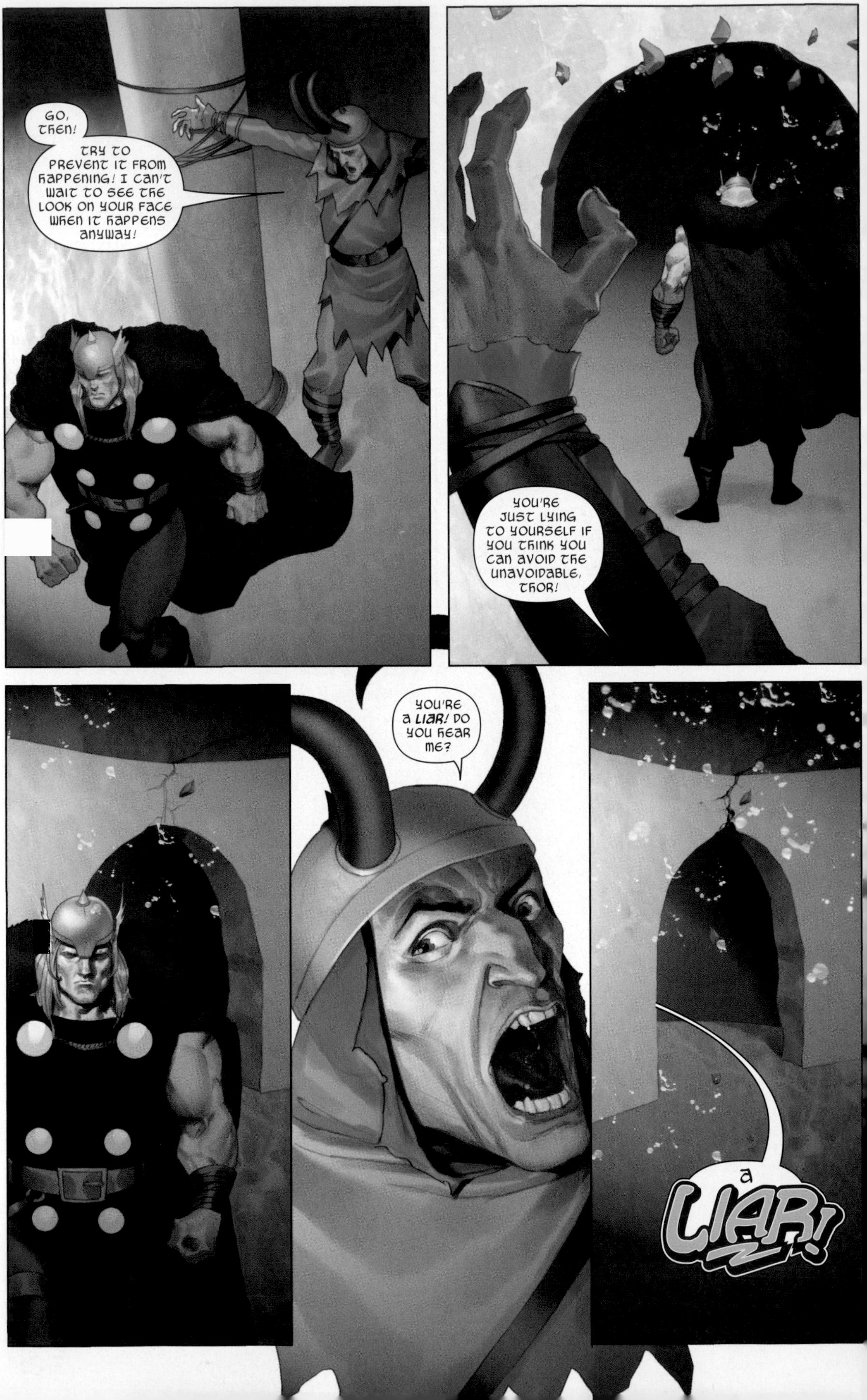
GO, THEN!
TRY TO PREVENT IT FROM HAPPENING! I CAN'T WAIT TO SEE THE LOOK ON YOUR FACE WHEN IT HAPPENS ANYWAY!
YOU'RE JUST LYING TO YOURSELF IF YOU THINK YOU CAN AVOID THE UNAVOIDABLE, THOR!
YOU'RE A LIAR! DO YOU HEAR ME?
A LIAR!

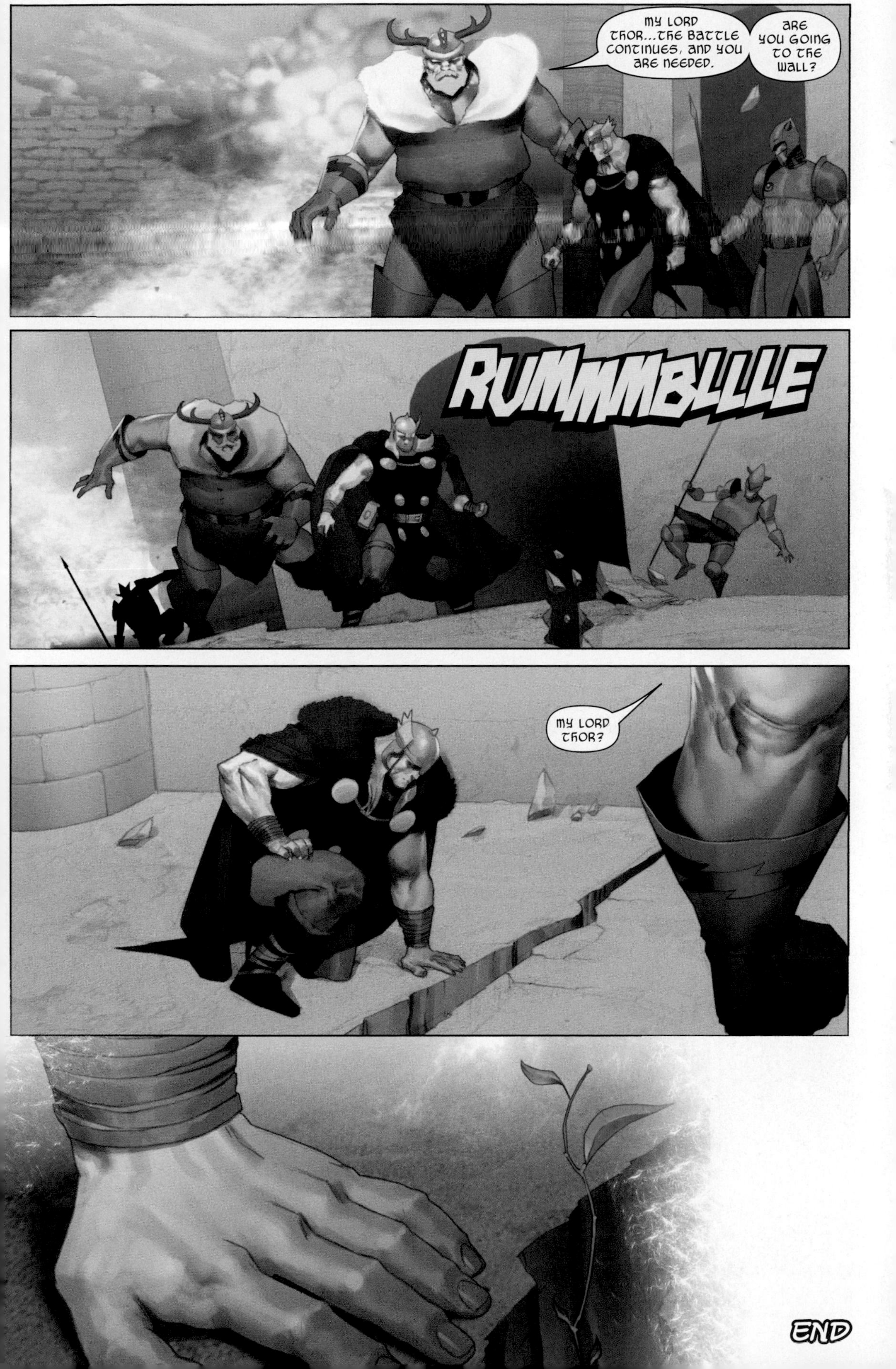
MY LORD THOR...THE BATTLE CONTINUES, AND YOU ARE NEEDED.
ARE YOU GOING TO THE WALL?
RUMMMBLLLE
MY LORD THOR?
END

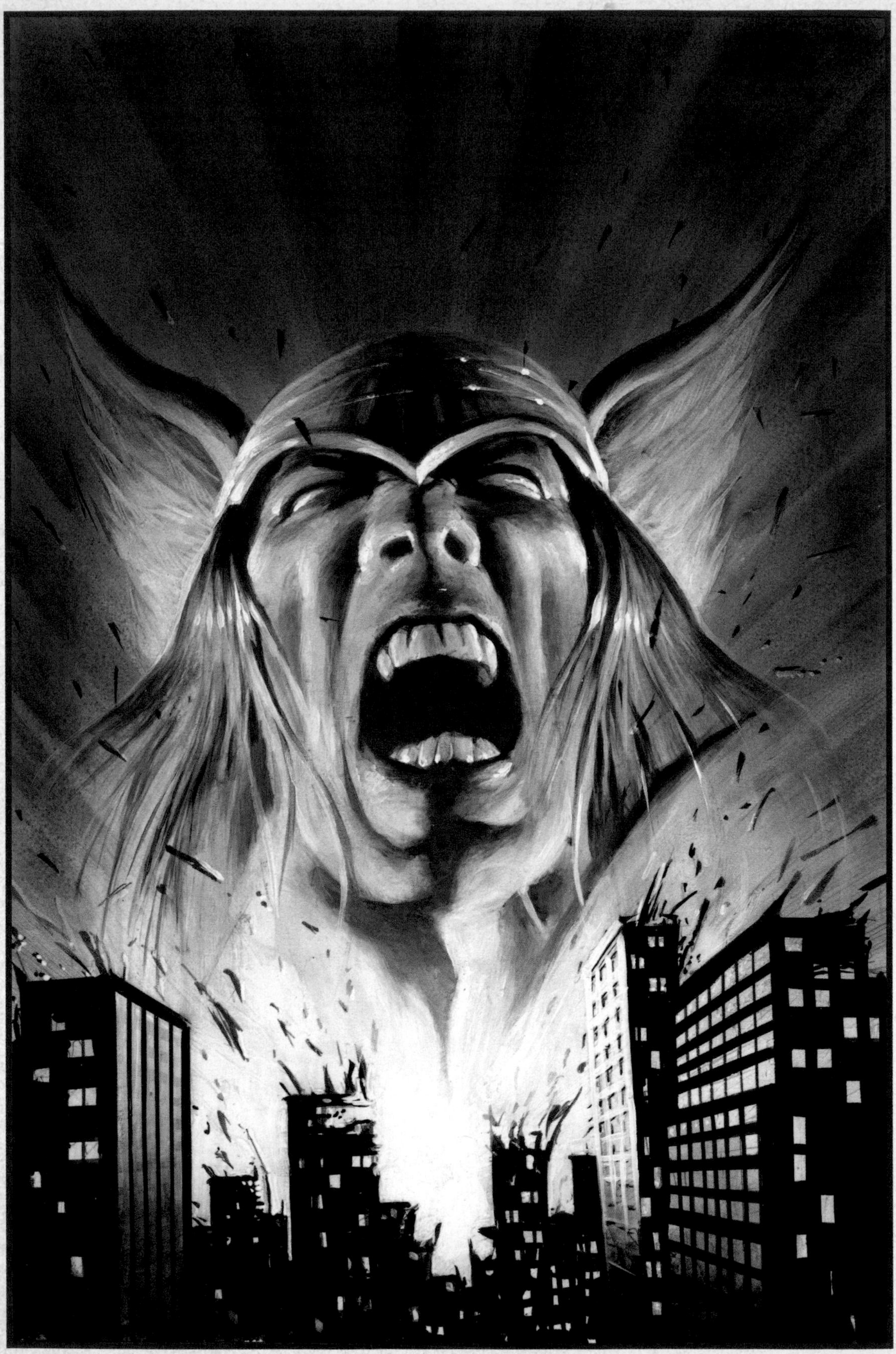

THOR: HEAVEN & EARTH #2

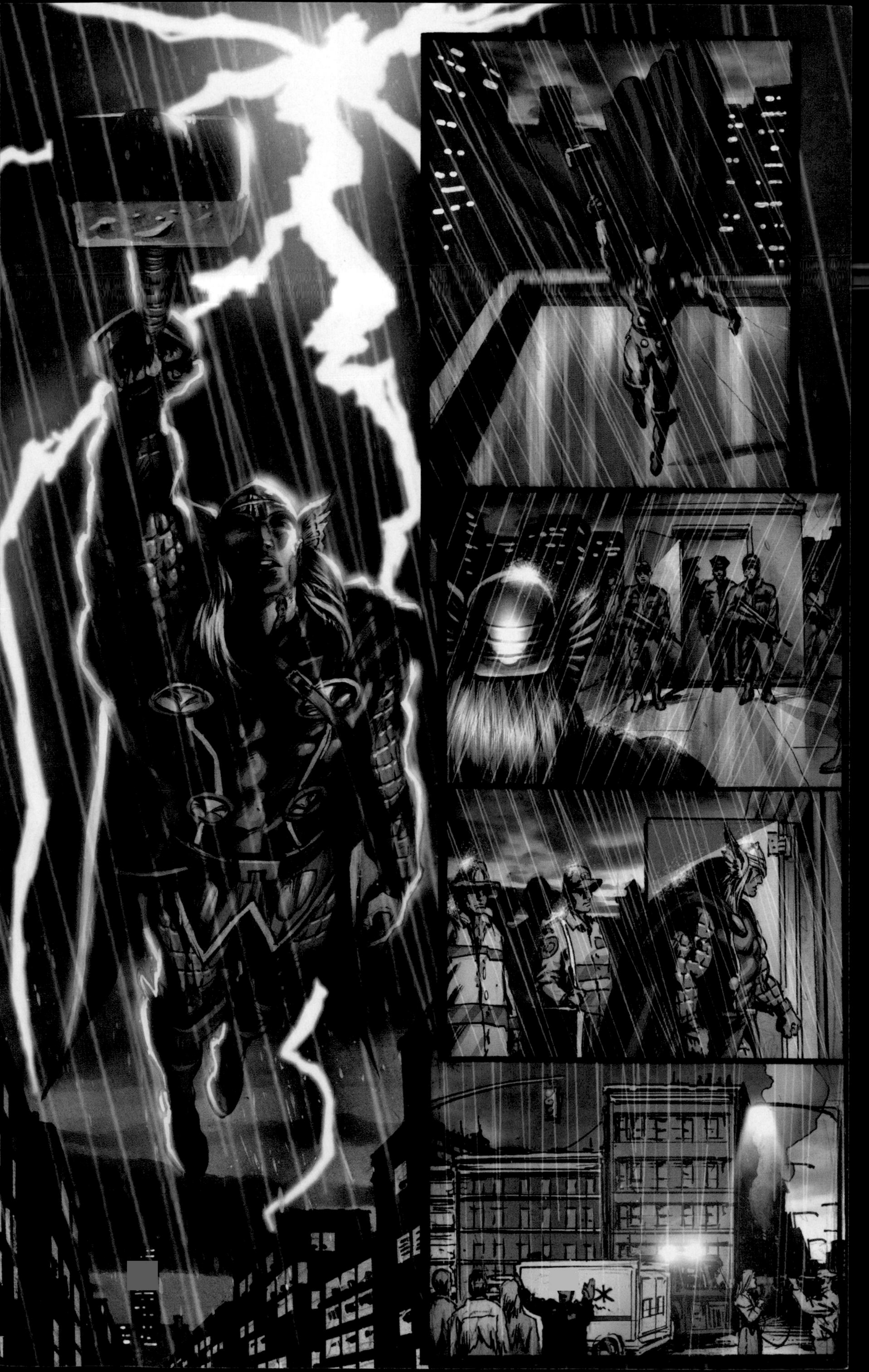

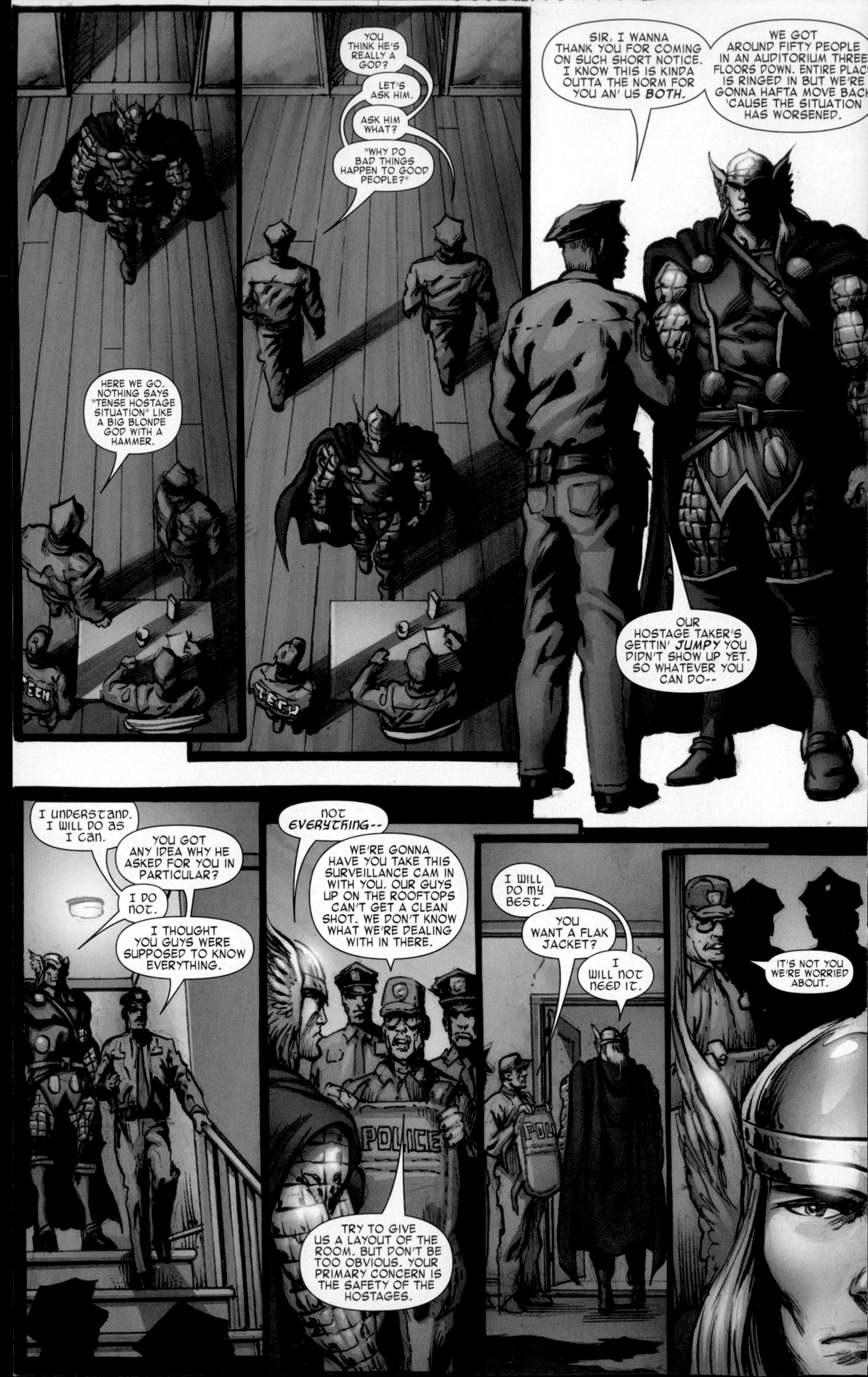

YOU THINK HE'S REALLY A GOD?
LET'S ASK HIM.
ASK HIM WHAT?
"WHY DO BAD THINGS HAPPEN TO GOOD PEOPLE?"
HERE WE GO. NOTHING SAYS "TENSE HOSTAGE SITUATION" LIKE A BIG BLONDE GOD WITH A HAMMER.
TECH
TECH
SIR, I WANNA THANK YOU FOR COMING ON SUCH SHORT NOTICE. I KNOW THIS IS KINDA OUTTA THE NORM FOR YOU AN' US BOTH.
WE GOT AROUND FIFTY PEOPLE IN AN AUDITORIUM THREE FLOORS DOWN. ENTIRE PLACE IS RINGED IN BUT WE'RE GONNA HAFTA MOVE BACK 'CAUSE THE SITUATION HAS WORSENED.
OUR HOSTAGE TAKER'S GETTIN' JUMPY YOU DIDN'T SHOW UP YET. SO WHATEVER YOU CAN DO--
I UNDERSTAND. I WILL DO AS I CAN.
YOU GOT ANY IDEA WHY HE ASKED FOR YOU IN PARTICULAR?
I DO NOT.
I THOUGHT YOU GUYS WERE SUPPOSED TO KNOW EVERYTHING.
NOT EVERYTHING--
WE'RE GONNA HAVE YOU TAKE THIS SURVEILLANCE CAM IN WITH YOU. OUR GUYS UP ON THE ROOFTOPS CAN'T GET A CLEAN SHOT. WE DON'T KNOW WHAT WE'RE DEALING WITH IN THERE.
POLICE
TRY TO GIVE US A LAYOUT OF THE ROOM. BUT DON'T BE TOO OBVIOUS. YOUR PRIMARY CONCERN IS THE SAFETY OF THE HOSTAGES.
I WILL DO MY BEST.
YOU WANT A FLAK JACKET?
I WILL NOT NEED IT.
IT'S NOT YOU WE'RE WORRIED ABOUT.

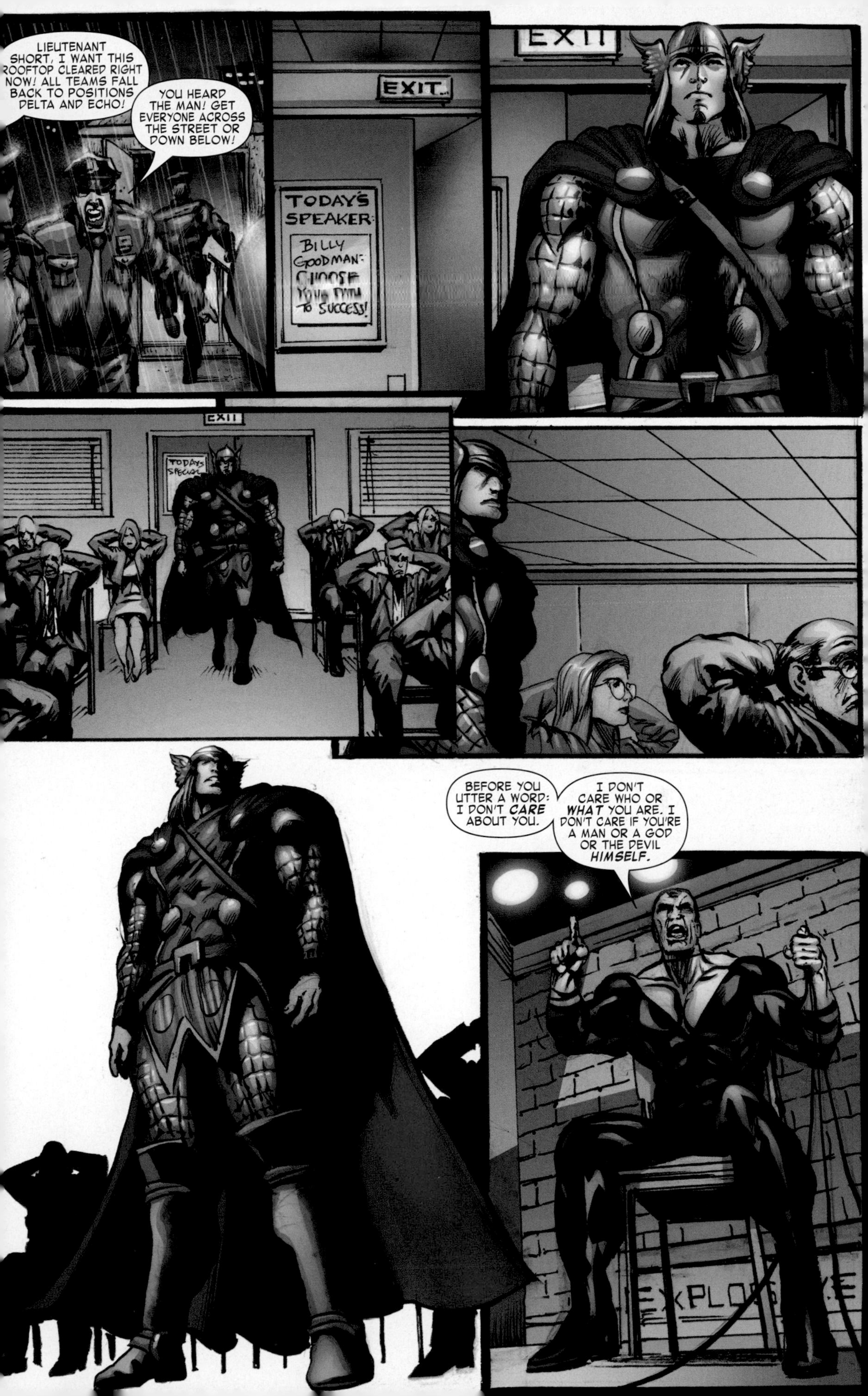
LIEUTENANT SHORT, I WANT THIS ROOFTOP CLEARED RIGHT NOW! ALL TEAMS FALL BACK TO POSITIONS DELTA AND ECHO!
YOU HEARD THE MAN! GET EVERYONE ACROSS THE STREET OR DOWN BELOW!
EXIT
TODAY'S SPEAKER:
BILLY GOODMAN: CHOOSE YOUR PATH TO SUCCESS!
EXIT
EXIT
BEFORE YOU UTTER A WORD: I DON'T *CARE* ABOUT YOU.
I DON'T CARE WHO OR *WHAT* YOU ARE. I DON'T CARE IF YOU'RE A MAN OR A GOD OR THE DEVIL *HIMSELF.*

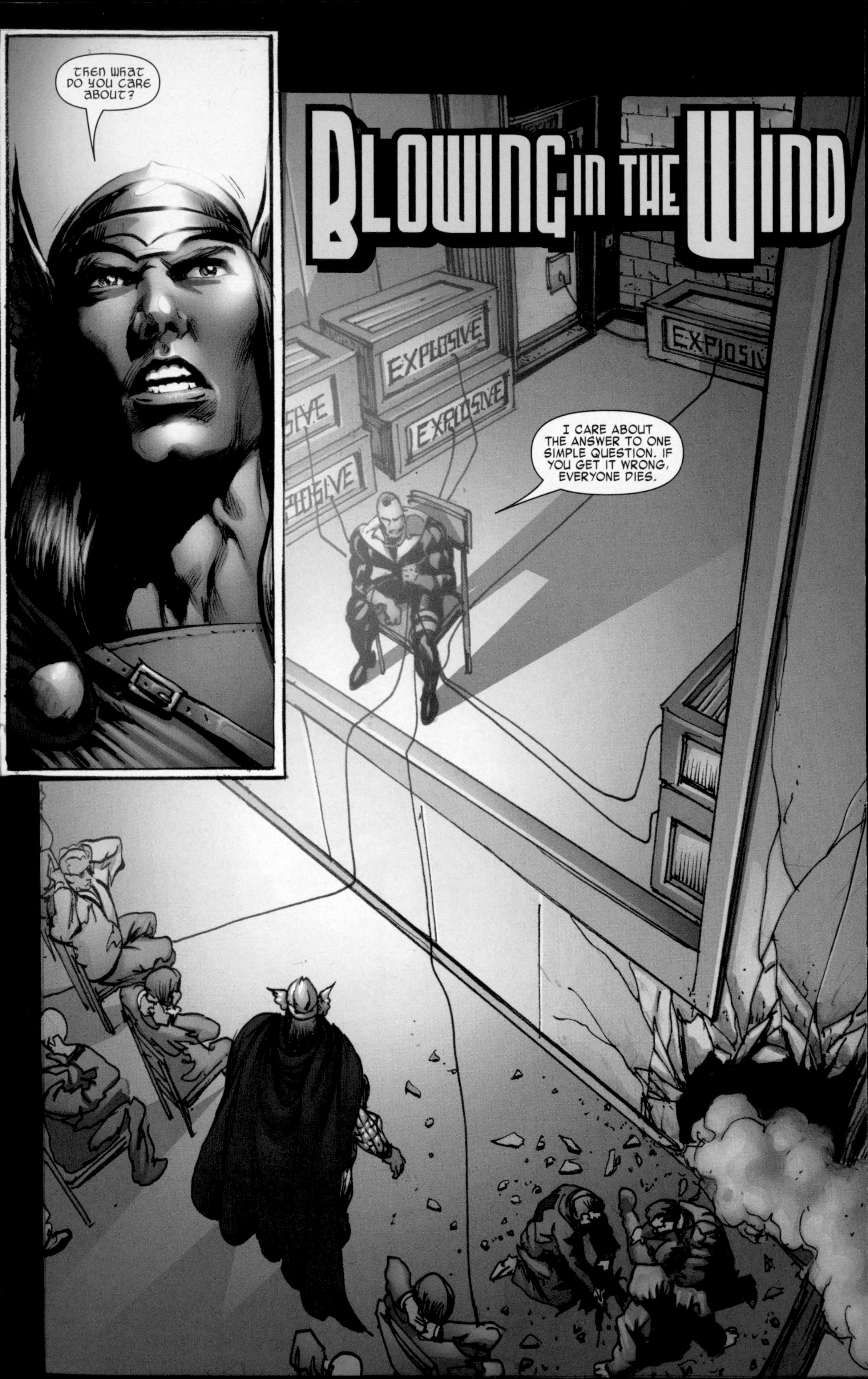
THEN WHAT DO YOU CARE ABOUT?
BLOWING IN THE WIND
EXPLOSIVE
EXPLOSIVE
EXPLOSIVE
I CARE ABOUT THE ANSWER TO ONE SIMPLE QUESTION. IF YOU GET IT WRONG, EVERYONE DIES.

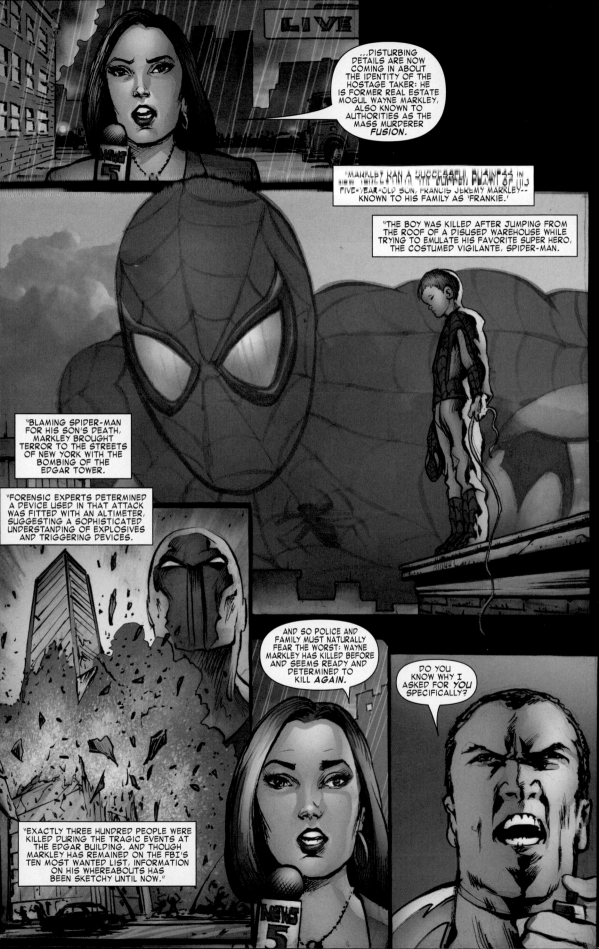

...DISTURBING DETAILS ARE NOW COMING IN ABOUT THE IDENTITY OF THE HOSTAGE TAKER: HE IS FORMER REAL ESTATE MOGUL WAYNE MARKLEY, ALSO KNOWN TO AUTHORITIES AS THE MASS MURDERER *FUSION.*

"MARKLEY RAN A SUCCESSFUL BUSINESS IN FIVE-YEAR-OLD SON, FRANCIS JEREMY MARKLEY— KNOWN TO HIS FAMILY AS 'FRANKIE.'

"THE BOY WAS KILLED AFTER JUMPING FROM THE ROOF OF A DISUSED WAREHOUSE WHILE TRYING TO EMULATE HIS FAVORITE SUPER HERO, THE COSTUMED VIGILANTE, SPIDER-MAN.

"BLAMING SPIDER-MAN FOR HIS SON'S DEATH, MARKLEY BROUGHT TERROR TO THE STREETS OF NEW YORK WITH THE BOMBING OF THE EDGAR TOWER.

"FORENSIC EXPERTS DETERMINED A DEVICE USED IN THAT ATTACK WAS FITTED WITH AN ALTIMETER, SUGGESTING A SOPHISTICATED UNDERSTANDING OF EXPLOSIVES AND TRIGGERING DEVICES.

AND SO POLICE AND FAMILY MUST NATURALLY FEAR THE WORST: WAYNE MARKLEY HAS KILLED BEFORE AND SEEMS READY AND DETERMINED TO KILL *AGAIN.*

DO YOU KNOW WHY I ASKED FOR *YOU* SPECIFICALLY?

"EXACTLY THREE HUNDRED PEOPLE WERE KILLED DURING THE TRAGIC EVENTS AT THE EDGAR BUILDING. AND THOUGH MARKLEY HAS REMAINED ON THE FBI'S TEN MOST WANTED LIST, INFORMATION ON HIS WHEREABOUTS HAS BEEN SKETCHY UNTIL NOW."

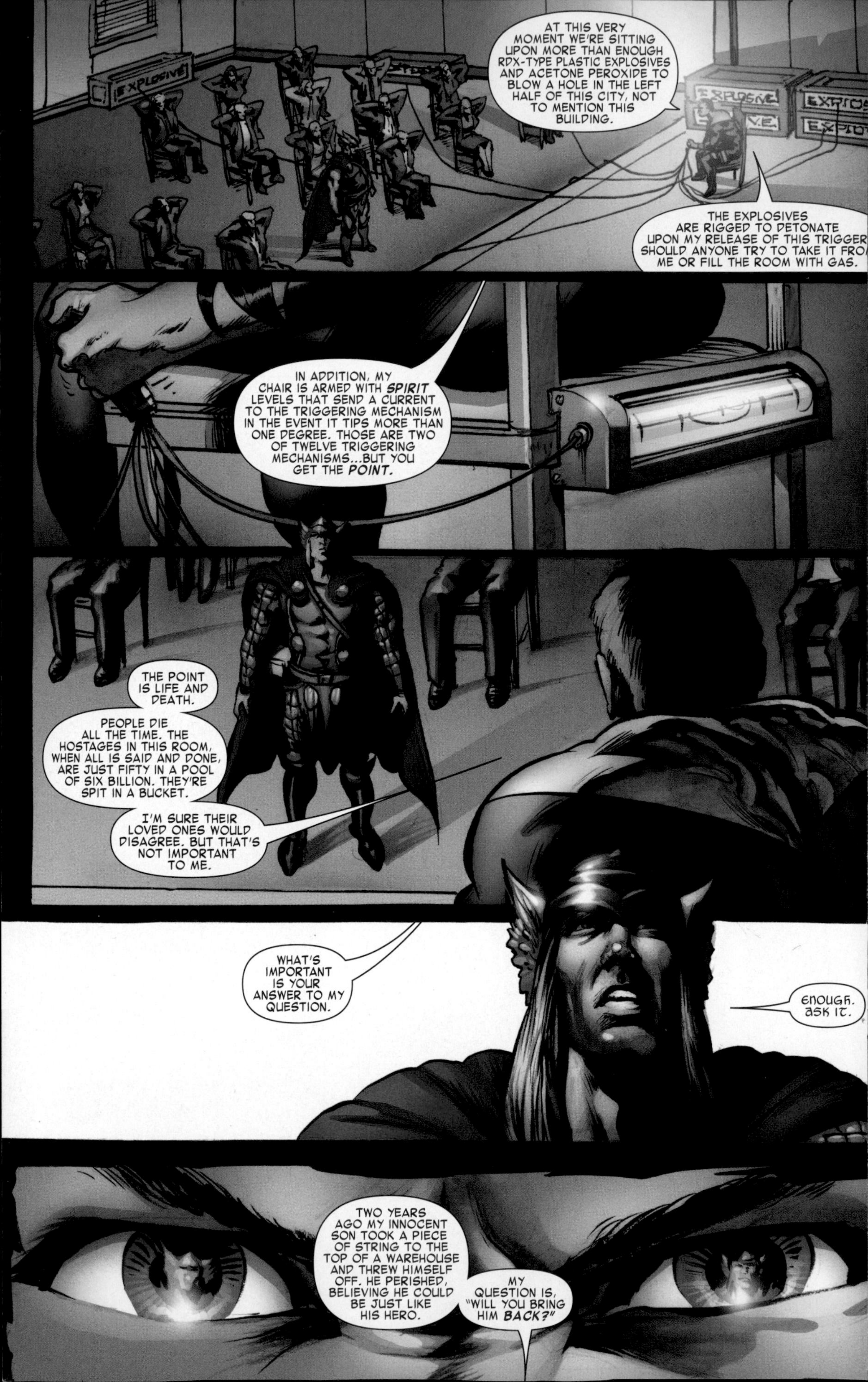
AT THIS VERY MOMENT WE'RE SITTING UPON MORE THAN ENOUGH RDX-TYPE PLASTIC EXPLOSIVES AND ACETONE PEROXIDE TO BLOW A HOLE IN THE LEFT HALF OF THIS CITY, NOT TO MENTION THIS BUILDING.
THE EXPLOSIVES ARE RIGGED TO DETONATE UPON MY RELEASE OF THIS TRIGGER SHOULD ANYONE TRY TO TAKE IT FROM ME OR FILL THE ROOM WITH GAS.
IN ADDITION, MY CHAIR IS ARMED WITH SPIRIT LEVELS THAT SEND A CURRENT TO THE TRIGGERING MECHANISM IN THE EVENT IT TIPS MORE THAN ONE DEGREE. THOSE ARE TWO OF TWELVE TRIGGERING MECHANISMS...BUT YOU GET THE POINT.
THE POINT IS LIFE AND DEATH.
PEOPLE DIE ALL THE TIME. THE HOSTAGES IN THIS ROOM, WHEN ALL IS SAID AND DONE, ARE JUST FIFTY IN A POOL OF SIX BILLION. THEY'RE SPIT IN A BUCKET.
I'M SURE THEIR LOVED ONES WOULD DISAGREE. BUT THAT'S NOT IMPORTANT TO ME.
WHAT'S IMPORTANT IS YOUR ANSWER TO MY QUESTION.
ENOUGH. ASK IT.
TWO YEARS AGO MY INNOCENT SON TOOK A PIECE OF STRING TO THE TOP OF A WAREHOUSE AND THREW HIMSELF OFF. HE PERISHED, BELIEVING HE COULD BE JUST LIKE HIS HERO.
MY QUESTION IS, "WILL YOU BRING HIM BACK?"

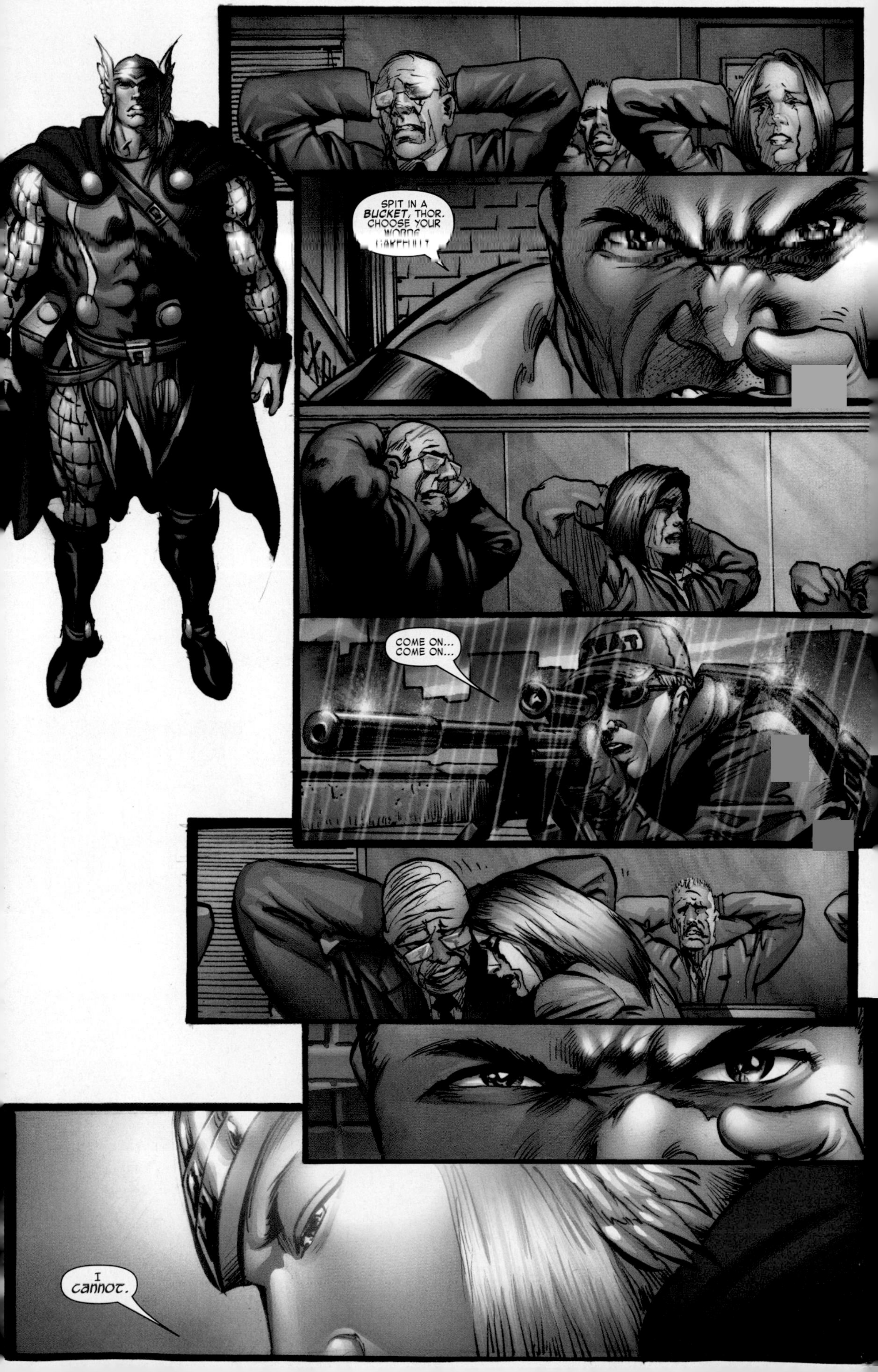
SPIT IN A **BUCKET**, THOR. CHOOSE YOUR
COME ON... COME ON...
I cannot.

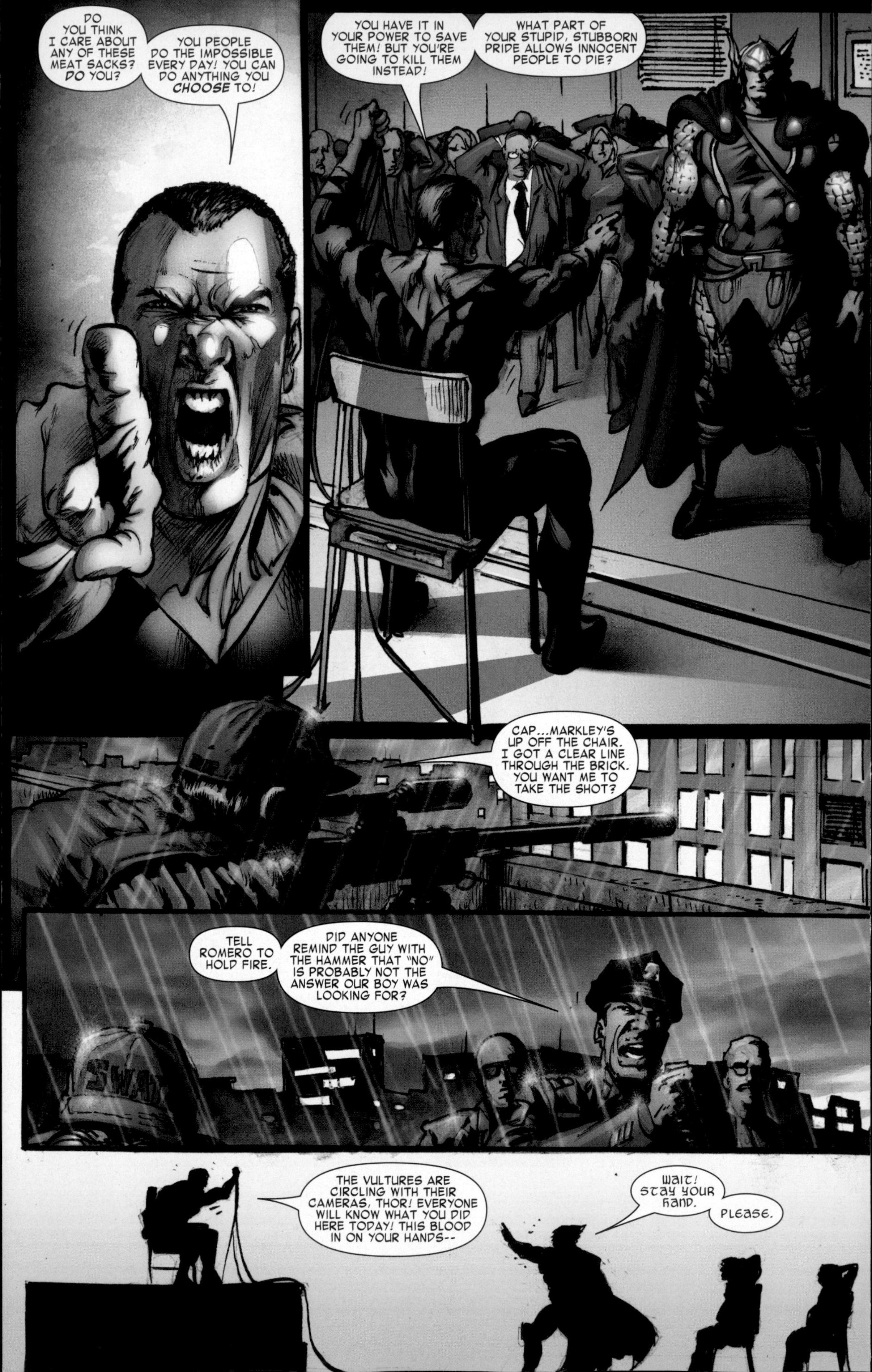
DO YOU THINK I CARE ABOUT ANY OF THESE MEAT SACKS? DO YOU?
YOU PEOPLE DO THE IMPOSSIBLE EVERY DAY! YOU CAN DO ANYTHING YOU CHOOSE TO!
YOU HAVE IT IN YOUR POWER TO SAVE THEM! BUT YOU'RE GOING TO KILL THEM INSTEAD!
WHAT PART OF YOUR STUPID, STUBBORN PRIDE ALLOWS INNOCENT PEOPLE TO DIE?
CAP...MARKLEY'S UP OFF THE CHAIR. I GOT A CLEAR LINE THROUGH THE BRICK. YOU WANT ME TO TAKE THE SHOT?
TELL ROMERO TO HOLD FIRE.
DID ANYONE REMIND THE GUY WITH THE HAMMER THAT "NO" IS PROBABLY NOT THE ANSWER OUR BOY WAS LOOKING FOR?
THE VULTURES ARE CIRCLING WITH THEIR CAMERAS, THOR! EVERYONE WILL KNOW WHAT YOU DID HERE TODAY! THIS BLOOD IN ON YOUR HANDS--
WAIT! STAY YOUR HAND.
PLEASE.

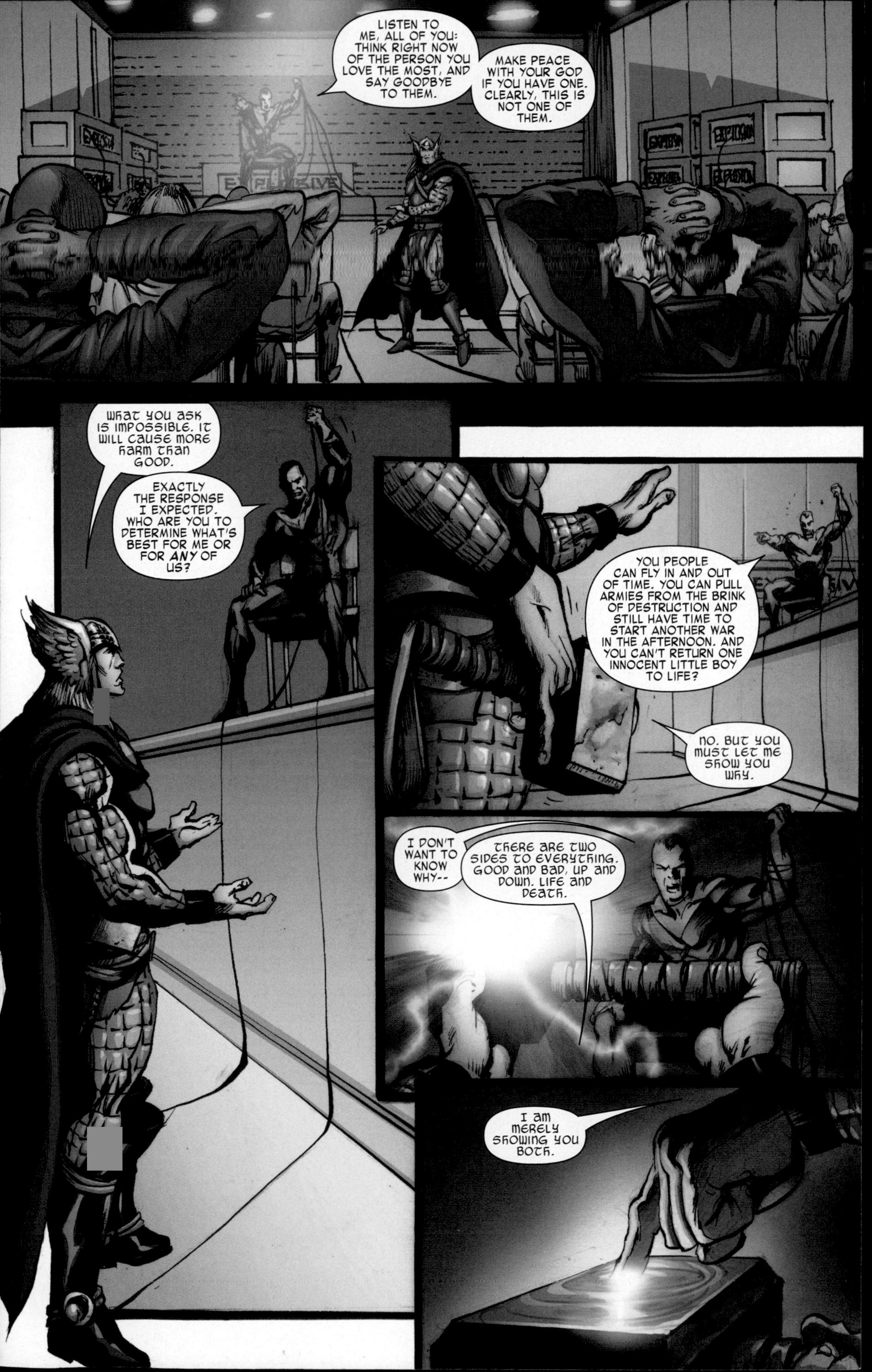
LISTEN TO ME, ALL OF YOU: THINK RIGHT NOW OF THE PERSON YOU LOVE THE MOST, AND SAY GOODBYE TO THEM.
MAKE PEACE WITH YOUR GOD IF YOU HAVE ONE. CLEARLY, THIS IS NOT ONE OF THEM.
EXPLOSIVE
WHAT YOU ASK IS IMPOSSIBLE. IT WILL CAUSE MORE HARM THAN GOOD.
EXACTLY THE RESPONSE I EXPECTED. WHO ARE YOU TO DETERMINE WHAT'S BEST FOR ME OR FOR ANY OF US?
YOU PEOPLE CAN FLY IN AND OUT OF TIME. YOU CAN PULL ARMIES FROM THE BRINK OF DESTRUCTION AND STILL HAVE TIME TO START ANOTHER WAR IN THE AFTERNOON. AND YOU CAN'T RETURN ONE INNOCENT LITTLE BOY TO LIFE?
NO. BUT YOU MUST LET ME SHOW YOU WHY.
I DON'T WANT TO KNOW WHY--
THERE ARE TWO SIDES TO EVERYTHING. GOOD AND BAD, UP AND DOWN. LIFE AND DEATH.
I AM MERELY SHOWING YOU BOTH.

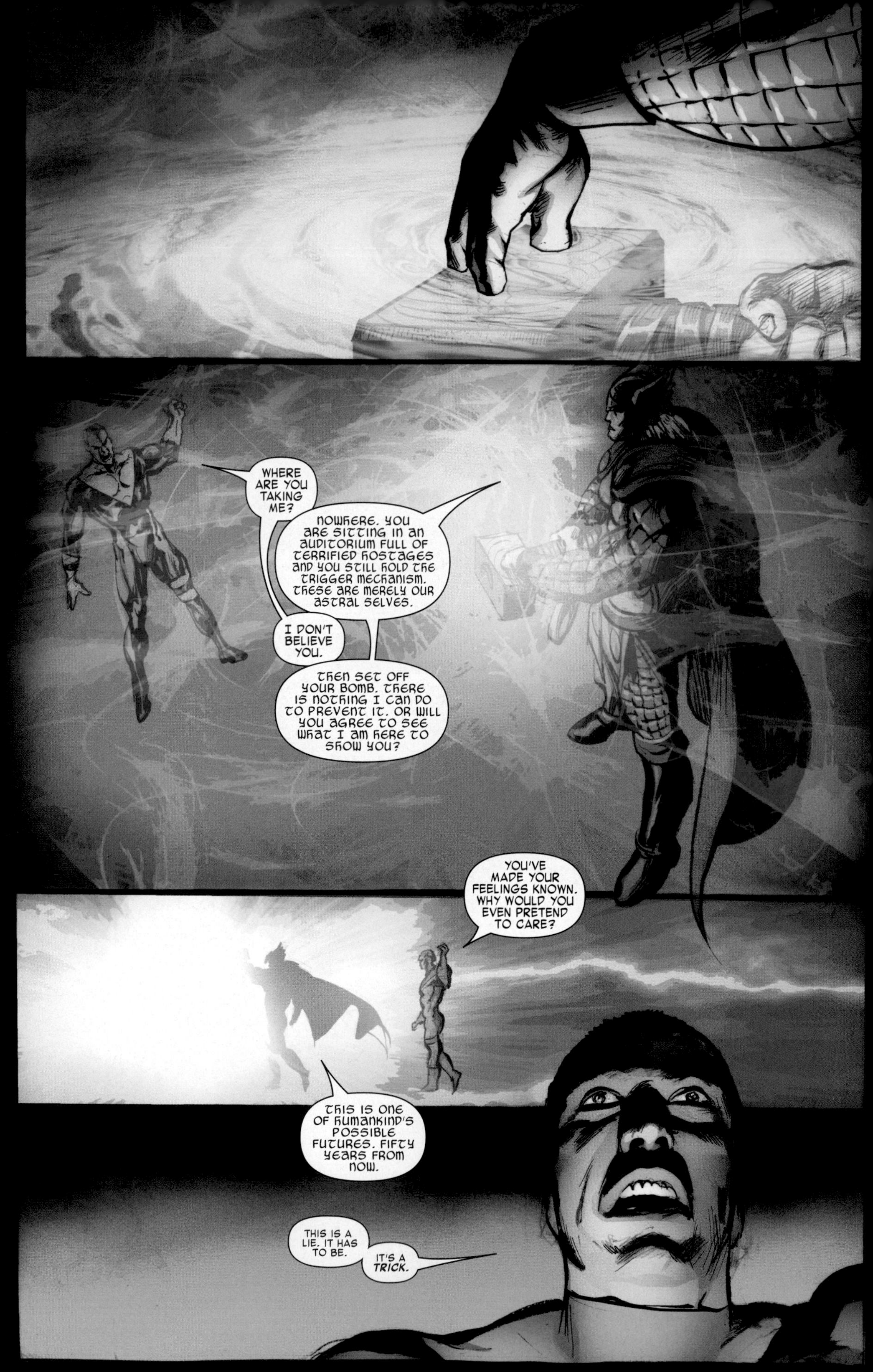
WHERE ARE YOU TAKING ME?
NOWHERE. YOU ARE SITTING IN AN AUDITORIUM FULL OF TERRIFIED HOSTAGES AND YOU STILL HOLD THE TRIGGER MECHANISM. THESE ARE MERELY OUR ASTRAL SELVES.
I DON'T BELIEVE YOU.
THEN SET OFF YOUR BOMB. THERE IS NOTHING I CAN DO TO PREVENT IT. OR WILL YOU AGREE TO SEE WHAT I AM HERE TO SHOW YOU?
YOU'VE MADE YOUR FEELINGS KNOWN. WHY WOULD YOU EVEN PRETEND TO CARE?
THIS IS ONE OF HUMANKIND'S POSSIBLE FUTURES. FIFTY YEARS FROM NOW.
THIS IS A LIE. IT HAS TO BE.
IT'S A TRICK.

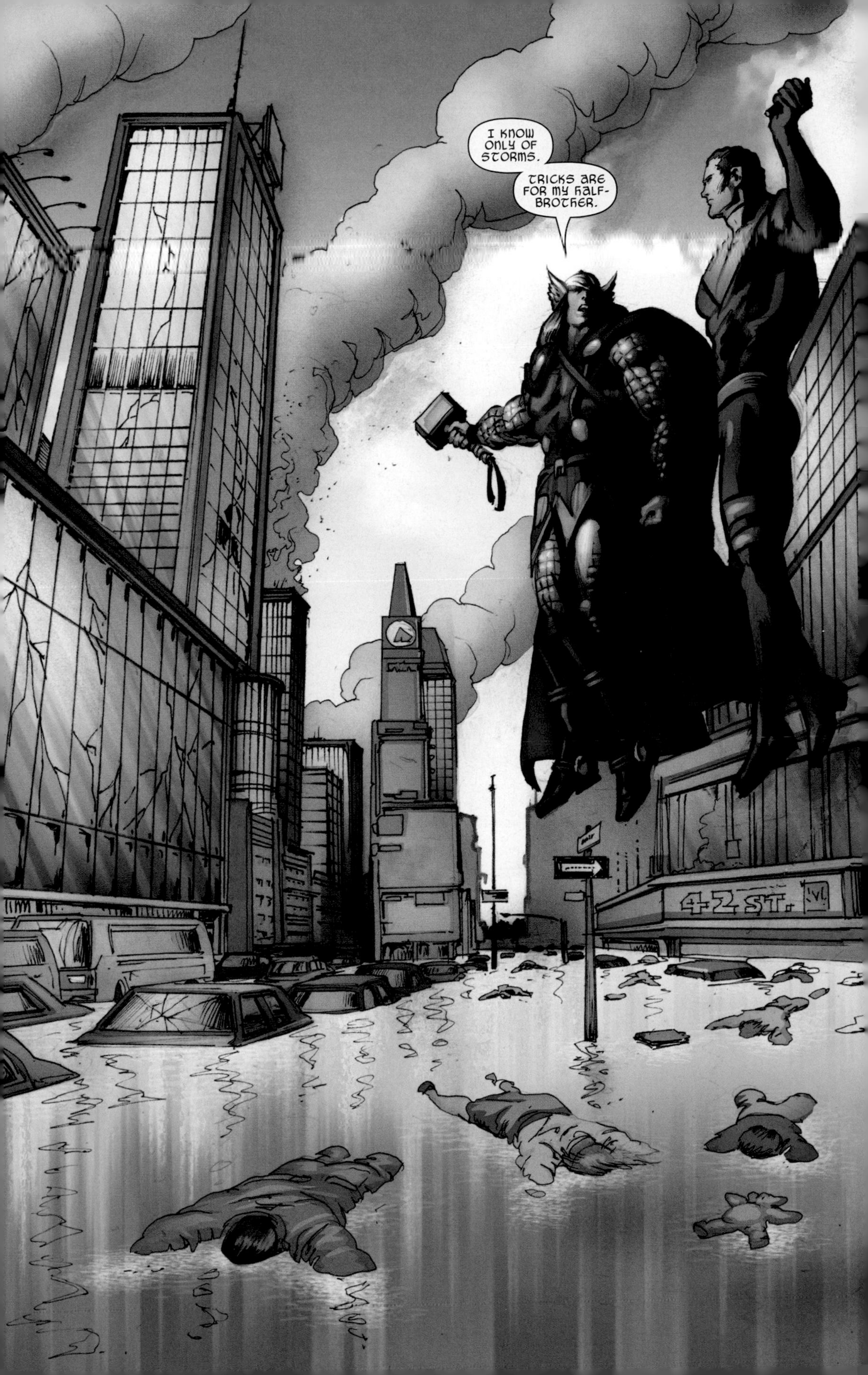
I KNOW ONLY OF STORMS.
TRICKS ARE FOR MY HALF-BROTHER.
42 ST.

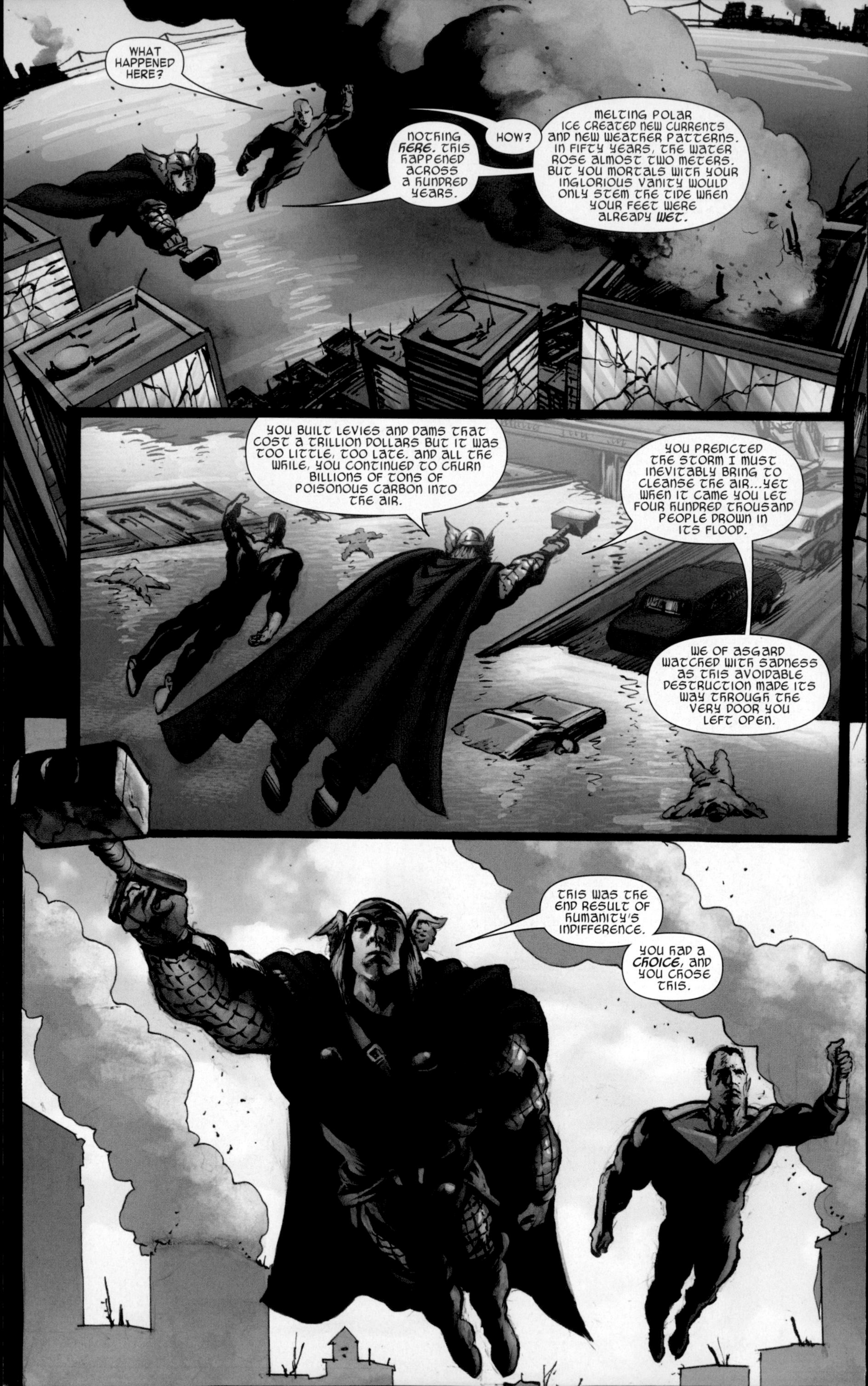
WHAT HAPPENED HERE?
NOTHING HERE. THIS HAPPENED ACROSS A HUNDRED YEARS.
HOW?
MELTING POLAR ICE CREATED NEW CURRENTS AND NEW WEATHER PATTERNS. IN FIFTY YEARS, THE WATER ROSE ALMOST TWO METERS. BUT YOU MORTALS WITH YOUR INGLORIOUS VANITY WOULD ONLY STEM THE TIDE WHEN YOUR FEET WERE ALREADY WET.
YOU BUILT LEVIES AND DAMS THAT COST A TRILLION DOLLARS BUT IT WAS TOO LITTLE, TOO LATE. AND ALL THE WHILE, YOU CONTINUED TO CHURN BILLIONS OF TONS OF POISONOUS CARBON INTO THE AIR.
YOU PREDICTED THE STORM I MUST INEVITABLY BRING TO CLEANSE THE AIR...YET WHEN IT CAME YOU LET FOUR HUNDRED THOUSAND PEOPLE DROWN IN ITS FLOOD.
WE OF ASGARD WATCHED WITH SADNESS AS THIS AVOIDABLE DESTRUCTION MADE ITS WAY THROUGH THE VERY DOOR YOU LEFT OPEN.
THIS WAS THE END RESULT OF HUMANITY'S INDIFFERENCE.
YOU HAD A CHOICE, AND YOU CHOSE THIS.

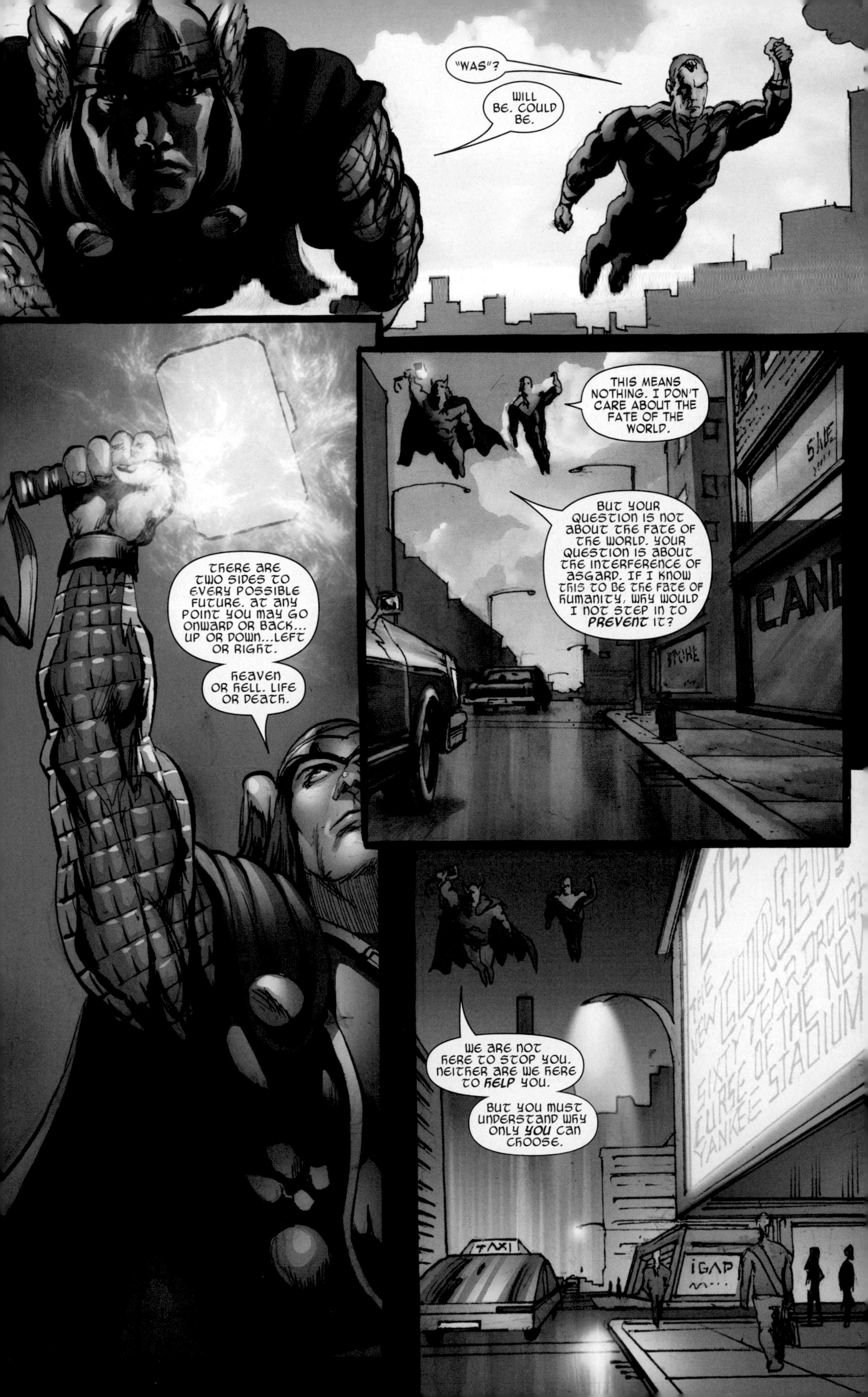
"WAS"?
WILL BE. COULD BE.
THERE ARE TWO SIDES TO EVERY POSSIBLE FUTURE. AT ANY POINT YOU MAY GO ONWARD OR BACK... UP OR DOWN...LEFT OR RIGHT.
HEAVEN OR HELL. LIFE OR DEATH.
THIS MEANS NOTHING. I DON'T CARE ABOUT THE FATE OF THE WORLD.
BUT YOUR QUESTION IS NOT ABOUT THE FATE OF THE WORLD. YOUR QUESTION IS ABOUT THE INTERFERENCE OF ASGARD. IF I KNOW THIS TO BE THE FATE OF HUMANITY, WHY WOULD I NOT STEP IN TO *PREVENT* IT?
WE ARE NOT HERE TO STOP YOU. NEITHER ARE WE HERE TO *HELP* YOU.
BUT YOU MUST UNDERSTAND WHY ONLY *YOU* CAN CHOOSE.
CAND
SIXTY YEAR DROUGH
CURSE OF THE NEW
YANKEE STADIUM
TAXI
GAP

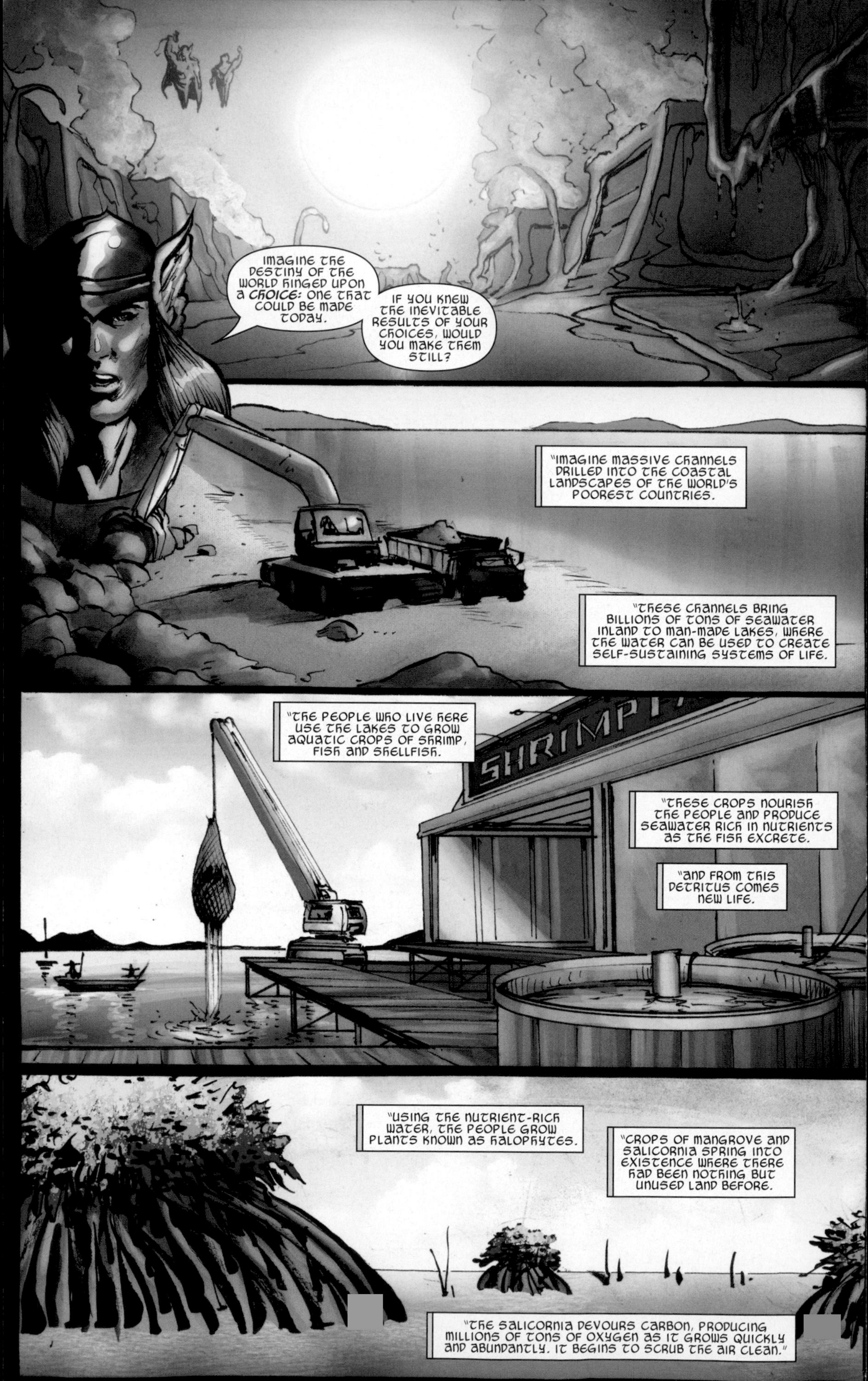
IMAGINE THE DESTINY OF THE WORLD HINGED UPON A *CHOICE:* ONE THAT COULD BE MADE TODAY.
IF YOU KNEW THE INEVITABLE RESULTS OF YOUR CHOICES, WOULD YOU MAKE THEM STILL?
"IMAGINE MASSIVE CHANNELS DRILLED INTO THE COASTAL LANDSCAPES OF THE WORLD'S POOREST COUNTRIES.
"THESE CHANNELS BRING BILLIONS OF TONS OF SEAWATER INLAND TO MAN-MADE LAKES, WHERE THE WATER CAN BE USED TO CREATE SELF-SUSTAINING SYSTEMS OF LIFE.
"THE PEOPLE WHO LIVE HERE USE THE LAKES TO GROW AQUATIC CROPS OF SHRIMP, FISH AND SHELLFISH.
SHRIMP
"THESE CROPS NOURISH THE PEOPLE AND PRODUCE SEAWATER RICH IN NUTRIENTS AS THE FISH EXCRETE.
"AND FROM THIS DETRITUS COMES NEW LIFE.
"USING THE NUTRIENT-RICH WATER, THE PEOPLE GROW PLANTS KNOWN AS HALOPHYTES.
"CROPS OF MANGROVE AND SALICORNIA SPRING INTO EXISTENCE WHERE THERE HAD BEEN NOTHING BUT UNUSED LAND BEFORE.
"THE SALICORNIA DEVOURS CARBON, PRODUCING MILLIONS OF TONS OF OXYGEN AS IT GROWS QUICKLY AND ABUNDANTLY. IT BEGINS TO SCRUB THE AIR CLEAN."

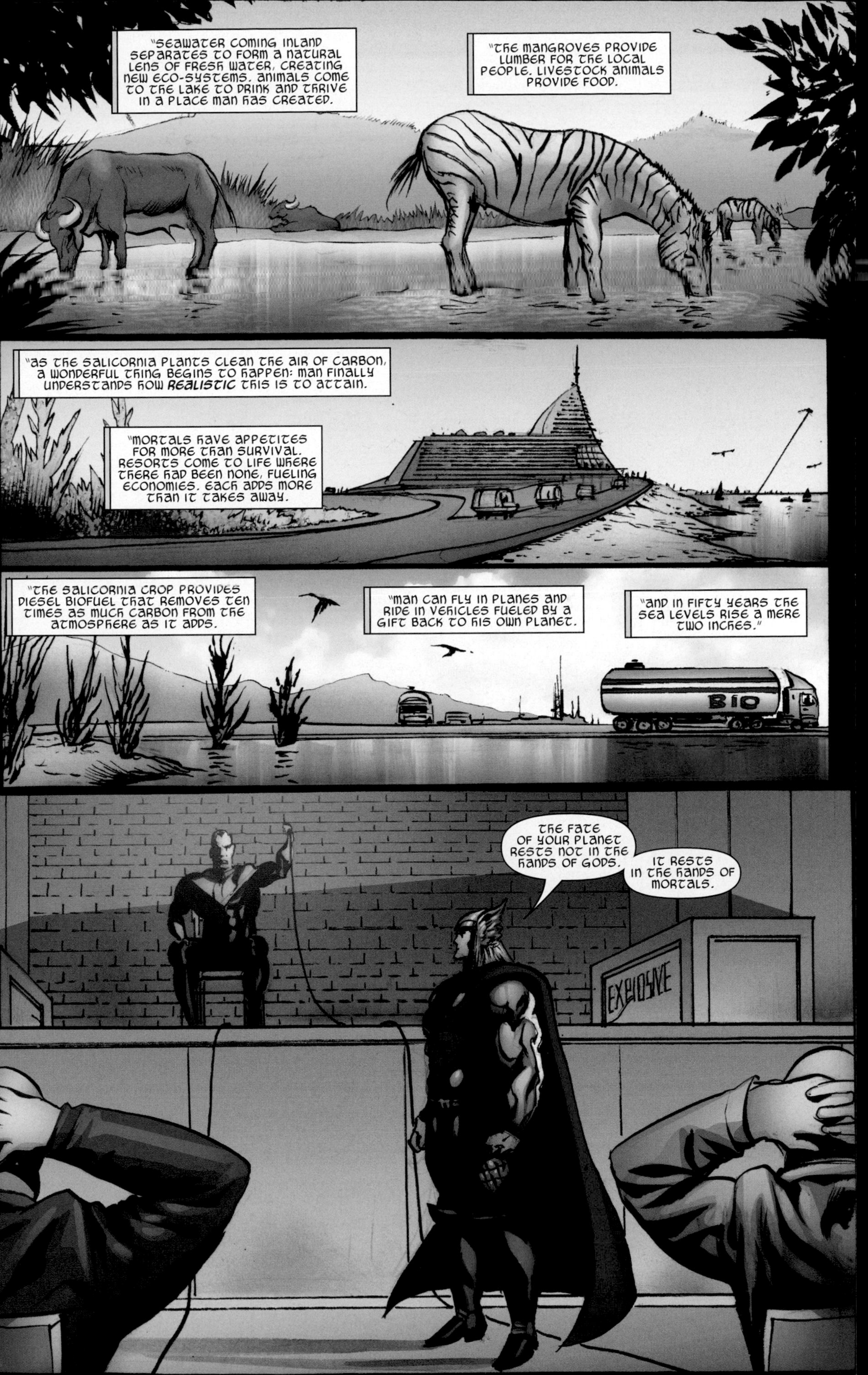
"SEAWATER COMING INLAND SEPARATES TO FORM A NATURAL LENS OF FRESH WATER, CREATING NEW ECO-SYSTEMS. ANIMALS COME TO THE LAKE TO DRINK AND THRIVE IN A PLACE MAN HAS CREATED.
"THE MANGROVES PROVIDE LUMBER FOR THE LOCAL PEOPLE. LIVESTOCK ANIMALS PROVIDE FOOD.
"AS THE SALICORNIA PLANTS CLEAN THE AIR OF CARBON, A WONDERFUL THING BEGINS TO HAPPEN: MAN FINALLY UNDERSTANDS HOW REALISTIC THIS IS TO ATTAIN.
"MORTALS HAVE APPETITES FOR MORE THAN SURVIVAL. RESORTS COME TO LIFE WHERE THERE HAD BEEN NONE, FUELING ECONOMIES. EACH ADDS MORE THAN IT TAKES AWAY.
"THE SALICORNIA CROP PROVIDES DIESEL BIOFUEL THAT REMOVES TEN TIMES AS MUCH CARBON FROM THE ATMOSPHERE AS IT ADDS.
"MAN CAN FLY IN PLANES AND RIDE IN VEHICLES FUELED BY A GIFT BACK TO HIS OWN PLANET.
"AND IN FIFTY YEARS THE SEA LEVELS RISE A MERE TWO INCHES."
BIO
THE FATE OF YOUR PLANET RESTS NOT IN THE HANDS OF GODS.
IT RESTS IN THE HANDS OF MORTALS.
EXPLOSIVE

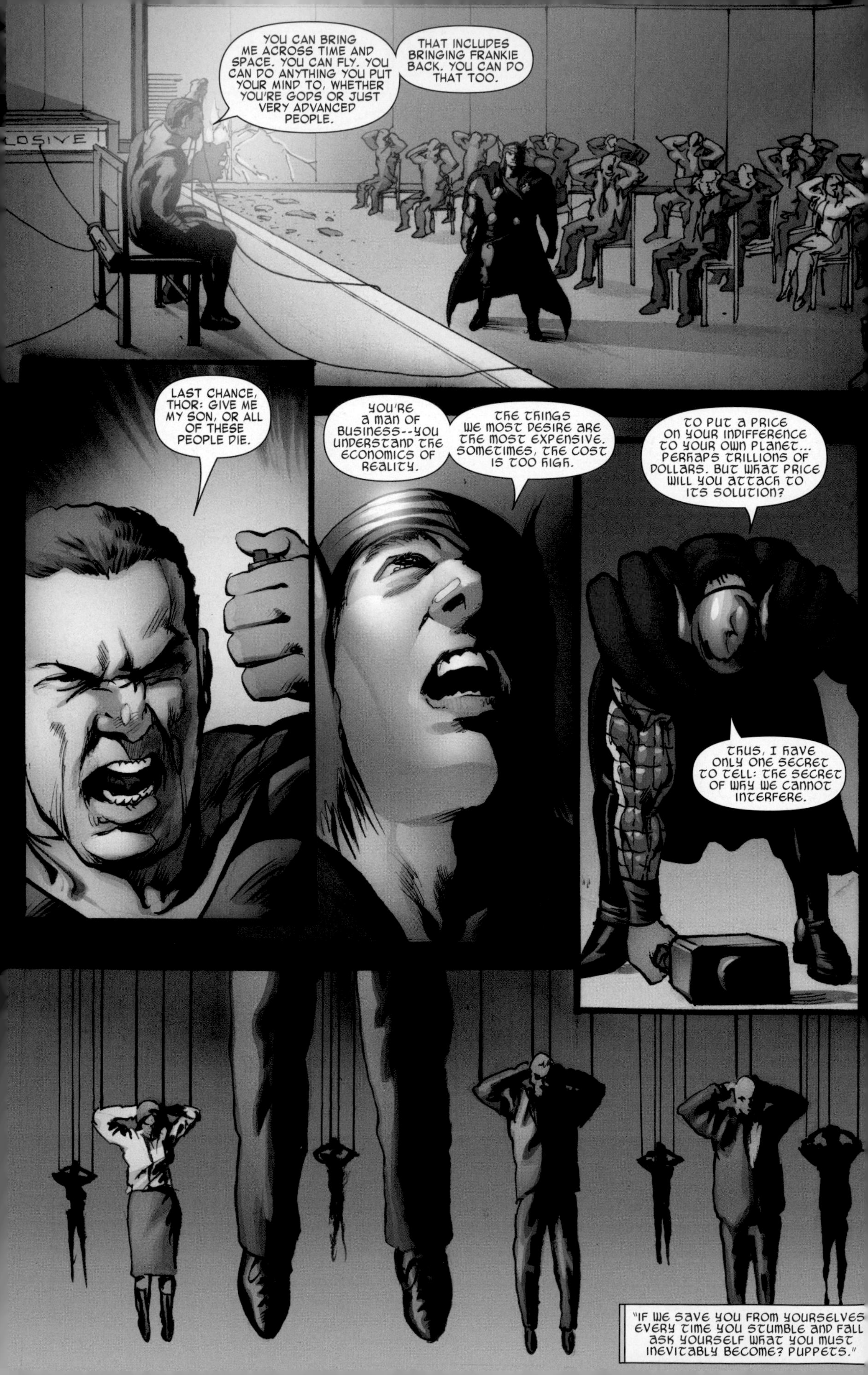
LOSIVE
YOU CAN BRING ME ACROSS TIME AND SPACE. YOU CAN FLY. YOU CAN DO ANYTHING YOU PUT YOUR MIND TO, WHETHER YOU'RE GODS OR JUST VERY ADVANCED PEOPLE.
THAT INCLUDES BRINGING FRANKIE BACK. YOU CAN DO THAT TOO.
LAST CHANCE, THOR: GIVE ME MY SON, OR ALL OF THESE PEOPLE DIE.
YOU'RE A MAN OF BUSINESS--YOU UNDERSTAND THE ECONOMICS OF REALITY.
THE THINGS WE MOST DESIRE ARE THE MOST EXPENSIVE. SOMETIMES, THE COST IS TOO HIGH.
TO PUT A PRICE ON YOUR INDIFFERENCE TO YOUR OWN PLANET... PERHAPS TRILLIONS OF DOLLARS. BUT WHAT PRICE WILL YOU ATTACH TO ITS SOLUTION?
THUS, I HAVE ONLY ONE SECRET TO TELL: THE SECRET OF WHY WE CANNOT INTERFERE.
"IF WE SAVE YOU FROM YOURSELVES EVERY TIME YOU STUMBLE AND FALL ASK YOURSELF WHAT YOU MUST INEVITABLY BECOME? PUPPETS."

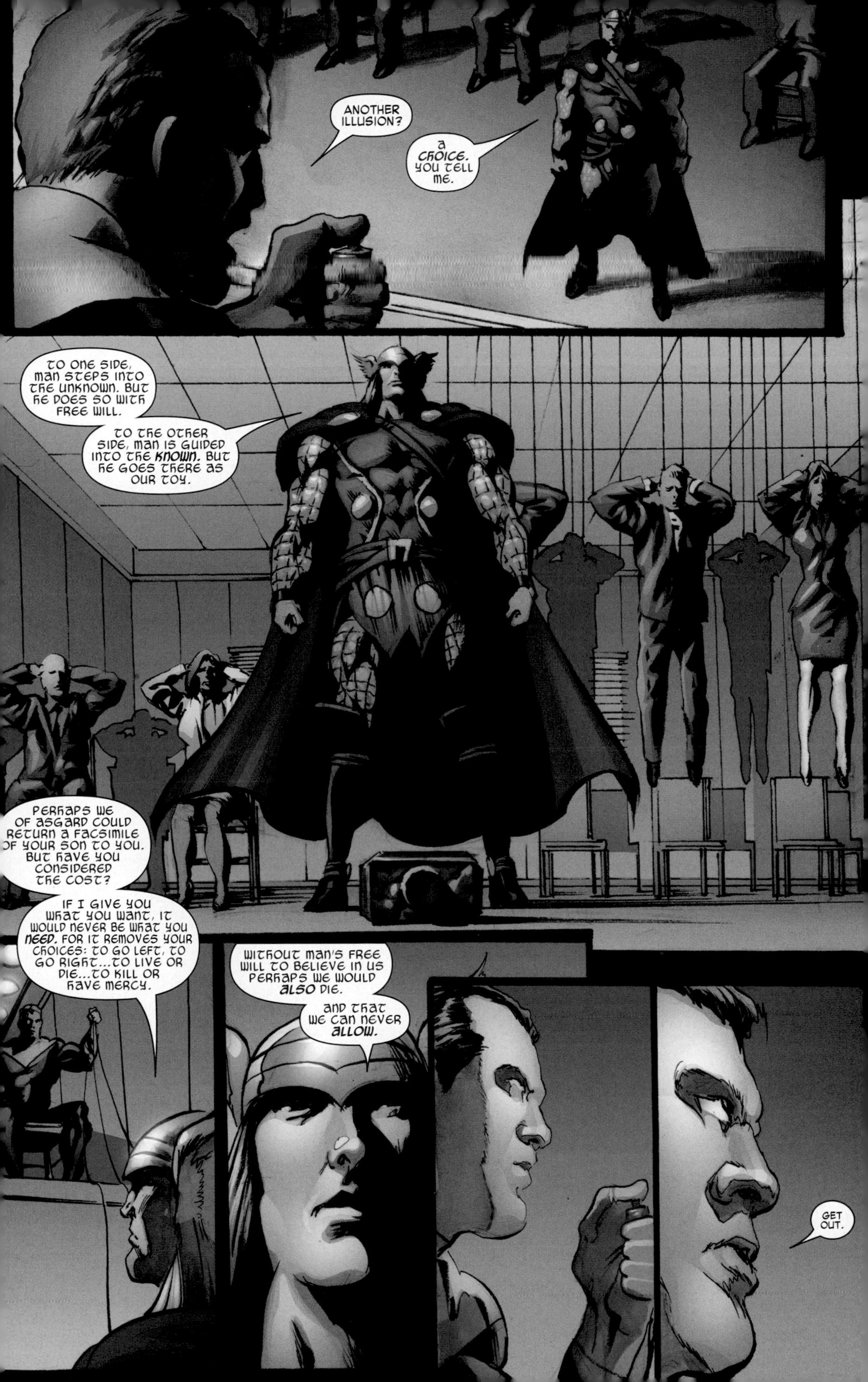
ANOTHER ILLUSION?
A CHOICE. YOU TELL ME.
TO ONE SIDE, MAN STEPS INTO THE UNKNOWN. BUT HE DOES SO WITH FREE WILL.
TO THE OTHER SIDE, MAN IS GUIDED INTO THE KNOWN. BUT HE GOES THERE AS OUR TOY.
PERHAPS WE OF ASGARD COULD RETURN A FACSIMILE OF YOUR SON TO YOU. BUT HAVE YOU CONSIDERED THE COST?
IF I GIVE YOU WHAT YOU WANT, IT WOULD NEVER BE WHAT YOU NEED. FOR IT REMOVES YOUR CHOICES: TO GO LEFT, TO GO RIGHT...TO LIVE OR DIE...TO KILL OR HAVE MERCY.
WITHOUT MAN'S FREE WILL TO BELIEVE IN US PERHAPS WE WOULD ALSO DIE.
AND THAT WE CAN NEVER ALLOW.
GET OUT.

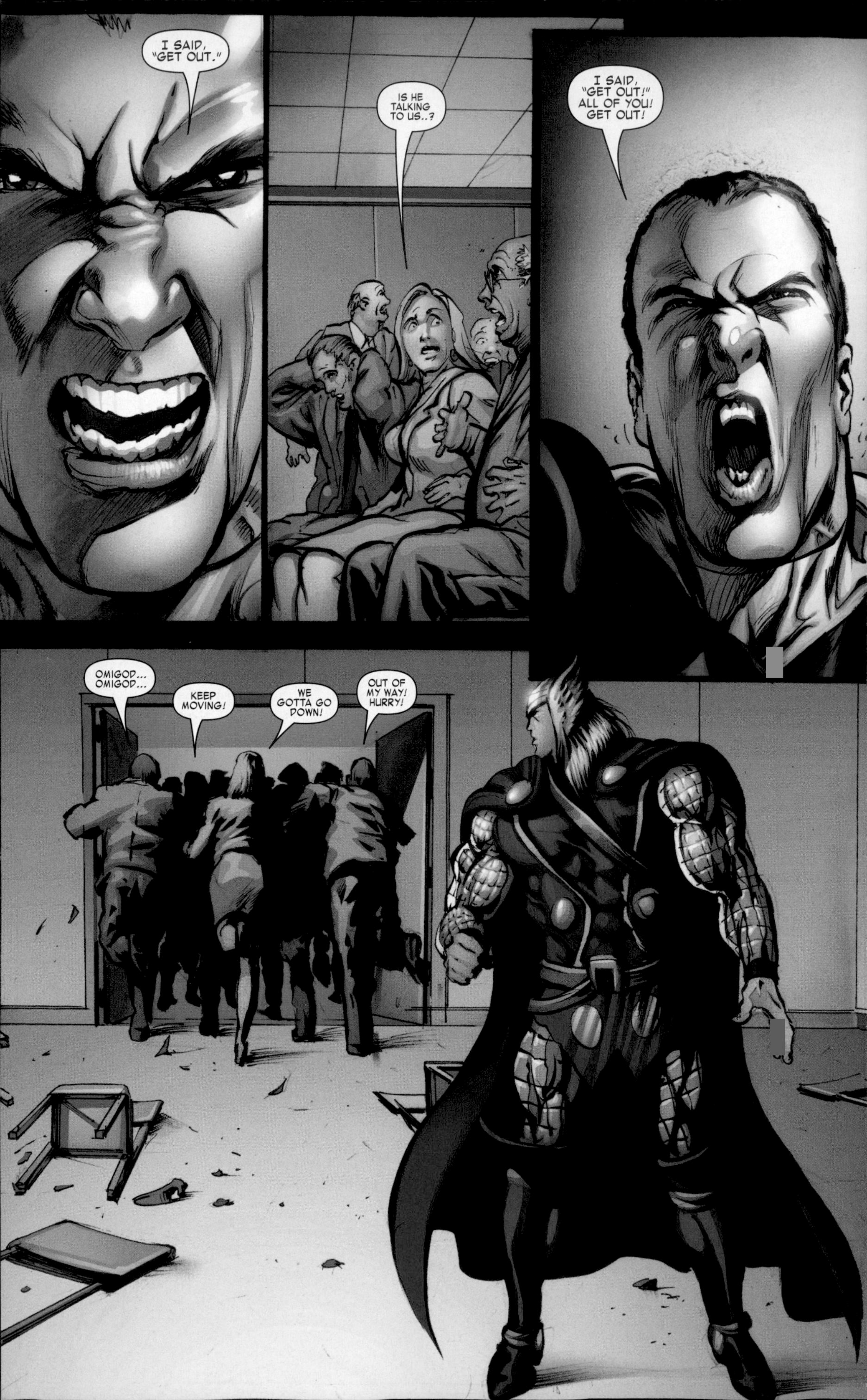
I SAID, "GET OUT."
IS HE TALKING TO US..?
I SAID, "GET OUT!" ALL OF YOU! GET OUT!
OMIGOD... OMIGOD...
KEEP MOVING!
WE GOTTA GO DOWN!
OUT OF MY WAY! HURRY!

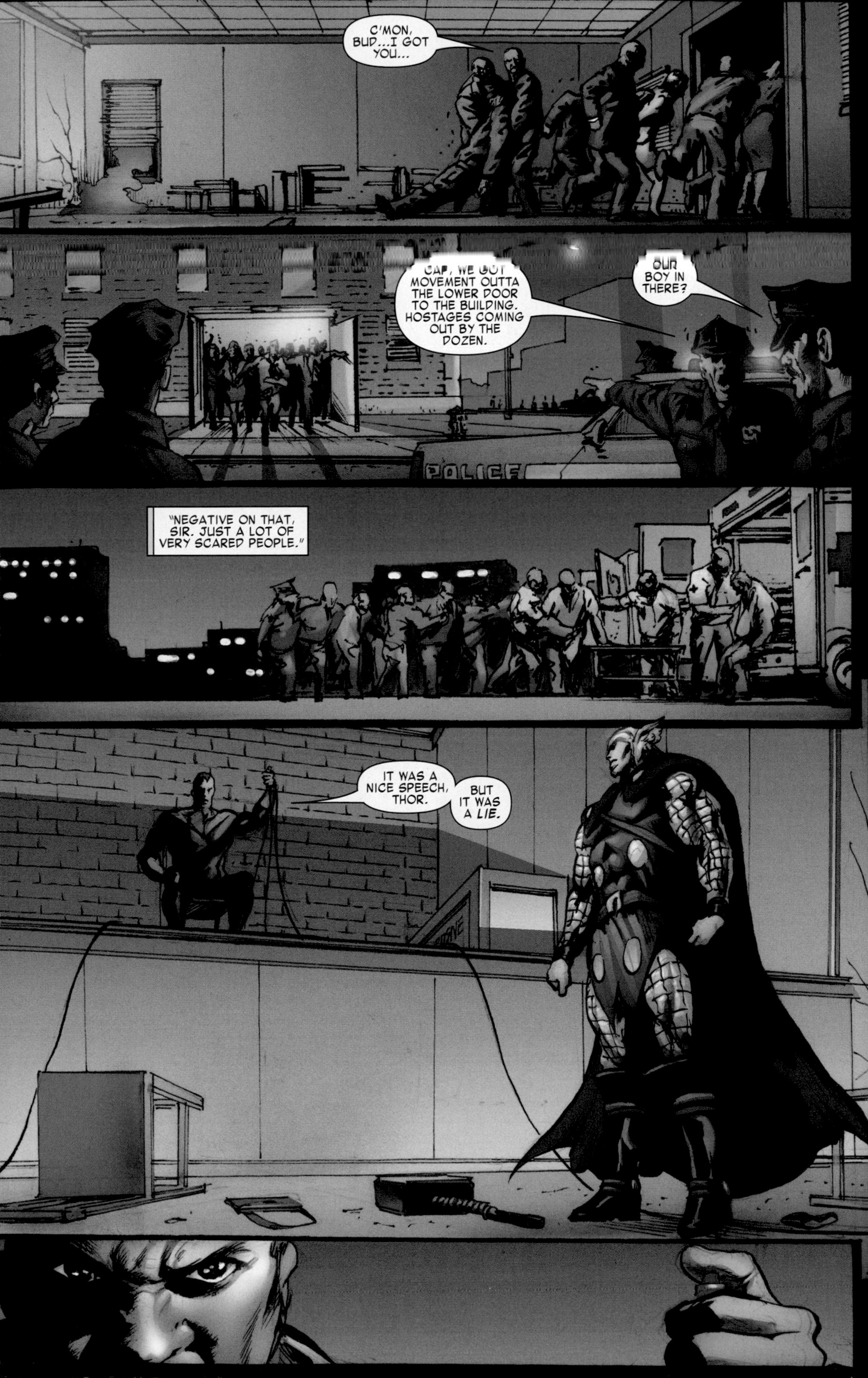
C'MON, BUD...I GOT YOU...
CAP, WE GOT MOVEMENT OUTTA THE LOWER DOOR TO THE BUILDING. HOSTAGES COMING OUT BY THE DOZEN.
OUR BOY IN THERE?
POLICE
"NEGATIVE ON THAT, SIR. JUST A LOT OF VERY SCARED PEOPLE."
IT WAS A NICE SPEECH, THOR.
BUT IT WAS A *LIE.*

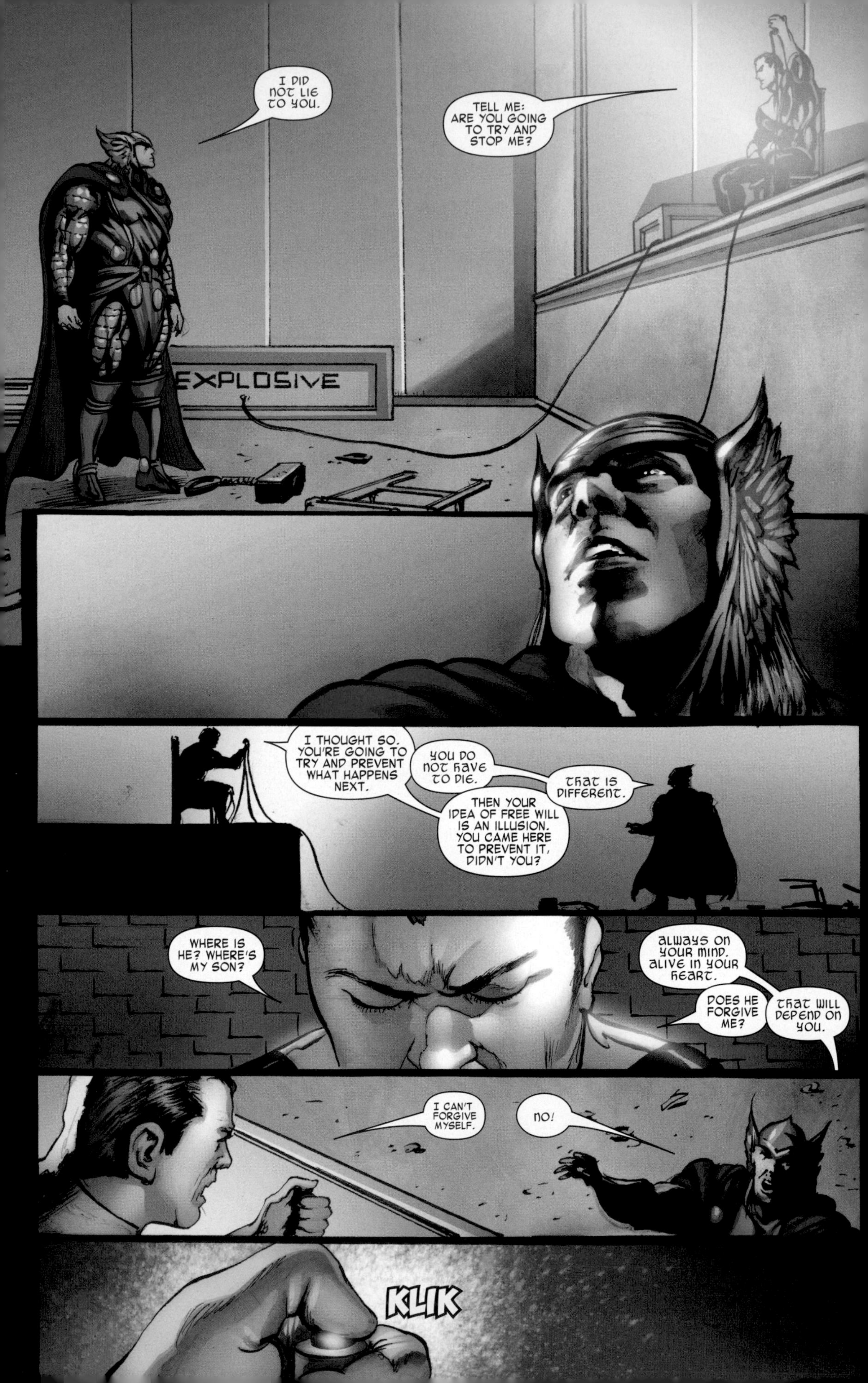
I DID NOT LIE TO YOU.
TELL ME: ARE YOU GOING TO TRY AND STOP ME?
EXPLOSIVE
I THOUGHT SO. YOU'RE GOING TO TRY AND PREVENT WHAT HAPPENS NEXT.
YOU DO NOT HAVE TO DIE.
THAT IS DIFFERENT.
THEN YOUR IDEA OF FREE WILL IS AN ILLUSION. YOU CAME HERE TO PREVENT IT, DIDN'T YOU?
WHERE IS HE? WHERE'S MY SON?
ALWAYS ON YOUR MIND. ALIVE IN YOUR HEART.
DOES HE FORGIVE ME?
THAT WILL DEPEND ON YOU.
I CAN'T FORGIVE MYSELF.
NO!
KLIK

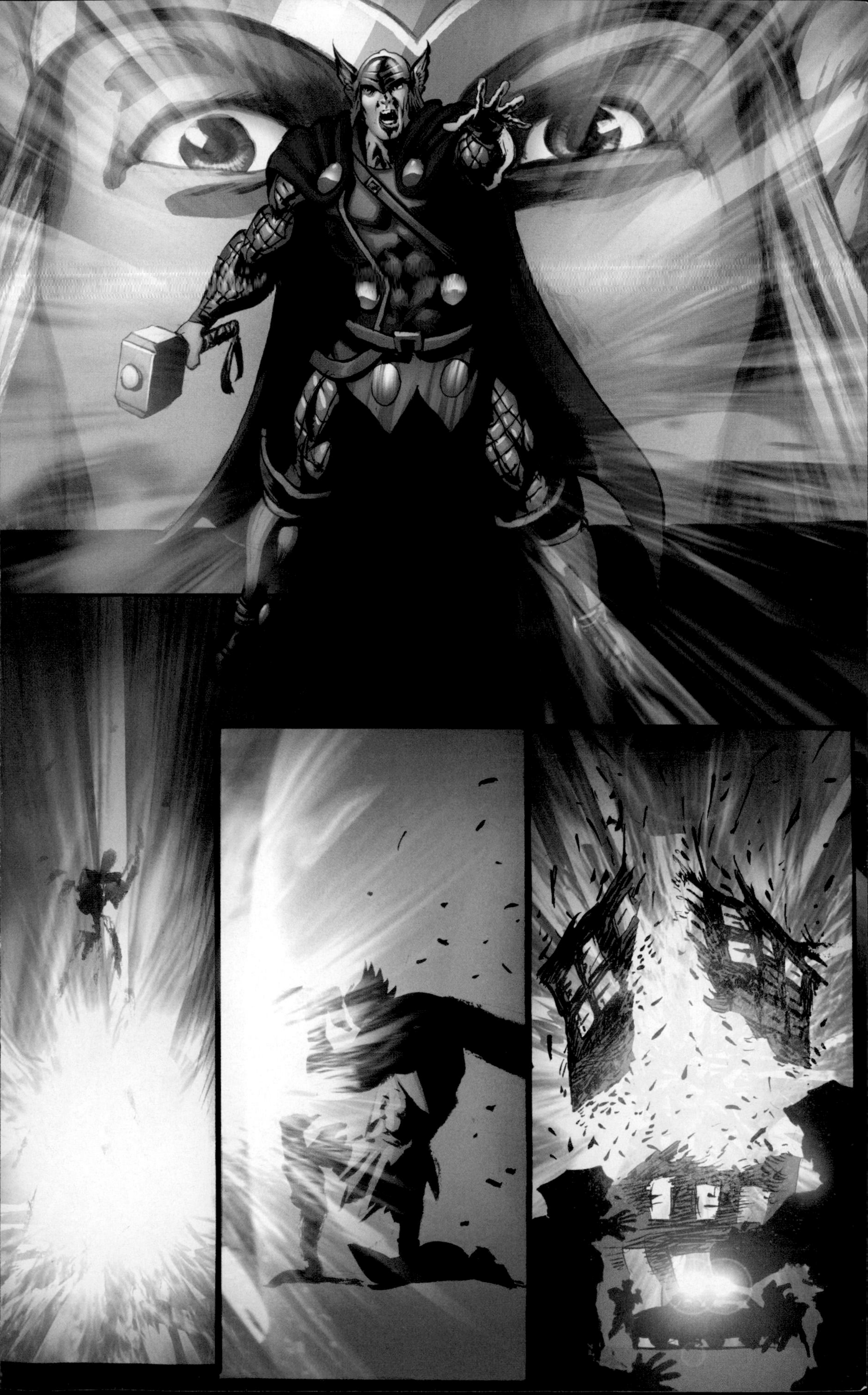

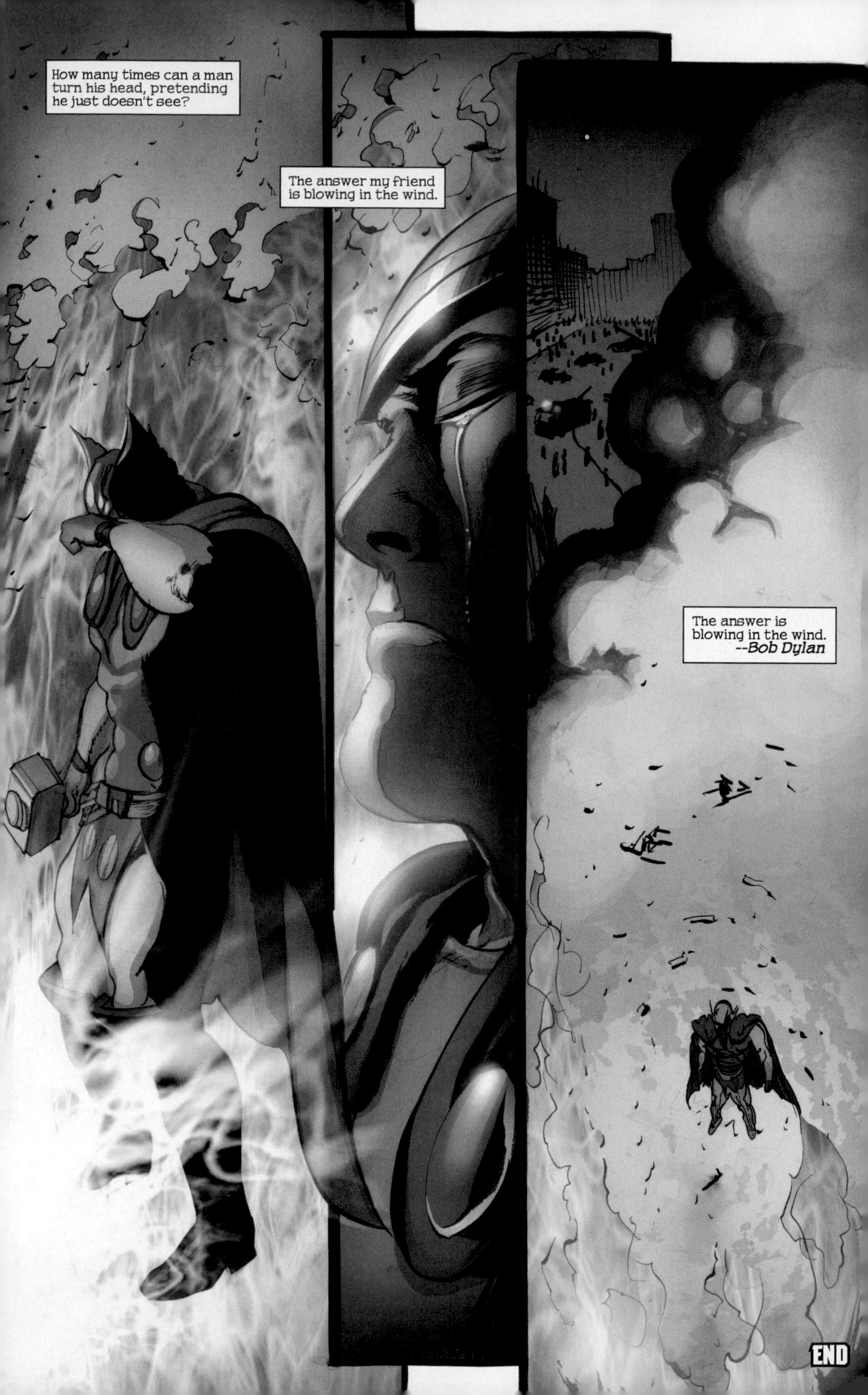
How many times can a man turn his head, pretending he just doesn't see?
The answer my friend is blowing in the wind.
The answer is blowing in the wind. --Bob Dylan
END

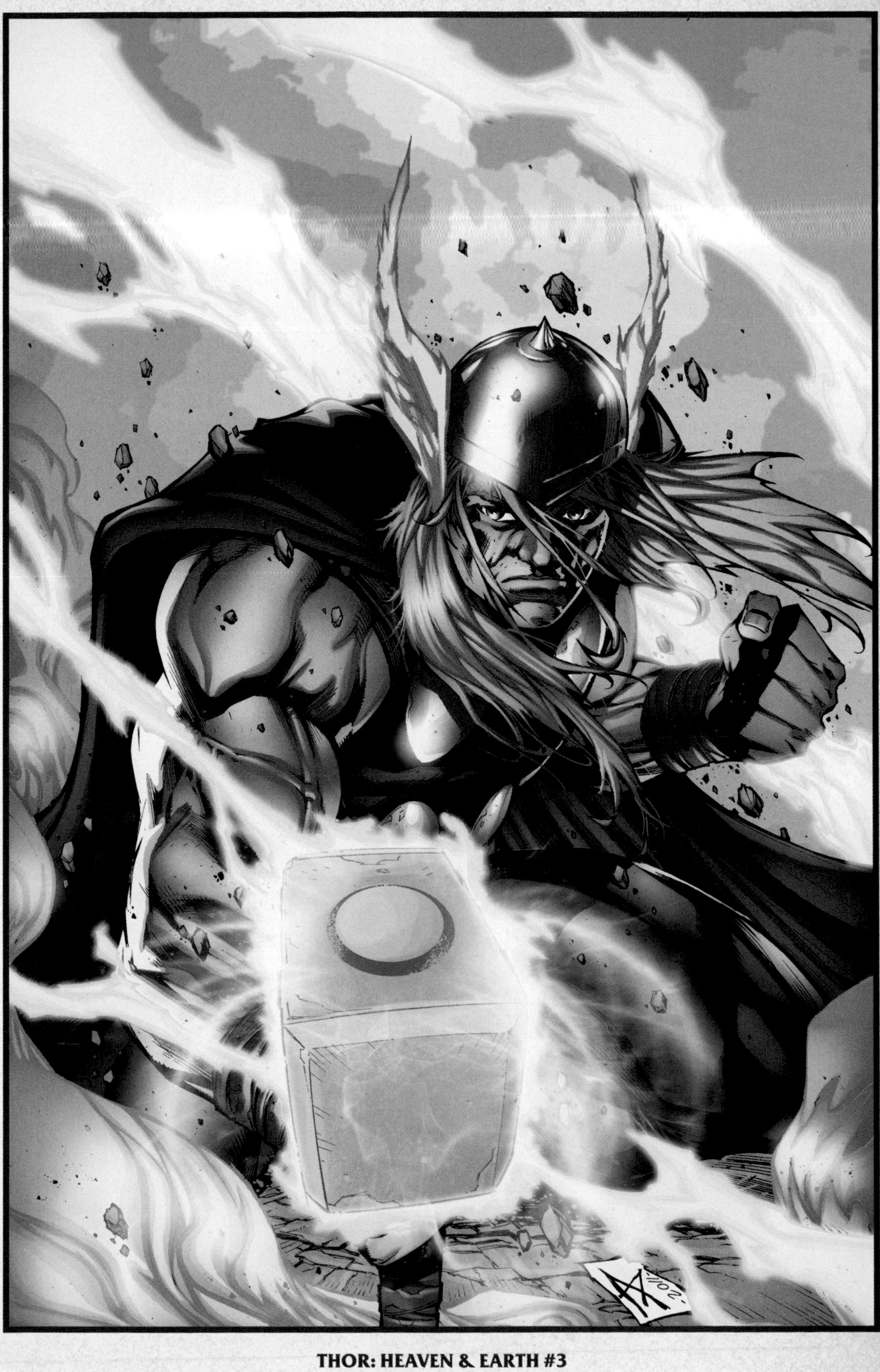

THOR: HEAVEN & EARTH #3

IT WON'T BE LONG NOW. IT'S PROBABLY JUST A MATTER OF HOURS.

IS IT GOING TO BE TONIGHT?

YES, I'M AFRAID SO.

"...CAN WE BE SURE HE ISN'T SUFFERING...?"

"...I'VE DONE WHAT I CAN TO MAKE HIM COMFORTABLE..."

"...DIFFICULTY BREATHING. YOU SHOULD GATHER TOGETHER AND SAY GOOD-BYE SOON, IF YOU CAN..."

"...A FEW MOMENTS TO CALL HIS SISTER IN CALIFORNIA..."

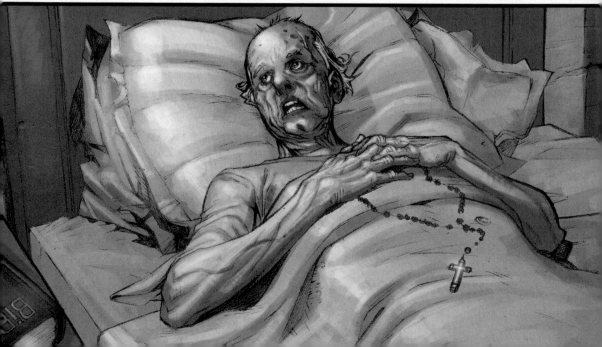

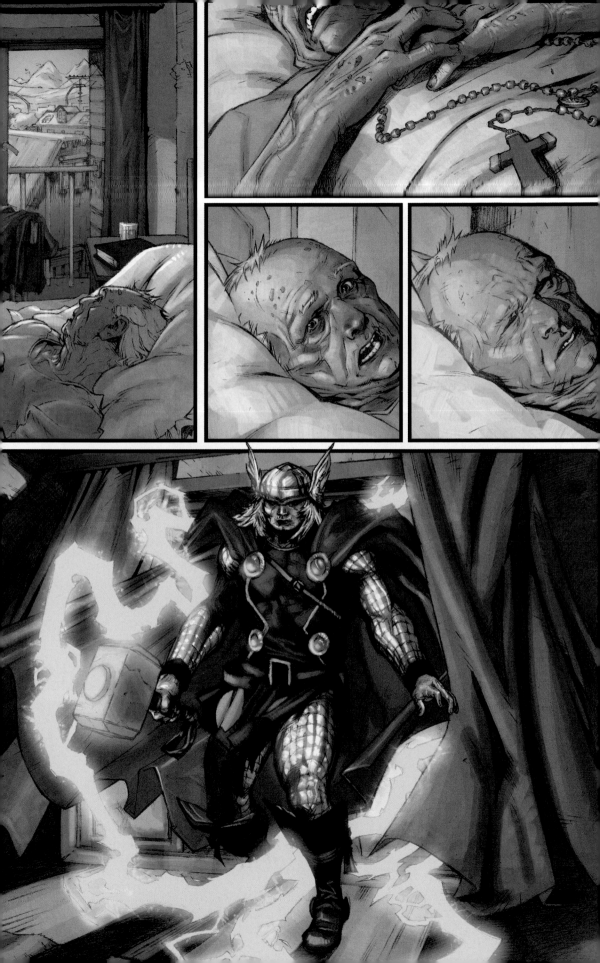

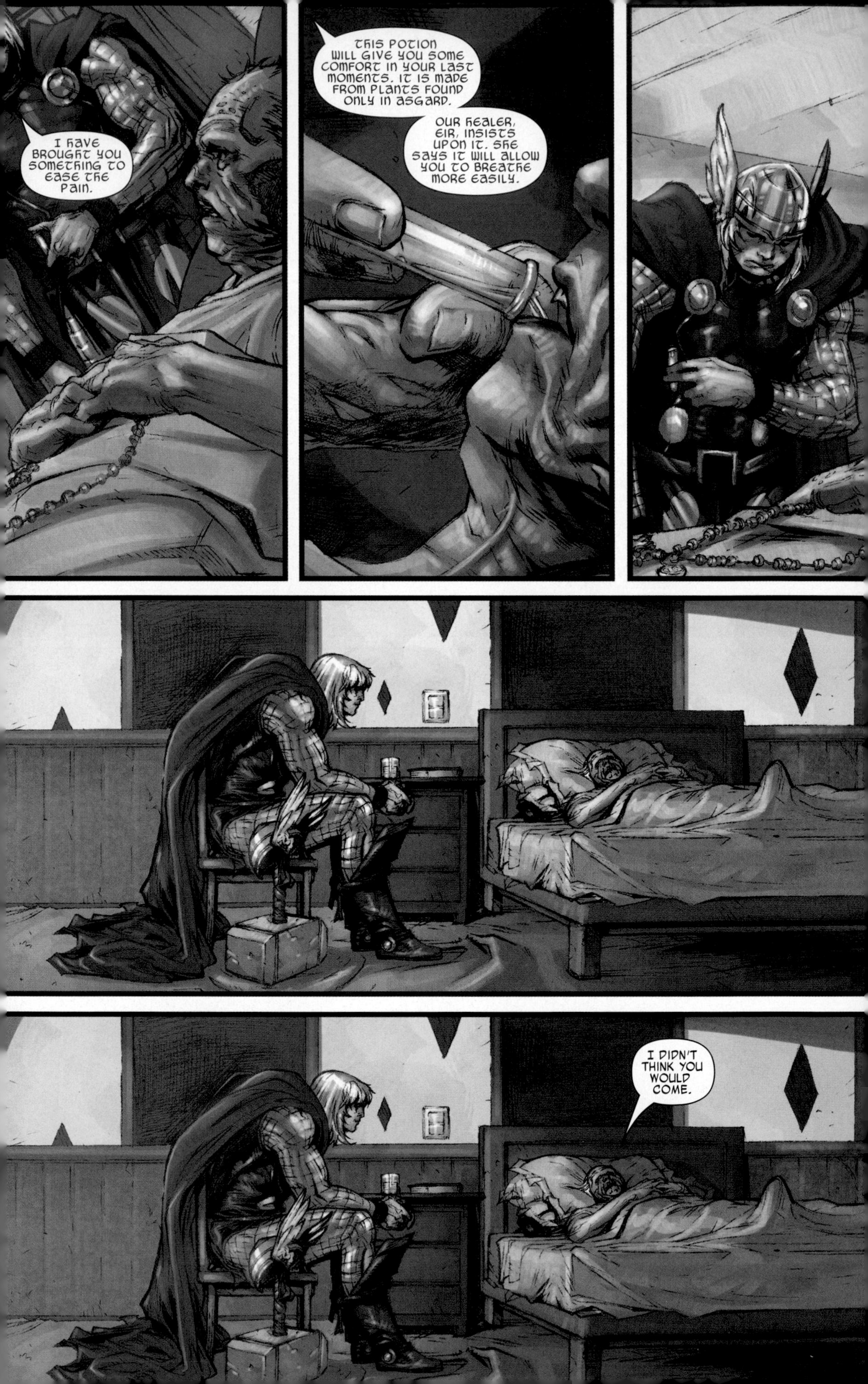
I HAVE BROUGHT YOU SOMETHING TO EASE THE PAIN.
THIS POTION WILL GIVE YOU SOME COMFORT IN YOUR LAST MOMENTS. IT IS MADE FROM PLANTS FOUND ONLY IN ASGARD.
OUR HEALER, EIR, INSISTS UPON IT. SHE SAYS IT WILL ALLOW YOU TO BREATHE MORE EASILY.
I DIDN'T THINK YOU WOULD COME.

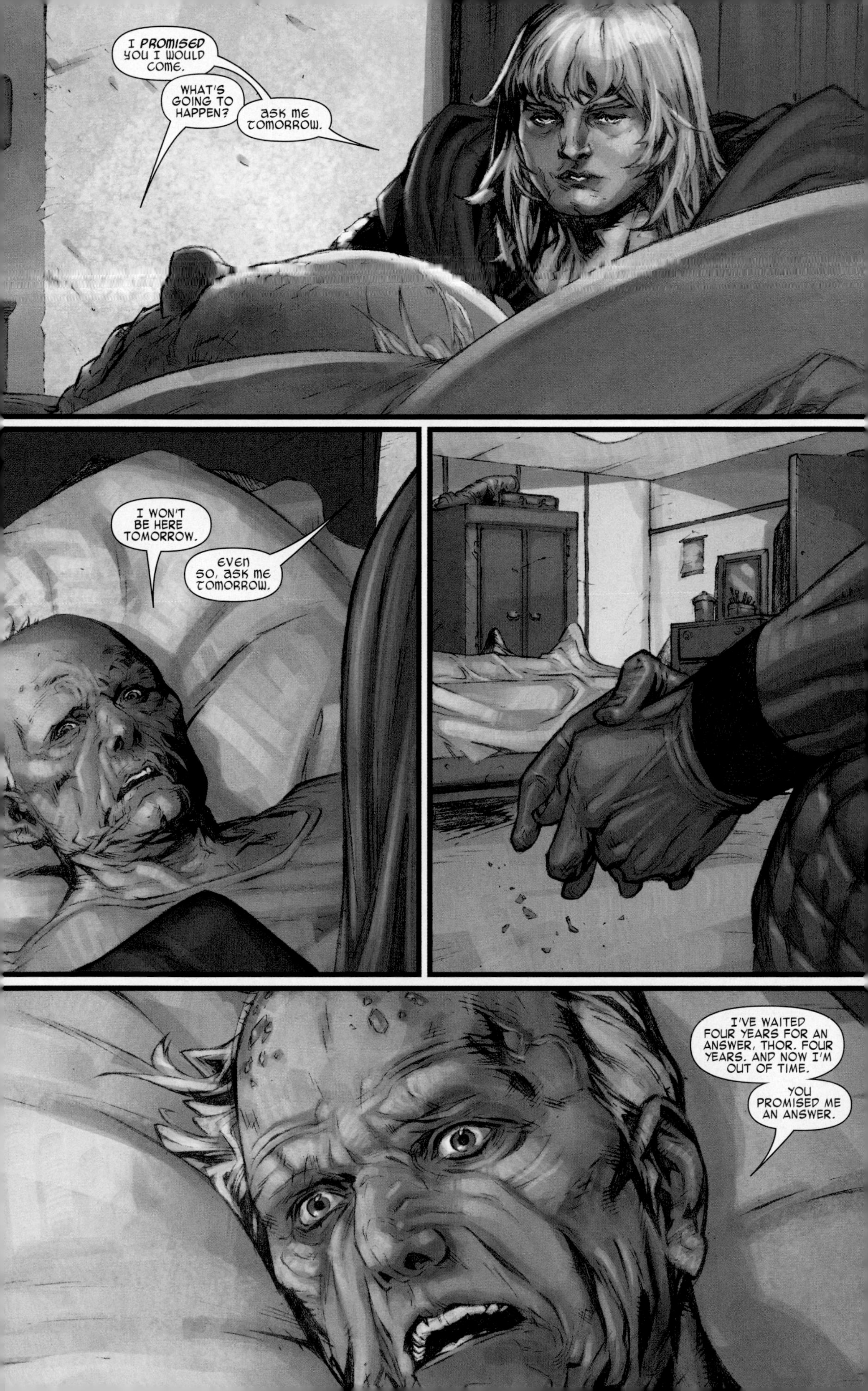
I PROMISED YOU I WOULD COME.
WHAT'S GOING TO HAPPEN?
ASK ME TOMORROW.
I WON'T BE HERE TOMORROW.
EVEN SO, ASK ME TOMORROW.
I'VE WAITED FOUR YEARS FOR AN ANSWER, THOR. FOUR YEARS. AND NOW I'M OUT OF TIME.
YOU PROMISED ME AN ANSWER.

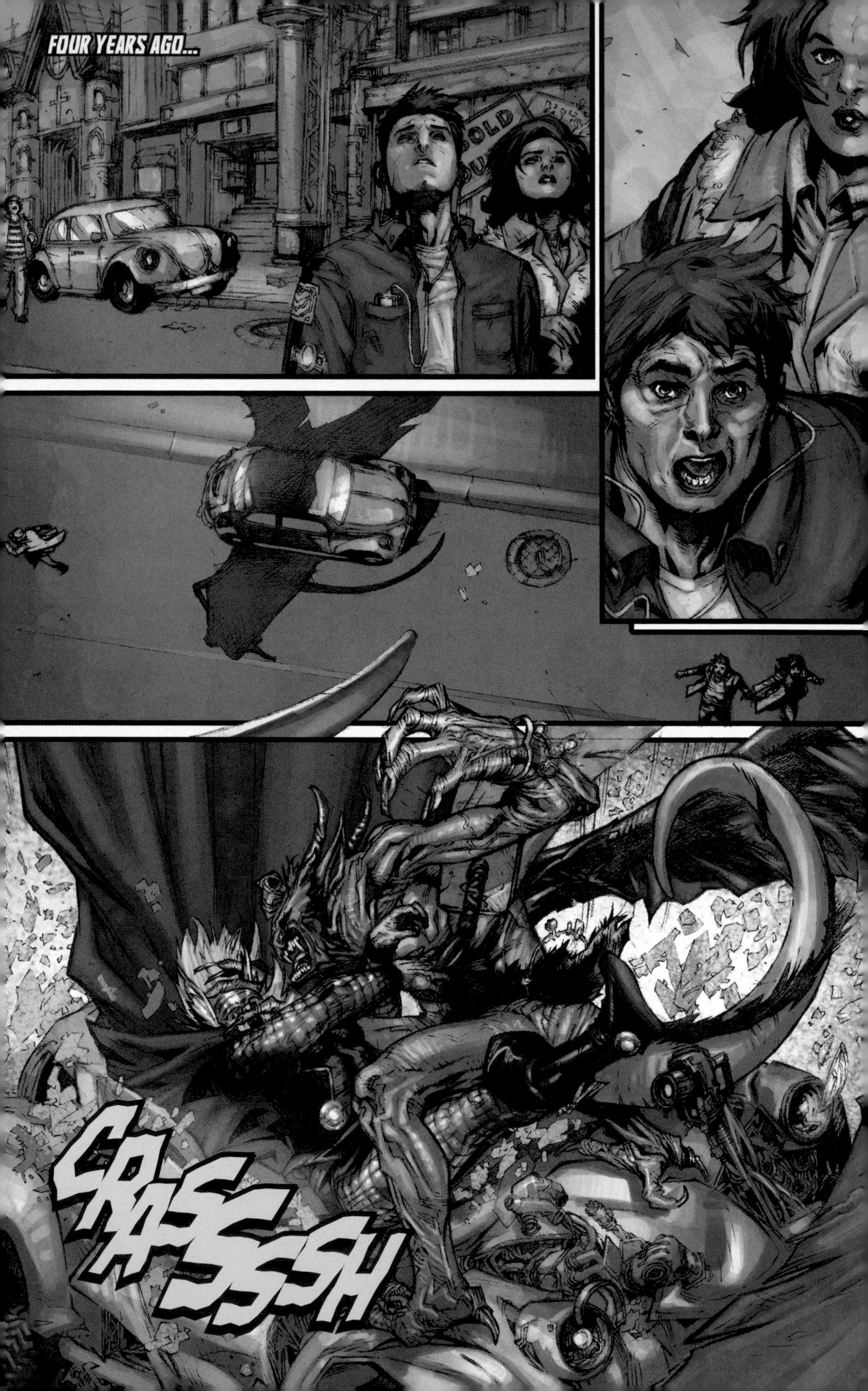
FOUR YEARS AGO...
SOLD
CRASSSSH

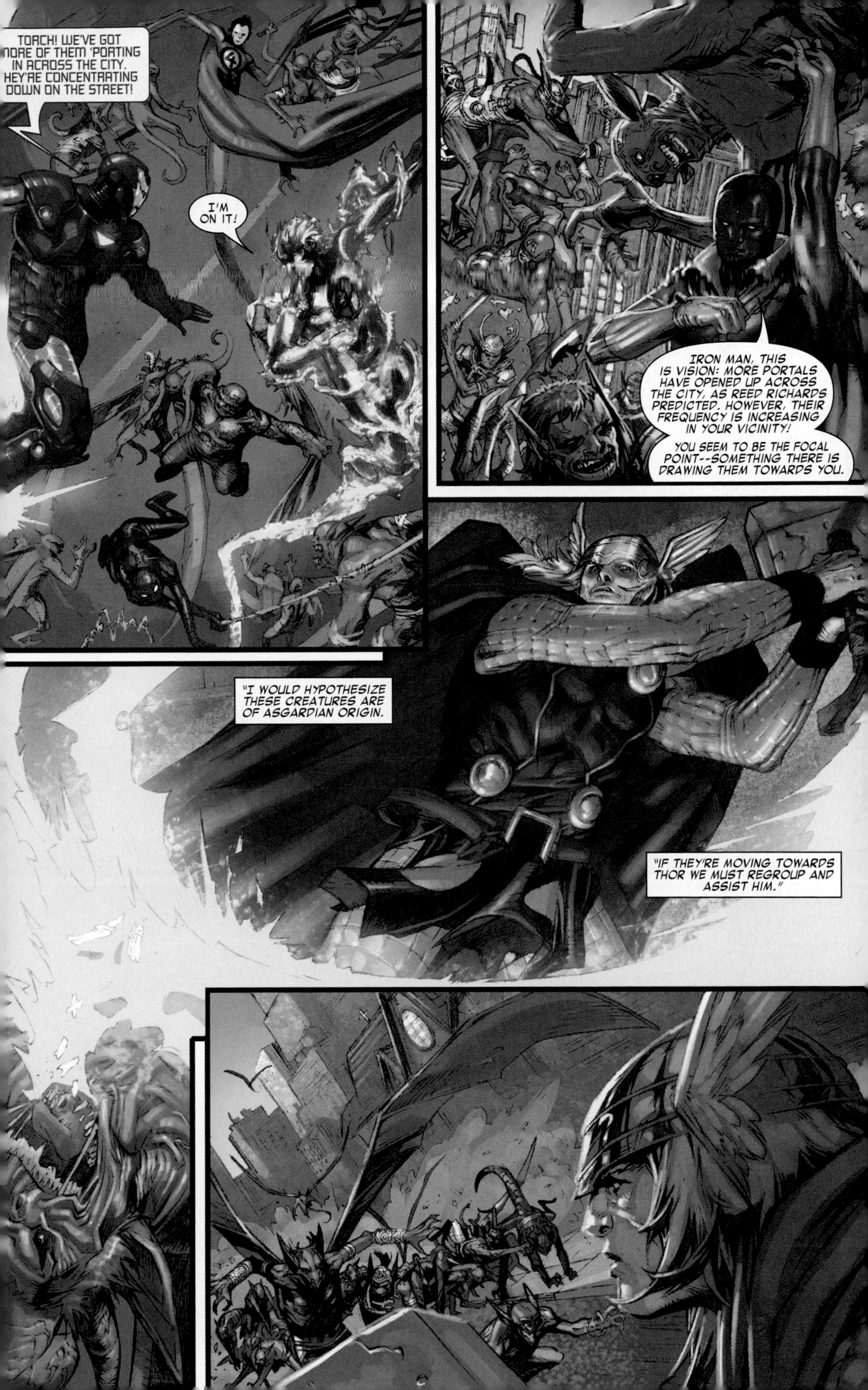
TORCH! WE'VE GOT MORE OF THEM 'PORTING IN ACROSS THE CITY. THEY'RE CONCENTRATING DOWN ON THE STREET!
I'M ON IT!
IRON MAN, THIS IS VISION: MORE PORTALS HAVE OPENED UP ACROSS THE CITY, AS REED RICHARDS PREDICTED. HOWEVER, THEIR FREQUENCY IS INCREASING IN YOUR VICINITY!
YOU SEEM TO BE THE FOCAL POINT--SOMETHING THERE IS DRAWING THEM TOWARDS YOU.
"I WOULD HYPOTHESIZE THESE CREATURES ARE OF ASGARDIAN ORIGIN.
"IF THEY'RE MOVING TOWARDS THOR WE MUST REGROUP AND ASSIST HIM."

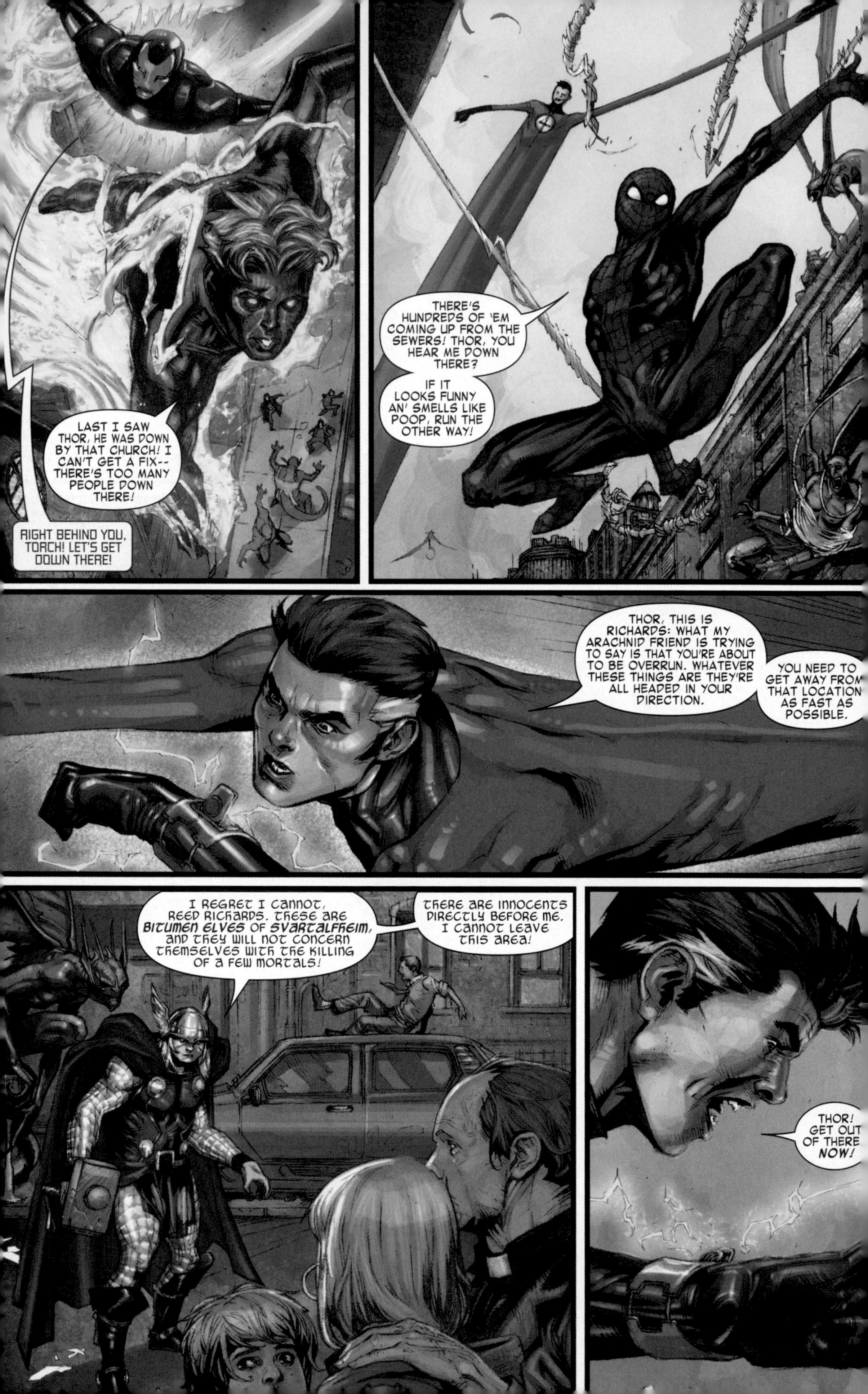
LAST I SAW THOR, HE WAS DOWN BY THAT CHURCH! I CAN'T GET A FIX-- THERE'S TOO MANY PEOPLE DOWN THERE!
RIGHT BEHIND YOU, TORCH! LET'S GET DOWN THERE!
THERE'S HUNDREDS OF 'EM COMING UP FROM THE SEWERS! THOR, YOU HEAR ME DOWN THERE?
IF IT LOOKS FUNNY AN' SMELLS LIKE POOP, RUN THE OTHER WAY!
THOR, THIS IS RICHARDS: WHAT MY ARACHNID FRIEND IS TRYING TO SAY IS THAT YOU'RE ABOUT TO BE OVERRUN. WHATEVER THESE THINGS ARE THEY'RE ALL HEADED IN YOUR DIRECTION.
YOU NEED TO GET AWAY FROM THAT LOCATION AS FAST AS POSSIBLE.
I REGRET I CANNOT, REED RICHARDS. THESE ARE BITUMEN ELVES OF SVARTALFHEIM, AND THEY WILL NOT CONCERN THEMSELVES WITH THE KILLING OF A FEW MORTALS!
THERE ARE INNOCENTS DIRECTLY BEFORE ME. I CANNOT LEAVE THIS AREA!
THOR! GET OUT OF THERE NOW!

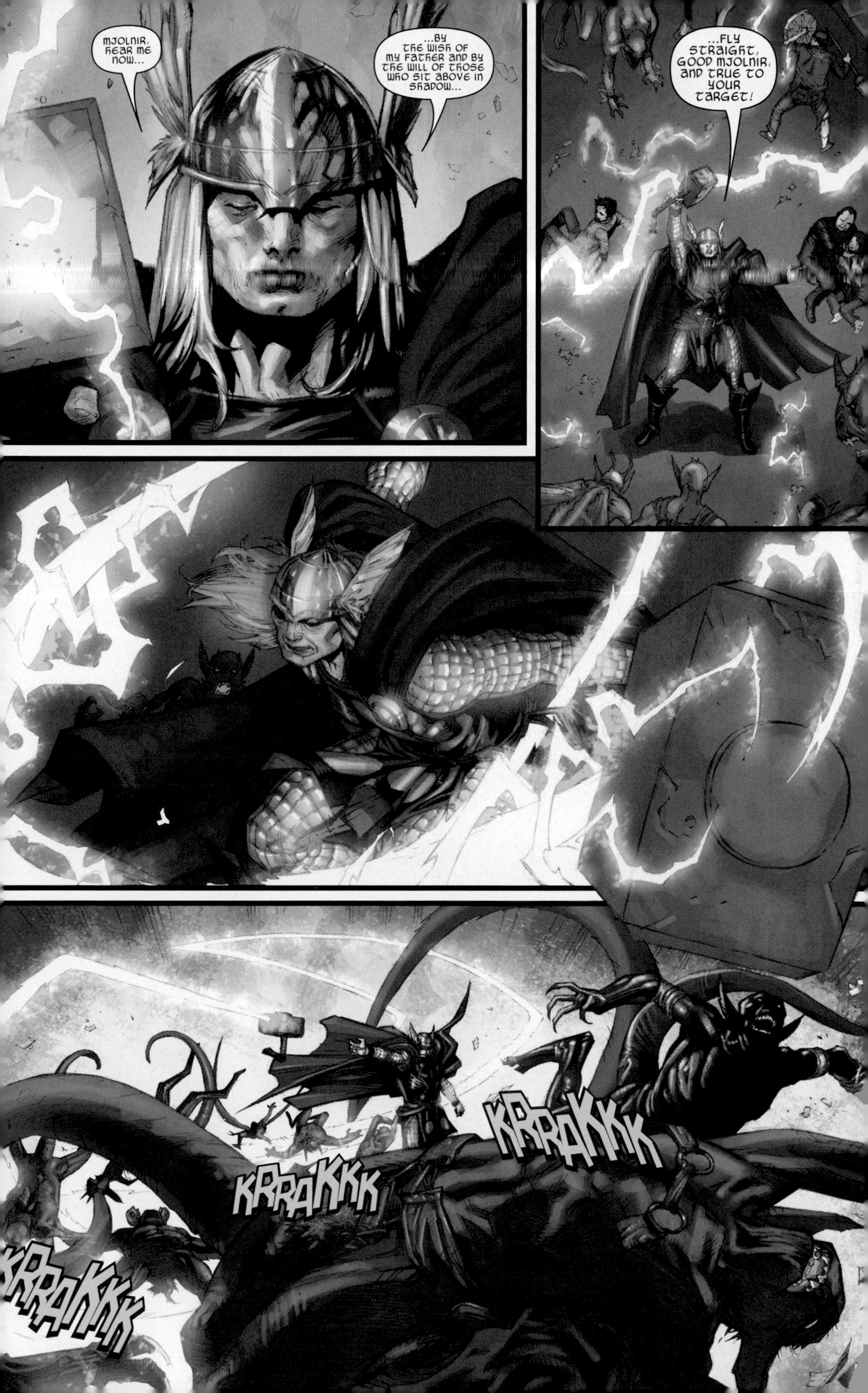
MJOLNIR, HEAR ME NOW...
...BY THE WISH OF MY FATHER AND BY THE WILL OF THOSE WHO SIT ABOVE IN SHADOW...
...FLY STRAIGHT, GOOD MJOLNIR, AND TRUE TO YOUR TARGET!
KRRAKKK
KRRAKKK
KRRAKKK

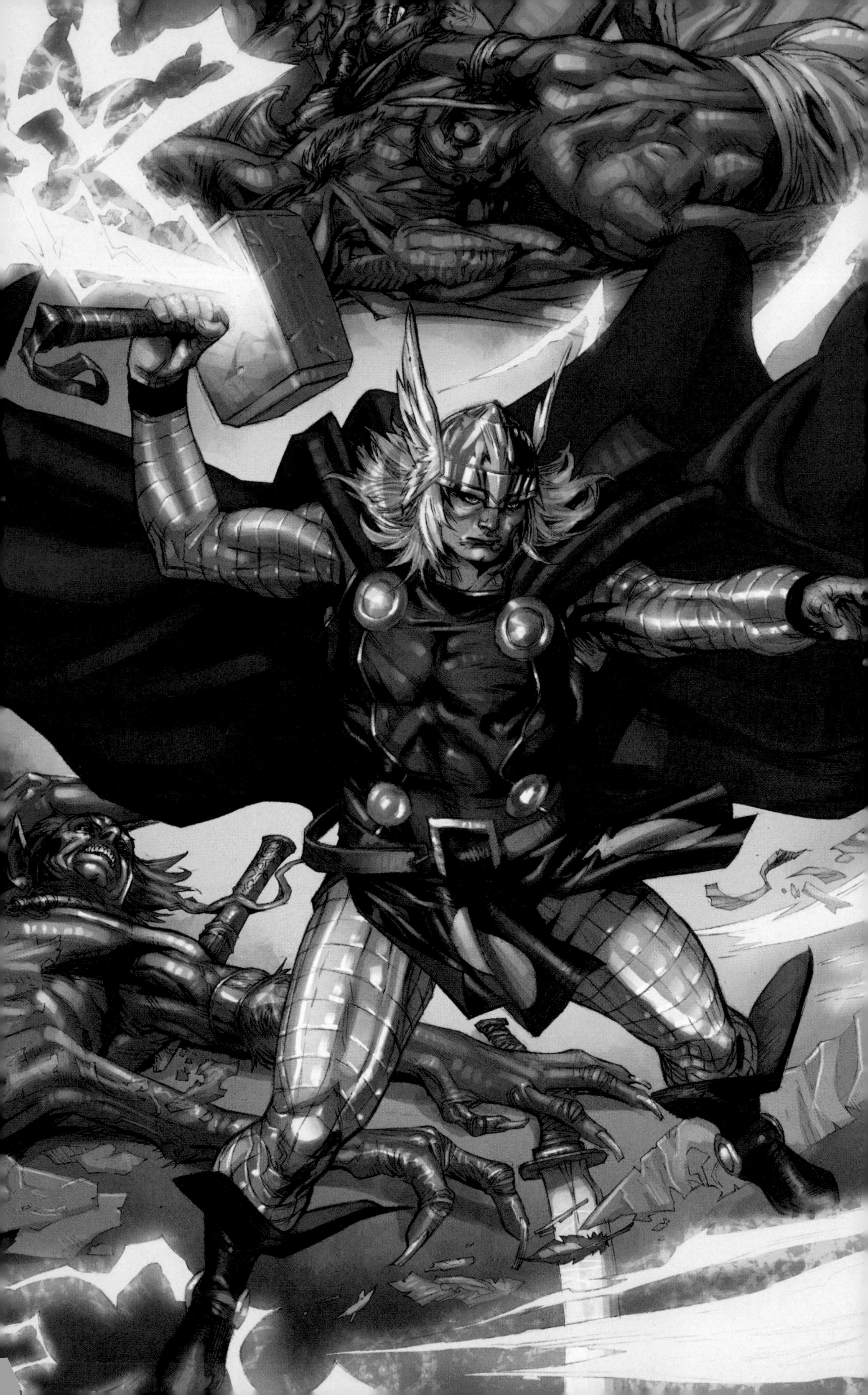

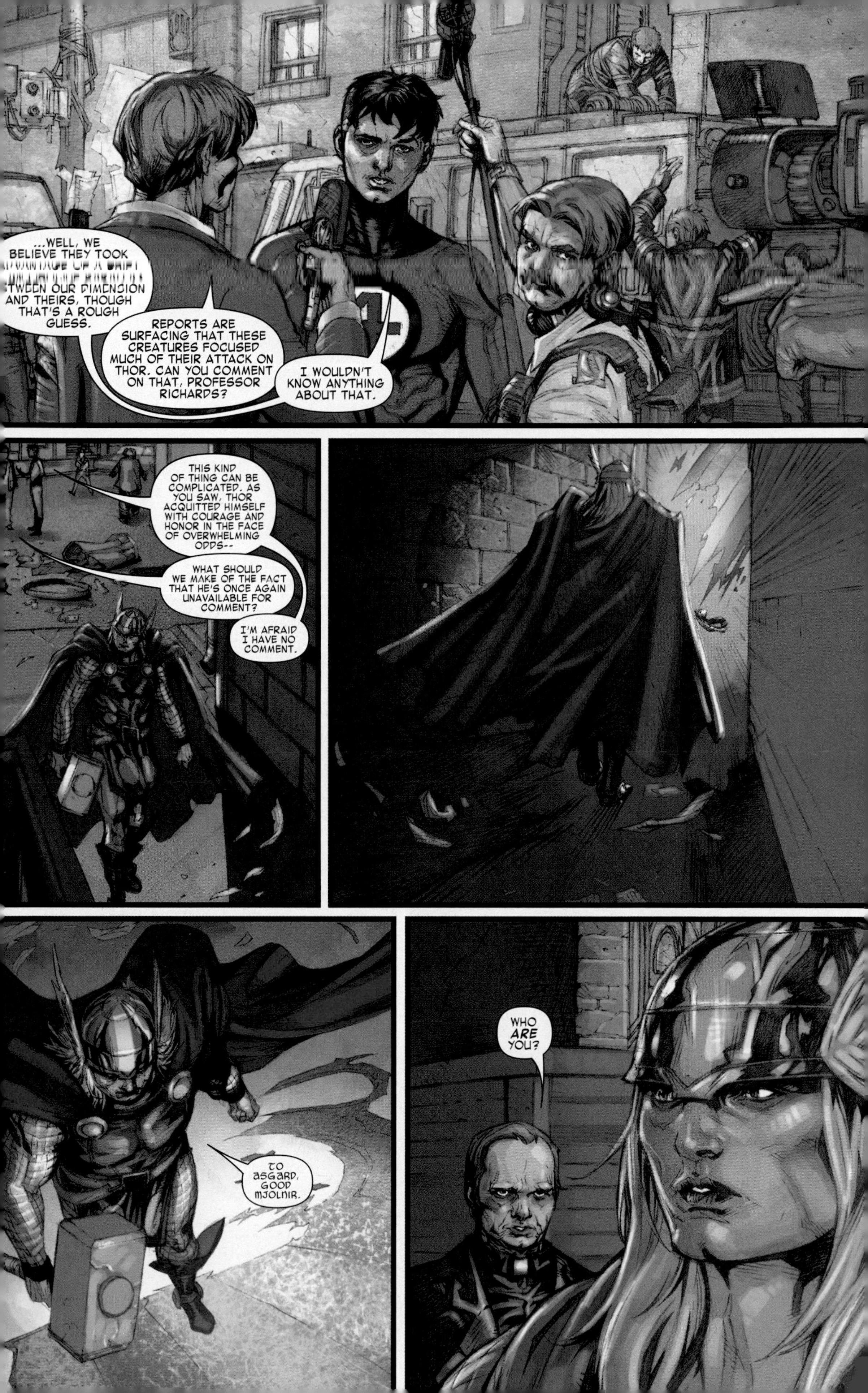
...WELL, WE BELIEVE THEY TOOK
TWEEN OUR DIMENSION AND THEIRS, THOUGH THAT'S A ROUGH GUESS.
REPORTS ARE SURFACING THAT THESE CREATURES FOCUSED MUCH OF THEIR ATTACK ON THOR. CAN YOU COMMENT ON THAT, PROFESSOR RICHARDS?
I WOULDN'T KNOW ANYTHING ABOUT THAT.
THIS KIND OF THING CAN BE COMPLICATED. AS YOU SAW, THOR ACQUITTED HIMSELF WITH COURAGE AND HONOR IN THE FACE OF OVERWHELMING ODDS--
WHAT SHOULD WE MAKE OF THE FACT THAT HE'S ONCE AGAIN UNAVAILABLE FOR COMMENT?
I'M AFRAID I HAVE NO COMMENT.
TO ASGARD, GOOD MJOLNIR.
WHO ARE YOU?

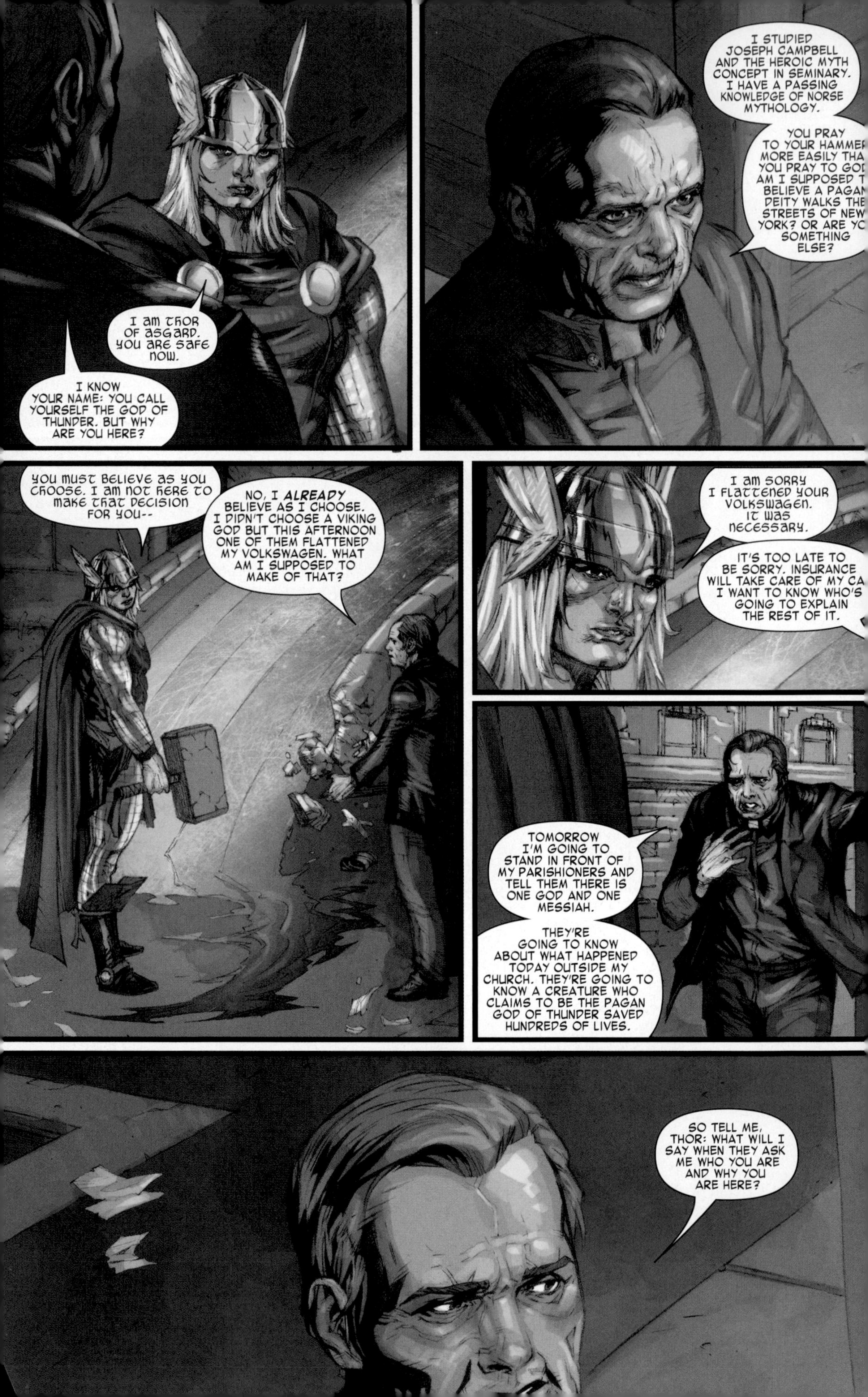
I AM THOR OF ASGARD. YOU ARE SAFE NOW.
I KNOW YOUR NAME: YOU CALL YOURSELF THE GOD OF THUNDER. BUT WHY ARE YOU HERE?
I STUDIED JOSEPH CAMPBELL AND THE HEROIC MYTH CONCEPT IN SEMINARY. I HAVE A PASSING KNOWLEDGE OF NORSE MYTHOLOGY.
YOU PRAY TO YOUR HAMMER MORE EASILY THA YOU PRAY TO GOD AM I SUPPOSED T BELIEVE A PAGAN DEITY WALKS THE STREETS OF NEW YORK? OR ARE YO SOMETHING ELSE?
YOU MUST BELIEVE AS YOU CHOOSE. I AM NOT HERE TO MAKE THAT DECISION FOR YOU--
NO, I ALREADY BELIEVE AS I CHOOSE. I DIDN'T CHOOSE A VIKING GOD BUT THIS AFTERNOON ONE OF THEM FLATTENED MY VOLKSWAGEN. WHAT AM I SUPPOSED TO MAKE OF THAT?
I AM SORRY I FLATTENED YOUR VOLKSWAGEN. IT WAS NECESSARY.
IT'S TOO LATE TO BE SORRY. INSURANCE WILL TAKE CARE OF MY CA I WANT TO KNOW WHO'S GOING TO EXPLAIN THE REST OF IT.
TOMORROW I'M GOING TO STAND IN FRONT OF MY PARISHIONERS AND TELL THEM THERE IS ONE GOD AND ONE MESSIAH.
THEY'RE GOING TO KNOW ABOUT WHAT HAPPENED TODAY OUTSIDE MY CHURCH. THEY'RE GOING TO KNOW A CREATURE WHO CLAIMS TO BE THE PAGAN GOD OF THUNDER SAVED HUNDREDS OF LIVES.
SO TELL ME, THOR: WHAT WILL I SAY WHEN THEY ASK ME WHO YOU ARE AND WHY YOU ARE HERE?

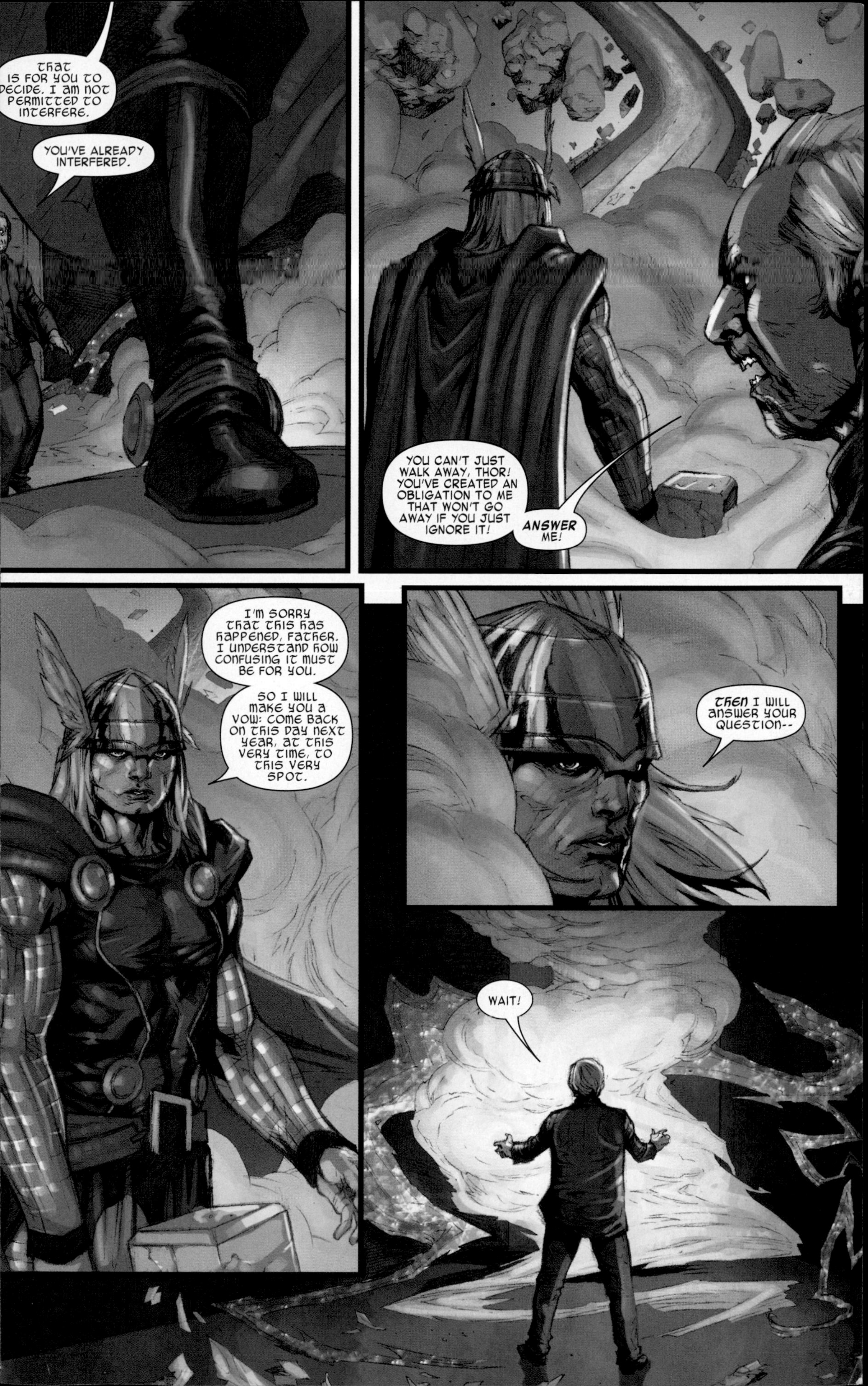
THAT IS FOR YOU TO DECIDE. I AM NOT PERMITTED TO INTERFERE.
YOU'VE ALREADY INTERFERED.
YOU CAN'T JUST WALK AWAY, THOR! YOU'VE CREATED AN OBLIGATION TO ME THAT WON'T GO AWAY IF YOU JUST IGNORE IT!
ANSWER ME!
I'M SORRY THAT THIS HAS HAPPENED, FATHER. I UNDERSTAND HOW CONFUSING IT MUST BE FOR YOU.
SO I WILL MAKE YOU A VOW: COME BACK ON THIS DAY NEXT YEAR, AT THIS VERY TIME, TO THIS VERY SPOT.
THEN I WILL ANSWER YOUR QUESTION--
WAIT!

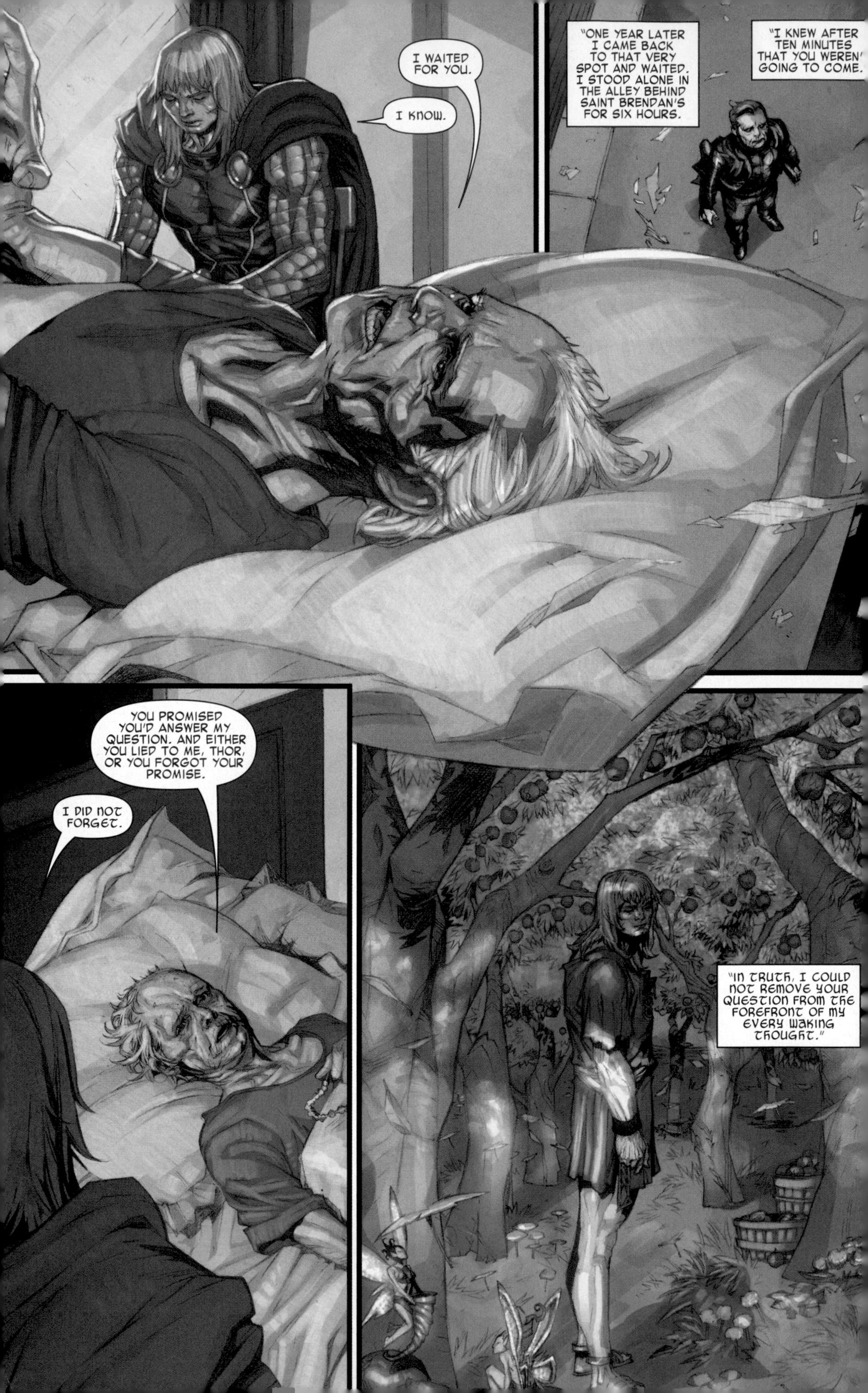
I WAITED FOR YOU.
I KNOW.
"ONE YEAR LATER I CAME BACK TO THAT VERY SPOT AND WAITED. I STOOD ALONE IN THE ALLEY BEHIND SAINT BRENDAN'S FOR SIX HOURS.
"I KNEW AFTER TEN MINUTES THAT YOU WEREN' GOING TO COME.
YOU PROMISED YOU'D ANSWER MY QUESTION. AND EITHER YOU LIED TO ME, THOR, OR YOU FORGOT YOUR PROMISE.
I DID NOT FORGET.
"IN TRUTH, I COULD NOT REMOVE YOUR QUESTION FROM THE FOREFRONT OF MY EVERY WAKING THOUGHT."

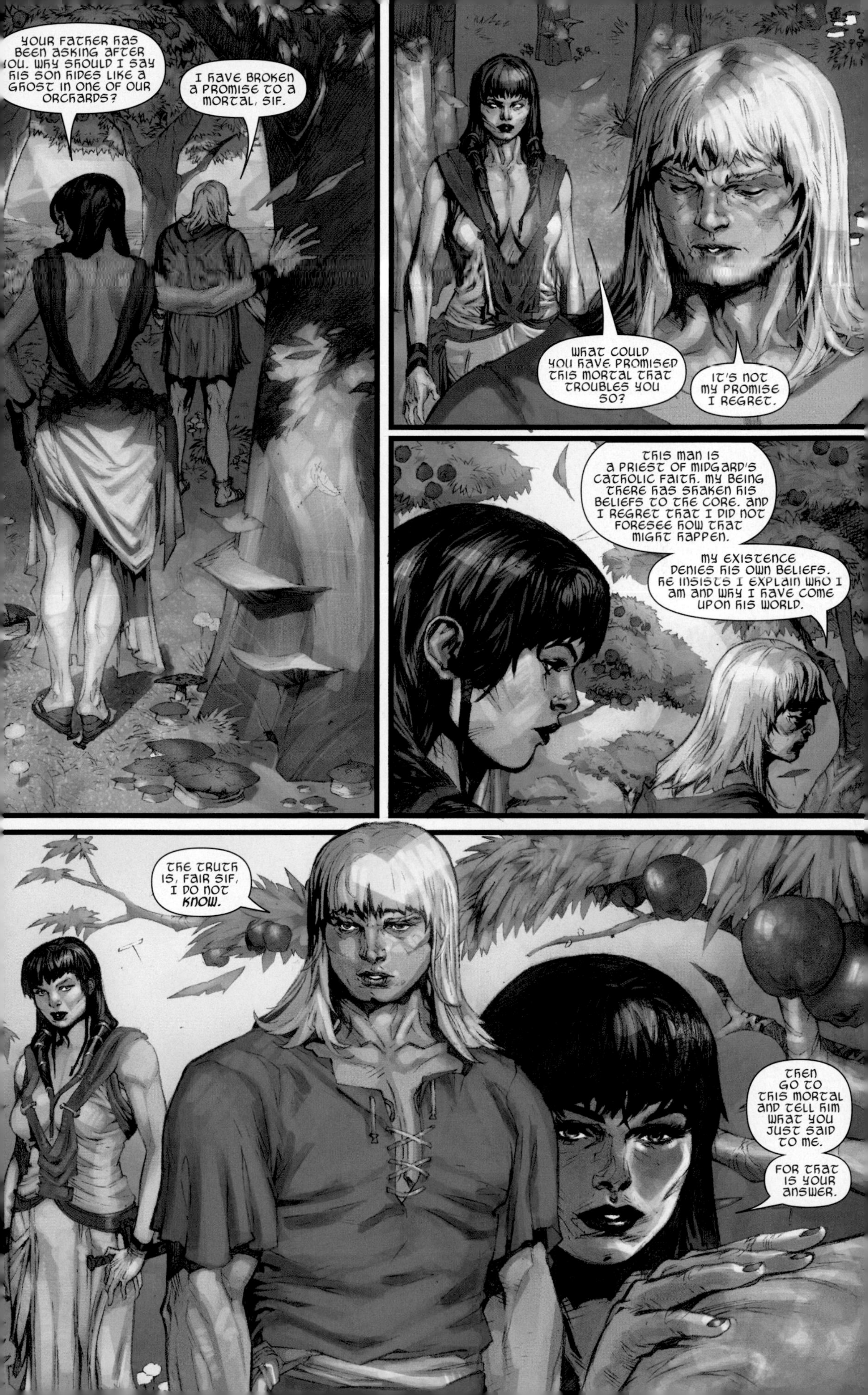
YOUR FATHER HAS BEEN ASKING AFTER YOU. WHY SHOULD I SAY HIS SON HIDES LIKE A GHOST IN ONE OF OUR ORCHARDS?
I HAVE BROKEN A PROMISE TO A MORTAL, SIF.
WHAT COULD YOU HAVE PROMISED THIS MORTAL THAT TROUBLES YOU SO?
IT'S NOT MY PROMISE I REGRET.
THIS MAN IS A PRIEST OF MIDGARD'S CATHOLIC FAITH. MY BEING THERE HAS SHAKEN HIS BELIEFS TO THE CORE. AND I REGRET THAT I DID NOT FORESEE HOW THAT MIGHT HAPPEN.
MY EXISTENCE DENIES HIS OWN BELIEFS. HE INSISTS I EXPLAIN WHO I AM AND WHY I HAVE COME UPON HIS WORLD.
THE TRUTH IS, FAIR SIF, I DO NOT KNOW.
THEN GO TO THIS MORTAL AND TELL HIM WHAT YOU JUST SAID TO ME.
FOR THAT IS YOUR ANSWER.

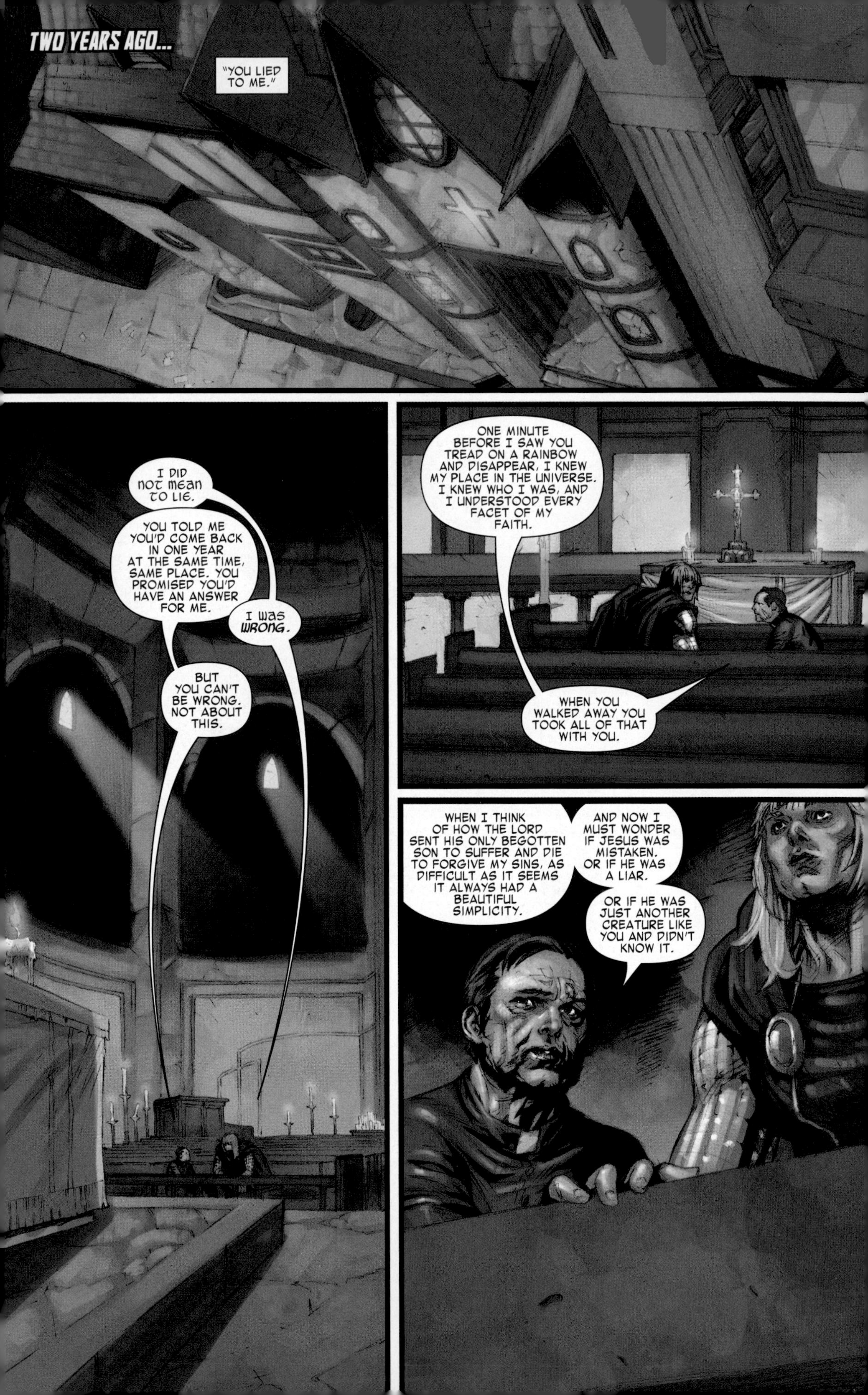
TWO YEARS AGO...
"YOU LIED TO ME."
I DID NOT MEAN TO LIE.
YOU TOLD ME YOU'D COME BACK IN ONE YEAR AT THE SAME TIME, SAME PLACE. YOU PROMISED YOU'D HAVE AN ANSWER FOR ME.
I WAS WRONG.
BUT YOU CAN'T BE WRONG. NOT ABOUT THIS.
ONE MINUTE BEFORE I SAW YOU TREAD ON A RAINBOW AND DISAPPEAR, I KNEW MY PLACE IN THE UNIVERSE. I KNEW WHO I WAS, AND I UNDERSTOOD EVERY FACET OF MY FAITH.
WHEN YOU WALKED AWAY YOU TOOK ALL OF THAT WITH YOU.
WHEN I THINK OF HOW THE LORD SENT HIS ONLY BEGOTTEN SON TO SUFFER AND DIE TO FORGIVE MY SINS, AS DIFFICULT AS IT SEEMS IT ALWAYS HAD A BEAUTIFUL SIMPLICITY.
AND NOW I MUST WONDER IF JESUS WAS MISTAKEN. OR IF HE WAS A LIAR.
OR IF HE WAS JUST ANOTHER CREATURE LIKE YOU AND DIDN'T KNOW IT.

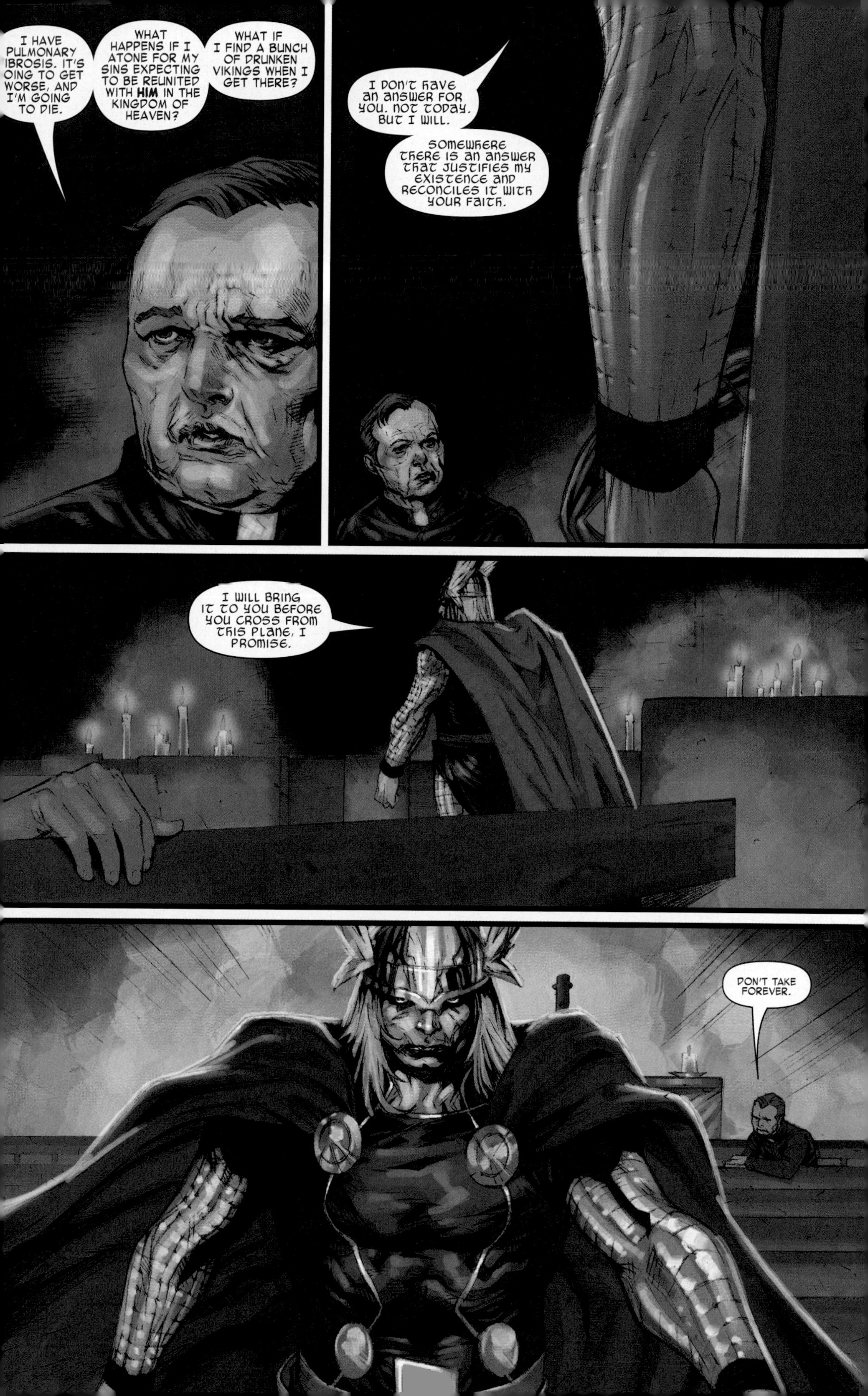
I HAVE PULMONARY FIBROSIS. IT'S GOING TO GET WORSE, AND I'M GOING TO DIE.
WHAT HAPPENS IF I ATONE FOR MY SINS EXPECTING TO BE REUNITED WITH HIM IN THE KINGDOM OF HEAVEN?
WHAT IF I FIND A BUNCH OF DRUNKEN VIKINGS WHEN I GET THERE?
I DON'T HAVE AN ANSWER FOR YOU. NOT TODAY. BUT I WILL.
SOMEWHERE THERE IS AN ANSWER THAT JUSTIFIES MY EXISTENCE AND RECONCILES IT WITH YOUR FAITH.
I WILL BRING IT TO YOU BEFORE YOU CROSS FROM THIS PLANE, I PROMISE.
DON'T TAKE FOREVER.

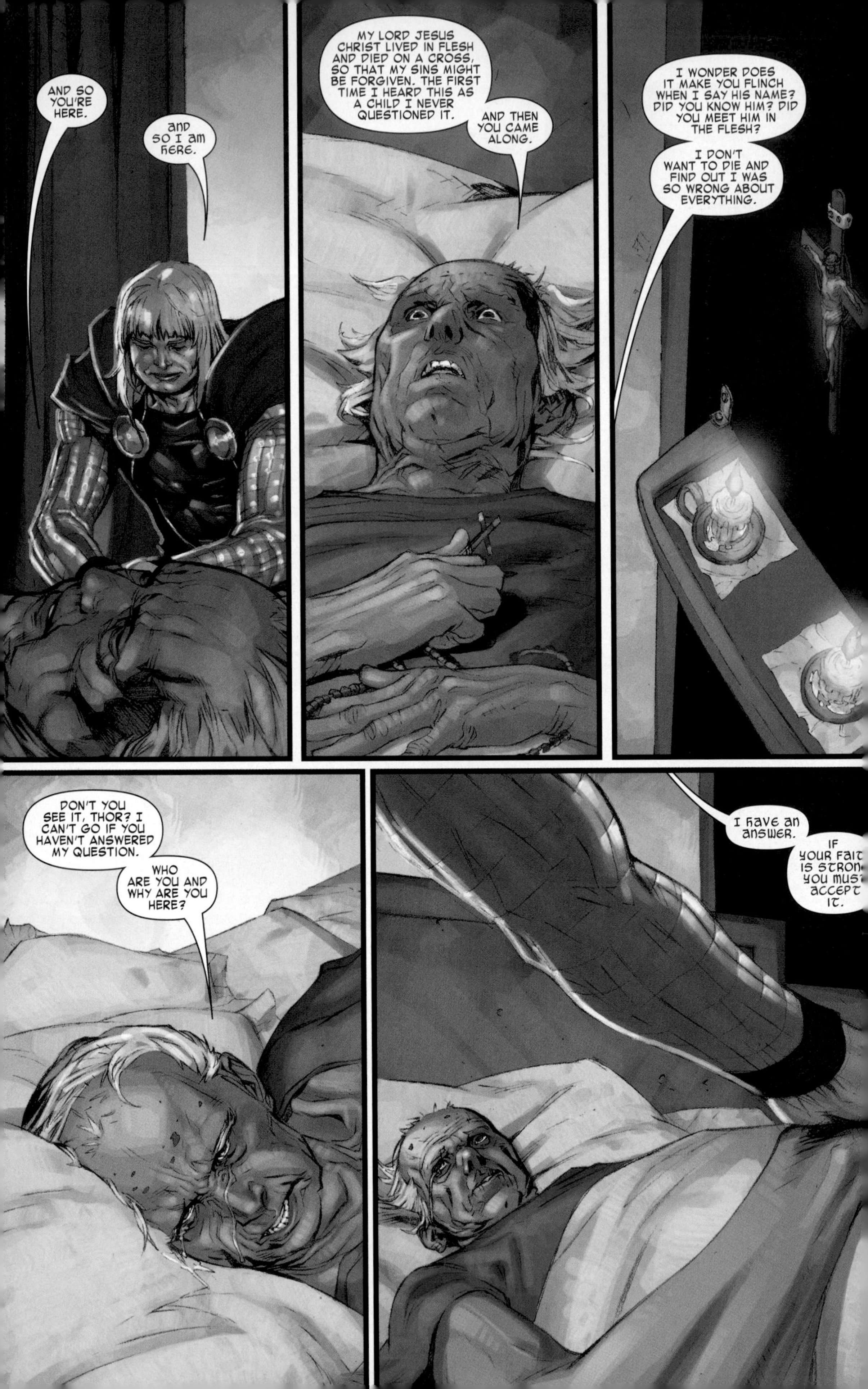
AND SO YOU'RE HERE.
AND SO I AM HERE.
MY LORD JESUS CHRIST LIVED IN FLESH AND DIED ON A CROSS, SO THAT MY SINS MIGHT BE FORGIVEN. THE FIRST TIME I HEARD THIS AS A CHILD I NEVER QUESTIONED IT.
AND THEN YOU CAME ALONG.
I WONDER DOES IT MAKE YOU FLINCH WHEN I SAY HIS NAME? DID YOU KNOW HIM? DID YOU MEET HIM IN THE FLESH?
I DON'T WANT TO DIE AND FIND OUT I WAS SO WRONG ABOUT EVERYTHING.
DON'T YOU SEE IT, THOR? I CAN'T GO IF YOU HAVEN'T ANSWERED MY QUESTION.
WHO ARE YOU AND WHY ARE YOU HERE?
I HAVE AN ANSWER.
IF YOUR FAIT IS STRON YOU MUS ACCEPT IT.

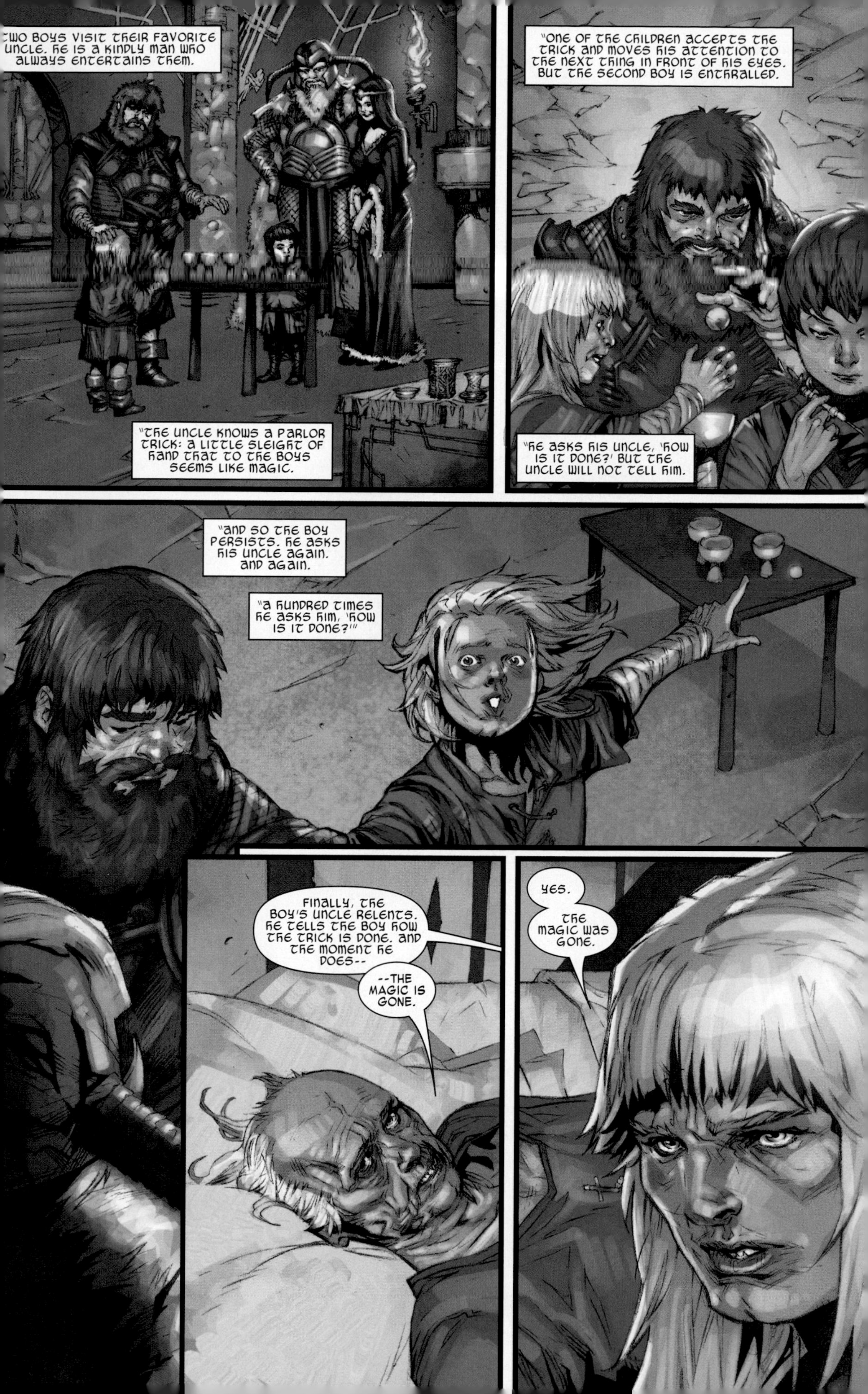
TWO BOYS VISIT THEIR FAVORITE UNCLE. HE IS A KINDLY MAN WHO ALWAYS ENTERTAINS THEM.
"THE UNCLE KNOWS A PARLOR TRICK: A LITTLE SLEIGHT OF HAND THAT TO THE BOYS SEEMS LIKE MAGIC.
"ONE OF THE CHILDREN ACCEPTS THE TRICK AND MOVES HIS ATTENTION TO THE NEXT THING IN FRONT OF HIS EYES. BUT THE SECOND BOY IS ENTHRALLED.
"HE ASKS HIS UNCLE, 'HOW IS IT DONE?' BUT THE UNCLE WILL NOT TELL HIM.
"AND SO THE BOY PERSISTS. HE ASKS HIS UNCLE AGAIN. AND AGAIN.
"A HUNDRED TIMES HE ASKS HIM, 'HOW IS IT DONE?'"
FINALLY, THE BOY'S UNCLE RELENTS. HE TELLS THE BOY HOW THE TRICK IS DONE. AND THE MOMENT HE DOES--
--THE MAGIC IS GONE.
YES.
THE MAGIC WAS GONE.

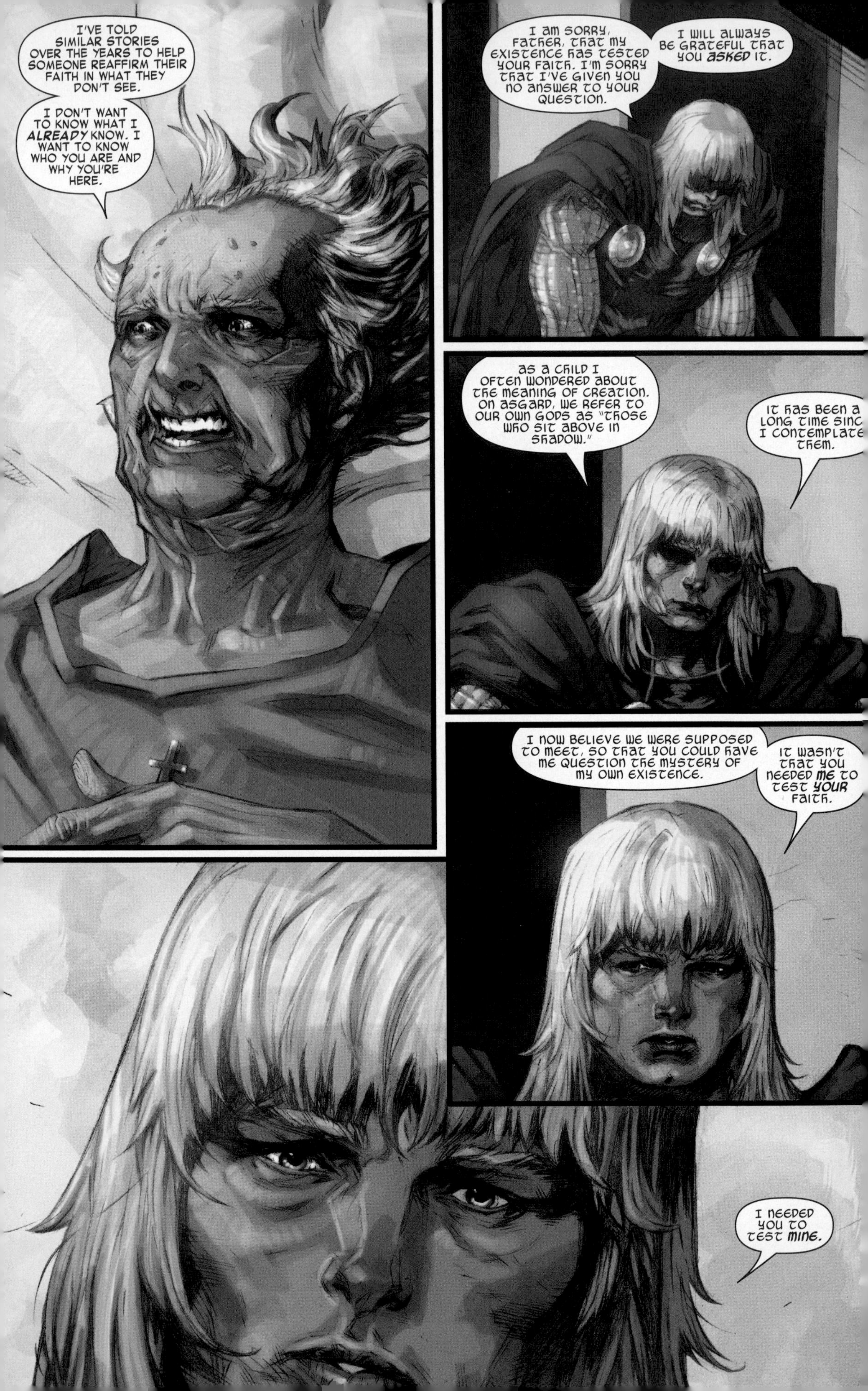
I'VE TOLD SIMILAR STORIES OVER THE YEARS TO HELP SOMEONE REAFFIRM THEIR FAITH IN WHAT THEY DON'T SEE.
I DON'T WANT TO KNOW WHAT I *ALREADY* KNOW. I WANT TO KNOW WHO YOU ARE AND WHY YOU'RE HERE.
I AM SORRY, FATHER, THAT MY EXISTENCE HAS TESTED YOUR FAITH. I'M SORRY THAT I'VE GIVEN YOU NO ANSWER TO YOUR QUESTION.
I WILL ALWAYS BE GRATEFUL THAT YOU *ASKED* IT.
AS A CHILD I OFTEN WONDERED ABOUT THE MEANING OF CREATION. ON ASGARD, WE REFER TO OUR OWN GODS AS "THOSE WHO SIT ABOVE IN SHADOW."
IT HAS BEEN A LONG TIME SINC I CONTEMPLATE THEM.
I NOW BELIEVE WE WERE SUPPOSED TO MEET, SO THAT YOU COULD HAVE ME QUESTION THE MYSTERY OF MY OWN EXISTENCE.
IT WASN'T THAT YOU NEEDED *ME* TO TEST *YOUR* FAITH.
I NEEDED YOU TO TEST *MINE*.

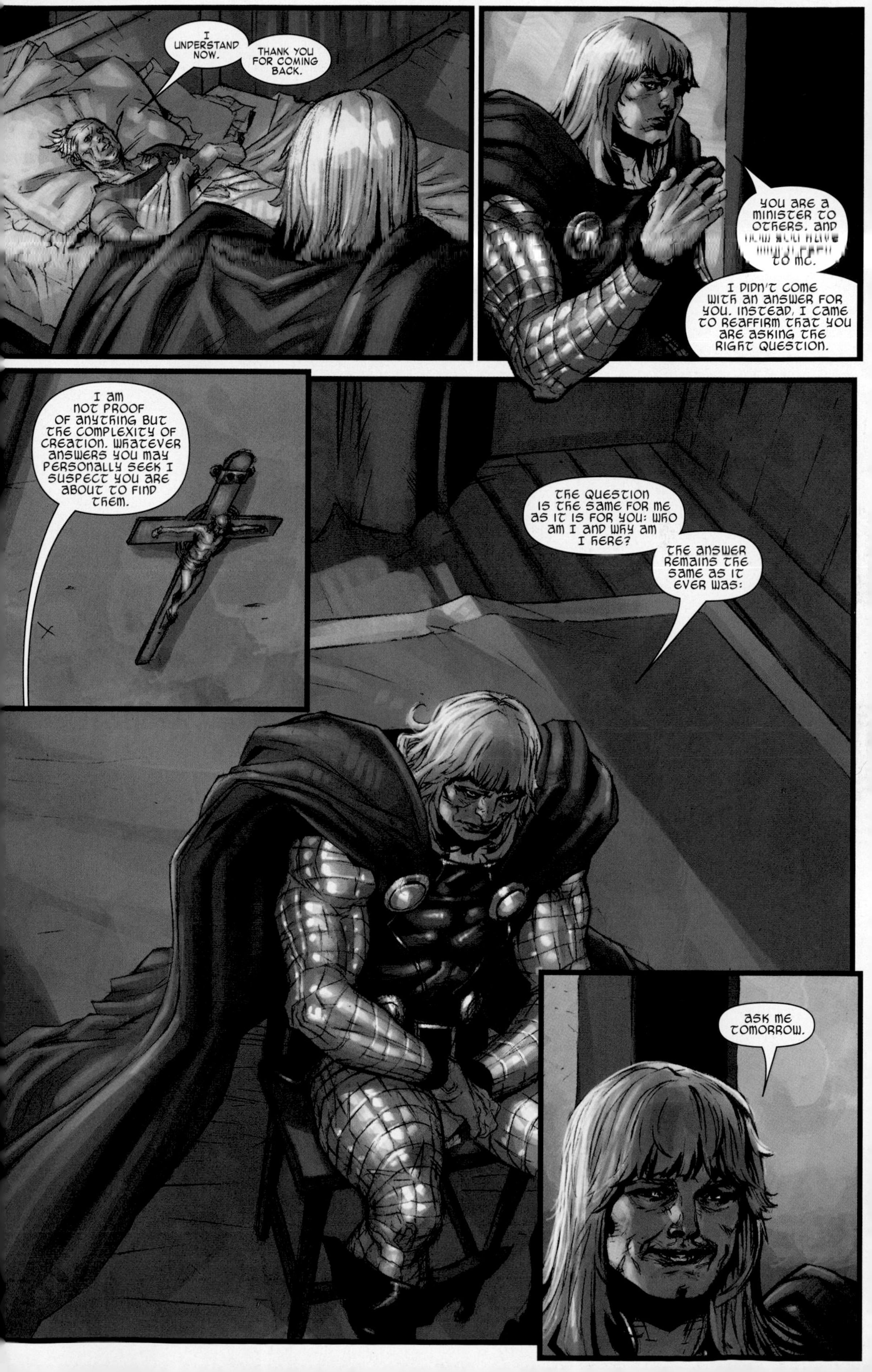
I UNDERSTAND NOW.
THANK YOU FOR COMING BACK.
YOU ARE A MINISTER TO OTHERS. AND
TO ME.
I DIDN'T COME WITH AN ANSWER FOR YOU. INSTEAD, I CAME TO REAFFIRM THAT YOU ARE ASKING THE RIGHT QUESTION.
I AM NOT PROOF OF ANYTHING BUT THE COMPLEXITY OF CREATION. WHATEVER ANSWERS YOU MAY PERSONALLY SEEK I SUSPECT YOU ARE ABOUT TO FIND THEM.
THE QUESTION IS THE SAME FOR ME AS IT IS FOR YOU: WHO AM I AND WHY AM I HERE?
THE ANSWER REMAINS THE SAME AS IT EVER WAS:
ASK ME TOMORROW.

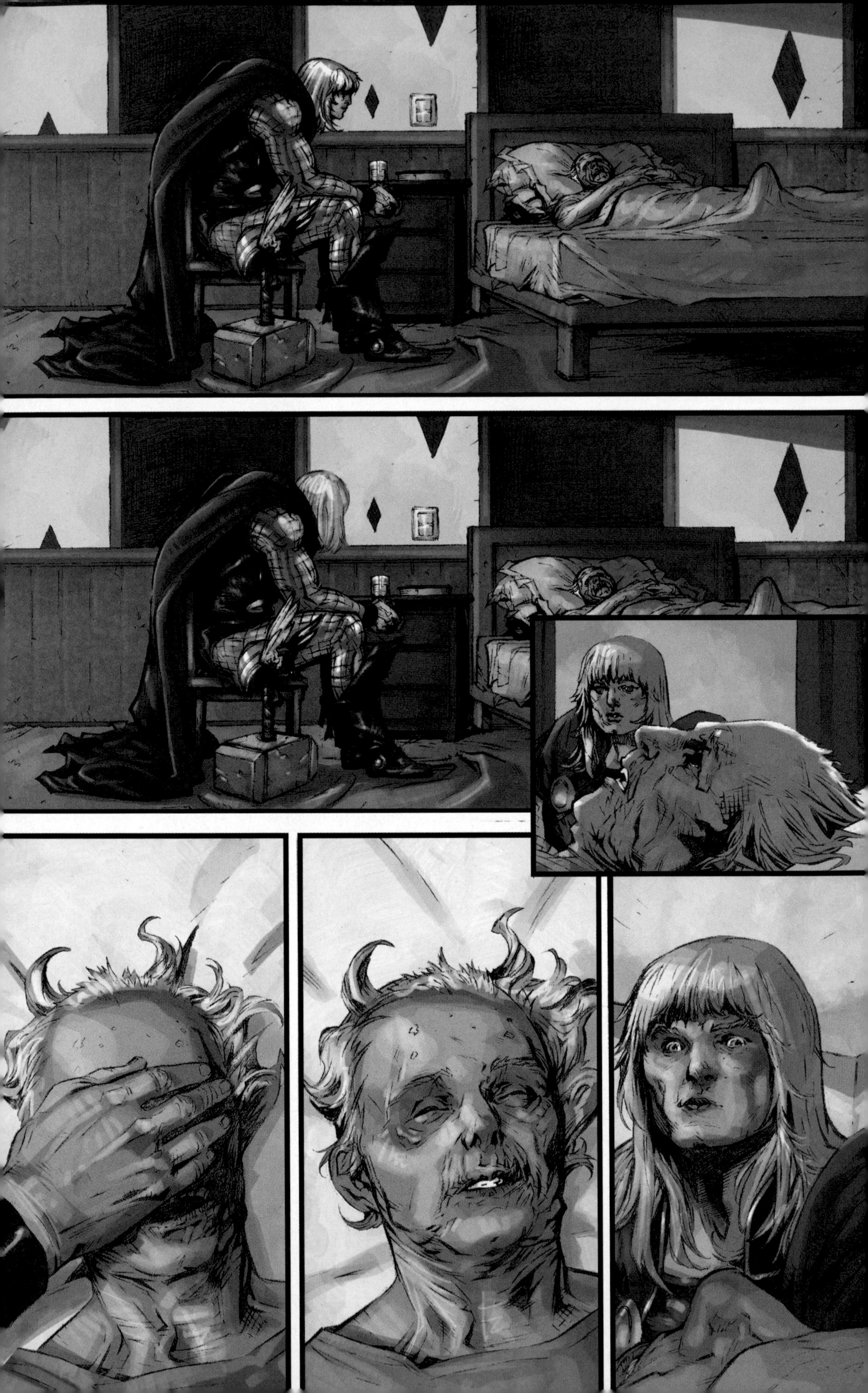

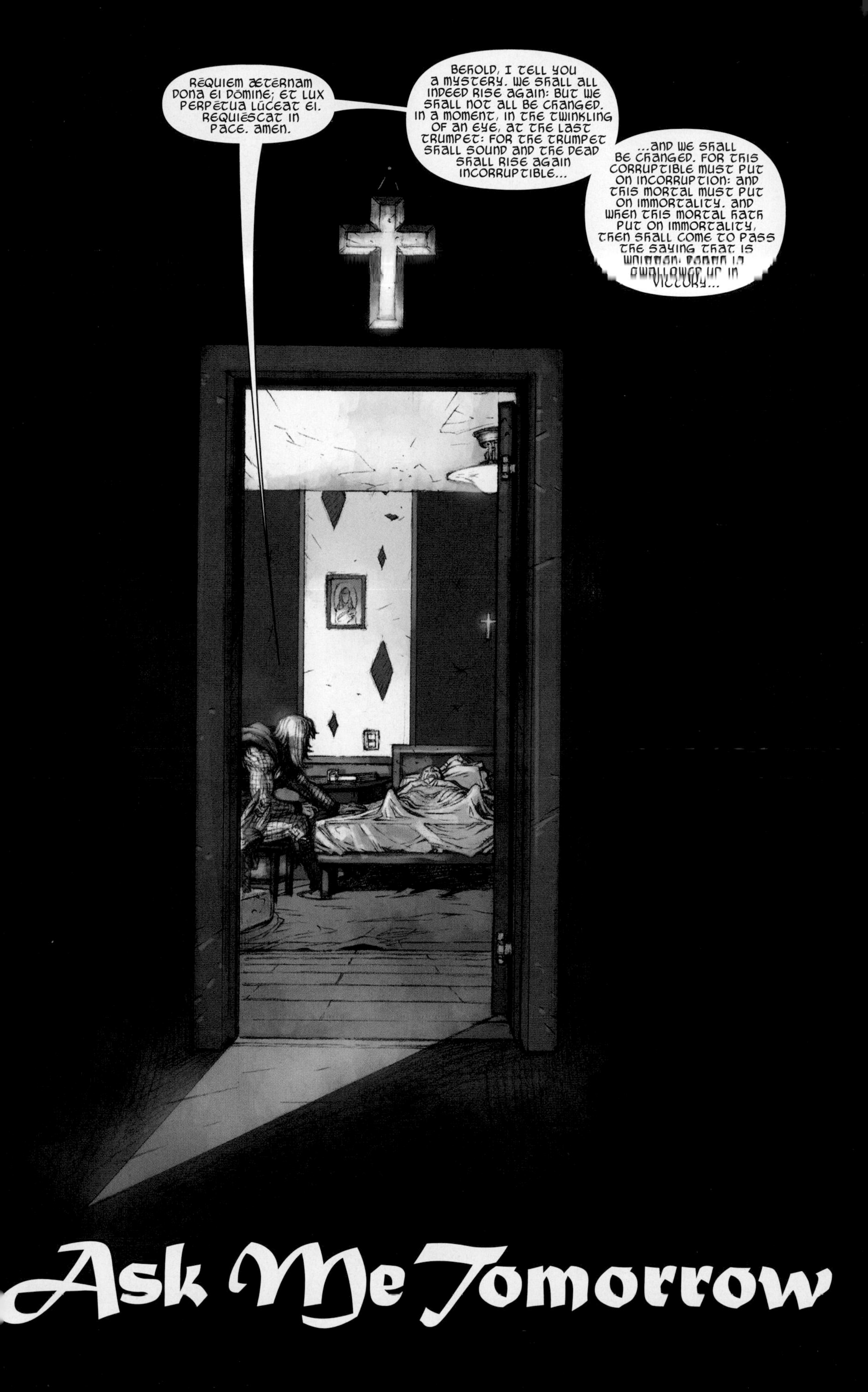
RĒQUIEM ÆTĒRNAM DONA EI DŌMINE; ET LUX PERPĒTUA LŪCEAT EI. REQUIĒSCAT IN PACE. AMEN.
BEHOLD, I TELL YOU A MYSTERY. WE SHALL ALL INDEED RISE AGAIN: BUT WE SHALL NOT ALL BE CHANGED. IN A MOMENT, IN THE TWINKLING OF AN EYE, AT THE LAST TRUMPET: FOR THE TRUMPET SHALL SOUND AND THE DEAD SHALL RISE AGAIN INCORRUPTIBLE...
...AND WE SHALL BE CHANGED. FOR THIS CORRUPTIBLE MUST PUT ON INCORRUPTION: AND THIS MORTAL MUST PUT ON IMMORTALITY. AND WHEN THIS MORTAL HATH PUT ON IMMORTALITY, THEN SHALL COME TO PASS THE SAYING THAT IS
VICTORY...
Ask Me Tomorrow

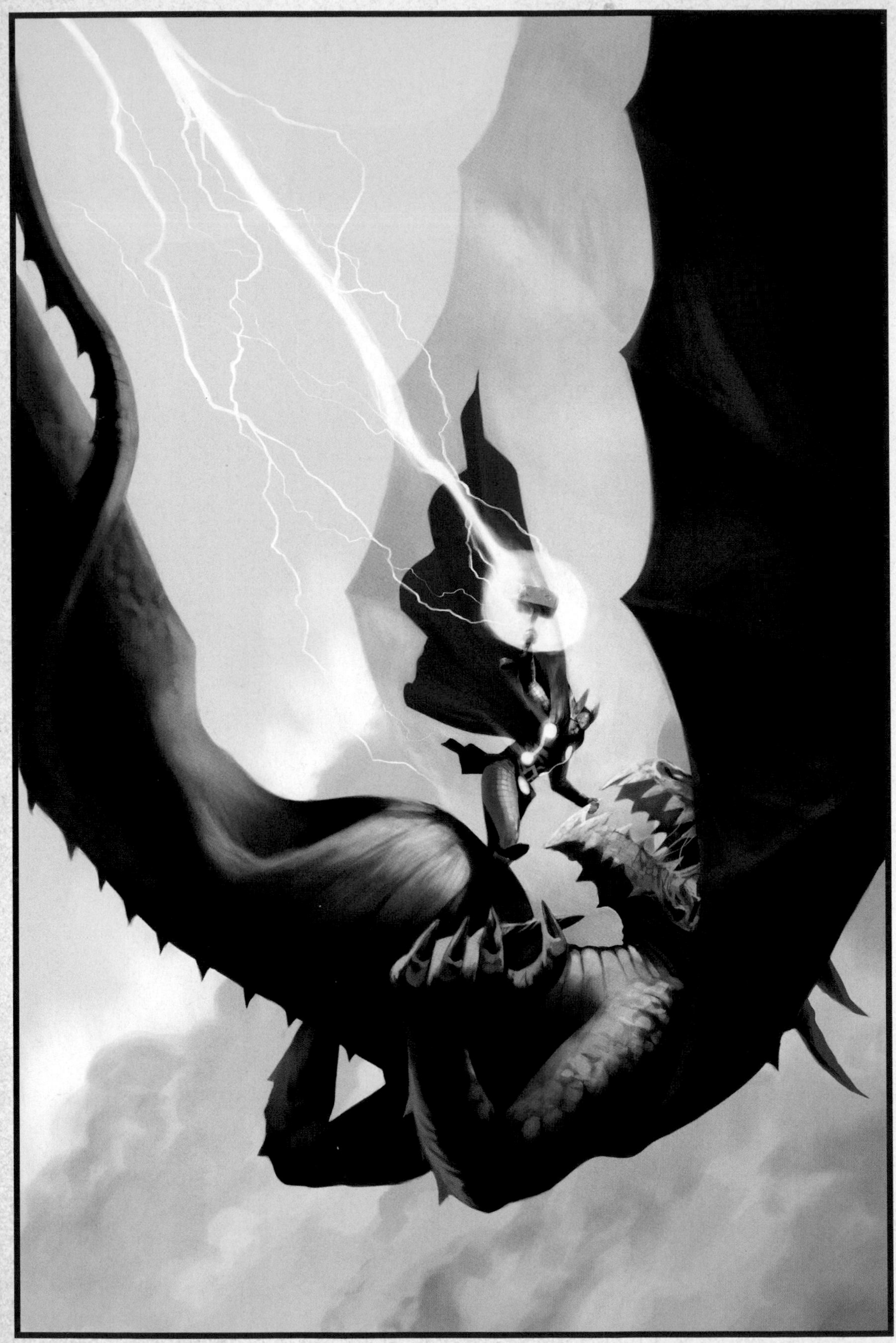

THOR: HEAVEN & EARTH #4

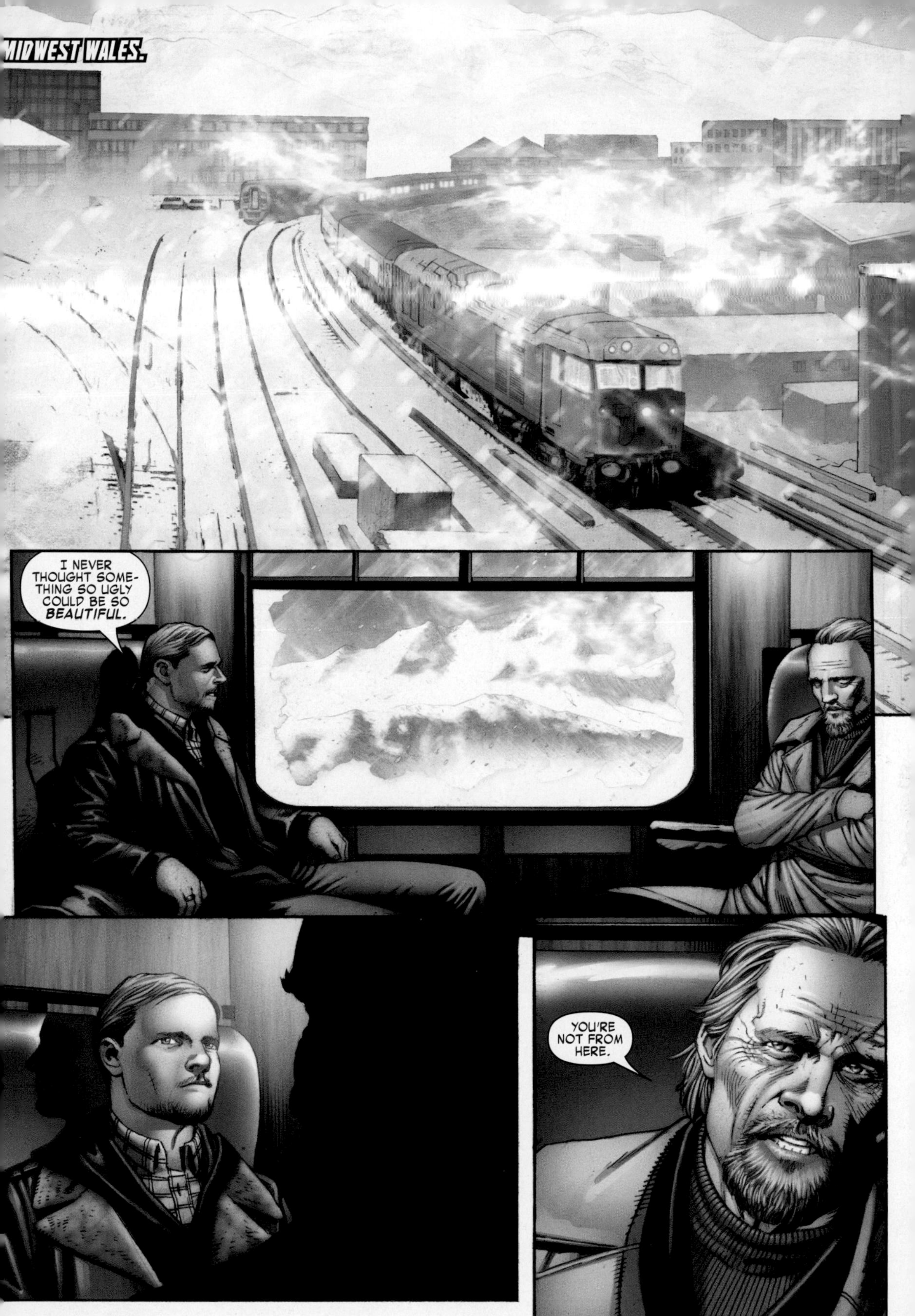
MIDWEST WALES.
I NEVER THOUGHT SOMETHING SO UGLY COULD BE SO BEAUTIFUL.
YOU'RE NOT FROM HERE.

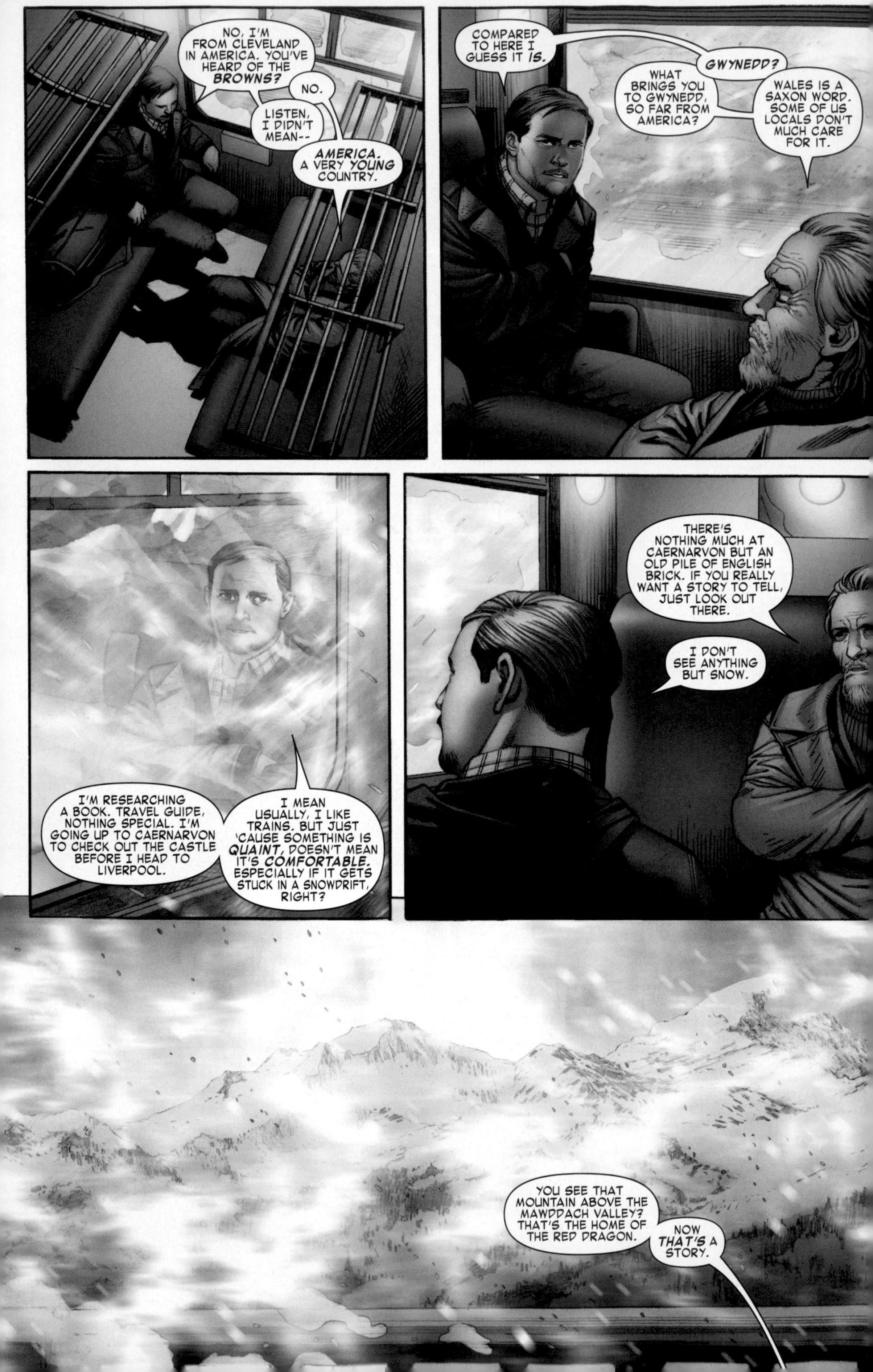
NO, I'M FROM CLEVELAND IN AMERICA. YOU'VE HEARD OF THE *BROWNS?*
NO.
LISTEN, I DIDN'T MEAN--
AMERICA. A VERY *YOUNG* COUNTRY.
COMPARED TO HERE I GUESS IT *IS.*
GWYNEDD?
WHAT BRINGS YOU TO GWYNEDD, SO FAR FROM AMERICA?
WALES IS A SAXON WORD. SOME OF US LOCALS DON'T MUCH CARE FOR IT.
I'M RESEARCHING A BOOK. TRAVEL GUIDE, NOTHING SPECIAL. I'M GOING UP TO CAERNARVON TO CHECK OUT THE CASTLE BEFORE I HEAD TO LIVERPOOL.
I MEAN USUALLY, I LIKE TRAINS. BUT JUST 'CAUSE SOMETHING IS *QUAINT,* DOESN'T MEAN IT'S *COMFORTABLE.* ESPECIALLY IF IT GETS STUCK IN A SNOWDRIFT, RIGHT?
THERE'S NOTHING MUCH AT CAERNARVON BUT AN OLD PILE OF ENGLISH BRICK. IF YOU REALLY WANT A STORY TO TELL, JUST LOOK OUT THERE.
I DON'T SEE ANYTHING BUT SNOW.
YOU SEE THAT MOUNTAIN ABOVE THE MAWDDACH VALLEY? THAT'S THE HOME OF THE RED DRAGON.
NOW *THAT'S* A STORY.

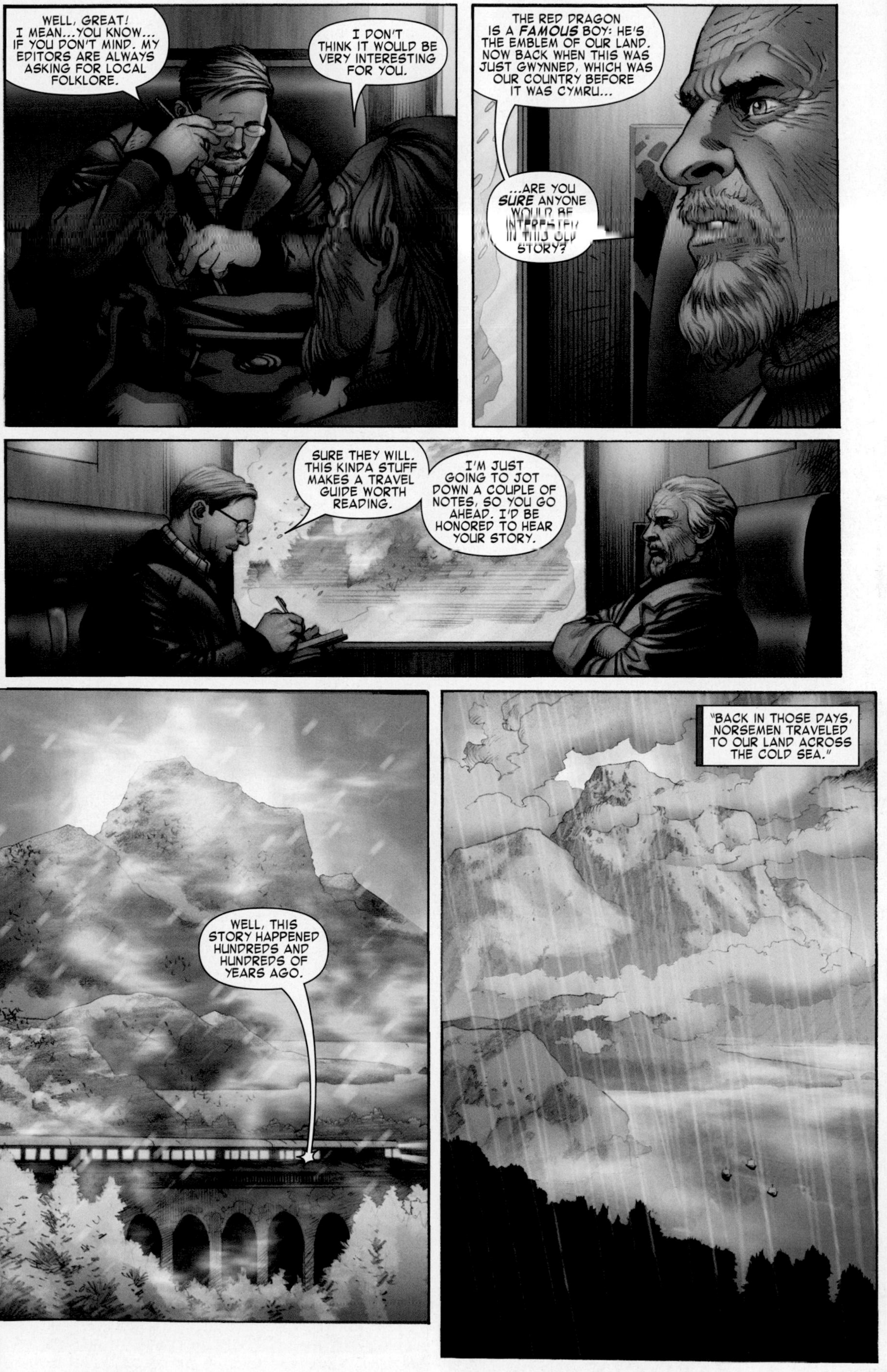
WELL, GREAT! I MEAN...YOU KNOW... IF YOU DON'T MIND. MY EDITORS ARE ALWAYS ASKING FOR LOCAL FOLKLORE.
I DON'T THINK IT WOULD BE VERY INTERESTING FOR YOU.
THE RED DRAGON IS A FAMOUS BOY: HE'S THE EMBLEM OF OUR LAND. NOW BACK WHEN THIS WAS JUST GWYNNED, WHICH WAS OUR COUNTRY BEFORE IT WAS CYMRU...
...ARE YOU SURE ANYONE WOULD BE INTERESTED IN THIS OLD STORY?
SURE THEY WILL. THIS KINDA STUFF MAKES A TRAVEL GUIDE WORTH READING.
I'M JUST GOING TO JOT DOWN A COUPLE OF NOTES, SO YOU GO AHEAD. I'D BE HONORED TO HEAR YOUR STORY.
WELL, THIS STORY HAPPENED HUNDREDS AND HUNDREDS OF YEARS AGO.
"BACK IN THOSE DAYS, NORSEMEN TRAVELED TO OUR LAND ACROSS THE COLD SEA."

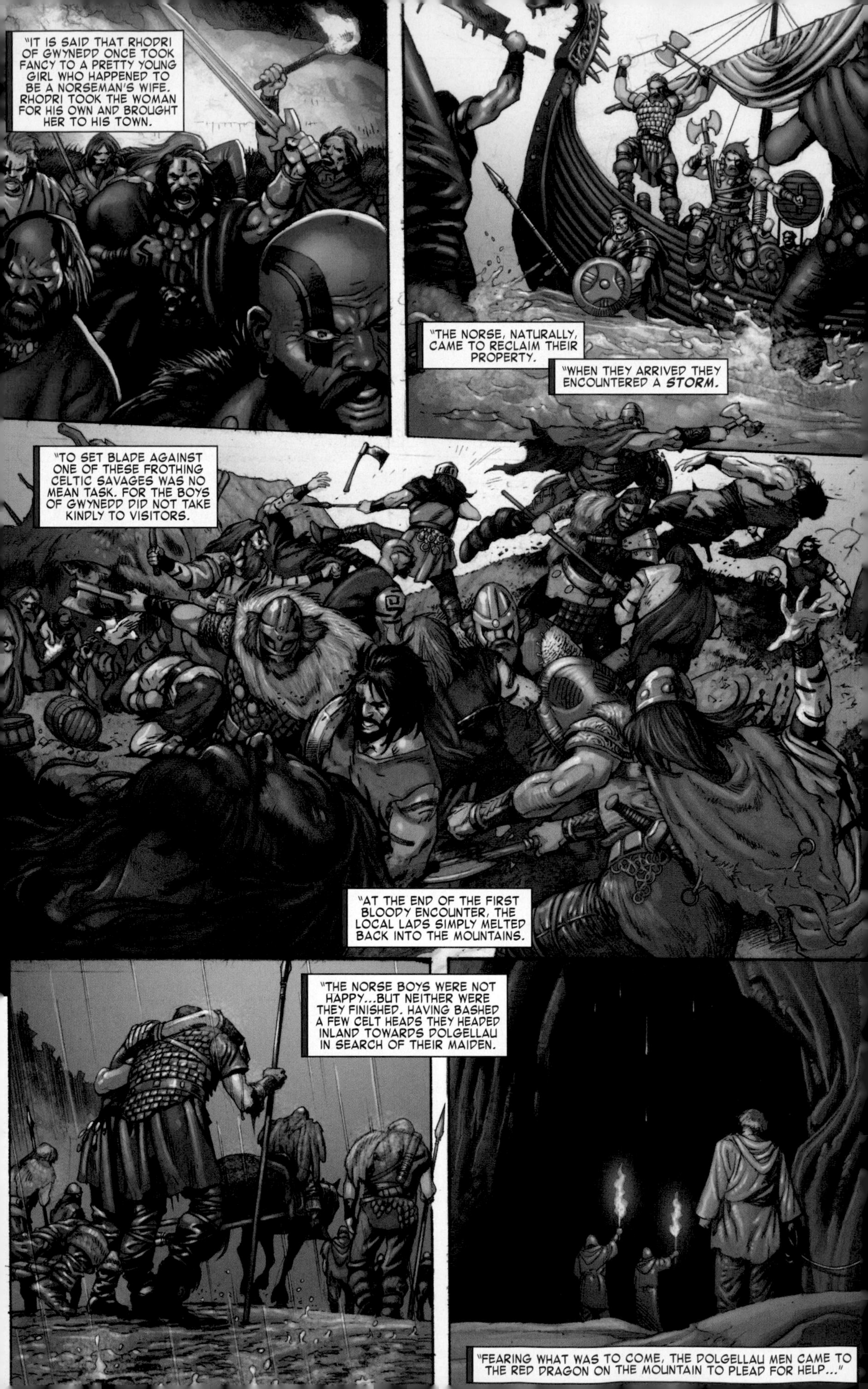
"IT IS SAID THAT RHODRI OF GWYNEDD ONCE TOOK FANCY TO A PRETTY YOUNG GIRL WHO HAPPENED TO BE A NORSEMAN'S WIFE. RHODRI TOOK THE WOMAN FOR HIS OWN AND BROUGHT HER TO HIS TOWN.
"THE NORSE, NATURALLY, CAME TO RECLAIM THEIR PROPERTY.
"WHEN THEY ARRIVED THEY ENCOUNTERED A STORM.
"TO SET BLADE AGAINST ONE OF THESE FROTHING CELTIC SAVAGES WAS NO MEAN TASK. FOR THE BOYS OF GWYNEDD DID NOT TAKE KINDLY TO VISITORS.
"AT THE END OF THE FIRST BLOODY ENCOUNTER, THE LOCAL LADS SIMPLY MELTED BACK INTO THE MOUNTAINS.
"THE NORSE BOYS WERE NOT HAPPY...BUT NEITHER WERE THEY FINISHED. HAVING BASHED A FEW CELT HEADS THEY HEADED INLAND TOWARDS DOLGELLAU IN SEARCH OF THEIR MAIDEN.
"FEARING WHAT WAS TO COME, THE DOLGELLAU MEN CAME TO THE RED DRAGON ON THE MOUNTAIN TO PLEAD FOR HELP..."

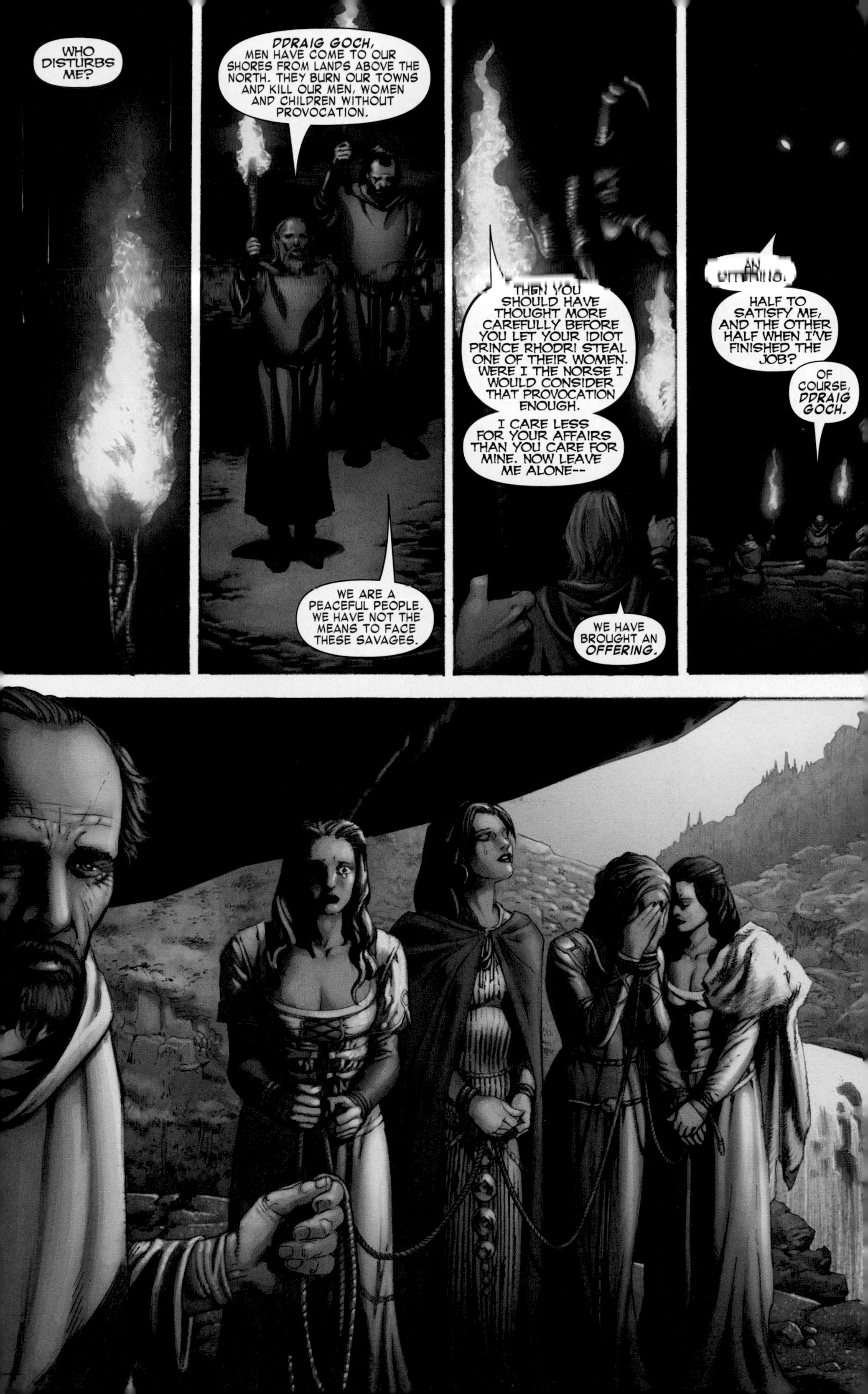
WHO DISTURBS ME?
DDRAIG GOCH, MEN HAVE COME TO OUR SHORES FROM LANDS ABOVE THE NORTH. THEY BURN OUR TOWNS AND KILL OUR MEN, WOMEN AND CHILDREN WITHOUT PROVOCATION.
WE ARE A PEACEFUL PEOPLE. WE HAVE NOT THE MEANS TO FACE THESE SAVAGES.
THEN YOU SHOULD HAVE THOUGHT MORE CAREFULLY BEFORE YOU LET YOUR IDIOT PRINCE RHODRI STEAL ONE OF THEIR WOMEN. WERE I THE NORSE I WOULD CONSIDER THAT PROVOCATION ENOUGH.
I CARE LESS FOR YOUR AFFAIRS THAN YOU CARE FOR MINE. NOW LEAVE ME ALONE--
WE HAVE BROUGHT AN *OFFERING.*
AN
HALF TO SATISFY ME, AND THE OTHER HALF WHEN I'VE FINISHED THE JOB?
OF COURSE, *DDRAIG GOCH.*

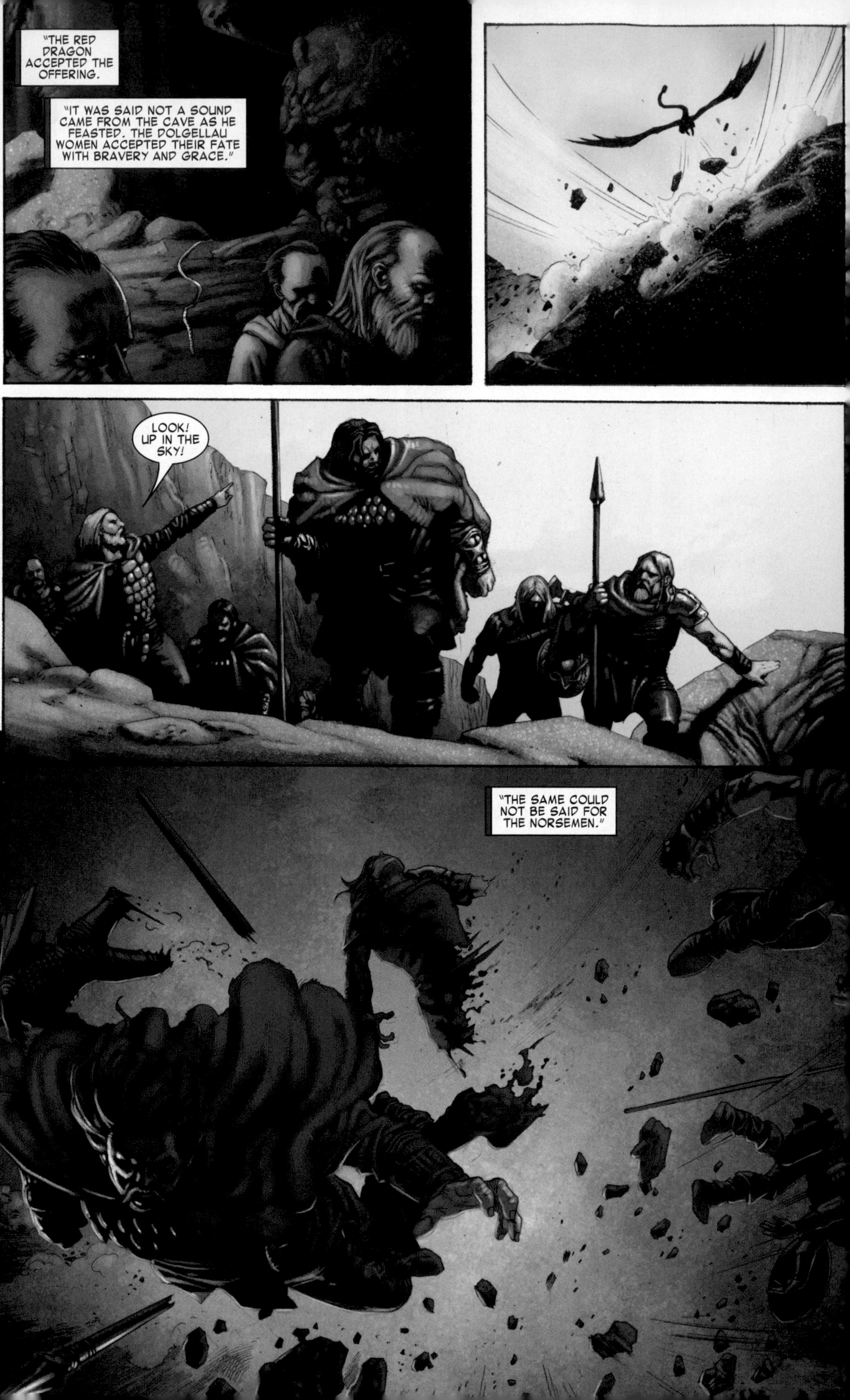
"THE RED DRAGON ACCEPTED THE OFFERING.
"IT WAS SAID NOT A SOUND CAME FROM THE CAVE AS HE FEASTED. THE DOLGELLAU WOMEN ACCEPTED THEIR FATE WITH BRAVERY AND GRACE."
LOOK! UP IN THE SKY!
"THE SAME COULD NOT BE SAID FOR THE NORSEMEN."

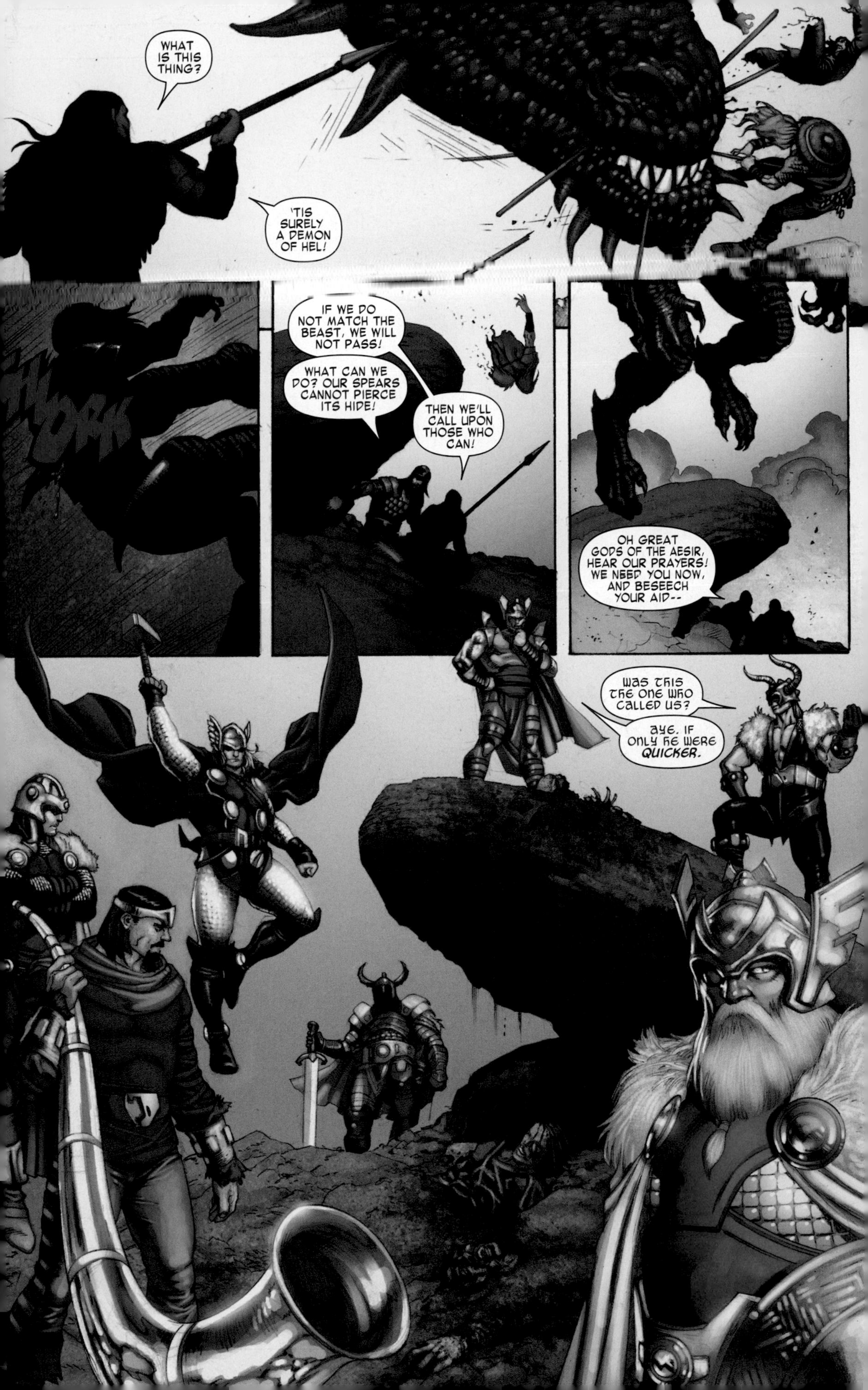
WHAT IS THIS THING?
'TIS SURELY A DEMON OF HEL!
IF WE DO NOT MATCH THE BEAST, WE WILL NOT PASS!
WHAT CAN WE DO? OUR SPEARS CANNOT PIERCE ITS HIDE!
THEN WE'LL CALL UPON THOSE WHO CAN!
OH GREAT GODS OF THE AESIR, HEAR OUR PRAYERS! WE NEED YOU NOW, AND BESEECH YOUR AID--
WAS THIS THE ONE WHO CALLED US?
AYE. IF ONLY HE WERE *QUICKER*.

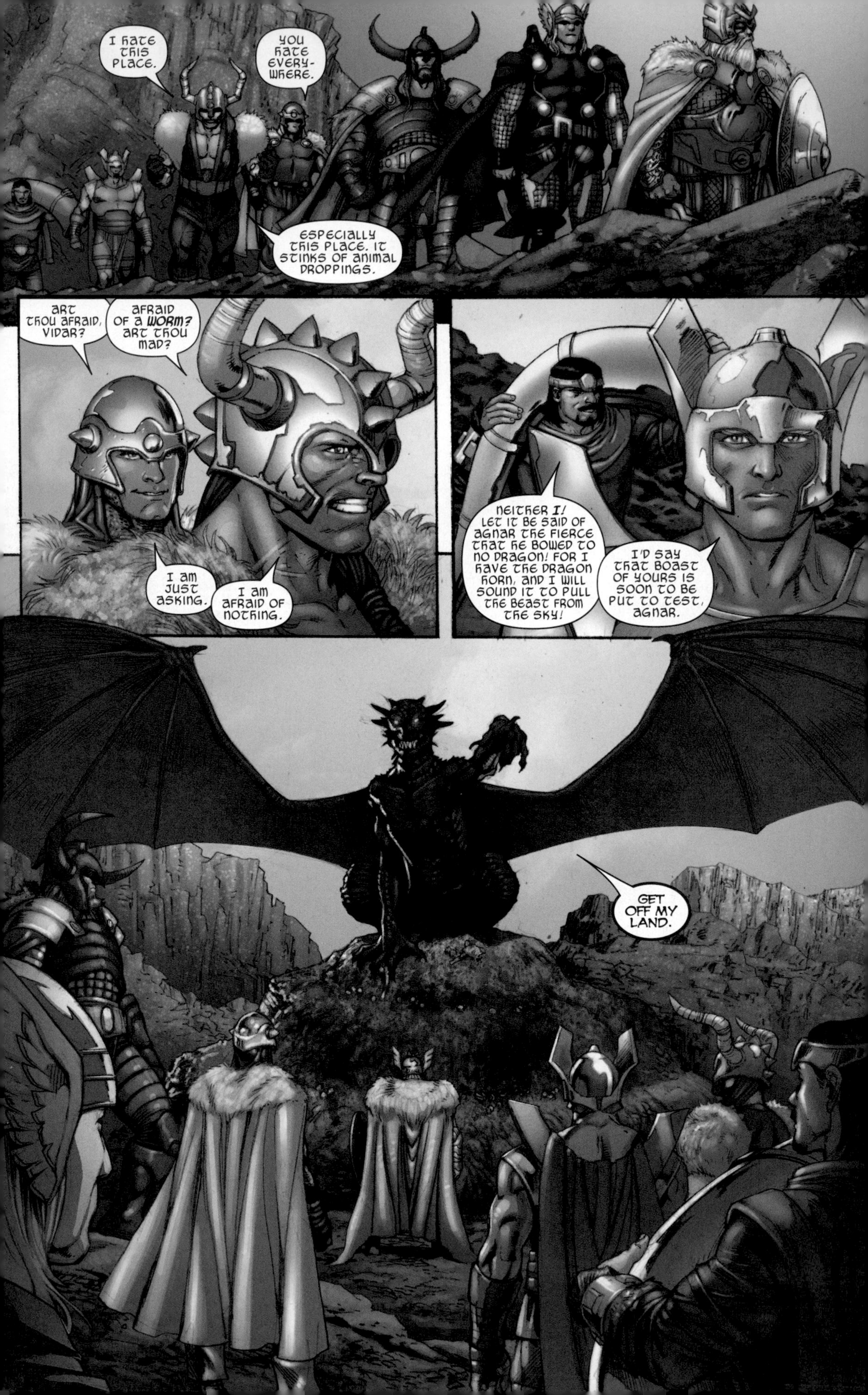
I HATE THIS PLACE.
YOU HATE EVERY-WHERE.
ESPECIALLY THIS PLACE. IT STINKS OF ANIMAL DROPPINGS.
ART THOU AFRAID, VIDAR?
AFRAID OF A WORM? ART THOU MAD?
I AM JUST ASKING.
I AM AFRAID OF NOTHING.
NEITHER I! LET IT BE SAID OF AGNAR THE FIERCE THAT HE BOWED TO NO DRAGON! FOR I HAVE THE DRAGON HORN, AND I WILL SOUND IT TO PULL THE BEAST FROM THE SKY!
I'D SAY THAT BOAST OF YOURS IS SOON TO BE PUT TO TEST, AGNAR.
GET OFF MY LAND.

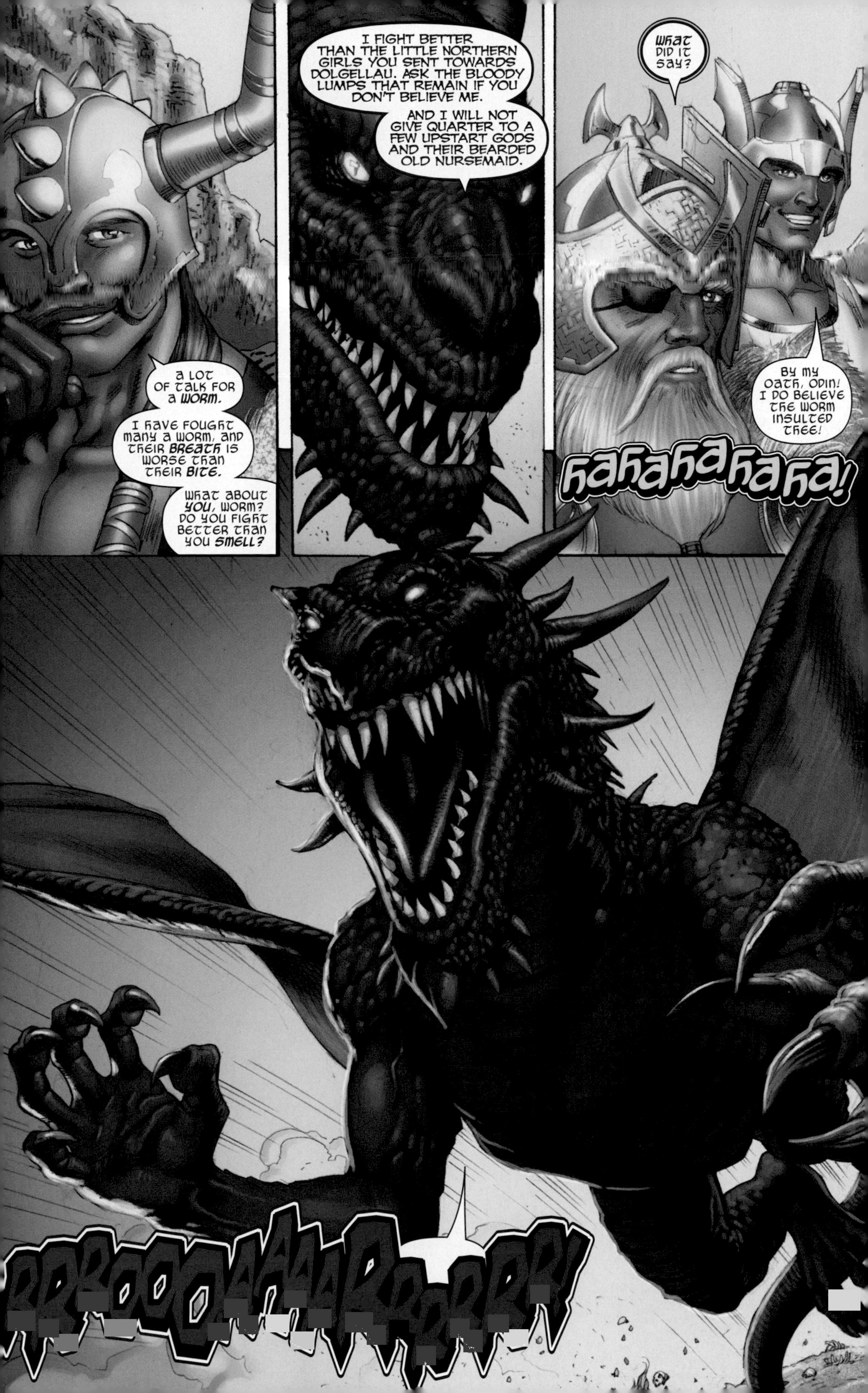
A LOT OF TALK FOR A WORM.
I HAVE FOUGHT MANY A WORM, AND THEIR BREATH IS WORSE THAN THEIR BITE.
WHAT ABOUT YOU, WORM? DO YOU FIGHT BETTER THAN YOU SMELL?
I FIGHT BETTER THAN THE LITTLE NORTHERN GIRLS YOU SENT TOWARDS DOLGELLAU. ASK THE BLOODY LUMPS THAT REMAIN IF YOU DON'T BELIEVE ME.
AND I WILL NOT GIVE QUARTER TO A FEW UPSTART GODS AND THEIR BEARDED OLD NURSEMAID.
WHAT DID IT SAY?
BY MY OATH, ODIN! I DO BELIEVE THE WORM INSULTED THEE!
HAHAHAHAHAHA!

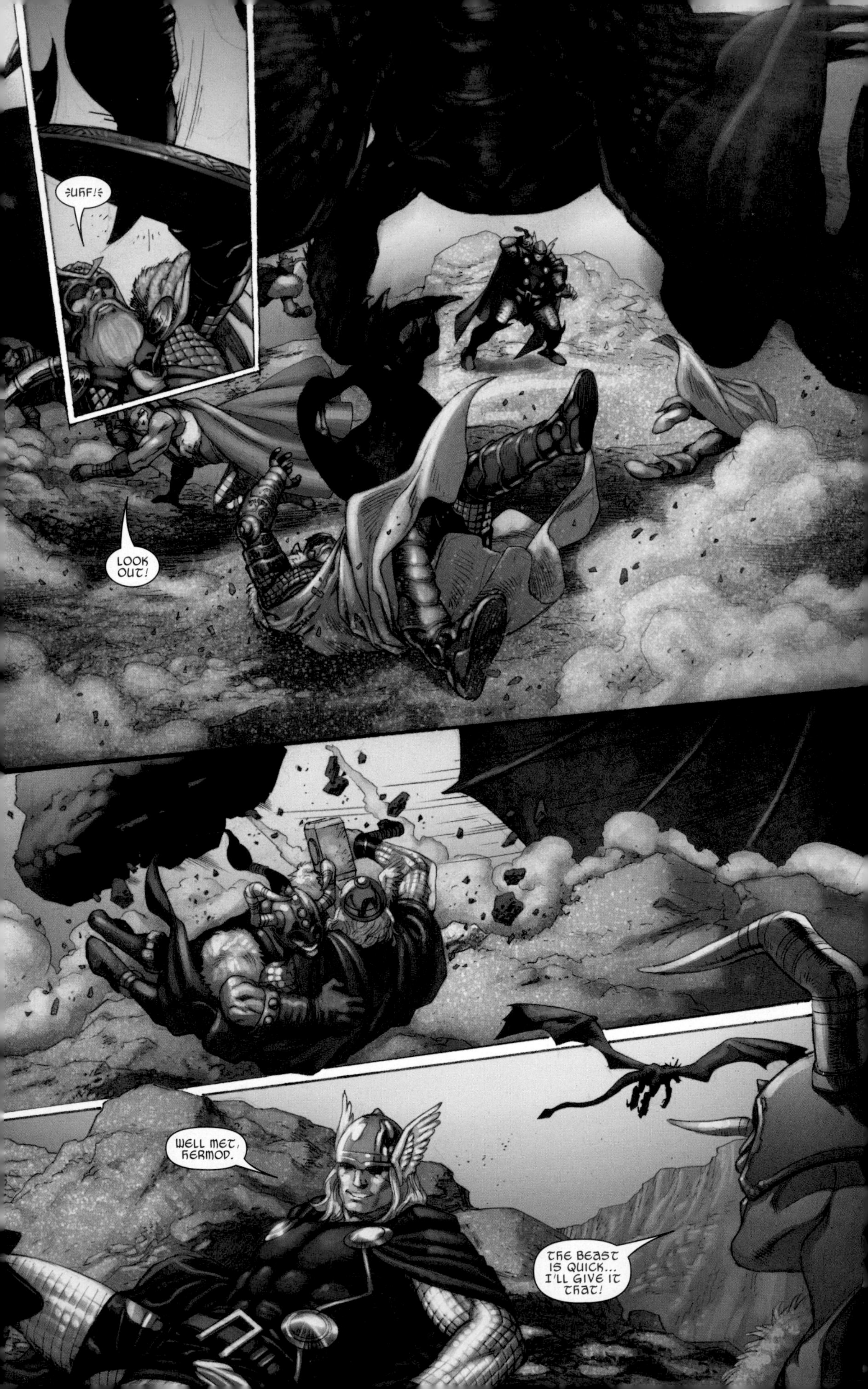
≥UHF!≤
LOOK OUT!
WELL MET, HERMOD.
THE BEAST IS QUICK... I'LL GIVE IT THAT!

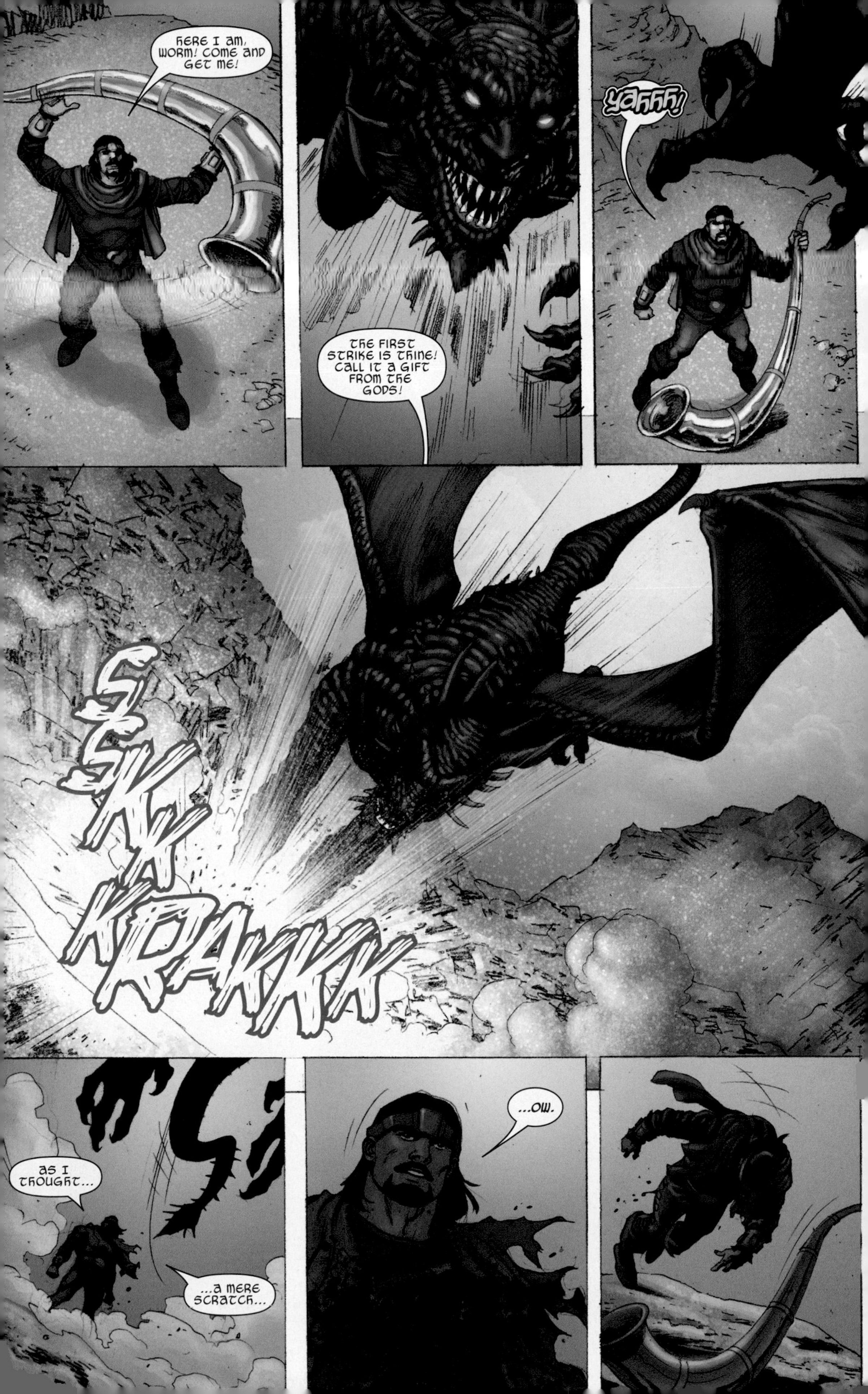
HERE I AM, WORM! COME AND GET ME!
THE FIRST STRIKE IS THINE! CALL IT A GIFT FROM THE GODS!
YAHHH!
SKKKRAKKKK
AS I THOUGHT...
...A MERE SCRATCH...
...OW.

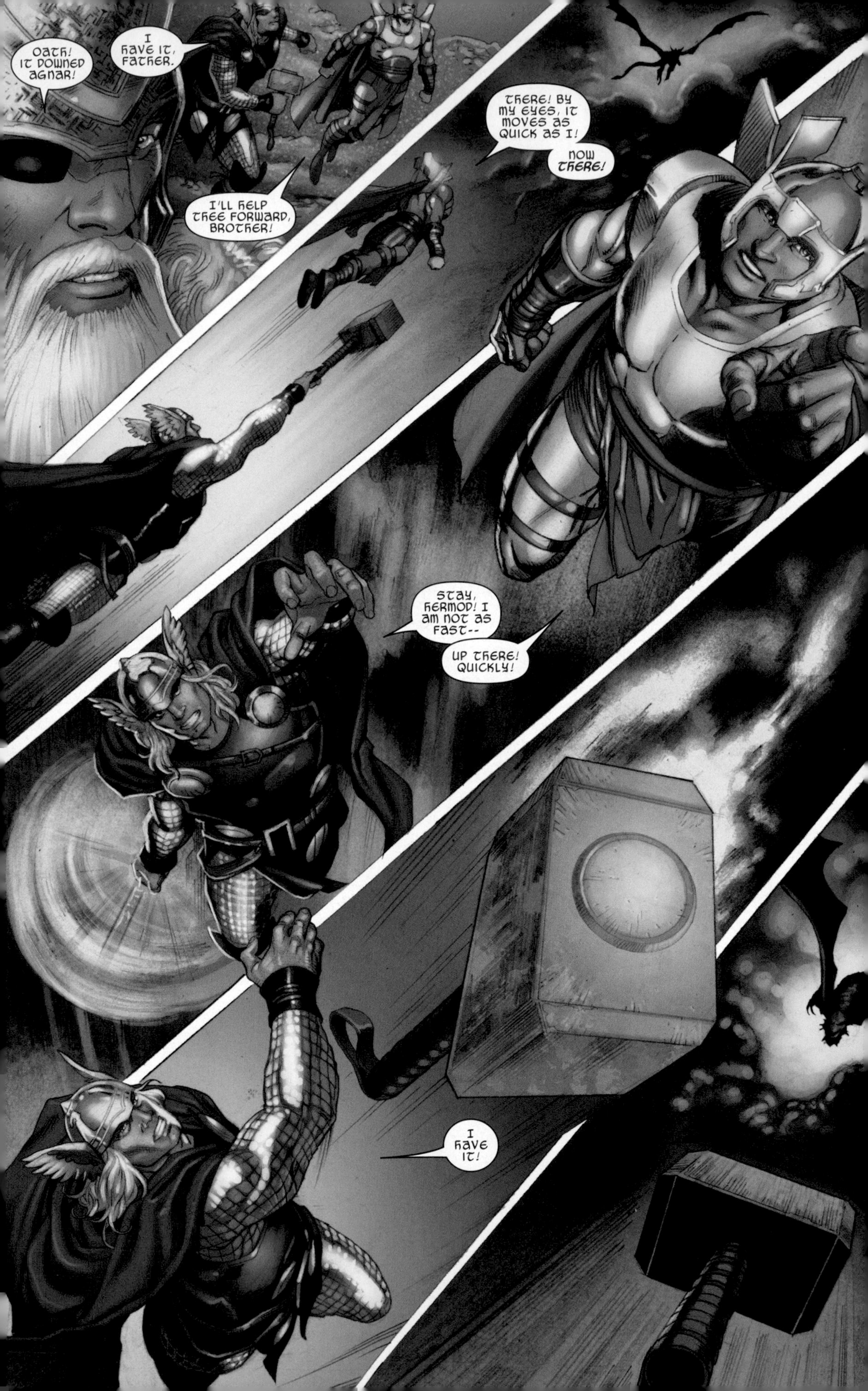
OATH! IT DOWNED AGNAR!
I HAVE IT, FATHER.
I'LL HELP THEE FORWARD, BROTHER!
THERE! BY MY EYES, IT MOVES AS QUICK AS I!
NOW *THERE!*
STAY, HERMOD! I AM NOT AS FAST--
UP THERE! QUICKLY!
I HAVE IT!

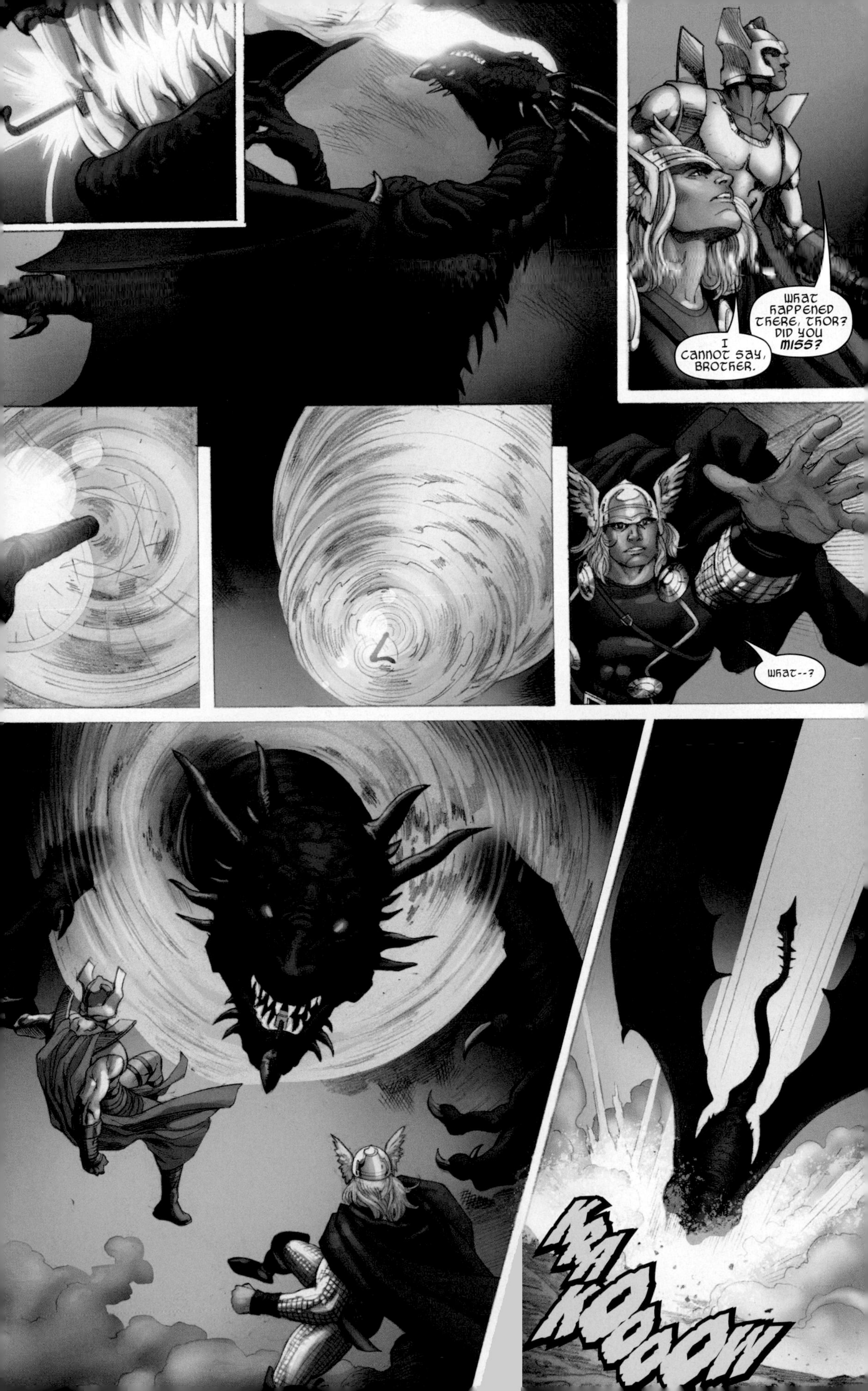
WHAT HAPPENED THERE, THOR? DID YOU MISS?
I CANNOT SAY, BROTHER.
WHAT--?
KRAKOOOOM

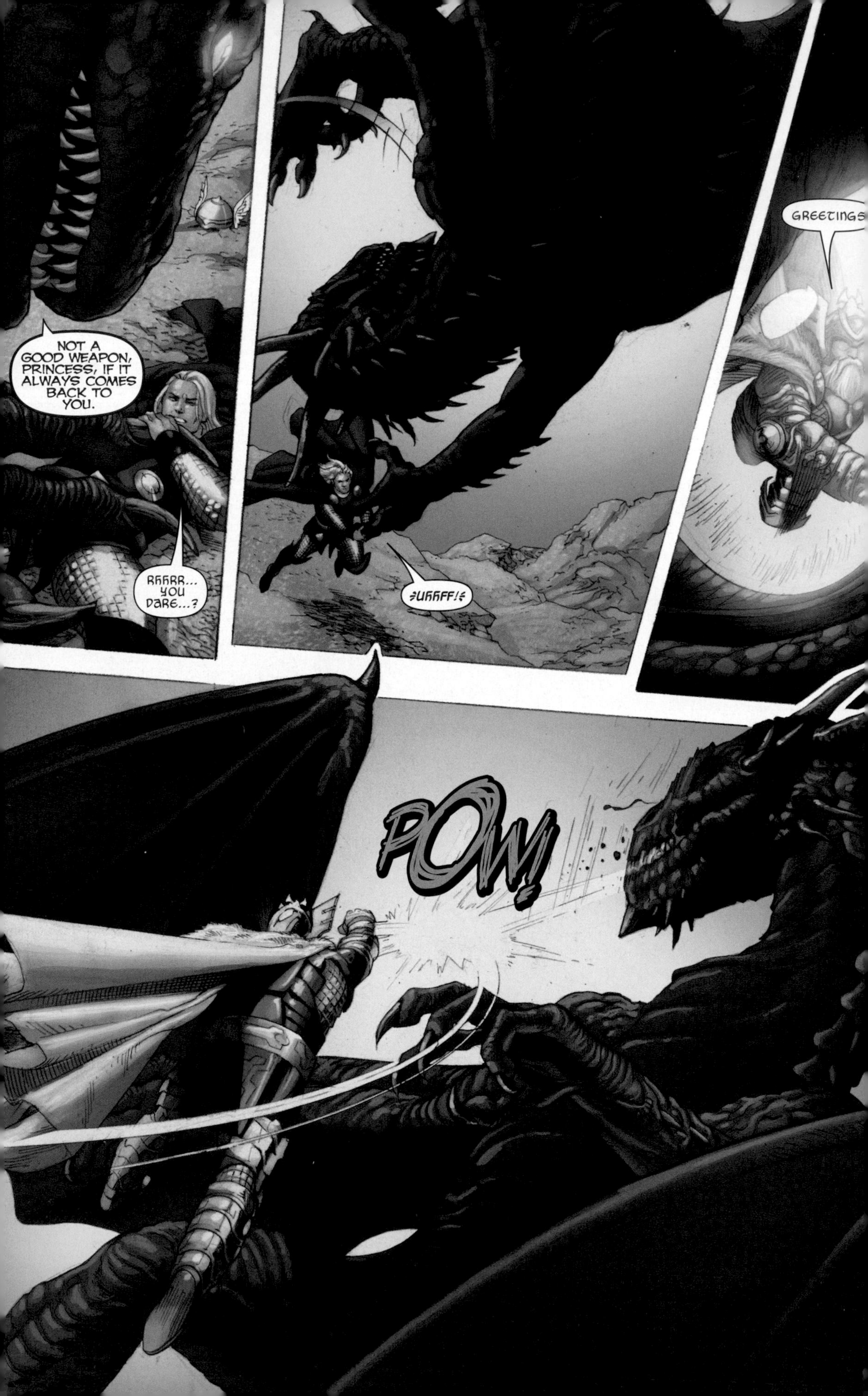
NOT A GOOD WEAPON, PRINCESS, IF IT ALWAYS COMES BACK TO YOU.
RHHRR... YOU DARE...?
GREETINGS
UHHFF!
POW!

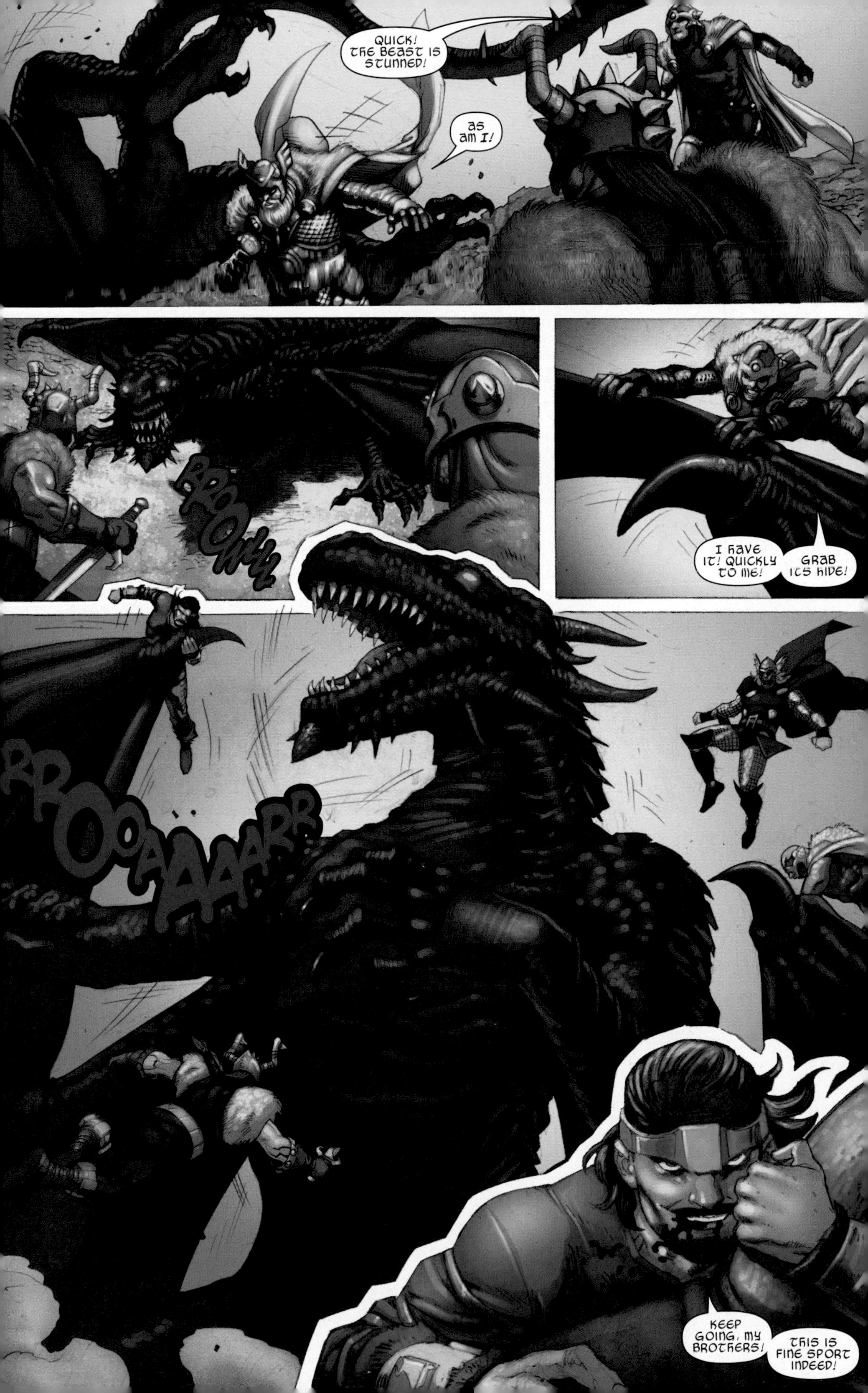
QUICK! THE BEAST IS STUNNED!
AS AM I!
RROOWW
I HAVE IT! QUICKLY TO ME!
GRAB ITS HIDE!
RROOAAAARR
KEEP GOING, MY BROTHERS!
THIS IS FINE SPORT INDEED!

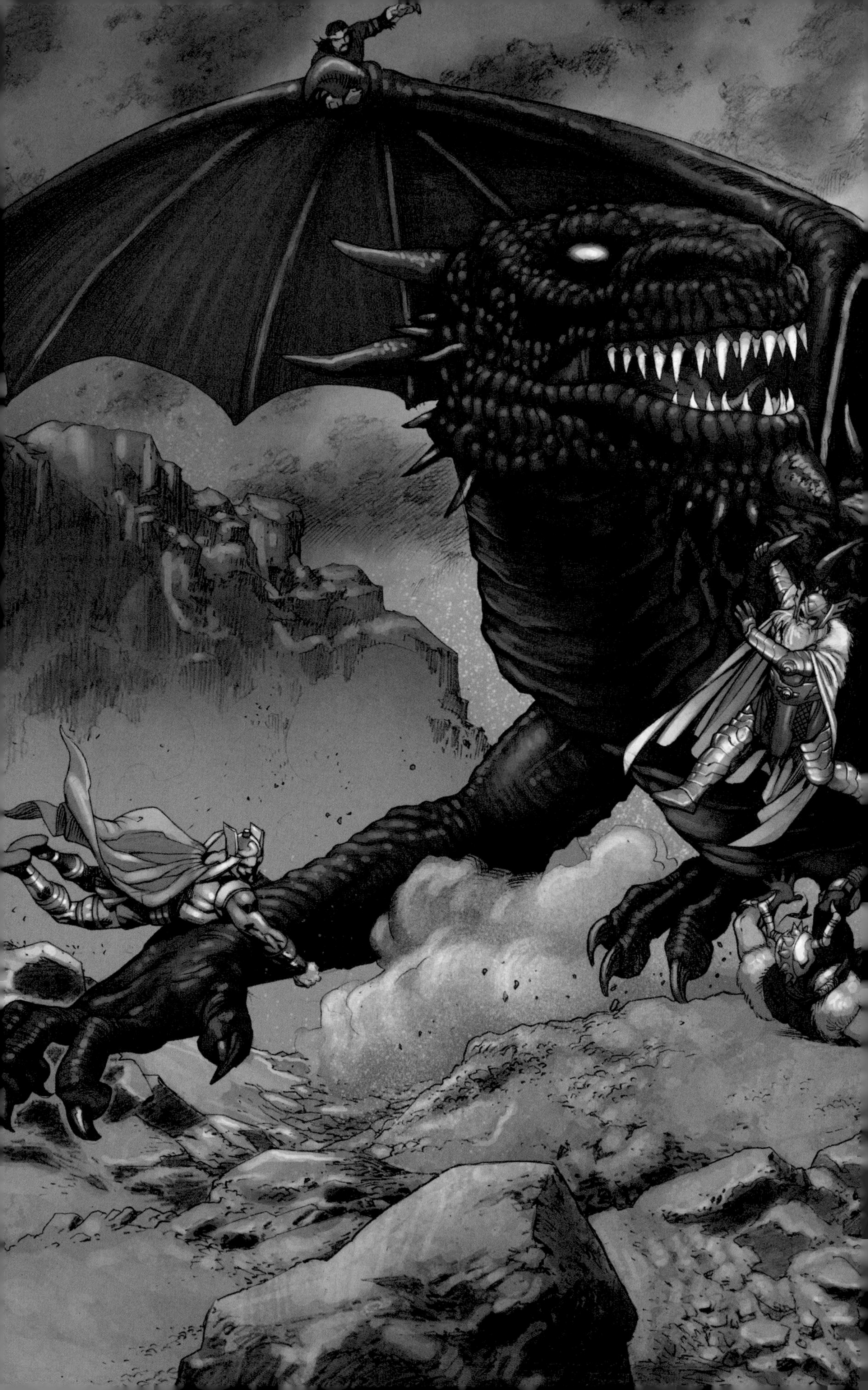

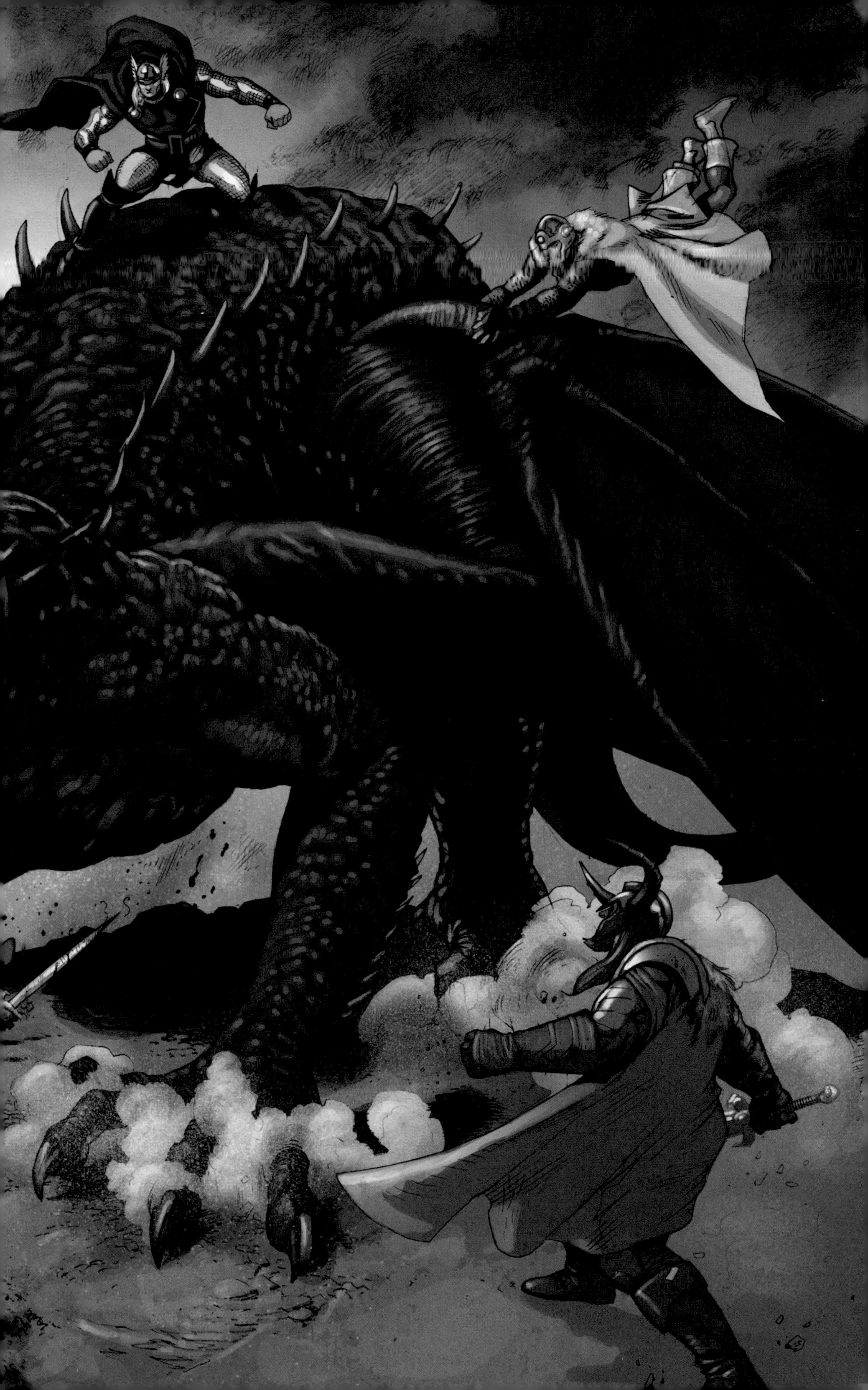

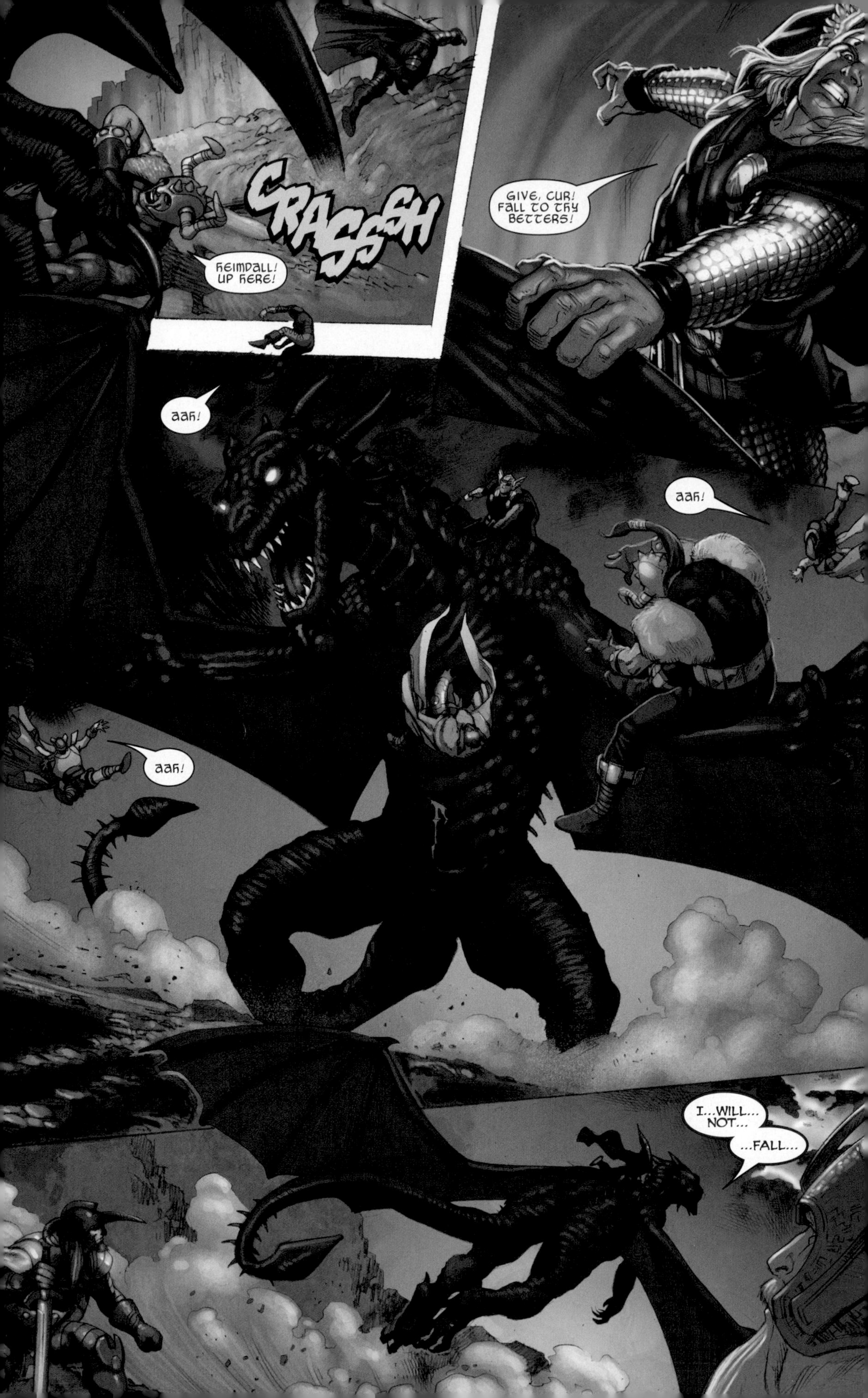
CRASSSH
HEIMDALL! UP HERE!
GIVE, CUR! FALL TO THY BETTERS!
AAH!
AAH!
AAH!
I...WILL... NOT...
...FALL...

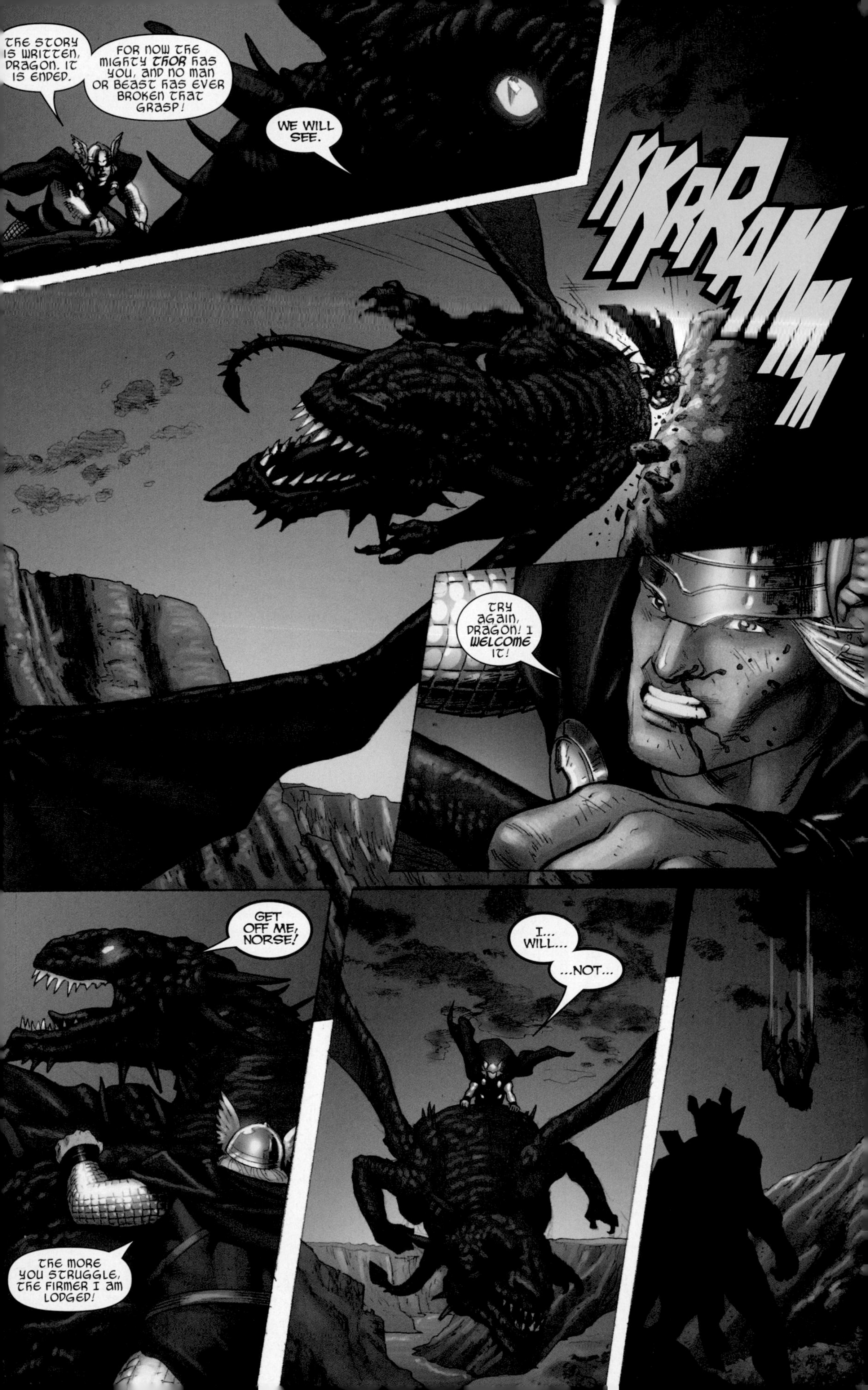
THE STORY IS WRITTEN, DRAGON. IT IS ENDED.
FOR NOW THE MIGHTY THOR HAS YOU, AND NO MAN OR BEAST HAS EVER BROKEN THAT GRASP!
WE WILL SEE.
KKRRAMM
TRY AGAIN, DRAGON! I WELCOME IT!
GET OFF ME, NORSE!
THE MORE YOU STRUGGLE, THE FIRMER I AM LODGED!
I... WILL...
...NOT...

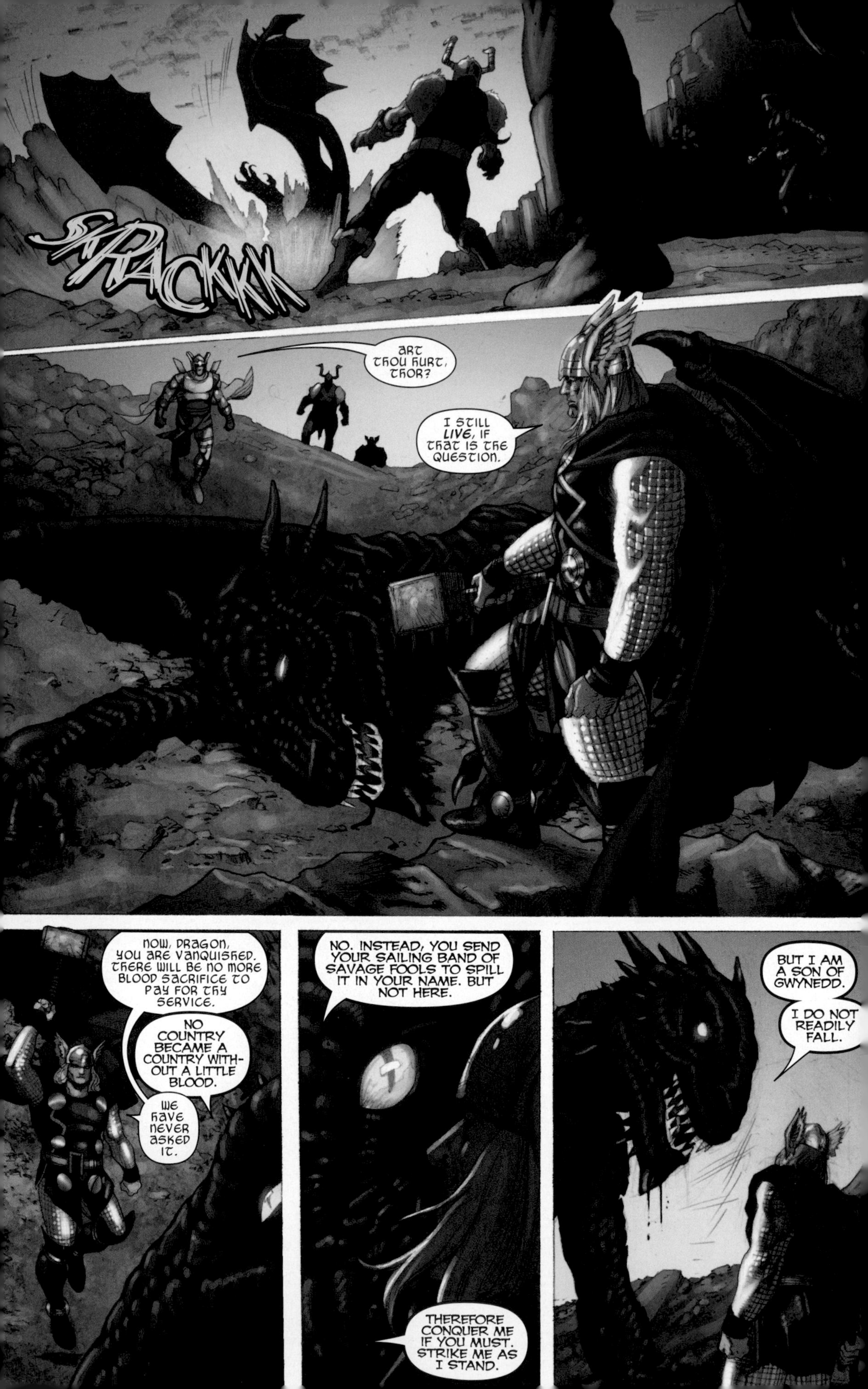
SKRACKKK
ART THOU HURT, THOR?
I STILL LIVE, IF THAT IS THE QUESTION.
NOW, DRAGON, YOU ARE VANQUISHED. THERE WILL BE NO MORE BLOOD SACRIFICE TO PAY FOR THY SERVICE.
NO COUNTRY BECAME A COUNTRY WITHOUT A LITTLE BLOOD.
WE HAVE NEVER ASKED IT.
NO. INSTEAD, YOU SEND YOUR SAILING BAND OF SAVAGE FOOLS TO SPILL IT IN YOUR NAME. BUT NOT HERE.
THEREFORE CONQUER ME IF YOU MUST. STRIKE ME AS I STAND.
BUT I AM A SON OF GWYNEDD.
I DO NOT READILY FALL.

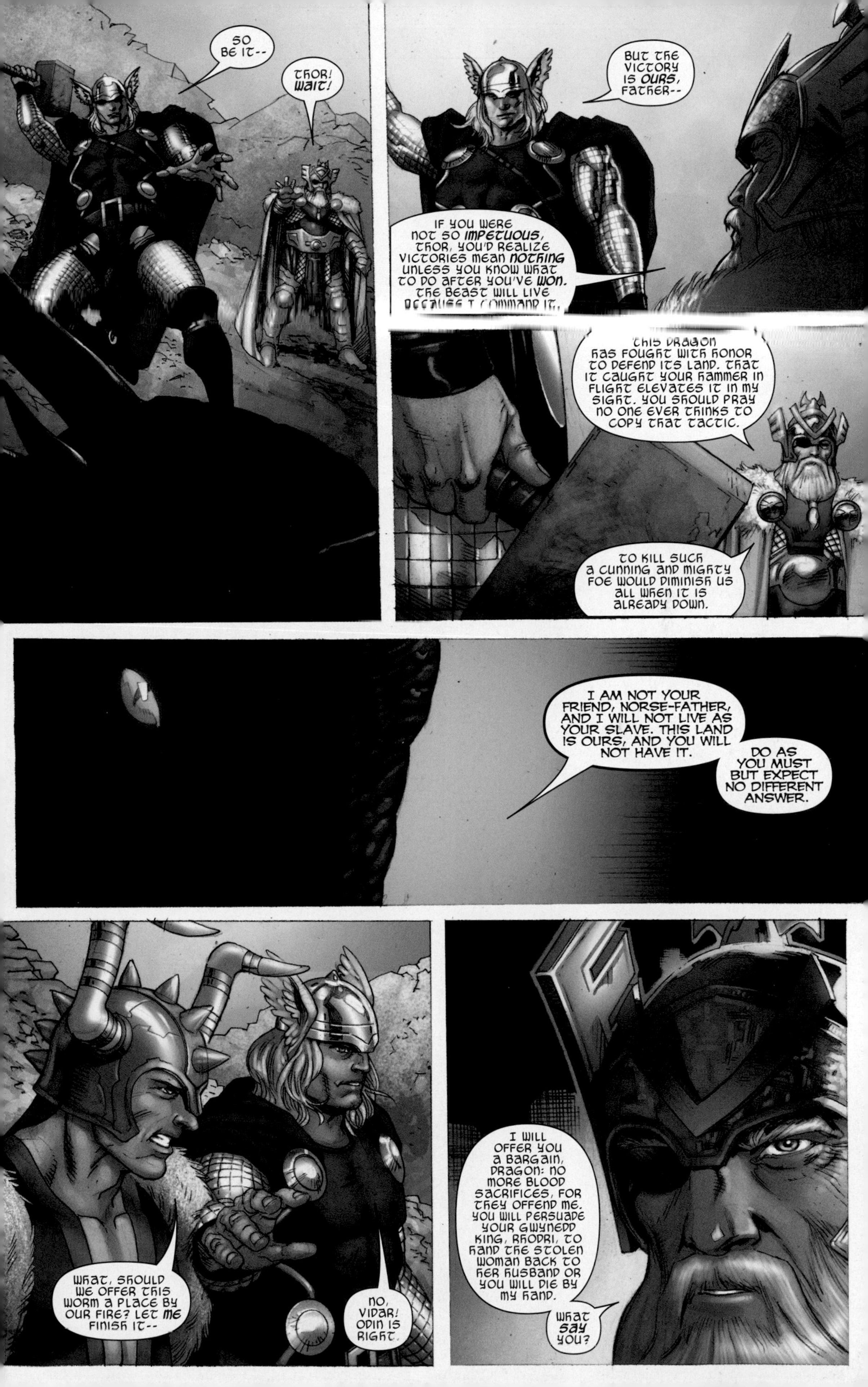
SO BE IT--
THOR! *WAIT!*
BUT THE VICTORY IS *OURS*, FATHER--
IF YOU WERE NOT SO *IMPETUOUS*, THOR, YOU'D REALIZE VICTORIES MEAN *NOTHING* UNLESS YOU KNOW WHAT TO DO AFTER YOU'VE *WON*. THE BEAST WILL LIVE BECAUSE I COMMAND IT.
THIS DRAGON HAS FOUGHT WITH HONOR TO DEFEND ITS LAND. THAT IT CAUGHT YOUR HAMMER IN FLIGHT ELEVATES IT IN MY SIGHT. YOU SHOULD PRAY NO ONE EVER THINKS TO COPY THAT TACTIC.
TO KILL SUCH A CUNNING AND MIGHTY FOE WOULD DIMINISH US ALL WHEN IT IS ALREADY DOWN.
I AM NOT YOUR FRIEND, NORSE-FATHER, AND I WILL NOT LIVE AS YOUR SLAVE. THIS LAND IS OURS, AND YOU WILL NOT HAVE IT.
DO AS YOU MUST BUT EXPECT NO DIFFERENT ANSWER.
WHAT, SHOULD WE OFFER THIS WORM A PLACE BY OUR FIRE? LET *ME* FINISH IT--
NO, VIDAR! ODIN IS RIGHT.
I WILL OFFER YOU A BARGAIN, DRAGON: NO MORE BLOOD SACRIFICES, FOR THEY OFFEND ME. YOU WILL PERSUADE YOUR GWYNEDD KING, RHODRI, TO HAND THE STOLEN WOMAN BACK TO HER HUSBAND OR YOU WILL DIE BY MY HAND.
WHAT *SAY* YOU?

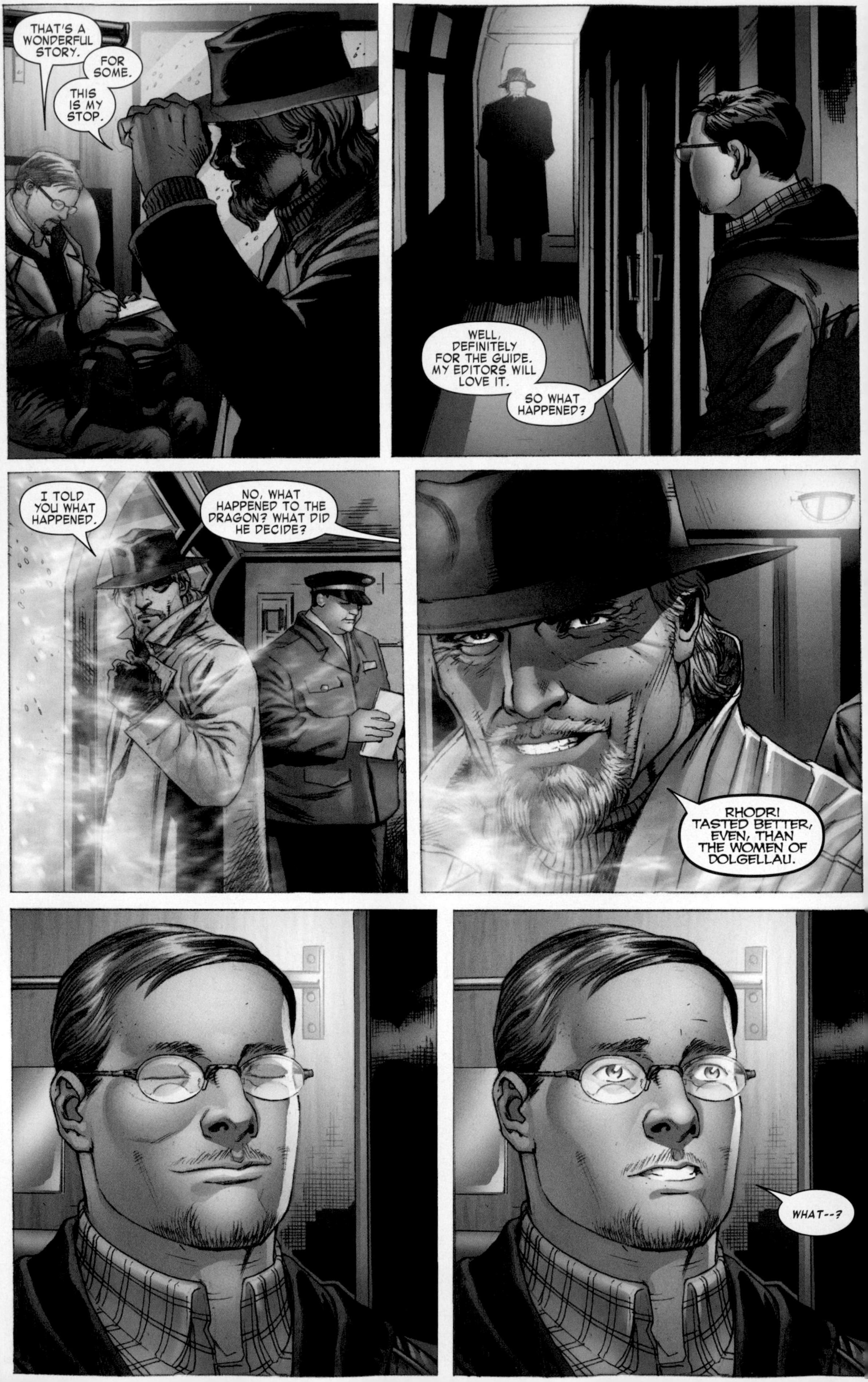
THAT'S A WONDERFUL STORY.
FOR SOME.
THIS IS MY STOP.
WELL, DEFINITELY FOR THE GUIDE. MY EDITORS WILL LOVE IT.
SO WHAT HAPPENED?
I TOLD YOU WHAT HAPPENED.
NO, WHAT HAPPENED TO THE DRAGON? WHAT DID HE DECIDE?
RHODRI TASTED BETTER, EVEN, THAN THE WOMEN OF DOLGELLAU.
WHAT--?

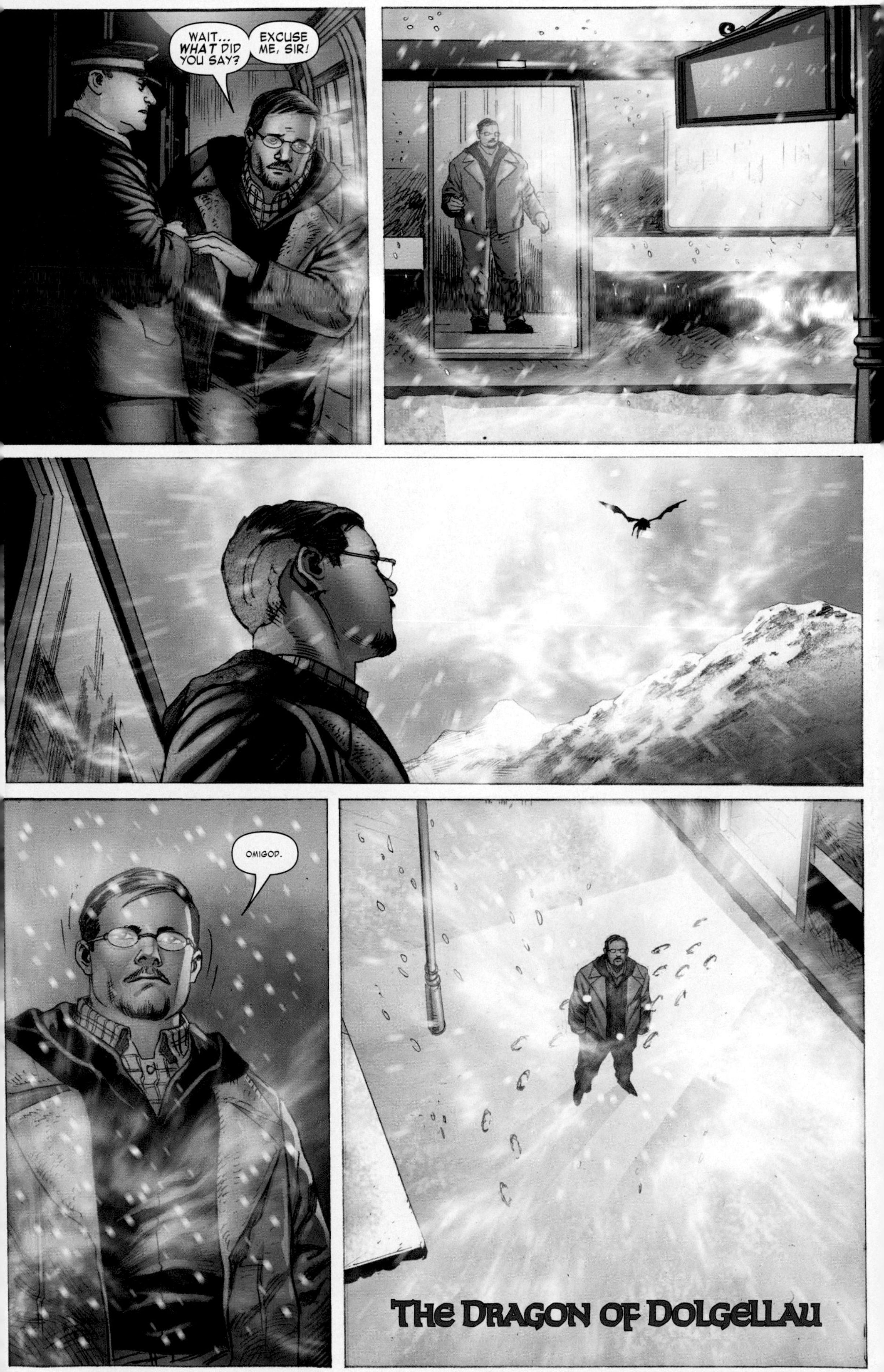
WAIT... WHAT DID YOU SAY?
EXCUSE ME, SIR!
OMIGOD.
THE DRAGON OF DOLGELLAU

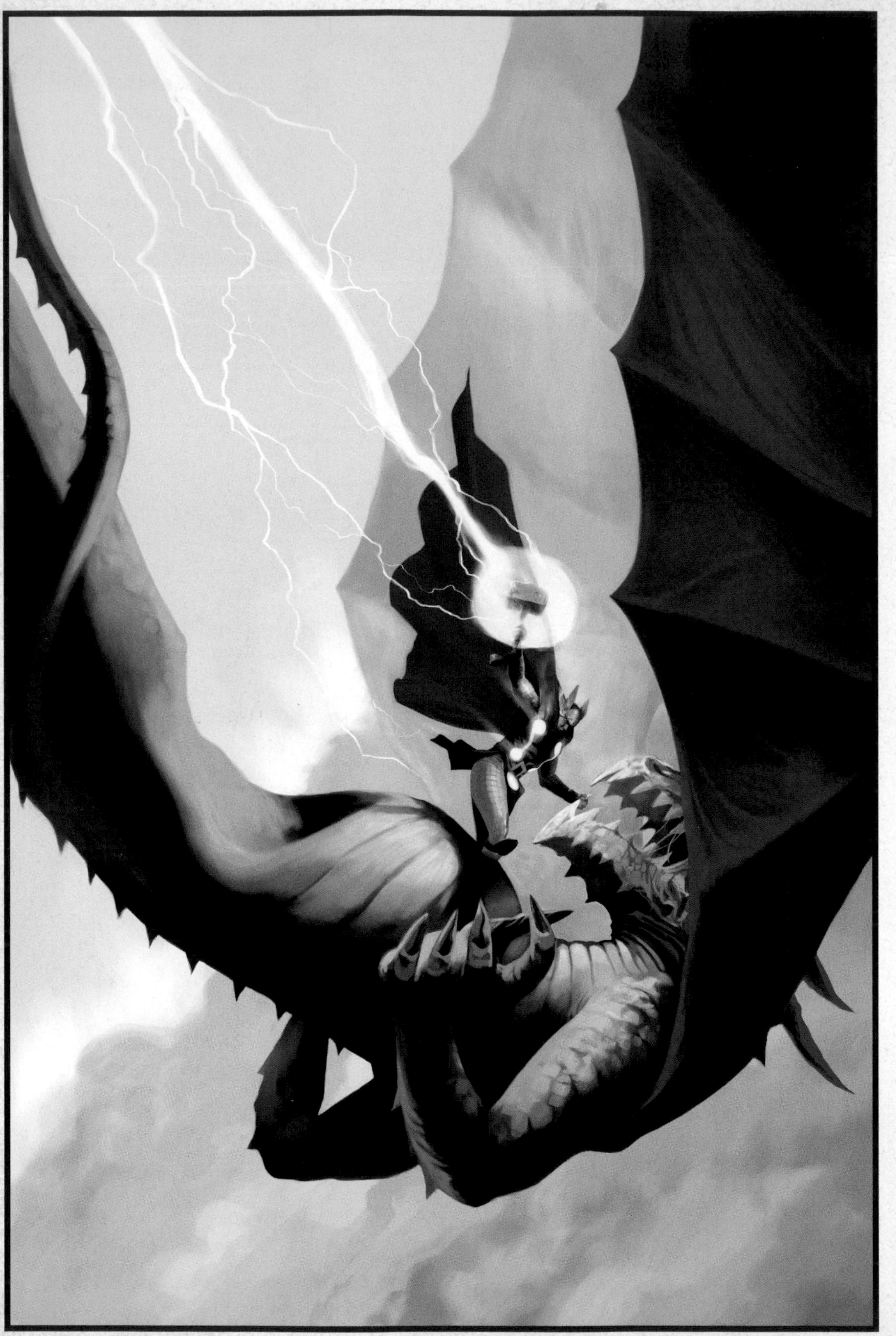

THOR: HEAVEN & EARTH #4 COVER ART BY **STÉPHANE PERGER,** WITH ORIGINAL COLORS

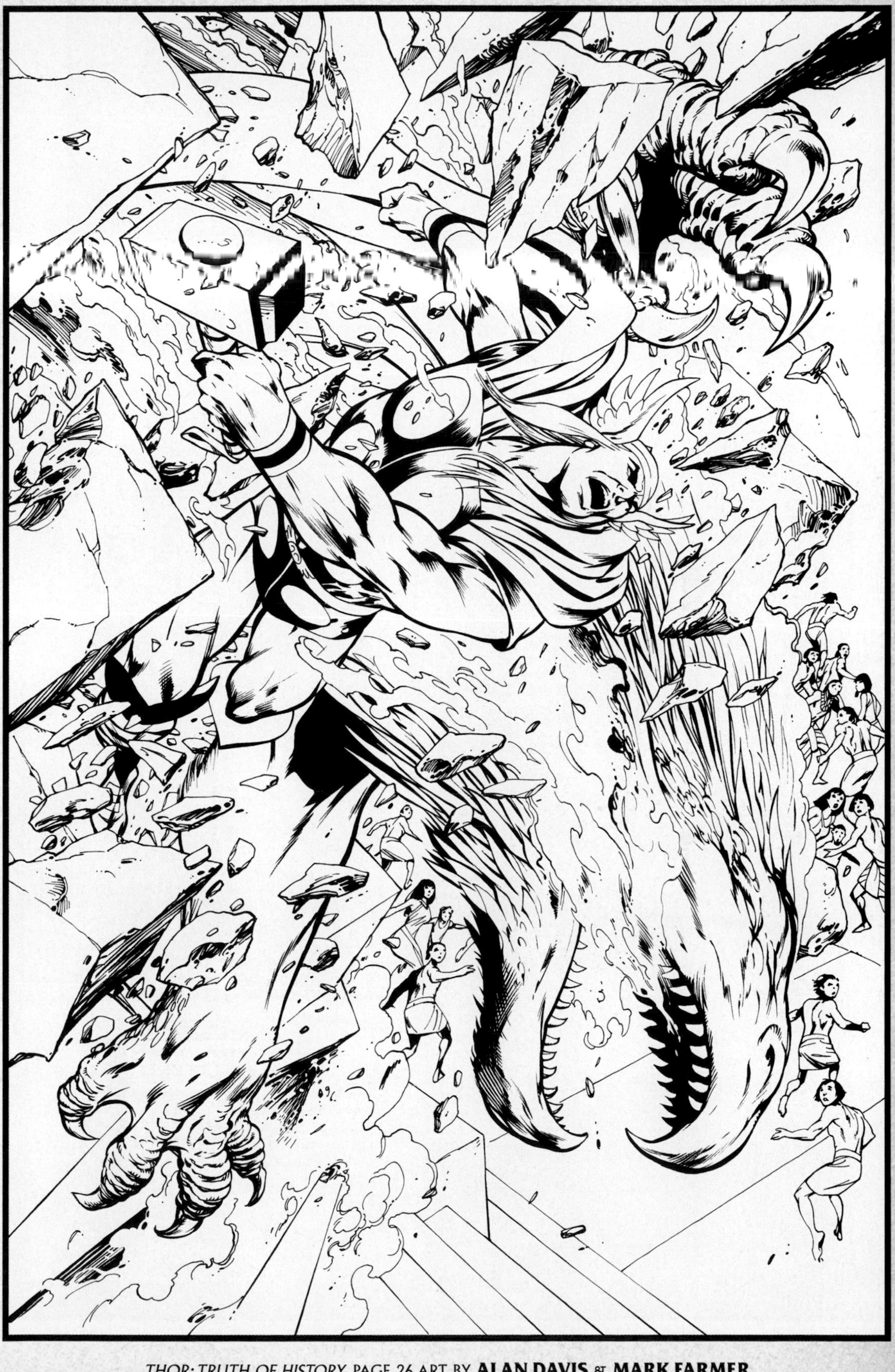

THOR: TRUTH OF HISTORY, PAGE 26 ART BY **ALAN DAVIS** & **MARK FARMER**

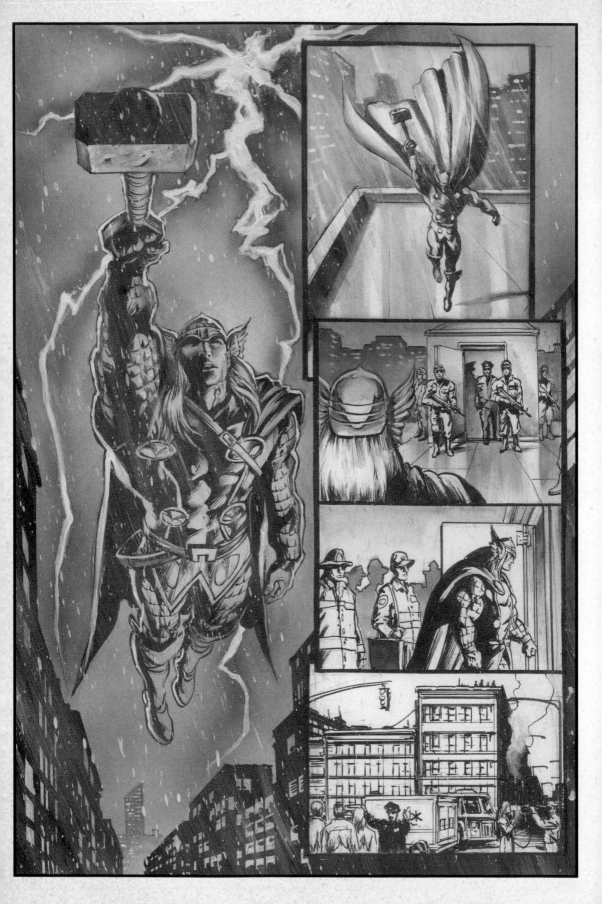

THOR: HEAVEN & EARTH #2, PAGES 1 & 11 PENCILS AND INKWASH BY **MARK TEXEIRA**

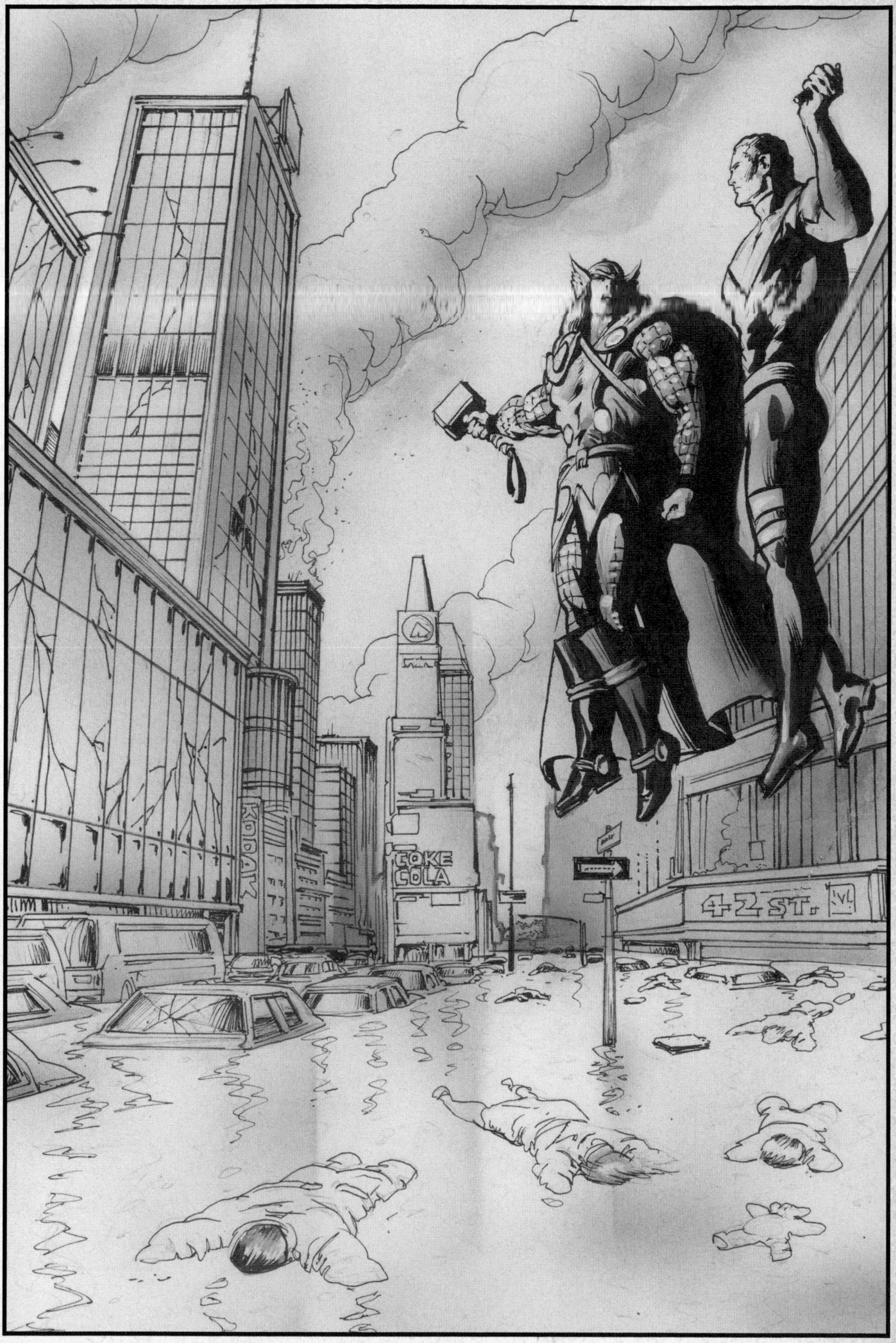
KODAK
COKE
COLA
42 ST.

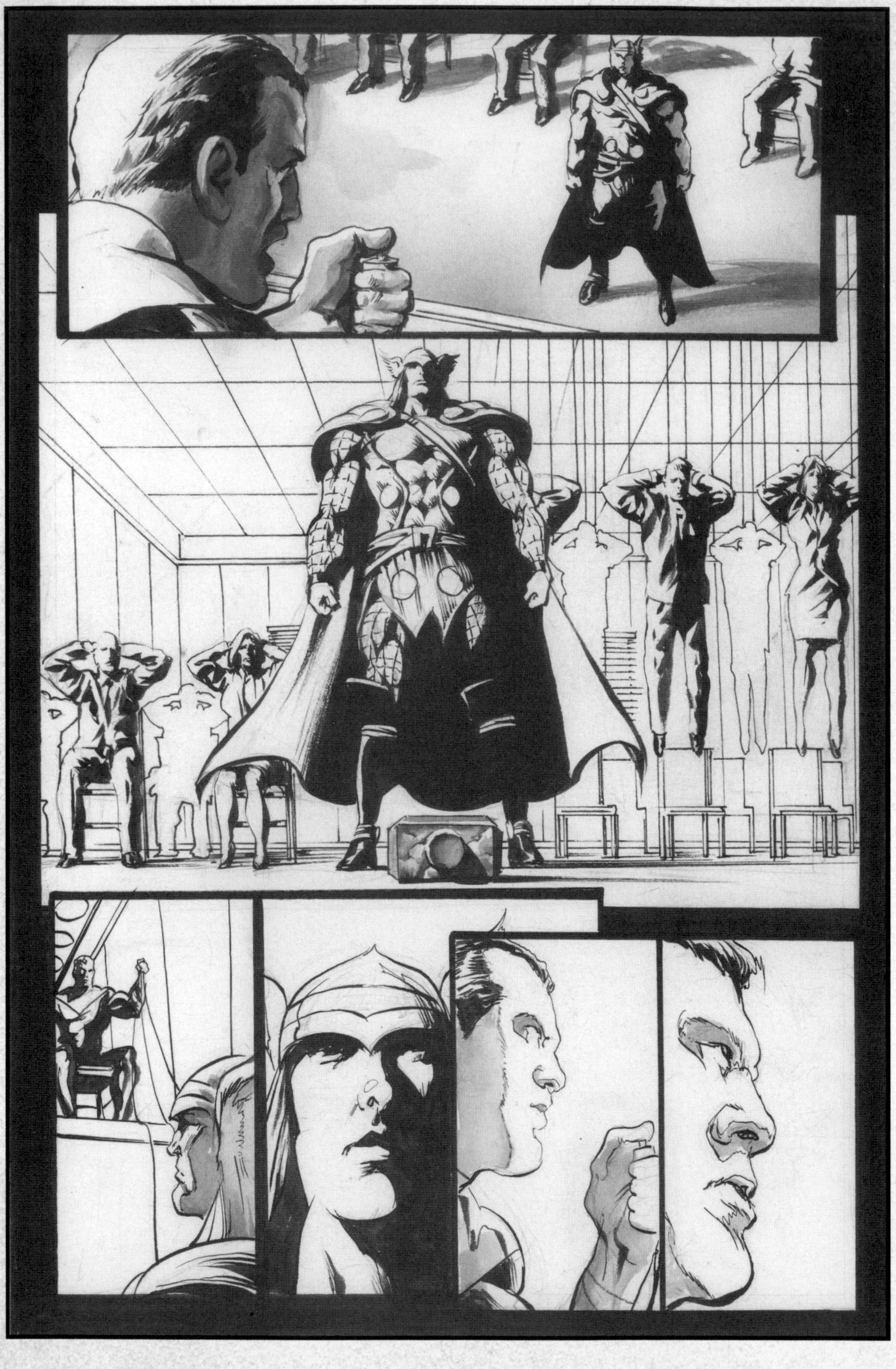

THOR: HEAVEN & EARTH #2, PAGES 17 & 21 PENCILS AND INKWASH BY **MARK TEXEIRA**

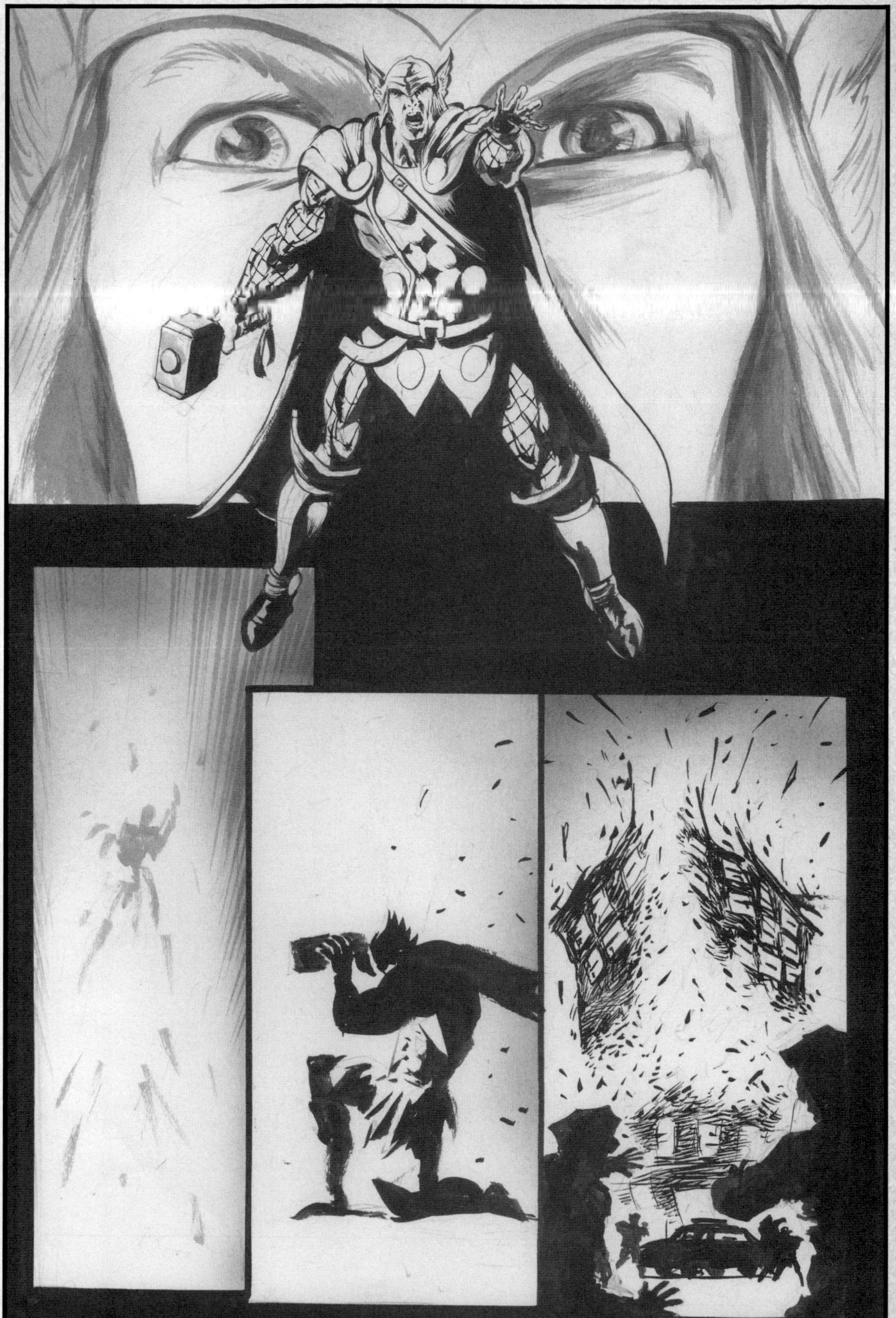

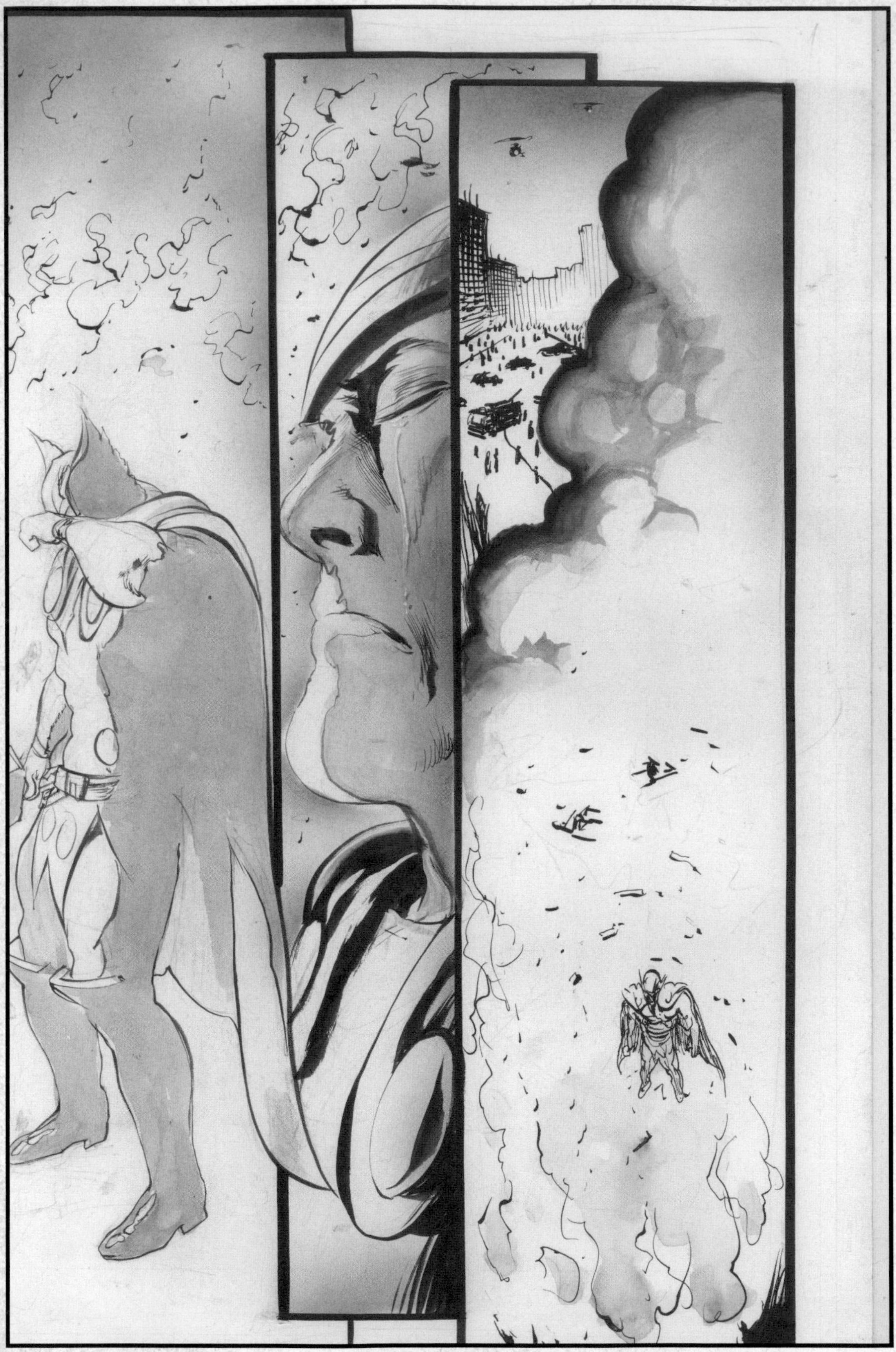

THOR: HEAVEN & EARTH #2, PAGES 21 PENCILS AND INKWASH BY **MARK TEXEIRA**

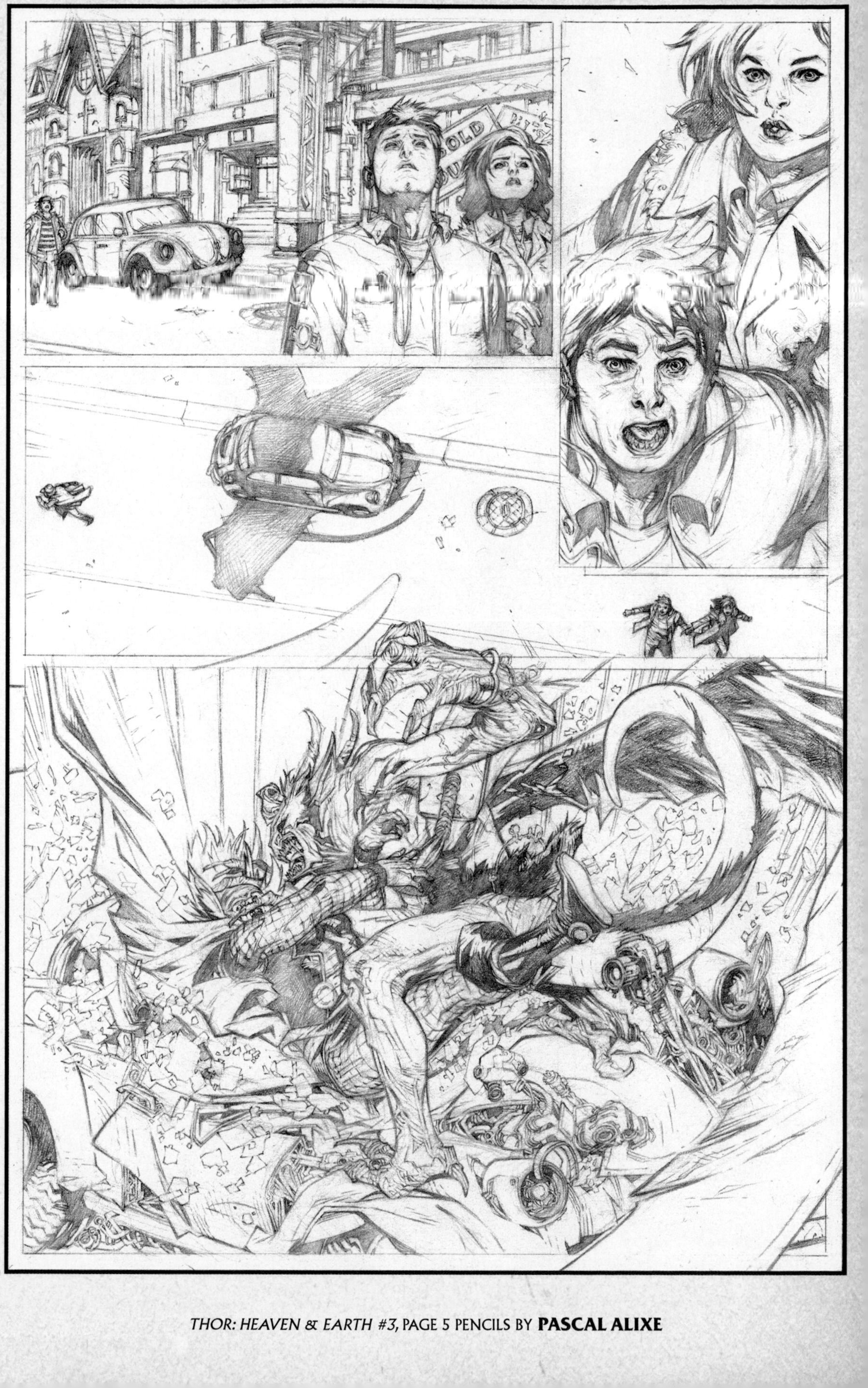

THOR: HEAVEN & EARTH #3, PAGE 5 PENCILS BY **PASCAL ALIXE**

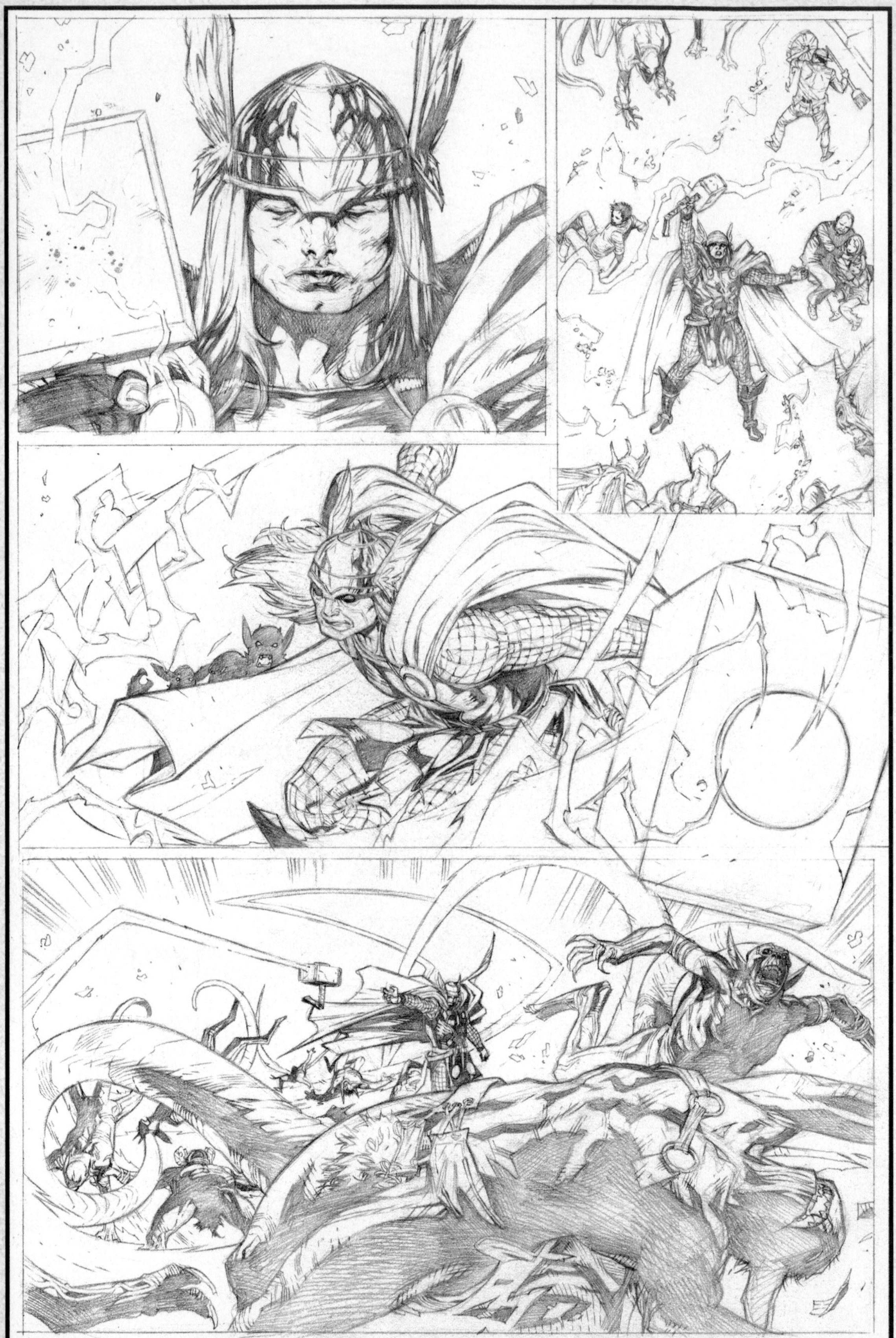

THOR: HEAVEN & EARTH #3, PAGES 8 & 9 PENCILS BY **PASCAL ALIXE**

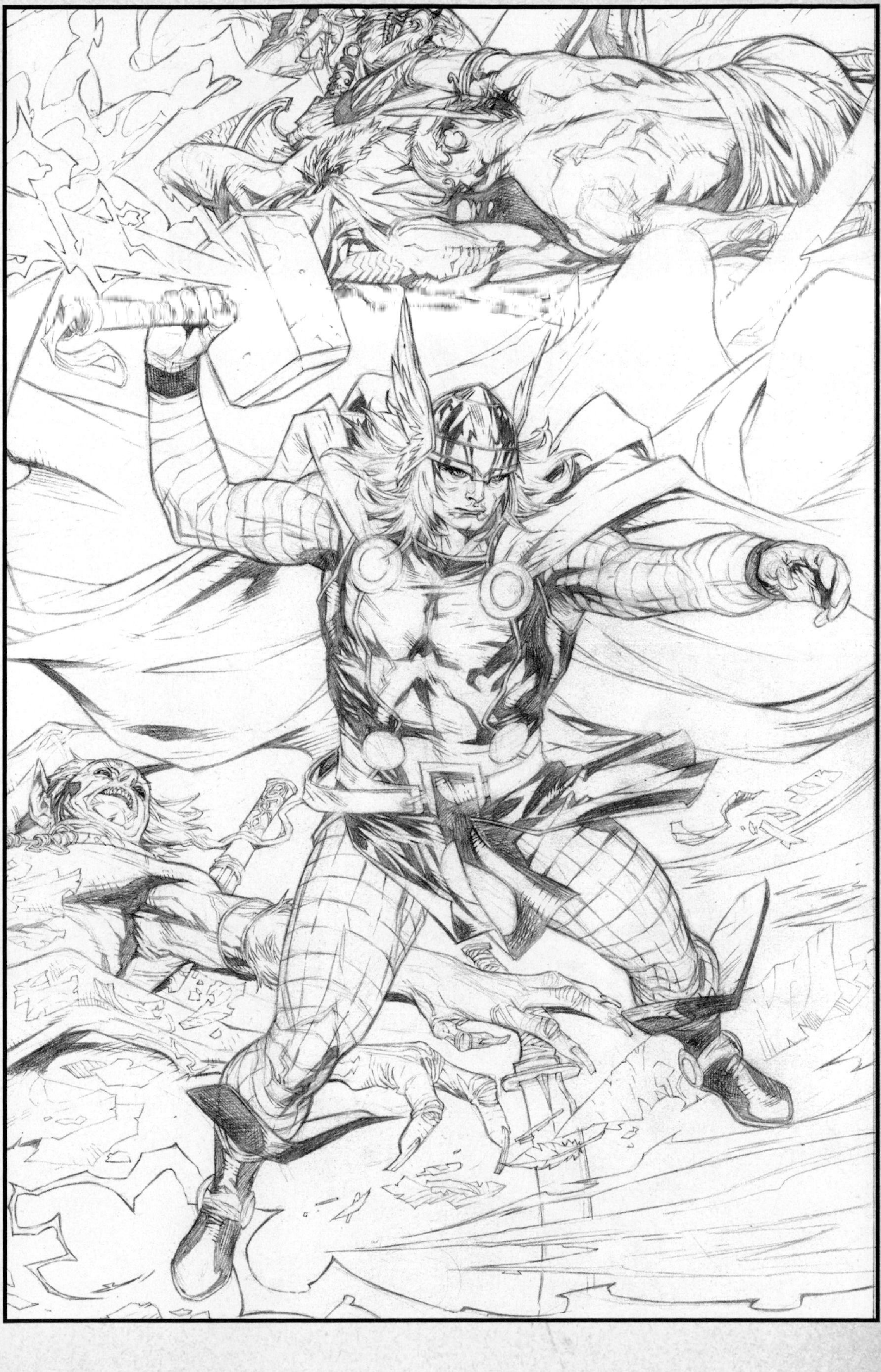

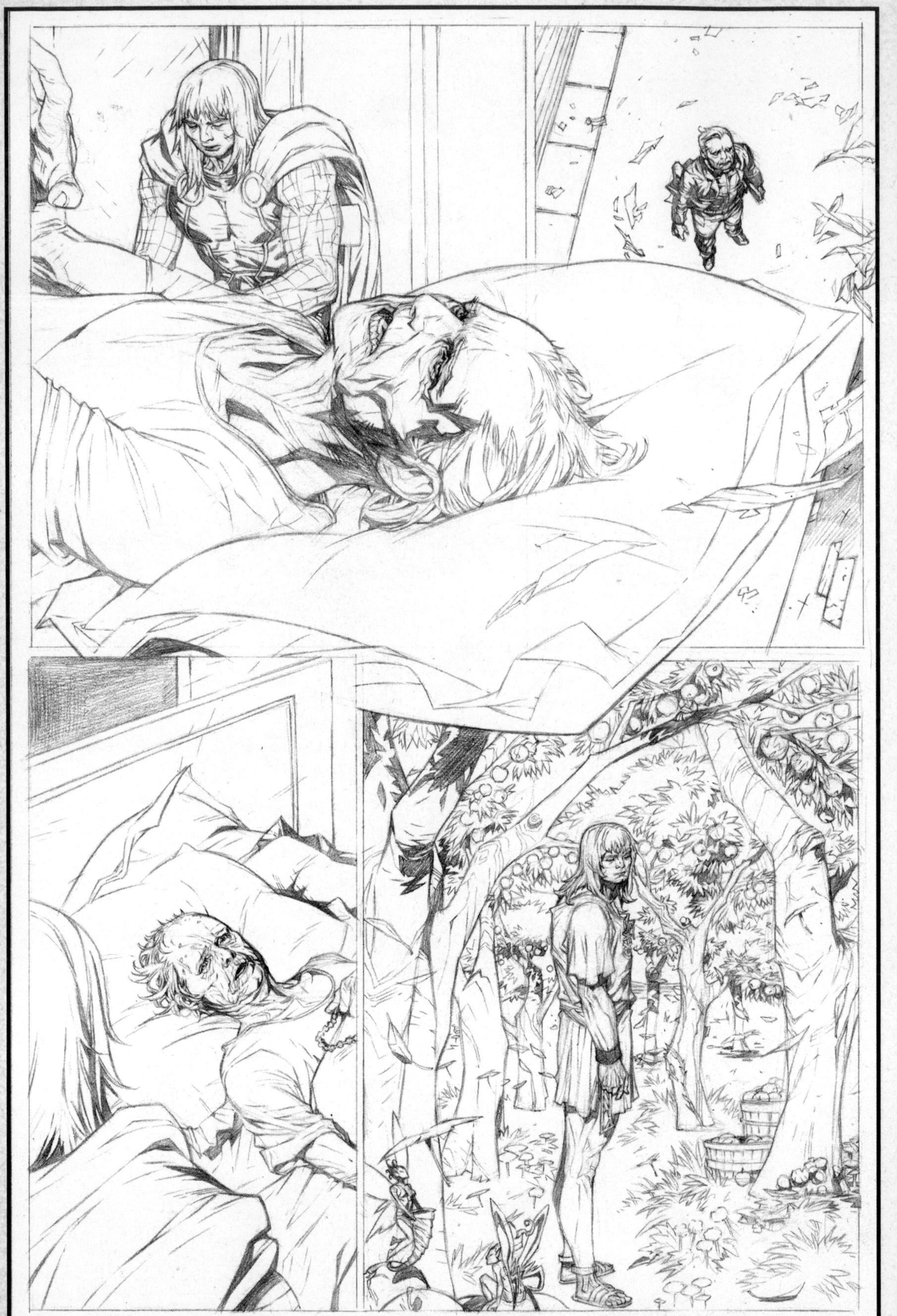

THOR: HEAVEN & EARTH #3, PAGES 13 & 20 PENCILS BY **PASCAL ALIXE**

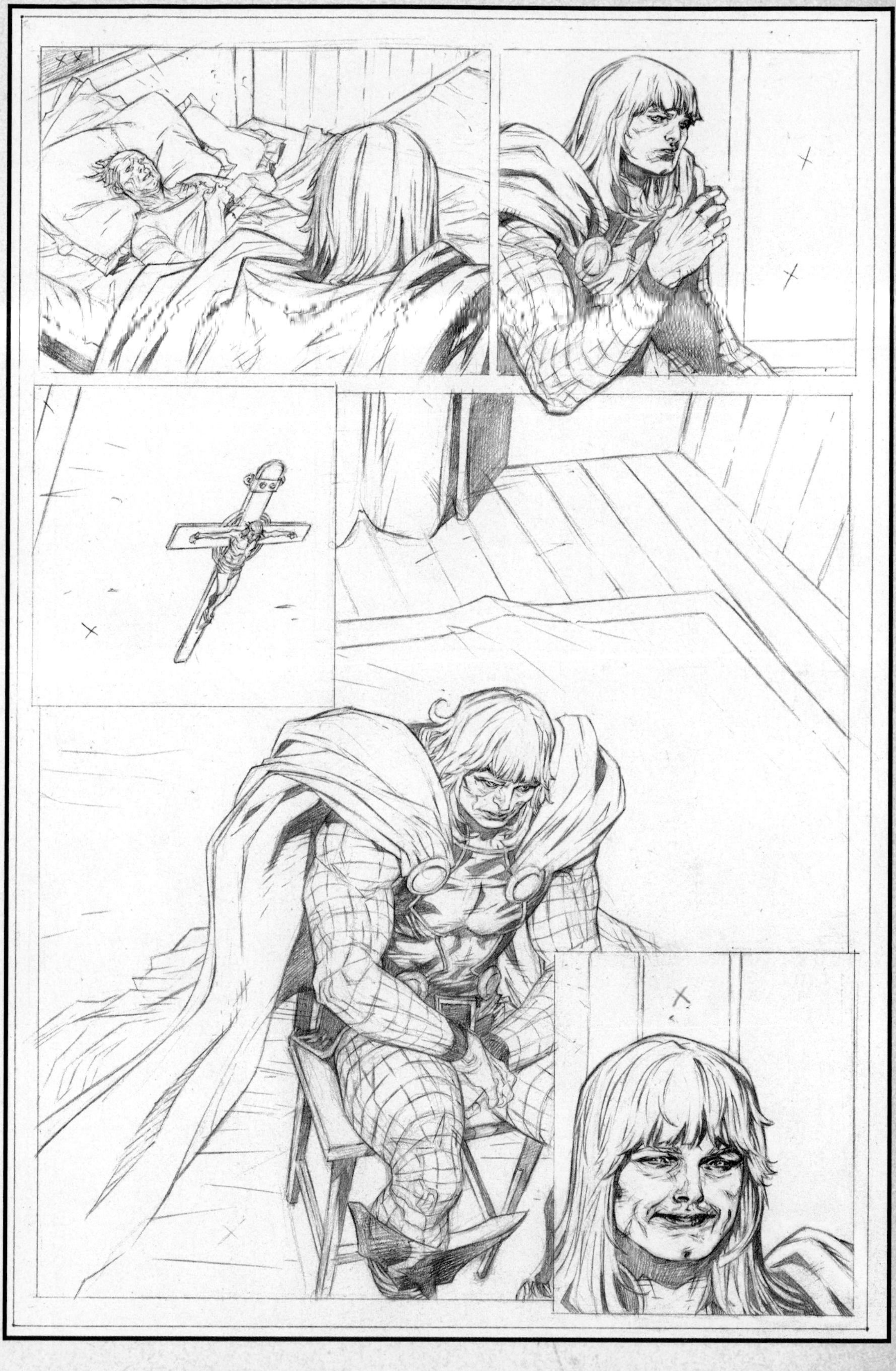

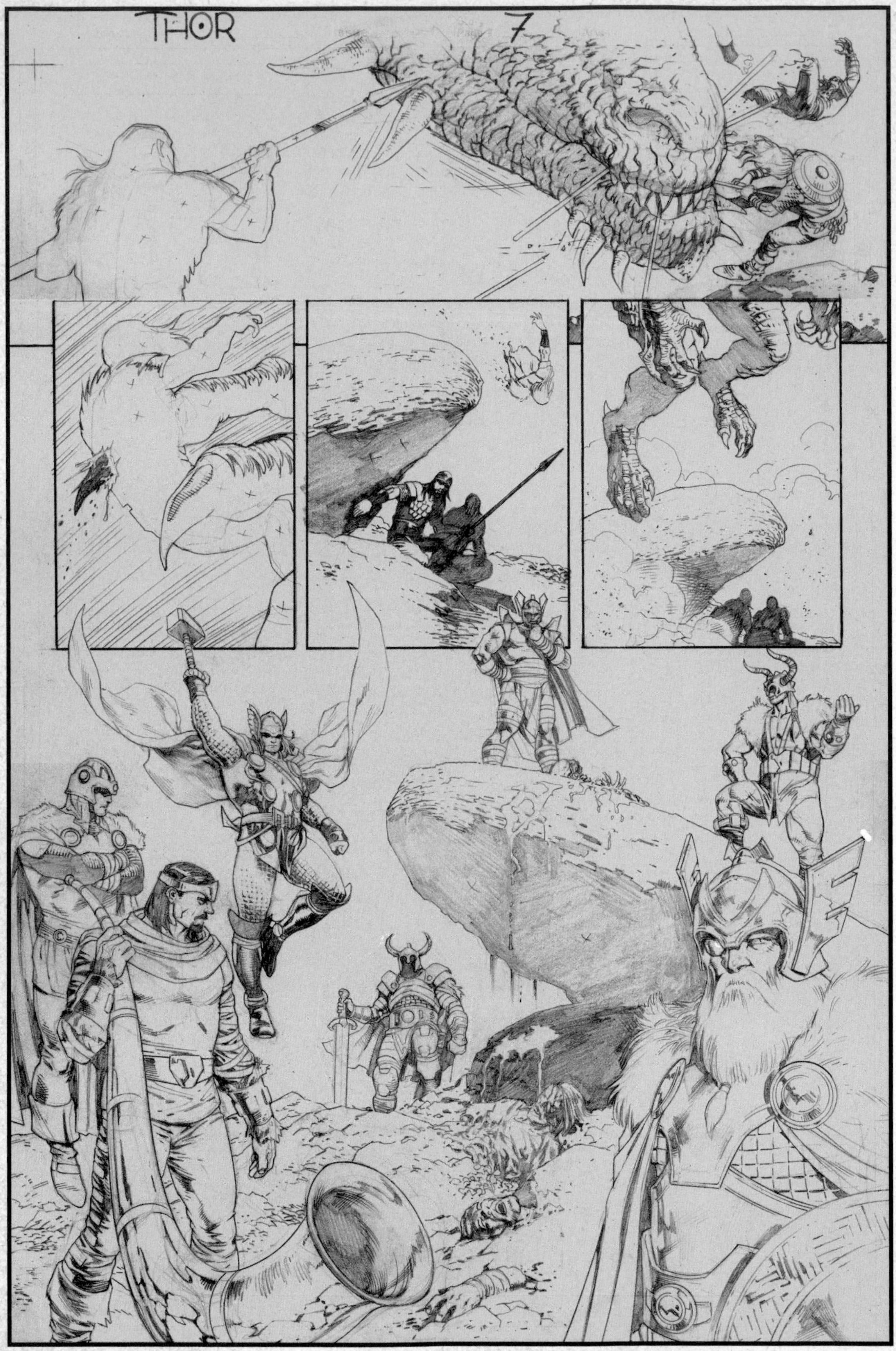
THOR
7

THOR: HEAVEN & EARTH #4, PAGES 7 & 8 PENCILS BY **LAN MEDINA**

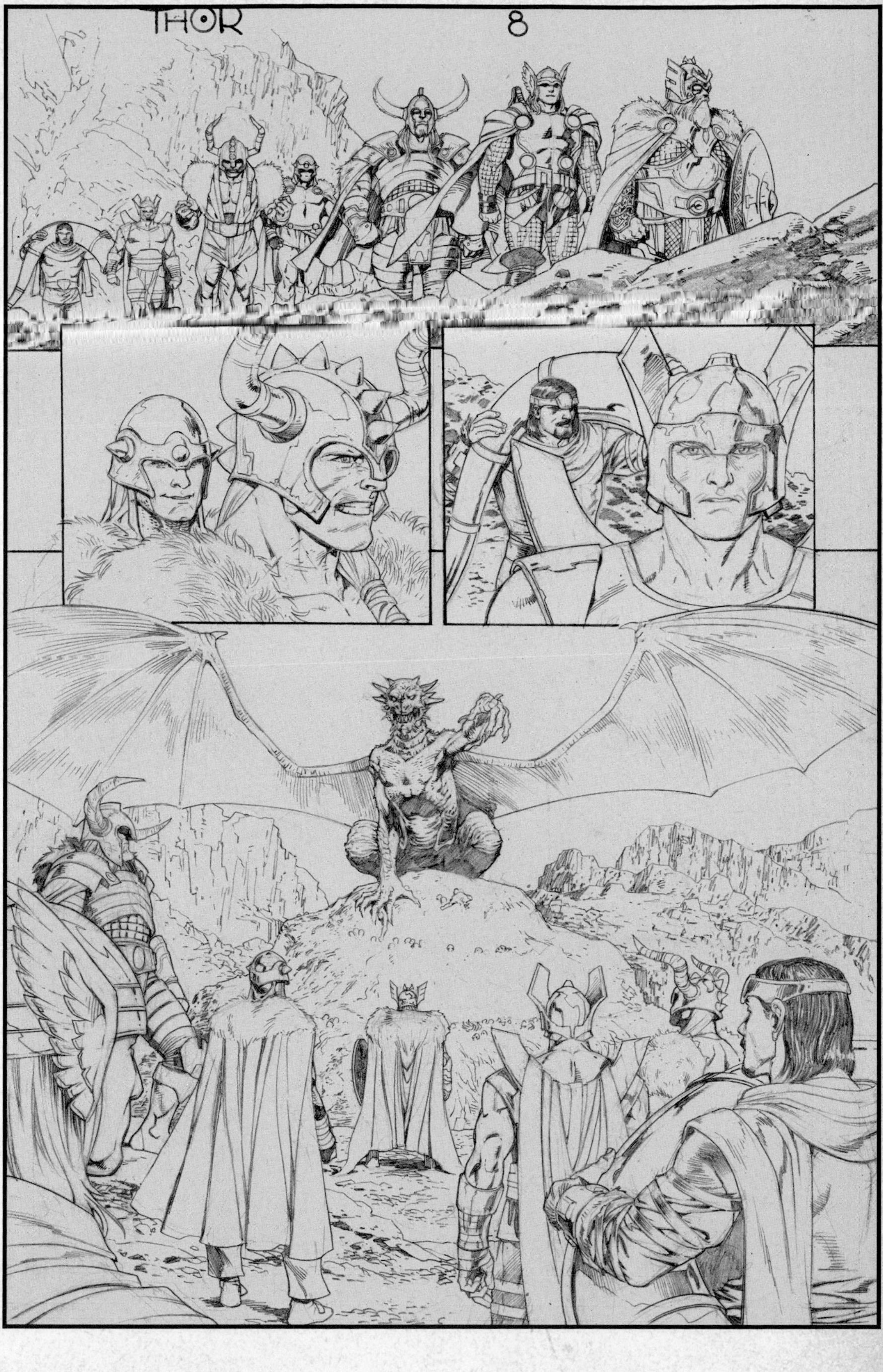
THOR
8

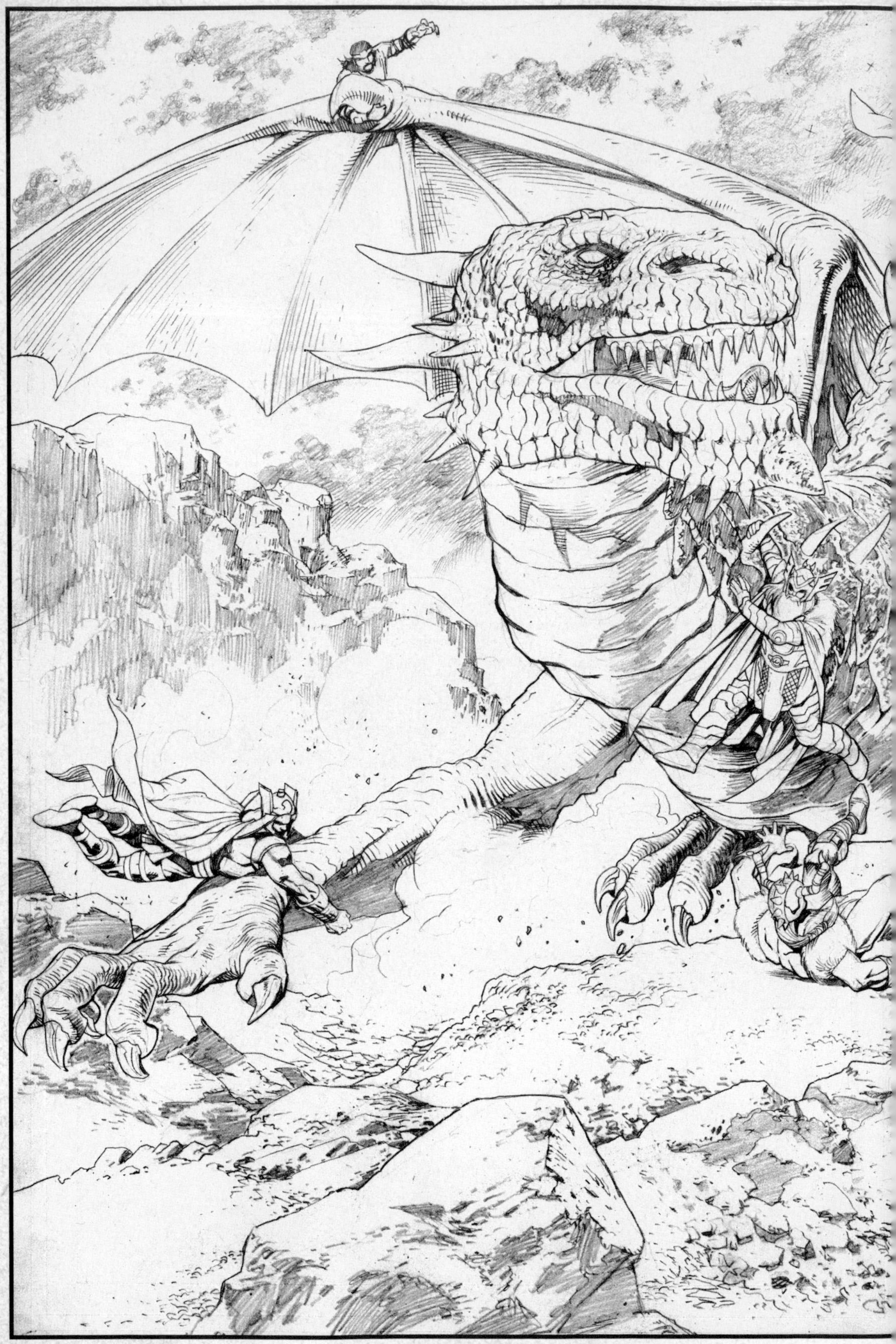

THOR: HEAVEN & EARTH #4, PAGES 16-17 PENCILS BY **LAN MEDINA**

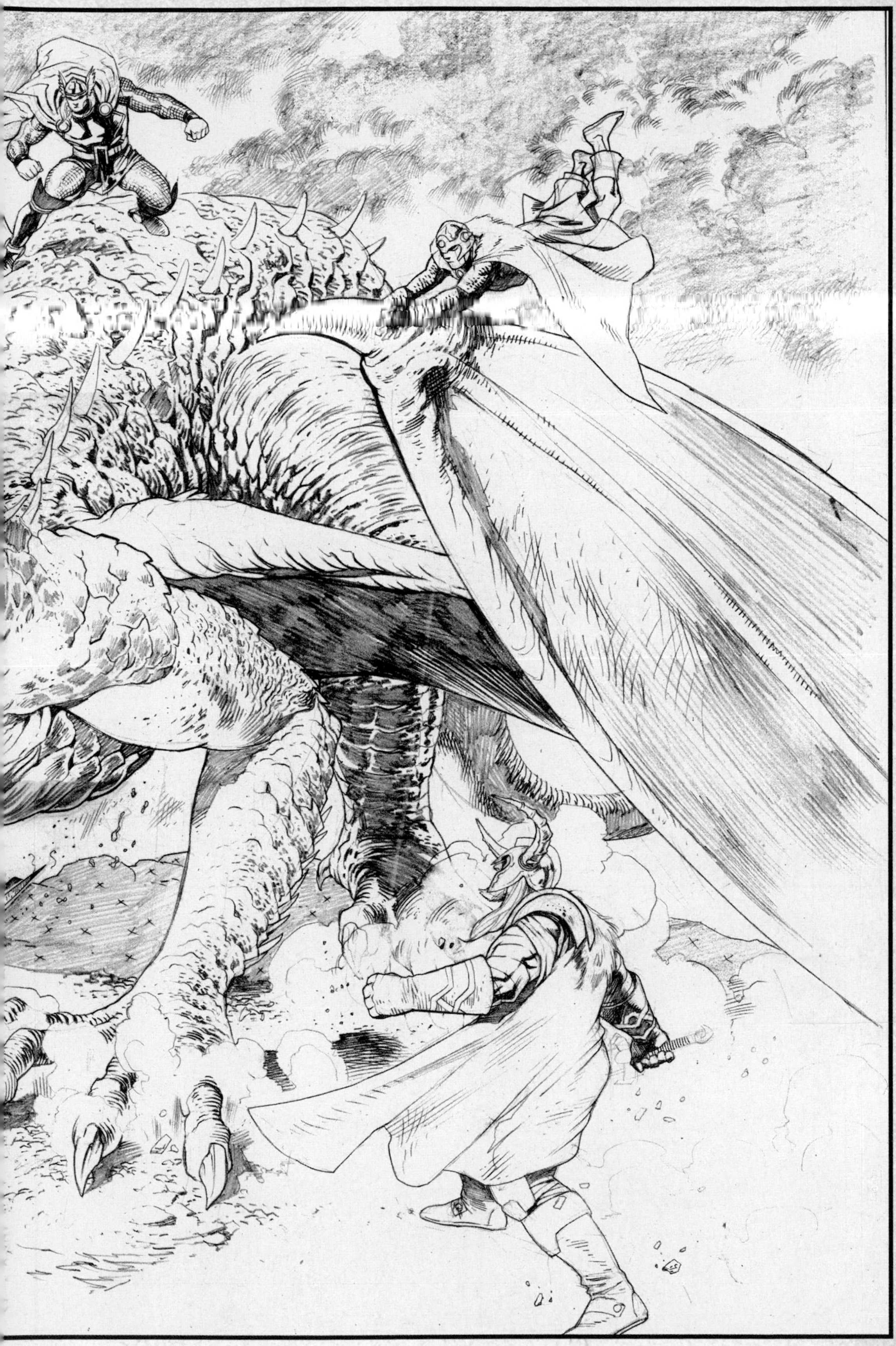

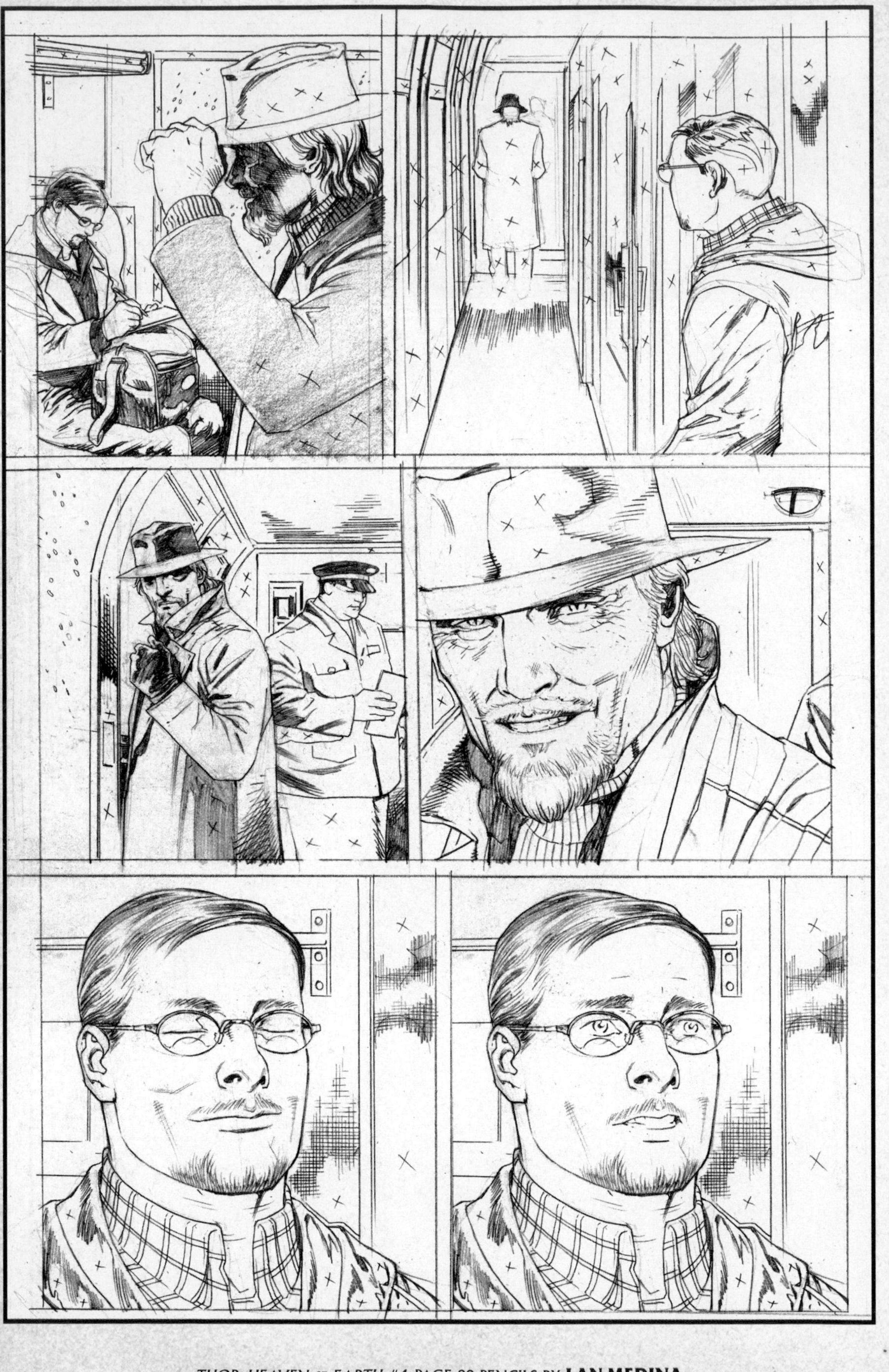

THOR: HEAVEN & EARTH #4, PAGE 22 PENCILS BY **LAN MEDINA**